MARITAL THERAPY
Moral, Sociological and Psychological Factors

MARITAL THERAPY
Moral, Sociological and Psychological Factors

Compiled and Edited by

HIRSCH LAZAAR SILVERMAN, Ph.D., Sc.D., L.H.D., LL.D.

Seton Hall University
Graduate Division, School of Education
South Orange, New Jersey
Past President, Academy of Psychologists in Marital Therapy
Past President, New Jersey Association of Marriage Counselors
Chairman, New Jersey State Board of Marriage Counselor Examiners

With a Foreword by

EDWARD J. RYDMAN, Ph.D.

Executive Director
American Association of Marriage and Family Counselors
Dallas, Texas

CHARLES C THOMAS · PUBLISHER
Springfield · Illinois · U.S.A.

Published and Distributed Throughout the World by

CHARLES C THOMAS • PUBLISHER

BANNERSTONE HOUSE

301-327 East Lawrence Avenue, Springfield, Illinois, U.S.A.

NATCHEZ PLANTATION HOUSE

735 North Atlantic Boulevard, Fort Lauderdale, Florida, U.S.A.

© *1972, by* CHARLES C THOMAS • PUBLISHER

ISBN 0-398-02415-4

Library of Congress Catalog Card Number 70-161185

With THOMAS BOOKS *careful attention is given to all details of manufacturing and design. It is the Publisher's desire to present books that are satisfactory as to their physical qualities and artistic possibilities and appropriate for their particular use.* THOMAS BOOKS *will be true to those laws of quality that assure a good name and good will.*

Printed in the United States of America

N-1

CONTRIBUTORS

Hirsch Lazaar Silverman, Ph.D., Sc.D., L.H.D., LL.D., *Editor*

Wesley J. Adams, Ph.D.

Gerald Albert, Ed.D.

Ben N. Ard, Jr., Ph.D.

Panos D. Bardis, Ph.D.

Rev. James R. Becherer

Mary S. Calderone, M.D., M.P.H.

William Langley Carrington, M.D.

LeMon Clark, M.S., M.D.

John W. Crandall, Ed.D.

William F. Eastman, Ed.D., A.C.S.W.

Albert Ellis, Ph.D.

David Goodman, Ed.D.

Robert J. Goodstein, B.A.

Rev. Matti Joensuu, D.D.

Merle R. Jordan, Th.D.

Sr. M. Catherine deRicci Killeen, O.P.

Joseph C. Landrud, Th.D.

Ruth Leder, Ph.D.

Eugene B. Linton, M.D., F.A., C.O.G.

David R. Mace, Ph.D.

Rev. Paul Marx, O.S.B.

Donald J. McCulloch, M.D., F.R.C.P.(C)

Thomas G. McGinnis, Ed.D.

John O. Meany, Ph.D.

David O. Moberg, Ph.D.

Donald D. Moore, Ph.D.

Ethel M. Nash, M.A.

A. E. Keir Nash, Ph.D.

Stephen Neiger, Ph.D., M.D.

Msgr. John J. O'Sullivan, S.T.O.

Lloyd G. Phillips, B.A.

John G. Quesnell, A.C.S.W.

Clifford B. Reifler, M.D., M.P.H.

Ira L. Reiss, Ph.D.

Isadore Rubin, Ph.D.

Charity Eva Runden, Ph.D.

Tatsuo Samejima

Gerald Sanctuary, J.D.

Rev. Frank A. Sargent, Jr., Th.M.

Patricia Schiller, M.A., J.D.

Emanuel K. Schwartz, Ph.D., D.S.Sc.

John Seymour, Ph.D.

Alfred Stern, M.D.

Joseph B. Trainer, M.D.

Rev. Ace L. Tubbs, Ed.D.

Rev. Alfred Vail, B.D.

Leland Foster Wood, Ph.D.

To My Wife Mildred
and Our Children Hyla, Morton and Kineret, Stuart

BIOGRAPHICAL NOTES

WESLEY J. ADAMS earned his B.S. degree from the University of Wisconsin, his M.S. also from Wisconsin, the Marriage Counseling Certificate from the University of Minnesota, and his Ph.D. from Oregon State University. Since 1969 he has been Assistant Professor of Family Life in Central Washington State College, Ellensburg, Washington. During 1966-67 he was a marriage counselor with the Family Service League of Waterloo, Iowa, and in 1964-65 he was a Psychiatric Social Worker with the Manitowoc County Mental Health Center in Wisconsin. He holds memberships in the American Association of Marriage and Family Counselors, National Association of Social Workers, National Council on Family Relations, and Phi Kappa Phi.

GERALD ALBERT received his B.A. from the City College of New York, his M.A. in Psychology from the New School for Social Research, and his doctorate (Ed.D.) in Counseling from Columbia University. He is Director of Counseling and Associate Professor of Counselor Education at the C.W. Post College of Long Island University; Executive Coordinator of the Institute for Testing and Guidance, a division of the Long Island Consultation Center in Forest Hills, New York; psychological consultant to Dunhill Personnel Service in New York City; and in private practice in Queens, New York City. He is a member of the American Association of Marriage and Family Counselors, the American Psychological Association, the American Personnel and Guidance Association, the National Council on Family Relations, the American Association for the Advancement of Science, the Medical Correctional Association, and several local professional societies. His papers have appeared in such publications as the *Columbia Teachers College Record*, the *Personnel and Guidance Journal, Psychotherapy*, the *Journal of Marriage and Family Living*, and the *Journal of Contemporary Psychotherapy*. He has recently completed a book entitled *The Marriage Prediction Handbook*.

BEN N. ARD, JR., is Professor of Counseling at San Francisco State College. He is also a psychologist in private practice in San Francisco. He received his B.A. from the University of California at Los Angeles, his M.S. from Oregon State University at Corvallis, and his Ph.D. from the University of Michigan at Ann Arbor. He is President of the Northern California Association of Marriage Counselors (a regional division of the American Association of Marriage and Family Counselors). He is a Fellow and member of the Board of the California State Marriage Counselors Association. He has taught at Michigan State University, the University of Michigan, and Central Michigan University. He was formerly a Fellow in marriage counseling and family life education at the Merrill-Palmer Institute in Detroit. He has edited *Counseling and Psychotherapy: Classics on Theories and Issues* and co-edited, with his wife, a *Handbook of Marriage Counseling*.

PANOS D. BARDIS earned his B.A., magna cum laude, from Bethany College, his M.A. from Notre Dame University, and the Ph.D. from Purdue University. He is a Fellow of the American Association for the Advancement of Science. Among his memberships are American Association of University Professors; Board of Advisors, American Society for Neo-Hellenic Studies; Fellow and Membership Committee, American Sociological Association; Group for the Study of Sociolinguistics; Advisory Council, Institute for Mediterranean Affairs; Life Fellow, International Institute of Arts and Letters, Geneva, Switzerland; Board of Trustees, Marriage Museum, New York; Board of Directors, National Academy of Economics and Political Science; Consultant, National Association on Standard Medical Vocabulary; National Council on Family Relations; and Professional Member, National Writers Club. He is Editor and Book Review Editor, *Social*

Science; Book Review Editor, *International Review of History and Political Science;* and Associate Editor of eight other international journals. He is listed in *American Men of Science, Community Leaders of America, Dictionary of International Biography, Leaders in American Science, Who's Who in American Education, World Who's Who in Science, 1700 B.C.-1968 A.D.,* and six others. Among his numerous publications are many poems, a novel, *Ivan and Artemis; The Family in Changing Civilizations,* second edition, 1969; over a hundred anthropological, historical, mathematical, medical, psychological, sociological, and statistical articles in various journals. He is Professor of Sociology and Anthropology at The University of Toledo.

REVEREND JAMES R. BECHERER of the Chancery, Diocese of Cleveland, Ohio, attended St. Gregory Seminary, in Cincinnati, and St. Mary's Seminary, in Cleveland, Ohio. He earned his M.A. in Sociology, with a minor in Psychology, from the Catholic University of America. In World War II he served in the United States Army Finance Corps. His past clerical assignments were at St. Francis, Medina, Ohio; St. Martha's in Akron, Ohio; and at Immaculate Conception, Akron, Ohio. His present assignments include Diocesan Director of Family Counseling, since 1967; Diocesan Chaplain Christian Family Movements; Lecturer, St. John's College, in Cleveland, Ohio; Instructor, St. Mary's Seminary, also in Cleveland; Part-time Assistant, Holy Family Parish, Cleveland; Instructor, Notre Dame College, Cleveland, Ohio; Consultant, Educational Research Council of America; and Special Assistant to the Chief of Chaplains, United States Air Force in the Far East in 1969.

MARY S. CALDERONE has been the Executive Director, since 1964, of the Sex Information and Education Council of the United States (SIECUS), in New York City. From 1953 to 1964 she was Medical Director, Planned Parenthood Federation of America; from 1949 to 1953 she was School Physician, Public Schools of Great Neck, New York; and from 1942 to 1943 she served the American Public Health Association's Merit System Examination Service in New York City. She earned the B.A. from Vassar College, and her M.D. from the University of Rochester Medical School. Her M.P.H. was earned from the Columbia University School of Public Health. She is the recipient of many honors, including "Spirit Of Achievement" Award, Women's Division, Albert Einstein College of Medicine in 1969; "Woman of Conscience" Award, National Council of Women of the United States, in 1968; University Citation to Alumni, University of Rochester, in 1968; Doctor of Medical Science (Hon.), Women's Medical College of Pennsylvania, in 1967; 1966 Personality-of-the-Year; Collier's 1967 Year Book; Certificate of Honor, The American Association of Planned Parenthood Physicians, New York, in 1964; and Distinguished Service Award, Mental Health Association of Nassau County of New York, in 1958. She is listed in *Who's Who in America, Who's Who of American Women,* and *Current Biography.* Her memberships include American Medical Association; New York County Medical Society; Fellow, American Public Health Association; American Medical Women's Association; Affiliate, American Association of Marriage and Family Counselors; and Affiliate, American Orthopsychiatric Association. She is a member of the Board of Directors, American Association for World Health Organization, Inc., and United States Committee for WHO. Among her numerous publications are *Abortion in the United States, Release from Sexual Tensions,* and *Manual of Contraceptive Practice.*

WILLIAM LANGLEY CARRINGTON is the older of two sons of an Episcopal Minister. He qualified in Medicine and Surgery at the University of Melbourne, Australia, in 1923 and obtained his senior medical degree, M.D., in 1925. After one and one-half years of internship at the Royal Melbourne Hospital, one year as Lecturer in Pathology at the Melbourne University, and three years as Medical Tutor at Trinity College attached to the University, he accepted the appointment of Medical Superintendent at the Alfred Hospital, Melbourne, which he held for more than three years. From 1930 to 1952 he conducted a Family Doctor practice but found himself becoming more and more involved in psychological medicine and in marital problems. He became associated in 1948 with the Marriage Guidance Council of Victoria. From 1953 to 1957 he was Foundation President of the National Marriage Guidance Council of

Australia. In 1952 he visited Great Britain for Post Graduate Study in Psychiatry at Maudsley Hospital, London, and attended Tavistock Clinic and other institutions. From 1935 to 1964 he acted as Honorary Lecturer in Pastoral Psychology at Ridley College, the Episcopal Theological Seminary of Melbourne, and was one of the pioneers of this work in Australia. His first major work, *Psychology, Religion and Human Need,* grew out of that experience. Since 1943 he has been a regular broadcaster over national and commercial stations in Australia and is in constant demand as a speaker and lecturer. He is still in full-time medical practice in Melbourne, dividing his time between emotional disorders and marital difficulties. His second major book, *The Healing of Marriage,* was published in 1961. He has been a Foreign Affiliate of the American Association of Marriage and Family Counselors.

LeMON CLARK, M.S., M.D., is in private practice as an obstetrician and gynecologist in Fayetteville, Arkansas. He served as instructor in economics and social science at Cornell University for six years before going to the University of Chicago and Rush Medical School. He is a member of the American Association of Marriage and Family Counselors, and served as vice-president of the organization in 1969. He is a Fellow of the Society for the Scientific Study of Sex, the American Geriatric Society, and the Royal Society of Medicine in Londan, England. For the past ten years he has served as Correspondence Editor for *Sexology* Magazine. He has written six books in the field of sex education and marital adjustment.

JOHN W. CRANDALL earned his B.A. from Columbia College of Columbia University, the B.D. from Princeton Theological Seminary, and the Ed.D. from Teachers College of Columbia University. He is an ordained minister of the Presbyterian Church, and is currently pastor of First Presbyterian Church, Whitestone, Long Island, New York. He is a clinical member of the American Association of Marriage and Family Counselors; Staff member of Community Guidance Service, in New York City; Staff member of the Long Island Consultation Center, in Forest Hills, New York; and his practice includes marriage counseling, parent counseling, family therapy and individual psychotherapy.

WILLIAM F. EASTMAN, Ed.D., A.C.S.W., is Assistant Professor of Marriage Counseling, Department of Psychiatry, University of North Carolina Medical School, and Marriage Counselor in the Student Health Service at the University of North Carolina in Chapel Hill. In these capacities he offers a premarital and marital counseling service for the 16,000 member student body; teaches and supervises marriage and family counseling with medical students and psychiatric residents; researches the problems and needs of student marriages and premarital relationships; and consults with administrators regarding mental health aspects of campus life. He served as President of the North Carolina State Association of Marriage Counselors from 1967 to 1969, holds memberships in the American College Health Association, the American Personnel and Guidance Association, the American Public Health Association, and the National Council on Family Relations; and is a member of the Admissions Committee of the American Association of Marriage and Family Counselors.

ALBERT ELLIS has M.A. and Ph.D. degrees in Clinical Psychology from Columbia University and has been a psychotherapist and marriage and family counselor for over twenty-five years. He was formerly Chief Psychologist of the Department of Institutions and Agencies of the State of New Jersey and is now Executive Director of the Institute for Rational Living and Director of Clinical Services of the Institute for Advanced Study in Rational Psychotherapy in New York City. He has been President of the Division of Consulting Psychology of the American Psychological Association, President of the Society for the Scientific Study of Sex, and Vice-president of the American Academy of Psychotherapists. He is also a Fellow of the American Sociological Association, the American Association of Marriage and Family Counselors, the American Orthopsychiatric Association, and the Association for Applied Anthropology. He is the author of over two hundred and fifty articles and of many books, including *Sex Without*

Guilt, A Guide to Rational Living, Creative Merriage, The Encyclopedia of Sexual Behavior, The Art and Science of Love, and *Reason and Emotion in Psychotherapy.*

DAVID GOODMAN was a Pulitzer scholar at Columbia University where he earned his A.B., A.M. and Ed.D. degrees. For twenty-five years he was principal of the Rhodes School, the largest private school in New York City. His column, "What's Best for Your Child," now retitled "Marriage, Children and You," was started fifteen years ago in the Bergen Evening Record and is now syndicated and published in forty-five newspapers from coast to coast. His book, *A Parents' Guide to the Emotional Needs of Children,* was "recommended first purchase for psychology sections, college and public libraries" by the Library Journal. He is also the author of *What's Best for your Child—and You, Guidelines for a Healthy Marriage, Living from Within—the Art of Appreciation.* He is a member of the American Association of Marriage and Family Counselors, the National Council on Family Relations, and the Society for the Scientific Study of Sex. He has contributed to the *Encyclopedia of Sexual Behavior.*

ROBERT J. GOODSTEIN is a counselor in Student Personnel Services in South Brunswick Public Schools. He attended Panzer College, now a school affiliated with Montclair State College, and graduated with a B.A. degree in Physical Education. He was a health teacher for six years in Rahway, New Jersey. He was awarded a Fellowship to the University of Connecticut in 1967 for Family Life Institute and is presently working towards his Master's degree in Family Life and Sex Education. He is involved with in-service training for teachers, adult sex education and counseling pregnant teen-agers, frequently lecturing in central New Jersey areas to provide information about how to institute sex education programs. He is a member of the New Jersey Education Association and the National Council of Family Relations.

REVEREND MATTI JOENSUU, D.D., is Executive Secretary of the Board of Family Questions of the Lutheran Church of Finland, Helsinki. He is the founder of the church family counseling services in Finland and has worked in family counseling since 1944. He served from 1965 to 1968 in the headquarters of the World Council of Churches in Geneva, Switzerland, as expert of family counseling and family education. He is a Foreign Affiliate of the American Association of Marriage and Family Counselors and of the American Association of Pastoral Counselors. The AAPC honored him with its annual Distinguished Contribution Award in 1968.

MERLE R. JORDAN is a "Down Easter" from the State of Maine. He grew up in South Portland, Maine, and received his A.B. from Bowdoin College. Following his theological education at Andover Newton Theological School, he served churches in Maine and California. Later he received his Th.D. degree from the School of Theology at Claremont, California, in the field of pastoral counseling. He spent a one-year internship in marriage counseling and psychotherapy at the Merrill-Palmer Institute in Detroit. He served for almost five years as the assistant director of the Pastoral Counseling Service of the Los Angeles Baptist City Mission Society. From 1966 to 1969 he served as Associate Professor of Pastoral Care and Counseling at the Divinity School of Silliman University in Dumaguete City, Philippines. In 1969 he became an Associate Professor at the Boston University School of Theology in the Department of Psychology of Religion and Pastoral Care. He is a member of the American Association of Marriage and Family Counselors and American Association of Pastoral Counselors and is a licensed family counselor in the State of California.

SISTER M. CATHERINE deRICCI KILLEEN, O.P. is the Elementary School Supervisor for the Dominican Sisters of Caldwell, New Jersey. She has been an educator of nineteen years experience and has taught in the elementary and junior high schools of New Jersey; she has also been a lecturer in the Department of Educational Administration and Supervision, School of Education of Seton Hall University. Her school was one of the original pilot schools to implement a sex education program on the junior high level. She also served as one of the coordinators for developing an in-service curriculum for teachers of sex education in New

Jersey at Montclair State College in Montclair, New Jersey, under the direction of Dr. Charity Runden, head of the Human Sexuality Institute. She received an A.B. degree from Caldwell College and an M.A. from Seton Hall University. She did postgraduate work in Clinical Psychology at Loyola University in Chicago and is presently a doctoral candidate in School Psychology. She is a member of the National Council of English Teachers, American Personnel and Guidance Association, New Jersey Education Association, Department of Elementary Administrators, and the National Association of College and University Teachers.

JOSEPH C. LANDRUD is a clinical psychologist in private practice of individual and group psychotherapy, marriage and family counseling in El Monte, California. He is an ordained minister on the staff of Lutheran Church of the Cross, Arcadia, California (The American Lutheran Church) ; and is President of the Southern California Association of Marriage Counselors. He obtained his B.S. from the University of Oregon, the B.Th. from Luther Theological Seminary in St. Paul, Minnesota, the M.Th. with a major in Psychology and Counseling from the Southern California School of Theology, Claremont, California, and his Th.D. also from the Southern California School of Theology. His professional memberships include American Psychological Association, American Association of Marriage and Family Counselors, American Academy of Psychotherapists, American Association of Pastoral Counselors, California State Psychological Association, National Council on Family Relations, International Transactional Analysis Association, and Academy of Religion and Mental Health.

RUTH LEDER is Assistant Director of Training and a member of the teaching and supervising faculties at the Postgraduate Center for Mental Health in New York. She is the author of numerous articles in the mental health field. She earned her B.A. from Hunter College of the City University of New York, her M.A. degree from Columbia University, and her Ph.D. degree from Yeshiva University. Since 1962 she has also been in private practice in psychotherapy, psychoanalysis, and group therapy in New York City.

EUGENE B. LINTON was born in Kunsan, Korea, where his parents were missionaries of the Presbyterian Church of the United States. He earned his B.S. degree from Davidson College, and his M.D. from Medical College of Virginia. From 1959 to 1962 he was Chief of the Department of Obstetrics and Gynecology in the Acuff Clinic, Knoxville, Tennessee, and served as Assistant Clinical Professor of Obstetrics and Gynecology at the University of Tennessee. From 1962 to 1965 he was Instructor in the Department of Obstetrics and Gynecology, Bowman Gray School of Medicine, Wake Forest University, in Winston-Salem, North Carolina. Since 1965 he has been Assistant Professor in the Bowman Gray School of Medicine, Wake Forest University, and is Chief of the Gynecologic Service and the Gynecologic Oncology Service. He is certified by the American Board of Obstetrics and Gynecology. Among his memberships are Medical Society of the State of North Carolina, American Medical Association, North Carolina Obstetrics and Gynecology Society, and the Continental Gynecologic Society. He has published widely in professional journals.

DAVID R. MACE, Ph.D., is currently Professor of Family Sociology and a staff member of the Behavioral Sciences Center at the Bowman Gray School of Medicine of Wake Forest University in Winston-Salem, North Carolina. He was a founder of the Marriage Guidance Council in England and its Executive Director for seven years before coming to the United States; and has served in this country, also for seven years, as Executive Director of the American Association of Marriage and Family Counselors. In addition he has been President of the National Council on Family Relations, President of the Sex Information and Education Council of the United States (SIECUS), Vice-president of the International Union of Family Organizations, and Consultant in Family Life to the World Council of Churches. He has published numerous books and articles in professional journals and has traveled throughout the world lecturing on marriage problems.

REVEREND PAUL MARX, O.S.B., is Professor of Marriage at Saint John's University and the College of Saint Benedict at Collegeville and Saint Joseph, Minnesota. Ordained in 1947, he received his doctorate in sociology from the Catholic University of America in 1957. Besides lecturing on marriage to groups across the country, on radio and television and writing articles on family life, he is an experienced marriage educator and counselor. In collaboration with John Quesnell, he has made several series of tapes on updating marriage and parenthood in the twentieth century for Audio-Education and Argus.

DONALD J. McCULLOCH, M.D., F.R.C.P. (C), is a psychiatrist and Director of the Advisory Bureau of the University of Toronto. For nine years he was Director of the Out-Patient Department of the Ontario Hospital in Toronto. He is an Associate Professor in the Department of Psychiatry of the University of Toronto.

THOMAS G. McGINNIS, Ed.D., is Director and sponsor of the Counseling and Psychotherapy Center, Fair Lawn, New Jersey, and a psychotherapist and marriage counselor in private practice. He is Associate Professor and specialist in human sexuality, marriage and family life education, New York University's Graduate School of Education. He is the author of *Your First Year of Marriage* and *A Girl's Guide to Dating and Going Steady.* He is President-elect of the American Association of Marriage and Family Counselors; Vice-president, American Association of Sex Educators and Counselors; Executive Board, International Union of Family Organizations (Paris, France) ; and a member, Board of Marriage Counselor Examiners of State of New Jersey. Among offices formerly held, he was President, New Jersey Association of Marriage Counselors and Chairman, New Jersey State Community Mental Health Advisory Council. He is President-elect, New Jersey Association of Mental Hygiene Clinics. He is a member of the American Psychological Association, American Academy of Psychotherapists, Academy of Psychologists in Marital Counseling, and National Association of Social Workers. He is a licensed psychologist and marriage counselor in the State of New Jersey. He has delivered professional papers abroad and has traveled widely in Europe, Russia and other Iron Curtain countries, studying patterns of sexual behavior, marriage and family life.

JOHN O. MEANY is an Associate Professor of Education at the University of Notre Dame where he is the Coordinator of the (Graduate) Counseling and Guidance Program. He has a Ph.D. degree in Psychology. He was formerly a partner in the Associated Psychological Consultants of Los Angeles. He was a psychologist with Metropolitan State Hospital in Los Angeles and the System Development Corporation in Santa Monica, California. He is a member of the American Academy of Psychotherapists and the American Psychological Association, and is on the Editorial Board of the *Catholic Psychological Record.*

DAVID O. MOBERG is Professor of Sociology and Chairman of the Department of Sociology and Anthropology, Marquette University, Milwaukee, Wisconsin. Prior to joining that department in 1968, he was a member of the faculty of Bethel College, St. Paul, Minnesota, for nineteen years and Chairman of its Department of Social Sciences from 1952 to 1968. During sabbatical leaves, he was a Fulbright Professor in The Netherlands (1957-58) and West Germany (1964-65) . He earned his M.A. degree from the University of Washington and his Ph.D. degree in Sociology from the University of Minnesota. He is a member of numerous professional societies, including the American Sociological Association, Gerontological Society, Religious Research Association, Society for the Scientific Study of Religion, and the American Scientific Affiliation. He is the author of *The Church as a Social Institution; Inasmuch: Christian Social Responsibility in the Twentieth Century; The Church and the Older Person* (with Robert Gray) ; and of a large number of professional articles in many journals and books. He is the current editor of the *Review of Religious Research* and is an associate editor of *Sociological Quarterly* and *Social Compass.*

DONALD D. MOORE is a psychologist and marriage counselor and holds the degrees of B.S.

from Davidson College, B.D. from Southeastern Baptist Theological Seminary, M.A. from Appalachian State University, and the Ph.D. from the University of North Carolina at Chapel Hill. He is currently Director of Counseling and Associate Professor of Pastoral Care at Southeastern Baptist Seminary, and maintains a limited private practice (marriage counseling) in Wake Forest, North Carolina. His memberships include the American Association of Marriage and Family Counselors, American Psychological Association, and Phi Delta Kappa. He has published articles in the areas of interpersonal relationships, problems of school desegregation, techniques of premarital and marital counseling, and sex education.

ETHEL M. NASH is Clinical Associate Professor of Obstetrics and Gynecology at the University of North Carolina School of Medicine. She is also a member of the Faculty of University of North Carolina Population Center and formerly served as President of the American Association of Marriage and Family Counselors, and a Member of the Board of SIECUS. She is currently a member of the Board of Directors of the National Council on Family Relations.

A. E. KEIR NASH earned his A.B. from Harvard College, the M.A. from University of North Carolina, and the Ph.D. from Harvard University. He is Assistant Professor of Political Science, University of California at Santa Barbara. He is a former Fellow of the Federal Republic of Germany and a Woodrow Wilson Scholar and has published numerous articles in legal journals.

STEPHEN NEIGER, Ph.D., M.D., is a psychologist and marriage counselor in private practice. For eleven years he was a senior psychologist at Toronto Psychiatric Hospital (Department of Psychiatry, University of Toronto). He is a Fellow of the Society for the Scientific Study of Sex, and Co-Editor of the *Journal of Sex Research* and the Founder of the Sex Information and Education Council of Canada.

RIGHT REVEREND MONSIGNOR JOHN J. O'SULLIVAN, S.T.D., is formerly Dean of Studies at St. Paul Seminary, St. Paul, Minnesota. He also taught a marriage course at St. Catherine's College and earlier taught at the Catholic University of America in Washington, D.C., where he was chaplain to the students and taught in the School of Arts and Sciences. He is presently pastor of The Church of the Visitation in Minneapolis, Minnesota.

LLOYD G. PHILLIPS has been Director of the Marriage Guidance Council of Victoria, Australia, since 1966. Following graduation from the University of Melbourne, he pursued theological studies and was ordained as a Methodist Minister in 1945. He was trained as a marriage counselor in 1954 and soon became a leader in marriage counseling and family life education in Australia. He was Secretary of the National Marriage Guidance Council from 1960-67 and has been Secretary of the Conference of Marriage Guidance Organizations since its inception in 1962. In 1964 he conducted a special series of seminars in New Guinea. In December, 1966, he was one of the Australian representatives to the I.U.F.O. Conference on the Family in New Delhi, India. He is a Foreign Affiliate of the American Association of Marriage and Family Counselors.

JOHN G. QUESNELL, A.C.S.W., is a marriage counselor, lecturer, an instructor at the Saint Paul Seminary, and President of the Minnesota Association of Marriage Counselors. He received his Master's degree from the University of Minnesota's Graduate School of Social Work and the certificate for a year's special training at the Family Life Center of Minnesota. He is presently Director of Family Services at the Catholic Welfare Services of Minneapolis.

CLIFFORD B. REIFLER, M.D., M.P.H., is Assistant Professor of Psychiatry, University of North Carolina Medical School, Assistant Professor Mental Health in the School of Public Health, and Senior Psychiatrist for the University of North Carolina Student Health Service. His duties include administrative responsibility of development and operation of programs relating to Student Mental Health in the University and teaching at graduate and postgraduate levels in both the Medical School and in the School of Public Health. His particular research interests are in the epidemiology of college mental health and in the social psychiatry of late adolescence. He is a Fellow of the American Public Health Association, holds memberships in the American Psychiatric Association, the American College Health Association, the American Medical Association, the American Psychosomatic Society, and the American Association for the Advancement of Science.

IRA L. REISS received his Ph.D. degree in sociology from the Pennsylvania State University. After teaching at colleges in the East, he went to the University of Iowa in 1961. In the fall of 1969, he joined the Department of Sociology at the University of Minnesota as Professor of Sociology and Director of the Family Study Center. He has published two books and many articles and has received several research grants from the National Institute of Mental Health. He is presently working on a book on the American family system.

ISADORE RUBIN, Ph.D., had been Editor of *Sexology* since 1956 and was an officer and a member of the Board of the Sex Information and Education Council of the United States (SIECUS) from its inception until January, 1969. He obtained a doctorate in Public Health from the New York University School of Education, with a dissertation in the field of adolescent sex education. His book, *Sexual Life After Sixty,* has made an important contribution and has been reprinted in nine foreign editions. His articles have appeared in many professional journals and books. He was an affiliate of the American Association of Marriage and Family Counselors, a Fellow of the Society for the Scientific Study of Sex, a member of the Advisory Committee of the American Association of Sex Educators and Counselors, a member of the SIECUS Publications Committee, and Book Review Editor of the SIECUS *Newsletter.*

CHARITY EVA RUNDEN, M.A., M.S.P.H., Ph.D., is Executive Director of the Educational Foundation for Human Sexuality and Professor of Psychology and Education at Montclair State College. She was formerly Acting Dean of the Graduate Division of Western Illinois University and has been Associate Chairman of Graduate Studies at Montclair State College. She is the author of *Twentieth Century Educators,* has edited *Selected Readings for Sex Education,* and produced a tape, "Why Sex Education in the Schools?" A number of her articles have appeared in professional journals. She has lectured widely on subjects concerned with human sexuality and sex education.

TATSUO SAMEJIMA studied marriage counseling in 1956-57 at the Marriage Council of Philadelphia, Division of Family Study, Department of Psychiatry, School of Medicine, University of Pennsylvania. On his return to Japan he continued to practice marriage counseling at Tokyo Family Court. In 1961 he was appointed by the Supreme Court the Training Supervisor in all of forty-nine Family Courts as Professor of Research and Training Institute for the Japanese Family Court Workers. He is a Foreign Affiliate of the American Association of Marriage and Family Counselors.

GERALD SANCTUARY is the International Representative of Sex Information and Education Council of the United States, Solicitor of Supreme Court in England, and was Executive Director of the National Marriage Guidance Council from 1965 to 1969. He is qualified as a marriage counselor and family life educator in Britain and is the author of comparative study of marriage conciliation, *Marriage Under Stress.* He is a widely recognized contributor to international conferences on marriage and family life.

REVEREND FRANK A. SARGENT, JR., earned at Wheaton College his B.A. degree, the B.D. from Westminster Seminary in Philadelphia, and the Th.M. from Princeton Seminary, and is a Ph.D. candidate at Boston University in the area of psychology and religion. He is a member of the American Association of Pastoral Counselors, and an Associate Member of the American Association of Marriage and Family Counselors. From 1967 to 1969 he was Assistant Director of the Counseling Center, Inc., of Willow Grove, Pennsylvania; in 1969 he was Associate in Pastoral Care at The Pastoral Institute of Lehigh Valley, Allentown, Pennsylvania, and from 1968 to 1969 he was Pastor of First Presbyterian Church of Kutztown, Pennsylvania.

PATRICIA SCHILLER, M.A., J.D., is currently Director of a Title III Project in the District of Columbia which is concerned with training doctors, nurses, counselors, psychologists, social workers, and other professionals in dealing with sex, personal and family problems in a school setting with youth and parents. She is a lawyer, clinical marriage counselor, and certified psychologist whose areas of specialization are sex, marriage and family relationships, and concerned with education, research and counseling. In addition, she is currently Clinical Assistant Professor at Howard University, College of Medicine, and Executive Director of the American Association of Sex Educators and Counselors. Since 1954 she has been concerned with marriage and family relations as a marriage counselor with the Legal Aid Society, Washington, D.C.; private work in marriage counseling; advisor and group therapists to Parents Without Partners, Inc.; consultant to church and social agencies; assistant director of a research project in Personal and Family Living at Cardoza High School, D.C.; clinical psychologist and group therapist at the Webster School for Pregnant School Aged Girls, and Ionia Whipper Home, Washington, D.C. She has published articles and book reviews in *Journal of Marriage and the Family, Journal of Guidance and Counseling, One Parent Magazine, NEA Journal,* and *Sexology.* She is President of the Middle Atlantic Division of the American Association of Marriage and Family Counselors, Inc., and a member of the American Psychological Association, American Group Psychotherapy Association, National Education Association, member of the D.C. Legal Bar and D.C. Psychological Association. She is listed in *Who's Who of American Women,* and *Who's Who of the Southeast;* and is a member of Psi Chi and Pi Gamma Mu.

EMANUEL K. SCHWARTZ is Dean and Director of Training at the Postgraduate Center for Mental Health in New York; Adjunct Professor of Psychology, Graduate School of Arts and Sciences, New York University; and Clinical Professor of Psychology, Postdoctoral Program in Psychotherapy, Adelphi University. He has lectured widely and contributes articles to professional journals worldwide. He earned the B.S.S. and M.S. degrees from the City College of the City University of New York, the Ph.D. from New York University, and D.S.Sc. degree from the New School for Social Research. Since 1937 he has been in private practice in New York City. His major interests are in projective techniques, psychopathology, and personality theory. He holds Diplomate status in both Clinical Psychology, American Board of Professional Psychology, and American Board of Examiners in Psychological Hypnosis.

JOHN SEYMOUR obtained his bachelor's degree from Paterson State College and his Master's and Ph.D. degrees in Clinical Psychology from New York University. He has had five years of postdoctoral training in psychoanalysis at the National Psychological Association for Psychoanalysis in New York City. He has held the positions of Staff Psychologist at Willowbrook State School, Bird S. Coler Hospital, and the Veterans Administration Hospital in Lyons, New Jersey. He has been Chief Psychologist at the North Essex Child Guidance Center, Lakeland Guidance Center and Essex County Guidance Center, all in New Jersey. Most recently he has been Director of Psychology Training for the State of New Jersey Department of Institutions and Agencies. Presently he is Assistant Professor of Psychology at Montclair State College and Clinical Assistant Professor of Psychiatry at the New Jersey College of Medicine. He has been in private practice since 1958 and specializes in individual psychotherapy and marriage counseling. Presently he is President of the Essex County Psychological Association and is Secretary of the New Jersey Psychological Association. He is a Fellow of the American Orthopsychiatric Association. For the past three years he has been Chairman of the Psychology Section of the New Jersey Academy of Science.

HIRSCH LAZAAR SILVERMAN is a college teacher, university administrator, educational consultant, marital therapist and clinical psychologist. His many articles and essays have appeared in professional journals throughout the United States and abroad. He is the author of twelve published volumes, including the text, published in 1967, entitled *Marital Counseling: Psychology, Ideology, Science*. He presently serves as Professor and Chairman at Seton Hall University's Department of Educational Administration and Supervision. Prior to Joining Seton Hall's faculty in 1965, he served as Professor of Psychology (1959-65) and Chairman (1959-61) of the Department of Educational and School Psychology in the Graduate School of Yeshiva University. He received his baccalaureate degree from the College of the City of New York and has been awarded three Master's degrees, in areas of advanced educational study and psychological services, from New York University, City University of New York, and Seton Hall University. He earned a doctorate degree in psychology from the Graduate Division of Yeshiva University. In addition to his Ph.D. degree, he has been awarded the Sc.D. by Lane College and the LL.D. degrees by Florida Memorial College. He was secretary of the Essex County (N. J.) Psychological Association, past-president of the Academy of Psychologists in Marital Counseling and the New Jersey Association of Marriage Counselors, and past vice-president of the New Jersey Academy of Science. He is presently Chairman of the New Jersey State Board of Marriage Counselor Examiners and Treasurer of the International Council of Psychologists. He holds Fellow status in eighteen national and international professional and learned societies. In addition to inclusion in *Who's Who in America, Who's Who in American History, Who's Who in American Education, Directory of American Scholars, Who's Who in the East, American Men of Science,* and other directories, he was elected to Phi Beta Kappa (Scholarship), Psi Chi (Psychology), Phi Delta Kappa (Research), Pi Gamma Mu (Social Sciences), Sigma Xi (Science), Kappa Delta Pi (Education) and Phi Sigma Tau (Philosophy) honor societies. He is an elected member of MENSA.

ALFRED STERN, gynecologist, earned his medical degree from the University of Cologne, Germany. After completing his postgraduate years of special training at the Obstetrics and Gynecology Department of the Goethe University in Frankfurt, Germany, he practiced gynecology in Cologne, where he was named Head of the Obstetrics and Gynecology Department of the Jewish Hospital. Forced to emigrate in 1937, he went to Berkeley, California, with his wife and their two children. He fulfilled the State requirements and since 1939 has practiced his profession in Oakland. He became a diplomate of the American Board of Obstetrics and Gynecology. His practice and his activities as President of the County Mental Health Association, as Vice-president of the American Association of Marriage and Family Counselors, and as Founder and first President of the Northern California Association of Marriage Counselors, have involved him in clinical and literary work in the fields of his medical specialty and of marriage counseling. His professional memberships include American Medical Association, American College of Obstetrics and Gynecology, Deutsche Ges. f. Gyn., International Fertility Association, International College of Surgeons, American Association of Marriage and Family Counselors, and California Mental Health Association.

JOSEPH B. TRAINER earned at the University of Washington his B.S. and M. S. degrees, and his M.D. at University of Oregon Medical School. He was a University Fellow in Zoology at the University of Washington; University of Oregon Medical School, Student Assistant in Physiology and Pathology; Walter Reed Army Medical Center, Instructor in Basic Science for Medical officers. He served as Associate Professor of Physiology and Medicine at the University of Oregon Medical School, Student Health Physician with some referral practice in Internal Medicine, Fertility Problems, Sex and Marriage Counseling. His writings include Section on "Endocrinology" in *Basic Medical Physiology* by W. B. Youmans; *Human Mating and Marriage* (Physiologic Foundations for Marriage Counseling); *Decalog of Medical Marriage Counseling,* National Clearinghouse for Mental Health Information Monograph, National Institute of Mental Health; *Sex, What are the Questions* (with Gerald Egelston of Lederle Laboratories); *The Human Dimensions of Sex; Medical Marriage Counseling in Sexual Incompatibilities.* Consultant in the preparation of a Marriage Counseling Handbook by the American Medical Association, his professional societies include Phi Sigma, Sigma Xi, A.O.A., Portland Academy of Medicine, Oregon Medical Association; Multnomah County Medical Society; Staffs of St. Vincent and Physicians and Surgeons Hospitals. His civic activities include the Medical Society Committee on Public Policy, School Health Committee, Sub-committee on Sex Education, Division of Continuing Education; Oregon State System of Higher Education, Ad Hoc Committee on Sex Education for Teachers; Governor's Committee on Children and Youth, Task Force on Family Life; American Social Health Association, Past Regional Director; Oregon State Health Service Directors, Past Chairman; Honorary member, Long Beach, California Society of Obstetrics and Gynecology. He is a consultant to the Legislative Committee of State Board of Education on Sex Education in Primary and Secondary Schools.

REVEREND ACE L. TUBBS earned the B.A. degree from King College in Bristol, Tennessee, and the B.S. from Union Theological Seminary, Richmond, Virginia. He earned the Ed.D. from Teachers College, Columbia University, in Family Life Education and Counseling. He is a Chaplain (Major) in the New Jersey Air National Guard. He is a member of the American and New Jersey Association of Marriage and Family Counselors, National Council on Family Relations, Synod of New Jersey Counseling Committee (Chairman), Presbytery of Elizabeth Evangelism Committee (Chairman), Presbytery of Elizabeth Marriage Committee, Westfield Ministerium (Past President), and the Union County Mental Health Association.

REVEREND ALFRED VAIL earned the A.B. from Hobart College, the B.D. from Seabury-Western Theological Seminary, and trained at the University of Pennsylvania, School of Education (Marriage Council of Philadelphia Training Program in postgraduate counseling and family life education), University of Indiana Plan for Adult Education, Trainer Certificate, and National Training Laboratory, Community Leadership Laboratory and Program for Community Change Specialists. He is an Associate Member of the American Association of Marriage and Family Counselors, The National Council on Family Relations, and an Affiliate of the NTL Institute for Applied Behavioral Sciences. He is the Rector of The Church of the Redeemer (Episcopal), Cincinnati, Ohio; Chairman, Committee on Clergy Salaries and Pensions, Diocese of Southern Ohio; Chairman, Talent Bank Task Force Committee, Diocese of Southern Ohio; and Member, Parish-Diocese Urban Task Force (Cincinnati Group).

LELAND FOSTER WOOD has bachelor's and master's degrees from the University of Rochester, the degree of B.D. from Colgate Rochester Divinity School, and his Ph.D. from the University of Chicago. He has served as a missionary in the Congo, as Professor of Religious Education at Bucknell University, and as Professor of Social Ethics at Colgate Rochester Divinity School. He led the work of the Commission on Marriage and the Home of the Federal (now National) Council of Churches for nineteen years, and, concurrently, was Secretary of the Church Conference of Social Work for many years. His lectures and conferences took him to all parts of the United States and into Canada. He is author of many pamphlets and books, among them *Pastoral Counseling in Family Relationships, Harmony in Marriage, How Love Grows in Marriage,* and *Beatitudes for the Family.* He is now serving, part-time, on the staff of the Lake Avenue Baptist Church of Rochester, New York. He is an affiliate of the American Association of Marriage and Family Counselors.

FOREWORD

Drawing upon the interests, therapeutic activities, conceptualizations and ruminations of many contributors, Dr. Hirsch Lazaar Silverman has assembled a provocative book with a wide range of topics in the field of marriage counseling and therapy. Some of the authors are well-known marriage and family counselors, while others are clergymen, educators, physicians, sociologists and other professionals who have special interests and concerns in this interdisciplinary field. While most of the contributors are from the United States, there are representatives of other nations. This is as it should be in a book concerned with moral issues. This country is a melting pot of ideas in every area of human relationships, and it is important to keep information, ideas and perspectives flowing from scholars in other cultures and other countries.

This book is published at an important time in the development of the field of marital therapy. Differences of opinion exist over the use of the term "family therapy" rather than "marriage" or marital counseling. Some practitioners who are traditionally oriented, feel that "therapy" belongs to medicine and more specifically, psychiatry. Others with rigorous training in nonmedical fields, declare that such training makes them equally or more qualified to engage in psychotherapy. Still others insist on using the more traditional term "counseling." As editor, Dr. Silverman has avoided the pitfalls of such semantic differences, and his contributors touch upon and clarify some of these concepts in a manner which aids the reader in understanding the broad and dynamic aspects of the field of marital therapy.

Much has been written in the popular and professional press about the sexual revolution of our period in history. Increasing numbers of people, young and old, are experimenting with life styles that were considered scandalous less than a generation ago. Divorce is more frequent at every socioeconomic level according to the recent publications of the U.S. Bureau of Vital Statistics. In and around college campuses and apartment complexes, young people are experimenting with communal living, new forms of families, consensual unions without legal or ecclesiastical sanction, etc. Traditional marital and family styles, while still practiced by the majority, are being questioned and hardly a family exists without facing some problems of change. Birth control, abortion, divorce, homosexuality, extramarital liaisons, sexual adjustment, orgasm frequency, etc. have become topics for discussion in the news magazines, women's periodicals, student newspapers and religious publications as well as radio, television, and the movies. Films that were considered "stag movies" may be seen in theaters in almost every city and town. With topics that were formerly discussed only in the privacy of the therapist's office or the clergyman's study or the physician's examining room now out in the open, it is most timely that the contributors to this volume have provided such a variety of perspectives on the moral, sociological and psychological factors in contemporary marital therapy in a clear and lucid way.

This book will be useful not only to students in the fields represented but to practicing professionals and the informed lay public. In fact, the latter group would be well advised to read this volume in order to understand what goes on in marital therapy and counseling. For too long, some trained professionals in every discipline have given the illusion that they possessed secrets such as those possessed by the shaman, the medicine man and the priest. Esoteric communication, jargon and initiation rites supported this stance. The educated layman is now more capable of reading and understanding, and with increased understanding, he will be more capable of choosing a well-qualified, carefully trained therapist to join him in finding not only the roots of his marital difficulties but also greater fulfillment and satisfactions within himself, his marriage and his family. To this end the forty-seven authors join in bringing together a wide-ranging and fascinating volume about marriage, the family and about life itself. It is worthy of careful reading.

EDWARD J. RYDMAN, PH.D.

PREFACE

My own interest now, as always, is the way people organize their lives. That is why I particularly enjoyed the work of editing this volume and contributing my thinking to it.

This is a book on marriage counseling and therapy. It deals with human beings. In this sense, this is a subjective book. There is, of course, no possible attempt at being fully representative of the field in all aspects (despite the fact I did invite all branches of thought-practitioners to contribute chapters).

This volume is concerned with the development of marital therapy, especially in the United States, its present status and significant trends that are already manifesting themselves to the point of reshaping the field. Consideration also is given to those significant innovations that are influencing constructive thought in marriage counseling.

As Editor I was often tempted to revise radically the phrasing, expressiveness, even format of the text and bibliographic references; but, for the most part, I have not taken the liberty to alter the emphasis, the outlook, the modes of expression, and the like, of each of the contributors. Not that I necessarily agree with all that has been written or implied by all the writers; but, again for the most part, each of them certainly has a message worthy of study and rumination.

In a sense, this volume is an effort in conceptual itinerary, a formula, a theorization. It is a kind of guided review of a field which encroaches upon the self-consciousness of most people.

I hope this book may be widely read by younger as well as older people, by clinicians as well as laymen, by students as well as teachers in the field of marital counseling and therapy.

The book certainly has shortcomings. As Editor I recognize this fact, but I hope they are minimal. Perhaps some paragraphs here and there may need additional revisions, more accurate editing, more amplification, more correction. But, in any case, this volume presents a series of interrelated investigations, all bearing on a common set of problems.

The chapters in this book are different in length, format, emphasis—hopefully adding flavor to the volume, and making it more readable, challenging and provocative.

Again, in the revision of the individual chapters, the Editor sedulously tried to maintain each author's own flavor of presentation—even at the risk of allowing at times some obsolescence of expression, some abstractions of viewpoints, even some inconsistencies in logic, in some cases. Some chapters are brilliant in concept; others are fluent in expression mostly. It is hoped that the strength of this volume may be judged rightly in a broad, intelligently-emancipated manner, with enlightened viewpoint and conceptualization.

This is an unpretentious book, written intentionally without jargon or pedantry, with descriptive and illustrative material cut to a minimum. But I hope it will be among the books which will change men's minds about the field of marital therapy. If some of the ideas developed in these chapters may in time (if not now) seem self-evident, it is because, hopefully, they may become part of our thinking in the field.

HIRSCH LAZAAR SILVERMAN

ACKNOWLEDGMENTS

IN THE COMPLETION of this volume I am grateful to a number of individuals. My colleagues and associates in the New Jersey Association of Marriage and Family Counselors have kindly suggested from time to time areas of emphasis in this book, and I am appreciative for their interest.

My publisher deserves special thanks for consistent encouragement and for remarkable patience with me as Editor. Particular gratitude goes to Mr. Payne Thomas for helpful advice. I express personal thanks to Mrs. C. E. Hildreth, Associate Editor, for suggestions that were always intelligent and valuable. In fact, the entire staff of the Editorial Department of Charles C Thomas, Publisher, has been most cooperative, and I thank them sincerely, individually and collectively.

I am indebted to the authors of the individual chapters for their cooperation and unfailing interest.

I am appreciative for the patience and understanding of my wife and children for their reasonableness and thoughtfulness in the many months of work and time spent in the editing of this volume. Humbly do I dedicate this volume to them in love.

In the preparation of this manuscript, I have had the valuable assistance of Mrs. Catherine Sedlak, for whose secretarial help and sound suggestions I am indeed grateful.

To Dr. John H. Callan, Dean of the School of Education of Seton Hall University, am I appreciative for thoughtful inspiration to continue research and contribute to knowledge.

To the distinguished writer of the Foreword to *Marital Therapy: Moral, Sociological and Psychological Factors,* I am personally appreciative for friendship and professional interest. Dr. Edward J. Rydman, Executive Director of the American Association of Marriage and Family Counselors, has helped the national Association enhance the profession of marriage and family counseling not only in the United States but internationally.

H.L.S.

CONTENTS

SECTION II
SOCIOLOGICAL FACTORS

SECTION III
MORAL FACTORS

SECTION IV
COMPREHENSIVE EVALUATION:
MARITAL THERAPY CONCEPTS

MARITAL THERAPY
Moral, Sociological and Psychological Factors

By the same author

SECTION I
PSYCHOLOGICAL FACTORS

Chapter 1

SEX EDUCATION IN THE UNITED STATES:
A FRESH LOOK

MARY S. CALDERONE

M UCH IS BEING DISCUSSED and written about sexual behavior in the United States: depending on the source, some of these things may be true, but many are not. Those that are true often bear no statistical relevance to the thousands of husbands and wives who live hard-working monogamous lives as full and equal partners in planning, bearing and educating their children, homemaking, working, worshipping, and recreation. And certainly for every ten young people who might smoke marijuana, bear illegitimate children, become hippies, drop out of school, or get into trouble with the law, there are ninety who do none of these things but work hard to stay in school, finish college, take jobs, and prepare themselves for life.

Yet it has for some time been obvious that sexual patterns are changing as rapidly as are other factors today. All over the world as well as in the United States, men and women are changing in their natures as men and women, in their roles and relationships to each other, and in their erotic interchanges. Certainly attitudes about sex acts and sexual behavior as mirrored in the motion pictures, television, and magazines—even in the home magazines—are also changing. To observe these changes, in an endeavor to make some sense out of their patterns, so that incoming generations might be helped towards an orientation about the role of sex in life that would be more relevant to today's needs and times, the Sex Information and Education Council of the United States, SIECUS, was founded in May of 1964 as a nonprofit organization that would seek support from foundation grants and from private contributions. The six founders were a Protestant clergyman, a lawyer, a family life educator, a sociologist, a public health educator, and a physician also trained in public health. Soon afterwards representatives of other professions joined the group: psychiatry, gynecology, pediatrics, education at all school and university levels including medical education, psychology, marriage counseling, publishing, the communications media, Roman Catholic and Jewish clergy, and business. These approximately fifty leading men and women serve three-year terms and work in committees, meet together periodically, and engage themselves closely in the policies and activities of the organization.

The basic purpose of SIECUS is clearly stated, and to read it carefully is to understand some of the questions about sex that SIECUS believes need clarification: is it simply a basic animal drive, as so many profess to believe, or does it manifest itself in ways specific to the human condition? If so, in what kinds of different ways? The mating of animals is governed by such clearly identified forces of nature as climate, temperature, length of day, state of nutrition, etc., but the human sexual urge manifests itself independently of such factors. Perhaps the most striking difference is that, whereas in lower mammals the urge to copulate relates, with few exceptions, specifically to the time of ovulation, the human female can and does receive the male at any time during her monthly cycle, with such peaks of desire as have been observed occurring for the most part just before and just after the menstrual period rather than in mid-cycle when ovulation is most likely to take place.

There is certainly no other integral and universal function of the human body that is regarded or treated so differently in different parts of the world, by different people, by different social classes, by different religions, and by the two sexes: it is looked upon as only for procreation, for recreation, as a right, a privilege, an obligation; it is used as an expression of love, of hate or hostility, of violence, as a form of communication, a status symbol, or a means to sell goods.

Furthermore, in spite of its intensity and universality, it is nevertheless one physiological function that is not essential to remaining alive, and it can be so influenced by any one of many factors that its exercise may not ever manifest itself at all (as in the "frigid" female), or may manifest itself to the point of obsession (as in compulsive promiscuity), or may be postponed at will and indefinitely (as in self-imposed continence), or may be so profoundly altered in its nature by external or internal circumstances that its manifestation may appear in forms that do not conform to the norms of the immediately surrounding society (as with incest). It is also the one physiological function that man has universally subjected to rigid laws, proscriptions, discussions, deliberate panderings, deliberate stimulation, deliberate denial; and as one of the normal physiological functions it has been observed to have more differences in expression and moralities that are related to social class than any other. Additionally it is the physiological function whose use or abuse is or has been most keyed into the morality value systems of every society and regarding whose employment or enjoyment external authorities, primarily ecclesiastic in Western societies have provided the often rigid rules.

Now man finds himself in the era of democracy, in which the individual human being is more and more expected to take full responsibility for himself, his decisions, his behavior. It is an age in which science and religion have been moving ever closer together to find rational bases for patterns of human living. In the face of the chaotic confusion of sexual behavior now observed in many societies, of diametric differences of personal belief about sex and its role in life, and particularly in the face of the almost instant communication that now takes place across the face of the world, it becomes imperative that thinking men and women should together consider this universal and central area of man's life.

DEFINITIONS

First, what do we understand by the word "sex"? Aside from its gender meaning, to each one of us it can mean something different at different times and circumstances in our lives, but generally speaking, for most people sex means coitus, the *act* of sex. But increasing numbers of people are seeking to discover new meanings more relevant and more revealing to our needs as evolving human beings. The old Christian concept that sex was an act to be performed by conjugal partners for the specific purpose of reproduction was in hard actuality never consistently validated by the way in which human beings really used it. The begrudging religious admission that an ancillary purpose was "to allay concupiscence" clearly applied only to males and simply served to relegate erotic sex to an animal-like, male-dominated status. Today, all religions affirm clearly the bipartite and co-equal roles of sex: for reproduction, and for establishing and deepening the all-important relationship between a man and a woman joined in the life partnership of marriage.

But this does not go far enough for those skilled in the sciences relating to human behavior to document a fact that simple human beings have long demonstrated in their daily existence: we do not suddenly become sexual persons on the day of marriage, nor even at puberty; we are legitimately and normally sexual from the very day of birth, although the terms in which we express sexuality vary greatly from age to age and circumstance to circumstance. Anna Freud, the great child analyst, put it this way in 1935:

> The sexual instincts of man do not suddenly awaken between the thirteenth and fifteenth year, i.e. at puberty, but operate from the outset of the child's development, change gradually from one form to another, progress from one state to another, until at last adult sexual life is achieved as the final result from this long series of developments.

If we, as citizens of different societies, do not like the "final result" as we observe it around us in "adult sexual life," and if we recognize that the old, simple rules of behavior, which never operated very well anyway, now operate even less well in our ever more complex world—then, if we want to change the results we shall have to take the trouble to understand the long, psychodynamic process by which the child evolves as a sexual being. If we do not understand the process, then how shall we become capable of modifying it so that the final results would please us better, or teach husbands and wives their roles as parents?

In point of fact, as today we study the psychosexual evolution of the human being, we see that it is not a single process but rather a complex of a number of processes, each one of which proceeds at its own rate, sometimes independently of, and at other times influencing or being influenced by, one or more of the others as well as by many external factors. If we call the entire process one of *sexualization,* by which the individual develops his sexuality, his sexual identity, then we must establish where and when that one part of sex that is so nodal, that is, erotic or genital pleasure, fits in to the whole.

PROCESSES

On the physical or physiological side we begin with the establishment at birth of the biological sex, not only in terms of the external genital anatomy that enables us to assign to the baby the gender of male or female, but also in terms of its internal anatomy, chromosomes, and hormones. During infancy and childhood growth of the genital organs parallels growth of the other body organs, until the onset of puberty when a new physiological process begins, namely reproductive maturation. The changes occurring in this process are not one of size alone, but profoundly affect the nature and functions of the genital organs, so that the boy now has the capacity to impregnate as signalized by his ability to ejaculate, and the girl of being impregnated as signalized by the onset of menstruation.

Another genital maturation process may already have been going on, may be just beginning, or may lie in the future: genitalization, or achievement of the ability to experience genital pleasure culminating in orgasm. By definition, it is apparent that the capacity for orgasm is always achieved by the male, either at puberty in ejaculation during nocturnal emissions, or earlier by the very common experience of masturbation. Thus by the age of eighteen practically 100 per cent of males have achieved genitalization. The same is not true of females, however, for in them the achievement of genitalization is not automatically assured but is subject to many cultural or other influences. While what would appear to be orgasm is observed even in very young female infants during masturbation, it may thereafter be suppressed or, depending on the culture, orgasm may not be learned until later in life, sometimes never. Here is a major difference between males and females which results in a second major difference: the female can function reproductively without ever functioning sexually, whereas the male's reproductive functioning depends entirely on his sexual functioning.

Meanwhile certain *social* processes are also taking place that will be critical in determining the kind of adult male or female the child will turn into: given the biological sex at birth, the child must eventually become aware of his gender identity, and this he does usually by the age of three when he can say with sureness, "I am a boy" or "I am a girl." This process of the development of gender identity then continues by constant accretion, both conscious and unconscious, of what is considered to constitute masculinity and femininity by the cultural setting in which the child lives. As the child continues to grow in consciousness he must then learn and accept the sex role behaviors that his particular society has designated as appropriate to the state of being male or female, as interpreted to him and acted out (or denied) by his parents.

On the *emotional* side there must also take place the profoundly important development of the capacity to relate to other human beings in various ways and degrees of affection and closeness; on the *intellectual* side the child is required to learn facts and skills, and to reason; and on the *spiritual* side during these critical years of evolution, the child must develop the capacity for ideals and aspirations, and is expected to recognize and accept certain moral values and standards. For all of these processes his society holds up to him certain guidelines for what it expects as to his behavior and achievement.

These and other related and important maturational processes, although going on more or less concurrently, do not necessarily proceed at the same rate, nor always in harmony with or reinforcement of each other. Disturbed family structure may deprive the child of one or both adequate parental role models, with resultant difficulties in the establishment of his own gender identity. Similarly emotional deprivation due to broken homes, wars, social stress or emotional cataclysms can so truncate the development of his capacity to give and receive affection that he may be rendered forever incapable of relating in any sustained and meaningful way to another human being.

Among difficulties that have been observed are those relating to distortions in the process of genitalization. Because of its power, authorities have in the past taught fear and distrust of the genital sexual drive, a fear which adults tend to displace onto the young. Thus the process of genitalization has, in most Western cultures, been subjected to many antagonistic forces, in particular to hostility, guilt, and anxiety. These attitudes have been especially focused on masturbation which, formerly met with punishment, threats, and shame, is now very generally accepted by authorities in psychiatry and religion as a form of private communication of the individual with himself, certainly not to be regarded as ever physically harmful, but rather as a way-station in his psychosexual evolution, to be left behind when more mature sexual expression becomes appropriate.

The feelings of affectional or even of erotic attraction to a member of the same sex that are common before and during adolescence are now also being recognized as ordinarily being passing stages in evolution and not necessarily as manifestations or precursors of fixed homosexuality. Yet, while it is now clear that erotic feelings and actions can be regarded as a normal and indeed integral part of growing up, we still need clarifications; just which erotic feelings and actions, and at what moments and in what circumstances, are to be looked upon as other than "normal"? Indeed, what does constitute normality in sexuality? The range of qualified opinions is here broad, with little consensus.

In the face of these and many other as yet unanswered questions, educators, physicians, sociologists, and religious leaders in the United States are recognizing and enunciating the importance of providing for children and youth the kinds of environment and education that will enable them, while understanding and accepting their own erotic feelings and those of others, yet to learn how to manage them responsibly in harmony with the moral values and ideals of their culture. It can truthfully be said that, in view of the chaotic and changing conditions of society, and the poor example of erotic stimulation and exploitation set by adults, never before have the young had to face such a gigantic task, for what kinds of moral values can they be expected to develop in a society that extols and highlights physical sex at every turn of the road—in advertising, on the newstands, in the movies, in the magazines, the "home" magazine included, and in the lives of the few adults whom they might look upon as heroes. What is the message they get from a famous sports figure when, in an interview by a well-known sports writer published in a subscription magazine that comes into many New York homes—*not Playboy*—he declares, "The night before the. . . game I grabbed a girl and a bottle and went to the. . .hotel and stayed in bed all night. . .same thing before the. . .game. It's good for you. . ."On seeing her some months later he remarks, "You know, I only was with that girl one night? We had a few drinks and we balled and I took her phone number and that's it. Never saw her again. Only one night with the girl. And I come up with the right name. A real memory job!"

The complex of sexual maturational processes and forces can be summarized in one comprehensive term—*sexualization*. As was pointed out, much of these maturational processes lies in the realm of the unconscious, and in the days when instant communication via television and radio, etc. did not exist, parental sexual roles as acted out before the children in the home and the community were clear and unequivocal and played the major role in the sexualization process. Today in the United States instant communication brings into practically every home sexual messages that are confused and often entirely at variance with those of the parents. In particular, they emphasize erotic and genital sex at the expense of the many other aspects of sexuality. These messages constantly get through to children at the youngest ages, even before the establishment of core gender identity: the four-year-old boy in a fatherless home sits in front of the television set and watches a rock group, a western, a murder mystery, a spy chase, an anguished soap opera episode, gang violence, or the ads—"the closer he gets," "take it off, take it *all* off," "I'm not his *date,* I'm his *mother"*—which male role image will he lean to?

Each society sexualizes its children in ways characteristic of that society or sub-society: in some, the male dominates sexually and socially, and the female is neither expected nor permitted to be sexual except in prostitution or childbearing. In other cultures the male dominates sexually but the female dominates socially. The sexual natures and behaviors of the adults resulting from the differing sexualizing impacts of the two societies will differ markedly.

In the United States we have experienced two major sexual changes: we see now an open and increasing emphasis on the erotic and the genital, and we have also seen a marked evolution in the roles and natures of women—as individuals and as persons, as well as sexually. This era has been termed the era of the resexualization of woman, when women have justly come to experience erotic sexuality as an accepted part of being a woman. Yet many men feel challenged by this evolution, are hostile to it, feel sexually threatened by it, not understanding that these changes in women are part and parcel of the profound changes taking place in the world's entire social structure: man cannot any longer accept that, in the world he must build, there can exist any group that, *as a group,* is rated and treated as inferior, whether because of color of skin, religious background, nationality, or gender.

Young human beings have to be taught the proper use for their faculties, and the sexual faculties are no exception. Man will not, can not, use his sexual faculties any better or more responsibly than he has been taught in childhood and youth. If we wish man to use his sexual faculties constructively, creatively, responsibly, maturely, and lovingly, then we must so construct the educational institutions of society (home, school, church) as to produce constructive, creative, responsible, mature, and loving human beings. For, of all man's universally-endowed physiological and psychological functions, this one, his sexuality, is the one that is the most likely to be used or misused in such a way as directly and consistently to reflect either the distortions, the deprivations, the brutalizations or the joys, the securities, and the wonders of his life surroundings during his first fifteen years. The Jesuits enunciated what Wordsworth phrased in poetry: "The child is father of the man."

Thus, to enter marriage without a clear understanding that the creation of a child will require more of the two people involved than mere provision of a sperm and an egg, or of food, shelter, clothes, recreation, education, is to miss one of the fundamental moral obligations of marriage. What it will require of the marriage partners is investment of *themselves* in the person who is their child. Today this is a most awesome responsibility, to be entered into only in full knowledge and awareness of the many critical factors, positive and negative, that play a role in the eighteen-year span during which the child's character and personality unfold, and during which he should be acquiring the knowledge and attitudes to assure successful fulfillment of himself in his sexual role as male or female. To enter into parenthood should be in full awareness of the high moral commitment that this requires of man and wife.

SELECTED BIBLIOGRAPHY

Broderick, Carlfred B., and Bernard, Jessie: *The Individual, Sex and Society: A SIECUS Handbook for Teachers and Counselors.* Baltimore, The Johns Hopkins Press, 1969.

Erickson, Erik H.: The concept of identity. Daedalus, Journal of the American Academy of Arts and Sciences, Winter, 1966.

Normal Adolescence: Its Dynamics and Impact. Group for the Advancement of Psychiatry. New York, Charles Scribner's Sons, 1968.

Sex and the College Student. Group for the Advancement of Psychiatry. New York, Atheneum, 1966.

Chapter 2

PSYCHOLOGICAL IMPLICATIONS OF MARITAL THERAPY

HIRSCH LAZAAR SILVERMAN

IN ALL LIKELIHOOD, casual and unconventional marriage counseling has existed from time immemorial, perhaps for as long as the institution of marriage. People have always been ready to advise others and to seek advice, to consult and be consulted; and there is no reason for assuming that marital problems would not have come under the fascination of this natural tendency of man. In any form remotely resembling a profession, however, marital counseling is no more than four decades old in the United States.

It reflects a degree of academic pedanticism to set the exact date when marriage counseling had its origin as a profession, but the approximate date can be set and the major currents in which it originated can be noted. Albert Ellis is of the opinion that marriage counseling began in the 1920's "with the investigations and teachings of Professor Ernest R. Groves." Emily Mudd avers that, "in the United States, formalized marriage counseling services whose chief focus is the promotion of partner adjustment before and after marriage began when two clinics opened in 1928." Abraham Stone states that he, together with Hannah Stone, opened the first marriage consultation center in the United States in 1929. (This pioneer venture was followed by the founding of the American Institute of Family Relations in 1939 with Paul Popenoe as Director, and the Marriage Council of Philadelphia in 1932 directed by Emily Mudd.)

Very shortly after the founding of the aforementioned marriage counseling centers, the American Association of Marriage Counselors was formed in the year 1942.

Marriage counseling is here regarded as a specialized field of family counseling which centers largely on the interpersonal relationship between husband and wife. It involves many disciplines and is interprofessional in character. Those who wish to qualify for this field, however, whether psychiatrist, physician, clergyman, psychologist, or social worker, require a common body of scientific knowledge, techniques, and qualifications.

The "practice of marriage counseling" means the rendering of professional marriage counseling services to individuals and marital pairs, singly or in groups, whether in the general public or in organizations, either public or private. "Marriage counseling" is a specialized field of counseling

which centers largely upon the relationship between husband and wife. It
also includes premarital counseling, pre-divorce and post-divorce counseling, and family counseling which emphasizes the spousal relationship as a
key to successful family living. The practice of marriage counseling consists
of the application of principles, methods, and techniques of counseling and
psychotherapy for the purpose of resolving psychological conflict, modifying
perception and behavior, altering old attitudes and establishing new ones in
the area of marriage and family life. In its concern with the antecedents of
marriage, with the vicissitudes of marriage, and with the consequences of
the failure of marriage, marriage counseling keeps in sight its objective of
enabling marital partners and their children to achieve the optimal adjustment consistent with their welfare as individuals, as members of a family,
and as citizens in society.

Marriage is today, as it has always been, part of the social fabric, and its
structure, strengths, weaknesses, and values arise out of the particular cultural and psychological climate in which we live. In a society or group
where divorce carries limited social sanction or moral stigma, it seems probable that, given conditions of unhappiness and tension, the possibility of
divorce as a solution will arise in the individual's thinking more quickly
than were divorce still regarded as it was in our own country fifty years ago.

In order to evaluate marriage counseling, we need definitions. Marriage
counseling is different from individual (and is usually distinguished from
family) counseling in that it centers primarily on the marriage pair and the
problems arising from this paired relationship. Marriage counseling involves
two individuals plus the *relationship* between them, and is concerned not
only with the growth of two individuals as separate persons, but with growth
of these individuals as they relate to each other in a very special and intimate
way involving close emotional interaction plus a sexual relationship.

It is sometimes said that counseling is different from education in that
marriage-education and guidance involves the process of giving information, presenting new material, and correcting misconceptions; that it is usually a group situation, and is preventive rather than therapeutic. Counseling is more often individualized and tends to be concerned with problems
involving a conscious decision-making process. Therapy goes beyond and
deals primarily with the unconscious, deeper probing into what may be
crippling neurotic or psychotic conditions. It is difficult to draw any kind
of dividing line between these processes and to know with certainty when
the client is involved in an educational rather than a therapeutic experience. Marriage counseling includes from time to time and, within one
client, all three different levels.

There is little question that the key to all counseling is the counselor
himself and that counseling skill (or art) is no entity apart from the coun-

selor as a person, his knowledge and training, his life experience, his attitudes, values, perceptions and feelings.

The marriage counselor, of course, brings to the session his *self*, plus his ideas about what *man* is, what counseling is, and his set of values and attitudes specifically toward marriage and families. The counselor himself faces enough questions: Does marriage have a value in itself such that it should be preserved? Are the marriage vows fully sacred? Is it "wrong" for the mother of young children to work outside the home? Is it "bad" to be in debt? Who should compromise if a husband and wife do not share the same interests and activities? Who should give in when the pair is deadlocked in conflict? What about attitudes toward children—when is a father too strict and a mother too lenient? What standards should the parents agree on with regard to an adolescent? He faces these *not* in order to take a stand himself or to sell his special brand of beliefs, but in order to be aware of how his own feelings are entering into the relationship between him and his clients.

An awareness of one's self in terms of needs and the ways he seeks to fulfill his needs is an essential to the counselor as his awareness of his social role with all its expectations. The counselor understands his own set of values and beliefs and knows how these may enter into his perceptions of his clients and of the situations in which they find themselves. A great deal of *knowledge of self* is the prerequisite for the counselor's wise use of himself. And knowledge of self exists only where there is a sense of acceptance and comfort *with* one's self. The counselor of necessity is a person of integrity and maturity; to the extent that these are lacking, there will be flaws in his counseling relationships.

The most important aspect of counseling is the degree of quality of communication that takes place. Communication not only reveals the client's problems and feelings but provides the clues to the counselor's feelings; it is the way in which the counselor makes himself known to his client. It is the way in which the counselor takes his client "unto himself."

All the factors that we have here indicated as being pertinent to counseling situations in general are pertinent to marriage counseling—the counselor's knowledge, training, and philosophical orientation, his maturity and image of himself in the counseling realtionship. There are, however, additional factors to be considered in dealing with a couple and their marriage problems.

In contrast to individual therapy in which the counselor centers his attention primarily on the individual, the marriage counselor must keep track of *two* personalities with not only the *intra* conflicts but also those between the two; there are two sets of inconsistencies, indecisions and interpretations; and there is a whole array of perception in the interplay of feeling and action between the spouses.

Because of this complexity some counselors prefer to work with only one of the married pair; counselors with a psychoanalytic orientation almost always work with one spouse, and only if it is absolutely necessary will they have contact with the other or his therapist. However, counselors who consider themselves primarily *marriage* counselors usually want to work with *both* of the partners, and in cases where only one spouse comes for help, the counselor will encourage the other to come in. By experiencing the *interaction* between the partners as well as learning of the perceptions and expectations that each partner has, the marriage counselor has much more knowledge of his case and has much better "feel" of the situation. (Some counselors believe that to counsel only one of the married pair is as ridiculous as it would be to read only the lines of one character in a Shakespearian drama!)

Each partner needs to be evaluated or "diagnosed" as if he were an individual counseling case. The counselor enters into each individual's feeling, his perceptions and his needs. Marriages are sometimes out of kilter because one partner's neurotic demands cannot be met, or because one spouse may be psychotic or on the verge of a psychotic episode.

In addition to the assessment of each individual, the counselor looks at the couple as a *pair*—noting what each "does to" the other and in what kinds of situations. He notes how they support and encourage each other and how and where they destroy. Probably the most important area the counselor concerns himself with is that of the clients' *perceptions*.

Each spouse has a set of perceptions a) of himself, b) of his spouse, and c) of his spouse's perceptions of him. In other words, he holds three sets of ideas: there is a) his own self-concept, b) his concept of his spouse, and c) his concept of what the spouse's concept is. These may be in close agreement or widely disparate.

The client also holds a set of *expectations* of a) what he "ought" to be, b) what his spouse ought to be, c) what their relationship ought to be, and d) what his spouse's expectations are on all these.

The counselor has to keep track of the wife's perception of and expectation for herself and her feelings about herself, her perception of and expectations for and feelings about her husband, and what she thinks her husband's perception of her is, his expectations for her, and his feelings about her. The husband, too, has this same "field" in which to operate.

It is the meshing of these perceptions and expectations of both the individuals that is the basis of the *relationship:* these plus what might be considered the basic needs of each individual accounts for feelings and behavior of the couple. To encompass this tremendous amount of action as well as emotion means the counselor must be extremely alert and himself be *open* to the experiences of the counseling sessions.

A family is a collection of individuals, differing in roles, ages, and biological attributes, but nevertheless having the same fundamental needs and wants. Every individual has a need for *survival,* and in addition, wants for *productivity, intimacy, making sense and order,* and *uniqueness.* We distinguish survival *needs* from *wants.* In times of stress, the *wants* may be experienced as *needs,* as though necessary for survival. Nevertheless, as a husband of a couple in therapy expressed it, "Needs are what our three-year-old has. Wants are what we have."

Problems of many different kinds may be cited as the immediate cause of marital difficulties—money, sexual maladjustments, in-laws, children, infidelity, etc. However, the problems essentially complained of fall within the broad category of lack of consideration by one spouse for the other. The lack of consideration may be in the handling of money—selfishness about money or failure to support; it may be in the area of affection and sex—failure to respond or perform adequately sexually or undue demand or withholding; it may be in the area of work or recreation-overactivity which leaves out the spouse or laziness in meeting responsibilities; it may be in ineffectual communication or complete absence of attempt to let the partner know what is going on. But essentially, the basic complaint is that a person fails to consider his spouse's feelings, needs, values, and goals, or acts in disregard of them.

To be sure, the factor of sex is significant in the marriage relationship. Sex involves powerful feelings. Sexual conflict arising from child-of-the-past influences, which are or are not directly concerned with sex, can jeopardize or destroy the mutual-respect balance so vital to successful marriage and rearing of children. Deviations from mutual respect in the sexual area produce deep, at times irreparable, wounds. And these wounds can not only wipe out the affection, trust, and sought-after fulfillment of marriage, but can be a contributory factor of considerable significance in development of pathogenic attitudes toward children.

Unfortunately, there has been no widespread dissemination of marriage prediction information, although a number of research studies of considerable significance have been published during the past thirty-five or forty years. Several writers (among them Burgess and Wallin, and H. J. Locke) have included summaries of major, prior studies in their published reports of their own investigations. There does not, however, appear to have been any recent effort to summarize and interpret the broad range of marriage prediction studies to date, for use by psychotherapists and counselors who are not sufficiently familiar with the literature in this area.

Although most people of marriageable age consider "falling in love" the prime ingredient in any recipe for a happy marriage, the majority of counselors may agree with Ogburn and Nimkoff when they write that ". . .even today in this age of romance, it is rather in the stories on film or pulp that all practical considerations are thrown to the wind, in favor of love. Among college youth, particularly, there appears to be a growing regard for the importance of traits of personality and character in the choice of a mate." Or, as Linton puts it, "The real problem is that of providing young adults with the knowledge and especially with the point of view required for the intelligent selection of permanent partners." If therapists and counselors can be armed with predictive knowledge of factors most likely to affect marital success or failure, some ill-fated marriages may be averted.

Awareness of characteristics likely to cause trouble also prompts one to seek help from someone professionally qualified in the field of interpersonal relationships. Such a person has the knowledge and skill needed to help in the development of those capacities which promote successful relationships with others—whether in marriage or out.

Discussion, dialogue, or communication, in short, the *therapeutic process* in marriage counseling, takes for granted that the persons concerned and involved have experiences and insights which may contribute something of value to the overall problem.

Dialogue in marital therapy uses the language of the experimenter, the individual trained and competent to confront new things, seeking enlarged areas of understanding, expanding knowledge, deepening insights. Dialogue and therapy then consist of both *transmission* and *reception*.

Professional dialogue in marriage therapy includes conversation and discussion with a purpose. It is reason's only real weapon. It is a civilized procedure and operation, democratic and constructive. To take useful part in reaching decisions is to seek understanding through consideration of alternatives; and through it individuals attain insight and understanding.

Such dialogue requires *common substance,* and requires a large measure of goodwill. It begins in an act of faith; the assumption that those who are in marital counseling will speak in honesty for the purpose of reaching understanding, and with a balanced generosity toward one another. It is by comparison of views that we reason our way toward truth. We increase the odds of finding the best and most feasible solution to a marital problem by considering alternatives.

The wife and husband in a marriage relationship who believe in dialogue through marital therapy do not necessarily come to the counselor's office with a fistful of fast deals but hopefully with heads full of constructive ideas. But "facts" are worse than useless unless they are accurate. (Inaccuracy does not mean deceitfulness, but may take the form of not being particular enough to be exact.) Also, facts are different from opinion. Truly, it is not things, but people's opinions *about* things, that trouble mankind.

Mutual understanding, of course, is helped by clear definition. It often helps in marital therapy to define conflicting arguments with clarity, so as to arrive at the critical point free of nonessentials. To be sure, if at all possible early enough in the therapeutic process, the real problem is to be brought out into the open. For there are no solutions to unknown problems. (Einstein once indicated that, "The formulation of a problem is often more essential than its solution.")

The truly basic elements in a sound marital therapeutic session are unity and simplicity. Small problems are necessarily more easily solved than larger ones, but at the same time the gestalt, the pattern of the whole, must be kept in mind. The center of the answer to a marital question should be the point of the question, and the circumference no wider than is needed to answer the question adequately at the time.

After all, dialogue is seeking truth. St. Thomas Aquinas said, "An angel perceives the truth by simple apprehension, whereas man becomes acquainted with a simple truth by a process from manifold data." In marriage counseling the search involves having willingness of mind to reach out to that which is not yet fully understood, or even to something which at first repels the wife or husband, or both. When one idea supplements another, as in professional marital therapy, often a joint truth emerges from the dialogue of persons who started even with divergent beliefs.

In marital counseling there are, of course, modes of silence: that of listless ignorance even, and that of intelligent attention. It is sometimes well for the therapist, as well as the counselee, to remain silent for a brief time during a session—and think out a problem for the time. But silence is not to be confused with listening. Every participant in a marital dialogue has the duty to listen *with* interest *and* attention; for listening *intently* and asking pertinent and relevant questions provide needed information for orderly mental processing.

There have been many treatment procedures for disturbed marital interaction. Traditionally, the major form of treatment has been *individual therapy* for one of the spouses. In Eisenstein's *Neurotic Inteaction in Marriage,* the individual psychoanalysis of one of the marriage partners is almost the exclusive form of treatment. According to this approach, successful therapy for one of the partners, tends to produce a greater maturity on the treated patient's part. This often leads to a greater tolerance of the spouse's irrational behavior as well as a marked lessening of mutual destructive interaction. However, a frequent consequence of the successful treatment of one of the partners may be the termination of the marriage itself. (The treated patient apparently develops sufficient maturity and courage to break up a bad marriage.) In some instances, the improved behavior of the treated spouse may cause a rupture of the stabilized neurotic interaction of the marriage, resulting in increased disturbance and divorce.

A common, although less frequently employed procedure for handling marital interaction, is through *concurrent* therapy. Here, a separate therapist sees each of the partners. Usually the therapists work independently of each other, or they may fleetingly compare notes during some period together. Occasionally, as in the Bird and Martin "stereoscopic technique," the husband's therapist and the wife's therapist hold regularly scheduled conferences, at which time each therapist presents his view of the patient's dynamics and discusses countertransference problems.

A third form of treatment is that of *conjoint* therapy, in which the same therapist sees *both* the husband and wife in separate as well as joint miniature group therapy meetings. In this form of therapy, a much greater emphasis is placed directly on the disturbed marital *interaction* itself, although the intrapsychic forces within the individual are not ignored. (Conjoint marriage therapy has received its major impetus from the increased use of family therapy techniques as well as from the studies of Jackson, Bateson, and Haley on family interaction and communication among schizophrenic patients.) Conjoint therapy has a number of unique features. With the marriage partners present, one can immediately observe and deal with the distorted perceptions and defensive behavior that characterize so much of the disturbed marital interaction. Since the active theater of operations of the marriage is in full view, the therapist can readily see the biases and the distortions of each participant, and can bring them to their attention. In moments of crisis, one can enlist the aid of one partner in helping the other. In conjoint therapy, there is also the advantage of reduction of costs and time involved when couples are seen together.

Conditions best treated by psychotherapy are supposed to be anxieties, difficulties in adjustment, psychosomatic disorders, phobias, disturbed interpersonal relationships, marital upsets, hesitancies to engage in life's activities, behavior socially disapproved of, inability to establish contact with people, confusions, conflicts with parents, disturbed behavior manifestations, personality difficulties, and the field of psychic phenomena generally, including the area of marital counseling. But what conditions are not truly conducive to such therapy, according to the theoretical views of therapists? Psychotherapy, then, developed out of the need of modern man for direction and guidance in his stressful and complicated way of life.

Wolberg's systematic approach, in dividing all psychotherapy in three categories, appears to be rather appropriate for marital therapy, with categories of: a) supportive therapy, b) insight therapy and reeducative goals, and c) insight therapy with reconstructive goals. As the objectives for the three kinds of therapy, Wolberg sets forth:

> . . .a) Strengthening of existing defenses. Elaborating of new and better mechanisms to maintain control. Restoration to an adaptive equilibrium. b) Insight into the more conscious conflicts with deliberate efforts at readjustment goal modifications and the living up to existing creative potentials. c) Insight into unconscious conflicts, with efforts to achieve extensive alterations of character structure. Expansion of personality growth with development of new adaptive potentialities.

Psychotherapy is a form of treatment, then, for problems of emotional nature in which a trained person deliberately establishes a professional relationship with a patient with the object of removing, modifying, or retarding existing symptoms, of mediating disturbed patterns of behavior, and of promoting positive personality growth and development, in marriage problems and malfunctioning no less.

Personality growth takes into consideration the aspect of personality maturation, to assist the individual to achieve a more gratifying relationship with people in his environments. The term "personality growth" brings one back to the more philosophical aspects that deal with the potential of the human being to achieve happiness and complete fulfillment.

A person *with* difficulties is the product *of* the causes of his difficulties, mostly environmental, patterns of living, and interpersonal relationships. Summarily, psychotherapy should be looked upon—by both the patient and the therapist—as repair work on a basis of science and art, and not as a complete rebirth of the personality. For the results of therapy are necessarily limited by such factors as the caliber of the original material, as well as the individual himself (constitution plus young ego), the degree of damage (infantile traumata and adult frustrations), and what remains to be worked with (adult ego plus the reality situation). Again, the implications here for marital therapy are wide and broad and deep.

By definition, finally, "psychotherapy" is the treatment of disorders by the use of suggestion, counseling, persuasion, advising, educational direction, occupational techniques, and the like, with the purpose or goal of relieving the patient of distressing neurotic symptoms or discordant personality characteristics which interfere with his satisfactory adaptation to a world of people and events. Enough therapists have pointed out that in practice there is no sharp demarcation or delineation between effective counseling and psychotherapy. Perhaps it is not so much how marital therapy is done, but how effective it is professionally and scientifically, that is the ultimate criterion of psychotherapy. *Cure,* then, is the main relief of the patient's current difficulties, and not paramountly a life-long freedom from emotional conflict and psychological problems.

Adjustment in regard to marriage counseling must be judged and evaluated in terms of an individual's capacities to change and to meet the demands imposed on her or on him; and psychologists know that these capacities will vary with the individual's personality and with his developmental level. Adjustment is again relative, and most assuredly in marital counseling, because its qualities vary to some extent with the society or culture in which it occurs, and also because of certain individual variations.

When psychologists speak of morality, what we essentially mean, in great part at least, deals with *moral considerations,* in effect pertaining to or concerned with *right conduct* or the *distinction* between right or wrong. In this sense, psychologists may well be concerned with the *principles* or *rules* of right conduct; and are expected to express or convey truths or *counsel* as to right conduct. Scientifically, then, marital counseling by a psychologist competent in his field is founded on the fundamental principles of right conduct rather than an enactment or custom, implying at the same time, as a logical corollary perhaps, the virtuous individual, or being virtually or practically such through the effect on the mind or feelings, or on results generally. Accordingly, what is being indicated is the multifaceted areas involved in marital counseling on a psychological level, involving an almost ortho-psychiatric emphasis multidimensionally.

In essence, then, in the psychological sense *morals* and *ethics* refer to rules and standards of *conduct* and of *practice,* with *morals* referring to generally accepted customs of conduct and *right living* in a society, and to the individual's practice in relation to these, with *ethics* implying high standards of honest and honorable dealing, of methods used, and of quality of product. Right-thinking, intelligently-emancipated psychologists may then find themselves in sufficient agreement with such an interpretation.

In the practice of marital counseling, time and time again it is established that moral laws are an important aspect of reality in living; and morality itself is an essential part of the functioning of human nature. Emphasized, therefore, is the importance of moral principles for effective living and mental health. The individual with an intelligent sense of morality is the person with a volitional disposition to *accept* and to *act* in terms of *self-imposed* moral laws and principles.

The concept of marital adjustment, then, in terms of the moral issues involved in the counseling process, refers essentially to the art of living *effectively* and *wholesomely* within the framework of responsibilities, relations, and expectancies that constitute the state of marriage, coupled with appropriate and intelligent compatibility of sexual, psychological, and religious factors, consistently requiring continuous personal growth, predicated on respect, love, trust, autonomy, recognition, and integrity in the lives of each of us as human beings.

Early adjustments are, of course, to be expected in every marriage. Differences in tastes and interests, minor likes and dislikes, must be ironed out. For emotionally mature men and women these are relatively easy. This requires *maturity*, and the mature person is considerate of the failings and shortcomings of the husband or wife and tries to make a constructive contribution to his or her development. The person respects the rights and the personality of the other and is willing to effect the compromises necessary in obtaining a finer relationship. When a problem arises, both parties contribute to its successful solution even though it may involve some mutual sacrifices. Neither party dominates and neither party submits, but both parties submit to the common cause, namely, success in their joint enterprise—marriage.

People of every psychological type and of every degree of psychic normality or abnormality may suffer from marital conflicts. Consequently, the marriage counselor must be trained and competent to recognize severe mental disturbance in his clients. Referral for psychiatric diagnosis and possible treatment may be appropriate; at other times, marital counseling may still be very appropriate, even in the presence of deep intrapsychic disturbance in one or both spouses. Many combinations of marital counseling and individual therapy are possible and appropriate in handling certain situations. The counselor must be particularly alert in the presence of depression or other psychiatric conditions predisposing to suicide, in his clients. Marital counseling and joint psychotherapy offer new insights and perspectives on many psychiatric problems.

The first of these is that any person attempting to do marital counseling needs comprehensive psychological training and knowledge as part of his professional skills. Also, psychiatrists and psychologists, who are usually more accustomed to dealing only with individuals, should have a good deal of knowledge and training in marital interaction and problems, to equip them well for their work. Thirdly, there is a need for close cooperation between all the helping professions and this should be reflected in the more widespread use of psychological and psychiatric consultations and referrrals by marriage counselors. Here again, it would also be highly desirable if psychiatrists more often availed themselves of the possibility of referring their patients for marital counseling, concomitant with or subsequent to individual therapy. Finally, it is always best to have completely flexible approach to any marital therapeutic or counseling situation. Rigid, sharply delineated systems of psychotherapy or counseling which set down "rules" as to the manner in which people can be worked with and *what* people we can work with may be comforting and reassuring to the therapist or counselor, but the best interests of the individual who consult us are served when we devise and improvise our approaches to fit *them* and their special, often unique situations.

Psychologists, psychiatrists, sociologists, and marriage counselors are keenly aware of the most serious psychological crisis in contemporary society, namely, the *identity crisis*. This identity crisis has its roots in many facets of recent history, and in many changing sociological patterns; and it has been nourished by the changing needs and aspirations of contemporary man and woman.

Similarly, the impact on family life, on marriage, and on society itself of the values created by affluence, and by increased emphasis on material things and their importance to our way of life, has certainly played a leading part in our definitions of basic roles. As Cottrell says in his *Roles and Marital Adjustment:*

> We are interested in marriage as a problem of adjustment of roles that people tend to play, these roles being conceived of as results of the past experiences of the marriage partners. We shall go a step farther in defining our problem and limit it to a study of marriage as an adjustment between roles that have developed in the childhood and adolescent family experiences of husband and wife. . . . Such a concentration of attention is due to the fact that so many of our case studies, both of well-adjusted and of poorly adjusted marriages picture people who seem to be seeking to reenact in their marriages, relational systems or situations which obtained in their parental families. These efforts are sometimes conscious and sometimes unconscious.

Other outcomes of role confusion and role diffusion are increased homosexuality, psychic impotence, and frigidity in marital relationships. The mechanism of this development need not concern us at this point. But experts in family life and in psychosexual development know from clinical experience and from well-accepted theory that *role confusion* in the areas of masculinity or femininity is a strong determinant of homosexual tendencies, of inadequate sexual relationships, and of orgastic inadequacy. (This is particularly true in situations where there is *role reversal,* and the mother becomes the dominant figure in the family pattern, and the father passively accepts the role of a meek follower.) It is this kind of psychosocial matrix that generates role confusion in children, particularly adolescents, who are striving for self-identity and a reduction of the identity crisis.

There is, therefore, the real need for, and a precise function of, role definitions in marriage. They are necessary to the satisfactory fulfillment of the most basic commitments of marriage. There are several such commitments that stand out prominently in the ongoing process of continuing marital adjustment. First of all, there is the commitment to love, to cherish, and to be faithful to the marital partner. Secondly, there is the commitment to protect and to nourish, to complement as much as possible the loved one's needs and characteristics, to communicate effectively with one another, and to support the other partner in sickness and in health. There is thirdly the commitment to gratify the most basic sexual and affectional needs of husband or wife, and thus in all respects to function effectively as a friend, a lover, and as a companion. And finally, there is the commitment, by implication if not by outright promise, to function effectively as a father or a mother when children become part of the family structure.

Members of the helping professions—in psychology, psychiatry, and social work— must assume increasing responsibility in marriage and divorce for protecting the child's developmental processes and ensuring as far as possible an atmosphere of love and continuity to minimize the child's inevitable feeling of abandonment. The practice of automatically giving custody to the mother must be challenged. The importance of flexibility in custody and visiting arrangements must be stressed.

In summary, then, the marital process is an integral part of the human life process. As the core institutional arrangement that binds people together, it is the basic fabric of social structure. If the weave is too tight it may create stress factors that result in a break. If the pattern is too compressed it may lack breathing space and decay. If the weave is too loose it may fall apart from lack of substance. Statistically, about one out of four marriages culminates in legal divorce; but nonstatistically, a much larger number of marriages close in *emotional* divorce. This knowledge of the frequency with which the marital process runs a terminal course to a condition of alienation or disjointedness, has been manifested in reevaluations of our traditional values and a search for new understanding and meaning with regard to both marriage and divorce. On a deeper level, people are growing and grasping for meaningfulness in relatedness; for apprehension of relatedness, oneness and separateness; for a sense of integrity in an inferno of contradictions, hypocrisies and illusions. If this seems somewhat critical, it is so intended as an expression of hopefulness: For this is part of the process of disintegration and growth. Old tissue may die in order that untapped potential may be drawn from it and new life generated.

Fundamentally, of all the characteristics that separate adults from children, probably the most important for the marital relationship is the ability to give of oneself—the very thing which makes human attachment desirable. This is different from the imperative attachments developed by infants and children. Their attachments are necessary for survival. Adult attachments express the luxury of choice. The difference can be recognized easily enough provided we do not allow ourselves to become romantically overwhelmed. In the latter instance, *need* dominates the relationship. This itself should make it suspect. But once out of hand, we do anything to justify the decision made. More rational choice involves *fact* more than it does *promise*. Grown-up loves do a great deal for each other and have a good time with each other *here and now* rather than merely in the happy never-never-land of the future.

Marriage is based on characterful living. We mass-produce almost everything in this country, but we cannot mass-produce character, because that is a matter of personal identity. It belongs to those who have found the part they are to play; who are doing the work for which they are best endowed; who are satisfied that they are filling a vital need; who are meeting their obligations and standing up to their tasks. Character is a positive thing. It is not protected innocence, but practiced virtue; it is not fear of vice, but love of excellence.

To push up from colorless mediocrity toward superiority is the way of the person of quality. All satisfying human life proceeds along this line of action—from below up, from minus to plus. To be successfully what we are, and to become what we are capable of becoming, is true ambition, no less a marital factor. This is a question of deep seriousness, and sometimes it demands courage in the asking and in the answering. Finding the point at which a value begins to totter is an authoritative guide as to how high we really rank it.

Among the things needed by the person in search of excellence are these: wide view, curiosity, courage, self-discipline, enthusiasm, and energy. Marriage counseling must deal with the factors. We have in mind the attributes needed to survive errors, to keep marching on a road that seems to be without end, to rise above disappointment and distress, to lie awake at night staring at broken hopes and frustrated plans and at a future that seems wholly dark—and to get up in the morning and go about our business with determination. All of these are part of education in marital relationships.

Only an imaginary line separates those who long for excellence and those who attain it, and enthusiasm is the quality needed to carry one over the border. This means having interest, zeal, and a strong feeling of the desirability of success. Enthusiasm provides the perseverance that overcomes impediments both real and imaginary.

One obstacle in the way of progress is resistance to change. It remains for the marriage counselor to explain this factor also to his clients. We must develop a sense of the pulse-beat of this changing life. We need to observe what is going on around us and filter it through a layer of common sense in order to decide in what direction and to what extent we have to alter course.

Sometimes practical experience is more harsh than school and home. It is ruthless, but effective. We do not merely need to learn things by chance or under compulsion but to develop the ability to extract the broadest meaning from our observation of the *how* and the *why* of things. One of the most valuable human rights available to the person seeking excellence in marriage is the right to correct errors revealed by experience.

Most of life is lived by batting averages, not by perfect scores. (The research scientist does not expect that every hypothesis he sets up will prove out. The financier does not expect that every investment will return a maximum dividend.) People live by making plans and by putting forth efforts that are, so far as they can see, in line with the results they want. Then they revise their plans and improve their performance as experience dictates. We need fear only one failure in life: not to be true to the best quality we know, in ourselves, in others, in life and in living.

SELECTED BIBLIOGRAPHY

Ackerman, Nathan W.: *Psychodynamics of Family Life.* New York, Basic Books, 1958.

Ackerman, Nathan W.: *Treating the Troubled Family.* New York and London, Basic Books, 1966.

Ard, Ben and Constance: *Handbook of Marriage Counseling.* Palo Alto, California, Science and Behavior Books, 1969.

Ardrey, Robert: *The Territorial Imperative.* New York, Delta Books, 1966.

Bach, George: *The Intimate Enemy.* New York, Morrow, 1969.

Bassett, William T.: *Counseling the Childless Couple.* Englewood Cliffs, N.J., Prentice-Hall, 1963.

Bateson, G., and Ruesch, J.: *Communication: The Social Matrix of Psychiatry.* New York, W. W. Norton, 1951.

Bauer, William: *To Enjoy Marriage.* Garden City, Doubleday, 1967.

Berne, Eric: *Games People Play.* New York, Grove Press, 1964.

Beier, Ernest G.: *The Silent Language of Psychotherapy.* Chicago, Aldine Publishing, 1966.

Bell, John E.: *Family Group Therapy.* Public Health Monograph #64, U.S. Department of Health, Education and Welfare, 1961.

Bell, N. W., and Vogel, E. F.: *A Modern Introduction to the Family.* Glencoe, Illinois, Free Press, 1960.

Berkowitz, Leonard: *Aggression: A Social Psychological Analysis.* New York, McGraw-Hill Book Co., 1962.

Bettelheim, Bruno: *Love is Not Enough.* New York, Free Press, 1955.

Biderman, A. D., and Zimmer, H.: *The Manipulation of Human Behavior.* New York, John Wiley and Sons, 1961.

Bier, William C. (Ed.): *Marriage: A Psychological and Moral Approach.* New York, Fordham University Press, 1965.

Blanck, Rubin and Gertrude: *Marriage and Personal Development.* New York, Columbia University Press, 1968.

Bonaparte, M.: *Female Sexuality.* New York, International Universities Press, 1953.

Bossard, James H. S.: *Ritual in Family Living.* Philadelphia, University of Pennsylvania Press, 1950.

Bossard, James H. S.: *One Marriage, Two Faiths.* New York, Ronald Press, 1957.

Boszomenyr, M. D.: *Intensive Family Therapy.* New York, Harper and Row, 1965.

Boszormenyi-Nagy, I., and Framo, James L.: *Intensive Family Therapy.* New York, Hoeber Medical Division, Harper and Row, 1965.

Breenton, Myron: *The American Male.* New York, Coward McCann, Inc., 1966.

Broderick, C., and Bernard, J.: *The Individual, Sex and Society.* Baltimore, John Hopkins, 1969.

Buckley, Walter: *Sociology and Modern Systems Theory.* Englewood Cliffs, N.J., Prentice-Hall, 1967.

Bugenthal, James T.: *The Search for Authenticity.* New York, Holt, Reinhart and Winston, Inc., 1965.

Burke, Judge Louis H.: *With This Ring.* New York, McGraw Hill, 1958.

Butterfield, Oliver M.: *Sexual Harmony in Marriage.* New York, Emerson Books, 1953.

Cady, Ernest, and Cady, Frances: *How to Adopt a Child.* New York, William Morrow, 1956.

Cahnman, Werner J.: *Intermarriage and Jewish Life in America, A Symposium.* New York, Theo. Herzl Press and Jewish Reconstructionist Press, 1963.

Calderone, Mary S.: *Release from Sexual Tensions.* New York, Random House, 1960.

Callaghan, Sidney: *Beyond Birth Control.* New York, Sheed and Ward, 1968.

Caprio, Frank S.: *Marital Infidelity.* New York, The Citadel Press, 1953.

Chesser, E.: *Unmarried Love.* New York, McKay Co., 1965.

Corsini, Raymond J.: *Methods of Group Psychotherapy.* New York, Blakiston Division, 1957.

Couch, Elizabeth: *Joint and Family Interviews.* New York, Family Service Association, 1969.

Cuber, J. F., and Harroff, P. B.: *The Significant American, A Study of Sexual Behavior Among the Affluent.* New York, Appleton-Century-Crofts, 1965.

DeMartino, Manfred F.: *The New Female Sexuality.* New York: The Julian Press, 1969.

DeMartino, Manfred F.: *Sexual Behavior and Personality Characteristics.* New York, Citadel Press, 1963.

Denton, Wallace: *The Role of the Minister's Wife.* New York, Westminster Press, 1960.

Deutsch, Helen: *The Psychology of Women* (2 Volumes). New York, Grune & Stratton, 1944.

Dicks, Russel L.: *Premarital Guidance.* New York, Prentice Hall, 1960.

Dominian, J.: *Christian Marriage—The Challenge of Change.* London, Darton, Longman and Todd, 1967.

Draper, Elizabeth: *Birth Control in the Modern World.* Baltimore, Penguin Books, 1965.

Duvall, Sylvanus M.: *Before You Marry.* New York, Association Press, 1959.

Eisenstein, Victor W.: *Neurotic Interaction in Marriage.* New York, Basic Books, 1956.

Ellis, Albert, and Harper, Robert: *A Guide to Rational Living.* Englewood Cliffs, N.J., Prentice-Hall, 1961.

Epstein, Cynthia: *Woman's Place.* Berkley, University of California Press, 1970.

Erikson, Erik H.: *Childhood and Society.* New York, W. W. Norton, 1950.

Eysenck, H. J.: *The Effects of Psychotherapy.* New York, International Science Press, 1966.

Farber and Wilson: *The Challenge to Women.* New York, Basic Books, 1966.

Festinger, Leon, and Kelley, Harold: *Changing Attitudes Through Social Controls.* Ann Arbor, Michigan, Research Center for Group Dynamics, 1951.

Fisher, Esther O.: *Help for Today's Troubled Marriages.* New York, Hawthorne Books, 1968.

Frank, Jerome: *Persuasion and Healing.* Baltimore, John Hopkins Press, 1961.

Freud, Sigmund: *New Introductory Lectures on Psychoanalysis.* New York, W. W. Norton, 1933.

Fried, Edrita: *The Ego in Love and Sexuality.* New York, Grune and Stratton, 1960.

Fromm, Eric: *The Art of Loving.* New York, Harper and Bros., 1956.

Glasser, William: *Reality Therapy: A New Approach to Psychiatry.* New York, Harper and Row, Inc., 1965.

Goldman, George D., and Milman, Donald S.: *Modern Woman—Her Psychology and Sexuality.* Springfield, Illinois, Charles C Thomas, 1969.

Goldstein, A. P., Heller, K., and Sechrest, L. B.: *Psychotherapy and the Psychology of Behavior Change.* New York, Harper and Row, Inc., 1966.

Goodman, Philip and Hannah: *Jewish Marriage Anthology.* Philadelphia, Jewish Publication Society, 1965.

Goodrich, Frederick: *Preparing for Childbirth.* Englewood Cliffs, N.J., Prentice-Hall, 1966.

Gordon, Albert J.: *Intermarriage.* Boston, Beacon Press, 1964.

Gottlieb, Sophie, and Barnhardt. *What You Should Know About Marriage.* New York, Bobbs-Merrill, 1962.

Gray, Madeline: *The Normal Woman.* New York, Scribner, 1967.

Greene, Bernard, (Ed.): *The Psychotherapies of Marital Disharmony.* New York, The Free Press, 1965.

Hamilton, Eleanor: *Sex Before Marriage.* New York, Meredith Press, 1969.

Hamilton, Eleanor: *Partners in Love.* New York, A. S. Barnes & Co., 1961.

Hastings, Donald W.: *Impotence and Frigidity.* Boston, Little, Brown & Co., 1963.

Hudson, R. L.: *Marital Counseling.* Englewood Cliffs, N.J., Prentice-Hall, 1963.

Hulme, William: *Building a Christian Marriage.* Englewood Cliffs, N.J., Prentice-Hall, 1965.

Huret, Morton M.: *Her Infinite Variety.* New York, Harper and Row, 1962.

Hunt, Morton: *The World of the Formerly Married.* New York, McGraw-Hill, 1966.

Heider, Fritz: *The Psychology of Interpersonal Relations.* New York, John Wiley & Son, 1958.

Jackson, Don: *Human Communication.* Palo Alto, California, Science & Behavior Books, 1968.

Jackson, Don: (Ed.): *Communication, Family and Marriage, Therapy, Communication and Changes.* Palo Alto, California, Science & Behavior Books, 1968.

Johnson, Dean: *Marriage Counseling: Theory and Practice.* Englewood Cliffs, N.J., Prentice-Hall, Inc., 1961.

Johnson, Warren R.: *Human Sexual Behavior and Sex Education.* Philadelphia, Lee and Febiger, 1968.

Kinsey, A. C.: *Sexual Behavior in the Human Female.* Philadelphia, Saunders, 1953.

Kinsey, A. C.: *Sexual Behavior in the Human Male.* Philadelphia, Saunders, 1948.

Kirkendoll, L.: *Premarital Intercourse and Personal Relationships.* New York, Julian Press, 1961.

Krenhausen, Phyllis and Eberhard: *The Sexually Responsive Woman.* New York, Grove Press, 1964.

Kubie, L. S.: *Practical and Theoretical Aspects of Psychoanalysis.* New York, International Universities Press, 1950.

Laing, R. D., and Esterson, A.: *Sanity, Madness, and the Family.* New York, Basic Books, 1964.

Leder, William, and Jackson, Don: *The Mirage of Marriage.* New York, W. W. Norton, 1968.

Lenski, Gerhard: *The Religious Factor.* Garden City, Doubleday, 1961.

Lewin, Kurt: *Field Therapy in Social Science,* Ed. Derwin Cartwright. New York, Harper & Brothers, 1951.

Lidz, Fleck and Cornelisen: *Schizophrenia and The Family.* New York, International Universities Press, 1965.

London, M. D.: *Sexual Deviations in the Female.* New York, Julian Press, 1957.

Lorenz, Konrad: *On Aggression.* New York, Harcourt, Brace & World, 1966.

Lowen, Alexander: *Love and Orgasm.* New York, Macmillan, 1965.

McGinnis, Tom: *Your First Year of Marriage.* Garden City, Doubleday, 1967.

Mace, David: *Success in Marriage.* New York, Abingdon Press, 1958.

Masters, William H., and Johnson, Virginia E.: *Human Sexual Inadequacy.* Boston, Little, Brown & Co., 1970.

Masters, William H., and Johnson, Virginia E.: *Human Sexual Response.* Boston, Little, Brown & Co., 1966.

Masters, William H., and Lea, Edward: *The Anti-Sex.* New York, Julian Press, 1964.

Mead, Margaret: *Male and Female.* New York, William Morrow & Co., 1955.

Meares, Ainslie: *Marriage and Personality.* Springfield, Ill., Charles C Thomas, 1957.

Menninger, Karl: *Love Against Hate.* New York, Harcourt, Brace, 1942.

Morris, J. K.: *Marriage Counseling: A Manual for Ministers.* New York, Prentice-Hall, 1965.

Mudd, Emily H., and Krich, Aaron: *Man and Wife.* New York, Norton & Co., 1957.

Nash, Ethel M., Jenner and Abse: *Marriage Counseling in Medical Practice.* Chapel Hill, North Carolina, University of North Carolina Press, 1964.

Nengarten, B.: *Middle Age and Aging.* Chicago, The University of Chicago Press, 1968.

Packard, Vance: *The Sexual Wilderness.* New York, McKay, 1968.

Pepitone, A., and Reichling, G.: *Group Cohesiveness and the Expression of Hostility.* New York, Human Relations, 1955.

Perls, Frederick S., et. al.: *Gestalt Therapy.* New York, Julian Press, 1951.

Petersen, James A.: *Married Love in the Middle Years.* New York, Association Press, 1968.

Petersen, James A.: *Marriage and Family Counseling.* New York, Association Press, 1968.

Petersen, James A.: *Education for Marriage.* New York, Charles Scribner's Sons, 2nd ed., 1964.

Piaget, Jean: *Language and the Thought of the Child.* London, Kegan Paul, 1926.

Pike, James A.: *If You Marry Outside Your Faith.* New York, Harper, 1954.

Rapoport, Anatol: *Strategy and Conscience.* New York, Harper & Row, 1964.

Reuben, D.: *Everything You Always Wanted to Know About Sex.* New York, McKay, 1969.

Rubin, Isadore: *Sexual Life After Sixty.* New York, Basic Books, 1965.

Reik, Theodore: *The Need to Be Loved.* New York, Farrar, Straus & Co., 1966.

Reik, Theodore: *The Many Faces of Sex.* New York, Farrar, Straus & Co., 1966.

Rogers, Carl R.: *Client Centered Therapy.* Boston, Houghton-Mifflin, 1951.

Rosen, John N.: *Psychoanalysis Direct and Indirect.* Doylestown, Pa:. Doylestown Foundation, 1964.

Rosenbaum, S.: *The Marriage Relationship: Psychoanalytic Perspectives.* New York, Basic Books, 1968.

Ruesch, Jurgen, and Kees, Wheldon: *Non-Verbal Communication*. Berkley and Los Angeles, University of California Press, 1956.

Rutledge, Aaron L.: *Premarital Counseling*. Mass., Schenkman Publishing Co., 1966.

Sarbin, T. R.: *Role Theory*, in G. Lindsey (Ed.) *Handbook of Social Psychology*, Vol. 1, Cambridge, Mass., Addison Wesley, 1954.

Satir, Virginia: *Conjoint Family Therapy*. Palo Alto, California, Science and Behavior Books, Inc., 1964.

Saul, Leon: *Fidelity and Infidelity*. Philadelphia, Lippincott, 1967.

Schofield, W.: *Psychotherapy: The Purchase of Friendship*. Englewood Cliffs, N. J., Prentice-Hall, 1964.

Schur, Edwin M.: Editor. *The Family and the Sexual Revolution*. Indianapolis, Indiana University Press, Inc., 1964.

Senn, Milton, and Hartford, C.: *The Firstborn*. Cambridge, Mass., Harvard University Press, 1968.

Silverman, Hirsch Lazaar: *Marital Counseling: Psychology, Ideology, Science*. Springfield, Illinois, Charles C Thomas, 1967.

Soddy, Kenneth, and Kielson, Mary C.: *Men in Middle Life*. Philadelphia, Lippincott, 1967.

Stewart, Charles W.: *The Minister as Marriage Counselor*. New York, Abingdon Press, 1960.

Storr, Anthony: *Human Aggression*. New York, Antheneum, 1968.

Taylor, Donald L.: *Marriage Counseling*. Springfield, Illinois, Charles C Thomas, 1965.

Terkelson, Helen E.: *Counseling The Unwed Mother*. Englewood Cliffs, N. J., Prentice-Hall, 1964.

Trainer, Joseph B.: *Physiologic Foundations for Marriage Counseling*. St. Louis, Missouri, C. V. Mosby, 1965.

Trobisch, Walter: *I Loved a Girl: Young Africans Speak*. New York, Harper & Row, 1965.

Van de Velde, Th. H.: *Ideal Marriage*. New York, Random House, 1943.

Wallis, J. H.: *Sexual Harmony in Marriage*. New York, Roy Publishers, 1965.

Wynn, J. C.: *Sex, Family and Society in Theological Focus*. New York, Association Press, 1966.

Winch, Robert F.: *Mate Selection*. New York, Harper, 1958.

Winnicott, D. W.: *Aggression in Relation to Emotional Development, Collected Papers*. London, Tavistock, 1958.

Young, Leontine: *Out of Wedlock*. New York, McGraw-Hill, 1954.

Chapter 3

MEDICAL MARRIAGE COUNSELING AND SEXUAL INCOMPATIBILITIES

JOSEPH B. TRAINER

> The doctor's job is to help people die
> young as late as possible.
> DONALD COOPER

T HERE IS more to marriage than sex, but sex is the heart of marriage. We may have many relationships to others involving love and commitment. They will be valuable and valued, they will be sexless, and they may be long sustained. But the marriage that is not well based in sex will never be a satisfying and cherished personal union. What may endure is a meaningless legal formalism, shrouding two souls without life.

Sex derives its singular position in the social arrangements of marriage from two dissimilar directions. Physiologically, sex, like hunger, is a repetitive urge or drive. Both are based in the brain stem and in the absence of repetitive reduction of the urges, both produce characteristic searching activity in the individual. Unsatisfied sexual urges and hunger urges induce restless, seeking, motor activity, an enormous cunning in pursuit of an object, and variable degrees of aggression in attaining it. The social animal, man, loses the best parts of his social nature when beset by sexual or food deprivation.

The male reacts much more strongly to these disequilibria than the female. Anyone listening to marriage problems is aware of the large number of husbands who express strong resentments about even the failure of meals to be ready on some regular schedule. The corresponding sexual situation is well described by a thirty-five-year-old man. "When we have gone maybe about a month with no sex—she's tired, or has a headache, or a crampy belly or is having her period—I begin to get picky and feisty or I wont talk to her. Usually I'm pretty quiet and agreeable, but this begins to get to me."

The second major direction of sexual importance is related to the essential social, herd, pair-forming primate nature of man, with the special human overlay of personal relating and emotional attachment. Sex is the only basic biologic urge (as distinguished from hunger and anxiety) dependent upon another person for its satisfaction. This requires that one relate well enough to another to evoke sexual behavior in order to have the sexual self-feeling gratified. Sex thus governs the smallest social grouping in a social animal—the couple. Since it does that, it necessarily conditions family formation, a universal to human societies. It accordingly gives rise to the concepts of kinship and becomes the basis of societal organization.

The combination of a deep-seated physiologic drive and a universal society organizer are not equaled in overriding force by any other human experience to date.

The sexual urge demonstrably is a common source of trouble when it continues to exist unmet. And, it is a source of trouble when its manifold delicate arrangements go awry. Both troubles are compounded when hedged around with the social sanctions of monogamous marriage which tend to constrict alternate choices of drive reduction. In marriage, sexual matters reflect the other areas of agreement or disagreement within this special framework. Sexual relationships are *closely personalized,* and are probably the most intimate conjunction of two people. In the formal values of monogamous western marriage they are presumed to be *uniquely restrictive* as a person-to-person relationship. The conduct of sex involves more *personal acceptance-rejection* than other aspects of marriage. There is a basic enormous *emotional intensity* about sexually relating which is multidimensioned, embracing excitement, joy, love, hate, fear, anger, pleasure, shame, disgust, and guilt.

Moreover, sexual solicitation is not so much a quest for reward as it is an *offering of the self.* Because of this it is potentially *ego-threatening* when removed from the unquestioned mutual acceptance of early love. Correspondingly, it does not make a subject for ready verbalizing or conversation between the pair. It is an unusual person in our culture who is able to speak freely to the partner on sexual problems even if things are going well. Sexual discordance thus becomes a focus of marital problems of all sorts. The label of sexual incompatibility may mean different things either in different marriages or in different stages of the same marriage.

The *sexual urge* does not stand alone. Two other basic biologic functions, each prepotent at its own time, have a closely intertwined relation. These are the *parental urge* and the *domestic urge.*

The *parental urge* seizes people in the strongest way and there are probably no more frantic people seen by the doctor than those who fear they are infertile. Having a child confers on one his terrestrial immortality —a very tangible kind. Our very own DNA has stamped out its unique and priceless replicate! Moreover, people quite simply love children, especially infants. They provide a continuum of being needed and present the basic sort of teaching challenge. Only contemporary technology in a small fraction of the world has made it possible to separate the *parental urge* from the *sexual urge.*

The *domestic urge* is the human equivalent of the ubiquitous territoriality of the animal world. "A man's home is his castle" expresses both a sentiment and a fundamental tenet of the *common law*. The man establishes and maintains his territory. It requires a woman to tend it and to make of it a refuge from the hostilities of the world. The relationship of the *domestic urge* to the *sexual urge* is self-evident.

Much marital discord can be traced to *frustrations* of these three urges. They are all likely to manifest as sexual dysfunctions on the surface because sexual activity is the closest relationship demanding a positive response from the other.

Frustration in any of the urges usually means the inability to get the other one to see your own concept of your basic images. It may occur from recognition of the inability of the partner to make allowances for your image. These imply a not-loving or a not-caring-enough to do it. Either represents a failure to get a suitable response from the other. The frequent reaction pattern to that is to withdraw into a closely self-oriented attitudinal state. This may be partly a determination to exert a dominance in behavior toward the mate. The wedge created by frustration of the *domestic or parental urges* reflects directly in diminished sexual activity or in an incompletely satisfying kind of sexual relationship. Western society, as pointed out, has not created an acceptable means for relieving the unsatisfied *sexual urge* outside the household. The problem accordingly becomes focused as a sexual problem bearing his and hers labels.

EARLY MARRIAGE

In early marriage sexual discordance itself is likely to really occur. The variance in strength or repetitiveness of drive quickly emerges in a new household. Even with the relatively high degree of premarital sexual activity seen today, a truly free rein to the drive mechanism becomes available only when the couple occupy their own territory. But the drives are rarely equal. We are all distributed along a regular bell-shaped population curve in sex as in other characteristics. A discordance between partners spells inevitable trouble. The inability of one to meet the rate of the other additionally involves the acceptance-rejection machinery acutely.

Male-female orientation differences rise quickly to the newly married surface. The male has a culturally and anatomically conditioned easy familiarity with his genitals. He has to handle his own a half dozen times a day just to keep an empty bladder. The female grows up surrounded still by multiple taboos, her genitals sensitive, unknown, and unfamiliar. Each sex provides the other with some degree of mutual surprise and a variable degree of incomprehension and dismay. Both are victims of sexual ignorance, although in decidedly different ways and neither understands sex as it appears to the other.

Sexual ignorance is pervasive, perhaps magnified by the aura of sex in advertising, television, magazines, and novels. The level of real information of any sort—physiological, medical, psychological or sociological—is discouragingly low.

Contraception plays an old part in a new way. For a long time the mechanical and aesthetic nuisances of diaphragms and jellies obtunded a free and easy sex expression. Currently the pill is taking its own toll. Between 30 and 40 per cent of women have an appreciable degree of depression from the estrogen excess. Depression depletes libido and many new marriages face the immediate hurdle of a depressed bride with a poor sex drive and an uncertainly bad disposition.

Primary sexual incompatibility is only one face of *early marriage*. The peculiarities of the new *paired-relationship* carry indeterminate hazards. If I ask a couple when the marriage went wrong, a most frequent response is, "The day I got married," or "The first night I was married," or "The first week I was married." Two unexpected personalities emerge when the title of "husband" and "wife" are assumed. This is a mixture of *adult interaction* and *child reaction* resurrected from the dimmest recesses of childhood. New self-images related to the status of marriage appear, and role playing takes on a serious cast. The new *paired relationship* establishes very early and once established tends to endure in that form for a very long time. Sexual problems may suddenly appear in the context of this new married configuration.

Fatigue states are the common denominator of much *early marriage*. The usual household today begins with both partners working, and many attending some classes as well. Child raising adds an additional burden. The first child increases the workload about 40 per cent; and a second child adds another 20 per cent. Tired people are like tired children—dispositions sour, tempers short, imprecations ready. Fatigue is a natural enemy of sex and ordinary individual differences in fatiguability may easily precipitate sexual discordances.

MIDDLE MARRIAGE

Middle marriage is a period when the *personal incompatibilities* of a pair become well-defined. They involve not two people but six, as Clark Vincent adapted so cleverly. There are husbands self-image, his image-of-wife, and his image-of-wife's image of husband, with a similarly disposed trio on the distaff side. The conflict may be between any pair of the three "people." This is the foundation of all the "misunderstanding" situations seen by the counselor. This leads to conflict and sex becomes both a victim and a focus of the conflict itself.

Progressive alienation is one of the most visible phenomena of *middle marriage*. It may be based on increasing awareness of *dislike* of the partner, or *disapproval* of the partner. Sometimes it rests on the quieter frame of *boredom* with the partner. Very often, especially in the middle and upper middle classes *preoccupation* is the divider. The wife becomes preoccupied with the children and the husband with his work. These too may be expressed overtly as sexual difficulties when the real problem is well removed.

Psychiatric states play a larger part in the dissatisfactions of middle marriage than commonly thought. *Schizoid personalities* emerge with increasing stress of any kind. *Depressive states* are among the frequent abnormalities—perhaps so much they should not be called abnormal. People with *chronic anxiety states* place an enormous burden on their marriages, and *hysterics* place an intolerable one, although these personalities are often superficially engaging and sexually attractive. The neurotic personalities take their toll of each relationship they make. The closeness and persistence of a married living situation is likely to uncover psychiatric disease before it is apparent anywhere else. The fact that these problems too, may be expressed by one of the couple as a sexual problem should not mislead the counselor.

Disease states emerge in force during middle marriage. Diabetes and Multiple Sclerosis frequently appear in the male as impotence. Uterine and breast disease in the female may cancel a prior interest in sex. Worry over disease and disability induce the same sexual losses as other preoccupations, only perhaps more acutely related to sex. Obesity and somnolence may be the hallmark of the highball-and-lunch, highball-and-dinner routine. No sleepy fat partner is a sex pot! He is well on his way to becoming an obituary notice from myocardial disease or at best presenting the problem of allowable sexual function in the postcoronary patient. Again, a look further in to see what underlies this pattern will be revealing.

ADVANCED MARRIAGE

So many problems ripen with advancing age both in the person and the marriage that sex often gets overlooked. It should not be, for cultivating what can be done sexually may well be the thing that makes living with age tolerable to desirable.

Aggravated incompatibilities are the universal hazard of advanced marriage. Neither can really bear the other and each can predict all the responses of the other. Long practice has made self-isolation in the union an art. Keeping the peace is a highly developed activity, but with the surface concealing multiple explosive resentments. One of the pair is likely to deny or deride the sexual aspirations of the other.

Disease states produce a host of sexual difficulties and misunderstandings. Coronary disease and hypertensive disease carry anxieties directly impinging on or related to sexual activity. Malignancies and surgery around the genitals have a special pertinency to the sex life. The psychological blocks so frequently seen are essentially informational lacks, which can be filled.

Iatrogenic dys-sexuality has emerged. Libido and potentia both are victims of the frequently prescribed anti-hypertensive and the tranquilizing medications. Here since the doctor participates in creating the sexual problem, the patient should have the opportunity to weigh the alternative benefits!

Mutual dys-attraction degenerates into a compounded state during this era. The men get slow and portly, putting up a large if not good front to their wives. They overeat, overdrink, and overlounge, becoming fat, sleepy, incompetent lovers. The women get menopausal, are thereby confronted with aging through a sexually-associated failure of function. They become anxious, overeat, overdrink, and overlounge. They become devoted clients of beauty parlors and cosmetics. They become artificial, fat, sleepless, but likewise incompetent mistresses in the conjugal bed. Sex with such a pair loses interest, excitement, variety, then comfort, and finally existence. The unrelieved tensions remain.

Involutional states may readily entail a loss of sexual activity by one of the partners. The sense of sexual loss may be acute in the unaffected partner. The paranoia of senility aggravates the sexual loss into a full-blown hostility.

PHYSICIAN FUNCTIONS IN MARITAL SEXUAL SITUATIONS

Doctors come—almost straight—out of the middlest of the middle class. This makes them good physicians, as a group. They tend to follow the best middle class precepts of honesty, integrity, hard work, and self-improvement. They are dedicated to an unusual degree to service. Such a background also makes for difficulties when they are called upon to act as sex or marital counselors. They individually share the restrictive sexuality of their class, they feel they have inadequate information (compared to their medical information) and they tend to be disease oriented. As physicians they examine, cogitate and take definitive action or give orders for action. As counselors they require a completely different approach. The same man who inspects with confidence and decision a vulva bearing an infected Bartholin cyst is undone if he has to look at the same structures and tell the patient how to use the components for more sexual fun.

These characteristics almost define the strengths and weaknesses of the doctor as a counselor. He is called upon often—about a sixth of office visits revolve in this area; his patients tend to look on him as the first and perhaps only person to whom they can turn with a sexual problem. Yet he answers laggardly and unwillingly. He was not prepared by his upbringing, his class association, his professional education nor his experience to feel comfortable with questions of sex and of marital relatingness. For the most part, the doctors greatest contribution has consisted of suggesting the name of a book, usually one of the old sex manuals.

Fortunately, the medical as well as the social scene is rapidly shifting and a major educational change is taking place both in the medical school and in the postgraduate field. As a part of this change I would like to capsulize some appropriate functions for the physician to bring his special learning and capacities to bear in counseling.

Sex Education

The doctor should take the lead in examining sexual structures at least as well as he examines noses and throats. He should accompany the examination (especially in young people) by a running commentary and explanation of parts—whether the function is excretory, (e.g. the female urethra) sexual (the penile corona) , or reproductive (ovaries or testes) . He should explain the sensory modalities, the response pattern, and the usual hygiene of the parts. Above all he should assure the patient about the quality or normality of the genitals.

Such an approach is done as simply and matter-of-factly as the approach to an eye or a hand. This at once removes the sense of mystery and the blight of ignorance. It makes the genitals acceptable to the patient as just another body structure. Most significantly, it constructs the communications route between doctor and patient for future use.

That kind of sex education is direct, personal, and highly effective and rates as first-class preventive medicine. No one but the physician is privileged to carry it out.

Related to individual education is the physician's function in group sex education. Doctors who feel they have developed a competence here should work with school systems. They can be very effective, both directly as teachers, and as resource people for the health education teachers, who carry the major load. Good sex education can minimize subsequent sexual problems in marriage.

Premarital Counseling

Physicians as a whole have not yet undertaken premarital examinations and counseling in any but the most fragmentary way. The examination is usually limited to a legalistic and ineffective search for hitherto undetected and unknown syphilis by way of a blood test. It is a travesty carried out by an unwilling doctor on a patient who comes equally unwillingly. The results are unsatisfactory to both.

Ideally, the couple should be seen in four visits. The first should be scheduled at least two months before the wedding for mutual acquaintance, to start the woman on contraceptives, and to quickly run down the major categories of potential problems. These might be money, relatives, housing, school, sex, personality structures, children and genetic diseases. The second session about a month later includes a general medical examination with a particular attention to sexual structures and any corrective measures such as circumcision or hymeneal dilatation. As with sex education earlier, good education should thread verbally through the procedure. Laboratory work should include a hematocrit, white and differential count, the required serologic test for syphilis, and blood typing for the major ABO group and Rh factor. A urine analysis should be done. Sometimes special tests may be indicated on the basis of the medical history and examination.

A final joint visit should include the reports on the examinations and a discussion with *both* of any abnormalities or potential problems found. By this visit the doctor should have been able to make some kind of assay of this particular couple. Suggestions now become pertinent for anticipating or forestalling sources of trouble. The couple will be friendly and relaxed at this stage. They now may be able to bring out things which would have been impossible before. The necessary papers can be signed by all and copies of the physical examinations can be given to them for future reference.

I am certain this approach is of the greatest value in establishing a successful new household. My patients have amply confirmed that the sexual life of the pair gets off to a resounding start. Most of them avoid the usual bumbling, and fumbling, and disappointments that have characterized many marriage starts. A six-week postmarital visit is an appropriate follow-up.

Dealing With Sexual Problems as Conflict Generators

It is not at all remarkable that sexual problems should arise so frequently and in turn give rise to an interminable assortment of personality conflicts. The gap in world view between the male subculture and the female subculture nearly defies bridging. The variation of individual placement on the population curves of sexuality are very often unknown before marriage. The male erotic and the female romantic arousal mechanisms are culture-conditioned attributes with a biologic underpinning. While they are obviously vastly different, the differences are rarely grasped by the opposed partners, leading to mutual frustrations. Beyond that, the need to evoke a positive response in the partner, or, conversely, to ignore the partner's needs entirely generates frustration and anger. The tendency to equate sexual response with an ego-feeding emotion of love compounds the conflicts.

The results of the conflicts, rather than the sexual problem, are the precipitators which bring the patient to a physician. *Frustration* may then express itself as a duodenal ulcer, complete with enough blood loss to demand transfusion—or as any of a host of other diseases. *Anger* and *rage* liberate enough epinephrine not only to blanch the face for all to see, but can also precipitate a heart attack. *Jealousy* changes a person from a simple neurotic to a homicidal psychotic.

The sexual offer being the social offering of the self, its rejection is therefore a rejection of the self. The inability to respond to an offer becomes an inability to respond to the person. The drooping penis in the marital bed implies disinterest. It cannot be hidden by overt or covert action, nor stiffened by the words of language. It arouses profound alarm in its owner, and self-doubt and anxiety in the partner. Such people come to their doctor with often visible tension and somatic symptoms ranging from dermatitis to those mimicking brain tumors.

The sensitized and perceptive physician must carry a high index of suspicion in dealing with the married. He must be able to take the presenting symptoms at face value first, assay them and be prepared to deal with them as representing secondary disease entities. The bleeding ulcer demands treatment as a bleeding ulcer first and foremost. But beyond this, he must hold that symptom up to the bright translucency of insight and begin to prod around in the scrap heap of the patient's life for the clues that lead to a basic explanation.

A sexual history will often tell the story. It requires more skill than other system histories. It is easier for most physicians to ask how the patient gets short of breath than how the patient gets an orgasm. For his part, the patient considers the events of his own sex life too personal and private even for the doctor's office. Both are constrained by the lack of suitable and easy language. Indeed, the language factor may have been the predominant contributor to the generation of the conflict for want of an easy way to say, "I love you dearly, but I don't want to make love right now." Or, "That way doesn't turn me on much, let's try this way instead." There is no language of sex for sociability, nor are there manners in, for example, the way we have manners about eating. All this complicates the doctor's problem. Fortunately the conversational freedom of the new generation, with their openness and honesty is drastically reducing the problem. With the "over twenty-five" population it still exists.

A sexual history is usually an interpersonal relational history with a nonexclusive tendency to be focused on sexual activities. I believe it must be taken firsthand by the doctor and not relegated to any of the testing devices. These tests have an appropriate use later on, but the investigative encounter must be personal.

The details of such a history are not germane to a short chapter but the inquiry must ascertain the following:

1. What motivates the pair, is it a utilitarian, with neutral, parallel, divergent, or hostile partners, or is it an intrinsic marriage with intimate partners?
2. How does each partner rate himself and the other on a sexuality scale?
3. What was the natural history of their sex life from the beginning to the present in terms of enthusiasm, frequency, satisfaction and the like?
4. What is the new situation which appears to be unsatisfactory, such as a change by one partner in frequency, or "impotence" (male) or "frigidity" (female).
5. Is there any extramarital sexual activity and if so do similar problems arise there; or does the mere existence of the extramarital sex contribute to or alleviate the marital conflict.
6. Are there discoverable medical situations, basically nonsexual, which bear on the sexual conflict? For example, is there a menopausal wife with a fragile, thin, easily broken vaginal lining due to estrogen deficiency? Such a vagina responds with pain to the normally pleasant rubbing of copulation. Or does the husband have mild angina pectoris which induces oppressive, frightening, vise-like chest pain on attempting a sexual approach?

A careful and conscientious search must be made for not merely genital abnormalities but significant disease in all other systems. These may be as diverse as disease of the lumbosacral cord, endocrine disorders, or emphysema of the lungs from smoking.

Among the executive and professional classes, chronic preoccupation and pressure with the accompanying fatigue state may be the very basic fault.

At some point, the doctor will have disposed of the easier problem of the presenting symptom. The ulcer will be on its way to healing. He should have analyzed the underlying sexual problem to a point where it is in some way recognizable. It may well have one appearance from the viewpoint of the husband and another from that of the wife. From both of these he must construct his own idea of the probable difficulty, verbalize it, and set up a plan of approach to its relief. To begin with, he must reassure them about all the aspects which appear to be intact. He then must get both oriented in those facets which he sees as not normal. If this is, for instance, a divergence in basic sexual appetite, it can be explained meaningfully in terms of similar variations in food appetite. The object is to get the pair to learn and accept their personality differences—to give to the other the same acceptance they themselves would like to receive. There may often be a problem of uncomplicated biologic ignorance. Most people know little of any body function (or structure) and even less about sexual structures or functions. Plain education is indicated, in terms and patient readily understands. The physician should instruct, he should get the pelvis and genitals out of their old taboo garments, and help the patient accept the genitals as easily as any other part of the body. He may give them a new insight to provide the excitement of variety. He can impart the attitude of look, try, experience, experiment, and above all, savor.

Cultural antipathies may exist. A recent example was the conflict generated in the mixed Catholic-Protestant marriage over use of anovulatory pills. But other old parental originated attitudes often reappear in the married couple and come to cross-purposes.

Perhaps our most pervasive hang-up is the residuum from one aspect of the puritan background of the United States. It could be epitomized thus:

Sex is sin, but fun
Home is good, and without sin
Therefore, sex can't be good *and* fun at home.

The epitome is the sad seed of measureless evil.

The doctor has an obligation to help people in sexual and marital disorders as well as in his ancient and more usual spheres. People now expect the doctor to be as knowledgeable in matters of sex, as he is in other bodily processes. They continue to look to him for counsel despite the technicization of a scientific medicine. They expect his role to be consonant with his vast experience of dealing with his patients on the most intimate basis. In matters of sex, human relationships, and reproduction, the doctor ought to be the guardian of the biological rights of the person just as the lawyer is guardian of his legal rights.

SELECTED BIBLIOGRAPHY

1. Hastings, Donald W.: *A Doctor Speaks On Sexual Expression In Marriage.* Boston, Little, Brown and Co., 1966.
2. Klemer, Richard H.: *Counseling In Marital And Sexual Problems.* Baltimore, Williams and Wilkins, 1965.

3. Lloyd, Charles W.: *Human Reproduction And Sexual Behavior.* Philadelphia, Lea and Febiger, 1964.

4. Masters, William H. & Johnson, Virginia E.: *Human Sexual Response.* Boston, Little, Brown and Co., 1964.

5. Nash, Ethel M.; Jessner, Lucie, and Abse, D. Wilfred (Eds.): *Marriage Counseling In Medical Practice:* A Symposium. Chapel Hill, N.C., The University of North Carolina Press. 1964.

6. Rutherford, Jean J., and Rutherford, Robert N.: *Consultation With Your Doctor For Personal Understanding Of Marriage.* Chicago, Budlong Press Co., 1964.

7. Trainer, Joseph B.: Human Mating and Marriage: Physiologic Foundations For Marriage Counseling. St. Louis, The C.V. Mosby Co., 1965.

8. Trainer, Joseph B.: A Decalog Of Medical Marriage Counseling: An Introductory Monograph. The National Clearinghouse for Mental Health (NIMH), 1970.

9. Vincent, Clark E. (Ed.): Human Sexuality In Medical Education And Practice. Springfield, Charles C Thomas, 1968.

Chapter 4

SEX ETHICS, SEX EDUCATION AND MORALITY

DONALD D. MOORE

T HE ENTIRE area of sex ethics is in need of periodically being reviewed and sometimes revised. Now is the time for the latter emphasis, especially in view of the current sexual revolution. There exists a direct relationship between the need for revised sex ethics (Christian and secular) and the lack of an adequate sex education for so many people. An exact relationship also exists between the lack of sufficient sex education and some people's inability to free themselves from an unpractical and visionary morality which hinders their progress in making necessary adjustments to life's demands. One psychotherapist believes that the *basic moral issue* in marriage counseling is to help clients to free themselves from a stagnant and unrealistic morality which blocks progress in love (4).

At the outset, it may prove helpful to define the key terms to be used in this chapter as we examine the relationships mentioned above.

Morality, as used herein, refers to that quality of behavior that makes it right or wrong, i.e. it refers to conformity to the rules of right conduct.

Sex ethic refers to the principle of morality in total sexual expression, including both the science of the (sexual) good and the nature of the (sexual) right. Reference is made to the rules of conduct recognized (or recognizable) in respect to the sexual class of human actions.

Sex education is the act or process of teaching and instructing about sex; the term is used to describe both the imparting and acquisition of knowledge about sex. This knowledge includes facts about general matters, vocabulary, anatomy, and physiology, and the psychology of human sexual relationships. Sex education should also ideally include information about such specific topics as: possible causes of poor sexual adjustment; conception and contraception; sex-act techniques; pregnancy; childbirth; sterilization and circumcision; menstruation; superstitions, misconceptions, and misinformation; masturbation; veneral diseases; and the effects of menopause on sex life.

SEX EDUCATION AND THE SEXUAL REVOLUTION

Marriage counselors, as much or more so than any other professional group, are becoming more keenly aware of the broadening impact of the contemporary sexual revolution and its necessitation of our redefining sex ethics. According to Joseph Fletcher, the history of Christian influence in sex ethics, for the most part, has been one of repression and rigid regulation, at least in the theory as set forth from pulpits and in manuals of moral and ascetical theology (2).

Secular Sex Ethics

With this sexual revolution, there are also growing awareness that it has produced an impetus toward the growth and development of an emerging secular sexual ethic. There are many causes of these needs for redefinition, among which are the obvious influences of technological advance and social changes with their resultant moral confusion and unsureness (7).

A lucid example of this uncertainty is the type of faulty conclusions drawn by some recent authors in their statements regarding the implications of technological and medical advances for premarital sexual conduct. Harvey Cox may have been in error when he assumed that advances in contraception and antibiotics "will soon remove the last built-in deterrents to premarital coitus" (1). The published evidence is to the contrary (7).

SEX EDUCATION

There have been recent research findings in sociology and psychology which demonstrate with clarity that those individuals with the most extensive and accurate information about their own sexuality have fewer mental and emotional problems (5). Furthermore, the evidence indicates that these enlightened individuals make a better overall adjustment to life than those with less adequate information and knowledge in the sexual sphere. McCary speaks of the many approaches to sex education ranging along a continuum (5). This continuum ranges from the ostrich-like approach (no sex education is good sex education) to the extreme of "sexual anarchy" and includes various stages and/or phases in-between. In between the extremes are such phases as the "thou shalt not" approach and one in which the learner is inundated with facts.

Probably the best solution is a course of selective compromise in which the most pragmatic approaches are utilized from among all the approaches. There are no pat answers to the dilemma, but answers can be worked out by each family as they seek to find an approach that is workable within their family. This same principle of selective compromise could work in churches and the schools which seek to provide programs of sex education.

Social Ethics

There are, nevertheless, implications of the need for redefining our sex ethics and a pressing need for a reexamination of what we have (and/or have not) been doing in the area of sex education. This latter concern is the main focus of this chapter. Although the topic will not be dealt with in detail, there are some direct implications for this matter (sex ethics and sex education) and its relation to a very pressing question in social ethics.

> . . . it is due to the marvelous successes of medicine that the problem of population pressure looms so large . . . Birth control and family planning have to be incorporated in an ethic of population control . . . We need a contemporary conscience about lovemaking and parenthood. People cannot suppose that they have a right to produce as many children as their desires and resources allow, because the social welfare has to be considered, as well . . . What an irony of successful medicine adds to human squalor and misery, as it is actually doing in many lands, and threatens to do even in rich America (3).

Moral Obligations

Some modern parents feel *morally* obligated to provide their children with a sufficient sex education. Marriage counselors are in a unique position to assist some of these parents in fulfilling these moral obligations. If there is ever marriage counseling with a didactic function, it is probably here.

Currently there exists an eminent need for a more rational sex ethic. Similarly there is a growing awareness that a more adequate sex education is proving useful in helping people to free themselves from a stagnant and unrealistic morality which heretofore has blocked their progress in love. Recent literature in the field is illustrative of that fact.

Normalcy and Naturalness

Sex education should begin in the home because it is there that parents have normal and natural opportunities to initiate the process. When a child asks the first question regarding sex, the question should be answered with the truth in terms that the child can comprehend. The question should not, of course, be over-answered. Too many parents think that they have to explain in minute detail the entire process of procreation when their child asks his first sex question, e.g., "Where do babies come from?" Answers should be given in carefully measured doses and in response only to the question asked. If the question is well-handled, the child will feel free to come back later for more information.

Chief Parental Tasks

Parents would also do well to remember that their chief task in sex education is to assist their children in gaining a thorough, complete grasp of facts, while remembering that sexual attitudes are mostly taught by example. What parents teach their children early in childhood about sex will often determine sexual attitudes which they (the children) will bring to their marriage years later.

Case 1

Alice, a twice-married female in her late twenties, confided that she divorced her first husband primarily because she thought that he was sexually perverted. These childhood sweethearts had married in middle adolescence; he was a high-school dropout who had enlisted in the Navy (in an apparent attempt to escape a bad home environment); she quit school when she became pregnant early in the marriage. (Two children, one girl and one boy, were born to this young woman before she was seventeen.) Alice was still a teenager (19) at the time of the divorce. She based her *diagnosis* of his perversion on the fact that he sought oral-genital stimulation as a non-exclusive part of foreplay. The divorce, for which she sued, was granted on the grounds of mental cruelty. The client was several years into her second marriage before she matured sufficiently (and *learned* enough) to believe that oral-genital contacts were normal and natural expressions between marital partners, when they (the expressions) are mutually desirable and satisfying. Unfortunately, it was also about then that Alice realized that she was "still in love" with her first husband who, by that time, had also remarried—and who (according to the client) was "very happy and obviously well-adjusted" in his second marriage. The client said, ". . . if only I could have gotten an adequate sex education early in life, maybe I wouldn't have been so shocked by my ignorance and by my shallow religious beliefs. Perhaps my life would have been different . . . if I had known earlier what is moral and good . . .

The set of circumstances in the above case is distinctive, but the case is not an isolated one. It is illustrative of the devastating effect of what Harper called a stagnant and unrealistic morality; moreover, it suggests what might be additionally advantageous when there is an adequate sex education.

Challenging Parents

Parents need to be challenged to be natural in their approach to the topic in assisting their children in obtaining a sound sex education. Care should be exercised by parents to avoid references to "stork" stories and the like, because they serve no useful function. Furthermore, they may only confuse a child and make more difficult his grasp of serviceable sexual attitudes.

The use of correct, specific words by the parents in programs of sex education also helps a child in his quest for truth. Too many parents, out of ignorance, naivete or whatever, resort to the use of incorrect, nonspecific words and terms in their crude attempts at sex education, e.g. the use of "pet names" for parts of the external reproductive anatomy. The following case reference is illustrative.

If the attainment of a functional sex education is a factor in alleviating the discomforts of too restrictive, outmoded and obsolete moral codes, then we ought to do what we can to help people obtain that education. Although ideally the concept that an adequate sex education is best provided in the home is true, too many parents are unequipped and unprepared for providing that education. Consequently, other institutions might be *morally* obligated to fulfill that function, for example, public school and churches.

Case 2

> The client, a white, married female, complained that her husband resorted to the use of "pet names" in his *teaching* about sexual anatomy to their two preschool sons. She said that he was teaching the boys to refer to their penises as "taliwhackers."

This case refers to an extreme example, but it is not by any means an isolated case. This father, whose intentions were honest enough, substituted what could be a four-syllable word (if it were in fact a word at all) for a two-syllable word which denotes correctly and specifically a part of the sexual anatomy. Too many modern parents, fettered by ignorance, superstition, and the like make superficial and unsuccessful attempts to provide their children with better than they (the parents) had, and the result is more often than not the passing on of an unlighted torch.

Sex Attitudes

Marriage counselors realize that attitudes about sex can serve to harm, impede, and even emotionally block a person's normal development in the area of sexual expression.

Case 3

> Lorna, a married mother-of-two, was thirty-five when she initiated a program of marital counseling. The children, a girl and a boy, were a high school senior and sophomore respectively; the daughter was seventeen and the son fifteen. The stated problem proved to be the real problem: the client was experiencing a great deal of difficulty showing emotion and in relating emotionally (romantically) to her husband. She had married young (age seventeen) and had her children early in the marriage, i.e. when she was eighteen and then twenty-years-old. There were aspects of mild psychosexual maladjustment in her case. However, part of the problem arose from there having been so poor an example of demonstrative affection in the parental home when Lorna was growing up. Lorna could (and did) recount too many episodes like the following one. "I remember so well that often, late in the day, Daddy would come in from working (in the fields) and he would try to embrace Mother and maybe try to kiss her on the cheek. Mother would glance at us children and turn away from Daddy, embarrassed and ashamed . . . I suppose that all of this has something to do with the fact that now I can't show my affection as well as I would like to—to my husband or the children, especially to our son. Now that I think about it, the whole matter of sex and its expression was pretty much negated in our home. We weren't *intentionally* taught that sex was wrong; we just weren't taught anything about sex. The entire subject was hush-hush—like it wasn't something to be discussed in public . . . No! on second thought like it wasn't to be discussed at all."

RESEARCH PROJECT

The fact has been empirically demonstrated that effective courses in sex education can be executed at all grade levels in the schools. The writer is annually involved in one such program for visually handicapped high school students (6).

Ideally, a program of sex education will be initiated long before a young person gets to high school. Unfortunately, however, the idea is seldom the norm. Knowledgeable persons may be all the more morally obligated to assist older young people and adults with sex education—especially if there has been no prior sex education. Some sex education may be appropriate for this latter age group to assist in clarifying misconceptions and in an updating of general sex knowledge. In the study cited above, the researcher found some rather dramatic and desirable changes in perceptible differences between the results of the pretesting and posttesting data on two multiple-choice sex knowledge inventories.

Methodology

Thirty visually handicapped high school students (16 males; 14 females) participated in a six-week sex education course, meeting two nights a week for two hours each session. The course included emphases toward better understanding of anatomy, physiology, vocabulary, and of the psychology of human sexual relationships. Methodologies used permitted the subjects to deal with sex attitudes and feelings in some detail and at length.

Progression

These subjects mastered much of the sex knowledge assessed by the two multiple-choice inventories which were completed under rigorous testing conditions at the first and final meetings of the class. The differences between the pretest and posttest group-scores were statistically significant without regard to academic class, sex, or race classifications. Most of the comparisons showed statistical significance at the .001 level of confidence. All of the groups made remarkable increases from the pretest to the posttest.

Statistical Evidence

In this limited study, the statistical evidence was conclusive; these students learned something in the course, i.e. they comprehended more of the material tested by these two instruments. These findings must, of necessity, be interpreted cautiously because of the small sample; the findings do, however, have some rather broad implications. This type of study needs to be replicated among other populations and on other campuses. Research needs to be conducted with other types of samples, e.g. with comparable groups of nonvisually-handicapped high school students. If these results were obtainable with visually handicapped students, what might research reveal if accomplished in a replication of this type of study for *sighted* students?

Interest Levels and Fatigue

Experience indicates that this type of course, offered even as late as the high school level, is well-received and generally appreciated by the participants. In the course cited earlier, there was a high interest level for the subject matter. Without this high interest level, there could have been a fatigue factor since the course was taught in the early evenings, after the regular school day's activities. Furthermore, the students participated in the course on their own time, at their own choosing, and the course was *non-credit.*

There were other less-easily documented evidences that the students needed and wanted the course, e.g. the questions asked and statements made indicated that the course was well-liked and that it was needed in this particular school. An oft-repeated statement was: "I surely have enjoyed the course; I only wish that I could have had some such course ten years ago . . . before I had learned so much that I am now having to unlearn."

Case 4

When she began psychotherapy, this mother-of-two was still severely encumbered with a massive guilt borne largely out of psychosexual maladjustment. Two aspects of her maladjustment are worthy of mention here. Seven months pregnant with her third child, the woman had agreed with her husband (a year prior to beginning treatment) that they really couldn't afford another child and that an illegal abortion would be in order. He assisted her in the procedure; they used a coat hanger. Only emergency hospital action saved the mother's life. The baby lived for a couple of hours and the mother heard the baby cry; in fact, she still hears the baby cry, and she has visions and she hears voices. The experience precipitated a psychotic break, and the prognosis is quite poor for this woman's case. There were other factors in her case, some of them occurring years earlier. It is here that her concern about and disgust with obscene, pornographic literature figures into her case. As an adolescent girl, she had been raped by a brother ten to twelve years her senior, whose passion (so averred this woman) had been aroused and heightened by his reading obscene and pornographic literature. This became just one more straw in the muddled haystack of this woman's development of intense psychosexual difficulties.

It was significant to note that in both her own case and in reference to her brother, this woman in her more rational moments talked at length (and with considerable intellectual and emotional insight) regarding the lack of adequate sex education in their early lives.

MORALITY

A morality which plays safe, by subjecting itself to an unconditional authority, is suspect. It has not the courage to take guilt and tragedy upon itself. True morality is a morality of risk (9).

Morality and Guilt

The whole problem of guilt and its management (or mismanagement) becomes a sticky problem when one considers all of the ramifications. Since sexual attitudes and moral attitudes are often so closely linked, the really difficult problem is the mixture of real and neurotic guilt. No attempt will be made here to deal with this aspect of the problem in any detail. Other writers have recently spoken of the topic in great depth and with much articulation, e.g. Stein, *Guilt: Theory and Therapy,* 1968 (8).

Because of the frequent linkage between sexual and moral attitudes, more attention should be given to the factor of guilt as it arises from ignorance, naivete, and conflicting feelings and attitudes. It might be helpful here to adopt a working definition of guilt for these intents and purposes. As viewed in the present context, guilt is meant to be a sense of wrong-doing, as an emotional attitude. As such, guilt involves emotional conflict and usually arises out of real or imagined contravention (of social or moral standards) in behavior or thought.

Alleviating Guilt: A Moral Problem

Closely related to this definition of guilt is an overriding realization that many parents are compounding guilt (as well as fear, etc.) reactions in their children by failing to provide them with adequate sex education. For many of these persons, the guilt is further amplified by their own mismanagement of these feelings after the persons reach adulthood. Some people develop intense guilt reactions even when they "try to get above their raising." These individuals often feel that they are going against their parents' teachings when they try to break away from the shackles of their ignorance and naivete. For some of these persons, the bands are too tight and they do not break away. They have been so well-indoctrinated that they cannot escape. For some of these in this latter group, their guilt is extended with their realization that they would even try to be free from thess parental influences—even though the parental teaching were permeated by superstitions, misconceptions, and outright lies. For such peop'e there needs to be some work done in the working through (acting out) of these guilt feelings. Marriage counselors are in unique positions to help at this point—to assist guilt-ridden persons in working through their guilt.

Learning, Unlearning, and Relearning

In many instances, the people who learn incorrect sex information early in life find that it is improbable or impossible for them to accept truth later in life. This statement is especially applicable to those for whom the learning of misinformation is conditioned by other factors (e.g. popular public opinion or beliefs, old wives tales, etc.). Of course, our best (and easier) work in this area is going to be preventive as we assist the present and future generations of youngsters to be spared of this guilt. One way that we can help to alleviate the guilt is to avoid it altogether by better teaching, and one area in which better (and more) teaching is needed is sex education.

REFERENCES

1. Cox, Harvey: *The Secular City*. New York, The Macmillan Company, 1964.
2. Fletcher, Joseph: *Morals and Medicine*. Boston, Beacon Press, 1960.
3. Fletcher, Joseph: Medicine's scientific developments and resulting ethical problems, In *Dialogue in Medicine and Theology*. (Dale White, Ed.). Nashville, Abingdon Press, 1968.
4. Harper, Robert A.: Moral issues in marital counseling, In *Marital Counseling*. (H.L. Silverman, Ed.). Springfield, Illinois, Charles C Thomas Publishers, 1967, pp. 325-335.
5. McCary, James Leslie: *Human Sexuality: Physiological and Psychological Factors of Sexual Behavior*. Princeton, N.J., D. Van Nostrand and Company, Inc., 1967.
6. Moore, Donald D.: Sex education for blind high school students, In *Education of the Visually Handicapped*. March, 1969, Vol. I, No. 1., pp. 22-25.
7. Oates, Wayne E.: *Pastoral Counseling in Social Problems: Extremism, Race, Sex, Divorce*. Philadelphia, The Westminster Press, 1966.
8. Stein, Edward V.: *Guilt: Theory and Therapy*. Philadelphia, The Westminster Press, 1968.
9. Tillich, Paul: *Theology of Culture*. London, Oxford University Press, 1959.

Chapter 5

THE ESSENCE OF SEXUAL MORALITY
ALBERT ELLIS

Before you can define sexual morality, some kind of a stand must be taken on what is general morality: for the former is logically derived from the latter. Let me, therefore, first make my stand on general morality clear.

I take the heretical view that the first principle of morality is: To thine own self be true; or be, primarily, kind to yourself. This principle, I insist, should be closely—in fact, very closely—followed by the second principle of morality: namely, Do not commit any deed that needlessly, definitely, and deliberately harms others. Or, as Immanuel Kant stated in his famous categorical imperative, Do not commit any act that you would not want to see adopted as a universally performed activity. Let me strongly state, however, that this second law of morality is only a corollary of, and in fact a logical deduction from, the first principle, which still is: To thine *own* self be true.

Why is this so? Because I cannot imagine any reason why you should be *consistently* kind to others and do your best to refrain from needless harming them other than the fact that you would like to insure, thereby, that they will be reasonably kind to you and will not harm you. You can, of course, *sometimes* be nice to others, even at your own expense, because you just happen to like or love these others and take genuine pleasure in pleasing them. But this is only *sometimes* likely to be true and can therefore hardly be stated as a *general* law of morality. Besides, being kind to others because you happen to like or enjoy them is hardly involved with any moral law whatever, but depends on your personal whim. If you treat a person well because you love him, you may indeed be a loving person, but are not necessarily either moral or immoral.

Morality has to do with principles of right social conduct and not with personal like or dislike. We preferaby should treat other people properly, or at least refrain from needlessly harming them, whether we personally like them or not. And we should do so, primarily, because *we* want to be, in our turn, treated properly by others; *we* want to help create, by our right conduct, the kind of a world that is safe and beneficial for *us* to live in; and *we* want to avoid reprisals, in case we do treat others badly. In the final analysis, then, morality is based, when it is sensible, on the golden rule: we try to do unto others as we would like them to do unto us. Consequently, far from being self-sacrificing, morality is based on highly rational, self-interested motives.

Would it not be more sensible, it may be asked, to do what many religionists, mystics, and do-gooders have asked us to do by putting the second rule of morality first? Would we not have a better, more loving society if we *first* did well by others, lovingly sacrificed ourselves for them, and *thereby* ensured that they, gratefully and humanly, would then do well by us? No, we would not—unless we happened to live, as few of us seem to do, among a group of angels. For angels, clearly, *would* be the kind of creatures who, when one loved and made sacrifices for them first, would invariably return love with love and kindness with kindness.

In *non*-angelic society, however, all that would assuredly happen if we *did* decide to sacrifice ourselves to others first and reap our moral rewards from these others second, would be that *some* of the others would love and sacrifice themselves for us—but many doubtless would not. Indeed, some people to whom we were most kind would surely be nasty, knife us in the back, and exploit our kindness in various nefarious ways. For, whether we like it or not, literally millions of people *are* stupid, ignorant, or emotionally disturbed, and definitely can *not* be relied upon to behave charmingly and morally.

When self-sacrificism, therefore, is made the first law of morality, the assumption underlying this creed is that those to whom we sacrifice our own interests will invariably sacrifice their interests for us when a suitable occasion arises. This assumption is clearly false. Self-sacrificism, in point of fact, encourages dependency and emotional illness. In most instances, the self-sacrificer senses that he is a self-defeating patsy, begins to hate himself for his weakness, and also ends up by hating the person or persons to whom he is being unduly ingratiating.

Moral sanity still consists of the primary axiom: To thine own self be true. For only in this way, obviously, can you be sure that at least *one* person in the world will be truly looking after your *own* interests. And also, by employing the immediate corollary of this first principle—namely, Do not commit any deed that needlessly, definitely, and deliberately harms others— you will be then ensuring, as much as any human can realistically ensure in this competitive world, that you will receive *minimal* reprisals from others on whose toes you might otherwise step.

Other corollaries to the first principle of morality can easily be derived; and I have derived several of them in my book, *The Case for Sexual Liberty* (Tucson, Arizona: Seymour Press, 1964). Here are some of these major corollaries:

1. The most desirable, and at present most needed, human desideratum is individual and social happiness: meaning the good health, well-being, satisfaction, freedom from fear and hostility, and genuine pleasure of the greatest possible number of individual men and women.

2. Individual-social happiness is the most desirable state for humans to achieve; and all other assumed virtues—such as duty, piety, spirituality, purity, self-sacrifice, artistic achievement, progress, patriotism, Aryanism, Christian science, fascism, pan-Slavism, sensuality, Shakerism, or Mumbo-Jumboism—are valuable only insofar as they contribute to human happiness, and are not in any way (in some esoteric, mystical, or "higher" sense) desirable in themselves.

3. To be real, human happiness should include the well-being of maximum number of *individual men and women,* rather than the "happiness" of some abstract community, state, government, nation, fatherland, county, city, race, creed, or religion. However honored their history or sacred their background, institutions and ideologies should be designed to serve mankind. As soon as they are maintained for their own mystical sakes, or for that of some ruling clique, they become perversions and foci of inevitable dangers.

4. Happiness realistically consists of human satisfaction that is to be achieved *now* and in the *foreseeable future:* during present humanity's existence in *this* universe. It is to be divorced from hypothetical beatitudes that, according to some theorists, exist and from even more hypothetical shades, heavens, or existences. We can realistically only ask for the happiness of living and in-time-to-live *human beings,* and not for any possible disembodied souls or gods.

5. Human happiness is likely to exist to a maximum degree when all normal and competent persons are permitted, and even encouraged, freely and fully to propagate any ideas, to present any productions, and to perform any actions which do not specifically harm, in a gratuitous, needless, unfair, and uninvited manner, other competent persons and which do not take unfair harmful advantage of minors or incompetent individuals.

If a certain act, whether it be sexual or nonsexual, is performed by a competent adult with another capable, reasonably mature person; if it does not specifically, needlessly, unfairly, and uninvitedly harm the individuals involved or any third parties; then, no matter what various statute books, religious teachings, or authoritative persons may say about it, I would hold that it is not a truly unethical and immoral deed.

These, briefly stated, are the rules of general morality to which I subscribe. It should also be made very clear that I strongly believe, as I have stated in *Reason and Emotion in Psychotherapy* (New York: Lyle Stuart, 1962) and various other writings, that when an individual violates these rules and clearly does act in an immoral or unethical way, he still should never be *blamed* or *punished* for his misdeeds but should have them objectively, nonpunitively brought to his attention and helped to accept himself as a wrongdoer rather than a sinner and to do his best to be less wrong in the future. Devaluing him as a person, just because he has shown himself to be a fallible human being, is just as wrong, and clearly immoral, as his own mistaken behavior has been.

The foregoing general rules of morality can easily be applied to sexual conduct. Let me now very briefly make a few such applications in regard to some of the serious sexual questions of our day.

Masturbation. Since masturbation refers to genital self-stimulation, it is not really a social act and hence cannot possibly involve immorality in the sense of the masturbator's harming another human being. He may possibly harm himself—though this would be exceptionally rare; and if he did so he would self-defeating and emotionally disturbed but would hardly (if he were seriously disturbed) even be responsible, let alone blameworthy, for his wrong-doing.

Petting. Petting between consenting adults (or, even for that matter, teen-agers) is again rarely even a wrong or mistaken act, since it is practically never harmful, as long as it is continued up to and including orgasm. Being a social act, it can be immoral if the petter forces his partner to engage in sex relations with him; or gets her to do so by some form of lying; or takes advantage of a minor. But in the manner in which it is usually practised in our society, it is rarely immoral.

Premarital intercourse. When premarital intercourse exists between freely consenting partners who are mature enough to know what they are doing, and when it is done discreetly enough so as to prevent the partners from getting into legal or other difficulties, it is obviously nonharmful and sane. And as long as the fornicator does not lie to his sex partners, deliberately subject them to the dangers of pregnancy or veneral disease, or use any degree of force or coercion to induce them to have sex relations, he can hardly be immoral. His partners are free agents, presumably able to make their own decisions. And if they make such decisions wrongly and later regret fornicating with him because, say, he does not love them enough, does not marry them, or is a poor sex partner, that is the prerogative which he, as a free human, must always give to other free people: the right to err, the freedom to make the wrong move—and presumably to learn about themselves and others thereby!

Adultery. Adultery is often unethical behavior, at least on the part of an adulterer who himself is married, because marriage in our society is normally supposed to be a trust relationship; and the adulterer often has to breach the trust which his mate has placed in him and is consequently unethical in regard to the overt and tacit marital agreement he has with this mate. If his wife knows about his adultery and consents to it, that is another thing entirely. Also, an unmarried individual who has an adulterous affair with a married person may be perfectly ethical, as long as he does not know the mate of the married partner and has no specific responsibility to him or her.

Sex deviations. True sex deviations include acts where the deviant fearfully or angrily, usually on an obsessive-compulsive, fixated, rigid basis, engages in a special kind of sex activity, and generally foregoes all other kinds of acts. Thus, the exclusive exhibitionist or the fixed homosexual is a deviant. Sex deviations do *not* truly include, today, noncoital sex relations between men and women, even when these are substitutes for penile-vaginal intercourse rather than merely preliminaries to this type of intercourse. True deviants are emotionally disturbed and self-defeating but they are not socially immoral, as long as they engage in their deviations with mature, willing partners.

Sexual assault and rape. Sexual assault and rape are clearly immoral acts, since they involve force or coercion, attacks on an unwilling sex partner, and some kind of real harm, in many instances, to the attacked person. Even though clearly immoral, however, acts of rape should be penalized sensibly and equitably, just as acts of nonsexual assault are dealt with, and should not be put in a very special category because they happen to be *sexual* immoralities. The man who nonsexually attacks a woman, and perhaps physically maims her for life, should be given the same kind of legal treatment (and, preferably, psychotherapeutic treatment) as the man who rapes a woman, and perhaps actually harms her very little; and the sex offender should not be cruelly punished, as today he is likely to be, just because he has wrongly and foolishly engaged in a certain kind of assault.

These, then, are some of the applications of the rules of general and sexual morality. To summarize: an act may rationally be considered to be unethical or immoral when it involves an individual's specifically, gratuitously, needlessly, unfairly, or uninvitedly harming another competent person or his taking advantage of a minor or an incompetent person to the specific detriment of this other. It is difficult to conceive of any acts being truly socially immoral if they do not fall within this definition. Sexual acts are immoral when they are generally immoral; and are never unethical simply *because* they are sexual. When an individual commits an immoral or wrong act, he is never a bad person but one who is fallible and whose *act* rather than whose *self* is deplorable. If he refrains from blaming or punishing himself for being immoral, and focuses on the possibility of his being less fallible and mistaken in the future, there is every reason to believe that he will be able to be less, though never entirely or perfectly, unethical and wrong.

Chapter 6

POWER WITH RESPONSIBILITY

LLOYD G. PHILLIPS

POWER HAS been defined as "influence, authority (over), in one's power, under one's control," and powerful as "having great power or influence" (1). To one who received basic training in marriage counseling, or counseling in general, in the early fifties (as did the writer) when the great new "in word" was "nondirective," the concept that the counselor has power in the counseling relationship may be difficult to grasp. While those trained in the Rogerian method were, on the whole, quick to accept the term "client centered" and to recognize that to be strictly "nondirective" required the kind of time which neither the counselor nor the clients had available, it was often a basic assumption that even though the counselor might be a facilitator he did not possess any real power.

Does the counselor, in fact, have power? A recent article by Stanley R. Strong (2) has described counseling as an "interpersonal influence process." Drawing on research on opinion-change he states, "In opinion-change research, a communicator attempts to influence his audience in a predetermined direction; in counseling, the counselor attempts to influence his client to attain the goals of counseling. Verbal communication is the main technique used by an opinion changer in influencing his audience; verbal communication is also the counselor's main means of influencing his client. For both, these communications present opinions or conceptions different than or discrepant from the opinions or conceptions of the audience or client. Finally, characteristics of the communicator as perceived by the audience, characteristics of the audience, and characteristics of the communication affect the success of influence attempts" (3).

There can be little, if any, doubt that when a counselor is working with clients he is attempting to bring an influence to bear on their particular interpersonal relationship. Irrespective of his theoretical background or the particular discipline from which he comes, a marriage counselor enters into counseling because he believes that it is possible, somehow, to effect changes in the relationship of the clients. This may lead to a decision on the part of the clients either to continue the relationship because positive gains are made or to move on to a divorce or separation because it seems now clear to them that the relationship cannot meet their basic needs.

Writing of the caseworker-client relationship, Helen Harris Perlman makes the point that to deny authority is to leave the client in a sorry plight (4). At times marriage counselors have been thought of as "interferring busybodies," moving into areas which are very personal and private to two people. In an attempt to justify their existence counselors have tended (the writer included) to overstate the situation in some such terms as the following—Marriage counselors only go in when they are invited by either one or both the spouses making an approach to seek help. The counselors effectiveness is limited strictly by the degree of motivation in the clients themselves. They have their own rights and powers and the counselor is unable to intervene unless they want him to do so. Even then he does not exert any direct control. He continues to be very client centered.

Maybe what counselors should be saying is—Yes, we recognize that in the counseling situation we may be directly in control. We do try to develop motivation in the clients. We do try to help clients look at areas they desire to avoid because they may be hurtful, or because they feel it will put them in a bad light with the counselor, or for some other reason. Finally, however, any decisions are made by the clients themselves, but in the light of all the influences which we have brought to bear in the counseling process (5).

Even a casual examination of the recorded counselor responses in any interview will reveal that the counselor has power and uses it far more frequently than he may believe. Suppose that he is simply making noises—"ah huh," "hm, hm"—by so doing he is conveying a message to the client which may go something like this—"I am with you in what you are saying. This could be an important line to follow for it seems important to you. Please continue the way you are going!" The result is that the client continues with the particular chain of thought which he has been pursuing. However, if the counselor moves from the encouraging noises to a reflection of something which has been expressed it is as though he said, "Wait a moment here. This appears to be very significant. Let's explore this feeling more deeply." The consequence of the reflecting back is that the client stops the general flow of his story and considers the nature of the feeling he has expressed. He responds to an influence exerted by the counselor. He does not consider the importance or significance of the feeling merely of his own accord. Occasionally it may be that as the client verbalizes his feelings something becomes clear to him without any intervention on the part of the counselor; however, such occasions would be rare.

Whether a counselor will openly admit it or not, the very decision to reflect something back to the client is a tacit admission that he has power in the counseling situation. All counselors would agree that counseling has a goal and a mode, a method, a technique, a skill is used to achieve that goal!

If counseling was thought to be purposeless, how many counselors would continue?

A counselor chooses what he will reflect. The skilled counselor will not just reflect something back because it was expressed in the last words of the client. He may well choose to reflect back to the first part of the client's statement and not the last, because it appears that it could be a more profitable line to follow. He is in fact saying to himself—"I have influence here. I have power to change the direction of the client's thinking." In response to his reflection the client does change direction just as surely as if he were a train following a track and the signalman switched the points and diverted it on to another line. It may be a dead end; it may be a detour; it may be a branch that does not lead to the desired goal; it may be the vital switch which enables the train to proceed to its true destination. The counselor has the power to do it if he so chooses. Maybe if he fails to use his power he is a bitter disappointment to his clients.

Quite clearly the counselor is recognizing his power in such instances as when he invites the client to talk about his early background or his family of origin, when he uses confrontation, and when he lends support to one partner rather than the other in some instance. In numerous ways the counselor is giving direction, not only to the course of a particular counseling interview, but also to the clients in their thinking, their behavior, and the pattern of their interaction with one another.

Jay Haley has expressed it in this way. "It is convenient for some therapists to argue that they do not take sides in a marital struggle but merely "reflect" back to the couple what they are expressing. Such an argument requires considerable naivete. If a therapist listens to a wife's complaints and then turns to her husband and says, "How do you feel about that?" he cannot make his classic statement without his inquiry being in some sense directive. A therapist cannot make a neutral comment; his voice, his expression, the context, or the mere act of choosing a particular statement to inquire about introduces directiveness into the situation. When the therapist is being directive, coalition patterns are being defined and redefined, and a crucial aspect of this type of therapy is continually changing coalition patterns between therapist and each spouse. The wife who drags her husband into marriage therapy soon finds that the therapist does not join her in condemnation of the fellow, and the dragged-in husband discovers with some relief that the focus also shifts to how difficult his wife can be" (6).

The counselor may feel that he has no desire to be an authority figure or a great influence either in or over the lives of others, but his decision to become a counselor inevitably sets him on the path to becoming such a person. It may well be that his power is as great as that of a witch doctor among a primitive people. Like it or not, the counselor has power. What then are the sources of his power?

Lest the previous comparison be pushed too far, let it be said quickly that whereas the witch doctor frequently built his power and influence by fostering fear, this is not so in the case of the counselor! Although fear may well play a part, that is fear on the part of one or both spouses that unless outside help is received their marital relationship will break down completely and there will be no alternative except separation or divorce, which neither of them may desire. Perhaps the major source of the counselor's power lies in the fact that the client gives it to him.

As part of the on-going research of the Marriage Guidance Council of Victoria, (7) an attempt is made to elicit from the client, early in the initial interview, what his expectation from the counselor really is. After discussion with the counselors a record face sheet was compiled by the research committee and used in a trial run. Further modifications were then made and the current sheet was put into use. Eight typical client expectations were listed and counselors are asked to record under one of these. If none is applicable the counselors are asked to record the expectation separately.

The listed client expectations are that the counselor will accomplish the following:

1. Bring deserting partner back.
2. Reconcile marriage.
3. Agree marriage is irreconcilable.
4. Give moral support or arbitrate.
5. Listen to unburdening of problems.
6. Tell client what to do.
7. Assist clients to find their own solution.
8. Give help with personal difficulties.

All of these expectations, with the possible exception of number 5 (listen to unburdening of problems) , actively attribute power to the counselor. While the research project is far from complete it would appear from counselor's comments that frequently they hear a plea from a client in some such terms as these, "Tell me what to do and I'll do it." The client is feeling helpless in the situation and he turns to someone he perceives as an authority for direction.

The feelings of the client in approaching a marriage counselor will be mixed. Despite improvement in recent years, consulting a marriage counselor is still far from a socially accepted practice—at least in Australia. When a client decides to seek help he probably feels very anxious. Out of his fear and desperation he has summoned up sufficient courage to make an appointment and get himself into the counseling room. He is there, despite all his contrary feelings—maybe even feelings of disloyalty—because there is an overriding hope that here is someone who can help. The very fact that this person is practicing as a marriage counselor gives the impression that here is a person with special training, skill, and experience in dealing with marital difficulties, who is obviously stronger and more powerful than the client. The client may at times overvalue the counselor.

> To come for help signifies weakness, despite the fact that the recognition of the need for help and the decision to come for it require strength. One is acknowledging that another person is wiser or stronger and taking the first step in allowing oneself to come under the influence of another unknown or little known person. Such feelings are almost universal, but the intensity with which they are experienced will vary. Anxiety will be greater, for instance, when the client is consulting the worker about matters in which he has a vital interest than about peripheral matters; it will also vary with the degree to which the client consciously or unconsciously believes himself to be at fault, and with the intrinsic nature of the matters about which he must talk (8).

If the basic source of power comes from the attitude of the client the continuance of the power comes also from the perception the client has of the counselor. Here many factors enter in, including the counselor's training, his knowledge, his developed skills, his integrity, his attitude, his whole personality—the kind of person the counselor is.

> We know of no disagreement to, or contrary evidence on, the assertion that the development of an emotionally warm permissive, understanding relationship is a first step in the counseling process. The development of such a working relationship characterized by mutual liking, trust, and respect is one of the first tasks of the counselor. It is as if the counselor must build a bridge or pipeline through which the client perceives the counselor as a powerful ally in his struggle with himself and his world (9).

Power is, at least initially, in the hands of the counselor and if he is competent it remains with him by tacit mutual agreement with his client. However, there are many different ways in which his power can be used. The choices open to him at any given moment are multiple.

Power may be used for diagnostic purposes. Obviously no marriage counselor can proceed to the treatment of a disturbed marriage relationship unless he is able to make a diagnosis of what, in fact, is wrong within the relationship. He may then exert his power to determine the cause of the disturbance. It is possible that this may become his chief end, if he has an overriding interest in research into the nature and causation of marital difficulties. The diagnosis may thus become an end in itself. Important as research into these areas undoubtedly is, this is not the main purpose of marriage counseling, although it is an obvious incidental gain.

At a particular stage in the counseling process the counselor may choose to throw his power on the side of one spouse as against the other because, in his professional judgment, he deems that spouse to be in need of support. At a later moment he may exert his influence on the side of the other spouse. This is not unusual. However, maybe because of deep-seated feelings within himself he believes men (or women) too often have things their own way. He may say that in his experience it is usually the man (or the woman) who is at fault in marital disturbances. He therefore sees his role as siding with the one against the other. He may not go as far as this but he may feel that there is always one that deserves more blame than the other. Therefore he uses his power to change the blameworthy partner.

If the counselor feels that the all-important goal of counseling is to enable each partner to grow as an individual, he will exert his power in this direction. He may go on seeing both of the spouses, and it may be deemed marriage counseling, but in fact he concentrates far less on their interaction as a marital dyad than he does on their individuality as persons. He uses his power to engage in what is virtually individual psychotherapy. This is right and proper in the appropriate place and an element is in all counseling. However, if the clients have no opportunity of developing insight or self-awareness in relationship to each other the result can be that the relationship is in a state of greater imbalance than ever and the marriage breaks because it is stifling the individual's growth.

Marriage counseling has become a practice in various parts of the world because it is recognized that in most societies marriage is an institution worthy of preservation. The pressure of society is on the side of saving marriages. Divorce is rarely simple and a high rate of divorce tends to be seen as a social disaster. The need to "save marriages" was the original impetus which gave rise to marriage counseling as a specialized skill. Consequently it may be that a counselor throws his power on the side of keeping two people together in marriage at all costs. Perhaps this is a particular temptation to the priest or clergyman counselor. The effects on the two persons directly concerned and the consequences for the children, are glossed over. It is amazing how often an attempt is made to save a marriage for the sake of the children. The notion that, as long as the couple stay together it is best for the children, must surely be outdated.

It is equally possible for a marriage counselor to exert his power to destroy a marriage. As the counselor gets deeper into a counseling situation he finds his earlier diagnosis confirmed and the causes so complex that he prognosticates a hopeless situation. Whether he is aware of it or not, the counselor, from this point on, may be using his power to convince not only himself, but the two clients in particular, that the marriage has no future. The only sensible thing for them to do is to dissolve the marriage in as amicable a way as possible. Of course, the counselor may not put this into direct words, but his attitude and the direction he gives to the counseling process lead inevitably to the confirming of his prognosis. Counselors need to be aware of the danger of prognosis actually creating a disease. If a person is esteemed of little worth, is consistently treated as of little worth, his fears that he may be of little worth are confirmed. He then behaves as if he were in fact so and ends up being a person of little worth.

The counselor's power can be used in many ways to meet needs within himself. These may arise from deep-seated personality factors such as obsessions or feelings of aggression. They may arise out of the deep need in every individual to feel himself esteemed and to feel himself worthy of esteem. Consequently he uses his power to gain the esteem of his clients and at the same time to prove to himself that he is worthy of their esteem.

Moral values are important to every individual. The upholding of personal values is at the very heart of a man's integrity. History is filled with examples of men and women who have accepted imprisonment, deprivation, suffering or even death, rather than be disloyal to what they have held important. Luther's words at the Diet of Worms are typical, "Here I stand. I can do no other!" Moral values are just as important to society. The whole rule of law is based on the fact that there are certain basic values which a society desires to preserve and that if you live within the society you are expected to abide by the law until, through exercise of the right to protest or by other democratic processes, you are able to change the law. Because moral values are so central to being, the counselor can use his power consciously or unconsciously to impose either his own moral values or those of society on his clients.

The central issue for a counselor in any given counseling situation is how to use his power, the determination of the direction in which change is desired and the application of his influence to achieve the required goal.

Either therapists can successfully influence behavior or they cannot, and they have little choice of what to claim. If they wish to say they cannot do so, or may not do so in just those areas where human concern is greatest, and are therefore not at all responsible for the behavior of their clients, one must ask what right they have to be in business. The very validity of the disclaimer destroys their most important function, so the help they can give must then be very narrowly defined. But if, on the other hand, they affirm some technical expertise and wish to claim a genuine ability to influence people, then they must also assume some responsibility for the nature of that influence. In that event, they must ultimately see themselves as moral agents as they are confronted with moral problems. And the extent to which they are confronted with moral problems depends on the significance of the problems with which they deal, for morals are the ultimate values we assign to our acts (10).

The counselor has power. He uses his power. He must use his power with responsibility, i.e. as one who is "liable to be called to account, to be answerable to a person for his actions, to be morally accountable for his actions" (11). As has been discussed elsewhere, (12) in the realm of morality there is a responsibility to one's self (one's own integrity), a responsibility to other individuals directly or indirectly involved, and a responsibility to society. To these which are generally accepted, the Christian man adds yet another—responsibility to God. In a counseling situation the counselor has a responsibility for his actions—the way in which he uses his power—to the clients, to himself, to his agency (if he works in this setting), to his profession, and to society. Here, too, some will want to add a final responsibility to God.

It, surely, would be accepted by all counselors that there is a primary responsibility to the client for his welfare, and in marriage counseling this cannot be completely dissociated from the welfare of the other partner in the relationship and that of any children of the marriage. There is a responsibility to work within the accepted moral framework of the partners. For example, if a couple are practicing Christians, a counselor does not behave responsibly if he exerts his influence to turn them away from their faith. Clients cannot be treated as numbers or objects, as just another case. Clients are individual persons with all the capacities which that implies in feeling, thinking and doing. There will be times when the needs of the clients conflict with the counselor's pursuit of knowledge. In such instances the validity of being "client-centered" must be emphasized.

The counselor has a responsibility to himself and his own integrity. Involved in this is a clear recognition of his own limitations. He is neither omniscient nor omnipotent. Referral of clients who need some specialized skill or knowledge beyond that of the counselor is both being concerned for the welfare of the clients and being honest with himself. Carl Rogers gives an excellent illustration of the therapist being responsible to himself in a case of extreme transference attitudes.

> S: I think emotionally I'm dying for sexual intercourse but I don't do anything about it . . . . The thing I want is to have sexual intercourse with you. I don't dare ask you, 'cause I'm afraid you'd be nondirective.
> C: You have this awful tension, and want so much to have relations with me.
> S: (goes on in this vein. Finally) Can't we do something about it? This tension is awful! Will you relieve the tension. . . . Can you give me a direct answer? I think it might help both of us.
> C: (gently) The answer would be no. I can understand how desperately you feel, but I would not be willing to do that.

S: (pause, sigh of relief) I think that helps me. It's only when I'm upset that I'm like this. You have strength, and it gives me strength.

As in setting any limit in the therapeutic experience, this is something which is purely the responsibility of the therapist, and he takes that responsibility. He does not attempt to evaluate the client's experience by some such statement as "That really wouldn't help you." He simply takes responsibility for his own behavior, at the same time indicating understanding and acceptance of the client's experience of the situation (13).

If a counselor is working within an agency then he has a responsibility to work within its framework. The agency may have certain policies concerning the nature of the initial interview or the intake service. It may have set ways of recording to facilitate research. It may have policy concerning the types of clients retained and those referred elsewhere immediately. It may have clearly defined policy about fees and rules about many other issues. While he remains within the agency, the counselor represents the agency to the client and must represent it responsibly.

Every professional person has a responsibility to all other members of his profession to see that he behaves in a manner which brings credit to the profession. The counselor will use his power in such a manner as will not leave his colleagues open to a general criticism. In behaving responsibly to his profession he will use every opportunity of increasing his understanding and developing his professional competence by endeavoring to keep up to date with the literature and entering into dialogue with his colleagues in seminars and conferences.

A counselor, like any other individual, cannot be part of a society without having a responsibility to society. Obviously he will not use his power to encourage his clients to behave contrary to the law. At the same time he has no responsibility merely to throw his weight on the side of conventional morality, simply because it is conventional. There will be times when he feels a conflict between his responsibility to clients and his responsibility to society. This could be a difficult decision where, for example, there is prior knowledge of a contemplated murder. Where marriage counselors in Australia are concerned, the Commonwealth makes it clear that there is a basic responsibility to confidentiality. The law provides that the marriage counselor is "not competent or compellable" to give evidence in any court of law (14).

Basically, it would seem that whether the counselor uses his undoubted power responsibly or not depends on the relationship he has with the client and the kind of person he, in fact, is. Much has been written about the relationship between therapist, caseworker or counselor, and client, and the qualities in the counselor which are necessary conditions to effect a change in the client (15).

Three characteristics of an effective counselor have been summarized by Truax and Carkhuff (1967) as follows:

1. An effective therapist is integrated, nondefensive, and authentic or genuine in his therapeutic encounters.
2. An effective therapist can provide a nonthreatening, safe, trusting or secure atmosphere by his acceptance, unconditional positive regard, love, or nonpossessive warmth for the client.
3. An effective therapist is able to "be with," "grasp the meaning of," or accurately and empathically understand the client on a moment-by-moment basis (16).

The mere possession of academic qualifications is no guarantee that the holder possesses the necessary personality characteristics to be an effective and responsible counselor. No one would deny that adequate training is important to the marriage counselor but experience shows that much depends on the kind of person who is counseling. Truax and Carkhuff suggest that while "essential therapeutic skills can be learned, it must also be clear that one way of producing more effective therapists is to be more selective in reviewing prospective trainees" (17).

Since its inception in 1948, the Marriage Guidance Council of Victoria has insisted that selection is a prerequisite for training as a marriage counselor. Processes have become more rigid as time has gone by in an endeavor to select those who will become effective counselors. The path to becoming a marriage counselor has several clearly defined steps: selection, training, supervision, and accreditation. When a counselor is accredited, supervision continues and increasingly is playing a part in reaccreditation. Throughout this process, counselors are ranked in each stage. Two groups have been followed through from selection to accreditation and their rankings at each stage have been compared in an endeavor to improve selection procedures.

There is little to guide in this area of the selection of counselors and such as there is points up the difficulties (18). However, the results which have been obtained in Victoria over the years appear to justify both the continuance and the further refining of selection processes.

Marriage counseling demands the use of power with responsibility. An adequate selection process for all counselors would therefore seem to be an essential step towards that goal.

REFERENCES

1. *Concise Oxford Dictionary.*
2. Strong, Stanley R.: Counselling: An interpersonal influence process. *J Counseling Psychol, 15:*215-224, No. 3, 1968.
3. Strong, Stanley R.: Counselling: An interpersonal influence process. *J. Counseling Psychol, 15:*215, No. 3, 1968.

4. Perlman, Helen Harris: *Social Casework*. Chicago, University of Chicago Press, 1957, 1957 pp. 69-70.
5. Arbuckle, Dugard S.: *Counseling Philosophy, Theory and Practice*. Boston, Allyn and Bacon, 1965, pp. 234-252.
6. Haley, Jay: *Strategies of Psychotherapy*. New York, Grune and Stratton, 1963, p. 138.
7. Since 1966, the Marriage Guidance Council of Victoria, in conjunction with the Mental Health Research Institute (Victoria), has been engaged in an extensive research program. Final results not yet available.
8. Hollis, Florence: *Casework—A Psychosocial Therapy*, New York, Random House, 1964, p. 150.
9. Brammer, Lawrence M., and Shostrom, Everett L.: *Therapeutic Psychology*. Englewood Cliffs, N.J., Prentice-Hall, 1960, p. 94.
10. London, Perry: *The Modes and Morals of Psychotherapy*. New York, Holt, Rinehart and Winston, 1964, pp. 14-15.
11. *Concise Oxford Dictionary*.
12. Phillips, Lloyd G.: *Individual Responsibility and Morality*. Paper presented to S.C.M., Monash University, 1967. Unpublished.
13. Rogers, Carl R.: *Client-Centered Therapy*. Boston, Houghton Mifflin, 1951, p. 211.
14. Commonwealth of Australia, Matrimonial Causes Act, 1959-66.
15. Rogers, Carl R.: The necessary and sufficient conditions of therapeutic personality change. *J Consulting Psychol, 21*:95-103, 1957; The interpersonal relationship: the core of guidance. *Harvard Education Review, 32*:416-429, 1962; Bugental, J.F.T.: *The Search for Authenticity*, New York, Holt, Rinehart and Winston, 1965.
16. Traux, Charles B., and Carkhuff, Robert R.: *Toward Effective Counseling and Psychotherapy*. Chicago, Aldine, 1957, p. 1.
17. Truax, Charles B., and Carkhuff, Robert R.: *Toward Effective Counseling and Psychotherapy*. Chicago, Aldine, 1957, p. 232.
18. Halmos, Paul: *The Faith of the Counsellors*. London, Constable, 1965, pp. 126-130.

Chapter 7

THE GYNECOLOGIST'S INVOLVEMENT IN COUNSELING

ALFRED STERN

By JOINING in the contemplation of "Moral Issues in Marriage Counseling" a gynecologist indicates that in his practice, founded on the natural sciences and directed by science, other considerations enter into decision-making.

While scientific testing must be expected to lead eventually to only *one* correct result, moral issues lend themselves to various alternative answers depending on the ethical values of the individuals involved and of society as a whole. It has been tried over and over to conquer this disturbing element of electivity either by establishing one code of ethics as the domineering one or by eliminating moral considerations in favor of expediency. Both attempts can be successful for a limited time only. The spiritual dictator cannot rule forever unchallenged. The pragmatist will realize that he himself by his high valuation of expediency is adherent to a distinct code of ethics to which valid alternatives exist. Choice, therefore, will continue to remain and to disturb and test man—and especially painfully the one who is called upon to give advice.

A prerequisite for the adviser who is to assist in the solution of complex problems is his familiarity with the problem. His understanding will help him to better apply his scientific and his philosophical armament to the finding of an adequate answer. An attempt is made to demonstrate in this chapter the rise and the many-faced nature of such problems (Examples #1 through #11) which engage the gynecologist's personal values as much as his technical professional training.

*   *   *

CONTRACEPTION

The upsurge in the development and in the use of reliable birth control devices has—like all great discoveries—desired, undesired, and unpredictable consequences. The gynecologist is faced with the task of foreseeing and evaluating these effects in every case.

Case 1

A university coed, during her first term away from home, comes to the office to ask for contraceptive advice.

You decline. She becomes pregnant with all the depressing ensuing possibilities: abortion, illegitimate motherhood, forced marriage, disillusionment. Her parents, her friends, she herself will blame you—and you will blame yourself, not without cause.

You comply. You have helped launching her on a career of nonmarital intercourse—psychologically, by conniving with her attitude, and in very deed, by eliminating the most embarrassing sequel. The threat of two possible developments is obvious: if the girl rates complete bodily intimacy as the supreme expression of a binding union she may squander it immaturely on an uncommitted partner, with all the later disappointment; if, however, she deflates the sexual experience and plays the market lightly she may block her way to the emotional and factual security of total commitment. In either case her parents, her guardians, her future husband or husbands, she herself may well blame you—and you yourself will, too.

You make your service dependent upon the consent of her parents. She may refuse to take them into her confidence; then you have practically declined getting involved, come what may. And still you are sharing the consequence, by default. You may instead, troubled by her underage status, proceed to inform her parents. This amounts to breaking the relationship of protected confidence between client and physician, counselor, spiritual adviser; it would be deadly to counseling. (The twilight of legal inconsistencies places additional difficulties upon the relationship between the minor and her medical adviser: manipulating a minor, as a gynecological examination and even the temporary interference with her fertility may well be called, is prohibited, unless sanctioned by parents or guardian. Statutory underage ends at legal age or at the moment of marriage, strictly seen therefore not at the premarital examination; underage ends automatically with the beginning of pregnancy.) *

You confine yourself to explaining, technically, the workings of the different contraceptive devices, their immediate and their long-range effects on the body, their reliability, and the status of research in the direction toward improvement. By this you are furnishing your client with all the useful mechanical knowledge available. You count yourself out as a counselor.

Case 2

You are asked by a *married woman* to furnish her—not for compelling medical reasons—a contraceptive device.

By doing so you violate the tenet that intercourse has the sole purpose of procreation. Powerful forces hold strictly to this attitude. You cannot al-

---

*Legal provisions are handled in this article in most general terms since the legislation varies in different countries and in different states. When for clarity's sake the author has to be more specific, the legal references are patterned after the California situation (which, however, at this writing is also in flux).

leviate their fear of hedonism by pointing at the ennobling effects of responsible freedom.

This orthodox conviction is not generally shared by our present-day society, yet its puritan message is buried in many a rational liberal mind and works on a subconscious level fostering ambivalent feelings about the acceptability of artificial birth control. Such ambivalence is often hidden behind the patient's complaints that "the pill" or other devices do not agree with her. One does not necessarily create ease and security in a woman's mind by crusading for contraception.

On the other hand, in cases where her mind is made up and contraception opted for, the habit and convenience of using it invites postponement of the decision to make their marriage fertile. The agewise, adventure-wise, harmony-wise best time for parenthood may be missed. A single child may remain deprived of brother or sister for valid reasons which, however, in the long run, may not outweigh the loss. The initiation of contraceptive procedures should be coupled with the reminder that the presently domineering indications should be reevaluated from time to time and that the proper time for reappraisal should not be conveniently passed by.

The denial of the request for birth control can lead to personal breakdown, to economic ruin, to the loosening of family ties. The advising gynecologist should weigh well whether the price for upholding a shiny principle is not too high. He should consider this even more since not he but the patient pays the price.

Instead of denying or going along with the request you use your expert medical knowledge to delineate to the patient statistically the comparative unreliability of the rhythm method, the possible irritating effects of the intra-uterine device, the percentagewise occurrence of short and long-range side effects of the "pill." You hope to have done your share. You have done it merely as a clinical pathologist, you have compared the pro's and con's of methods, but you have not faced the vexing problems of philosophy which may disturb your patient. You have kept aloof of the dichotomy of opinions which can be reconciled neither by decree nor by majority vote.

Case 3

You are approached with the request for contraceptive help in cases where the protection is sought for *extra-marital* purposes: by *adult* single women, widows, divorcees, or in triangular set-ups.

You provide the protection. By doing so you challenge the tenet that intercourse is the prerogative of people only when they are bound in marriage. You may also aid with the violation of an existing marriage by facilitating adultery.

You deny your assistance. You may be instrumental in depriving a woman, capable of giving and taking the full and mature experience of complete intimacy, of this blessing. You may finalize her frustration.

FERTILITY

Case 4

In cases of *infertility* the frustration is most tangible. The desire for a child is part of the human fabric. The gynecologist is asked to give advice and help toward this goal.

Various considerations, however, may suggest the denial of help. Few will hold up against genuine urge for parenthood. Except in clearly established instances of serious hereditary handicaps, it is still presumptuous to try "eugenic engineering." It is rather timid to invoke economic insecurity against the positive experience of parenthood. It does injustice to the deserving couple to discourage them by the specter of population explosion. Valid as these considerations may be they should not be abused to interfere with the also valid desire of a couple to perfect their marriage through progeny.

Giving help is sufficiently justified by the woman's wish to be healthy enough to conceive. But by correcting her infertility you do not necessarily become her benefactor. Your help can be of questionable value when the aspiration to parenthood rests on dubious motivation. The wish for an offspring is not always the result of the combined desire of a harmonious couple to have a child by each other.

The husband who presses for fatherhood because his predominant goal is the perpetuation of his family name by his son, the religious fanatic who owes a first-born to God, think less of their wives than of the tribe. The gynecologist in this case gives his service to another institution than to marriage.

The woman, married or unmarried, who yearns for pregnancy because she believes by this experience to become emotionally and sensually better capable of reacting than in her present nulliparous status thinks less of her husband than of her own therapy. Her contribution to parenthood will be egotistic and immature. Before giving gynecological advice the counseling professional should give her time and maybe direction to develop into a wife and potential mother first.

The couple who is anxious to produce a child in order to cement their cracking marriage expects from the newborn third party what they have been unable or unwilling to achieve. The counselor should hesitate before advocating or approving of childbirth as a cure of marriage. Harmony should precede, it does not necessarily follow, procreation.

This fallacy is even more painful in the case of the unmarried girl who believes in "hooking" her man into matrimony or fidelity by her pregnancy.

It does harm to the unmarried mother and to the extra-marital or premarital child. (This constellation is especially trying. The pregancy is not always aspired to by clear scheming; it begins often as the result of ambivalent, half-conscious omission of precautionary contraceptive measures. The gynecologist has to sense this trend and in the given cases he has to verbalize it bluntly. He may even replace the contraceptive pill for safety's sake by an intra-uterine device. This subterfuge is, however, merely a technical instead of an educational protection.)

STERILIZATION AND INSEMINATION

Two therapeutic procedures in the field of fertility and sterility are fraught with problems of a nonmedical nature.

Case 5

Contraception is most safely obtained by *sterilization*. Informed consent by the patient and the spouse removes the operation from the category of mayhem.* The existence of a Society for Voluntary Sterilization indicates that requests and consent will be forthcoming in increasing number. While the legal question is thus being answered in the most permissive way, the threat of a later change of the patient's mind remains. If unforeseen circumstances (death of children, new marriage) rekindle the wish for children the virtual irreversibility of the operative effect makes correction nearly impossible. The surgeon should be utterly sure of the present and future features of his case before he undertakes without dire necessity final inroads in his patient's fertility—if he does so at all.

Case 6

Conception can be achieved in adequate cases by artificial *insemination*. Here, too, informed consent has to be given in writing by husband and wife.

Opinions and feelings are divided as to whether in case of donor insemination (AID) the introduction of a stranger's sperm constitutes adultery. While this concern can be eliminated legally, uneasiness may still linger in the couple's mind and grow to destroy their affection for the child.

The question of paternity does not arise when the husband's sperm can be used for insemination (AIH). Since, however, the sperm is generally obtained by masturbation, religious restrictions may prohibit the procedure or interfere with its undisturbed acceptance.

---

*Legal provisions are handled in this article in most general terms since the legislation varies in different countries and different states. When for clarity's sake the author has to be more specific, the legal references are patterned after the California situation (which, however, at this writing is also in flux).

Artificial insemination can be a highly satisfactory method of overcoming infertility if all participants—wife, husband and physician—are fully aware of and reconciled with its logical and its irrational implications before the procedure is attempted.

ABORTION

Among the cases in which the question of abortion comes up, one finds a multitude in which the medical emergency is too serious to leave any acceptable alternative to the immediate termination of pregnancy. In turn, there are often cases in which the health conditions are so precarious that they preclude the interruption. Both these groups become rarely charges of the counselor; they require the surgical expert, and they may well need sympathy.

The situations in which the medical indication is less clear cut create agonizing problems for the gynecologist. He has to take a stand when his patients present him with their case and frequently he has to act as a judge in a less immediate personal encounter when he is a member of the Therapeutic Abortion Committee of his hospital, installed to approve or disapprove of applications.

Case 7

A *married* couple requests the interruption of a pregnancy. For this they present in fact reasons which are sufficient to give *legal* license for the operation, but which are not equivocal enough to rule out a different, more conservative answer.

You choose to approve of and to perform the abortion. By making this decision you admit that, in this arguable case, you rate the objections lower than the reasons for the interruption of the pregnancy. Yet, among the objections are such important ones as the protection of the unborn child, the preservation and strengthening of the maternal instinct, the readiness for risk and sacrifice as a parent, the habit for perserverance at an important enterprise. By deciding for abortion you may furthermore convey to the parents the feeling that the continuation of a pregnancy is negotiable. You may foster the later outbreak of dormant guilt feelings in your patient. Finally, you disregard the many cases where early pregnancy rejection changes later into urgent desire for the child.

You turn down the application for abortion. In so doing you impose upon the patient hardships which may damage seriously her bodily or mental health, her family life, her social situation, and you ask her to accept these severe wounds in order to uphold yours, the outsider's standards above hers. You set yourself as the judge against a free persons; and if you err she has to pay. You may condemn an unborn to a life of debility, misery, and indignity.

Case 8

A woman, married or unmarried, requests the abortion of her *illegitimate* child. Sufficient reasons can be stated to cover the operation *legally*. But physical and mental recovery can be visualized also if she carries her pregnancy through.

You proceed with the abortion. Like in the case of the legitimate pregnancy, by so deciding you devaluate, compared with other necessities, the child's right to live and the preeminence of motherhood. Moreover, you cannot escape the suspicion that in this case you add another devaluation: you appear to conform with the claim of the sheltered ones that illegitimate motherhood is intrinsically inferior to legitimate motherhood. You stigmatize the girl's or woman's experience as something invalid which should be eliminated. This may be very degrading to a pregnant woman who already feels troubled by insecurity, but who loved very seriously when she conceived. But suppose the pregnancy happened to be really the result of superficial casualty and neglect; then you may wonder whether by eliminating the consequence you are not helping the attitude that caused it to be perpetuated.

You decline the abortion. In this case the hardships to which you condemn the illegitimate mother and her child may far exceed the distress of the legitimately pregnant woman to whom abortion is denied. In addition, by trapping a girl forever with the result of her error you may stifle her chance of turning back and of recovering toward a new style of life. When in the case of doubt one votes for carrying the pregnancy through one better ask oneself to what extent punishing tendencies have influenced one's decision.

You submit the known facts about the case without your positive or negative recommendation to the Therapeutic Abortion Committee where the final decision of approval or disapproval belongs anyway. By thus withholding your own partisanship you may not even change the outcome of the Committee's deliberations. But the patient expects from the physician in whom she confides to have an opinion of his own, to make it clear and to defend it—sometimes even against herself. You fail her as a counselor because you demote yourself to the level of a subordinate who divests himself of his own responsible opinion.

Case 9

You are confronted with a pregnant patient who requests an abortion in the *absence of any legally recognized indication*.

You provide or help her to obtain an illegal abortion because of your deep personal conviction that in her situation every evil is less deleterious than carrying this pregnancy to the bitter end. For good and widely shared reasons you may consider the law inadequate and in need of change. But you are making yourself guilty of breaking the law.

You decline assistance. You may turn down the applicant because you find her case invalid. You may also refuse help because you rate law abidance higher than the illegal correction of inequities. You choose the protection and the security which legality provides for yourself, your family, and the social order of which you and your patient are part. If you convince your patient of the sincerity of your claim that this is to her greater interest she may follow your guidance confidently. If you have, however, primarily your self-protection in mind you will have to admit to this in all honesty before yourself and before your patient hoping but by no means expecting that your patient will accept your decision.

CHILDBIRTH

The obstetrician's procedure is determined by the combination of clinical circumstances. When all considerations of safety for mother and child are fulfilled there remains mostly still a margin of freedom of approach, unimportant for the physical outcome of childbirth but important for the woman's experience of it.

Case 10

You are asked by the couple to *admit the father to the delivery room.*

You comply. You may even have suggested it because you thus open the door to the sharing by the couple of one of the decisive moments in family life. While you wish to tighten the bond between the couple you may find you are serving quite different trends. The woman who resents going through pregnancy or having been impregnated by the husband, may want him to be crushed by witnessing the "suffering caused by him." This will not improve the relationship. The man who wishes to watch the birth of the child may be induced by sensationalism, he aims his glance and possibly his camera at a physiological "happening" not at the arrival of his and his wife's offspring. His presence will give no comfort to the mother. Yet, comfort and togetherness are the only valid reasons for his admittance. If these purposes are not dominant or when the woman is under anesthesia the cause for the father's attendance at delivery collapses.

You deny entry to the delivery room to the prospective father in your endeavor to keep out every disturbing or damaging element. But you should be aware that by regarding the obstetrical suite as the sole sterile domain of the professional you may also sterilize the human relationship between husband and wife. Mechanization to perfection of labor and delivery may keep the family unit from reaching perfection. Obstetrics is more than a skilled mechanic's function.

Case 11

A prenatal patient wants to come to an agreement with you on the issue of being *awake at childbirth versus anesthesia* during delivery. This problem can arise in those cases merely where no overriding medical indications tip the scale toward one method.

You agree with your patient who prefers being awake when the child is born because she wants to experience this decisive hour in her life as a woman with all her senses alert. This decent and basically uncomplicated, healthy attitude becomes often corrupted by inflating it. The claim that the mother who went through "natural chldbirth" will love her baby more than the one who delivered under anesthesia is unproven. Rather, one might reverse the statement and suggest that the wish to participate awake in the act of giving birth will be found in women eager for motherhood rather than in indifferent ones.* Anyway, you will hardly arouse her maternal love by denying her relief from pain. The crusader for "natural (sometimes unrealistically called: painless) childbirth" can defeat the noble purpose of this endeavor, namely naturalness, by overemphasizing procedural technicalities. By over-insistence on months of preparation, breathing classes, or pedantic exercises one runs the danger of replacing common sense by a method. If one props up one's own or the patient's self-confidence by institutionalizing and delineating the delivery program with Australian, French or other names, one may end up selling brands instead of an uncomplicated approach to childbirth. Here, as in every human endeavor one needs to be careful that the procedure will not overgrow its goal. The purpose of natural childbirth is not to enhance pride in childbirth but to deepen the joy of motherhood.

You go along with the patient who wishes to be "put out" by anesthesia when her baby arrives. You save her from a good deal of anxiety, you spare her painful sensations. However, you "shield" her also from conscious and active participation in the birth of her baby as though she would undergo the removal of a diseased organ. The laboring birth-giving woman is relegated to passivity; you take over by the authority of your professionalism. This is safe because one is usually well inclined as a physician to keep up one's professional competence. But one has also to check one's eagerness lest one take away too much of the patient's own control over her life and actions.

---

*The same confusion of cause and effect has entered the debate about breast feeding versus bottle feeding.

The list of issues where philosophical orientation influences the use of pure medicotechnical means is legion. The question of appetite-curbing prescription versus self-motivated dieting, of tranquillizing medication versus unmitigated confrontation with the patient's disturbing problems provide additional examples of the gynecologist's perpetuous dilemma and challenge. Maybe there is no decision on omission and commission altogether which is not the result of factual knowledge and personal philosophy combined.

Knowledge is acquired by learning and experience, personality is shaped by background and living. It is not presumed in this chapter to mold the counselor's character. The author also refrains from trying to proselytise and from crusading for his own preferences which can never be universal; starting to promote one's personal way of reacting is not an act of scientific deduction but a try at persuasion. This chapter is dedicated and confined to the task of making known some real situations to which answers have to be found time and again.

THE IMPORTANCE OF ETHICO MORALISTIC CONSIDERATIONS IN COUNSELING UPON SEXUAL MATTERS

JOHN SEYMOUR

MARITAL counseling presents many issues of an ethicomoralistic nature but nowhere might these be so intense as in the area covered by the term, sex. No field is so fraught with perplexing problems involving moral issues as the handling of sexual questions in counseling. It is reasonably safe to say that on no other subject can the counselor feel more shaky, more anxious and concerned than when the client begins addressing himself to conflicts of a sexual character. The counselor's own sexual risibilities often become affected, and his sentiments will begin to color his statements, interpretations, and reflections. He is prone to lose his objectivity and exhibit problems of a personal nature.

The position represented here is that, in reference to morality of situations, the counselor must respect his client's right to choices, his own goals, standards of behavior and his own solutions, while the counselor remains in objective control of the case through awareness of his own biases, attitudes, prejudices and needs, and restrains his natural impulses to direct the situation. When the client is told what his morality should be, his moral values become shattered with some consequent loss of identity. Paul Tillich has said, "*Person* is a moral concept, pointing to a being which we are asked to respect as the bearer of a dignity equal to our own, and which we are not permitted to use as a means for a purpose, because it is purpose itself." (24) Choice and responsibility are at the very heart of ethics.

Some authorities exhort counselors to adopt another attitude. Harper distinguishes between morality and the nonmoral ideal stating that the former is concerned with good or bad conduct in reference to specific cultural standards (19). The latter is seen as the utopian ideal in that the criteria of right and wrong are not helpful in their application to problems. He states that "a sex ethic should be constructed solely for the welfare of living . . . human beings and not to please our ancestors . . ." He goes on to say that Moses' and Jesus' points of view should be subjected to the same rational inspection as any other points of view. "And any scientific evidence available . . . should take precedence over opinion from any source." Philosophically and abstractly speaking the wisdom of these statements is comprehended. However, should we engage in such logistics with clients who may bow to our superior knowledge, but unconsciously and sometimes consciously feel that their individuality has again, as in childhood, oozed away, and the values by which they have lived, been lost without replacement.

The literature abounds with the approach that the marriage counselor or psychotherapist must face up to his own set of values. That is fine, and we will have something to say about countertransference problems. But when it is further stated that the client has to face up to them too, then it seems to me we become less professional and the counseling relationship changes to a social one. Hudson contends that even if the counselor does not consciously reveal his values, they will be exposed unconsciously, and therefore favors the more spontaneous situation whereby the counselor rams his values down the client's throat (20). There is a tremendous difference in impact upon the client when the communication is conscious rather than unconscious. Although the client may at some level be aware of the counselor's other attitudes, he will feel respected for what he is as a distinct human being.

Integrity therapy is derived from the Judeo-Christian ethic of the commitment of sins, and has been championed by O. Hobart Mowrer (3). Psychopathology stems from misbehavior in violation of one's conscience. Cures are achieved by admitting one's mistakes and thereafter practicing honesty. Not surprisingly, cases illustrating success are chosen. Forcing confessions can also redound to the poorest interests of the client.

These methods may be rationalizations of the therapist's power needs, under the guise of a necessity for frankness. Usually the counselee before seeking help has impressions about the general value systems held by counselors and may have deferred getting involved because of fears and resistance to upheavals within his own philosophical framework. If their fears are realized by blunt therapy, they may react with antipathies at various levels of consciousness.

Should the marriage counselor have definite values about divorce, abortion, homosexuality, premarital and postmarital sex, masturbation, etc? Or should he have values about a specific divorce situation rather than divorce per se? In a thoroughly destructive, sadomasochistic relationship divorce becomes a necessity if no changes are possible within the relationship itself. In a situation where some personality alterations and/or interaction between two people may possibly be modified, the counselor may work towards maintaining the marriage. Also if one is treating a member of a religious group, for example, a devout Catholic, one must work within the framework of the marriage. If there are indications of a change in the client's view towards his religion, then the counselor's goals change too.

The therapist who has a definite view about the general phenomenon, divorce, most likely will perform ineffectively.

No system of therapeutic endeavor should be rigid, and there are occasions when information and advice-giving are necessary. Direction is surely in order when it becomes necessary to ameliorate the effects of destructive acts upon the self or others. It is also essential to be informative so that the client, armed with knowledge that he may not have had before, has a greater freedom of choice in arriving at better decisions for himself. This is particularly pertinent in the realm of sexual difficulties because, as a tabooed subject, lack of information and misinformation has been rife. Individuals involved premaritally or postmaritally seek counseling for a great variety of problems including impotence and frigidity, homosexuality and other deviations, and playing a lively part is the interplay of moral codes and religious values in a constant state of flux. The therapist must often clarify for the person seeking help that which is going on out there. Lerner discusses a model of existence which states that Americans may be said to live in three universes: a natural or biological universe composed of unrestrained impulses, a social universe with rather well-defined patterns towards life goals, and a moral universe that gives meaning to life (21). It may be important, surely helpful, to indicate that in reference to the moral universe there are two codes involved, a formal and an operative one, and that Americans may inveigh against shaky sexual morals and yet accept them in practice. In effect then, it would be of significance to point out the risk of exposure versus the attained satisfactions of well-hidden "immoral" sexuality. Discretion becomes a virtue at the present time while our formal code is in such a fluctuating state, most particularly for the American girl who, although ostensibly free in most areas, continues to be closely watched on her sexual behavior. Although the inconsistency of the two codes is required to be indicated to the client, a careful evaluation of his conscience level needs to be made. That is, to what degree would the evasion of sexual taboos become a source of inordinate anxiety and guilt.

A familiarity with parental codes that have contributed to a client's problems, sexual and otherwise, is taken for granted by the therapist. Less often is the need seen to be conversant with the values represented by him. This should be considered an ethical responsibility. Whether stated or not, each individual has a kind of graded value system set up for himself, and most often this will include spirituality whether it be of a formal religious nature or of an informal one. Until comparatively recent times, religion has been the chief vehicle of morals and moral opinion. The relationship then between maintaining self worth, and one's value system and religion (spirituality) is integral. Karl Menninger has stated, "Living by spiritual standards is more valuable than life maintained at the cost of demoralization and depersonalization" (15). A knowledge of the values that religion contains, pertaining to sex, is of importance in understanding the person we are trying to help, and our evaluation of him should include some enlightenment about his religious set. Clients might be classified on the following continuum—rigid religiosity, religious but not in all areas, religious but extremely open to change, and extreme readiness to change.

What has been the attitude of religion toward sex? A stated position would acclaim its beauty and virtues. More importantly are the subliminal communications which in effect have stated that sex is filthy and revolting. Orthodox Christians and Jews have developed distasteful and prudish attitudes at a less than conscious stance towards the whole notion of sex; and religious morality regards it as something to be engaged in furtively or avoided. The word "obscenity," associated with sex, is derived from "that which is not represented on the stage," that which is kept off scene (Watts, Alan—*Nature, Man and Woman,* New York, Pantheon, 1958). Very consciously, fornication, masturbation, and homosexuality have all been labeled as evil. A vociferous minority conviction for seven hundred years has been that fornication is not a sin if love is part of the relationship. Studies have been made of the prelogical thought processes that might account for the Judeo-Christian taboos on sexuality, and anthropologists and students of comparative religious indicate that these are the same processes that gave birth for example to the Orphic taboo on eating beans (25).

In America, up to the early part of the 19th century, churches and courts engaged in religious and legal regulation of sexual behavior. As the court became less involved in its control of sexual practices which began to be taken for granted, the ministers, missionaries, and moralists proceeded to be very loud indeed, and preempted for reform. While the influence of major religious groups has been to discourage examination and experimentation in the area of sexuality, this has not been true of minor religious groups. Theodore Schroeder writing in the early part of this century hypothesized that many a religious movement originated during a period when an individual has been under stress while wrestling with erotic desires, and then has found a tremendous need to deny these (25). It is of interest to speculate upon the unconscious denial of sexuality manifested by the names given to Pennsylvania towns—Blue Balls, Intercourse, and so on. American Shakerism was founded by Mother Anne Lee in 1774. It is described that even though she was married she was concerned about her "sinful" sexual impulses. Her manner of resolving this problem was to form a community which practices celibacy (25). The Rappites allowed married couples to live as man and wife for one year in seven. Other sects reduced aggravated sexual tensions by monagamy or polygamy. Contemporary observers of religious revivals of the 18th and 19th centuries say that religious excitement resulted in sexual arousal (25).

The more rigid Puritan tradition restricted sex to procreation, because of its emphasis upon Biblical rectitudes. This then led to repression and frustrations, roadways to neuroses. It was challenged by sexual uprisings in the 1840's, finally flaring forth into the flagrant revolt of the 1920's. There was a demand to break formal sexual codes, to deviate from majority sexual patterns, with a feeling of freedom that one should lead a fully expressive life in the pursuit of happiness. For many, however, changes in sex mores were circumscribed by the attitudes of the formal religion to which they belonged. Although the major religions are in a continuing state of change in its effort to adapt to the new needs of each succeeding generation, there remains a hard core based upon strong tradition which is not as amenable to modification (25). Marriage counselors would do well to gain an understanding of the religious value systems of their clients whose sexual orientation is so often bound up with their orthodoxy.

CATHOLIC DOCTRINE

Of the major religions, Catholicism has the most to say in guiding the sexual ways of its adherents. Sex was originally conceived as being "good, noble, dignified." In the Garden of Eden, Adam and Eve had no sense of shame since they were subject to God's will; but after the Fall a rightful sense of shame was incurred since reason was now impaired, i.e. it was no longer Godlike and therefore one could succumb to temptation. Sex was still seen as a "noble" act when properly used; it was an expression and intensification of love, and its correct management created worshippers of God. This view is unlike that of Puritanism for it does not derogate sexual pleasure. As a matter of fact, Catholicism extols the pleasures of sex indicating that it was keener before the Fall, and that marital couples do nothing wrong in enjoying its pleasure. The production of children results in "sex imitating the love of Christ for his Bride (the Church) whom he fructifies to spiritual offspring" (9).

Catholicism apprehends the possibility of using sex in three ways: a) as an animal impelled by no other motive than sensual thrill, b) As a human being in which sex becomes a union of mind, heart, and will as well as of body to be used primarily for the purpose of propagation and secondarily for personal development, and c) as a Christian in which the sex act reflects the union of Christ with his church, and propagates worshippers of God. Sex is seen to be derived from God, and its purpose is to create and enlarge the human race which eventually will inhabit Heaven. Thus we are able to comprehend the rationale behind many of the church's edicts.

Premarital and extramarital sex does not fulfill the Creator's goal. One cannot interfere with the birth of a child because procreation is primary. However, sex may also be engaged in to advance "psychological and physical prosperity" for it is considered to be basic as an aid to the growth of the total personality in that it reduces sexual tensions, intensifies love, and helps the human being become empathic and less narcissistic. A man who "loveth his wife, loveth himself" (St. Paul). Divorce, then, is out of the question because of the profundity of the relationship. Christ states, "Whosoever shall put away his wife . . . and shall marry another, committeth adultery." (Matthew 19:9).

Catholic morality asserts that sex is a natural act, and therefore any unnatural pattern is immoral. Artificial insemination and masturbation become immoral. Contrivances that would prevent natural copulation and birth such as contraceptives, sterilization, and abortion are corrupt. Onan was struck dead on the spot for unnatural prevention of childbirth (Genesis). Sex between parties of the same gender is contrary to nature's plan. One may however, cooperate with nature through periodic continence known as rhythm, for there is no artificial implementation. Even here, just and not selfish reasons are needed, such as physical or emotional problems of some severity, and both parties must consent to the method.

As a preventive to infidelity and masturbation, spouses may not depart from each other for any length of time unless mutually agreed upon. Sexual intimacies other than intercourse are encouraged because affection and closeness are desirable, but these intimacies may not culminate in orgasm. This does become a problem in counseling with Catholic adolescents because for one or more college years, or even in high school "steady dating" of the same partner, which leads to heavy petting to climax and sometimes to intercourse, is the tendency in American society. The Catholic Church has taken a stand against prolonged dating at least for the high school parochial child.

As part of the Divine Plan, sex is supernatural as well as natural. In its ascetic doctrines Catholicism teaches that virginity or celibacy is more sanctified when it is pursued as a dedication to God. Generally then, the proper use of sex is an act of religious virtue which "redounds to the praise of God."

Catholics have continued to try to maintain a religious rather than a secular control over morals; their religious laws are peculiarities when compared with the civil laws of lands, and they have become an island albeit a large one. Alterations of interpretation of doctrine vary from one diocese to another and although in a state of flux, certain issues have remained relatively unchanged.

JEWISH THEOLOGY

Judaism as a general concept is seen as a religious civilization, a religiously oriented culture, or an ethnic group rather than a "religion" or a "faith." Because of its interaction with many different cultures, sexual attitudes will vary from one community to another. According to Rabbi S. Glasner, the excessive number of Jewish authorities leans towards the right of center, inclined towards greater social control, with a negative attitude towards sexual behavior outside of marital coitus (17). He further goes on to state that contradictory material may be illustrated by the statement of Moses Maimonides, "We ought to limit sexual intercourse altogether, hold it in contempt, and desire it only rarely . . . The act is too base to be performed except when needed" (Guide for the Perplexed, II, 49). On the other hand, he quotes Nachmanides "It is not (true) as our rabbi and master (Maimonides) asserted . . . praising Aristotle for teaching that the sexual urge is a source of shame to us. God forbid that the truth should be in accordance with the teachings of the Greek! The act of sexual union is holy and pure . . . The Lord created all things in accordance with His wisdom and whatever he created cannot be shameful or ugly . . . When a man is in union with his wife in a great spirit of holiness and purity, the Divine Presence is with them" (17). We note here that sex and godliness are related, similar to Catholic doctrine.

In the preexilic period there has been a definite lack of sermonizing on sexual matters, according to Dr. Louis Epstein (13). After that, Jewish history is replete with changes in attitude varying from the restrictive to the permissive. Jewish tradition has always given full recognition to the sexuality of women, even singling them out to have a greater sex drive than men. Therefore both in the Bible and Talmud, men are exhorted to be aware of their wives sexual needs. In one example, a husband is cautioned against taking a long journey without first having intercourse with his wife, and he was required to resume sex relations immediately upon his return. Rather unique for the time in which it was written, the Talmud advises that the husband should be certain that his wife has achieved orgasm before attaining his own satisfaction. There was a belief that this might influence giving birth to sons (17).

Modesty and reticence are highly regarded virtues in the Jewish tradition. Yet a reading of the "Song of Songs" on Passover made sexual passion clear to the young hearer. The high standard of morality never went to the extreme of endorsing celibacy. Premarital chastity was praised, most particularly in the young woman, but no penalty was imposed for its violation. Within the marriage sexual freedom is notable although there

were precepts regarding frequency of intercourse with much divided
opinion about its duration and the use of byplay. Traditionally, intimacies
between the two sexes have been discouraged. Generally speaking, Judaism
has maintained control over sex mores by moral persuasion rather than
through religious laws. The Schulchan Aruch, a 16th century document
that deals with laws of marriage, divorce, and sex relations, recommends
great restraint during intercourse. Rabbi Moses Isserles, a contemporary
authority, states that sexually a man may do with his wife whatever he
wishes . . . "But although all these things are permissible, one who sanctifies
himself by (avoiding) that which is permitted him is considered holy."
This is the extralegal standard of morality that may characterize Jewish
practice to a far greater extent than legal permissiveness (17).

Before and during the Middle Ages any attempt at contraception was
considered sinful, and is still so considered by many Orthodox Jews.
Medical problems were valid reasons to employ contraception. The Jewish
attitude similar to the Catholic has never considered the function of intercourse to be for procreation only.

Masturbation has been rigidly prohibited. One Talmudic authority regarded it as a capital crime (Niddah 13a). As a precaution it was forbidden
for a man to hold his penis even while urinating, except by a married man
in preparation for intercourse. Adultery was forbidden even under threat
of death. The attitude toward abortion remains right of center. The chief
safeguard of sexual morality was that of early marriage. Eighteen was considered a maximal age for young men, and delay would result in being
called to account before the elders. Dowries made early marriages financially feasible (17).

To summarize, then, it is extremely difficult to generalize about Jewish
sexual attitudes and practices. The counselor must learn from his client the
extent of his orthodoxy. The Chassidim, for example, would represent an
extreme antisexual position (singing and dancing restricted to the men)
(17).Generally it is seen to lean in the direction of frank, nonpuritanical
attitudes accompanied by a rigid, self-imposed discipline of sexual restraint.

PROTESTANT THEOLOGY

Protestantism today relies even less upon religious authority than
Catholicism and Judaism, but this does not imply greater sexual freedom,
for secular law in sexual matters may often overcompensate when religion
transfers its authority over these matters to the law. It would appear that
the founders of Protestantism were going to create a more accepting attitude
towards the approval of sexual expression as a basic need, but in actuality
prudery and shame became the mental postures of the time.

At the end of the Reformation the clergy were forbidden to marry, and this ruling was changed perhaps not so much to obtain freedom from rigidity in this area, but to correct a grievous condition that existed, in that a sturdy number of the clergy were involved in sexual affairs and common-law marriage. Luther was convinced that "whoever does not marry must misconduct himself." He destroyed the distinction between the "higher" way of life of the clergy as against the "lower" existence of the laity. He denied that any man or woman could be free from lust, and in this manner foreshadowed Freud in his insistence upon the overwhelming strength of the libido. Marriage becomes a remedy for concupiscence (8).

Calvin's stance towards sex in marriage indicated that it was no sin but must be proper and decent, not lustful. Catholic moral theology had seen sex as doubly motivated and the reformers continued to recognize the necessity of marital intercourse as a relief from libidinal tension.

After Freud and Havelook Ellis threatened puritanical and Victorian sexual morality by stating that sex is a natural instinct to be accepted and enjoyed, and that sexual repression produces perversion and deceit, 20th century Protestantism found itself in a schizophrenic position with regard to sex. Supporters of traditional morality are overtly in the majority, contending that all sex outside of matrimony is sin. Various sects and groups run the gamut from acceptance of premarital expressions of affection to a frowning upon dancing and the cinema. The traditionalists see a return to decorum arguing that frankness has not helped, while a minority of liberals feel that we should continue to advance towards responsible sexual freedom. Planned parenthood and contraception are generally acceptable. No Protestant wants the breakdown of sexual responsibility or an anarchy of moral standards (8).

SEXUAL DEVIATIONS

Generally, counselors exhibit a liberal view towards so-called sexual deviations and reflect the opinion of present writers in this field. For example, some authors defend cunnilingus and fellatio if it is not carried to the point of orgasm, while others do not consider any sexual practice immoral if it is of benefit to the sexual adjustment of the marital partners (25). However, it is of moral importance to point out to the client that the law differs radically with usual therapeutic goals. State laws continue to carry statutes that may invoke penalties: Connecticut indicates thirty years for mouth-genital contacts, Georgia threatens life imprisonment at hard labor, and Ohio has a one-to-twenty-year term. It would not be an exaggeration to state that currently all sex but face-to-face relations between spouses is criminal in this country.

State laws relating to artificial insemination should be carefully checked out by the counselor. As a matter of fact, no state has passed legislation defining the status of children born in this manner. A suggestion has been made that artificial insemination is to be found in Leviticus in the Old Testament, and in the rabbinical materials of the Midrash (25). Alan Guttmacher of Johns Hopkins University found it was a known procedure in horse-breeding among Arab sheiks as early as 1322. Of the major religions only the Catholic Church has set forward a definite opinion. Catholic writers prohibit onanism. Even in testing the husband for fertility, the physician may not exercise the prostate gland.

Insemination may be of two different types: A.I.H. or homologous referring to that which is obtained from the glands of the husband; versus A.I.D. or heterologous, that which is secured from a donor. It is most particularly in situations of the latter type that questions have arisen sometimes culminating in legal suits. Disputes arise about the legal father, about the wife's act being considered an adulterous one, or even whether the donor's wife could sue him for adultery. To complicate the matter even further, consider the inquiries that could result from the present possibility of combining the sperm and ovum of husband and wife, and transplanting the fertilized egg to another woman as host for gestation.

These controversial areas lead many writers and physicians to show that such acts as contraception, sterilization, and artificial insemination can be justified morally, and they will argue against the Church (15). For example, Fletcher states that Catholic conception of natural law is questionable in that God intended that everything in nature should be accepted and regarded as good. He proves that natural sex does not aim at reproduction, for only one out of seven days in a person's life is fertile. Parenthood and birth are considered matters of personal responsibility rather than religious ones, and a view to the contrary is considered an attack upon the freedom of the individual. Hopefully clients will be exposed to both sides of such controversies, but not within the province of the therapeutic encounter.

Definite communication of value judgments to clients in many sexual areas are not only unwarranted on the basis of usurpation of his ethicomoral standards, but are unwise in reference to our present state of sexual knowledge. Homosexuality as symptom or disease entity has never been fully resolved, although the tendency has been to regard it as the former. Yet we continue receiving knowledge from the field of genetic biology informing us that the simple gene-chromosome model does not account for the whole range of genetic phenomena. The rigidly exclusive classifications of male and female are contradicted by the recognition of "at least seven genetic gradations of sex, from supermale at one extreme through various degrees of intersex to superfemale at the other extreme" (23).

Perhaps there are as many studies which claim that those who refrain from coitus until marriage find greater happiness than those who have premarital experiences, as the converse (4). Therefore, to be biased towards premarital coitus is not even necessarily supported by scientific evidence, and to smugly place a burden upon the client whose values and/or religion forbids it is nontherapeutic and additionally unscientific.

There remains an emotional hangover of Victorian standards in regard to masturbation, and despite the fact that Kinsey, Ellis, and others have pointed out that masturbation is not harmful, (12) sex information-dispensing publications continue to blush when discussing this topic. The Child Study Association of America in 1958 indicated that parents should ally themselves with the child's own conscience, and while assuring him that the practice is not harmful, find ways to help him grow out of it. Helen Manley's *Curriculum Guide in Sex Education* states, "Frequent handling of sex organs occurs with some children. The help of parents in preventing this is very valuable . . . Usually keeping the hands busy and diverting attention will be the necessary remedy . . . Masturbation, the term for this, is *usually* only harmful when the child is psychologically hurt by overanxious adults" (22). The italics are mine. What is the unusual nonpsychological harm that can occur? Both instances are illustrative of biases about this subject which may invade the counseling of the therapist.

COUNTERTRANSFERENCE

The whole issue of morality in counseling must be very closely tied in with the values and personality of the counselor. Countertransference relates to the triggering off in the psychotherapist of responses to the patient or client that are based upon problems and immaturities that either have not been resolved or have been unsuccessfully dealt with in his own therapy. This common phenomenon, while discussed at some length in psychoanalytic literature, is relatively neglected in the literature related to therapeutic-counseling efforts, and has its antecedents in Freud, who did not fully discuss countertransference. The notion that one's own therapy magically will dispel most of the counselor's problems is not based upon the pragmatic reality of the situation. A first generation of therapists and counselors can only partially combat the effects upon themselves of long-standing psychological problems that have been nurtured for centuries. We have become aware that no type of therapeutic endeavor will do more than modify the behavior of the individual. This modification is of tremendous value to humanity, and well worth the effort, but it indicates the impossibility of performing the whole task. We who are professionals recall the foibles of our teacher-dispensers of the art of therapy, including our own therapist, and the occasional contact with a renowned person in the field who himself is an example of irrational behavior. We become aware of inappropriate behavior, sometimes delinquencies, of colleagues in their behavior towards clients, or in fulfilling related functions such as expert witnessing in a court of law. Recently, (March, 1969) in a nationally publicized case involving a political assassin, a psychologist who was testifying as an expert, was accused of plagiarism when portions of his diagnostic report were found to resemble a report of a different case included in a book. The psychologist admitted "lifting" it to enrich his report.

Often therapists receive feedback from clients concerning sexual relationships that develop within the therapeutic hour. Given a human being's strong need for sensual experiences, the many nuances of meaning that sex can create, the counseling relationship with a client usually sexually frustrated, the secretiveness of the therapeutic intervention, it becomes virtually impossible for the counselor to prevent relationship fantasy. To handle your fantasies in a candid manner with your client would only be encouraging that which you need to suppress in yourself. Fortunately most professionals control the situation at this level. One way of coping with such a serious countertransference problem is to discuss this openly with colleagues. The writer was involved with a group of therapists who dubbed themselves, "The Truth Club," where many problems of this nature were elicited. Traditionally, therapists are reluctant to discuss their cases. Freud was quite clear on this subject and stated unequivocally that no erotic gratification on the part of the therapist was permissible (18).

Sexual issues continue to torment society, and therapists are not immune to the present state of confused thinking. Our clients come to us for help because they are dissatisfied with their existent mode of sexual and other interpersonal relationships. Changes in thinking and behavior are necessarily slow in evolving, since so many safeguards must be removed in the process. It is not a simple matter to give up in a day those precepts which have influenced us since the day we began to draw breath. However, the impatience of unempathic and egocentric counselors, who often hide behind what they consider a rational system of therapy, overrun and attempt to destroy defenses in as similar a fashion as the paternal systems of colonialism power drove their way into the lands of simple folk in order to elevate their standards of living.

It is not being suggested that the therapist should approach his clients in a pussy-footed manner. Often matters of daily living pursued by the client may be injurious to him or to others, and direct action must be taken.

We are not speaking here of the necessity of using a particular technique, be it called psychoanalysis or existentialism. The system is not as important as the counselor's emotional and moral stability-strength of character they once tritely called it. Basic to the therapeutic counseling relationship is the need to treat with honor and esteem the human being who places his life in our hands.

REFERENCES

1. Barnette, H.H.: *The New Theology and Morality.* Philadelphia, Westminster Press, 1967.
2. Bassett, M.: *A New Sex Ethics and Marriage Structure.* New York, Philosophical Library, 1961.
3. Bassin, A.: IRT therapy in marriage counseling. *Marital Counseling,* H.L. Silverman (Ed.). Springfield, Illinois, Charles C Thomas, 1967.
4. Benson, P.H.: *Religion in Contemporary Culture.* New York, Harper, 1960.
5. Blanck, R., and Blanck, G.: *Marriage and Personal Development.* New York, Columbia University Press, 1968.
6. Bowman, H.A.: *A Christian Interpretation of Marriage.* Philadelphia, Westminster Press, 1959.
7. Brav, S.R. (Ed.): *Marriage and the Jewish Tradition.* New York, Philosophical Library, 1951.
8. Cole, W.G.: *Sex in Christianity and Psychoanalysis.* New York, Oxford University Press, 1955.
9. Clemens, A.H.: *Marriage and the Family: An Integrated Approach for Catholics.* Englewood Cliffs, New Jersey, Prentice Hall, 1957.
10. De Fabriguis, J.: *Christian Marriage.* New York, Hawthorne Press, 1959.
11. Ditzion, S.: *Marriage, Morals and Sex in America.* New York, Bookman Associates, 1953.
12. Ellis, A.: *The American Sexual Tragedy.* New York, Twayne Publishers, 1954.
13. Epstein, L.M.: *Sex Laws and Customs in Judaism.* New York, Bloch Publishing Co., 1948.
14. Fletcher, J.: *Moral Responsibility: Situation Ethics at Work.* Philadelphia, Westminster Press, 1967.
15. Fletcher, J.: *Morals and Medicine.* Princeton, Princeton University Press, 1954.
16. Genne, W., and Genne, E.: *Christians and the Crisis in Sex Morality.* New York, Association Press, 1962.
17. Glasner, Rabbi S.: Judaism and sex, *The Encyclopedia of Sexual Knowledge.* Ellis, A., and Abarbanel, A. (Eds.), New York, Hawthorne Books, 1961.
18. Greenson, R.R.: *The Technique and Practice of Psychoanalysis, Vol. I.* New York, International Universities Press, 1968.
19. Harper, R.A.: "Moral Issues in Marriage Counseling", *Marital Counseling,* H.L. Silverman (Ed.). Springfield, Illinois, Charles C. Thomas, 1967.
20. Hudson, J.W.: "Value Issues in Marital Counseling", *Marital Counseling,* ed. H. L. Silverman, Springfield, Illinois, Charles C Thomas, 1967.
21. Lerner, M.: *America as a Civilization,* New York, Simon and Shuster, 1957.
22. Manley, H.M.: *Curriculum Guide for Sex Education,* St. Louis, State Publishing Co., 1967.

23. Stone, L.J., and Church, J.: *Childhood and Adolescence,* New York, Random House, 1968.
24. Tillich, P.: *Love, Power and Justice: Ontological Analyses and Ethical Applications,* New York, Oxford University Press, 1960.
25. Wilson, R.A.: Modern Attitudes Toward Sex. *The Encyclopedia of Sexual Knowledge.* Ellis, A., and Abarbanel, A. (Eds.), New York, Hawthorn Books, 1961.
26. Wynn, J.C.: *Sex, Family and Society in Theological Focus.* New York, Association Press, 1966.

Chapter 9

HIDDEN VALUE JUDGMENTS IN THE COUNSELING OF COMMON SEXUAL MARRIAGE PROBLEMS

STEPHEN NEIGER AND DONALD J, McCULLOCH

S N.: DON, I have come to you today for help in examining some of the ethical dimensions of the type of counseling I do. I know that a great deal of "ethical decision making" enters my counseling each day. And yet, to make explicit the types of judgments I use is a different thing again. I also know that you have been doing a lot of counseling, some of which may be similar to the type of counseling I do. Last but not least, I know you as a man of profound ethical concern, a person who lives ethics in his everyday life. I thought it might be as interesting to you, as it would be to me, to take a look together at the probably hidden ethical judgments we make in what I call sexually oriented marriage counseling.

D.McC.: Suppose you try and define first, Stephen, what you mean by sexually oriented marriage counseling.

DEFINITION

S.N.: This again seems deceptively simple. In an article written for general practitioners (8) I described the types of complaints I tend to receive as, "the presenting symptoms of comparatively healthy adult patients in which a great deal of suffering to patient and spouse results from a symptom that will often yield to a well planned but relatively simple therapeutic line of attack. Such common problems include the psychological difficulty of obtaining and maintaining erection, premature ejaculation, 'frigidity,' so-called sexual incompatibility (of sexual needs, techniques, and appetites), false fear of abnormality, and many more."

After distinguishing these from more complex types of sexual problems, especially gross sexual deviations, I went on describing my method of treatment, which consists mainly of the alleviation of guilt and fear by supplying knowledge both in the treatment session and in the periods in between through reading materials. A great deal of emphasis is put on such factors as the restoration of the patient's self-confidence, the building of a positive attitude to sex, the induction of relaxation and an atmosphere of nonexpectation, the breaking of the vicious circle of failure expectation, facilitation of communication between the couple, and so forth. There is more, of course, to this method of treatment, but for our purposes today this brief introduction may perhaps do.

D.McC.: Your remarks raise a whole host of interesting questions. One that I hope we can discuss is the various philosophies of counseling that underlie different counselor methods. However, I'd like to stay for a moment on the question of the definition of patient populations. Your patients appear to present with rather specific complaints and problems in the sexual area. Mine, often, do not. A good many of the married couples I have seen have rather global concerns. They have reached a point where, much of the time, they just don't feel very good with each other. Of course, if they are forced to be specific, they will usually list sex, probably along with the handling of money, child-rearing, and in-laws as their areas of difficulty. So, I can't but wonder about your patient population. Are they really so different or has previous therapist contact persuaded them to focus their difficulties narrowly to the sexual area?

S.N.: I rather *do* tend to think of my patients as suffering from a sexual problem—whatever other *additional* problems they may or may not have. In fact, it has always been my contention that a common marital sexual problem such as impotence or frigidity will yield best to *direct* attack on the symptom and that all the relationship therapy in the world, sometimes going on for months and years, will not necessarily resolve the sexual problem.

Of course, I do not go as far as to say that this may be their only problem. All I am saying is that this is a problem in its own right that needs treatment in its own right.

Frequently I encounter a situation in which a couple are referred to me by another counselor. They had made excellent progress with that counselor in all areas of their marriage except the sexual one.

They then begin insisting that this is now their only problem and are in turn referred to me. What typically happens in these situations is that they experience a sort of honeymoon in their treatment situation with me and begin making very rapid progress towards their maximum potential in love making. Once they have approached or reached this potential, they often realize that the sexual problem was not quite as important as it loomed in their minds. Yes, the woman now *does* have orgasm, even multiple orgasms. Yes, the man now *can* last as long as he wishes to. As a result, they now really enjoy themselves in bed, but there are still other important problems. Not infrequently, they end up going back to their old counselor in order to continue working through these with him, although their attitudes to each other are much improved.

Sometimes, however, I see couples who insist that there *are* no other problems. The couple assures me that they are quite capable of operating harmoniously in such decisions as finances, children, in-laws and what have you. Their relationship is good and quite visibly rewarding in all areas but the sexual. And yet, in many cases, attempts were being made (sometimes for years) to treat their "problem" on the "relationship level" on the assumption that faulty sexual knowledge or technique is secondary and the problem will solve itself somehow in the "contex" of some mystical "improvement" in their personalities or their relationship.

Emily H. Mudd, in her article, *Sex Problems in Marriage Counselling* (Mudd in Brecher and Brecher, 1966) (1) divided her cases into four categories: a) difficulties in sex adjustment which reflect inadequate information; b) sex difficulties as part of a total marital difficulty; c) sexual problems regarded as the focus of marital difficulty; d) complex problems. Regardless of which category my cases belong to, I feel that the sexual problem can be and *must* be treated as an independent entity.

D.McC.: But I would argue that this is only one of several possible approaches. My point is that if a couple begins to work cooperatively on almost any area of their relationship, and if this work should prove rewarding, things will start to happen for them which will have generally good effects for the total relationship. The advantages of selecting the sexual relationship as your target area are many. It is an area on which two people can work without it having too many consequences for other people. By contrast, if they start experimenting with their child-rearing, it might have adverse effects on a third person, the child. In the sexual area, they can experiment as a "self-contained unit" so to speak.

Another advantage is that it is an area that can bring high immediate reward. What I mean by this is that if you are successful in your counseling, the results are immediately apparent and the feeling is so good. The whole optimism, excitement, and joy of the process will tend to spread to other areas. Then your couple can behave as if sex *was* the problem. This isn't to say that a counselor couldn't take financial difficulties as the target area, or child rearing, but these do not carry the same high immediate reward prospects.

S.N.: I like what you said. I like it because it provides a very elegant explanation to my "successes," regardless of whether or not sex really *is* the central problem. What you seem to be saying is that it doesn't really matter whether or not sex "is" the central problem. What really matters is, to what extent the counselor estimates that he has the skills and his patients have the potential to make quick improvement in this one key area. If this decision is favorable and turns out to be correct, then regardless of how central you or I would judge the sex problem to be in this couple's situation, quick progress will be made. One reason, as you so well put it, is that these positive feelings which have been acquired through cooperating in this area, will quickly spread to others. A second reason may lie in the special nature of the sexual area which probably focuses and summarizes the feelings of tenderness and affection which you would hopefully like to see the couple carry over to some other dealing during the day, and to some of their problem solving approaches to difficulties that are other than sexual. Last but not least, I firmly believe that a couple who have learned to communicate with each other about sex should have little problem in communicating with each other about everything else.

D.McC.: But there is at least one important disadvantage in picking the sexual area as the one on which to focus attention: your methods may have to be quite indirect.

For contrast's sake, let us assume that your counseling is focused around the handling of money. It is not such a high immediate reward area as is sex, but it has the advantage that you can sit down with the couple and work openly and directly on the problem with them, possibly with paper and pencil. At the end of each month you can all look at their accounts as well as their feelings, and so check the effects of your counseling.

In sex you can make suggestions, but in order to have the things happen which you would like to happen, and to check if indeed they did happen, all you can use is words. After you questioned and added to your clients' sexual knowledge, they go home, and in the privacy of their own place they try to work out what has been discussed and suggested. Then they may come back and say that it didn't really work. But you weren't there to see what they did, and you weren't there to instruct them. And there is a growing sense that, my God, if I only could be present, if only I could do these things myself, or at least if I could take his hand or hers and place it in this way and show them how to do it, they could make great progress. And you really could do something analogous to that if you were counseling around financial matters.

S.N.: Yes, and if you were dealing with them about child rearing, you could put them behind the one-way screen and see what they actually do with their kids and then rerun the whole thing on video tape and analyze with them what was actually happening.

But you cannot do it in sex counseling. I doubt that even Masters and Johnson (6) have gone that far. And this raises the problem of just what you actually *can* do. There is a continuum here ranging from verbal description to pictorial presentation—the using of an anatomical atlas—and I sometimes catch myself imitating the relative position of the sex organs with my hands and fingers and wonder if my patients feel embarrassed about that. And some people go still farther and this is where "sense relaxation," whirlpool baths, massage, and nude encounters come in, and still farther along this continuum the "laying on of hands" practiced by some Reichians—until nothing else is left except to make the decision whether or not you actually take the patient to bed with you and show her how to achieve an orgasm and what it may be like.

. **D.McC.:** There is a lot more of this happening than many people think, and there is some reason to believe that the results are not always altogether negative. If they are, it may be mainly because it has been done surreptitiously and with guilt, rather than the counselor raising this possibility openly with the couple. However, I cannot see the day coming soon when this type of approach would become open. There are all sorts of social and biological forces at work which make it just too dangerous for the counselor to suggest this type of demonstration.

I wonder if this might be a good point at which to perhaps begin taking a look at some of the assumptions which the counselor and the counselee bring the "counseling process."

S.N.: Yes, you mentioned these before and I am intrigued. I imagine that what you mean is some sort of an implicit "philosophy of counseling" or a statement of what counseling is really all about.

BIAS 1: THE COUNSELOR'S CONCEPT OF WHAT COUNSELING IS ALL ABOUT

D.McC.: Yes, this is what I meant. Theoretically, perhaps, the counselor or the therapist is a neutral facilitator who helps people to clarify what their own postitions are. He helps them to become aware of the contradictions between what they want and what they are doing towards achieving their goal. In effect, he is supposed to be a kind of liberator by creating situations in which some kind of free dialogue or discussion may occur. Do we really believe that?

S.N.: No, I don't. I don't know which famous sculptor it was, perhaps it was Michelangelo, who said that the statue is always there in that block of granite, and all the sculptor does is free it with his chisel from all that superfluous material. Now, I don't think it is like that at all. Before touching that block of granite with a chisel, the sculptor has some very strong presupposed opinions as to what he wishes to "find" in that block.

D.McC.: Quite true. Just like the sculptor has a presupposed notion as to what the statue is going to be like, so the counselor usually does have a strong idea of what normal or ideal sexuality or mental health or whatever it is should look like. We all know the "heroic" things which some psychiatrists may do to people in order to bring them to their concept of health, often regardless of what the patient says he wants. They may shock them, cut their brains, and do all sorts of other things in order to bring about in the patient what the psychiatrist considers health. The patient, in his turn, may be desperate enough that he may give himself fully into the hands of the psychiatrist to make him into something else, because all he knows is that he cannot live with himself the way he now is.

Similarly, in the sexual area, it is important that the counselor should realize that he brings to the counseling process more or less strong, clear-cut notions of what he wants the patient to be like at the end of the counseling process. I suppose we could even distinguish a dimension of how badly the counselor *wants* to have a certain outcome in the patients, how far he is willing to go, how directive or forceful he is willing to be in order to make the patient into what he wants him to be like.

And he has many means to achieve this end. Some of these are quite subtle, but no less powerful.

Even the giving of information, "objective," "undistorted" information, is not in itself a value-free position. There would be a number of people who would feel that it is dangerous to give this information or to allow free discussion because that may bring to the surface all sorts of problems and contradictions that may threaten the institution of marriage itself. The probability is that the counselor who feels that the institution is more important than the individual will not likely encourage free discussion, and will not likely give certain types of information such as the possible positive effects of extramarital liaisons.

Now, if we would imagine counselors on a continuum from those who feel that the marriage must be preserved, whatever it will cost the individual, to those who feel that the individual must be upheld, regardless of the cost to the institution, you could probably also get a continuum of the type of information that is being given and the type of action taken. For example, just as the institution centered counselor may censor certain types of information, so the libertarian counselor, who has some strong ideas about what constitutes "growth" for the individual within or outside marriage, may emphasize individual enhancements and withhold the information that a good many people may have trouble with this kind of freedom.

Presumably, most counselors are somewhere in between the extremes of this continuum; they are fairly nondirective and fairly encouraging in trying to bring out into the open their counselees' value system. But the point I was trying to make is, that it would be extremely naive for the counselor to suppose that he himself brings no values to bear in the counseling situation.

S.N.: I strongly agree with you that the ideal of the counselor as a passive catalyst "bringing out whatever there is in the counselee" and "letting him take it from there" is probably a myth and that certain basic value positions do enter the picture. The important thing then is to become aware of these. I wonder if we now could become a bit more specific and see what are the dimensions of bias, other than the bias of what counseling is all about, in which the counselors value system may effect the outcome of the counseling. I suggest that a good place to begin would be the counselors bias about marriage itself. For example, just a moment ago you mentioned the "individual centered counselor" as opposed to the "institution centered counselor." I think we have adequately made the point that there is a lot of room for bias right here. I wonder if we could now take some time to look at another possibility of the counselors bias with regard to the institution of marriage. What I am refering to is the counselors belief as to the importance of sex in marriage.

BIAS 2: THE COUNSELORS CONCEPT OF WHAT MARRIAGE IS ALL ABOUT. IS IT EXCLUSIVELY, PRIMARILY, OR MAINLY A SEXUAL UNION?

Walter Stokes, a prominent marriage counselor (and one for most of whose views I have the utmost respect) stated fairly recently: *(Sexology,* March, 1965) (10) "I am convinced that for a woman to function at her best as either wife or mother she must have the rich emotional experience of guiltless capability to enjoy orgasm in intercourse. I find something deeply significant in the fact that, during all my practice as a counselor, I encountered only two instances in which a woman regularly achieving orgasm with her husband came to me contemplating divorce." Implicit to this type of statement, (which is by no means unique to Walter Stokes but can be found in a number of marriage manuals) is the idea that sexual satisfaction is somehow so central to marriage that the lack of the former is almost inevitably bound to result in the death of the latter.

My experience is in rather sharp contrast with these views. Compatibility of outlooks in major areas of life such as religion, values, society; in major areas of marital interaction, such as the raising of children, the expression of affection, the handling of finances, the very meaning of marriage itself; and last but not least, in major dimensions of personality; have, in my opinion and experience, at least as strong a bearing on success or failure of a marriage as do sexual techniques or even attitudes.

Far be it from me to minimize the importance of the role of sex in marriage. However, I would like to protest what I feel amounts to its maximization. In earlier stages of mammalian, and even human, evolution sex has indeed played such a crucial role in the formation and maintenance of a stable man-woman union. Yet it seems to me that the higher one progresses in (at least our western type of) civilization, the more sex tends to yield to, or at least share its exclusive place with, some of these other powerful variables in keeping the couple together. Certainly, faulty sexual outlooks and techniques may be *one* of many things likely to cause a sick marriage.

A faulty heart functioning will cause a sick organism. Yet it would be hardly justified to single out the heart as the "only important" or even "the most important" organ in the human body. A sick kidney or a sick artery may kill the person just as surely and in many cases just as quickly. I have seen quite a few marriages in which sex was the only rewarding area of communication that was left and yet the marriage has fallen apart because of intolerable conflicts in other areas. Similarly, I have seen a number of marriages which were, and apparently remained for many years, most rewarding for the individuals involved, in spite of very little or no sexual expression between the couple. This, of course, is not my ideal. But who is to enforce the ideal in any field! I think that regardless of whether Stokes is right or I am (or whether we are both right and have just seen different types of patient populations) the important lesson to learn might be how the counselors bias on the role and on the importance of sex in marriage may have a very important bearing on his attitudes and on his counseling in general. To mention only the most obvious area, it will effect the zeal, in one case, with which he may attack a particular sexual problem and, in another case (or perhaps the same one), the outlook with which he may terminate counseling if the sexual problem does not yield to his therapeutic attack. This attitude is not likely to go unnoticed by the couple. Any comments, Don?

D.McC.: No, I agree with you. And I know that both of us tend to prepare our patients for the possibility that, contrary to their and our expectations, the sex symptom will not disappear by the end of the counseling. It is important that the therapist secure himself a base for "withdrawal" and not leave the counselee with a sense that nothing has been accomplished and that the marriage is now doomed.

S.N.: I am sure that no one would wish to do that. One of the passages in the Kinsey report (5) which I keep earmarked for quick reference is the table showing the incidence of complete lack of orgasm after a number of years of marriage. It indicates that 25 per cent of all women in Kinsey's sample were completely unorgastic after one year of marriage. After the fifth year this figure was still 17 percent but by the fifteenth year of marriage it declines to 10 per cent. In other words, the majority of those who "don't," after the end of the first year, probably "will," sometime between the first and the fifteenth year.

Yet at the same time it is important to point out to the woman the existence of that stubborn 10 per cent. In other words there is no absolute guarantee that she will ever necessarily achieve orgasm. And to tell her, that if she doesn't, such a great deal still remains to be enjoyed in sex! The analogy I like to use is how much art there remains to be enjoyed by a person who is colour-blind.

However, time presses and we have yet to discuss a still richer source of bias, that of the counselors attitude to sex itself. Would you like to open the discussion in this area?

BIAS 3:   THE COUNSELORS CONCEPT OF WHAT SEX IS ALL ABOUT

D.McC.: I will try. Let us suppose that we have a counselor who does not accept exclusivity as an essential feature of sexuality and who believes that it is possible for a human being to love two people simultaneously. Let us suppose further that this counselor is consulted by a couple who have found that whenever they encounter a strong attraction towards another nonmarital partner, they are full of guilt and wonder whether the attraction means they don't love their spouse.

Now, if this type of confession occurs in the course of counseling and if it is really upsetting then there is a warning signal, chances are that the upset couple are people who *do* believe in the exclusivity principle. Perhaps even more important, they are frightened that the meaning of a real or imagined extramarital adventure is that, possibly, "I am not loved any more." Now, it is quite possible for the counselor at this point to disregard these danger signals and to proceed with what he honestly believes is simply the giving of up-to-date information, "facts" and to proceed "enlightening" the couple. Strictly speaking he may be right. It is quite possible that the evidence that the counselor has in support of his own theory of sexuality is more accurate than that possessed by the couple. But in sharing it with his clients, he is obviously trying to shift very much his clients conceptions of their marriage and their values about sexuality.

It is possible, of course, that he may succeed and end up with a couple that are much better adjusted, that have quite different and freer notions about sex and about exclusivity than they had before. But it is also possible, and even more likely, that during the period of transition some pretty disturbing and disturbed behavior may appear in the couple who are being counseled. They may separately begin to experiment, to explore extramarital relations and feel that they have in effect the go-ahead from the counselor. When the whole thing blows up, the counselor may find himself the target of attack from both, in effect saying to him: "You told us that this is a good thing to do and now look what is happening to our marriage."

It is also possible, that the counselor's value system may effect the one partner in the couple more than the other. That one partner may make a major shift in view and in practice and the other may not. Quite conceivably, at that point, you may end up with a very much worsened marital situation. It is, therefore, clear at least to me, that the counselor faces a decision, a rather ethical decision, at many points during the counseling process, whether or not to give out "objective," "factual" information to the couple. And the giving or withholding of this or any other type of information may be very often the function of his own value system. But let me go one step further in this.

As you know, Isadore Rubin (9) has divided the spectrum of beliefs as to how people ought to behave sexually, into six philosophies. Now it is pretty clear to me that some of the spokesmen for various beliefs feel fairly strongly about how other human beings ought to behave sexually, at least from the way they talk. For example, if you take the extreme traditional point of view about sexuality being only in the service of reproduction, you can find in the church strong sanctions against any other kind of behavior. It is not just a question that they would *like* people to be that way but some of them feel that if they aren't that way, then they can go to hell or we will punish them in some way, they are sinful, evil, or something of the sort. You may have, in effect, a spiritual counselor coming on as kindly and loving but if the client doesn't accept his advice, if he prefers to move in another direction, the counselor's own values may come out pretty strongly and pretty punishingly. And I rather suspect that this is equally true for the representatives of the extreme left. How do you see it?

S.N.: Yes, the left can put on the pressure just as strongly. I have seen clients coming from libertarian counselors and feeling pretty guilty for being so "square." There is a strong value system implicit in all of Isadore Rubin's six schools of sexual philosophy. One would expect more pressure on the extremes such as the "traditional conservative" position in which sex is strictly for reproduction, or the extreme "anarchistic" position which wishes to do away with marriage and the family as the breeding ground of authoritarianism. However, there are rather strong value judgments inherent even in the so-called "middle of the road" philosophies.

Take, for example, the relativistic "situational" or "interpersonal" ethical school, in whose judgment no act is inherently right or wrong but must be judged by its effects on the total relationship. I would suspect that this school would frown on advice given by another counselor who attempts to train the patient to masturbate ("how antisocial!"), unless the masturbation is strictly a stepping stone towards a more "rewarding" interpersonal relationship. As you know, this is often the first step taken with an unorgastic woman. Very often, however, masturbation has a value in itself for the client as an emergency outlet when the husband is away or as a source of variety even if he is at home. Also, in some cases one has to be content to bring the patient to the point where he or she can have a "rewarding" orgasm by masturbation or by the use of a vibrator and no other goal of the treatment may be achieved.

Here, however, I must recognize my own value judgment entering the picture. In effect, I just said, that an orgasm achieved by masturbation, while less valuable than an orgasm achieved in interpersonal sharing, is still better than no orgasm at all.

Just how punitive a counselor is towards his client who does not follow him in his philosophy is probably a different dimension of his personality altogether. Here a best selling marriage manual is first to come to mind which, although written decades ago, is unfortunately still widely being sold on the book stands and continues driving many women to the marriage counselor because of the book's highly punitive, intolerant demands of what it considers "normal." The *sole* theme of this book is to persuade women that "clitoral orgasm" is neurotic, immature and shallow and that they must, repeat *must,* strive towards the incredible delights of the one and only normal "vaginal orgasm" if they are to grow up and to become healthy. Now this type of opinion has its foundations in the Freudian theory of sexuality. Yet, there has always been a wide range of opposition to this theory and also a wide range of tolerance for other opinions, even among psychoanalysts themselves. This particular book was written before Masters and Johnson (6) had conclusively proven that, physiologically speaking, there is only one orgasm and "differences" are due to psychological conditioning, but at a time when the facts about the innervation of both clitoris and vagina were quite well known already and *after* the two Kinsey reports (4), (5) were available showing, in effect, that so-called "clitoral orgasm" is quite "normal." In fact, the author quarrels with the findings of the Kinsey report and pleads on page after page throughout the whole book with his female readers not to succumb to this feeling of "false normalcy" but to fight their "immature" and neurotic" ways of sexual satisfaction.

Here you have a very good example of a theoretical philosophy of what sex *should* be like, used in most *intolerant* way. To many of my patients who are being made ill by this book, the simple fact that this book is in print and is available makes it an equivalent authoritive statement to Masters and Johnsons finding which are also in print and also available.

We have, so far, identified three almost independent dimensions in which the counselor's philosophy on sex have a bearing on the type of counseling he does. We discussed the traditionalism versus radicalism continuum, we mentioned the personal versus interpersonal continuum, and now the "clitoral versus vaginal" continuum. Are there others?

D.McC.: I can think of one more. This would be the counselor's position along the continuum of the still unresolved question of how much of the sex drive is biologically set and how much is environmentally determined. Let us assume that there are two counselors on the extremes of this continuum and each is consulted by a couple in which the one partner wants sexual expression far more frequently than the other. I think that the counselor who assumes that he is dealing with a different *biological* rhythm in these two people, a situation not very modifiable, may focus his attention on the frustrated party, the person who wishes for *more* sexual expression, and help him work out ways in which additional outlets could be obtained. On the other hand, the counselor who assumes that these differences are due to different *social* and psychological experiences of the less active person may concentrate almost fully on *this* person to try to increase his responsiveness.

S.N.: Yes, the whole question of differences in sexual appetites between the marital partners is a rich field of value judgments as well as an excellent opportunity to demonstrate the relativity of these value judgments in historical perspective. When the double standard was at its highest peak, in the Victorian period, prostitution flourished and took care of the male part of the problem. The female part of the problem was socially controlled by simply ruling out an orgastic female as normal (9). Women appeared to accept this situation without too many overt signs of unhappiness, just as they do accept it in some contemporary primitive societies. (3, 7).

Later on, when we began developing the egalitarian notion that both male and female are entitled to sexual satisfaction, the advice given to couples with discrepant sexual appetites was that it is a "marital duty" and it just "doesn't matter how much you feel like sex, you simply must if the other wants to." This definition of "marital duty" was, of course, much more easily forced on the female who simply had to lie there while the male, of course, was dependent on his erection.

The modern version of this advice, given generally these days, reinterprets the concept of marital duties slightly. The advice given by most of my colleagues these days in cases of discrepant sexual appetite is that the less desirous partner does not have to fully involve himself in the sexual activity but, if the other partner desires, he or she has to respond in some manner such as, for example, by the use of oral-genital or manual-genital techniques or both. Of course, we still find that in the case of the wife "passive" intercourse may be more enjoyable. The wives in some of my couples describe this as an act of "giving" similar to that of "nursing a baby."

We have discussed how biases in the counselor's attitudes towards counseling, marriage, and sex itself may strongly influence the outcome of his counseling. However, we did not discuss whether or not the counselor can do something about these attitudes. I feel that, unless we wish to leave nihilistic impressions, we owe it to our readers to add at least a few sentences on the constructive side. How do you feel?

KNOW THYSELF—LOVE THY FELLOW COUNSELOR

D.McC.: Indeed there is a great deal the counselor can do about his own biases. The first thing he can do is to recognize and to make clear to the patient that he is not God. Not only is he not God, but he is also not a "scientist" in the sense that the physicist or even the biologist are scientists. There are many theories of marriage counseling, just as there are many theories of psychiatry. The patient is entitled to this information. I am not quite sure how it should be communicated to him in order to avoid confusing him, but in some way he must learn that the counselor's personality approach and opinions are just one of many possible.

Secondly, the opposite of the God-like posture must be recognized and avoided by the counselor. He cannot sit there and entirely disclaim his own importance. He must recognize and let the patient know, in some manner, that he realizes his own importance in what happens. Whether he is obtrusive or unobtrusive about his own directiveness, he cannot possibly engage with another human being in a discussion about an important aspect of living without significantly altering things. He may try and play the I-am-not-really-important role, but he is only deceiving himself and his client.

Certainly, if you suggest to a couple that, for example, they might go into a basic encounter group, you are putting them in an environment where certain things are going to happen. It is not a neutral environment. I can't see any patient who enters a counseling situation as coming to a totally neutral environment. The client may change, almost certainly will change, and even the counselor himself will change. He, too, will make a number of important discoveries about himself.

S.N.: It is a very delicate balance then which seems to be required between the counselor's knowledge of his unimportance and of his importance. He must be aware of his position on the continuum of different philosophies of counseling and he also must be keenly aware of how he, with his value position, may continually affect the client, regardless of whether or not he consciously tries to.

I think it is possible to demand of him that he be aware of the broad spectrum of philosophies and methods coexisting that differ from his own, in the community in which he lives. He must be receptive to the patients value system and he should be aware of approaches in counseling which, while he is not practicing them, may more beneficially affect his patient than his own. In plain English he must avoid feeling that if he refers his patient to a counselor whose approach is very different, in fact the opposite of his own, it is like sending this patient to the "enemy."

Of course, these are only things which most ethical codes in psychiatry, psychology, and social work demand of the counselor anyway. But it is one thing to officially subscribe to these ethical codes and it is another thing *not* to feel morally wrong with oneself if one moves a patient towards another counselor whose philosophy is very different from one's own. One might suspect that most counselors in fact feel that they have to protect their clients from even knowing about those kinds of philosophies.

The client may come to the counselor and say, "I have heard from so and so about a method of approach which is quite different from yours. What do you think of that method?" The true test of the counselor's self-knowledge and humility may come at this point. Will he be defensive or will he explain that there are a great many possible views on how to reach sexual contentment of which his is only one?

REFERENCES

1. Brecher, Ruth, and Brecher, E. (Ed.) : *An Analysis of Human Sexual Response.* New York, Signet, 1966.
2. Farber, S.M., and Wilson, R.H.L. (Ed.) : *Sex Education and the Teenager.* San Francisco, Diablo Press, 1967.
3. Ford, C.S., and Beach, F.A.: *Patterns of Sexual Behavior.* New York, Ace Star Book, 1951.
4. Kinsey, A.C.; Pomeroy, W.B., and Martin, C.D.: *Sexual Behavior in the Human Male.* Philadelphia and London, W.B. Saunders, 1948.
5. Kinsey, A.C.; Pomeroy, W.B.; Martin, C.D., and Gebhard, P.H.: *Sexual Behavior in the Human Female.* Philadelphia and London, W.B. Saunders, 1953.
6. Masters, W.H., and Johnson, Virginia E.: *Human Sexual Response.* Boston, Little, Brown, 1966.
7. Mead, Margaret: *Male and Female.* New York, Mentor, 1955.
8. Neiger, S.: Common sexual problems and the general practitioner. *J College of General Practice of Canada, X, 3*:21-27, 1963.
9. Rubin, I.: Transition in sex values—Implications for the education of adolescents. *J Marriage and the Family, 27, 2*:185-189, 1965.
10. Stokes, W.R.: How important is the wife's orgasm? *Sexology, XXXI, 8*:512-514, 1965.

Chapter 10

SEX EDUCATION AND THE BATTLEGROUND
OF CONTROVERSY

TOM McGINNIS

I BELIEVE that family life education, encompassing sex education, should be included in public school curricula. My convictions on this matter have grown gradually as a result of some twenty years of practice as a psychotherapist and marriage counselor. I have observed over and over again the tragic results of the lack, on the part of many people, of a clear, broad understanding of the numerous aspects of sexuality, marriage, and family relationships. My convictions were further strengthened and crystallized when, a few years ago, I began to teach graduate courses in sex education, marriage, and family life education at New York University.

Most young people in our modern society, when they reach the middle or late teens, are flung into a life for which they are utterly unprepared. Their knowledge and preparation for what it means to be an adult man or woman, a mate for a person of the opposite sex, a family member, and a parent are gleaned in a most hit-or-miss fashion—by limited and often distorted sessions with their peers, by observation of the adults around them, by what they happen to read, by the movies they chance to see, or sometimes by the halting and embarrassing attempts of their parents to inform them of "the facts of life." The results are too often what one would expect: ineffectual human functioning, unhappiness, disrupted marital and family relationships, unsatisfactory sexual experiences, and ruined lives. This affects all of us. If we are not personally victims of such poor preparation for life, someone close to us may be; conceivably, it could be our own child.

Such a state of affairs is unnecessary in an enlightened society. Sexuality can enrich life instead of making a hell out of it. What is more joyful than the full, vigorous use of ourselves as men or as women? What is more important than the preparation of our youngsters for a happy, enduring marital relationship and family life?

Yet, until recently, we have been notoriously—perhaps inexcusably—negligent in preparing young people to assume their roles as mates and as parents. We have much more knowledge than previous generations have had about what makes human beings "tick," what makes for a fulfilling marriage and a happy family life—and what destroys them. We are now much more knowledgeable, not only about how to teach in a pedagogic

107

sense, but more important, how to convey to young people an understanding of the psychological dynamics that underlie their life patterns. We can even educate in human values by the use of free, open exchanges with young people.

SEX AND THE YOUNGER GENERATION—WHERE THEY ARE AND WHERE WE ARE

We of the older generation, because of our "head-in-the-sand" attitude, are in real danger of losing touch with—to say nothing of control over—the behavior, attitudes, and value systems of the young. A new society is emerging while many of us are still talking and thinking in terms of the old. Most of us were raised in the belief that life would always go on in more or less the same way, that patterns of living on which our whole moral structure rested would remain essentially unchanged. But there is ample reason to believe that this may not be true. Traditional morality is experiencing a far more severe and profound upheaval than most people are aware of. Young people have less respect and awe for the family and parental authority than was evident a generation ago. Suddenly, to our shock and dismay, we discover that we are either not being heard by the young, or that they are not listening. They are off somewhere in another age, so to speak, following paths we have never known (such as "grass" and LSD), and our voices do not seem to reach their ears. It is ironic that we can clearly and effectively communicate with Buzz Aldrin and Neil Armstrong on the moon 238,000 miles away, but we cannot seem to communicate with the teenagers in our own households on matters very close to our hearts and to theirs.

The consequences of our inability to communicate with our young people can be pretty grim—both for them and for us. Sex in our culture can be a powder keg. Adults know this but young people do not; and because they do not, and we are not helping them to find out, there are teenage sex and drug parties, increased premarital pregnancies, shocking outbreaks of gonorrhea and syphilis among teenagers, tragic marriages of immature couples followed by separations and divorces, illegal abortions, and evidences of dangerously distorted and incorrect conceptions of sexual matters. The reaction of some of our generation is to call for a return of authoritarian control, of rigid moral teachings, of stiff punishment, of censorship of movies and books. But this is as futile as the mythical attempt of a certain king to order back the tides of the sea.

The society we now see emerging is different in many respects from the one in which we have lived, and is probably different from any that has existed before. Vast changes—medical, social, cultural, ethical, and moral

—have caused us to develop different reasoning for many of the things we do. The loosening of restrictions on sexual behavior is just one result of these changes. The reasons for controlling the sex impulse today are really not the same reasons that once prevailed. That is not to say that there are no longer good reasons for restraining one's sexual behavior. There are very good reasons, but it is important to realize that they are not the same reasons we were once taught. The old reasons may be neatly summed up in a limerick:

> There was a young lady named Wilde
> Who kept herself quite undefiled
> By thinking of Jesus
> And social diseases
> And the fear of having a child.

In the new society now emerging which Professor Hans Zetterberg, in his recent study of sexual life in Sweden, calls "the contraceptive society," the fear of having a child is no longer paramount—and eventually it will cease to be. With even greater progress in medical treatment, the fear of social diseases will not be the horror it once was. We like to think that religion is still a significant restraining force; but reports of churches and synagogues are not reassuring in this regard. Many churchgoers are alarmed at what is happening among their own young people.

If I were an alarmist, I could draw a terrifying picture of a society losing all its moral restraints, with resultant instability in family life and the danger of the family's loss of ability to function as the social institution for the care and rearing of children. There would be elements of truth in this picture. But I am not an alarmist. There are available to us rarely tried resources, and now, perhaps for the first time, we are being impelled into using them. We tend to forget that our children are the harvest of our own teachings. Inadequate as we are in some ways, most of us are honest, sincere, concerned, reasonable, understanding, and negotiable. Because of these qualities, we have given our children much valuable psychological equipment. We have also taught them to speak out, to express their feelings and sometimes to act them out. And this too is salutary. Emotionally speaking, we have been more democratic and forthright in our relationships with them than our parents were with us. On balance, I believe they are a healthier generation of children and we are a healthier generation of parents. They just look less healthy to us because they don't fulfill many of our expectations of them and their lack of dedication to tradition or the *status quo* shocks and frightens us. Then, too, they may see us as unhealthy because our reluctance or unwillingness to exert parental authority naturally invites their confusion and uncertainty.

What I am saying is, let's not sell them or ourselves short. Both generations are making progress in accepting and understanding each other. How many of us have moved from a position of displeasure, even of revulsion, when we saw the first long-haired boy, to our present position of tolerance? How many youngsters have come to tolerate that old parental admonition, "Why, when I was your age, I . . ."

We have been afraid to call on the resources of intelligence, honesty, and moral responsibility in our young people because their use presupposes freedom, and we, as parents, have been fearful of allowing them that freedom. We believed they were incapable of its use. We lacked confidence in their self-confidence. Even now we are not giving it to them—but they are taking it. We cannot stop them because—let us face the situation realistically —parental prohibitions are becoming more and more unenforceable. Enforcement of strict codes in the past was based largely on feelings of guilt and on the fears of detection, conception, and infection. These deterrents in large measure no longer work very effectively. The automobile, job mobility, pockets full of money, and a torrent of information and misinformation pouring through the entertainment and news media, have taken the youngsters out from under their parents' effective control. We as well as the young people will be far better off if we cease trying to impose on them an authority we no longer possess; rather, we should grant them the freedom to take responsibility for their own acts, while at the same time we lend our energies to equipping them to use that freedom wisely. Quite frankly, I strongly believe that we adults have no alternative.

WHAT DO WE MEAN BY SEX AND SEX EDUCATION

Sex is much more than a biological phenomenon. It has deep psychological aspects rooted in culture, history, and religion. It has to do with the person's concept of himself—his entire self as a male or female, physically, mentally, emotionally, and spiritually. This is what is so little understood, not only by the young but by many adults as well—a person's sexuality is so basic to his nature that it permeates his entire personality. Failure to understand this is responsible for the treating of sex as something apart, separate from the personality—a thing, like a piece of cake to be eaten, or an appetite, a desire. This false concept is responsible for much tragedy. Therefore, we must distinguish between "sex," which is largely a biological and anatomical concept, and "human sexuality," which embraces the broader aspects of the whole personality.

When I speak of "sex education," I am talking about education, not indoctrination, in the nature and function of human sexuality in its broadest sense. Opponents jump to the conclusion that we are talking about "sex instruction," which has to do only with the functions of the various organs, or lessons in positions of sexual intercourse. On the contrary, all the leaders I know in the sex education movement favor and encourage a total approach to the complicated and interrelated biological, sociological, psychological, cultural, spiritual, and moral dimensions of human sexual functioning. One of our sex education teachers at N.Y.U. described it as follows, and I believe it would be hard to improve on her description:

> Sex education means helping the child to understand his own complete personality. This involves a knowledge of his maleness or femaleness—what it is; how it functions; and what part it will play in his life. It involves developing responsible attitudes in the use of his sexuality, so that he may develop his own code of behavior which will serve to guide him in his own actions, and in his relations with other people. It means developing an understanding and appreciation for the role played by the opposite sex, so that marriage and child rearing become an experience shared together in a happy, well-adjusted fashion.

NEED FOR SEX EDUCATION IN THE SCHOOLS

The concentration on sex by the mass media and the entertainment industry has stimulated an artificial and, in some respects, dangerous fascination with the genital and exploitive aspects of sex at the expense of an understanding of the real nature of human sexuality and its relation to the sense of self.

There is danger in looking upon sex as a mere appetite, and this misconception leads to the pursuit of sex for itself alone, without one's being aware of what the process can do to himself or to others. Girls, for example, sometimes use sex as a weapon for taking revenge on their parents by becoming pregnant, or their boy friends by teasing and then turning off; or they use it as a trap to lure a boy into marriage. Some boys use sex to gain a sense of manliness, virility, or power; to see how many conquests they can make, or to raise their status in the eyes of their peers. All these exploitive uses of sex tend to convert what could be a positive, joyous, and enriching experience for both partners, into a deadening, self-defeating experience for at least one of the partners, and often for both.

A true understanding of human sexuality is necessary for the strengthening and perhaps even for the survival of society, and in my judgment no group in our society today is adequately meeting the need for bringing about this undertaking. The home is the ideal place for sex education, for it goes on there all the time, whether we like it or not. How an infant is held, how a child is toilet trained, how an adolescent observes his parents giving and receiving affection—all these are components of his sex education. However, children need more help than experience and observation can provide. They need opportunities for open, honest, and realistic discussion and evaluation.

Today many of us, as parents, are not well enough equipped to do the kind of job we know is required. We are not doing an adequate job, perhaps, for the following reasons: a) Many of us have insufficient knowledge of human sexuality; b) we are so emotionally involved with our own children that we cannot be sufficiently objective; c) in many cases, we ourselves have been brought up to regard sex as private and "hush-hush," so that we cannot talk about it easily or teach it effectively; d) we often tend to be authoritarian in our attitudes towards the "right" and "wrong" of specific acts such as, for example, masturbation; e) communication between parents and children is often poor; and f) perhaps most important of all, the sexual lives of many parents themselves are dull, disappointing, and full of conflict.

Churches and synagogues have attempted in various ways to deal with the problem, but aside from the fact that many young people are not reached by them, the churches' approach to sex is often in terms of moral absolutes. These absolutist positions are being widely challenged, not only by other elements in the community, but within the churches themselves, as witness the present controversy in the Catholic church on the sinfulness of birth control. Such rigid moral positions with respect to human sexuality cannot be the *only* useful basis for preparing young men and women to live healthy and fulfilling adult lives. Let me back this up if I can: The assumptions of one generation are apt to be discarded by the next; the assumptions by one group in a multicultural society are not accepted by other groups; and rigid positions, religious or otherwise, cannot easily take into account the vast and rapid social changes of our time. Just as one example, let's note the position of women—the increasingly prevalent view among educated women that they should have the right to participate in premarital sexual intercourse or to use "the pill" and other contraceptives, if they wish. What is actually happening is that young people are widely ignoring these rigid moral positions and probably cannot be won back to them.

I have come to the conclusion that no one community resource can do the kind of qualitative job in sex education which most of us would want. Each of them—the home, the school, the church, local professionals, including the family doctor—all share in this important responsibility—and each should make his contribution. What we really need is a resource which can coordinate their contributions in a major educational effort. In my considered judgment, the school at this time is the most comprehensive and desirable choice. It is the only resource able to reach *all* the children in the community. It is the only resource with the knowledge, experience and educational wherewithal to accomplish a task of this magnitude.

Furthermore, the school is already in the business of teaching and is committed to the position that the more knowledge a person has, and the healthier his personality, the more successfully he can function in life. It is providing an increasingly improved atmosphere for open and honest communication among students, teachers, and parents. On the other hand, however, the school should not be expected or tempted to do this job alone. It must strive for and enlist the cooperation and active involvement of the community itself, as well as every interested and concerned community resource.

Up to this point we have taken a look at sex and the younger generation; where they are and where we are. We have defined what we mean by sex and sex education and we have focused on the need for sex education in the schools.

If time had permitted, I would have liked to explore more carefully the steady progress which we have made in the United States and, more specifically, in New Jersey; the job and qualifications of the teacher and some of the innovations we have developed in our teacher training, sex education program at New York University. But we will have to pass over them so that we can get to the most difficult and pressing problem in the field of sex education today. I choose to call it "the battleground of controversy over sex education."

Let's begin by reviewing the changes that have occurred in the strange and wonderful year just past. In this era of general controversy, we have suddenly witnessed the arrival of sex education at the very top of the controversy heap, right up there with Vietnam. And this is not at all a bad thing. Perhaps never before have the citizens of any country cared so passionately about what goes on in the classrooms of the nation.

I am reminded of the familiar story of the world's greatest mule trainer, who, it was said, could turn the most recalcitrant beast into a willing worker. When the owner of such an animal brought his mule in for training, he was appalled to see the great trainer lift a baseball bat and, without warning, strike a hefty blow between the animal's eyes. As the beast lay stunned, its owner turned on the trainer, demanding, "Is this any way to teach anything?" To which the trainer calmly replied: "First you gotta get their attention!" If the hue and cry over sex education accomplished nothing else, it at least got the attention of the people.

As sex educators, we cannot claim the credit for that feat. This was the one great service rendered to us by the opponents of sex education in the schools. Until the beginning of 1969, objections were mild and localized; not unlike the onset of a great many diseases that are virulent when full-blown. But objections which were mild enough in the beginning, escalated into a cause and a challenge when taken up and inflated by extremist groups. Today, every newspaper, every magazine, and virtually every television "talk-show" has given significant time and attention to this controversy. Only a short while ago, there were communities in the nation representing the full spectrum of acceptance or rejection of sex education in the schools. Now virtually every community is torn by arguments, some of them sincerely put forth by thoughtful and informed questioners, but more and more of them packaged as "instant arguments" and trotted out in all their catch-phrases by professional right-wingers. It is to this aspect of the controversy, this debasement of honest questioning, that I would like to address my remarks.

I think the time has come to try to get some perspective on what has happened, and why. Let's look back to just one year ago. At that time, the clamor about sex education took the form of a rapidly rolling bandwagon. Sex education enjoyed the dubious distinction of being an "in" course, almost a fad. Almost everybody wanted it without really having thought through what "it" amounted to in terms of *what* was to be taught, *when* it was to be taught, *how* it was to be taught, and *who* was to teach it. Many community groups seemed actually to feel that the lack of something called sex education in their particular school systems left them with the stigma of being old-fashioned and generally "not with it." In response to this, state after state saw its legislatures not only support such efforts, but, in some cases, actually mandate them. School administrators saw their hands being forced, and moved ahead without being certain that they had a firm foundation on which to build. This overenthusiasm had the effect of temporarily hushing the slight objections that were so hesitantly raised. The steamroller went full speed ahead.

Some schools found themselves with ill-defined curricula and a mass of hard-to-evaluate material. All this had to be sifted through and somehow "taught by" inadequately prepared and frequently frightened teachers who had been hastily recruited from rosters of gym teachers and school health nurses. Along with uncertainties about teaching methodologies, there was inadequate recognition of the need for coping with the dubious posture of the community. Parents, in particular, were short-changed in the area of information about what was happening and what was planned. There was a crucial breakdown in communication; and the vacuum was quickly filled by those individuals and organizations that saw sex education as a threat or as a means to an end. These people were not at all hesitant about talking to the parents—long, loud, and often. The shrillness of their arguments penetrated into the classrooms and administrative offices where, by mid-1969, many felt that they were in a "damned if we do and damned if we don't" situation.

Those of us entrusted with the formidable task of preparing teachers to operate in this field scarcely had time to anticipate the dangers—so preoccupied were we with the job at hand.

It was our experience with our graduate Fellowship Training Program in Sex Education at N.Y.U. which enabled us to reevaluate the total picture. In the process of their training, many of the fellows expressed increasing anxiety about their futures. They had begun to comprehend the vast scope of the field of sex education. They expressed concern about their ability to handle positions of heavy and premature responsibility which would require them to design and develop programs, train teachers and provide opportunities for wide parent participation. A few panicked at the thought of how they would respond to opposition.

This put those of us on the University level under even more pressure as we began to relate to these reactions. It also gave us more reason to explore what was going on. We tried to come out of our ivory towers and delve into what was causing all the pressure.

What *was* responsible for the urgency reflected in newspaper editorials, church and synagogue sermons, civic organization speeches, requests from parents and students? Certainly not the sudden realization that many of us had sexual hang-ups and wanted to save our children from our fate. There were more justifiable concerns than that. People were confused and upset by the rapid changes they could see taking place in the lives of youngsters. They were troubled by teen-age rebellion; tales of campus cohabitation; the erotic emphasis on sex in literature and the theatre; the sexual freedom supposedly offered by "the pill" and, closer to home, parents were frustrated by their own inability effectively to influence their children. Many people developed an affinity for sex education in the hope that it would help children to develop sorely needed personal guidelines that would enable them to build healthier and happier lives in the face of undermining influences. Parents wanted to offer their children, even their very young ones, a more qualitative preparation for life. Where, naturally, would they turn but to a program that gave promise to defining and providing understanding of human sexuality and promoting healthy personal, marital, and family relationships? Even the kids were asking to be taught it, an educational phenomenon that we are not likely to encounter again for a long time.

So, as we have said, sex education became the popular "thing" of its time. The idea was reinforced over and over again and the pressures to implement it swept us into establishing our program without first ensuring that we had all the ingredients for its success, as well as the time in which to do it well.

Now we find ourselves in a rather uncomfortable position. No sooner had we begun to realize that we might have to drop back a pace or two, do some evaluating and strengthening when the oragnized opposition began to take pot shots at sex education and at the character and integrity of individuals active in the movement. For the past several months, we've been blasted by the extremists from all sides, and to add to our discomfort and frustration in New Jersey, we are temporarily subject to a moratorium. I must admit it has been exceedingly difficult for us to accept.

Despite these setbacks, we must pick ourselves up, gather our available resources and work thoughtfully and diligently toward introducing and expanding programs with firm foundations.

I have some suggestions as to how we can go about this. Let's review, first, at least three necessary ingredients of good sex education programs: trained, qualified teachers; a well-planned curriculum based on appropriate subject matter; and, a community that has been involved in all facets of planning the program.

I should like to explain here that, while I certainly advocate well-qualified and trained teachers, I am not saying that we cannot begin our programs without them. Our programs do not have to be perfect to be helpful, and we must realize that even a trained teacher will need time to develop expertise. Correct information, no matter how amateurishly taught, is still infinitely better than pornography, gutter information, and the distortions found in much of our literature today.

Those communities which do not have many qualified teachers must realize that this is going to take time. If there is little opposition in their area, they might well spend much of their time on efforts to prepare teachers through university training programs, local workshops and seminars. They can also work on developing a program of parent sex education that will coordinate with the student program.

Areas with little controversy and some trained teachers can focus on gaining experience in the classroom—"on the firing line," strengthening their programs with this experience. In areas where opposition is strong, it's an entirely different situation. They will have to devote most of their energy to carrying out a determined public education campaign in order to cope effectively with the flood of criticism and protect their programs from being eliminated from the curriculum.

How does a school system at this point know what direction to follow? In tackling this problem, each district must try to determine the degree of acceptance and rejection of sex education in the community. I would like to suggest some guidelines for making this assessment. May I invite your attention to the following diagram which outlines "major categories of response to sex education" in any community:

MAJOR CATEGORIES OF RESPONSE TO SEX EDUCATION

Left Wing "Gung Ho's"	Committed Supporters	Uncommitted	Committed Opposition	Right Wing Extremists
		Yes ⟷ Yes but No ⟷ No but		

On the extreme left, we have the left-wing thinkers. Let's call them the "gung ho's." They are "gung ho" over sex education or nearly anything that is new and presumably progressive. They do not need convincing that sex education in schools is a good thing—they are convinced. Let's accept this group but be a bit wary of how they might go about supporting the cause. Their approach is often too emotional and not backed up with thoughtful consideration. They can help us, but they can also do us a disservice by being vocal but not knowledgeable. At their worst, they can put us in the position of the old cliche: "with friends like those, who needs enemies?"

In the next column, we have what we can term the "Committed Supporters," who have rational and solid convictions. They can be sex education's most valuable and reliable asset. They have thought out and evaluated the situation and can speak convincingly in campaigns for public support.

Moving to the right, in the center, we draw a wide column for the Uncommitted. The Uncommitted is made up of a variety of people. In this group are parents who pay little attention to school activities unless it means a raise in their taxes. There are also people who have no children or whose children are no longer in school. Among them are retired citizens. We also find families with too-busy parents, working mothers, parents who are television sitters, families with severe financial or emotional problems. In general, these are people who have other concerns that to them are more attractive, pressing, or important than the question of whether or not we should have sex education in the schools. I am not condemning them. I am aware that there can be any number of appropriate forces that prevent them from being active and vocal. They may or may not have opinions about sex education, but they do not have or seek social or political channels through which they can communicate these to other people. Some have ambivalent feelings about the whole idea and could move in either direction. Others are vaguely against it but are not quite sure why. These people will remain silent until they are moved by fear or a threat to their security or, on the other hand, by an honest appeal for their help in a good cause. We could label some of them "Yes, buts" where the direction is toward acceptance, and others "No, buts" where the direction is toward rejection.

The next column I call the Committed Opposition. Like the Committed Supporters, these people also have rational and well-thought out reasons for their views. They are not extremists—but they are definitely against sex education. In terms of their personal lives, the idea of sex education is in conflict with the important basic values they have lived by as a result of cultural upbringing, religious training or moral teachings. They simply cannot expand their outlook sufficiently to accept anything they feel is different, radical, or reactionary.

In the right-hand column are the extremist opposition—the radical right wing. This is the only well-organized group in the spectrum, and I will spend more time evaluating them because their influence in some areas is enormous. While I am not out "to get," so to speak, any individual or organization, I will be trying as a psychotherapist to identify a particular personality style and approach to life. If not dealt with appropriately, this personality style can be destructive, not only to sex education but to the whole educational scene, and perhaps to our society.

In the vanguard of extremist activities directed against sex education in the schools is the John Birch Society. Their reasons for launching a nation-wide campaign are quite explicit. And I quote: "Sex education is a communist plot to promote sexual promiscuity and destroy one whole generation of American youth." Still quoting—"Deep-laid plans have been carefully initiated to spread this subversive monstrosity over the whole American educational system . . . . but a preponderant majority of the American people are not yet even aware of this filthy communist plot."

The society's active arm, MOTOREDE (Movement to Restore Decency), has established chapters in many communities in the United States which are working to bring about the demise of sex education.

Equally vociferous and damning are the charges leveled against sex education by the Christian Crusade. In their booklet entitled, *Is the School House the Proper Place to Teach Raw Sex?*, the author, Gordon Drake, misquotes and distorts numerous leading exponents of sex education, weaving an intricate mosaic purporting to reveal a diabolic and nefarious plot to seduce the minds and morals of little children. He charges educators, physicians, and clergy alike with intentional or unwitting complicity in a great plan for communist takeover. Their statements are quoted out of context and given an interpretation which implies an attack on the Bible and the churches, indeed on all religion, as superstitious, inhibiting, and detrimental to human fulfillment.

In addition to these two major organizations there are numerous small groups, each with its own particular reasons for opposing sex education. Most of these bear catchy alphabetical names such as ACRE (Association of Citizens for Responsible Education), MOMS (Mothers for Moral Stability), PAUSE (Parents Against Unconstitutional Sex Education), and POPE

(Parents for Orthodoxy in Parochial Education). On the other extreme there is a group with an even catchier title, which I am told is *for* sex education. It calls itself MENAPAUSE (Men Against Pause).

In general, the approach of the extremist is notable for its "scare tactics." His favorite weapons are distortion, accusation, name-calling, and personal abuse. He even resorts to "guilt by association," that old ghost dredged up out of the McCarthy era. He tends to be a self-styled defender of the faith, opposed to everything which seems contrary to *his* particular concept of the traditional "American Way," e.g. the civil rights movement, hippies, fluoridation, sensitivity training, and sex education. He plays on people's fears and prejudices by pointing up sinister lurking dangers in any new idea or program. To him it may even be an attempt at subversion —a "communist plan" to take over the country. His "righteous" campaigns are frequently vicious.

This personality type is very difficult to communicate with, as almost any clinician in the mental health field will attest to. Characteristically, he is rigid, stubborn, arrogant, suspicious, tenacious, repetitious, and hostile. Moreover, he is extremely perceptive to any hint of vulnerability in his opponent. He will maximize, beyond all proportion, even an insignificant error such as the misquoting of a date. He will sniff and snoop until he develops a clue—a means of "getting to" his victim—then pounce upon him, indulging in name-calling and other vituperative language. In a meeting of a school board or a community agency—perhaps even a political party committee—he can cause disruption and disablement of effective process. He is suspicious of any new or different suggestion and attempts to belabor it at great length. An argument with him will generally result in a power struggle.

Most people find this kind of attack overwhelming and frightening, as well as emotionally wearing. To escape it, they will often withdraw. Those unaware of this tactic may be impressed and overawed, but those who recognize it will be better prepared to deal with it and will less likely be intimidated, for they will perceive the clever and subtle distortions and fear-provoking threats.

It is an unfortunate fact that slanted propaganda, loudly pronounced, often tends to become more and more believable if it is repeated often enough. Eventually it becomes almost absolute. This was the technique employed by Nazi Germany three decades ago. The value, therefore, of teaching people to recognize the difference between truth and distortion is obvious. Of importance to us here and now is that it could preserve not only the idea of sex education but our whole educational system. The extremist's attack on sex education cannot be equated with any challenge to education that we have experienced in the past. Sex education has been deliberately made the object of an assault designed to destroy it and—if we allow it to be destroyed—it will not be the last victim. In his fear, the extremist feels he must achieve control of the whole educational system "to save the youth of our country" and sees in the vulnerability of sex education an opportunity to drive the opening wedge.

All right, now, if we have this understanding of the extremist and his threat, how do we relate to them? Quite frankly it is very difficult. First, we must accept that there is no such thing as rational negotiation and communication based on discussion. It is futile, for example, to set up a panel in the hope of educating the general public by airing pros and cons when that panel will include an extremist. I am told that David Susskind's attempt to discuss sex education on a recent Sunday evening television show resulted in panel members trying to outshout one another. The one extremist on the panel was so interruptive and dominating that balanced, and opposing views, were virtually impossible to be heard.

Where pro and con speakers *must* confront each other, the democratic process with fair and equal opportunity to all to be heard, must obtain. Certainly, parents have a right to hear all the facts and should be allowed to make their own judgments without melodramatic and irrelevant interference. The time allotted to any one speaker or questioner from the audience should be firmly limited. In this way, the inequity of one person dominating a public discussion may be lessened. But just limiting the time available to the extremist is in itself not sufficient. The audience should be aware of his ploy and not fall into the trap of responding when he indulges in name-calling and personal abuse. Often, the natural reflex action on the part of the person under attack results in a quarrel, rather than what should have been a constructive debate. There should, therefore, be a conscious determination to disregard such attacks and adhere strictly to issues. These attacks can sometimes be so destructive that it is frequently necessary to decide, on the spot, whether to disregard them or temporarily terminate the discussion. Generally, such drastic action is unnecessary; a tirade that develops one-sidedly can be self-defeating and leave publicly exposed he who indulges in it.

While we may be obliged to spend some of our time fighting for and justifying the purposes and values of sex education, we must at the same time be working toward a stronger support base by organizing forces in the community. As we plug the dike with one hand, we can fashion with the other a community action program of positive information that will reach out and educate the public. We should be open and honest about our mistakes; admit that we are, figuratively, just learning to walk in this field; and point up the need for the participation and involvement of people outside the schools themselves. It is a cold, hard fact that the success or failure of sex education will be decided at the grass roots level—by the voter—as he ultimately either accepts or rejects the program. The professional educator cannot "go it alone."

The campaigns or programs I call for will, of necessity, differ from community to community because of the unique characteristics of each location. Every community has its own particular socioeconomic makeup and cultural milieu. Each has its own political climate. Some areas readily accept innovative and progressive ideas. Others assimilate new ideas more slowly. Furthermore, organized opposition to sex education may vary in its influence and intensity. You know your own district. You can best set up specific guidelines for your program and tailor-make it to your own needs by an evaluation of the factors I have just mentioned.

Help and strength rest with the involvement and dedication of the people I called the Committed Supporters. They can be a powerful force because they comprise most of the leadership in the churches, service clubs, and political groups that make up every community. They are intelligent, concerned, and willing to further the cause of sex education. They can influence many people in the large uncommitted group in our diagram with their enthusiasm, sincerity, and honesty. It is to this group that we must address ourselves. In some cases, only a slight effort will be necessary to move them over into the committed column; others will require more painstaking effort.

Keep in mind that many national organizations have gone on record in support of sex education. To mention just a few, they are the National Congress of Parents and Teachers, American Medical Association, United Nations Educational, Scientific and Cultural Organization known as UNESCO, National Education Association, and the United States Department of Health, Education and Welfare. An Interfaith Statement on Sex Education was issued jointly in 1968 by working groups of the National Council of Churches, the Synagogue Council of America, and the United States Catholic Conference Family Life Bureau, containing this statement: "We urge all to take a more active role—each in his own area of responsibility and competence—in promoting sound leadership and programs in sex education. We believe it possible to help our sons and daughters achieve a richer, fuller understanding of their sexuality, so that our children will enter a world where men and women live and work together in understanding, cooperation, and love."

PREDICTIONS

In closing, I would like to make some predictions. I predict that parents, students, and teachers in 1980, looking back at the present storms of controversy over family living courses, including sex education, will regard our fears and reservations with amusement. The squeamishness and concerns which beset us now will be gone. Practically all schools by then will have included family life and sex education as a part of their curriculum. It will be accepted and taken for granted. The problems will not be those of whether or how to introduce the subject, but rather of how to improve its quality and effectiveness. There will be a unified, comprehensive, sequential, and well-defined pattern of education (not instruction) for all ages from kindergarten to twelfth grade; and sex, marriage and family life education will not only be taught as subjects in themselves but will be integrated with other subjects. We will move our educational focus from one of preparation for marriage and family life to one of *preparation for human experience*. Classroom interaction will highlight intellectual, emotional, and behavioral processes and will include open discussions of the development of values and morals. Increased understanding of self and others will allow specific course content to become more beneficial to the development of one's total life experience.

No longer will there be felt any need to segregate the sexes in these discussions or to select a male teacher for boys and a female teacher for girls. The personal qualifications of the teacher and his ability to communicate with his students will be the controlling factor in his selection, rather than his sex. Teacher training will have made great strides; we will be training teachers to teach teachers.

Chapter 11

THE AUTHENTIC MARRIAGE: AN EXISTENTIAL INTERPRETATION

JOHN W. CRANDALL

T HE MARRIAGE counselor, in his work with disturbed couples, is guided customarily by a set of therapeutic goals. He knows what he is trying to achieve with the persons under his care and bends his technical skill and knowledge accordingly. Implicit in this effort is an assumption, or set of assumptions, as to the nature of the ideal marital state, for without such, however subtle or latent, the therapy would become an aimless, hit or miss affair. "The ideal of health," says Sutherland, "holds the same relationship . . . to goals of therapy as the pole star holds to a trip northward. It defines the direction of our effort" (1) .

What is this ideal state? In this chapter, we approach the matter in the light of critical elements in the structure of the existence, or the human nature, of the persons in the marriage. The approach is ontological, that is, related to the being of marital partners. (Hereafter to be called MPs for simplicity's sake.) While other studies would generate models of the optimal marriage on the basis of statistically average behavior or on generalizations of conduct abstracted from the responses of informants, we propose to ask the question: "What are the implications of the human nature of MPs for the marital optimum?" Hopefully this approach will bring a greater dimension of depth into this area of research and tend, in some measure, to raise sights beyond the conclusions of researchers such as Terman (2) and Burgess and Cottrell (3) that the best marriages are related to norms of adjustment. Says Kolb in an evaluation of these re-searches: "The person best fitted for marriage is highly socialized, i.e. he is characterized by traits of stability, conventionality, and conformity" (4) .

The image of man that will inform this study will be drawn, for the most part, from the ontological thought of the existentialist philosopher, Martin Heidegger. The model of the optimal marriage based on this image will consist of three elements: specifically, a) the optimum as *ideal,* b) the optimum as *conditions* favorable to the fulfillment of the ideal, and c) the positive *mood* induced by progress toward the ideal. Examined, in the first instance, will be the question of what a marriage *ought* to be; in the second, of how a marriage *becomes* what it ought to be; in the third, of what is *experienced as benign emotion* in the process of a marriage becoming what it ought to be. These dimensions will be known henceforth as the *teleological, instrumental,* and *positive emotive-consequential* dimensions of the optimal marital setting. Taken together they are the logical structures of a perfect state conceived as a totality. The ought, the conditions of the ought and the resultant positive mood induced by intimations of the ought, all interrelate and combine to form an idealistic whole. An optimal meal, for example, includes an ideal of congruence between hunger and the availability of food. It also includes an adequacy of funds for the purchase of food, freedom from physical illness, and a being present in the vicinity of food: that is, conditions for the assurance of the idealistic congruence. It includes, too, a positive accompanying mood: for when the meal is done, a sense of well-being and fulfillment occur.

THE TELEOLOGICAL DIMENSION OF THE MARITAL OPTIMUM

In Heidegger's view, the telos, or the ideal of marital relationships, would be one in which MPs evolve *in the authentic mode of existence.* As those whose being it is to have a choice; as those, who by virtue of their human condition, are essentially unsettled and unfinished and never determined forever like a thing is, MPs exist one with the other as *possibility.* It is the possibility to decide and before them are two ways: inauthentic existence and authentic existence.

To exist inauthentically is to be closed off to the reality of things. It is to narrow down existence to what is manageable and safe even though this means a projection of a false self, a "they self" dictated by others (5), or an engagement in "idle talk" (6) where speech disguises truth, or that noninvolvement in life experiences which is "curiosity" (7). Inauthentic existence is life hidden in distortions, falsities, and ambiguities.

Authenticity, however, means an *openness to things as they are.* It is an openness to the fundamentalness of objects and realities: the silkiness of silk, the woodiness of wood—what lies at the heart. Most specifically it is an openness to the reality of one's own existence; of one's own unique possibilities and structures. What is discovered in such personalized openness is nothing alien to the self like a conformist or "they self," but an originative and distinctive reality. Authentic existence is *the taking hold of the world in one's own way* (8).

A marriage in which MPs choose the authentic style of ontological openness is a marriage *lived in the truth.* Coming from the Greek, *aletheia,* truth means literally, uncovering or revelation. Truth exists when what is hidden is no longer so. "To say that an assertion 'is true' signifies that it uncovers the entity as it is in itself. Such an assertion asserts, points out, 'lets' the entity 'be seen' . . . in its uncoveredness. The *being-true . . .* of the assertion must be understood as *being-uncovering*" (9).

In this marital style which *lets being be,* there are two features which typify its truthfulness. These are the following: a) *transfacadic movement* and b) *processuality.*

Transfacadic movement. MPs living in the truth as being-open, exhibit what could be called a transfacadic movement, that is, a movement in which MPs in the varied expressions of their life together go beyond the protective walls of pretense, beyond facades. They stand out and away from the defensive maskings which typify inauthentic marital interactions toward what is more fundamentally real.

Marital relationships are lived on a real basis. Feelings come forth, for example, as they really exist. This applies to feelings that are thought of as negative—resentment, jealousy, shame, anger, annoyance—as well as feelings that are thought of as positive—tenderness, love, admiration. They are expressed directly as they arise without benefit of facadic intricacies. Anger and resentment do not hide themselves behind the subtleties of civilized murder such as condescension or overprotectiveness nor do love and affection hide themselves behind the substitute striving of affection for animals. They come forth as they are. As Rogers puts it: "It is as though the map of expression of feelings has come to match more closely the territory of the actual emotional experience" (10).

Deep desire also emerges in its full honesty: the instinctual desires such as sex, the psychic desires such as the wish to be protected and, also, the more uniquely personal desires of MPs to be themselves in keeping with the original possibilities of their natures. In the ontological context, such desires do not lurk behind facades. Sexual interest does not mask itself in a wife's orgiastic dreams nor does the wish to be protected mask itself in the reaction formation of tyrannical dominance; neither does the urge to originality, the life dream, hide itself by day and come forth only in the dark when no one else is about. Such urges are openly avowed. Sex is a tempest or a passing caress, but in all instances a joyful gift of nature to be freely appropriated. The desire for protection is the open acknowledgement of MPs of a sense of inadequacy or helplessness freely given without the fear that others will want to gain by it. And the life dream—it is dreamed, so to speak, in waking hours—*and there is no laughter.*

Language too, comes to reveal, rather than disguise the truth, for in the transfacadic context, language is *speech* (authentic discourse) as contrasted with idle talk (inauthentic discourse). Speech is an Heideggerian term for discourse that *discloses being* (11). In speech, MPs come in touch with precisely what it is that is being talked about. If, at the core of the discourse, there is resentment, then it is the resentment that is the communicative focus. If it is the feeling on the part of the wife, tired after a week's work, "I want to go away to the country for the weekend," this is not masked in words of idle talk such as, "It's such a pretty day today"—a communication which hints at the truth, but does not express it; rather what is felt and desired is brought forth in words to the surface, into unconcealedness. Speech, says Heidegger, is akin to *poetical discourse* wherein "the communication of the existential possibilities of one's state of mind can become an aim in itself . . ." (12). Indeed, the authentic living in the truth manifested in transfacadic movement is essentially a poetic phenomenon of which speech is but one example. For MPs to live authentically is for them at the same time to live poetically, for in either case existence is disclosed. "To dwell poetically means: to stand in the presence of the gods and to be involved in the essence of things" (13).

PROCESSUALITY

On the basis of the context of transfacadic movement in which they live, MPs exhibit a still further evolvement in the truth which is called *processuality*. Here MPs in their collective capacity for letting being be, carry forward the movement away from facades in an ever-ramifying way. MPs are in a state of flux and seem content to remain in the flowing current. The striving for conclusions and end-states diminishes. They feel no compulsion to be always the same, today, yesterday, and forever. Within the context of basic identities and value structures, they refashion things. A variety of feelings are aroused in them for a particular person, a variety of attitudes toward a particular experience, rather than a rigid set of "proper" feelings and attitudes. The horizons of their lives are ever-expanding ones, with new possibilities of living, of relating, of experiencing and of fulfillment unfolding all the time. It is a marital estate wherein persons live the truth of the human condition, notably its unsettled, unfinished character. Each MP is aware that he is not fixed and finished as an object is. Rather, he knows himself as possibility thrown into the world. Accordingly, he does not expect himself or anyone else to reach an end-point of growth and development. Closure is put on the tendency to freeze the other in a mould of stereotyped expectation and perception.

Such a tendency, when acted upon, typifies the inauthentic marriage. Here impulses, acts, thoughts and feelings become subject to a restraining logic and repetitiveness in which all the poetry, drama, richness, and spontaneity of these behavioral possibilities become drained off. At its most demonic, the inauthentic marriage stabilizes itself through patterns of interaction which radically curtail and inhibit growth. In these instances, MPs fit together in such a way that the strength of the fit is derived from depressions, not extensions of personal being.

In a marriage lived in the truth, however, these patterns do not obtain. Human possibilities are not dimmed down, but accepted thankfully and joyfully as the raw material of existence. These possibilities present themselves as *challenging pregnancies:* biological dispositions of sex, aggression and curiosity, acquired possibilities born of contact with a given heritage which, when incorporated within the self as felt values, becomes a "position" to adventure in and upon and to defend, talents inborn, lying like sleeping beauties prone to awaken at the kiss of interest—such possibilities in the authentic mode are personally activated and in a processual manner. They become for each MP a personalized explorative context, a spur to becoming. Marital life thus becomes literally ahead of itself, never static, always reaching beyond what is to what could yet be. Its normality lies in its openness and flexibility.

THE INSTRUMENTAL DIMENSION OF THE MARITAL OPTIMUM

The Heideggerian concept of *understanding* is the key element in the instrumental dimension of the marital optimum. For it is understanding that opens up a marital relationship definitively to the possibility of truth and interactions based on it.

By understanding, Heidegger does not mean an attitude of sympathy or a mere theoretical understanding, but a *practical* understanding which relates to things on the basis of their use. Understanding is related to the being of each MP as that being which discloses itself. As a disclosing being he is unique. He exists, as do all other beings, but, unlike them, he *knows that he exists.* He is open to himself in his being. He is the one who can disclose being, who can experience not only his own being as being, but the being of all other persons and things as being.

This knowledge is the fundamental form of understanding, a practical understanding in which there is disclosed to MPs the ontological purpose of their existences. In understanding, each MP knows what he is ontologically capable of. He is a *lumen naturale* who exists in order that what is hidden may, through him, come to light (14). If a valley of flowers lies before him, he is to allow it to disclose itself by being aware of it. If a piece of wool slips through his fingers, he is to let the wooliness of the wool reveal itself through the apperceptiveness of touch. If he confronts his own existence, he is to let what is intrinsic to that existence unfold. If he confronts the existence of another, he is to let what the other is come forth and be. He exists, in short, that being might be, or in Heidegger's apt phrase, as *a servant and shepherd of being* (15). In understanding, he *knows* that he exists in this capacity.

With the dawning of understanding, the possibility of a marriage lived in the truth comes dynamically into focus. This is because MPs who understand become aware of themselves and each other, not simply in terms of familiar role obligations and expectations, but in terms of what each in the deepest functional sense is for. The focus is not upon functionality in terms of culturally derived expectancies: a wife there to clean and cook, a husband there to financially support. Rather, the focus is upon what each MP is ontologically for as a servant and shepherd of being. With such a vision of himself and the other, each MP can go to the other in the assurance that *no danger is involved in such an approach.* The other, as the servant and shepherd of being, will so serve and shepherd the being of the one who approaches. He will encourage the expression of the varied realities within him. He will not let his possibility waste itself, but will be for it a catylyst that it might emerge and be. Neither will he let the darker realities simmer within him. His angers and jealousies will likewise be permitted to come forth, for these, too, are aspects of what he is. He will listen to the other and to what his life is trying to communicate and respond in such a way that blockages to the communication become minimal.

MPs in understanding, not only come to serve and shepherd each others being, they come also to serve and shepherd their own beings. For the being of an MP is his unique life possibility. It is a calling of his nature, an ontological summons, as it were, to accept, appropriate, and assemble that which exists originatively for him. To honor being is to honor also his own being; to guard its course is to guard its development within himself.

Understanding, then, is a gateway to living maritally in the truth. When opened up in a marriage, it brings about a reality wherein each MP comes to regard himself and the other as one there to let being be. The awareness is a primordial, ontological awareness, and in its setting there is a possibility for love that can come about in no other way.

Take, for example, the need of MPs to be alone in the private dimensions of their existing. Here they resist interacting with each other. The urge is to be separate in their own world.

If an authentic development is to take place within a marriage, this condition must be accepted, for in such a development, MPs come to be in their own way and this requires, among other things, the freedom for the discovery and exploration of the self that is associated with a sphere of separateness. If this freedom is not experienced, then grave disasters can occur in the marriage. Here they would stem from an inauthentic fear of separateness. When this happens MPs view the own world of the other as threatening and as something that must be overcome. To the extent to which it is an own world, it is something that resists undue control or influence. It is the seat of that centrifugal movement which pulls one MP away from another. It is the seat of a possible rejection, of a potential upsetting of a homeostatic marital balance, of an anxiety-arousing strangeness. As such, separateness must be destroyed. Thus we observe, in such inauthentic marriages, the frantic effort to reduce distance by attempts to devour the other, to make him over, to incorporate him. Often this effort is associated with the dominant person in the marriage who insists that the other subordinate his will in a master-slave relationship. The dominant one, however, is often himself dominated by the seemingly passive one who utilizes his passivity as a method of control. In either case, separateness, as an authentic dimension for the personalized extension of being, is abrogated. The result is hate, suspicion, and alienation.

When understanding takes hold in a marriage, however, these difficulties are avoided. As servants and shepherds of being, MPs are constrained to relax their grip on the existence of the other and make room for the individual being that struggles to become in a context of distance. The resistance of the other to a communal approach is now viewed not from a perspective of anxiety which would seek an overwhelming of that resistance, but from a perspective of respect which acknowledges the right and the need of the other to be distant in his own world. Through such respectful acceptance of the ultimate inaccessibility of each other's wills, MPs provide, one for the other, a private sanctuary in which the secret of what is ownmost in them can be safeguarded. Here in these sanctuaries they can get the "feel" of their own uniqueness; they can find that breathing space in which a true exploration of their being becomes possible.

Or take the opposite of the need for distance: the *need for relation*. Here MPs reach out directly for each other. Each senses that his self cannot fulfill itself without the other. Standing out in the world in a process of becoming, his self needs the other to confirm the worth of itself. It needs the other in order to be heard, in order to discover the significance and value of its creative products. As Buber says:

> The human person needs confirmation, because man as man needs it. An animal does not need to be confirmed, for it is what it is, unquestionably. It is different with man: sent forth from the natural domain of species into the hazard of the solitary category, surrounded by the air of a chaos which came into being with him, secretly and bashfully he watches for a Yes which allows him to be and which can come to him only from one human person to another. It is from one man to another that the heavenly bread of self-being is passed (16).

When the bread is so passed in a marriage, the self of each MP finds its rest in the other. When it is not so passed, it is quite otherwise. The other becomes a dangerous other who, by his rejectiveness hinders the self's unfoldment, makes it suspicious, over-needful of defending itself, and prone to retaliatory measures. The self becomes diverted from its task of realizing itself in the midst of its originative possibilities and becomes involved, instead, in the self-saving stratagems of defensive armoring. The self, like the flower blighted by some outward force hostile to its growth, ceases to unfold in the truth of its being and curls up within itself under the protective blanket of the now closed petals. The real task of MPs becomes not one of self-realization, but one of defense and revenge.

Such a web of destructive interactions can once again be forestalled when understanding takes hold in a marriage. For understanding is the mood wherein the other is actually seen as one secretly and bashfully watching for a *yes* which allows him to be; it is also the mood wherein acts constitutive of such a *yes* take place.

One such act is a surrender of power over the other, or the need to establish a position of dominance out of the other's weakness. The point of the interpersonal relation now is to help the other to his own sense of mastery.

Another act is a surrender of the condemnative attitude, or the tendency to see the other only in the light of his failures. The point of the interpersonal relation now is to relate to the other on the basis of his strengths.

Still another act is the surrender of the perfectionist attitude, or the need to see the other as the sole cause of marital difficulties. The point of the interpersonal relation now is an affirmation of being that is both positive and *self-critical*.

In such ways the mood of understanding helps to resolve the crises inherent in the marital contexts of distance and relation and thus makes an authentic development within the marriage possible. When these crises are so resolved, MPs can proceed in the marriage on the basis of a forward rather than a backward look: *for they are secure.*

THE POSITIVE EMOTIVE-CONSEQUENTIAL DIMENSION OF THE MARITAL OPTIMUM

In the preceding pages, the optimal marital setting has been conceptualized as one in which MPs, in the context of understanding, come progressively to experience themselves and each other on the basis of the truth of being to the end of an authentically evolving existence. The analysis of the authentic marriage will now move a step further to a consideration of the positive mood accompanying such a development.

The development is basically individuative. In it, MPs stand out on the basis of a continuous enrichment and expansion of their originative possibilities, a movement processually forward toward a telos of self-fulfillment. Each comes to selfhood and as he does, there comes to be, as an accompaniment of the process, a sense of assuredness and well-being. A positive mood keeps pace with the individuative advance. It envelops the advance as an emotive phenomenon generated by the advance itself. It is a mood consequential to becoming and can best be described as *joy.*

HOMECOMING

Joyous marital relationships are constituted by what Heidegger calls *homecoming,* a term derived from the Holderlin poem of the same name. The poem's central figure, a wanderer, arrives at the soil of his homeland and meets again the country people of the district. As he does so, joy wells up in him *because he has returned to the source.* "The original essence of joy," says Heidegger, "is the process of becoming at home in proximity to the source" (17). By *source,* he means the actuality of being and by *joy,* the *feeling of self-fulfillment in the presence of being.*

Tillich says much the same thing: "Joy is nothing else than the awareness of our being fulfilled in our true being, in our personal center" (18).

Marital joy is a collective instance of this process. In drawing close or coming home to being, MPs experience that full flush of being which is self-realization and as an emotive consequence, the joyous sense, both in them and all about them in their varied interactions. The joyous feeling itself is related to various factors intrinsic to this fulfilling, homecoming process.

There is the *truth* factor. Having no need, as would be the case in the inauthentic marital context, to lose themselves in a maze of facadic, defensive maneuvers, MPs in their homecoming, are open to themselves, to one another and to all that would be disclosed to them. They are free to be themselves, and because they are, joy comes to them, for "it is reality that gives joy . . . Joy is born out of union with reality itself" (19).

There is, too, the *psychic safety* factor. Here we note the primal and pervasive sense that grips the members of an authentic, homecoming marriage to the effect that no harm will come to them if they emerge from behind facadic walls into the light of truthful interactions. It is the sense, not of an abstract freedom to be and become what theoretically could be, if a certain benign combination of factors were to take place, but an existential freedom, a literal being free. It is the safety sense that is the psychic underlay of this literality, for existential freedom is a product of security. It presupposes that "being for one" of things which removes the fearful bars of the human prison house. As the bars fall away and as MPs feel safe to move about in the world, to experience it widely and richly, to lay bare the deepest sensitivities of their being, as they *feel safe to be free,* this too brings joy to them and to their life together. They can exult, for the ridicule of being, the contempt for it, the fear of it and the scorn mocking its expression—these inauthentic attitudes which shatter safety have passed away. *It is alright to be real.*

There is also the *control* factor. In the collective process of homecoming, MPs *take charge of their own existences.* Encouraged by the many supports to a personalized becoming, each comes to that trust in his own being, that assuredness in the midst of his possibilities, that freedom to be himself which constitutes him the controlling agent of his life. In the authentic marriage, there is no other who seeks to bend life utterly to his will, to subjugate it by threats and conditional demands, to coerce it into being something other than what it is. The other, as the servant and shepherd of being, seeks not to bind, but to free and is the active supporter of life that would find itself in its own way. MPs, accordingly, come to live their lives; they are not lived by others, and therein, too, is their joy. "The first effect of happiness," says Nietzsche, "is the feeling of power . . ." (20). The continued effect, which is joy, is "the feeling of increased power" (21).

Such a joyous power sense, or the exultant feeling of mastery over the energies that are one's life, is most highly refined in the authentic marriage at the point of a *willed power loss*. Here, MPs, especially in acts of being-surrender in the interpersonal relationship, rejoice that they are strong enough to be weak, that their control is so great that they are free to limit it in the interest of the other's good. While remaining in control at all times and while able whenever necessary to will back the surrendered mastery, such willing is not normative. Life is characteristically lost that life may be found. Since the loss is freely willed and not forced by fear, it is the *summum bonum* of power. The accompanying joy is long-lasting, for the power related to it is benevolently used. It elicits nothing from the other that would menace the being-surrender context. It elicits no hate, jealousy, envy or other being-threatening moods. *It elicits nothing but the other's joy.* Joy surrounds the marriage in perpetuity. Constantly renewed, it remains in all the relationships of the authentic marriage as its emotive blessing.

Homecoming, then, is the source of marital joy, that positive emotive accompaniment to the self-fulfilling process. It is the source, because it brings existentially into being those realities which, in effect, comprise joy: truth, safety, and control. When these three exist in the psychic orientation of MPs, then the marriage, emotively speaking, becomes at its best.

REFERENCES

1. Sutherland, Richard L.: Therapeutic goals and ideals of health. *J Religion and Health, 3:*119, January, 1964.
2. Terman, Lewis M.: *Psychological Factors in Marital Happiness.* New York, McGraw-Hill and Company, 1938.
3. Burgess, Ernest W., and Cottrell, Leonard S.: *Predicting Success or Failure in Marriage,* New York, Prenitce-Hall, 1939.
4. Kolb, William L.: Sociologically established family norms and democratic values. *Social Forces,* 26:454, May, 1948.

5. Heidegger, Martin: *Being and Time*. Translated by John Macquarrie and Edward Robinson, New York, Harper and Row, 1962, p. 167.
6. Heidegger, Martin: *Being and Time*. Translated by John Macquarrie and Edward Robinson, New York, Harper and Row, 1962, pp. 211-214.
7. Heidegger, Martin: *Being and Time*. Translated by John Macquarrie and Edward Robinson, New York, Harper and Row, 1962, pp. 214-217.
8. Heidegger, Martin: *Being and Time*. Translated by John Macquarrie and Edward Robinson, New York, Harper and Row, 1962, p. 167.
9. Heidegger, Martin: *Being and Time*. Translated by John Macquarrie and Edward Robinson, New York, Harper and Row, 1962, p. 261.
10. Rogers, Carl R.: *On Becoming a Person*. Boston, Houghton Mifflin Company, 1961, p. 315.
11. Heidegger, Martin: *Being and Time*. Translated by John Macquarrie and Edward Robinson, New York, Harper and Row, 1962, p. 205.
12. Heidegger, Martin: *Being and Time*. Translated by John Macquarrie and Edward Robinson, New York, Harper and Row, 1962.
13. Heidegger, Martin: Holderlin and the essence of poetry, tr. by Douglas Scott, in *Existence and Being*, Chicago, Henry Regnery Company, 1949, p. 282.
14. Heidegger, Martin: *Being and Time*. Translated by John Macquarrie and Edward Robinson, New York, Harper and Row, 1962, p. 171.
15. Heidegger, Martin: *Uber den Humanismus*. Frankfort, V. Klostermann, 1947, p, 29.
16. Buber, Martin: Distance and relation. Translated by Ronald Gregor Smith, *Psychiatry, 20*:104, May, 1957.
17. Heidegger, Martin: Remembrance of the poet. Translated by Douglas Scott in *Existence and Being*, Chicago, Henry Regnery Company, 1949, pp. 260-261. sr
18. Tillich, Paul: *The New Being*. New York, Charles Scribner's Sons, 1955, p. 146.
19. Tillich, Paul: *The New Being*. New York, Charles Scribner's Sons, 1955, p. 146.
20. Nietzsche, Friedrich: *The Dawn of Day*. Translated by J.M. Kennedy, Edinburgh, T.N. Foulis, 1911, p. 286.
21. Nietzsche, Fredrich: *The Will to Power* Vol. 2. Translated by Anthony M. Ludovici, Edinburgh, T.N. Foulis, 1910, p. 168.

Chapter 12

MARRIAGE COUNSELING IN THE STUDENT HEALTH SERVICE

WILLIAM F. EASTMAN AND CLIFFORD B. REIFLER

In our nation today, nearly seven million students are enrolled in colleges and universities. One out of every twenty-three undergraduates and over half of all graduate students are married (1).

Prior to World War II it was a rarity to see a married student on campus. With the influx of returning veterans, the number of married students climbed rapidly. While in recent years the proportion of married students has declined to 20 per cent of all undergraduate and graduate students (2), every indication points toward the continuing presence of married students in significant numbers on our college and university campuses.

The wishes, drives, and justifications that make student marriage attractive are common to our nature and culture. There are educational, psychological, sociological, and financial factors encouraging students to marry while pursuing their degree.

The increasing graduate school enrollment reflects concensus among society, university, and students that extended education is not only valuable but increasingly necessary for one's immediate and future vocational pursuits.

The young adult, as Erikson has pointed out, has normal drives toward intimacy, productivity creativity, and generativity (3). While some persons need extended time to accomplish their earlier psychosexual tasks, the majority of young adults are prepared to move into marriage during the years normally devoted to graduate study. The median age at first marriage, for example, is currently twenty-three years for men and 20.1 for women (4), well within the college years.

The changing relationship between the individual and society also encourages marriage during student days. Keniston has written regarding the key role of the family today:

> Most unalienated young people want large families; they marry early and are prepared to work hard to make their marriages a success; they usually value family life far more than meaningful work. Families play a special role in American life today—and among the reasons for an increasing emphasis on them is that they provide a place where a man can be himself and enjoy himself in the present. A wife and children can be enjoyed in the here and now, and are dependent neither on traditional wisdom nor on future success. Furthermore, children constitute a

link with the future that, unlike vocational commitments, will endure regardless of how society changes. Naturally, parents are affected, and radically affected, by social change and how they reared their young; but the mere facts of children and family constitute a point of present stability and a link with history in a changing and apparently unmanageable world (5).

Contrary to expectation, financial capability also often encourages students to marry prior to graduation. While finances present less problem to married undergraduate and graduate students than is generally believed, worry about finances is a major problem for married students (6). For a number of years, according to both objective and subjective standards, married students have had reasonably satisfactory incomes, particularly in the absence of children (7). Aller, in a study of one western campus, reported that one-half of the married students indicated they had no financial problem (8). Among the married undergraduates, only the younger couples received significant financial aid from parents (9). Part-time students with family are the largest single category of graduate students. Seventy-six per cent of these families have incomes of 6000 dollars or more and one-fourth have incomes of 10,000 dollars and over (10).

College and university administrators forecast the continuing presence of substantial numbers of married students. The United States Office of Education reports that between 1965 and 1970 the number of institutions of higher education planning to provide residential accommodations for married students will be increased 20 per cent (11). In this five-year period the anticipated increase in married residential facilities will be 48 per cent with the private institutions projecting a greater increase than the public campuses in these living accommodations (12). Thus, available evidence confirms that on our college and university campuses marriage is here to stay.

THE RESPONSIBILITY OF THE STUDENT HEALTH SERVICE FOR THE MARRIED STUDENT

The university, through its student health service, carries responsibility for the health of all students—married as well as single. The concept of student health is broadly defined and is expressed in a program extensive in scope, which encompasses medical care, preventive medicine and psychiatry, health education, mental health care, and supervision of the environment (13). Clearly, the American College Health Association conceives of the marital relationship as a health entity.

Married students . . . may be under particular stress, although it is the usual experience that students who marry tend to be mature and that their marriages are psychologically supportive. Nevertheless, colleges should offer voluntary courses in premarital education, their physicians should be available for, and adept in, premarital and marital counseling and the health service should have contact with community resources of help to married students; for example, family counseling agencies, prenatal classes, well-baby clinics, and household help services (14).

The university's commitment to the present and future health of its students was articulated by the President's Commission on Higher Education in 1947 which listed among its eleven objectives of education these pertaining to individual and marital health:

1. To attain a satisfying emotional and social adjustment.
2. To acquire the knowledge and attitudes basic to a satisfying family life (15).

The college health service is an integral component of the institution and its academic purposes and is thus dedicated to the promotion of growth and change in the single and married students so that they may become more mature, effective adults able to utilize their knowledge productively and satisfyingly in their professional, social, and personal lives (16).

Survey and anecdotal information reveal that important medical and dental needs of student families are being neglected. A study in 1965-66 of medical care at Standard University probably reflects the general extent of medical and dental care in student families. On the Stanford campus, 26 per cent of the 10,600 registered students were married. Nonstudent spouses and children comprised 63 per cent of the members of student families, and the married students with their spouses and children comprised a population nearly equaling the number of single students. Stanford at that time did not include students' dependents under Health Service coverage. During the survey period, a high proportion of all family members saw a physician, with the rates of usage being as high or higher for wives and children than for husbands. Wives and children were more likely to be hospitalized, whether or not they were covered by insurance. A majority of the young children were not receiving regular dental care at a time when preventive dental care and education are of great importance. Nearly one-fifth of all families reported that their children were not receiving regular well-baby and child care. The relatively high proportion of inadequately immunized children appeared inconsistent with the general level of sophistication of this educated population. One-third of all families had no health insurance aside from the student's personal Health Service coverage and nearly 40 per cent of all wives and children had no hospitalization insurance. The lower income families spent as much for medical care annually as other families but had the poorest health and hospital insurance coverage. The principal barriers to optimum medical-dental care for student families were the relative lack of money and relative lack of information, with inability and/or unwillingness to pay for care being the more significant reason (17).

It seems appropriate that a major expression of the university's commitment to growth, change, and health be the delivery of at least a minimum of health services to nonstudent spouses, including the provision of a marriage counseling service. Optimally, health coverage would be extended to all dependents. Illness in the wife, whether pimarily physical or emotional, can be as devastating to the student husband's state of health, creativity, and productivity as illness in himself. Furthermore, the increasing costs of medical care often quickly deplete student financial resources or sometimes cause postponement of needed medical attention. If the working wife is stricken, the loss of work combined with the cost of medical treatment may be financially disastrous. A prepaid health fee covering both the student and nonstudent spouse would enable the college health service to treat the married student through his family unit. Furthermore, it is becoming increasingly important that students be covered by major medical and hospitalization insurance which would provide for service beyond the range and duration reasonably offered by the Student Health Service. Included in such benefits would be provision for private psychiatric treatment and private marriage and family counseling.

MARRIAGE COUNSELING SERVICE AT THE UNIVERSITY OF NORTH CAROLINA

The University of North Carolina at Chapel Hill offers marriage counseling in the psychiatric section of the Student Health Service. This large coeducational liberal arts institution, which enrolled its first student in 1795, is the oldest state-supported university in the country. The population of the town, including university students, approximated 30,000 in 1965. In 1967-68 the total student population averaged 15,355 of whom two-thirds were undergraduates. Among undergraduates, male students outnumbered females 3:1, while the ratio in the Graduate School was 1.7:1.

The Director of the Student Health Service has the responsibility for student health at the University. He has a staff of one part-time and eight full-time physicians and a well-equipped sixty-five-bed infirmary which is attached to a wing of North Carolina Memorial Hospital, the primary teaching hospital for the University of North Carolina School of Medicine.

The psychiatric section of the Student Health Service is staffed by members of the faculty in the Department of Psychiatry who devote the major portion of their clinical time to the area of student health. These staff members include two psychiatrists, a psychologist, and a marriage counselor. The position of marriage counselor was created in 1966 and, as far as is known, is the only such position in a college health service in the United States. In addition to these staff members, second and third-year psychiatric residents spend varying amounts of time in the Student Health Service as a required part of their training part of their training and are supervised by the staff psychiatrists. All professional services of the Student Health Service, including psychiatric consultations and marriage counseling, are provided without additional charge as part of the student's health fee.

Except for a service which provides solely vocational and educational testing and counseling, the Student Health psychiatric section represents the only formal psychological counseling service on campus designed primarily for students. The Student Health Service does not extend its services to non-enrolled persons except for marriage counseling when the nonenrolled spouse is seen.

Psychiatric treatment and marriage counseling in the Student Health Service are primarily characterized by a "conservation" approach directed toward treatment for the acute problem within a diagnostic framework, crisis intervention, and maintenance of a functional adaptive capacity. Consequently, students are usually seen for relatively few visits, and the psychiatric staff and marriage counselor generally limit themselves to evaluation, immediate therapeutic intervention, and referral when necessary. In practice this has been more true of psychiatric consultation than of marriage counseling. If a longer-term out-patient contact is indicated, the student is referred to either the staff or private clinics of the Department of Psychiatry in the North Carolina Memorial Hospital. If hospitalization, other than a brief stay in the University Infirmary is indicated, the in-patient service of the North Carolina Memorial Hospital is available, as are several other nearby state and private hospitals (18).

Student Clients

During the two years that the Student Health Service has specifically offered premarital and marital counseling, 190 clients have utilized the service, including 133 married and 57 single persons. In 83 per cent of all marriages represented, both partners were seen, and in one-third of the instances where only one partner was seen, the other was geographically unavailable. The undergraduates, of whom over one-half were single, composed the largest group of clients (Table I). The majority of nonstudents

TABLE I
ACADEMIC STATUS OF MARRIED AND SINGLE CLIENTS

Academic Status	Married Clients		Single Clients	
	Number	Percentage	Number	Percentage
Undergraduate	29	22	43	75
Graduate	48	36	12	21
Non-student	56	42	2	4
Total	133	100%	57	100%

were the wives of graduate students. During the second year the number of clients increased 60 per cent with the largest increase in requests for service coming from the graduate married men and their nonstudent wives.

The average number of interviews for married students was 6.6 with 80 per cent of the clients having less than ten interviews. The youngest married man was 18, the oldest 37, with 26 the median age. Sixty per cent of the married men were graduate students. The youngest married woman was eighteen, the oldest thirty-five, with twenty-three the median age. Sixty per cent of the married women were nonstudents. The median length of marriage at the time the clients were seen was three years. Couples were seen who had been married for as brief a time as one month and as long as fifteen years. Three-fifths of the married couples had no children, which underscores the excellence of the opportunity for improving family health prior to the arrival of children. Among the couples with children or where the wife was pregnant for the first time, over one-third represented forced marriages.

One-half of the couples were self-referred, i.e. they were desirous of consultation and either knew how to contact the marriage counselor or took initiative to learn the referral procedure (Table II). The referral sources remained similar during the two years with the most noteworthy increase coming from University administrators.

TABLE II

REFERRAL SOURCES OF MARRIED AND SINGLE CLIENTS

Referral Source	*Married Clients Percentage*	*Single Clients Percentage*
Self	51	38
Psychiatrist	14	7
Clergyman	11	7
Non-psychiatric physician	8	21
Faculty and residential counselors	7	9
University administrator	4	7
Other professional	4	2
Relative or friend	1	9
Total	100%	100%

The presenting problems most frequently mentioned by the married clients have been extramarital affairs, sexual incompatibility and the wish to separate or divorce (Table III). Those whose chief complaint was the wish to separate or divorce generally were not involved in extramarital affairs. In contrast, one-half of those with the presenting problem of an extramarital affair also were contemplating separation or divorce. In two-thirds of the instances it was the wives who were having the affairs, were frigid and/or wanted to end the marriage. Ten couples were separated at the time

Marital Therapy

TABLE III
PRESENTING PROBLEMS OF MARRIED CLIENTS

Presenting Problem	Number	Percentage
Extramarital affair	18	25
Sexual incompatibility	14	19
General marital incompatibility	12	16
Wish to separate or divorce	11	15
Husband's violence	6	8
Other*	12	17
Total	73	100%

*Includes psychosomatic conditions, depression, anxiety, relationship to parents, referral of spouse to psychiatrist.

of their first appointment and twelve additional couples separated during counseling. These 22 couples represented nearly one-third of all family units that requested counseling. The fact that these couples would request help when their relationships were fractured to this extent, in most instances, indicated concern and responsibility for constructive and supportive dissolution of the marriage as well as for understanding themselves and their partner. At least five couples reunited during or subsequent to counseling.

The total percentage of student families with major problems involving extramarital affairs, sexual incompatibility, and the wish to separate or divorce is not significantly higher than reported in a recent study of clients writing for marriage counseling help (19). Among the University of North Carolina student-clients, the predominance of women, rather than men, with these presenting problems is the noteworthy feature.

Eight married clients were referred for psychotherapy in addition to five other married clients who postponed or otherwise resisted referral to therapy.

The premarital clients represented 30 per cent of all clients. Three-fourths of the premarital clients were undergraduates, nearly one-half of them men. As would be anticipated among the unmarried clients, junior and senior women were seen in greatest numbers. Nearly one-half of all unmarried clients were seen as couples.

One-half of all premarital clients had only one interview and nearly one-fifth had five or more interviews. In addition there were collateral interviews with the parents of eight different students which presented opportunities for brief family therapy.

The principal referral sources for the single clients have been self-referrals and referrals from nonpsychiatric physicians who in most instances were physicians in the Student Health Service (Table II). In comparison with the married couples, the premarital clients had fewer self-referrals and were more dependent on referral by Student Health Service staff.

The premarital presenting problems most frequently mentioned were deteriorating relationship and indecision regarding marriage to one's fiancee (Table IV). Among the nine individuals whose stated problem was a pregnancy, four were men. Four of the single clients were referred for psychotherapy, which was similar to the proportion of married clients needing individual treatment.

TABLE IV

PRESENTING PROBLEMS OF SINGLE CLIENTS

Presenting Problem	Number	Percentage
Deteriorating relationship	13	23
Marital indecision	12	21
General information	10	17
Pregnancy	9	16
Relationship to parents	5	9
Dating anxiety	2	4
Other	6	10
Total	57	100%

CONCLUDING THOUGHTS

The availability of premarital and marriage counseling in the Student Health Service of the University of North Carolina at Chapel Hill over the past two years generally has served a need not otherwise met on this campus. The clients seen for premarital and marriage counseling have not slowed the increasing proportion of students requesting psychiatric consultations in the Student Health Service, indicating that the marriage counselor represents an additional service to students.

Several factors indicate that the premarital and marital counseling service is utilized by students who, in most instances, would not otherwise contact the psychiatric section of the Student Health Service. Only a few of the clients seen in counseling have required a psychiatric consultation or referral for psychotherapy or had previously contacted a psychiatrist. Also, the nature of their problem, focused as it was on a relationship, usually would not necessitate psychiatric consultation unless personal discomfort was severe enough to interfere markedly with academic functioning. In addition, the many nonstudent spouses and fiancees normally would not be eligible for psychiatric consultation in the Student Health Service.

Without the presence of premarital and marital counseling in the Student Health Service, most of these students seen during the past two years presumably would not have sought help anywhere. For their concerns, obtaining professional help is relatively difficult and/or expensive. Durham, nine miles distance, has a small private family service agency whose three staff members occasionally work with out-of-town students. In the near-future Chapel Hill's planned family service agency may provide service to some student families. Although the Chapel Hill-Durham area, has a high rate of psychiatrists per population, there are only a limited number of psychiatrists, psychologists, social workers, and other professionals offering private marriage counseling. Even when the professional services are available, the fees are prohibitively high for most students. The out-patient psychiatric clinic at the University of North Carolina has only recently been able to offer extended marriage counseling to a limited number of couples.

Colleges and universities currently offer needed and effective premarital and marital counseling services under various auspices. Our evaluation, based on a two-year experience, is that the logical administrative location for such counseling is within the Student Health Service. Our assessment confirms the recommendation of the American College Health Association that a successful college health program must be responsible to, or originate from, one department charged with implementing the program—the college health service (20). Colleges and universities are among the institutions well known for compartmentalization and the attendant communication problems. Therefore, any efforts to coordinate, integrate, and consolidate services and programs certainly can be encouraged.

The university health service has an opportunity not matched by any other component of the institution for recognizing students with significant premarital and marital relationship problems. No other department of the university sees as many students in privacy and protected by confidentiality. The university health service physicians, more than any other faculty or staff, exercise their professional knowledge and skills at the moment when students are primarily focused on their own needs, problems, and welfare. This represents an opportune moment for the process of change to begin since students, like other mortals, are more likely to shift their feelings, attitudes, and behavior when they are experiencing frustration and emotional pain. During the 1967-68 academic year, over two-thirds of the 15,000 member student body of the University of North Carolina at Chapel Hill requested a medical consultation at the Student Health Service and made 51,307 ambulatory visits. Such extensive student-physician contact presents an unequaled opportunity for the diagnosis of individual and campus needs in the areas of premarital and marital health.

The Student Health Service is charged with the responsibility of helping to maintain the highest possible level of physical and emotional health within the student body. As a staff member contributing to this objective, the marriage counselor, through his various clinical, teaching, research, and campus activities, can contribute to the understanding of premarital and marital relationships as health entities. Our experience indicates that the opportunity for preventive, nonclinical campus consultations is limited only by time and energy. During the past two years a significant segment of the marriage counselor's time has been spent in consultation with administrators, residential college advisors, and in group discussions with students in their residential settings. The requests to participate in preventive, educational programs in the residential settings have been numerous and varied. For example, a men's residential college invited a Student Health Service physician and the marriage counselor to discuss normal male-female sexuality. Three women's residential colleges organized panels focusing on the career versus family roles of women. Freshman women requested dialogue on the problems of college dating and relationships to parents. A men's residential college desired a discussion following a movie on premarital pregnancy. A sorority focused on the changing sexual behavior. College-age church groups planned programs on dating problems and interpersonal relationships. A fraternity requested a discussion of sexuality with its pledge class. Women's residential colleges sought programs on dating, sex, and contraception and invited the men from that residential college into the discussion. The in-service training program for women housemothers, hostesses, and graduate counselors discussed movies and issues related to dating relationships.

These efforts have met only a small portion of the students' needs for accurate information and group discussion. Such discussions are a vital process through which they can become more aware of the needs, expectations, and attitude of themselves and others and thus more appropriately claim their own sexuality and work out their own acceptable values. As a part of this effort, in response to a combined request from students and faculty, the marriage counselor also offered a course, "Anticipating Marriage," in the noncredit, student organized Experimental College.

The University Health Service also has the responsibility and opportunity to research the problems of college marriages and study the preventive aspects of these young marriages. Research possibilities in these areas are limited by the current complexities and relatively undeveloped status of research on successful-unsuccessful marriages. It is difficult to do research on prevention when one is not clear what he is striving to prevent or attain.

Another obstacle to research on college marriage is the difficulty some administrators may have in becoming committed to such an investment and in implementing the findings. It is also true that mental health professionals have created opposition to their own research interests in their tendency toward psychologizing and in overemphasizing the uncovering and labeling of illnesses. A more useful approach may be to attach less emphasis to diagnosis, or the labeling of limitations, and concentrate and conceptualize on increasing the strengths of the individuals and their marital relationships. Certainly the opportunities for field studies on new marriages are readily available in the college and university setting. The findings obviously could be reflected in the increased well-being of those young families as well as contributing, in general, to our understanding of the needs and problems within the process of a beginning marital realtionship.

The variety of premarital and marital clinical research and preventive-educational needs might best be met by a faculty position of marriage counselor and family life coordinator. In such a capacity, this professional person could meet the more acute clinical needs while reserving sufficient time to plan and coordinate the myriad of possible formal and informal programs and activities on campus in the area of family life education.

With the variety of responsibilities carried by faculty members, the marriage counselor and family life coordinator well may be the most aware, knowledgeable, and committed person on campus regarding the needs of single and married students in family life education. If not otherwise offered on our campus, who else is willing, and able to do the following:

1. Offer courses and seminars on human sexuality and preparation for marriage.

2. Offer a counseling practicum to other strategic persons doing the majority of campus counseling—faculty, housemothers, deans, residential hall counselors and chaplains.

3. Lead discussions on the wide variety of topics requested by residential groups.

4. Coordinate the procurement of the films, books, and pamphlets that could make an educational-emotional-attitudinal difference for the students.

5. Promote discussions of the mental health aspects present and future residential life on campus.

6. Assist in discovering and coordinating the specific programs, services, and discussion needs of married students and help them move toward articulating a more effective choice on their own behalf within student government and university policy arenas.

In terms of both short and long-range benefits, such a position of marriage counselor and family life coordinator offers the possibility of a unique educational input by the university health service. At present, it is doubtful if there is an area of greater importance for personal satisfaction and successful living that is accorded less attention than that given to this broadly defined area of preparation for family living.

Premarital and marriage counseling and family life programming within the university health service are legitimate and necessary components of responsible health care. As premarital and marital disharmony are prevented or lessened, as premarital and marital health are increased, the growth and development of both the student and his spouse can be fostered. Personal satisfaction and academic productivity and creativity can be increased and our society thereby enhanced. The unfortunate and costly waste of human potential and loss of satisfaction incurred by prematurely terminated education can be avoided, and healthier attitudes and behaviors can be integrated and subsequently transmitted to our next generation.

REFERENCES

1. Adapted from U.S. Bureau of the Census, *Statistical Abstract of the United States: 1967,* 88th ed. Washington, D.C., 1967, p. 132.
2. Adapted from the U.S. Bureau of the Census, *Statistical Abstract of the United States: 1967,* 8th. ed. Washington, D.C., 1967, p. 132.
3. Erikson, E. H.: *Childhood and Society.* New York, Norton, 1963, pp. 263-268.
4. U.S. Bureau of Census, *U. S. Census of Population: 1960-Subject Reports, Age at First Marriage—Final Report PC(2)-4D.* Washington, D.C., U.S. Government Printing Office, 1966, pp. 38-39.
5. Keniston, K.: *The Uncommitted: Alienated Youth in American Society.* New York, Dell, 1965, p. 227.
6. Lantagne, J. E.: Do married men succeed in college? College marriage inventory, *J Sch Health, 29:*81-91, 1959.
7. Nygreen, G. T.: Marital adjustment in the University of Washington married student community. *Dissertation Abstracts, 14:*1273-1274, 1954.
8. Aller, F. D.: Some factors in marital adjustment and academic achievement of married students. *Personnel and Guidance J., 41:*609-616, 1963.
9 Oppelt, N. K.: Characteristics and activities of married college students. *J Coll Stud Personnel, 6:*228-231, 1965.
10. U.S. Department of Health, Education, and Welfare: *The Academic and Financial Status of Graduate Students,* Spring 1965, Washington, D.C., 1967, p. 21.
11. U.S. Department of Health, Education, and Welfare: College and university enrollment and physical facilities survey, 1965-70, *College and University Physical Facilities Series,* Washington, D.C., 1967, p. 3.
12. U.S. Department of Health Education, and Welfare: College and university enrollment and physical facilities survey, 1965-70, *College and University Physical Facilities Series,* Washington, D.C., 1967, p. 6.
13. American College Health Association: *Recommended Standards and Practices for a College Health Program.* Coral Gables, Florida, American College Health Association, 1964, p. 7.
14. American College Health Association. *Recommended Standards and Practices for a College Health Program.* Coral Gables, Florida, American College Health Association, 1964, p. 28.
15. The President's Commission on Higher Education: *Higher Education for American Democracy.* Vol. 1, Washington, D.C., U.S. Government Printing Office, 1947, pp. 50-54.
16. American College Health Association: *Recommended Standards and Practices for*

a College Health Program. Coral Gables, Florida, American College Health Association, 1964, p. 7.

17. Osborne, M. M., Jr., and Dirksen, L. J.: Utilization and problems of medical care in student families. *Amer J Public Health, 59*:65-76, 1969.
18. Reifler, C. B., Liptzin, M. B., and Fox, J. T.: College psychiatry as public health psychiatry, *Amer J Psychiat, 124*:662-671, 1967.
19. DeBurger, J. E.: Marital problems, help-seeking, and emotional orientation as revealed in help-request letters. *Marriage and Family, 29*:712-721, 1967.
20. American College Health Association: *Recommended Standards and Practices for a College Health Program.* Coral Gables, Florida, 1964, p. 11.

Chapter 13

THE WOMAN IN THE FAMILY

EMANUEL K. SCHWARTZ AND RUTH LEDER

No subject in the history of man has been more controversial than that of woman, and the controversy continues to the present. It is a relentless struggle on the part of men and women to understand themselves and the nature of their relationship. Possibly the problem arises from the basic nature of the female role, as the bearer of life and because of the newborn being totally dependent upon her for nurturance. Possibly it is this factor more than all others that complicates, for men and for women, an understanding of each other. Will Durant suggested that men are, by nature, slaves to women and women are, by nature, slaves to children and the race. For him, marriage is not a relationship between a man and a woman, but a relationship between parents and their children (3). In this connection, it is amusing to note that the word matrimony means etymologically—a unity of mothers, *matri monium*, one mother, a union for mothering. In this presentation we wish to discuss the woman, then, the woman in the context of marriage and the family.

Aristotle and later Freud saw woman as a fault of nature, an error in the making of man, and therefore naturally subordinate to him, like slaves and animals. In earliest Biblical times, the bridegroom purchased his bride-to-be. On the other hand, the Mary cult in Christianity makes of woman the best, the most beautiful, the most powerful. What could be more important than to be the "Mother of God?" For Huxley, woman's virtue was man's most poetic fiction (9). Similarly, Santayana saw beauty in the idea that "there is no God and Mary is His Mother." Among other things, it is this projected esthetic quality which often obscures our efforts to understand the woman and to deal with the difficulties for which we "blame" her.

Edward Albee, the eminent American playwright, describes woman, the mother in the family as, "The Delicate Balance" in a play by that name. She is depicted as the hub which gives organization and structure to the family unit. At the same time she must be the recipient of the aggression of all the members of the family. Albee intuited here one of the primary functions of the woman as wife and mother. It is by her being the recipient of their aggressions and helping them work through these feelings within the context of the family that they can survive in the larger community

147

outside. The fact that we, the writers, think this is desirable certainly reflects our own "cultural orthodoxy" (14).

Western culture supports the view that women are inferior and that they exist to serve men. Human society is supposed always to have been basically patriarchal, that this was the social condition at the beginnings of mankind. However, that theory, according to Briffault, is "as erroneous as the geocentric medieval theory of the universe. . . . Human society . . . was originally formed around the mother and not around the father" (2). Briffault's hope for humanity is expressed in the statement, "The practical lesson which the true history of the relations between the sexes does seem to point is that mutual cooperation between them and social equality are more conducive to the smooth working of social organization than any form of sex antagonism" (2).

The question arises, then, What is the essence underlying these points of view which represent only an infinitesimal sample of the conflict of opinion concerning the woman and her role in the family! It is our position, based on psychoanalytic theory and practice, that the reactions to the woman on the part of the man as well as of the children, and her reactions to them are characterized by ambivalence. The prevailing state of interrelations within the family is ambivalent. Ambivalence is defined as an emotional condition in which contradictory feelings, positive and negative, the entire spectrum, are present and are directed toward the same object. If the relations between the woman and all others around her are embedded in ambivalence, at best only an atmosphere of antagonistic cooperation can be accomplished. At any moment only one extreme or another is felt, and double-bind signals are being expressed. Strife is the usual, the ordinary; conflict and tension are basic to the interactions between woman, man, and child.

The reason for ambivalence is not so much the real conditions of living as the illusory expectations projected upon the other out of one's own historical development. "What drives us into matrimony is clearly neither more nor less than the expectation that we shall find in it the fulfillment of all the old desires arising out of the Oedipus situation in childhood—the desire to be a wife to the father, to have him as one's exclusive possession, and to bear him children" (8). This process is generally referred to as transference. Transference, by definition, is always ambivalent, always uncomfortable, always automatic, always unconscious and derived from personal experiences within one's own nuclear family, that is, the woman and the man relate symbolically in terms of expectations arising out of her or his own parental family. The mother projects upon the father and the child expectations which she had with her own mother, father, or siblings; the man does the same.

Moreover, the parents may see the child not only as their child, but behave toward him also as their symbolic infantile selves, or as their own mother, father, or sibling. Should the children revive images and functions of the nuclear parents, the mother or the father may react to them as if they were their nuclear parents. Horney points out that the infantile fears attached to the father or mother may then be transferred by the parents to the children leading to basic feelings of insecurity with their own children. She stresses that there is an inexhaustible variety of indirect conflicts which the mother may feel toward the children or toward the husband arising out of her experiences with her own mother, her own father, and her own family (8). This is true also of the father with regard to the mother and the children. As a consequence the disguised forms of expectation become one of the most complicating and subtle forces in the disruption of family life. Added to the real and unreal expectations each brings into the marriage, there may be a cultural ideal, for example, that marriage can be for life, forever, and must be happy. It is this attitude which led Margaret Mead to suggest, that "the American marriage ideal is one of the most conspicuous examples of our insistence on hitching our wagons to a star. It is one of the most difficult marriage forms that the human race has even attempted" (13).

Eric Berne's method of transactional analysis may be schematically helpful in clarifying the nature of these distortions (1). He thinks that every human being relates to every other in three fundamental ways: as parent, as child, and as adult. These three roles are present in all of us at all times and may be acted upon out of our own necessities (expectations) as well as out of the necessities and provocations (expectations) projected upon us by the other. For example, the woman may see herself as parent, child, or adult. She may wish to relate to the man as her parent, as her child, or as another adult. In vector analytic terms, she sees the man hierarchically as being superior, a parent, or inferior, a child; and horizontally as being a peer, another adult. This kind of perception by the woman is countered by the man's prototaxic or parataxic perception of her as parent or child, rather than syntaxically as adult (21). It is as distorting for either parent to demand the child be parent or adult, as it is inapppropriate for the child to see the parent as child or adult.

This form of analysis stimulated by Berne and Sullivan is intended to throw light upon the general proposition we are presenting here, that at the core of family strife are the irrational expectations of its membership. This is true of all the members of the family. Moreover, the child's dependence brings him into conflict with his parents with consequent ambivalent feeling about them, just as they have conflicting feelings about him. The relationship between mother and child, for instance, cannot remain static or be fully satisfying to either for long. Similarly, the relationship between the parents can never be completely fulfilling for any length of time. Because good marriages are so rare, Horney is convinced that arranged marriages have a greater probability of success because such partners tend consciously and unconsciously to expect less of each other (8). Whatever gratification they can get from or give to one another is considered gratefully as a lucky break, a happy accident, a serendipity.

Frustration of the irrational demands bilaterally projected is a necessary consequence of the nature of human transactions. It has been said that the only successful marriage is one in which the partners have interlocking neuroses. As the joke has it, a good marriage is one in which the bumps in his head fit into the holes in hers. There is some truth in this piece of folk wisdom. If their neuroses match there may be a better chance for the survival of the marriage than where continuous antagonism exists as a result of unspoken demands to fulfill unconscious expectations. In transactional terms, if the wife wants to play parent to the child in the husband and the husband wants to play child to the parent in the wife, this may lead to some bilateral gratification. Complications, however, enter when a real child appears and he triangulates the situation. Triangulation results in the kinds of difficulties and conflicts which have been identified with competition, the struggle for attention, for centrality, for fulfillment, the desire to possess, the wish not to be separated, the fear of rejection or abandonment; that is, the usual neurotic forms of behavior found especially in the triad (22).

Our thesis is that each partner brings into marriage the historical expectations derivative of the original, the nuclear family, and that in order to convert the new family to the familiar, each will repeat those transactions previously experienced. Even where mates are self-selected, the decision to get married may be a consequence not so much of love, the desire for fulfillment, or any other conscious reason. For example, Pincus reports, "Many of the very young couples who reach helping agencies seem to have married out of conflicts with their parents rather than from any real feeling for each other . . . Once they are married the deep anxieties concerning the parental figures still have to be reckoned with, and they often find themselves unable to enjoy their relationship any longer. Either may be resentful of the other's dependence, or anxious about his indifference, and both equally furious at being 'landed for good' with a wife or husband or baby" (15).

Pollock offers a way of classifying intrafamilial difficulties; namely, "the marital system, the parents-and-children system, and the sibling system. Each of these three subsystems is composed of a plurality of interaction patterns: between husband and wife, between parents and children, and among siblings" (7). But problems in each of these subsystems occur not so much because of real factors, survival necessities, but rather because of projected expectations buried in the fantasies of the individuals involved. These fantasies are only tangentially related to contemporary reality. They are largely historically determined reactions to it, projections upon it, distortions and expectations of it.

The situation is best described, in our opinion, by Laing, Phillipson, and Lee, as the spiral of reciprocal perspectives. "Human beings are constantly thinking about others and about what others are thinking about them, and what others think they are thinking about the others, and so on. One may be wondering about what is going on inside the other. One desires or fears that other people will know what is going on inside one's self."

"A man may feel that his wife does not understand him. What may this mean? It could mean that he thinks that she does not realize that he feels neglected. Or he may think that she does not realize that he loves her. Or it may be that he thinks that she thinks that he is mean, when he just wants to be careful; that he is cruel, when he just wants to be firm; that he is selfish when he just does not want to be used as a doormat."

"His wife may feel that he thinks that she thinks he is selfish when all she wants is to get him to be a little less reserved. She may think that he thinks that she thinks that he is cruel, because she feels he always takes everything she says as an accusation. She may think that he thinks he understands her, when she thinks he has not begun to see her as a real person, and so on."

"One sees both that this area is the very heart of many relationships, and that we have in fact very little systematic and scientifically tested information about it" (10).

These fantasies, these imaginings are largely defensive operations in light of the anxiety that is experienced in the interpersonal transactions within the family. Moreover, there is little possibility for a woman and a man to relate to one another without anxiety. Furthermore, it is even less likely for a woman and a man to become involved with one another without additional and new kinds of anxieties in the presence of a third person, especially if that third object is their child. Since anxiety is always present, marriage partners will utilize defenses, mental mechanisms necessary to deal with these anxieties in order to gain a sense of security within the social context of the family. One of the most common ways of dealing with anxiety is by utilizing the mechanism of defense which we call familiarization, that is, transference. What transference does is to project the past upon the present moment; that is, to expect that "I and the other" will behave in the current situation as "I and the other" behaved in the familiar situation in which "I" grew up. This is one way uncertainty in front of the unknown and the unfamiliar is dealt with in order to avoid chaos or the overwhelmingly debilitating force of anxiety. The greater the anxiety the greater the necessity to project illusion. To project familiar expectations upon the other or others is necessary in order to give structure to the situation and not to be immobilized by the anxiety.

In a fascinating methodological analysis, Laing, Phillipson, and Lee assume three levels of distortion that the woman and the man impose upon a common situation by reason of a different repertory of fantasies. The first is, "They do not *see* the situation in the same way." The authors give this illustration.

"Mrs. Jones feels that her husband is greedy, lacks consideration, and has a violent temper, and that he has probably slept with another woman on a particular night (that he stayed out without calling) . . . . Contrary to her husband's view, she feels that her husband does not take her seriously, does not respect or love her, does not think a lot of her, is not honest with her, and is not able to face her conflicts. Each of these attributions was seriously reinforced by the single incident of staying out late . . ."

"Mr. Jones is 'astonished' over most of this. He says that he is less touchy, more detached, etc. presumably . . . because the things that touch him have not been touched. In his family not to report one's whereabouts was perfectly acceptable. Everyone is assumed to do this at some time or another. If this were so he would view it as a form of nonsense that his wife would be concerned about his absence. In his mind there is no issue involved at all."

"At first he maintains he has no complaints about his wife." But when one explores him more carefully a second level of distortion is seen in operation. "Nothing that she *does* is wrong—except to *say* that what he does is wrong. . . . He is not complaining that she stays out nights, that she doesn't report where she is going, and so on. His complaint is that she is complaining about him."

The third level arises out of the fact that both of these persons "come from families with different value systems. He states that in his family treats and attention were carefully limited. . . . In Mrs. Jones' family, on the other hand, to withhold treats and attention was considered a mark of punishment" (10).

It is useful to understand the three levels of distortive operations when conflict and strife occur in a marriage. Such distortions are based upon transference, unreal expectations, the familiarization of the relationship. First is the way each perceives the situation and reacts to the facts, the objective condition. Second is, "Everything she does is fine," said Mr. Jones. He is not concerned about how she sees the situation. What is difficult for him is the fact that she is complaining. Mrs. Jones, however, says it is what he does that causes difficulty, nothing that he says. He does not complain;

he is perfectly willing to accept everything at face value. But what he does is unacceptable to her, the affective reaction. The third level is the difference in values originating from what was considered "good" or "bad" in their original families, the ethical attitude. Variations in socioeconomic status, in education, and in religious and ethnic background play a part in the disjunctive perceptions, the cognitive dissonances which occur to provoke tensions and conflict in the marriage. Idealization puts inordinate demands upon each other and frustration must ensue.

To summarize, ubiquitous storm and strife in marriage occur not so much as a consequence of the actualities which are always useful as triggering mechanisms but rather as the result of distortions projected upon the participating individuals and upon the present situation and stemming from the original, the nuclear family. These unconscious expectations, projections, fantasies, and transferences color the ways in which the partners in marriage perceive each other, motivate the things they do and predetermine the values to which they adhere, which then may be further complicated by the overall value systems within the community in which the new family seeks to exist (20).

There is little to be gained in blaming woman or man for these social phenomena, as does Shainess in her charge that men have denied, for self-serving purposes, the truth about women, and that everything man has ever done with regard to woman has been an attempt to demean her (19). On the other hand, it would be equally useless to assert that women are always "the power behind the throne," that man is merely the executor of the unconscious, unspoken, nonobvious directives of the woman, namely, the mother in his life. Both these points of view only foster the already existing climate of antagonism.

We recognize with Ashley Montague that in every society there are tensions, insecurities, and difficulties and that also in every marriage these will occur (4). It helps little to avoid coming to grips with the problem and fall to philosophizing with Kubie that the problem of marriage is not new but has been "veiled for centuries because of the many marriages which have been terminated by early death" (4). It has not been so veiled. The novels and plays of world literature, the vital statistics, and the social history of modern society highlight the problems of marriage, the difficulties between man and woman in every community. Even if Kubie is correct that women and men "are infinitely ingenious in their ability to find new ways of being unhappy together" (4), our task is to try to understand some of the reasons for their discontent and seek ways and means to prevent or ameliorate such a state of affairs, where possible.

The scope of this social and personal problem brings it to the forefront of our culture today. The mounting divorce rates and the increasing number of suicides are attracting the attention of behavioral scientists and social historians in this country and elsewhere. The epidemic of filicides is becoming the concern of the helping professions as well as of government, although we do not have to go so far as Raskovsky in assuming that the wish to kill the child lies at the root of most destructive social operations such as war (look at the word *infantry!*) (16). We wish to take a more limited perspective of this problem and restrict our analysis to the pervasive difficulties in woman-man relations in marriage.

From the point of view of the helping professions, the question is posed repeatedly: Of what value is it to reveal what Kubie calls "the mysteries, the unconscious forces" that lie behind this state of affairs? Mead strikes a similar note in her inquiry, "What good is insight in changing this situation?" Perhaps the problem of human happiness whether in marriage or otherwise will always remain unsolved. Perhaps the analytic slogan, "Knowledge is power, and self-knowledge is the road to freedom," may be of little ultimate use in the battle of the sexes. On the other hand, some evidence is appearing in scientific psychotherapy which leads us to be somewhat optimistic about the possibilities of applying our knowledge of unconscious processes, of the transference phenonemon, to negotiating marital conflicts.

In an exceedingly instructive work, Malan offers the results of his quantitative studies of the efficacy of various modalities and interventions in brief psychotherapy with persons having difficulties, including marital partners. He opts for direct concern with transference, the irrational expectations projected upon the current situation out of one's familiar past. Malan is convinced that this is the most efficient way to break through the impasses of the repetition compulsion experienced in intimate interpersonal transactions. He says, "The mere fact that important transference work seems on the whole to be associated with favorable outcome is enough to contradict the hypothesis that transference interpretations intensify dependence—or at least they intensify it to the point at which termination becomes impossible without relapse. The detailed evidence on the relationship between transference interpretations and dependence overwhelmingly confirms this conclusion" (12).

In Ginott's method of teaching how to improve communication between parents and children (5) or in the Lederer and Jackson (11) attempts to facilitate communication between husband and wife, we have a very limited approach. Such self-help manuals as well as others (6, 18) offer detailed instructions on what to say or to do, but are of little use unless some break is made not in the communications equilibrium but in the immobilizing massive transference expectations. Only after there has been a breakthrough in the wall of resistance to change, in the rigid repetition of past patterns, can communications facilitation be useful. We would doubt therefore the efficacy of self-help manuals in moving the family forward to more successful operations, despite Wolf's cautionary that, "In our society very real problems exist in the man-woman relationship that cannot be solved by insight into and the resolution of transference alone" (17).

We maintain, therefore, that an understanding of the woman's role in the family and its complications due to her real and unreal expectations and the reciprocal rational and irrational expectations of the man and of the child is inexorably necessary. Only by grasping the unconscious, historical, deep-level meaning of these expectations in terms of how interpersonal situations are perceived, what one does with them, and the compulsive judgment of what is "good" and "evil," is it possible for a member of the helping profession, whether he is called psychoanalyst, psychiatrist, psychologist, counselor, clergyman, or teacher to make a proper evaluation as to where he shall place the fulcrum of his efforts to maximize positive outcomes.

Since help for problemed marital partners must be immediate rather than prolonged, brief treatment is much more appropriate for most ailing marriages, if help is at all to be successful. It is important for the professional, then, to be able to make exquisitely discriminative and appropriate transference interpretations so as to move the marriage forward, to release it from the chains of the dead historical past into the possibility of new ways of relating. It is the preferred and probably the unique way to relieve the marriage relationship of burdens out of the past. Techniques of communications facilitation in marriage which stem largely from the work of Bateson, Haley, and Jackson, for example, are of no great consequence so long as the massive defenses against the anxiety before the unfamiliar remain intact. Only by breaking through the wall of this mass of expectations arising from the defense of familiarization can we then begin to move forward to where the members of the family may be able to help themselves.

REFERENCES

1. Berne, E.: *Transactional Analysis in Psychotherapy.* New York, Grove Press, 1961.
2. Briffault, R.: *The Mothers.* New York, Macmillan, 1931, p. 312-314.
3. Durant, W.: *The Pleasures of Philosophy.* New York, Simon & Schuster, 1953.
4. Eisenstein, V.W. (Ed.): *Neurotic Interaction in Marriage.* New York, Basic Books, 1956, p. 8, 11, 15.
5. Ginott, H. G.: *Between Parent and Child.* New York, Macmillan, 1965.
6. Greenblat, B.R.: *A Doctor's Marital Guide for Patients.* Chicago, Budlong Press, 1968.
7. Greene, B.L. (Ed.): *The Psychotherapies of Marital Disharmony.* New York, Free Press, 1965, p. 17, 188.
8. Horney, K.: *Feminine Psychology.* New York, Norton, 1967, p. 87.
9. Johnston, J., and Karmiller, M.: *Family Tree.* Cleveland, World, 1967.

10. Laing, R.D.; Phillipson, H., and Lee, A.R.: *Interpersonal Perception.* New York, Springer, 1966, p. 23, p. 128-130.
11. Lederer, W.J., and Jackson, D.D.: *The Miracles of Marriage.* New York, Norton, 1968.
12. Malan, D.H.: *A Study of Brief Psychotherapy.* Springfield, Ill., Thomas, 1963.
13. Mead, M.: *Male and Female.* New York, Morrow, 1949, p. 342.
14. Mowrer, O.H. (Ed.) : *Morality and Mental Health.* Chicago, Rand McNally, 1967.
15. Pincus, L. (Ed.) : Marriage: *Studies in Emotional Conflict and Growth.* London, Methuen, 1960, p. 215.
16. Raskovsky, A.: *Personal Communication,* 1969.
17. Rosenbaum, S., and Alger, I.: *The Marriage Relationship.* New York, Basic Books, 1968.
18. Rutherford, J.J., and Rutherford, R.N.: *Consultation With Your Doctor for Personal Understanding of Marriage.* Chicago, Budlong Press, 1967.
19. Shainess, N.: *Images of woman. Amer J Psychother, XXIII:*77-97, 1969.
20. Silverman, H.L. (Ed.) : *Marital Counseling.* Springfield, Ill., Thomas, 1967.
21. Sullivan, H.S.: *The Interpersonal Theory of Psychiatry.* New York, Norton, 1953.
22. Wolf, A., and Schwartz, E.K.: *Psychoanalysis in Groups.* New York, Grune & Stratton, 1962.

SECTION II
SOCIOLOGICAL FACTORS

Chapter 14

MARRIAGE AS RELATIONSHIP-IN-DEPTH: SOME IMPLICATIONS FOR COUNSELING

DAVID R. MACE

LEO TOLSTOY, in *Anna Karenina,* says "All happy families resemble one another; every unhappy family is unhappy in its own fashion." This is another way of saying that as marriages become more successful, they converge upon a common goal and increasingly share common characteristics.

What is the essential quality that is to be clearly distinguished in all good, successful, satisfactory marriages? Lederer and Jackson divide all marriages into four types, and categorize the "best" as "Stable-Satisfactory." They consider that this ideal type represents only 5 to 10 per cent of all marriages. They add that they have found such marriages only between elderly men and women who have lived together for thirty years and more. The implication is that it takes that amount of time to build the "harmonious and collaborative union" that meets their criteria. They refer to the "hand-in-glove fit of the two spouses," and to the way in which "each partner clearly reads the other's signals, and in turn, responds with unambiguous messages (1).

To describe this quality of deep and stable harmony in a good marriage I have coined the term "relationship-in-depth." The full meaning of the term will emerge in the discussion that follows. In this chapter I wish to examine the concept in some detail, and then to suggest some of its implications for the marriage counselor.

MARRIAGE AS INTERPERSONAL INVOLVEMENT

The total range of interpersonal involvement of spouses in marriage can conveniently be divided into three sections—minimum involvement, limited involvement, and maximum involvement.

Minimum Interpersonal Involvement

Marriages of this kind are structured to serve utilitarian ends. The traditional marriage, which is still to be encountered in many of the developing countries, was not undertaken so that husband and wife might live happily ever after. It was embarked upon to serve ends that were of vital importance for the continuity of the family line, the preservation of the family property, and the passing on of the family tradition. In the patriarchial families that represent the most common pattern, a wife was sought for the son when he reached the age of marirage. Frequently he had no part in the choosing of his wife, and sometimes he did not even meet her until they were brought together for the wedding ceremony. After the wedding they lived together in the parental home. Often they would never set up a separate household of their own, but be incorporated into the extended family group, which might mean that the husband lived in the men's quarters and the wife in the women's quarters, and that they had little opportunity of being alone together and of developing what might be called a relationship. I have been a guest in such homes in the Orient, and have noticed that the married pair do little confiding in each other. If the husband has something on his mind, he talks it over with one of the men in the household; if the wife has troubles, she takes them to a confidante.

These marriages function very satisfactorily in terms of what is expected of them. They produce children, which is their primary purpose. The wife contributes her domestic skills to assure her husband's comfort, and the husband provides her with the security and protection she needs. Such marriages are not likely to get into serious trouble, because there is very little to go wrong. The major disaster occurs when the wife fails to bear children. Less serious disasters result from laziness or incompetence or disobedience on her part. Almost nothing the husband can do is regarded as blameworthy. There is simply no expectation that there will be any interpersonal relationship between the two. If mutual affection and companionship develop between them (and this often happens), it is regarded as a bonus; if not, the marriage can still meet the basic requirements.

Although the outward forms of patriarchalism and the extended family have virtually vanished from our midst, the inward attitudes they enshrined still linger on today. Especially in our lower socioeconomic subcultures, the concept of the marriage of minimal involvement still is frequently encountered. No longer supervised by the older generation, it takes the form of a mutually acceptable bargain for the exchange of needed services. The wife makes herself sexually available at all times to her husband, bears children for him, takes care of his home, cooks his food, washes his clothes, and performs other well-defined functions. He in turn provides a home and the money to maintain it, undertakes some of the heavy and technical tasks, and protects his wife and children when they need it. Provided the bargain is reasonably kept on both sides, nothing more is demanded. Problems which arise in this type of marriage usually involve violence, or failure to provide maintenance, in the husband; infidelity or gross neglect of the home and children in the wife. Such problems seldom come to the marriage counselor. The aggrieved spouses take their complaints to the courts and demand their legal rights.

Limited Interpersonal Involvement

The great majority of today's marriages are undertaken with the expectation, on the part of both husband and wife, that they imply an interpersonal relationship, which is interpreted both as a source of pleasure and fulfillment, and as a commitment to do what is possible to make the partner happy. The duties of marriage still remain, though they are not so rigidly specified; but the joys and satisfactions of a shared life are now seen as the primary goal. The proof of this is that when the modern couple fail to find together the happiness to which they consider themselves entitled, they usually feel justified in resorting to separation or divorce.

The trouble is that, while our romantic concepts point to a state of ecstatic bliss as the goal of marriage, we have not defined this goal in any but emotional terms. So the modern couple look for something they vaguely describe as "love" and "happiness," which has no precise definition; and even where it is made specific to some extent, husbands and wives are given little guidance about how to achieve it. Each married partner therefore establishes his or her criterion of marital success, and pursues his or her private fantasy. If these criteria and fantasies happen to correspond to a reasonable extent, as they are likely to do if the couple come from similar cultural backgrounds, they may be fortunate in reaching a state of more or less satisfactory equilibrium. Otherwise, they will strive to manipulate each other to play the roles which their individual fantasies assign, and meet in headlong collision and conflict.

There follows a period in which, through negotiation and pressure, compromise solutions are sought as a means of keeping the relationship tolerable to both. If these attempts fail, as they probably do in at least one-third of our American marriages, the result is either an open break or a tacit agreement to shut off the areas of unresolved conflict and live together in mutual tolerance. If the struggle for compromise succeeds, the marriage settles down to a more or less acceptable relationship, in which, for both partners, the assets decidedly outweigh the liabilities. The romantic dream is now abandoned, and a state of reasonable comfort and security is judged to be the best that can be hoped for.

All these people settle for a relationship of limited involvement. Sometimes this is all they ever expected or wished for. Sometimes they had higher hopes, but abandoned them when confronted with what appeared to be an intractable reality situation. This group undoubtedly represents the great majority of American marriages today. Some of them, as we have seen, find the attempt to adjust to their partners too difficult and discouraging, and give up, though in most cases, they try again later with another partner. Others manage to fulfill enough of their hopes to settle together for a lifelong partnership, which may get better as time passes, or may undergo little change. Between these extremes, there is a middle group who, unwilling either to quit or to settle for a disappointing level of achievement, decide to seek help. They go in large numbers to marriage counselors, to clergymen, to social workers, to psychologists and psychiatrists, and become involved in whatever brand of therapy represents the preference or the competence of the professional helper. Some of these couples are able to achieve with counseling help what they could not manage alone, and make enough further adjustments to tip the scales in favor of continuing with the marriage. Others, either because the therapy is superficial or because the gap between what they expect and what they can attain is too wide to be bridged, move out of marriage, consoling themselves with the assurance that at least they gave it a fair trial, and sought outside help, before they gave up.

Maximum Interpersonal Involvement

This group represents the really good marriages—the less than 10 per cent, according to Lederer and Jackson, who make their dreams come true. I do not care to make guesses if I can avoid it, but if I had to offer an estimate of the proportion of all marriages that are fully and deeply happy, I would agree that it was probably less than one in ten.

The characteristic quality of these marriages is what I call relationship-in-depth. We will discuss what this means, in more precise terms, later. But I am thinking of married couples who are able to maintain a close and secure relationship without serious conflict or disagreement, and to cooperate smoothly in all the areas of their shared life. From this happy and harmonious relationship they derive a deep sense of satisfaction and self-confidence that sustains and strengthens them not only in the marriage, but in all their other relationships and enterprises. To achieve this kind of success in one significant human relationship is probably the best assurance a person can have of his mental health and emotional maturity. To succeed in any other kind of achievement, but to fail to achieve any relationship in depth, is to be condemned to live always with a deep, gnawing uncertainty about one's adequacy as a person.

According to Lederer and Jackson, it takes at least thirty years to achieve a fully mature marriage. This I would not dispute. However, there is a perfection of the bud as well as of the flower; which means that a marriage can be as good as it may reasonably hope to be at the particular point in development it has reached. True, it will attain greater depth and quality later, as the accumulation of shared experience continuously extends and enriches the areas of mutual involvement. But what really matters is that a couple should be as fully involved with each other, in the experience of the shared life, as they can reasonably expect to be in their given conditions. Lederer and Jackson say they have "never observed a generally constant collaborative union between spouses during the period when they are raising children " (2). Their criteria may differ from mine; I would say quite positively that I *have* witnessed such unions, and that they are possible.

There are a few married couples who seem to move easily and gracefully into relationship-in-depth. They are unusually mature people, with great sensitivity and consideration for others, and well matched in having a great deal in common from the very start. But there are more who come to a deep relationship the hard way, through "blood and sweat and toil and tears," as Winston Churchill said in another connection. They have to achieve trust and unity through a long, determined process of working through their interpersonal conflicts. This is the hard way, but it is not a route to be despised, because what people have fought and struggled for they prize, as achievements that come easily can never be prized. So the way they arrive at relationship-in-depth does not really matter. All are blessed who arrive, by whatever path they travel. It may well be that the city of the truly happily married, like the New Jerusalem, has twelve gates, through any of which a couple may enter.

MAJOR MODES OF MARITAL INVOLVEMENT

The shared experiences of the married couple may cover a field as wide as life itself, and a full list of their areas of involvement could never be compiled. But for our present purpose I will select three modes of involvement which are quite basic for the achievement of relationship-in-depth. They are communication, sharing, and cooperation. The first is concerned with the proper recognition and identification of each other, without which there can be no real relationship at all. The second concerns their achievement of unity in the face-to-face relationship of their common life. The third has to do with their side-by-side relationship as they interact together with the outside world.

Communication

It is not true that every marriage failure is a failure in communication, because there are couples who are so incompatible that even full knowledge of each other could not provide enough in common for the building of a mutually shared life. But for all married couples who *do* have the necessary modicum of mutual affinity to achieve a workable marriage, the achievement of effective communication is more important than anything else. The key to relationship-in-depth is communication-in-depth. We marriage counselors know that a considerable amount of our effort to help couples in trouble has to be expended in the direction of clearing up the matted tangles of misunderstanding and distrust that result from the absence of communication.

There are couples who seem not to be able to communicate. But for every one of these, there are probably nine at least whose problem is that they are not *willing* to communicate. In our everyday social life we manage to get along with a good deal of deception of one another. Telling the whole truth to colleagues and associates is not necessary and at times not appropriate. But in the intimate life of marriage we are in a quite different situation. When two people live as close to one another as husband and wife do, it is impossible to maintain mutual trust without transparent honesty. It is my conviction that this is probably the greatest of all causes of marital failure. Lack of honesty leads to lack of understanding, which creates suspicion, resentment, and hostility. There may be a few rare situations in which husband and wife may legitimately withhold the truth from one another; but it is my view that this always, and inevitably, involves a misfortune. To have to censor your communication to your marriage partner, and close off a portion of your thoughts that cannot be shared, is fatal to the achievement of relationship-in-depth.

It is fatal also to the full enjoyment of marriage at its best. Probably the richest reward that marriage brings is the experience of being fully and completely known to the person with whom you live in the closest of all relationships, and to be loved nevertheless. No person can achieve full self-acceptance if in his mind there lurks the suspicion that if the people he loves knew the whole truth about him, they would recoil from him or reject him. There are men who pay therapists to accept them in the light of all the facts about them, who would gain far more if they could be confident of equal acceptance from their wives.

Communication in marriage, however, is not just a total disclosure of oneself. It is, in addition to that, an ongoing process of sharing thoughts and feelings openly and fearlessly. This includes hostile feelings toward the partner, which *should* be shared; but in a good marriage they are shared with appropriate apologies, and an appeal for help in getting rid of them; and that makes all the difference.

The vital clue to problems of sexual adjustment in marriage, I am sure, lies in the realm of communication. That is why I always make it my aim to deal with sex problems in conjoint sessions; though it may require individual sessions to prepare the couple for the kind of open discussion that facilitates therapy. Not only is it important that husband and wife should be able to communicate with one another about their sexual needs and responses. The sex life itself is a very important form of communication. When they are symbolically interpreted, the common psychosexual problems are all manifestations of communication problems. Vaginismus in the wife is a nonverbal way of saying "I won't let you come into my life. I must shut the door and keep you out." Impotence is the husband saying, "I can't give myself completely to you, because I'm not quite sure what you might do to me. So I'm afraid to go any further." Orgasm inadequacy may mean, "I'm not sure enough of you to let myself go completely and abandon myself to you." Infidelity is saying, "I don't feel you want me to come very close to you any more, so I will go to someone else instead."

Sharing

We often speak of marriage as a union. This does not mean that two people become one, because that is neither possible nor desirable. But it does mean, in its true sense, a complete pooling of possessions and the entering into a joint life, face to face, with nothing reserved or held back. Anything less than that is only a partial marriage, with the intention of limited involvement such as we have already discussed. Many marriages start on this basis and never go any further. These couples will never know the meaning of relationship-in-depth.

The most important thing for a couple to share is their "religion." I do not mean this in a rigidly institutional sense. I believe every man has a religion, whether he has ever given it precise formulation, or joined himself to a group of like-minded persons, or not. My religion is what I believe about myself, my nature and destiny; what my values and standards are; what constitute my motives and goals in life. Unless husband and wife can truly share their fundamental approach to human life, and their comprehension of its meaning and purpose, it will be very difficult for them to achieve relationship-in-depth. This is the final problem of the inter-faith marriage—there remains always, for the two people concerned, a central area of human experience where they are strangers to one another.

A true unity in marriage requires also a sharing of relatives and friends. The husband cannot fully share his wife's life unless he fully accepts her family, and vice versa. It is not necessary that he should think they are wonderful people, if they are not. But he must bind them to him so that he takes them into his life as if they were his own family; and she must do the same with his relatives. They do this not for the sake of the relatives, but out of love for each other. The same is true of mutual friends, except that in this case, there are no bonds of kinship, and in a close marriage friends of the one who cannot become friends of the other tend to recede to the periphery of the circle of acquaintances.

Sharing of money may be an acid test of relationship-in-depth. Money symbolizes our sense of worth, the value we place upon ourselves, and the means by which we strive to reach many of our most important goals; a home, the esteem of others, education, social life, and travel. It is no surprise to learn that the management of money is always the most highly checked item on any marriage problems list submitted to Americans. Money policy is the most sensitive indicator of how far husband and wife have really developed what Fritz Kunkel called the "we-feeling." I would go so far as to say that a married couple will never be able to achieve a completely workable money policy until they have attained relationship-in-depth.

The other major area of sharing is the children of the marriage. Every person conceives of his child as a projection of himself, and he will always treat it as such. So if the two selves of the parents are out of harmony, the task of parenthood cannot proceed smoothly. Every significant area of mal-adjustment in marriage becomes, consciously or unconsciously, a battle-ground on which the estranged spouses fight each other for control of their children; and this always communicates itself to the child, though general-ly not at the level of conscious awareness.

Cooperation

This is the side-by-side aspect of the marriage relationship. It is closely linked with the face-to-face relationship, so that a failure in the one will re-sult in the disturbance of the other. Ideally, the behavior of the couple as together they face the business of living, in all its aspects, will be governed by their close, intimate, mutual love and trust. When that happens, prob-lems seldom arise.

The running of the home is the major joint enterprise in which the married couple are engaged, and its magnitude and complexity must not be underestimated. The organization of a family in our world of today is at least as complex as the management of a small business. There are endless decisions to be made and duties to be performed. Even with good coopera-tion, it will often tax the resources of husband and wife to the limit to get everything done to their mutual satisfaction. There is a house to choose and furnish. There are the tasks of maintenance and home management to be fairly shared between them. There are relationships with neighbors to be handled with wisdom and skill. There are the wider church, community, and civic obligations to be met in such a way that the couple do not get in each other's hair. There are the children's schedules to be fitted in with their own needs and plans. There is the entertaining to be done. And along with the seemingly endless procession of routine tasks and duties, there are the unexpected crises—illnesses and accidents; special calls for assistance from relatives and friends; disagreements among the children and with the children, and between the children and their friends, to be ironed out; financial crises and work crises and weather crises and transportation crises.

At any point in this complex process of coping with events, husband and wife may find themselves in conflict. They may disagree about what should be done or how it should be done. They may get their signals crossed and be involved in a misunderstanding. One may be tired or irritable and snap at the other. One may feel an action of the other to be unfair or hostile or irresponsible or inappropriate. Sometimes there is no time for full explanation or clarification, because the show must go on. Only deep underlying trust in each other will keep the ship on an even keel at such times. If such trust does not exist, there will almost inevitably be mutual recrimination and quarrels and arguments, lasting far into the night when rest is sorely needed.

Without cooperative planning and execution, the life of the home can be badly disrupted, setting everyone on edge and producing anything but peace and harmony. All other human partnerships involve limited areas of cooperation, or close cooperation for limited periods with opportunities for recuperative withdrawal. But in a marriage, the closest and most intimate of all adult human relationships goes on and on without let-up or escape. If it is happy and harmonious, everything can be taken in stride. But if there is disagreement, competitiveness, and conflict, it can be really hell.

Conflict is, in fact, inevitable in marriage. Two people living so close together cannot expect to be in agreement all the time about everything. They are the products of different backgrounds, and they have consequently learned to approach the business of living in different ways—each has his own method, his own order of priority, his own pace. Thrown together in a common task, they will inevitably clash. And the business of marriage is to work on the differences that arise, analyze them, understand and respect each other's sincerity and goodwill, work out compromise adjustments; and then tackle the slow, discouraging task of changing habit patterns in order to achieve more harmonious cooperation. There is no easy way to do this. There are no short-cuts, no laborsaving gimmicks. It can be done only when two people have the resolute will to do it, because the goal is sufficiently important to them both.

OBSTACLES TO RELATIONSHIP-IN-DEPTH

The rewards of a truly happy and harmonious marriage are so obvious that you would imagine everyone who marries would make this his goal. We have in fact reached the point today at which people are less and less willing to tolerate a mediocre marriage. The traditional functions of the family—mutual protection, economic security, cooperative production of food, vocational training of children, and so on—have more and more been taken over by the community at large; and the major function of families today is to provide emotional security and fulfillment, and a sense of personal worth, in a vast and complex world. Failure to achieve a good relationship in marriage therefore means a major disaster today, comparable to a failure to beat off the Indians or raise enough crops for the winter in the past. The future of marriage will depend very deeply upon whether it can deliver the kind of personal fulfillment, to spouses and children alike, which has now become its primary task.

What then are the hindrances faced by couples as they attempt to carry out the now very difficult, but highly rewarding, task of marriage today? Let me select four of them for discussion.

Lack of Comprehension

I cannot escape the conclusion that most marital failures stem from ignorance about marriage and about how to approach the task of building a satisfying relationship. When I try to reconstruct, in counseling with couples, their concepts of the making of a marriage, I find that it adds up to a most confused hodge-podge of starry-eyed romanticism, superstition, superficial concepts, and *laissez-faire*. Seldom do I find any real understanding of the complexity of the task of bringing two separate individuals into a delicately balanced coordination of each other's thoughts, feelings, wishes, beliefs, and habit-patterns. There is little recognition on the part of each that they must make some radical changes in their way of thinking and acting in order to maintain the kind of close relationship which they imagine, once initiated by sexual attraction, will somehow be automatically self-perpetuating. There is rarely any clear realization that disagreement is inherent in a partnership as intimate as that undertaken by two people in marriage today; with the result that, instead of recognizing conflict as the raw material out of which the marriage must be fashioned, they flee from it as from some alien element that threatens to destroy their love. I find that they have generally entered marriage with little readiness for its demands, having spent the premarital period in a round of pleasure-making activities that bears little relationship, and even less resemblance, to the realities with which married life now confronts them.

What is evident, therefore, is that despite the excellent programs we have provided for the privileged few, we are doing a deplorably poor job of preparing young people generally for marriage, either corporately or individually. And in view of the difficulty of the marital task, and of the high rate of failure shown clearly by our statistical data, this is an act of incredible folly on the part of a supposedly highly developed culture.

The problem is not just one of lack of knowledge, however. At least equally important is the tragic fact that many of these people are utterly confused about what marriage involves, because they have been furnished no good models with which to identify. I find that those who come to me for counseling, surprisingly often, say they wonder whether marriage may not be greatly overrated. They are skeptical about what it has to offer. They even say they have never seen a really good marriage, and ask me whether such a thing exists. They admit that they cannot regard their parents as models, because in some cases their marriages ended in divorce; or if not, they communicated clearly to their children that they were living together in a state often far removed from warm affection, and sometimes no better than impatient toleration of each other.

If one has no personal experience of observing a good marriage functioning, how does one learn the skills necessary for this delicate task? How does a man know how to deal with his wife in a thousand complex situations, if he has never watched another man, skilled in the art? How does a woman know how to function as a good wife if she has no concept of how the role is played, because she has never seen it played?

Unwillingness to Venture

There are plenty of people who go into marriage with the definite intention of seeking limited involvement only. There are others who settle for this when they see what maximum involvement is likely to cost them in terms of the effort necessary to achieve it. What these people do is to relegate marriage to a relatively low position in their list of priorities; and then give it a corresponding amount of their time and attention.

This is predominantly a man's point of view. The attitude is widespread among men that, while one must devote a certain amount of special effort to the business of courtship, when once the girl is won and safely corralled in the split-level suburban home, the husband can again give his full attention to his previous preoccupations—his work, his men friends, his sports, his hobbies. This concept is fortified by the fact that boys in our culture are not prepared for depth relationships with anyone, and particularly not with the women in their lives. They are raised to consider that the manly role is that of rugged independence. The strong, silent type is the one held up for the boy to emulate—the self-sufficient male, able to cope with any situation. If he has dependency needs (and he has) he is expected to suppress them. So the concept of living in a relationship of complete openness with his wife, a relationship in which he may freely express his emotions and acknowledge his weaknesses, is abhorrent to his male pride. Yet in fact this is exactly what many American males need above all else; and if they had it, the result would be to increase, not diminish, their adequacy in their dealings with others; to fortify, not undermine, their self-confidence; and to foster, not arrest, their growth toward maturity. But American males do not yet see it that way. So they adopt the policy of keeping their emotional life clamped tightly down, and sitting on the lid; and of putting a safe distance between themselves and their wives so that there may be no danger of close interpersonal involvement.

Another deterrent, associated with the one we have been discussing, is the fear of losing personal freedom of action in a close relationship. This affects the woman as much as it does the man. After all, the women of our culture have not been so long emancipated that they have forgotten what their grandmothers suffered under the sovereign rule of the dominant male. So a relationship that is close and intimate is seen as a threat to autonomy, a trap that may deprive you of the freedom to think and act and plan in your own way. American culture, again, has encouraged a passionate devotion to the concept of individual freedom, a doctrine with which no one could quarrel in principle.

Yet freedom overemphasized can drive us into a tragic loneliness, an isolation from our fellows, which is stultifying rather than creative. The real meaning of human life is not to pry ourselves loose from our fellows, but to find ourselves in relationships with others that enhance our selfhood. Havelock Ellis was fond of saying, "To live is to love, and to love is to live," and without question he was right. Nothing more enhances and fulfills the growth of the individual toward maturity than to be involved in creative depth relationships; and nothing provides the conditions for this experience better than a warm and close affection between a man and a woman in marriage.

Psychological Barriers

In addition to those who *will* not make the venture of seeking relationship-in-depth in their marriages, there are those who *can* not do so. They are blocked by obstacles that are located deep in their own personalities. Inadequate and insecure, many of them are vividly aware of their need for the healing and protection of a close and loving relationship with another person; but paralysing fears hold them back from making the venture, and they defeat their own ends by generating hostility that causes the partner to retreat, or terror that causes *them* to retreat. So, like Tantalus in the Greek myth, they spend their married lives within reach of all they want and need, yet unable to grasp it.

These unhappy people have been traumatized in earlier life. As children, even as infants, their trusting love has been betrayed by insensitive or maladroit adults, who have rejected them, punished them inappropriately, or exploited them. They have had to build elaborate defences against becoming involved in relationship-in-depth, because they can trust no one to come too close without the ulterior intention to take advantage of their defenselessness. We have seen how these fearful attitudes create, and are symbolically represented by, the psychosexual difficulties in marriage. The sex act represents, for both male and female, a surrender of the self to the partner, a willingness to be open and naked and defenseless in an encounter with another self. These are just the things these disturbed people are unable to do.

They try to solve their problem in many ways. Some withdraw into themselves, and live their married lives shut up within the confines of an impenetrable shell. Some go from partner to partner, developing superficial relationships and, when the demand to face real involvement casts its threatening shadow, running away and starting all over again with someone else. Others enter into relationships on an aggressive, exploitative basis, staving off any real involvement by treating the partner as an object rather than as a person. They are all unhappy people, and they render their partners unhappy by being unable to put any substance into the shadowy encounters that represent all they are able to tolerate.

Some of these marriages achieve a certain spurious "success" because the respective neurotic needs of the partners are complementary and produce a kind of pathological interlocking. The sadistic man who finds a strongly masochistic woman is one example. The husband who needs to inflate his male ego by convincing himself of his adequacy will find it satisfying to take over and manage a nervous, cringing woman whose need is to be managed and manipulated. A roughly opposite pattern is that of the insecure wife who seeks to build a sense of adequacy by playing an indulgently maternal role toward a pampered and irresponsible husband, whose outrageous behavior she tolerates with the resignation of the martyr.

These and other interacting combinations of neurotic patterns may establish the marriages concerned on a basis of security. But this is not to be confused with relationship-in-depth. As Bela Mittelmann, in a discussion of reciprocal neurotic marriage patterns, has said, "The emotional patterns of the mates complement each other in such a way as to perpetuate their pathological reactions through an intrapsychic vicious circle" (3). In other words, the marriage is sustaining the neurotic patterns of both. Any movement toward emotional health, on the part of either, would disrupt the relationship.

Fear of Overdependence

There are some who take the view that to invest oneself too heavily in relationship may be undesirable. They are concerned not so much with the loss of individual freedom, as with the possibility that the personality may lose flexibility if it is geared too narrowly to a very deep relationship with one other person.

There is, of course, in the minds of some wives, the fear that they may become the victims of male dominance. Much more frequently, there is the suspicion in a husband's mind that if he becomes too deeply involved with his wife, he will either become less masculine or will be regarded as a henpecked husband. These things can happen; but when they do, the situation that results is not at all what I mean by relationship-in-depth. A healthy close relationship between husband and wife, far from diminishing their personality growth, will enhance it—a man becomes truly masculine by learning to play the proper complementary role toward a woman he loves; and the same is true in reverse for the woman. Anyway, full maturity in a human being does not consist in overdeveloping masculine or feminine qualities. The "he-man" is not man at his most mature, but more often a manifestation of an adolescent fixation; and the current concept of feminity as exemplified by the obtrusively "sexy" woman is very wide of the mark. The truly mature person represents a blend, in good proportion, of the qualities of both sexes—masculine aggressiveness tempered by sensitivity and tenderness, feminine modesty and sweetness balanced by firmness and self-assurance when the occasion requires it.

There are other married people who fear that, if they become too closely involved with one another, they will die of boredom! The truth is that when husbands and wives find each other boring (as they often do), it is generally because their relationship is so superficial, and so "guarded" against getting into real issues, that they have nothing stimulating to talk about and nothing exciting to do together. People who live at arms' length from each other, so that their talk is about trifles, and their actions routinized, inevitably grow weary of each other. These same people, in other relationships that reach down to deeper levels and touch reality, can suddenly "come alive." This is what happens again and again in the "affairs" to which married people resort to escape from their boredom. They will often admit afterwards that their paramours were not as attractive to them as their spouses; but in the atmosphere of adventure and excitement which the "affair" created, a quality of realism took over for a time that had been lacking in their marriages. As we counselors know, it sometimes takes a marital crisis of this sort to make a husband and wife fully aware of how much they really care for one another.

There is, however, a real danger of confusing relationship-in-depth with the altogether different concept of "togetherness." There is no more heretical doctrine about marriage than the idea that "spending time with one another," or "doing things together," necessarily contributes anything to improvement of the relationship. "Relationship-in-depth" refers to quality, and not to quantity. A wife who petulantly demands that her husband stay home with her three nights a week, and gets him to do so with the coercion of her pastor, is dangerously near to destroying her marriage, rather than saving it. The truth of the matter is that people who have a good relationship *want* to spend time together, and find ways and means to do so. But they also recognize each other's rights to spend time in other ways, because they have no fears, anxieties, or suspicions that their spouses will develop wayward tendencies as soon as they are out of each other's sight.

An excellent example of this was the marriage of Harold Nicolson, the distinguished English writer and commentator. In his memoirs, written by his son, appears the following letter he had received from his wife, "I was always well-trained not to manage you. I scarcely dare to arrange the collar of your greatcoat, unless you ask me to. I think that is really the basis of our marriage, apart from our deep love for one another, for we have never interfered with each other and, strangely enough have never been jealous of each other. And now, in our advancing age, we love each other more deeply than ever before" (4).

IMPLICATIONS FOR COUNSELING

Some implications for marriage counseling have already been incidentally touched upon, but there are many more. I will content myself, in concluding this chapter, with three rather obvious ones.

A Framework for Diagnosis and Therapy

There are many concepts which can be used to systematize marriage counseling theory, and in this chapter I am dealing with only one of them. I suggest, however, that it is a useful one. The idea of relationship-in-depth (which I have here merely sketched, and which needs fuller treatment), provides us with a goal which would, in all probability, be acceptable to most marriage counselors, as defining the conditions we would desire to create in every marriage, if we could. It is a goal that is in keeping with modern concepts of marriage, in which the quality of the relationship, and the happiness and fulfillment attained by the spouses, tend to become the optimum values; rather than the number of children born, or the contribution made to the maintenance of the family tradition, or simply the stability of the marital bond and its continuity—which were the values most highly sought and esteemed in the past.

I have proposed not only a goal upon which marriage counselors could agree, but also a continuum along which, at whatever point was appropriate, a particular marriage relationship could be charted. This could serve, if criteria of measurement could be worked out, as at least a rough scale for the evaluation of a marriage. Any given marriage could be placed somewhere along the line that stretches from minimal involvement, through various stages of limited involvement, to maximum involvement, thus providing a "marital involvement index."

I invite my research-oriented colleagues to explore this further. It would at least be a better criterion for measurement than that of marital happiness, which Terman and others tried to develop. It offers, I think, more promise than the concept of marital interaction, though there are close similarities between the two, and some might consider them identical. However, I perceive an important difference between them. Interaction simply expresses how two people feel and respond to one another—it is almost purely subjective. But involvement has about it an element of commitment as well—a purposeful decision to endure negative interaction because of an accepted obligation to push through a stalemate to a new relationship at a deeper level. It is this factor in the concept of involvement that is, of course, important for marriage counseling, which is concerned less with measuring the relationship, as it is, than with changing it into something better. There are conditions in which deep involvement could be very painful, and lead to interaction so negative that a subjective judgment would call for withdrawal. Yet from an objective viewpoint, enduring the pain may be the only way to reach ultimately the goal of greater depth in the relationship.

The concept of involvement may also serve as a guide for the counselor in formulating the immediate objective of his treatment plan—to move the couple along the continuum in the direction of the theoretical goal. To do this, he would have to determine for each spouse what was the desired degree of involvement in the marriage, and why. He would then know how much disparity existed between the husband's concept and the wife's concept of what was desirable, and he could get to work on the task of trying to close the gap, and to bring them, if possible, to a common definition of what might constitute a practicable and attainable level of involvement. With this agreed upon, the nature and direction of the counseling task would be clear to all concerned, and it would remain to be seen how far it could be achieved. If it could not it would have to be modified.

There would, of course, be couples who could not close the gap in their concept of marriage enough to make any progress; and this would have to be recognized and honestly faced. There would be couples who might have to travel backwards along the continuum in order to find a point at which, having regard to their limitations, they might have to settle. But with a frame of reference, these unusual situations could be seen clearly for what they were, and consequently, perhaps more readily accepted by those being counseled.

A Concept of the Counselor's Usefulness

We have failed rather badly, particularly in the United States, to see marriage counseling as a broad response to a national problem. In other countries, marriage counseling services have generally been organized on a national basis, often directed by a Government Agency, as an attempt to meet a general need manifested by the population. But the American counselor has tended to be preoccupied with his own personal and professional goals. As long as he could establish a practice or secure a position in an agency, and as long as people with marital troubles sought his help and paid the appropriate fees, all was well. The fact that he might in fact have been lavishing his hard-earned skills on the intensive care of a few marital couples who could make very limited progress, or who might well break up in the end, was perhaps a little frustrating, but it did not challenge his whole concept of the value of what he was doing. He was not too seriously perturbed by the fact that while he was treating these people, the next lot of disoriented marriages were shaping up to join the line and keep the supply coming. He did not consider very seriously the possibility that the real task of the marriage counselor is to put himself out of a job, by cutting off the stream of unsuccessful marriages further back.

There are evidences that the time may have come to look rather critically at what we marriage counselors are doing. Clark Vincent (5) has stressed the concept of "marital health," as a more positive goal than the "saving" of marriages from breakdown. Just as the treatment of mental disorder reached a point at which the emphasis had to swing from the remedial approach to the preventive, and the widespread adoption of the term "mental health," so a similar swing in emphasis may be due in our field.

This would mean that we marriage counselors might move out of our remedial routines and strive actively to get involved in two other directions. First, we should be doing much more in the area of marriage preparation, and in guiding the married couple through their first critical year, in which they come to know what interpersonal involvement in marriage really means. I become more and more convinced, in my premarital counseling, that some exciting possibilities exist in the direction of establishing a contact with engaged couples, and arranging to "service" their marriages for them during the early adjustment period, until they find their direction and get well established on the road to healthy growth of the relationship. They will not come to us and ask for this, because this represents a rather new idea; but it is an idea they accept very readily when it is persuasively presented to them, specially when it is coupled with the concept of the goal of relationship-in-depth as something well worth striving for.

The second new field of activity is that of "marriage enrichment," as it is most commonly described. This consists of working with married couples, not to "solve their problems," but to facilitate their growth toward the highest levels of marital health. The concept of relationship-in-depth makes its own appeal here also. There are large numbers of married couples who, while reasonably content with their existing situation, and certainly not thinking at all about breaking up, are wistfully aware that marriage has not really come up to their expectations, and wish they could move toward the "higher reaches" of the shared life; but who have no idea what to do about it, and who therefore take no action until something specific is offered to them.

My wife and I have been experimenting, for some years now, with week-end retreats for groups of not more than ten married couples; and with similar groups coming for a series of sessions to our home. It has been made clear that these meetings were not for problem couples, but for those with stable marriages who nevertheless were willing to consider how far they are developing the full potentialities in their relationship. Nothing in which I have been involved in my professional career has been more rewarding than these programs; the couples have been most responsive, and most grateful for the help they received from this experience.

The Counselor's Own Marriage

I raise this final point with some diffidence, yet I feel it is an inescapable implication of the issue I have raised in this chapter. I am well aware that the skill of a marriage counselor is something inherent in himself, compounded from his basic compassion for other people, his training, and his experience. I know that there are excellent counselors who are unmarried; some who are not happily married; some whose marriages have broken up. I am not suggesting that these circumstances incapacitate them in their work. I know some persons, in each of these categories, to whom I would not hesitate to send any married couple in need of help, confident that they would receive excellent service.

What I am raising is not a negative question, but a positive one. I am addressing those marriage counselors who have the good fortune to be very happily married themselves, and to have progressed a long way toward the achievement of relationship-in-depth. I am suggesting that such counselors have a hidden resource of which they may not be making the fullest use.

At a conference of the American Association of Marriage Counselors in Minneapolis a few years ago, I recall a demonstration interview conducted by a psychiatrist and his wife with a married couple. The psychiatrist explained, in the following discussion, that it was his custom for his wife to share with him in all his marriage counseling sessions. He made it clear that she was not, at least when they began this arrangement, qualified as a therapist in any way. The idea was not to provide the couple with two therapists, but to give them the opportunity to discuss their problem with a mature married couple. This seemed to me to have some very significant advantages. While struggling with their own problems of relationship, the patients were constantly confronted with a working demonstration of what they wanted to achieve. At the same time, the wife had access to another wife to whom she could turn with confidence that her difficulties with the role would be well understood. The husband had also the counselor's wife available to interpret to him how an independent woman, successfully married, thought and felt about the material he was presenting. At another level, both patients could use the counseling team as parent-surrogates to work through problems that represented carry-overs from their childhood experiences.

It seems to me that there are some interesting possibilities here that could profitably be further explored. I have encountered few marriage counselors indeed who have tried out the idea of working with their wives as co-therapists. Yet why not? We have come nowadays to recognize the great potentialities of conjoint interviews, with husband and wife together and the reality situation right there in the counseling office. Why not conjoint interviews conducted by conjoint counselors who are a well-adjusted married couple, offering the healing power of a healthy marriage to nurse a sick marriage back to health again?

There are other possibilities along the same lines. Many of us are now doing group counseling with married couples. Why not introduce into each group a married couple who have a relationship with each other of great depth and creativity, to share their experiences with the others and provide them with a model for identification and emulation? Seeing before them a marriage that really works, with full freedom to examine and investigate it, might awaken new hope in discouraged spouses. To weary travelers struggling along a rough and rocky road, what greater incentive could there be to persevere, than to round a bend and catch a glimpse in the distance of the shining peak, distant yet accessible, that is their final goal?

REFERENCES

1. Lederer, William J., and Jackson, Don D.: *The Mirages of Marriage.* New York, W. W. Norton & Company, Inc., 1968, pp. 129-131.
2. Lederer, William J., and Jackson, Don D.: *The Mirages of Marriage.* New York, W. W. Norton & Company, Inc., 1968, p. 130.
3. Mittelman, Bela: Analysis of reciprocal neurotic patterns in family relationships in Eisenstein, Victor W. (Ed.). *Neurotic Interaction in Marriage.* New York, Basic Books, Inc., 1965, p. 82.
4. Nicolson, Nigel: *The Diary and Letters of Harold Nicolson.* New York, Atheneum, Vol. III, p. 386.
5. Vincent, Clark: Mental health and the family. Vol. XXIX, No. 1, *J Marriage and the Family,* 1967, pp. 33-39.

Chapter 15

COUNSELING AND THE EVOLUTION OF THE CONCEPT OF SIN

PANOS D. BARDIS

"Magna pars hominum est quae
non peccatis irascitur sed peccantibus."

Seneca, *De Ira,* II, xxviii, 8.

THE SOCIOLOGY OF RELIGION

T HOSE WHO deal with the sociology of religion "have undertaken three main types of religious study. They have studied religion as a central theoretical problem in the understanding of social action. They have studied the relationship between religion and other areas of social life, such as economics, politics, and social class. And finally, they have studied religious roles, organizations, and movements" (1).

These researches have seldom been interdisciplinary. The present investigation, therefore, is interdisciplinary, placing main emphasis on the following four goals:

1. To organize and systematize most of the important ideas regarding sin which have dominated the Western world, and thus supply the counselor with that kind of knowledge which facilitates insightful and creative thinking about some of the problems with which he deals. In the area of marriage counseling, for instance, such knowledge is valuable, since, as a well-known authority has indicated, the concept of sin and marital adjustment are closely related (2).
2. To see if certain hypotheses or theories could be formulated concerning the "evolution" of the concept of sin.
3. To utilize such generalizations in the construction of a questionnaire or scale for the quantitative measurement of attitudes toward sin. The counselor would thus secure additional relevant information about his individual counselee.
4. To employ this quantitative information as a partial index of modernization.

METHODOLOGY

In order to obtain a fairly representative sample of data, the author prepared three somewhat complete lists of major thinkers—primarily theologians—who have speculated about sin, of important religious systems, and of religiously rather homogeneous historical stages or periods. At random, he then selected units from the three lists, and proceeded to investigate and scrutinize as impartially as possible, each of them both extensively and intensively.

The data are here presented geographically, chronologically, and topically. Of course, the problem of overlapping is unavoidable, but the writer has attempted a logical and unambiguous classification of the subject matter. The additional problem of summarizing complex and involved technical treatises is formidable and virtually insoluble.

SIN: ETYMOLOGY AND DEFINITION

The English "sin" is related to the Anglo-Saxon *synn* and the Old Norse *synd,* both of which mean "offense." The Latin origin is *sons,* or guilty. There is a definite connection between this word and the Latin *sum,* I am, as well as the Greek *eimi,* also I am. The implication here is—to be the one, that is, the guilty one. In other words, sin is common, or to be is to sin!

A universally acceptable definition of sin, which is a predominantly religious concept, is impossible, since each definition is influenced by the particular faith, viewpoint, and so forth of the definer. Nevertheless, two brief dictionary definitions should be sufficient here: "a breaking of the law of God deliberately" (3); and *"transgression volontaire de la loi divine, notion de faute, avec responsabilité personnelle"* (4), which is a primarily Christian definition.

Sin is not synonymous with *crime,* namely, the breaking of the civil law, or with *vice,* which is immoral behavior consisting in the violation of a society's ethicosocial norms. Sin further differs from taboo, which may be defined as a prohibition of various acts or contacts under the threat of supernatural punishment.

COUNSELING: ETYMOLOGY AND DEFINITION

"Counseling" comes from the Latin *consilium,* or consultation, deliberation—from *con,* together, and *salio,* I leap.

It has been stated that "counseling is a more general term that might be applied to any situation in which one person takes responsibility for advising or giving help or guidance to another. It may or may not be under agency auspices and may have more or less the qualities of a professional relationship—one characterized by the fact that the counselor takes conscious responsibility for bringing special knowledge and skill to help the other person to solve his problems" (5). Moreover, counseling consists of attempts "to rehabilitate the individual in reference to his personal problems, but those in which profound personality reorganization is not required" (6).

MODERNIZATION

A social scientist has asserted that "modernization is the current term for an old process—the process of social change whereby less-developed societies acquire characteristics common to more-developed societies" (7). Diminishing provincialism has accompanied this process. In early imperialistic times, for example, the colonial spirit could be detected in phrases such as "The 'Anglicization' of India." Late imperialism, however, witnessed what was known as "Europeanization," in view of the similarities among the various imperialistic nations. The dominant term during the third stage —World War II—was "Westernization," whereas after the war "modernization" referred to the entire planet.

In 1955, Lewis mentioned economic development as an exceedingly important component of modernization (8). A better analysis has been presented by Lerner, who has listed the following constituents: first, self-sustaining economic growth; second, public participation in the polity; third, a diffusion of secular-rational norms; fourth, increasing physical, psychic, and social mobility; and fifth, corresponding personality changes to facilitate adjustment to the new social system (9).

Although Lerner's list seems adequate, his definition of modernization appears to be slightly narrow. Indeed, modernization may refer to one and the same highly developed society—even the most modern one—when various forces generate a social system which is more developed than the one that it succeeded, and which has never existed in any other society. This dimension makes the study of social change more inclusive and fruitful. Needless to add, such change involves all major social institutions—the family, the church, the economy, and so on.

THE HEBREWS

Sin in the Old Testament

The ancient Hebrews, whose influence on the West is still considerable, dealt with sin repeatedly. Although this is a formidable task, their countless and complex ideas in this area may be rather satisfactorily organized as follows.

Such complexity is partly indicated by the many Hebrew words employed with reference to sin, and by the fact that the Septuagint, somewhat incorrectly, almost always translates most of them as *anomia* or *hamartia*. Usually, however, the Hebrews spoke of *hattat,* or missing the mark, and *het,* or unwilful sin (here the problems of transliteration and translation are insoluble). Less common were *asam,* guilt as liability bofore God (usually a ritual offense); *avon,* perversion; *marah,* rebellion against parents; *pasa,* rebellion against a political authority; *pesa,* rebellion against God; *ra,* evil indisposition; *resa,* wickedness (with emphasis on legal offenses) ; *segagah,* a straying; and *seker,* a lie (like the Platonic "lie in the soul," this was inclusive) .

The definition of sin was almost always religious, since sin was considered a *malum ipsius Dei,* stressing man's transgression of Jehovah's will. David confessed, "Against thee, thee only, have I sinned" (Psalm 51:4). The moral element found in Job 31 was rather exceptional.

Also exceptional was the separation of deed from thought with reference to sin. But even then the distinction was nebulous and incomplete. Similarly, as in the New Testament, the idea of conscience was virtually nonexistent. Indeed, the only reference to it is found in The Wisdom of Solomon: "they perished in trembling fear" (17:10) . Verses such as "God will circumcise thine heart" (Deuteronomy 30:6) , however, indicate that sometimes the Hebrews vaguely identified man with his heart—which was regarded as the organ of thought—and the heart with the seat of conscience.

Although "Noah was a just man and perfect" (Genesis 6:9) , the typical belief was that sin is universal: "the imagination of man's heart is evil" (8:21) .

In classifying sins, the Hebrews merely distinguished between serious offenses and less serious ones. Moreover, their inadequate classification usually emphasized the corresponding sanctions.

Their etiology of sin was also limited. For instance, the existence of the serpent was taken for granted and, particularly in later Old Testament times, Satan was frequently mentioned as a cause of sinful conduct.

Sin was considered inborn. Adam's fall, which included the elements of external disobedience and man's pursuit of independence through a filial protest, initiated such heredity. More specifically, Genesis 3 attempts an explanation of mankind's fate by discussing the universality of death, man's sweat and toil, and woman's sorrow in childbearing and her submission to the male. This theory, of course, was not always accepted, and its pessimism was not complete. Still, David gives us the seed of "original sin" when he laments, "in sin did my mother conceive me" (Psalm 51:5) . Similarly, "their origin was evil and their wickedness inborn" (Wisdom of Solomon 12:10) ; and "who can bring a clean thing out of an unclean? Not one" (Job 14:4) .

The collective aspect of sin, punishment, and reward was dominant. It is not only true that "Israel hath sinned" (Joshua 7:11) , but also that Moses accepted the communal sin of Aaron's calf (Exodus 32) . More importantly, the cases of Abimelech, David, and Ahab indicate that, although a person's social environment might tempt him, society was not blamed for his sin—since he was free to resist temptation—but, all the same, his offense hurt the entire community.

Moreover, because man was made in God's image (Genesis 1:26), sin could easily upset the harmony of nature. According to Isaiah, "instead of the brier shall come up the myrtle tree . . . for an everlasting sign" (55:13); and "cursed is the ground for thy sake" (Genesis 3:17).

Nevertheless, it was possible for man's sins to be forgiven, as God is "merciful and gracious, longsuffering, and abundant in goodness" (Exodus 34:6).

In primitive times, human sacrifices were not unknown. Indeed, Exodus 22:29 states, "the firstborn of thy sons shalt thou give unto me." Thus, Mesha "took his eldest son that should have reigned in his stead, and offered him for a burnt offering" (II Kings 3:27). Similarly, Jephthah did with his daughter "according to his vow" (Judges 11:39), whereas "Abraham went and took the ram, and offered him up for a burnt offering in the stead of Isaac" (Genesis 23:13—cf. Greece's Agamemnon and Iphigenia).

Other sacrifices were known as guilt offering and included an atonement made by a priest if a man "sin, and commit a trespass against the Lord, and lie unto his neighbor . . ." (Leviticus 6:2).

The sin offering was aimed at purification from ritual, involuntary, and other similar offenses—for instance, after the birth of a child, "when the days of her purifying are fulfilled, for a son, or for a daughter, she shall bring a lamb of the first year for a burnt offering, and a young pigeon, or a turtledove, for a sin offering" (Leviticus 12:6). This practice was introduced in the days of Aaron: "thou shalt cause a bullock to be brought before the tabernacle of the congregation: and Aaron and his sons shall put their hands upon the head of the bullock" (Exodus 29:10).

The law of Moses, in general, placed greater emphasis on moral responsibility and dealt with a longer list of sins.

Unlike the priests, whose concern with ceremonial offenses was criticized by Jesus, the prophets discussed moral sins. Amos, for example, condemned injustice: "I know your manifold transgressions and your mighty sins: they afflict the just, they take a bribe, and they turn aside the poor in the gate from their right" (5:12).

In later times, the priests identified perfection with the observance of the law. This automatically made all outsiders sinners.

The apocalyptic order of the Essenes, who opposed all forms of secularization, "practiced baptism and other lustrations, symbolizing repentance from sins and purification of soul" (10).

Scapegoats and Sin Eaters

An interesting practice pertaining to sin, which has given us the word "scapegoat," is described in Leviticus 16:7-9, 21-22, 26, as follows: "he shall take the two goats, and present them before the Lord at the door of the tabernacle of the congregation. And Aaron shall cast lots upon the two goats; one lot for the Lord, and the other lot for the scapegoat. And Aaron shall bring the goat upon which the Lord's lot fell, and offer him for a sin offering. . . . And Aaron shall lay both his hands upon the head of the live goat, and confess over him all the iniquities of the children of Israel, and all their transgressions in all their sins, putting them upon the head of the goat, and shall send him away by the hand of a fit man into the wilderness: And the goat shall bear upon him all their iniquities unto a land not inhabited: and he shall let go the goat in the wilderness. . . . And he that let go the goat for the scapegoat shall wash his clothes, and bathe his flesh in water, and afterward come into the camp."

Actually, "scapegoat," which is *caper emissarius* in Jerome's Vulgate and *bouc émissaire* in French, is a translation of the Hebrew *azazel*. The modern term was introduced by William Tindale (1484-1536), the English translator of the Bible. The Hebrew word, however, seems to mean "goat for Azazel," a desert demon. In Islamic mythology, Azazel has been described as a jin of the wilderness, while John Milton used this name for the standard-bearing leader of the fallen angels (*Paradise Lost*, I, 534). Among Christians, Jesus himself has been identified as a "divine scapegoat," since he took upon himself the sins of mankind.

This ceremony, which has been common in many parts of the world, is still found among some peoples (11). Similarly, "savage tribes have been known to slaughter an animal on the grave, in the belief that it would take upon itself the sins of the dead" (12). In Borneo, however, the natives have annually transferred their sins to a boat, which was then launched in the ocean. An analogous method was customary in Japan, where those "desiring to purify themselves took a bit of paper and rubbed it over the entire body. Then these papers were collected, placed in a paper boat, and with appropriate ceremony were sent away to sea" (13).

According to Howlett and many other scholars, it was the Hebrew scapegoat that gradually led to England's *sin eater* (14) (that sin eating developed from a cannibal ritual during which the mourners ate the corpse is a theory that has been rejected almost universally). An author has described the sin eater as "long, lean, ugly, lamentable," and sin eating as follows: "Bread and beer were passed to the man over the corpse, or laid on it; these he consumed, and by this process was supposed to take on him all the sins of the deceased, and free the defunct person from walking after death" (15). The custom was continued up to the 17th century, but as late as 1825, Professor Evans of the Presbyterian College studied the case of an English sin eater (16). The famous story of *The Sin Eater* (1895), by Fiona Macleod (pseudonym of William Sharp of Paisley, a novelist), was based on such cases. Sin eating is also mentioned by Mary Webb of Shropshire in her 1924 novel, *Precious Bane,* which won the Femina-Vie Heureuse Prize. Finally, some social historians have seen a connection between this practice and the drinking and eating at Irish wakes.

THE GREEKS

Terms for "Sin"

As in the case of Hebrew, premodern Greek included many words for sin.

The Septuagint and the New Testament, however, usually employed *hamartia* (missing the mark, wrongdoing) and *anomia* (lawlessness, violation of the law).

Other terms were *adicia,* unrighteousness; *agnoema,* error; *asebeia,* impiety; *epithymia,* lust; *hamartema,* sin, disobedience to the divine law; *hettema,* defeat, fault; *parabasis,* transgression; *paracoe,* failing to hear, disobedience; *paranomia,* lawlessness; *paraptoma,* a falling away; and *poneria,* depravity.

Human Sacrifices

In very ancient times, human sacrifices were not disapproved by Greek religion.

The most famous case, which recalls Isaac and Jephthah's daughter among the Hebrews, is that of Iphigenia. According to the tragedian Euripides (485-406 B.C.), the seer Calchas advised her father Agamemnon that Artemis would not allow the Greek ships to sail against Troy unless Iphigenia was sacrificed on the altar of the goddess of chase (*Iphigenia in Taurica,* 10-24). Another tragedian, Sophocles (496-406 B.C.), informs us that Agamemnon's sin was that, "while playing in the grove of the goddess, he frightened an antlered stag with spotted hide, and, as he shot it, he boasted loudly" (*Electra,* 566-569). The words of the chorus in the *Agamemnon* of the tragedian Aeschylus (525-456 B.C.) indicate that the young princess was actually sacrificed: "the things that happened next neither did I see nor do I tell; the arts of Calchas were not ignored. Justice tends to teach wisdom through suffering" (248-251). Euripides, however, has Iphigenia declare: "But Artemis stole me and, giving to the Achaeans a hind instead of me, sent me through the clear air to dwell in this Taurian land" (*op. cit.,* 28-30). Some evolution in punishing sins is revealed by the words of Athena, the goddess of wisdom, which refer to the new shrine of Halae after Iphigenia's return to Attica. Indeed, the more symbolic and less barbarous sacrifices, which involved the spilling of a few drops of blood only, are described in this way: "When the people observe a festival, in quittance for your slaughter, one must touch a man's throat with the sword and draw out the blood" (*ibid.,* 1458-1460).

Orphism

This ancient religion was the first Greek faith that had both a founder and texts of doctrines. The founder was Orpheus, perhaps a real Thracian, who lived in archaic times, while the texts were the celebrated Orphic poems, the greatest of which was the *Rhapsodic Theogony.*

The god of the Orphists was remarkable. Even Clement of Alexandria (150-215 A.D.), the Athenian theologian who often attacked Orphism vehemently, praised Orpheus for composing verses which described a god similar to that of the Christians: "There is one, self-created; from one all things proceed; and in these he moves around; none of the mortals sees him, but he sees all" *(Exhortation to the Greeks,* 64). Moreover, it seems that Plato (429-347 B.C.) was referring to an Orphic verse when he wrote: "God, according to an old saying, holds the beginning and the end and the middle of all things" *(Laws,* 715d). The old Orphic saying was the following: "Zeus in the beginning, Zeus in the middle, and from Zeus all things proceed."

As for human nature, the Orphists believed that it is both good and evil. According to Plato, they called the body *sema,* that is, an evil tomb, the soul being man's divine part which is liberated in the next world. Aristophanes (450-385 B.C.), the Athenian comedian, based some of his verses on this belief: "Men, leading a dark life below, similar to leaves, feeble, creatures of clay, shadowlike and spiritless tribes, wingless, ephemeral, suffering mortals, dreamlike people" *(Birds,* 605-607). Some say that Plato's famous allegory of the cave, dealing with human nature and education, was also borrowed from Orphism *(Republic,* 514-518). The great importance of this allegory is indicated by the following: first, it inspired Francis Bacon's "idols of the cave"; second, Thomas Huxley's discussion of "Jack and the Beanstalk," in his *Evolution and Ethics* (1893), is related to the same idea; third, when Sir Arthur Eddington made his well-known statement about a universe of shadows and the new physics, he was very close to this Orphic-Platonic concept; fourth, some have seen the beginning of the fourth dimension in this theory; and fifth, Carl Jung employed the allegory in his *Analytical Psychology.*

The Christian belief in life after death, plus salvation or punishment, was also taken from the Orphists, who had contributed this rather original doctrine—incidentally, wall paintings containing the image of the poet Orpheus were not unusual in the catacombs. In fact, the Christians merely added the idea of purgatory to the old Orphic dogma. Then, when Plato writes, "it is necessary to descend" (*Republic,* 520c), he is paraphrasing the Orphic "descent into Hades." Something analogous is mentioned by Pausanias, the Greek geographer of the second century A.D., namely, "the Lacedaemonians say that the cult of Demeter of the Lower World was given to them by Orpheus" (*Laconia,* XIV, 5).

Acceptance of reincarnation was another Orphic principle. This is implied by Plato when he refers to a swan that used to be Orpheus (*Republic,* 620a).

Regarding sin and Orphism, Plato further speaks of "having only inanimate food, and, on the contrary, abstaining from animate things" (*Laws,* 782c-d). Indeed, killing animals and eating their flesh were two of the most serious sins. The same philosopher informs us that the Orphists had developed ceremonies aimed at "the remissions of sins and purifications for unjust acts, by means of sacrifices . . . for those still living, and there are ceremonies . . . for the dead which deliver us from the evils of the next world, while dreadful things await those who have not sacrificed" (*Republic,* 364e-365a) —cf. Homer's reference to sacrifices and libations "when a man transgresses and sins" (*Iliad,* IX, 501).

Sin and Vampirism in Pagan and Christian Greece

There are literally thousands of documents dealing with this fascinating subject. One of the main ideas which these works emphasize is that certain deadly sins lead to some form of physical incorruptibility after death. The documents also reveal a definite association between classical themes and modern beliefs, as well as an evolutionary pattern in the sphere of doctrines concerning reward and punishment in the next world. In addition, most of these works stress the dreadful consequences of a curse that follows a heinous deed, but add that, even if a curse is not uttered, the penalty is still severe.

In prehistoric times, very few sins were mentioned in this connection. Chief among them was the slaying of a close relative. Hesiod, however, the didactic poet of the eighth century B.C., presented a somewhat longer list of offenses: stealing, doing wrong to a suppliant or a guest, sinning with a brother's wife, offending orphans, and abusing an old father (*Works and Days,* 321-332). He then advised, "sacrifice to the immortal gods purely and cleanly" (336-337). Aeschylus, on the other hand, discussed many more sins, but placed greater emphasis on the killing of close relatives and on miasma, or pollution. As time went on, the list of transgressions became much longer and included all forms of murder.

In Christian Greece, the Church expanded the list further, and reiterated more ominously that a curse was not necessary for a sinner's soul to be tormented after death. All violations of the "divine law" were mentioned. But as the number of punishable offenses increased, the Church, being the judge, understandably began to speak less of automatic punishment, and more of formal ecclesiastical excommunication. It is interesting to note that many of Aeschylus' ideas regarding sin are found in the Church's *Nomocanon,* an anthology of imperial laws and ecclesiastical canons (circa 600 A.D.).

In modern Greece, the belief in vampires, or *brycolaces,* was common, as is indicated by works such as *De Graecorum Hodie Quorundam Opinationibus* (1645), by Leo Allatius, a Greek historian and theologian (17). In fact, by the second half of the 18th century, the subject had become so popular throughout Europe that many theological treatises were written about it in German universities, particularly in Leipzig, for example, John Zopft's *Dissertatio de Vampiris Serviensibus,* Halle, 1733. As has already been mentioned, this theme is ancient—the Church simply increased the number of sins in this connection. Indeed, some of the most powerful, macabre, and frightful lines in all literature dealing with this theme are found in the *Eumenides* of Aeschylus, where the mother slayer is threatened thus: "You must pay! I will suck the red gore from your living limbs. I will feed on you—a fiendish feast! And when you have withered, I will drag you living down to hell so that you may pay for your murdered mother's anguish" (264-268). Similarly, those who slay close relatives are pursued by the Furies mercilessly and relentlessly "until they pass beneath the earth; and after death, there is not much liberty. Over our victim consecrate, this is our song: full of frenzy, full of rage, breaking the brain, the hymn of the Furies, magic to manacle the mind, untuned to the lyre, withering the life of mortals" (338-346).

Another pattern in this evolution involves the consequences of violent death and lack of burial. In other words, it seems that in antiquity, as in modern times, it has been the masses that have accepted the corporeal return of the deceased. The educated classes, however, have adopted a symbolic and more abstract principle, namely, the spiritual reentry of the dead into the visible world. Furthermore, acceptance of both beliefs has generally been inversely proportional to the advancement of education and science. The least obvious element in this generalization is that the intellectuals of classical times accepted the return of the spirit only. Nevertheless, ancient literature is replete with relevant evidence. Homer, for instance, describes Elpenor, the companion of Odysseus, as follows: "And first came the spirit of my comrade Elpenor; for he had not been buried yet" (*Odyssey,* XI, 51-52). About Patroclus, the friend of Achilles, the epic poet adds: "then came to him the spirit of hapless Patroclus, in all things looking exactly like him, in size and fair eyes, and in voice" (*Iliad,* XXIII, 65-67). In the *Eumenides* of Aeschylus, it is the spirit of Clytaemnestra, the wife of Agamemnon, that complains: "It is because of you that I am thus dishonored among the dead" (95-96). Then, in the *Hecuba* of Euripides, the volitant phantom of Polydorus, prince of Troy, laments: "unwept, tombless; and now over my dear mother Hecuba I flit, having left my body, hovering for three days" (30-32). Plato himself writes that it is the spirits of sinners that return after death: "such a soul is weighed down and pulled back to the visible world . . . wandering about the monuments and the tombs, where the shadowy phantoms of souls have actually been seen" (*Phaedo,* 81c-d). The *Philopseudes* of Lucian of Samosata (second century A.D.) reflects the belief that "only the souls of those who died violently wander" (29). Under the influence of the Greeks, Vergil (70-19 B.C.) states that "when cold death has separated soul from body, my shadow will haunt you in every place" (*Aeneid,* IV, 385-386). And so on. Finally, it is significant that passages indicating the opposite are not only exceedingly rare, but also relatively nebulous and indirect. Orestes and Electra, for example, beg their dead father Agamemnon thus: "Give me the lordship over your halls. And I, too, father, request the same of you" (Aeschylus, *Libation-Bearers,* 488-481). Electra also pleads: "and, falling upon your knees, ask him to come himself from the dead as our gracious ally against the enemies" (Sophocles, *Electra,* 453-454).

THE NEW TESTAMENT

To the Old Testament concept of sin the New Testament added three main ideas: first, sin as an individual act; second, as a condition; and third, as a force.

Jesus

The teachings of Jesus himself may be summarized thus:

The legalistic definition of sin by the scribes and Pharisees was condemned repeatedly: "ye reject the commandments of God, that ye may keep your own traditions" (Mark 7:9).

More common was his familial conception of sin, as is indicated by the parables of the prodigal son and the good Samaritan, and by his emphasis on God as a father and on all men as brothers.

To a certain degree, sin is innate: "That which is born of the flesh is flesh; and that which is born of the Spirit is spirit" (John 3:6).

The seat of sin is the heart: "Do men gather grapes of thorns, or figs of thistles?" (Matthew 7:16).

Sin appears to be more moral and less theological than in the Old Testament: "Inasmuch as ye did it not to one of the least of these, ye did it not to me" (Matthew 25:45); and "If a man say, I love God, and hateth his brother, he is a liar" (I John 4:20).

Similarly, conscience becomes more prevalent now than it was in Old

Testament times: "Beware of false prophets, which come to you in sheep's clothing, but inwardly they are ravening wolves" (Matthew 7:15); and if "the light that is in thee be darkness, how great is that darkness!" (6:23).

Both action and intention are taken into consideration: "first be reconciled to thy brother, and then come and offer thy gift" (Matthew 5:24).

Still, it is not frequently that the psychology of sin is discussed.

Personal responsibility for one's own sins is a dominant idea.

Sin is a type of slavery: "Whosoever committeth sin is the servant of sin" (John 8:34).

The immediate causes of sin are at least six: a) Satan: "He that committeth sin is of the devil" (I John 3:8), or "then cometh the devil, and taketh away the word out of their hearts" (Luke 8:12); b) mammon: "what shall I do? . . . I cannot dig; to beg I am ashamed" (16:13); c) desire: "when lust hath conceived, it bringeth forth sin" (James 1:15); d) weakness: "the spirit truly is ready, but the flesh is weak" (Mark 14:38); e) the will: "How often would I have gathered my children together . . . and ye would not!" (Matthew 23:37); and f) scandal: "And whosoever shall offend one of these little ones . . . it is better for him that a millstone were hanged about his neck" (Mark 9:42).

Although "thou art made whole: sin no more, lest a worse thing come unto thee" (John 5:14), Jesus opposed the Old Testament belief that physical suffering is generated by sin. His statement about the man who was born blind is more typical: "Neither hath this man sinned, nor his parents: but that the works of God should be made manifest in him" (9:3).

A person's sins tend to influence others. Even Jesus himself could be affected: "thou art an offence unto me" (Matthew 16:23).

With reference to forgiveness, Jesus rejected the contractual and quantitative concept of sin that dominated the Old Testament: "O thou wicked servant, I forgave thee all that debt" (Matthew 18:32).

As the same verse indicates, more startling and revolutionary was his emphasis on the value of asking forgiveness: "I forgave the . . . because thou desiredst me" (cf. the parable of the prodigal son).

It is love that can solve the problem of sin: "Thou shalt love the Lord. . . . Thou shalt love thy neighbour" (Matthew 22:37, 39).

Paul

St. Paul's writings on sin constitute the most systematic theology of this subject found in the New Testament. Virtually all of this theology is presented in the introductory section of Romans. His main thoughts in this area were as follows:

He usually preferred three terms: *hamartia,* with the definite article, or sin as a general state (Romans 5:12); and *hamartema,* or a sinful deed

(I Corinthians, 6:18), and *parabasis,* or transgression (Romans 4:15), both as an individual act.

His typical definition of sin emphasized anti-God attitudes and actions: "the carnal mind is enmity against God" (Romans 8:7).

Unlike the authors of the Old Testament, who took the serpent's existence for granted, Paul concentrated on Adam's fall: "by one man's disobedience many were made sinners" (Romans 5:19). However, his etiological analysis of this extremely difficult problem remained incomplete—Soren Kierkegaard's *Concept of Dread,* 1844, is one of the best discussions of this subject. Of course, Paul, too, spoke of the "man of sin" (II Thessalonians 2:3) as one of the causes of sinful conduct—by this he usually meant the Antichrist. Another cause is the flesh, which, in Paul's writings, ordinarily represents human nature: "they that are after the flesh do mind the things of the flesh" (Romans 8:5).

In the conflict between reason and the flesh, which is the seat of sin, defeat is not inevitable; for Paul, more than any other New Testament author, stressed victory through Jesus.

Freedom of choice is not excluded completely.

The flesh and the universality of death—which results from sin—explain why sin is universal: "death passed upon all men . . . all have sinned (Romans 5:12). Besides, since he was eager to spread the gospel beyond the Jewish nation, and since he constantly mentioned God's grace in relation to forgiveness, Paul could only assert: "There is none righteous"; "we have before proved both Jews and Gentiles, that they are all under sin" (3:9-10).

His famous list of sins included seventeen items, but he added "and such like"—"Adultery, fornication, uncleanness, lasciviousness, idolatry, witchcraft, hatred, variance, emulations, wrath, strife, seditions, heresies, envyings, murders, drunkenness, revellings, and such like" (Galatians 5:19-21).

Although its vague beginning may be found in Jesus and the Old Testament, one may aver that the celebrated *peccatum originis,* or original sin, for which Christ was sacrificed, was really invented by Paul: "the scripture hath included all under sin, that the promise by faith of Jesus Christ might be given to them that believe" (Galatians 3:22); and "by one man's disobedience many were made sinners" (Romans 5:19). This hereditary association between sin and Adam was developed more specifically by later theologians. Paul's further belief that original sin leads to concupiscence renders his theory of sinful behavior rather psychological.

Sin causes both physical and spiritual death: "in Adam all die" (I Corinthians 15:22); and "the end of these things is death" (Romans 6:21). Moreover, sin affects the entire cosmos, since man is God's vice-regent: "the creature was made subject to vanity . . . the whole creation groaneth and travaileth in pain" (8:20,22). Incidentally, it was his well-known statement, "the wages of sin is death" (6:23), that gave us the phrase, "to earn the wages of sin."

Paul rejected the Jews' ethnocentrism, which consisted in dividing mankind into Jews and sinners; for observance of the law cannot save the world.

On the contrary, without explaining the process, he added that only Jesus could save all men: "Christ, who gave himself for our sins, that he might deliver us from this present evil world" (Galatians 1:3-4).

POST-OLD TESTAMENT JUDAISM

In general, the Jews have regarded being aware of the sinful act and knowing its wrong nature as necessary components of sin. Furthermore, one of their basic classifications of wicked conduct has been sins against God only and sins against man. Of these, the first may be atoned by means of charity, prayer, repentance, and the like, while the second category requires an additional element, namely, that the victim has forgiven the sinner. Still, there is no sin that cannot be forgiven, since God's power to forgive is unlimited, whereas man's ability to transgress has certain limits.

At least two main principles concerning sin distinguish the Jews from the Christians. First, the Roman Catholic idea of confession is rejected; for sins must be confessed only to God, not to other humans. It is also significant that the Jews' public confession stresses the collective aspect: "We have sinned," not "I have sinned." Second, although it is admitted that Adam's sin had added a hereditary weakness to human nature, the concept of original sin is not really accepted by the Jews. Besides, at Mt. Sinai, Jehovah's people had become sinless once more, but sin returned to mankind through the image of the Golden Calf.

Today, the Jews of the United States still disapprove of the theory of original sin and stress salvation without any kind of human mediation. More significantly, they have discarded all traditional concepts of heaven and hell, and, instead, identify these two states with a terrestrial good life, or evil life, respectively. Similar ideas were expressed even many centuries ago by one of the greatest Jewish philosophers, Maimonides (1135-1204) — this is true of his later works, not of his "Thirteen Articles of Faith," primarily Article 11, which he wrote at the age of twenty.

The Talmud

The title of this great compilation of Jewish law and tradition is Hebrew and means "instruction." The work consists of two parts, the Mishnah (Repetition), which was published by Judah the Prince (135-217 A.D.) and his students, and the Gemara (Learning), which constitutes a commentary on the Mishnah. Its two editions are the Jerusalem or Palestinian Talmud, completed in 450 A.D., and the four times longer Babylonian Talmud, which was finished about fifty years later. The Talmudists' beliefs about sin are found in the following representative comments.

Since virtue is acceptance of the Torah (the Five Books of Moses and the Talmud), sin is a rebellion against the Lord by disobeying his will, which is revealed in the Torah. Such disobedience is more serious when a human being is wronged than when a precept that merely affects the God-man relationship is violated.

Regarding some of the causes of sin, the Talmud declares: "A man does not commit a transgression unless a spirit of madness has entered into him" (Sotah 3a); and "Be not wrathful and you will not sin; be not intoxicated and you will not sin" (Berachoth 29b).

As for human nature, the Talmud is replete with contradictions. In the second half of the first century B.C., for instance, Hillel I and Shammai agreed that man is essentially sinful. Then, when certain rabbis averred that the first patriarchs were sinless, another objected that, if God "had entered into judgment with Abraham, Isaac, and Jacob, they would not have been able to stand against the reproof" (Arachin 17a). Berachoth 4d, however, suggests that it is possible for humans to be sinless: "Happy the man whose hour of death is like the hour of his birth; as at his birth he is free of sin, so at his death may he be free of sin."

This last statement further indicates that the concept of original sin is rejected. Similarly, the Talmud speaks of "A child aged one year who has not tasted sin" (Joma 22b). It is true, of course, that the Talmudists agreed that Adam's disobedience made death universal, and that "There is no generation in which there is not an ounce from the sin of the Golden Calf" (Taanith 68c). Still, instead of stressing inheritance in this area, the rabbis constantly referred to man's free will and personal responsibility.

Because of certain persecutions, an early Jewish synod decided that the three most serious sins—a person should die rather than commit them— are "idolatry, unchastity, and bloodshed" (Sanhedrin 74a). Peah 15d adds a fourth, namely, slander.

This last is exceedingly serious. In fact, God took draconian measures against it: "I have surrounded you with two walls," he says to the tongue, "one of bone and the other of flesh" (Arachin 15b). Megillah 18a further states: "A word for a *sela*, silence for two" (*sela* means a coin). It is no wonder, then, that slander is called *lishan telitae*, or third tongue—because "it slays three persons: the speaker, the spoken to, and the spoken of" (Arachin 15b).

The rules regarding sex are extremely strict: "A man should never walk behind a woman along the road, even his own wife. . . . A man should walk behind a lion rather than behind a woman" (Berachoth 61a). Similarly, adultery—even lusting with one's eyes—is virtually synonymous with denying God's existence.

If a man were sinless, he would never die, since sin leads to death: "There is no death without sin" (Shabbath 55a).

To avoid sin, one should have pure thoughts and engage in honest labor. Reading the Torah is especially helpful: "I have created the evil impulse," God says, "and I have created the Torah as an antidote to sin" (Kiddushin 30b). When this antidote does not work, one must pray, but if this, too, fails, speculating on death should prove to be more effective (Berachoth 5a). If, however, all this does not generate righteous conduct, one should dress in black and go and sin where one is unknown (Chagigah 16a). Needless to add, such behavior will still be sinful.

The psychology of reinforcement is found in many Talmudic passages; for instance: "If a man commit an offense and repeat it, it becomes to him something permitted" (Joma 86b).

The Cabala and the Zohar

The cabala (Hebrew for "tradition") is a theosophical and theurgical system that developed in France and Spain between the 7th and 18th centuries. Its climax was the Zohar (Hebrew for "splendor"), a mystical commentary on the Five Books of Moses, probably written by the Spanish cabalist Moses de Leon (1250-1305).

The Zohar takes the existence of sin for granted and personifies it in Samael, or "Venom of God," who is the prince of death and evil spirits (2:34b). The book explains that God permits the existence of such forces for the sake of testing man's moral strength (2:163a).

This classic further states that man has three souls: first, *neshamah,* the divine soul which never sins; second, *nefesh,* the natural soul which can sin and, therefore, may be punished in the next world—the third soul may also be punished there; and third, *ruah,* the spirit which gives life and inspiration to man (1:81b, 206a; 2:141b; 3:70b).

Het kadmon, the cabalists' original sin, disrupts the harmony of the cosmos in Old Testament fashion (1:12b). The extreme view thus is that man's history is a struggle to return to the sinlessness that characterized the world before Adam's fall.

ISLAM

The Moslems have usually distinguished two kinds of sins: first, *kabirah,* or great, sins—the sinner who does not repent is sent to purgatorial hell;

and second, *saghirah,* or little, sins—these are of the venial type and result from man's fallen nature.

Ordinarily, the *kabirah* list includes seventeen items: infidelity, disobedience to parents, committing venial sins habitually, despairing of God's mercy, disregarding God's wrath, cowardice in battle, magic, false witness, false oath, accusing an innocent Moslem of adultery, adultery, drinking wine, theft, usury, taking the property of orphans, murder, and unnatural crime.

Another famous statement recommends that the followers of Mohammed (570-632 A.D.) "Abstain from seven destructive things, namely, associating anything with God, magic, killing anyone without reason, taking interest on money, taking the property of the orphan, running away on the day of battle, and charging an innocent woman with adultery" (Mishkat 1:2) .

EARLY CHRISTIANITY

It seems safe to assert that the main innovation of Christian theology was a large number of formal distinctions, since its basic ideas had already been stated, directly or indirectly, in the Bible. "The theme of human imperfection," for instance, "is sharply accented in Judaism and became the basis of the Christian doctrine of sin" (18) .

Another author has stated that, while Christianity "made the first attempt to unfetter women by preaching equality between the sexes, it also introduced the concept of sin into love" (19) . It is interesting to note, however, that adultery and fornication were ordinarily condemned less than other sexual offenses, for example, zoophilia, since the former are physically identical to conjugal coition, and that adultery was considered more serious than fornication, obviously because marital infidelity effects property matters.

As for the Romans' influence in this area, we are told that the sadistic element in their civilization "was bound up with sexual guilt, and in their culture we can see the first glimmerings" of certain aspects of the Christian concept of sin (20) . In other words, such guilt generated a strict code of ethics which was imposed on the liberal peoples of Europe. Accordingly, the sexual energy of the masses "was transformed into every kind of undesirable form of psychoneurotic behavior—hysterical attacks, erotic illusions, incubi and succubi, witch-hunts and witchcraft (in that sequence) , flagellomania, psychic impotence, etc." (21) .

All this gradually led to the development of soteriology, namely, the theological discipline dealing with man's salvation. In general, the following are the most characteristic ideas concerning the concept of sin in early Christian times:

Irenaeus (130-200 A.D.). The bishop of Lyons discussed original sin in a manner that recalls St. Paul's assertions.

Tertullian (160-220 A.D.). Like Paul and Irenaeus, this African church father merely identified Adam with his descendants rather mystically, without even attempting to explain the transmission of original sin. He further averred that grave sins committed after one's baptism could be forgiven only once—this extreme viewpoint was later rejected by most theologians.

Hermas (2nd century A.D.). A similar philosophy regarding postbaptismal sins was formulated by Hermas—a slave owned by a Roman lady —who wrote *The Shepherd*.

Athanasius (296-373 A.D.). In his *De Incarnatione,* the patriarch of Alexandria introduced the idea that Adam's fall, namely, his misuse of human freedom, resulted in mankind's reduction to a natural state. He was also convinced that, both before and after Christ, some men were sinless.

Ambrosiaster. It is now certain that, despite what most medieval authors believed, Ambrosiaster, who wrote the famous collection of Latin commentaries on Paul, was not the same as Ambrose (339-397 A.D.). In this collection, we read that mankind's unity is found in Adam's fall itself, as well as in its results. Moreover, the transmission of original sin is explained in terms of natural generation. (Here the influence of Romans 5:12 is obvious: "as by one man sin entered into the world, and death by sin; and so death passed upon all men.")

Pelagius (400 A.D.). The most violent logomachy about original sin was initiated by Morgan, or Pelagius, a British (perhaps Irish) monk, against whom St. Augustine wrote *De Peccatorum Meritis et Remissione* (411 A.D.). The Pelagian heresy included the following ideas: first, the freedom of the will and individual responsibility are too important and real to disregard; second, Adam's mortality existed even before his fall; third, his transgression affected himself, but not his descendants—man merely follows Adam's wicked example and perpetuates it habitually; fourth, infants are born sinless; fifth, man's mortality did not result from Adam's disobedience; sixth, Jesus' resurrection will not be accompanied by man's resurrection; and seventh, even in pre-Christian times some men were perfect. Needless to add, all this still remains an abstruse and recondite problem in logic and theology.

St. Augustine (354-430 A.D.). The rather Platonic bishop of Hippo, who attacked the Manichean theory of sin and thus influenced medieval theology considerably, defined sinful conduct as "any thought, word, or deed opposed to God's law." Unlike Pelagius, he further believed that man's moral disability is complete. He also distinguished two kinds of sins, namely, *mortalia seu capitalia* and *levia.*

In general, his chief contributions to the theology of sin were two. First, he formulated "the doctrine of the decrees, by which he asserted that God foreordained some to salvation and some to eternal loss" (22).

His second contribution, which renders the church's services necessary, dealt with original sin more extensively than all previous theories. His contention was that, since infants themselves have not committed any sins, since the Church baptizes infants, and since baptism purifies from sin, it is obvious that sin must be inherited from Adam. In his *Simplicianus* (397), he explains this by emphasizing concupiscence, which diminishes the freedom of choice and changes the human race into a *massa damnata*. Lust itself makes coitus sinful, since it frees the reproductive organs at the expense of the will. According to his *On Marriage and Concupiscence*, "That alone was not sinful flesh which was not born of such concubinage" (I, 13).

MEDIEVAL CHRISTIANITY

The early Christians had already established original sin as a fact. In medieval times, therefore, theologians discussed primarily its nature and inheritance.

As was mentioned previously, the Church adopted the Orphic doctrine concerning the next world and gradually contributed one main element to it, purgatory. This involved the purification of venial, or pardonable, sins through prayers, good works, and the like.

As time went on, however, the early Christian belief in salvation by simple faith in Jesus was replaced by a formalized, ritualized, legalized, and institutionalized penitential system, which stressed forgiveness through the sacraments, chiefly baptism. In other words, sin became more external now, and its purification necessitated an amount of penance directly proportional to its seriousness. This system finally developed into the most important source of ecclesiastical power.

Anselm of Canterbury (1033-1109). Unlike St. Augustine's followers, the archbishop who became famous for his ontological argument for God's existence divorced original sin from concupiscence, thus anticipating scholastic philosophy. Furthermore, he averred that mankind's seminal presence in Adam explains why original sin is inherited in the process of generation.

Albert the Great (1200-1280). In dealing with original sin, the brilliant Dominican philosopher, who was known as *Doctor universalis,* contributed a formal component, that is, privation of original righteousness. This he opposed to concupiscence, which is the material element.

Thomas Aquinas (1225-1274). According to his *Summa Theologica* and

De Malo, St. Thomas saw two elements in Adam's state before his transgression. One was his *pura naturalia,* or pure nature, which had been perfected by the second component, namely, his supernatural gifts. The loss of these gifts constitutes original sin, which is inherited through generation. Much less pessimistically than St. Augustine, he added that man's will and reason have retained their natural powers.

Some of the Angelic Doctor's most famous statements about sin are the following: "Sins are not imputed to people out of their mind" (*Summa Theologica,* II-II, Question 142, Article 3); "The sins that do personal hurt are more grievous than sins against property" (Question 73, Article 3); "A man must not commit one sin to avoid another" (Question 113, Article 1); and "When a whole people sins, vengeance is to be taken upon them" (Question 108, Article 1).

RENAISSANCE AND REFORMATION

The Renaissance rejected the idea of purgatory, while the Protestants abandoned Pelagianism, the external view of sinful conduct, and the concept of man's dual nature. Instead, they followed St. Augustine and stressed the radical sinfulness of the human race. They also tended to define sin in terms of various local customs and mores.

Martin Luther (1483-1546). Since Luther identified original sin with concupiscence, and since he asserted that Adam's fall annihilated man's freedom entirely, and even that its consequences were not eliminated by baptism, his theory of sin may be described as extremely pessimistic. Nevertheless, his emphasis on *justificatio* (justification) indicates that, in Luther's theology, because of God's mercy and Jesus' sacrifice, a man's sins may go unpunished. This is possible on the basis of *sola fides* (faith alone).

Luther's association of sin with Satan is revealed by the fact that, as he often confessed, he "lived in a constant consciousness of contact and opposition to the Devil" (23). This partly explains why, in a famous caricature, "the bloated head of Luther, stored with naught but wind, is represented as a fitting object for the Devil's bagpipes" (24).

John Calvin (1509-1564). Equally pessimistic was Calvin, the French theologian who wrote *Institutes of the Christian Religion.* His doctrine of predestination included the dreadful results of sinful conduct, while his arguments concerning original sin were similar to Luther's.

John Milton (1608-1674). In a myth that recalls the birth of Athena, the English poet identifies sin with a woman who sprang from Satan's head and now guards hell's gates. In *Paradise Lost,* which, like his *Paradise Regained,* was inspired by the Bible, the woman is described as follows:

> The one seemed Woman to the waist, and fair,
> But ending foul in many a scaly fold
> Voluminous and vast, a Serpent armed
> With mortal sting (II, 650-653).

Jacques Bossuet (1627-1704). Like St. Augustine, the French bishop of Meaux dealt with original sin rather pessimistically.

EARLY MODERN TIMES

English Puritanism "emphasized the danger of sin attached to love with all the implications of eternal damnation and endless suffering for the unrepentant" (25). The similar ideas of American Puritanism found their best expression in the tragic lives of Hester Prynne; her lover, Arthur Dimmesdale; and their child, Pearl (in Nathaniel Hawthorne's most famous work, *The Scarlet Letter,* 1850).

Beginning with the 18th century, however, the doctrine of sin was developed less and less. Enlightenment leaders like Gotthold Lessing (1729-1781), for instance, conceived of sin less religiously and more morally and philosophically, stressed reason at the expense of supernaturalism, and advocated secularism, religious toleration, and happiness in this world. Some of these ideas are seen in Lessing's *Nathan der Weise* (1779), especially in the character of the benevolent and gentle Jew of Jerusalem and his answer to Saladin in the form of the beautiful story of the ring—it is no wonder that the Nazi regime banned the drama!

Such rationalism, reinforced by modern science, gradually made the doctrine of original sin much less tenable, particularly among liberal Protestants. Most Roman Catholics, however, and Karl Barth, the Swiss dialectical theologian who wrote *The Word of God and the Word of Man* (1928), have defended various traditional aspects of this doctrine.

In 1798, Thomas Malthus, an English clergyman and economist, published *The Essay on the Principle of Population.* Its author asserts that sociopolitical revolutions will not eliminate sin, and recommends sexual abstinence and prohibition of marriage among the lower classes.

In the 19th century, the prevailing optimism and liberalism made the concept of sin secondary, if not tertiary, in most theological thinking. More ascetic and conservative was Soren Kierkegaard, the philosopher-theologian of Copenhagen, who inspired Karl Barth's dialectical theology and Martin Heidegger's existentialism. In his *Begrebet Angest* (1844), Kierkegaard avers that *Angst,* or the feeling of dread, causes both sins of the flesh and sins of the spirit.

THE 20TH CENTURY

Some of the new ideas regarding sin are seen in the following developments.

Religio-psychiatry, one of the movements that appeared in the 20th century, deals "with the relation between religious and scientific approaches to mental, emotional, or spiritual healing" (26). Its clergymen and psychiatrists, who disapprove of traditional therapeutic techniques in their respective fields, prefer a curative system that is both psychiatric and religious. Quite significantly, certain Roman Catholics have distinguished "between 'scrupulosity,' a compulsive neurosis leading to detailed confessions of partly imagined misdeeds, and the appropriate confession of sin, a religious concern" (27).

In 1912, Frederick Tennant published *The Concept of Sin,* in which he contends that sin is relative. Two and a half decades later, Reinhold Niebuhr asserted that religion often promotes sin through its absolutistic conceptions (*Moral Man and Immoral Society,* 1936).

Additional developments indicate a new interest in salvation here and now by improving this world, and a change in emphasis from sins of the flesh to sins that are civic, political, psychological, and social. A few randomly selected examples should suffice.

The incomplete portal towers of the second largest church in the world, New York's Cathedral of St. John the Divine—which its Manhattan neighbors call "St. John the Unfinished"—reveals part of this change. Indeed, Bishop Donegan, influenced by the liberalism of modern theologians and current social conditions, is interested in present human needs rather than in spectacular cathedrals.

This gradual change becomes more obvious when we consider the still traditional rural South. One of the best descriptions of the fundamentalist churches and their revival meetings in this area is found in Erskine Caldwell's 1968 book, *Deep South.* Despite the fact that "rural camp-meetings have been replaced by brick-walled auditoriums and revival tents by rainproof sheds," writes the author of *Tobacco Road,* he still heard countless sermons damning sins of the flesh, and saw numerous congregations engaging in glossolalia. He further found that salvation has nothing to do with prejudice against the Negro, and that Biblical miracles—from the creation of the universe in six days to Jesus' walking on water—are interpreted literally, not symbolically.

Many men and women, however, would agree with the San Diego youth who wrote: this is "the death of the church. The young people with whom I communicate do not want a reformed church, a free church or an open church. They don't want any church, because they have grown free enough, mature enough not to need it. They have the best of its values without its fears, its hang-ups, its commitments to bastard structures. They can live honestly in or out of community, deal with present poverty, suffering, injustice—without the church. The liberals who suggest a church without compelling dogmas, stifling rituals and unreal moral codes will find that such a church already exists. It's called the world, and its adherents are called men" (28).

Less radical, but still modern, were the attitudes of the delegates to the 180th General Assembly of the United Presbyterian Church, in May 1968. Besides recommending that their church donate fabulous funds to satisfy some of the needs of the poor, the delegates adopted a communion litany that was somewhat ecumenical and stressed civic sins: "Forgive us for pretending to care for the poor, when we do not like poor people and do not want them in our houses. Forgive us for bypassing political duties; for condemning civil disobedience when we will not obey You. Forgive us for cheering legislators who promise low taxes, but deny homes and schools and health to those in need. Forgive us when we deplore violence in our cities if we live in suburbs, where lawns are clipped and churches large." The delegates also commissioned a new hymn, "When the Changes Come," which included the following verses:

> Dusty creeds, lonely prayers,
> Where are you, where are you?
> At the edges of our sight,
> Visions taunt us in the night,
> Men kill other men at war.
> Hungry children lying on the floor.
> Religion won't protect us any more.

Various Faiths

Finally, here are the teachings of a random sample of faiths dealing with sin and salvation.

Agnostics

According to Bertrand Russell, the main ideas of agnosticism about this subject are six: first, the concept of sin is rejected; second, human conduct may be desirable or undesirable; third, punishment is not good in itself; fourth, the doctrine of hell is unacceptable, since it involves vindictive punishment; fifth, the traditional theology of sin is harmful; and sixth, punishment must be deterrent or reformatory (29).

Catholics

In general, Roman Catholicism has taught that the deliberate breaking of God's law leads to eternal damnation, but salvation may be achieved through good works and faith. Moreover, as "sin is removed from one cell of the Body, the rest of the Church profits accordingly. . . . What happens is not merely the checking of bad influence, in this case the effects of sin, but the transmission of new vitality in the form of grace from one part of the Church's body to all the others (30). Another feature of Catholicism is that its moral theology, especially since the 16th century, has developed a remarkable typology of sins—the mortal and venial kinds are the chief ones—as follows (not all types presented here are of Catholic origin; besides, despite the nature of this classification, it is not implied, for instance, that original sin and actual sin do not constitute an exhaustive dichotomy; also, although, as is indicated below, the terms "capital"—Latin *caput*, or head—"deadly," and "mortal" have sometimes been employed synonymously, such usage is technically inaccurate—still, in a study of the present nature, the popular aspects must not be neglected; then, there are the conflicting definitions and interpretations within one and the same religion or church; finally, such problems do not obscure the tendency to make punctilious distinctions among various forms of sin).

Original Sin. This is not a sin in itself, its main component being the loss of sanctifying grace, which is regained through baptism. According to the doctrine of "immaculate conception," however, Mary was kept free from original sin (Pius IX, *Ineffabilis Deus*, December 8, 1854).

Sins Against the Holy Ghost. There are six sins in this category, the unforgivable one being, in Matthew's words, "blasphemy against the Holy Ghost . . . it shall not be forgiven him, neither in this world, neither in the world to come" (12:31-32). This, St. Augustine interpreted as God's rejection even when death is near, namely, final impenitence. The forgivable sins against the Holy Ghost are presumption, despair, resistance to truth, obstinacy in sin, and envy.

Sins Crying to Heaven for Vengeance. These are four and involve our neighbors: willful murder (such as Cain's fratricide in Genesis 4:9-10: "Where is Abel thy brother? And he said, I know not: Am I my brother's keeper? And he said . . . thy brother's blood crieth unto me"); perversion, or the sin of Sodom ("the cry of Sodom and Gomorrah is great, and because their sin is very grievous," 18:20); oppression of the needy ("Thou shalt neither vex a stranger, nor oppress him. . . . Ye shall not afflict any widow, or fatherless child," Exodus 22:21-22); and keeping a worker's pay ("the hire of the labourers who have reaped down your fields, which is of you kept back by fraud, crieth," James 5:4).

Deadly Sins (also known as mortal or capital). This distinction is partly based on the one and only similar classification found in the New Testament: "There is a sin unto death: I do not say that he shall pray for it . . . and there is a sin not unto death" (I John 5:16-17). The Catholic list, however, was prepared by Pope Gregory the Great (590-604) and, despite Luther's opposition, was approved at the Sixth Session of the Council of Trent (1545-1563). The people's concern about the seven deadly sins in medieval times is partly revealed by *Le Livre de la Chasse,* a copy of which used to be owned by Spain's Ferdinand and Isabella but now is in Manhattan's The Cloisters. Gaston Phébus, the French knight who wrote this little masterpiece in 1387, says: "By hunting, one avoids the sin of sloth"; and, "According to our faith, he who avoids the seven mortal sins will be saved; therefore, the good sportsmen will be saved." This type of sin, which must be confessed to a priest when possible, may be defined as a grave transgression, involving full consent and knowledge, and leading to the loss of sanctifying grace and eternal damnation. The seven deadly sins are anger, avarice, envy, gluttony, lust, pride, and sloth.

Venial Sins. As their name indicates (Latin *venia:* pardon), such sins, unlike the deadly ones, result in a partial loss of sanctifying grace and, therefore, are pardonable, or may be purged in purgatory. Confession to a priest is not necessary.

Actual Sins. When a violation of God's law involves a thought, word, or deed, arises from the free will, and is one of malice or weakness, of commission or omission, or of ignorance, it is considered an actual sin.

Material Sins. Such offenses are sinful in themselves, but the sinner is not aware of their nature or he commits them involuntarily.

Formal Sins. These free and voluntary violations of ecclesiastical or divine laws include knowledge of their sinful nature, as well as their deliberate placing.

Sins by Silence. Referring mainly to property matters, such sins are committed when a person's silence promotes another's sinful behavior or does not diminish its harmful consequences.

Habitual Sins. Actual sins become habitual when repetition has reinforced them.

Disciples of Christ

Walter Scott (19th century), a relative of the great novelist, and the other founders of this faith rejected the concept of original sin completely.

Episcopalians

While a very nebulous idea about "purgatory" seems to have been retained by some of them, Episcopalians in general have abandoned "physical" resurrection as a reward and the traditional doctrine of heaven and hell—these are now regarded as states of being. Instead, religious conduct is rewarded not only in the next world, but also in the present one in the form of a wholesome life. Sin, on the other hand, is something similar to a sociopsychological "illness." The authors of the "Articles of Religion" have written: "Original sin standeth not in the following of Adam. . .but it is the fault and corruption of the Nature of every man, that naturally is engendered of the offspring of Adam" (IX) ; man "is such, that he cannot turn and prepare himself, by his own natural strength. . .to faith. . .without the grace of God" (X) ; "Not every deadly sin willingly committed after Baptism is sin against the Holy Ghost, and unpardonable" (XVI) ; and the "Doctrine concerning Purgatory. . .and also Invocation of Saints, is a fond thing, vainly invented, and grounded upon no warranty of Scripture" (XXII) .

Methodists

Besides many other ideas, this religion emphasizes John Wesley's (1703-1791) concept of "social holiness," namely, to love and serve mankind.

Presbyterians

No physical resurrection is possible. Moreover, sins cannot be forgiven through the mediation of a minister or priest, since between God and man there is only Christ.

Protestants (in general)

Unlike the Greek Orthodox and Roman Catholic Churches, almost all Protestant groups have discarded confession. Influenced by the natural and social sciences, they have also defined sin in rather modern ways, while some liberal branches now disregard virtually all traditional definitions of sin.

Quakers

Adam's transgression is not inherited, since man is good by nature and evil is not really prevalent. George Fox (1624-1691) himself spoke of an "ocean of light over the ocean of darkness."

Unitarians

Original sin, a physical heaven and hell, eternal damnation, and ecclesiastical ritualism aimed at salvation have no place in this faith. Yes, evil does exist in our world, but a great deal of it has been caused by man himself, who, influenced by heredity and environment, is potentially good and evil, as well as individually responsible. Since salvation is identified with the creation of a peaceful and just society by means of scientific knowledge and superior moral values, one may aver that, to a great extent, the ideals of Unitarianism are expressed by Edwin Markham's following lines:

We men of Earth have here the stuff
Of Paradise—we have enough!

CONCLUSION AND GENERALIZATIONS

It seems, then, that much of the past is still living in the present, and that, in view of its widespread influence, neither the counselor nor the counselee can ignore such information with impunity. More importantly, the sociohistorical approach leads to certain generalizations—hypotheses and theories, but not laws—which may be employed rather fruitfully when an effort is made to understand and solve various individual and social problems. Needless to add, such generalizations are impossible when we parochially and ethnocentrically stress knowledge of the present exclusively.

In this essay, for instance, on the basis of the data discussed here, as well as those omitted, many generalizations are relatively obvious. Of course, *at least some of these may be supported or rejected through additional research.* Moreover, it must be stated explicitly that no orthogenetic emphasis is implied by such formulations, since most historical stages overlap or are mixed; since, even when a major trend is conspicuous, a few, several, or many pendulum oscillations are usually present; and since glimmerings of modern thought occasionally did appear in the past, but were frequently extirpated as "heresies" for which the people were not ready as yet.

Finally, the most appropriate generalizations are employed in the somewhat theoretical construction of a quantitative device for the measurement of attitudes toward sin. This technique may be used by counselors in order to secure additional information, as well as by researchers as a partial index of modernization among individuals or groups.

In brief, the main generalizations are as follows:

1. As time goes on, the tendency is to make fine, precise, and punctilious distinctions among more and more kinds of sin.

2. The definition of sin has been moving from absolutism to relativism.

3. Condemnatory attitudes toward the corrosive consequences of sinful behavior have at first included only the local, then the national, and finally the international community.

4. Sin has been increasingly examined on the basis of more branches of human knowledge.

5. Physical resurrection has been stressed less and less.

6. Abstract, intellectual, and symbolic conceptions of sin, reward, and punishment have been less prevalent in ancient times, and more typical of the educated classes in general.

7. In the Old Testament-New Testament-modern times sequence, the view concerning sin has become less religious, theological, and supernatural, and more moral and philosophical.

8. Man's filial relationship to God influenced the Old Testament definition of sin considerably, but such influence has been steadily declining.

9. The nature of sinful conduct itself, especially with regard to motives, has been scrutinized more and more.

10. The aspects of guilt and individual conscience, and the concomitant distinction between thought and deed, have gradually become more dominant.

11. In general, the psychological component of the concept of sin was limited in the Old Testament, but more conspicuous in the teachings of Jesus, and seems to have reached its climax at the present time.

12. Increasing emphasis has been placed on the etiological analysis of sin, while at the same time its metaphysical causes (Satan and the like) have been virtually discarded.

13. Society has been blamed more and more as a cause of various transgressions.

14. The notion that sin is inherited (original sin and the like) has become less popular, while the belief in general environmental causation has gained greater approval.

15. Civic, political, psychological, and social sins have been attracting attention at the expense of sins of the flesh.

16. The concept that physical suffering constitutes a punishment for sin has been common in the Old Testament, less common in the New Testament, and much less common in the modern world.

17. The conviction that sin disrupts the entire cosmos has been constantly losing ground.

18. The cleansing of sin by means of magical and nonmagical rituals (for example, baptism) has been moving from almost universal acceptance to almost universal rejection.

19. The role of saints and priests as mediators between God and man is slowly becoming a thing of the past.

20. The formalization, legalization, and ritualization of institutions concerned with sin and spiritual reward and punishment have faced growing resistance—Christ opposed the laws of the scribes and Pharisees, Luther attacked medieval ceremonialism, and today's liberals are criticizing the religious establishment.

21. Man's solution of the sin problem has been moving away from sacrifices to the divinity and closer to social planning.

22. The ancient theory that the community is punished for the individual's sins and the accompanying collective catharsis have been more or less replaced by the idea of individual punishment and personal psychological treatment.

23. The old rules enacting vindictive penalties for sin are being slowly superseded by efforts to deter and reform.

24. The rigor of moral codes and the incidence of mental aberrations involving incubi, succubi, and the like are positively and proportionately related.

25. Typologies of sins stressing sanctions are becoming exceptional.

26. The philosophy of terrestrial reward or punishment in a peaceful or chaotic society has been winning support at the expense of the theology of a physical heaven and hell.

27. Finally, the old hypothesis that the historical process is an attempt to return to the perfection that prevailed before Adam's sin is becoming practically obsolete.

A PARTIAL INDEX OF MODERNIZATION: MEASUREMENT OF ATTITUDES TOWARD MORALITY

(Score equals sum total of ten numerical responses. Theoretical range: 0, least modern, to 100, most modern.)

Below is a list of issues concerning morality. Please read all statements very carefully and respond to all of them on the basis of your own true beliefs without consulting any other persons. Do this by reading each statement and then writing, in the space provided at its left, only one of the following numbers: 0, 1, 2, 3, 4, 5, 6, 7, 8, 9, 10. Zero means the lowest amount of agreement, and 10 the highest. You may write any of these numbers.

(For research purposes, you must consider all statements as they are, without modifying any of them in any way.)

_____ a. Sin is never inherited (original sin is a myth) .

_____ b. No mediators (saints, priests, etc.) are needed between God and man.

_____ c. Morality is a matter of individual conscience.

_____ d. Sin is not caused by Satan.

_____ e. The religious study of sin is less important than its psychological and sociological study.

_____ f. Physical resurrection after death is impossible.

_____ g. The concept of sin changes from time to time and from place to place.

_____ h. Reward and punishment take place in this world, not in heaven and hell.

_____ i. Extremely strict moral codes often cause mental illness.

_____ j. Religious rituals cannot remove sin.

REFERENCES

1. Bellah, Robert N.: Religion: The sociology of religion, in David L. Sills, Ed. *International Encyclopedia of the Social Sciences.* New York, Macmillan, 1968, Volume 13, pp. 406-407.
2. Silverman, Hirsch Lazaar: Morality and marital counseling, in *idem*, Editor, *Marital Counseling: Psychology, Ideology, Science.* Springfield, Illinois, Thomas, 1967, p. 445.

3. Barnhart, Clarence L., Ed.: *The World Book Dictionary.* New York, Doubleday, 1969, Volume 2, p. 1928.

4. Thiollier, Marguerite-Marie: *Dictionnaire des Religions.* Paris, Larousse, 1966, p. 197.

5. Wiltse, Kermit T.: Counseling in public assistance, in Ernest Harms and Paul Schreiber, Eds. *Handbook of Counseling Techniques.* New York, Macmillan, 1963, p. 195.

6. Britton, Joseph H.: "Counseling with older adults, *ibid.,* p. 357.

7. Lerner, Daniel: Modernization: Social Aspects, in Sills, *op. cit.,* Volume 10, p. 386.

8. Lewis, W. Arthur: *The Theory of Economic Growth.* Homewood, Illinois, Irwin, 1955.

9. Lerner, Daniel: Modernization: Social Aspects, 1968, p. 387.

10. Lyon, Quinter Marcellus: *The Great Religions.* New York, Odyssey, 1957, p. 605.

11. Thiollier, Marguerite-Marie: Dictionnaire des Religions, Paris, Larousse, 1966, p. 198.

12. Puckle, Bertram S.: *Funeral Customs.* London, Laurie, 1926, p. 69.

13. Braden, Charles Samuel: *The World's Religions.* Rev. ed., New York, Abingdon, 1954, p. 155.

14. Puckle, Bertram S.: *Funeral Customs.* London, Laurie, 1926, p. 70.

15. Ditchfield, P. H.: *Old English Customs.* London, Methuen, 1896, p. 202.

16. Puckle, Bertram S.: *Funeral Customs.* London, Laurie, 1926, p. 69.

17. Polites, Nicolaus: *Paradoseis.* Athens, 1904, Volume 1, p. 576; Alexandrus Moraitides, "Cuccitsa." in N. Apostolides, Ed., *To Diegema Anthologemeno.* Athens: Rodes, no date, pp. 319-332.

18. Parsons, Talcott: Christianity, in Sills, Ed. *International Encyclopedia of the Social Sciences.* New York, Macmillan, 1968, Vol. 2, p. 427.

19. Brussel, James A.: The psychiatric implications of love, in Silverman, Hirsch Lazaar, *Marital Counseling.* Springfield, Illinois, Thomas, 1967, p. 46.

20. Partridge, Burgo: *A History of Orgies.* New York, Bonanza, 1960, p. 87.

21. Partridge, Burgo: *A History of Orgies.* New York, Bonanza, 1960, p. 87.

22. Braden, Charles Samuel: *The World's Religions.* New York, Abingdon, 1954, p. 197.

23. Wall, J. Charles: *Devils.* London, Methuen, 1904, p. 14.

24. Wall, J. Charles: *Devils.* London, Mathuen, 1904, p. 131.

25. Brussel, James A.: *The Psychiatric Implications of Love.* Springfield, Illinois, Thomas, 1967, p. 47.

26. Klausner, Samuel Z.: In Sills, David L.: *International Encyclopedia of the Social Sciences.* New York, Macmillan, 1968, Volume 12, p. 632-633.

27. *ibid.,* p. 633.

28. *Time,* December 6, 1968, p. 19.

29. Russell, Bertrand: "What Is an Agnostic?", in Leo Rosten, Ed., *Religions in America.* New York, Simon and Schuster, 1963, p. 197.

30. Hardon, John A.: *Religions of the World.* Westminster, Maryland, New man, 1965, p. 334.

SELECTED BIBLIOGRAPHY

1. Atiya, Aziz S.: *History of Eastern Christianity.* Notre Dame, Indiana, University of Notre Dame Press, 1968.

2. Bardis, Panos D. :*The Family in Changing Civilizations.* 2nd ed., New York, Associated Educational Services Corporation, Simon and Schuster, 1969.

3. Barnes, Harry Elmer: *A History of Historical Writing.* 2nd ed., New York, Dover, 1963.
4. Brockelmann, Carl: *History of the Islamic Peoples.* New York, Capricorn, 1960.
5. Bury, J. B.: *History of the Late Roman Empire,* New York, Dover, 1958.
6. Finkelstein, Louis, Ed.: *The Jews: Their History, Culture, and Religion.* 3rd. ed., New York, Harper, 1960.
7. Glover, T. R.: *The Conflict of Religions in the Early Roman Empire.* Boston, Beacon, 1960.
8. Harnack, Adolph: *History of Dogma.* New York, Dover, 1961.
9. Hatch, Edwin: *The Influence of Greek Ideas on Christianity.* New York, Harper, 1957.
10. Hoult, Thomas Ford: *The Sociology of Religion.* New York, Holt, Rinehart, and Winston, 1958.
11. Lessa, William A., and Evon, Z. Vogt: *Reader in Comparative Religion.* 2nd ed., New York, Harper, 1965.
12. Marias, Julian: *History of Philosophy,* New York, Dover, 1967.
13. McKenna, Marian: *History of Catholicism.* Paterson, New Jersey, Littlefield, 1962.
14. Papamichael, G.: *He Orthodoxus Anatolice Ecclesia.* Athens, Apostolice Diaconia, 1954.
15. Rosa, Peter De: *Christ and Original Sin.* Milwaukee, Bruce, 1967.
16. Silverman, Hirsch Lazaar, Ed.: *Marital Counseling: Psychology, Ideology, Science.* Springfield, Illinois, Thomas, 1967.
17. Soper, Edmund Davison: *The Religions of Mankind.* 3rd ed., New York, Abingdon, 1951.
18. Thiollier, Marguerite-Marie: *Dictionnaire de Religions.* Paris, Larousse, 1966.
19. Tsirpanlis, Emil C.: The immortality of the soul in 'Phaedo' and 'Symposium'. *Platon.* 1965, pp. 224-234.
20. Yinger, J. Milton: *Religion, Society and the Individual.* New York, Macmillan, 1957.

METHODOLOGICAL APPENDIX

The empirical tests of the scale may be summarized as follows:

Criterion of Internal Consistency

The sample involved in this criterion* consisted of males and females; parents and children; college students and nonstudents; whites and Negroes; and Catholics, Greek Orthodox, Jews, and Protestants. These one hundred subjects came from various parts of the United States, but primarily from the midwest.

Of the one hundred scores secured, the ten highest and ten lowest were used to ascertain the discriminatory power of each scale item. Thus, for each statement, the difference between the sum of the ten highest and the sum of the ten lowest responses was obtained, for example, eighty-five minus twenty equals sixty-five (the artithmetic mean, 6.5, was not necessary for the ranking that followed). Of all possible items, it was decided to retain only those

*Likert, Rensis: A technique for the measurement of attitudes. New York, *Arch Psychol, 140:*11-53, 1932.

whose discriminatory power was represented by a value of at least thirty. In this way, the ten scale items (see list above), together with their respective values, were as follows: h-85, a-82, f-81, e-77, i-77, b-62, d-62, c-56, j-43, and g-30.

Validity

The well-known difference between Catholics and Protestants in the sphere under consideration was employed as an independent criterion of the scale's validity. The sample included twenty Catholic college students (ten of each sex) and twenty Protestant ones (also ten of each sex). The arithmetic means of the scale scores were Catholics 59.65, and Protestants 80.45. This difference was significant beyond the .001 level (t 3.65, df 38).*

Another similar sample gave the following values: Catholics 61.92, Protestants 83.29; t 3.87; df 38; also significant beyond .001.

Reliability

A sample of thirty Catholic, Jewish, and Protestant parents and college students gave a raw Pearsonian coefficient of correlation† of the split-half type that was as high as .78. When this value was corrected by means of the Spearman-Brown prophecy formula,‡ the resulting reliability coefficient proved to be .88, that is, significant much beyond the .001 level (df 28).

Another similar sample, and a split-half test of the odd-even type, gave the following values: raw r, .84; corrected r, .91; df 28; also significant much beyond .001.

---

*Miller, Delbert C.: *Handbook of Research Design and Social Measurement.* New York, McKay, 1964, pp. 79-81.

†Szulc, Stefan: *Statistical Methods.* London, Pergamon, 1965, pp. 495-497.

‡Carrett, Henry E.: *Statistics in Psychology and Education.* 4th ed., New York, Longmans, Green, 1955, pp. 333-341.

MARRIAGE AND FAMILY COUNSELING AS LEGAL INTERVIEWING AND COUNSELING OF FAMILY LAW CASES

TATSUO SAMEJIMA

> The greatest contribution of Social Work to law may be the gathering and presentation of facts and insights that will enable our courts to decide cases and issues within appropriate social context and the greatest contribution of law to Social Work may be the insistence that the rule of law apply to all public endeavor.
>
> HENRY H. FOSTER JR.

THESE WORDS of Henry H. Foster would, I believe, be one of the best answers to my subject "Marriage and Family Counseling as Legal Interviewing and Counseling of Family Law Cases." The gathering of facts and insights could not be separated theoretically, but they could be divided into two concepts: the gathering of facts and the establishments of insights.

The establishment of insights would be the goal and content of the adjustment activities of marriage and family counseling. The establishment of insights could be facilitated by the gathering of facts. Furthermore, if this could be done under the rule of law, marriage and family counseling would be recognized as a technique of legal interviewing and counseling. Facts and insights are the soul and essence of family law practice.

In the subject "Marriage and Family Counseling of Legal Interviewing and Counseling of Family Law Cases," there are four concepts: family law cases, gathering of facts, adjustment activities, and marriage and family counselors.

Family Law Cases

Family law cases deal with matters regarding the establishment, administration, and reorganization of legal relationships between husband and wife and between parents and child.

The object of judicial procedure is to establish legal effect by court decision. In civil procedure, parties hope to get a judgment favorable to them. On the contrary, in non-litigious procedure (Freiwillige Gerichtsbarkeit), the court develops legal protective activities with consideration of public interest.

Gathering of Facts

Whether in civil action in a regular lawsuit court or in noncontentious procedure of a family court, the judgment or determination is formulated upon a basis of fact.

In family law cases, we handle the problems of family members in respect to matters of the establishment, administration, and reorganization of relations between family members.

The legal relations of family members are included in their interpersonal relations. In other words, the interpersonal relations of family members will have some definite influence on their legal relations. Therefore, facts having meaning in legal relations are inseparably related to interpersonal relations. In order to gather facts having some meaning in legal relations, it is necessary to gather facts which have some meaning in the interpersonal relations between family members.

Adjustment Activities

In a broad sense, the judgment of the court is legal adjustment. The judgment or determination of matters regarding the establishment, administration, and reorganization of family members are legal adjustment.

The adjustment activities of family law cases have not only a legal aspect, but also a social aspect and psychological aspect.

Social adjustment as a manipulation of environment will be done to the accompaniment of legal adjustment.

Psychological adjustment is included, to some extent, in legal adjustment. Some family law cases can not be resolved without psychological adjustment.

Divorce cases can be called "cases of adjustment between husband and wife." Trouble which arise between family members are resolved in "cases of adjustment between family members."

Marriage and Family Counselor

The legal aspects of family law cases belong exclusively to the function of the law. The social and psychological aspects of the family are the area of professional activities such as marriage and family counseling. This is the reason why activities of marriage and the family counselor are attracting attention of people in every country both in the East and the West.

Factors of Problem Solving in Family Law Cases

Family law cases may be settled under the dictates of the law, however, family law cases should be dealt with not as cases, but as living members of a family. With this purpose in mind, each case needs to be resolved individually and objectively with the use of individual treatment of marriage and family counseling under the rule of law.

The gathering of facts is done to determine the exact situation and true need of each case. This is only made possible when a good relationship is established between counselor and client.

The object of family law cases is primarily the relationship between husband and wife, and parent and child, but in handling these cases, there is another problem regarding such a relationship, that is the relationship between counselor and client.

From the above we can see that facts and the relationships between parties concerned are two factors in problem solving in family law cases.

If problem solving in family law cases is possible by the gathering of facts and adjustment activities in an authoritarian setting of the court under the rule of law, the marriage and family counseling would be used as legal interviewing and counseling.

Direct and Indirect Facts

The way of thinking of a client and his actions are facts. In the area of law there are two kinds of facts: direct fact and indirect fact. Direct facts are those with which requirements of law are fulfilled, for instance, direct facts of divorce are those with which a ground for divorce as laid down by the law is fulfilled. Indirect facts are those with which primary facts required by law are inferable.

In civil action, the requirements of a law are provided strictly in detail, as indicated above in divorce cases, but in non-litigious procedure the requirements of law are not provided in detail as in civil procedure, but facts which are existing in a situation are taken into consideration by the court from a legal point of view in order to attain the object of the law. Facts taken into consideration in non-litigious procedure are indirect facts.

These indirect facts are judged in the individual treatment of court, but these same facts are treated by social science and counseling effectively.

Relationship

Interviewing always involves a relationship between people—the interviewer and the interviewee. The success or failure of the interview depends on how quickly and how positively the relationship is formed. However, there is a condition in authoritarian setting of the court which is likely to make the formation of the relationship more difficult than in other fields of counseling.

Interviewing techniques in counseling have been developed to overcome difficulties of this kind, even in the authoritarian setting of the courts.

People come to the courts with a particular intention. What is the client conscious motive in turning to the Court? What are his ideas as to what he wants and expects from it, and what is his role and relationship to it?

In the court operation, cases which are suitable to assign to counseling services should be selected upon the basis of the client's motives, desire, and agreement. But counseling services are gradually becoming popular among people, and counselors have become engulfed by a wave of requests for their service even during the court procedure.

Chapter 17

CONCEPTS OF SEXUAL ABNORMALITY AND PERVERSION IN MARRIAGE COUNSELING

ISADORE RUBIN

CONCEPTS RELATING to sexual "abnormality," "perversion," and "deviance" have loomed large in all discussions of sexual behavior and, consequently, of counseling dealing with that behavior. Any counselor in the field of sexuality and marital problems is made keenly aware—from the number of questions constantly addressed to him by single individuals and by married couples—of the fact that the discussion is not one of abstract theoretical interest but of immediate practical concern.

Large numbers of individuals in our society are deeply concerned about whether their sexual desires and actions are "normal" or "perverse." Their anxieties cover a very wide spectrum: the frequency, circumstances, and fantasies of masturbation, the desire to adopt other positions than the "missionary position" during sexual intercourse, the desire for oral-genital acts, homosexual feelings on the part of a happily married husband or wife, sexual initiative on the part of the wife, fantasies or dreams of affairs with other partners, assorted kinds of fetishistic feelings, desires for mate-swapping and involvement of other individuals in a couple's sexual life, the continuation of strong sexual needs and feelings in the later years of life, to mention but a few.

Counseling in many of these areas no longer represents any special problem for the qualified and knowledgeable counselor. There is general consensus, for example, that such terms as abnormal or perverse have no application to either the desire for, or the adoption of, those coital positions which are most pleasurable and satisfactory to the partners concerned. Far from attempting to limit a couple in their choice of coital positions, marriage counselors today encourage them to abandon rigid repetition, in the interests of attaining greater mutual pleasure in intercourse, of encouraging a search for variety in order to keep alive the spirit of sexual adventure for a longer period of time, and of encouraging the flexibility which may be necessary at various periods of life, such as pregnancy illness, or other eventualities.

Although a medical professor of the University of Prague just a half century ago could attribute the sexual desire that continued in some women after the menopause to psychological disturbance or to physical pathology and warn against a woman's marrying a still virile man at this period (1), few marriage counselors today are unaware of the normality of sexual desire and activity in the later years of life. Although there is still a great deal of resistance on the part of the public to accept the fact of sexuality in the older years—just as there was resistance in Freud's time to accepting the fact of childhood sexuality—counselors are sufficiently aware of the longitudinal research at Duke University (2), the laboratory work of Masters and Johnson (3), and the studies of a number of others, to recognize the fact that there is no automatic cutoff to a couple's sexual life (4).

The investigations of Kinsey and his colleagues have shown that mouth-genital actions on the part of both husband and wives are far more common than were ever suspected in the past and are reported most often by those with higher educational backgrounds and presumably of higher social classes (5). Although very many couples show great concern about this as a result of traditional condemnation and popular association of mouth-genital acts with homosexual acts, there is no special problem for counselors to recognize such acts as perfectly acceptable and normal. Although such acts are prohibited by law in almost all states—even for married couples—there is an almost unchallenged tendency among leading marriage counselors to stress the fact that such decisions belong to the couple concerned and are to be made in the light of the feelings of the particular individuals and their mutual needs. Seward Hiltner, a leading pastoral theologian, in regard to the forms of sexual stimulation among married couples, has pointed to "the joint criterion of self-fulfillment and fulfillment of the other" (6). "No form of such stimulation prior to coitus is wrong from the Christian point of view," he said, "if both partners desire it and if it does not involve the personality-injuring cruelties of sadism or masochism. The intensity proper to a marriage relationship is likely to be aided by some novelty, whether this be in the sexual play prior to intercourse or the form of intercourse itself." It is true that there is present in this statement the implication that all forms of sex play should culminate in penile-vaginal intercourse in order to be acceptable, an implication which is made quite explicit by Catholic counselors. For example, John R. Cavanagh, in his book, *Fundamental Marriage Counseling—A Catholic Viewpoint,* asserts that "any act which is desired or acceptable to both partners is permissible as part of the sex play prior to intercourse as long as the act ends properly with the deposition of the semen in the vault of the vagina in such a way that there is no interference with the primary purpose of the act" (7).

Although these religious spokesmen are discussing what they consider morally right or wrong rather than what they consider normal or abnormal, the transition from one to the other is often made by counselors who are ostensibly not speaking from a religiously-oriented point of view. Actually, there seems to be no basis for making the normality or abnormality of a sexual act dependent on whether it culminates in intercourse.

Wardell B. Pomeroy has pointed to the many meanings of the word "normal" and emphasized the need to avoid confusion in the use of it (8). There are many ways in which the concept of normal or abnormal sexual behavior is used, according to Pomeroy. These are the following:

1. The Statistical Definition

By this standard, that which is commonplace or frequent is "normal" and that which is uncommon or infrequent is "abnormal." According to a statistical definition, masturbation, nonmarital intercourse, and mouth-genital contact (among better-educated persons) would be called normal. Male homosexuality would be almost but not quite normal, but female homosexuality would be abnormal. In our society, intercourse with the male above is the most usual position and hence called the normal position. But there are less than 15 per cent of the cultures of the world in which this is the usual, preferred or "normal" position.

2. The Phylogenetic Definition

Since humans are a species of mammal and since we often speak of "natural" sexual behavior, another definition of normal behavior is based on examination of whether the behavior is also found among various mammals. If this definition were applied, very few of the kinds of sexual behavior that humans engage in would be considered phylogenetically abnormal.

3. The Moral Definition

For most people, including professionals, this is the most common definition of normality. According to Pomeroy, in comparison to other cultures, we have inherited as restrained and inhibited a set of sexual codes as anthropologists can find on this earth. By this definition, almost every sexual act except marital intercourse is considered morally wrong and hence abnormal.

Defining normality in this way is today complicated by another problem —the reappraisal now taking place about sexuality by large sections of the church and consequently conflicting definitions of morality within various religious groups.

4. The Legal Definition

Since most laws grew out of church codes, in most cases the laws defining sexual behavior are duplicates of the moral definitions of the church. However, as Dr. Pomeroy notes, there are curious differences. Masturbation is considered morally wrong but is not proscribed in any of the states; on the other hand, mouth-genital activities are considered acceptable behavior in marriage in all the major religions, but is legally proscribed in forty-nine of the fifty states.

5. The Social Definition

By this definition, sexual behavior which does harm to society or any of its members is abnormal, that which does no harm is normal. According to this definition, behavior involving force or directed toward a child by an adult would be against the interests of society and be socially abnormal, while any sexual behavior involving two consenting adults in private would not be so considered.

6. A Psychological Definition

A psychological definition has also been proposed, based on how a person felt about his behavior. Thus, sexual behavior leading the individual to have feelings of low self-esteem would be abnormal.

Since any particular act may be considered normal by some of the definitions and abnormal by others, Pomeroy suggests that "it makes more sense to banish the entire concept from our vocabulary and our thinking." "At the very least," he adds, "it is important to designate which of the various definitions one is using before labeling a given sexual act. I feel, rather that our concern should be with individual well-being rather than with the illogical, irrelevant, and psychologically-damaging labeling of sexual behavior as normal or abnormal."

Albert Ellis, in an analysis of what is "normal" sex behavior, also has noted that, whichever of the various definitions of the term normality we use, "normal" sex behavior still boils down to socially accepted and culturally learned behavior and that it is human cultures and subcultures that make sexual acts healthy or unhealthy, mature or immature, adjusted or maladjusted, disturbing or nondisturbing (9).

Psychoanalyst and sociologist Hendrick M. Ruitenbeek declares, "Currently, most sociologists and psychoanalysts would agree that what is considered as normal sexual practice in one culture may be considered a perversion in another. They would also agree that it is extremely difficult to define sexual normality even within the limits of a specific culture and its social structure. Since it is thus difficult to define the norm, defining perversion, departure from the norm, presents that much more of a problem" (10). However, this does not prevent him from proceeding, in the same book in which he makes this statement, *Psychotherapy of Perversions,* as if the term perversion is indeed a medical and psychological evaluation of an objective condition.

Kinsey and his colleagues, on the other hand, on the basis of their own data as well as on available cross-cultural data, concluded without equivocation that "perversions are simply a measure of the nonconformity between an individual's behavior and the mores of the particular society in which he lives" (11). They argued that "current concepts of normality and abnormality in human sexual behavior represent what are primarily moral evaluations" with "little if any biologic justification."

There is little doubt that both psychiatric and popular thinking about what is perverse or normal has been given its scientific sanction from Freud's analysis of "perversions" and his insistence that genital primacy was "the final outcome of sexual development." This idea has been one of the anchoring points of libido theory. In his classic work, *Three Contributions to the Theory of Sex,* Freud defined perversions in the following way, "Perversions are sexual activities which either a) extend beyond the regions of the body that are designed for sexual union or b) linger over the immediate relations to the sexual object which should normally be traversed rapidly on the path towards the final sexual aim" (12). According to the psychiatrist Thomas Szasz, this definition of a perversion is "nothing short of a disguised introduction into psychoanalysis of the official Roman Catholic view of 'normal' and 'abnormal' sexual behavior" (13).

Social psychiatrist Martin Hoffman, in an analysis of Freud's concept of genital primacy, is also struck by the similarity between Freud's views on perversions and the Roman Catholic views predominating in this day (14). Hoffman argues that the idea that the genitals are "designed" for certain activities, as Freud puts it, is not only clearly a relic of natural law theory, but also points the way to the idea of divine law, which is the real basis of natural law theory.

There is even greater similarity, as Hoffman notes, between the Roman Catholic view on the purpose of sex and Freud's statement, "The final outcome of sexual development lies in what is known as the normal sexual life of the adult, in which the pursuit of pleasure comes under the sway of the reproductive function." Hoffman also finds a striking similarity between Thomas Aquinas' list of sexual sins and Freud's list of perversions. What we witness here, he concludes, is "a translation of moral theology and the consequent infiltration of ethical values into psychoanalytic theory."

Thus, we are brought up sharply to this question, Are we in a discussion of the perversions dealing with objective scientific analysis, or are we dealing with disguised value judgments? If the latter is true, then we are faced with a dangerous form of circular logic, in which prevailing religions and moral judgments are introduced in carefully disguised form into scientific analysis, and then the conclusions derived from this analysis are used as "scientific support" for the prevailing religious and moral judgments.

With the decline of the power of the label "sin" to stigmatize and control sexual behavior and with the rise in authority of psychiatry, it has been primarily the term "mental health" which is used to evaluate sexual behavior. For most persons—professionals as well as laymen—this term is considered a medical term and the use of it is considered to be an objective, scientific evaluation of a mental condition or of behavior rather than an evaluation based on disguised moral judgments. Actually, as many careful analyses have shown, it is not possible to define "mental illness" in an objective, scientific value-free way. In recent years, Szasz has raised this problem most sharply, but others have done so over the years as well (15). "There can be no definition of mental illness," said psychiatrist Seymour L. Halleck in 1967, "outside of the value judgments of psychiatry and the society. As of this date the profession of psychiatry has not been able to come up with a consistent definition of mental illness which is acceptable to all of its members" (16). Other professions have been no more successful.

In a thorough and comprehensive analysis of the definitions of "mental health" and "mental illness" appearing in leading textbooks published in both England and the United States, the British sociologist Lady Barbara Wooton showed that all of these definitions expressed, not scientifically established facts, but the personal value positions of their authors (17). Psychiatric definitions of mental health, this sociologist asserted, are suspiciously like "an attempt to increase the appeal of a purely ethical judgment by clothing it in the fashionable medical dress favored by a scientifically minded age." Lady Wooton notes that the concept of adjustment is particularly prominent in the literature of mental health and adds, "Fine phrases cannot, however, obscure the fact that adjustment means adjustment to a particular culture or to a particular set of institutions; and that to conceive adjustment and maladjustment in medical terms is in effect to identify health with the ability to come to terms with that culture or with those institutions—be they totalitarian methods of government, the dingy culture of an urban slum, the contemporary English law of marriage or what I have elsewhere called the standards of an 'acquisitive, competitive, hierarchical, envious' society."

The well-known American sociologist Kingsley Davis, in an important analysis of the concept of mental health, presented a persuasive body of evidence to support his conclusion that "mental hygiene can plunge into evaluation, into fields the social sciences would not touch, because it possesses an implicit ethical system, which since it is that of our society, enables it to pass value judgments, to get public support, and to enjoy an unalloyed optimism. Disguising its valuational system as rational advice based on science, it can conveniently praise and condemn under the aegis of the medico-authoritarian model" (18).

A clear example of the problems inherent in the attempt to use terms like mental or emotional health or illness as terms of objective medical diagnosis may be seen in the contradictory statements about homosexuality made by psychiatrists. In his book *Understanding and Counseling the Male Homosexual*, Stanley E. Willis, II declared, "If their homosexual patterns are neither promiscuous nor compulsive, if their relationships are based on a homophilic admiration for a compatible same-sex partner and undertaken in the privacy of their own society with fidelity and consideration, then their adjustment is responsible and healthy. Society would be well advised to accept such situations and not try to impose a useless sense of neurotic guilt on such people" (19).

A sharply contrasting view was reported by the press on March 16, 1969, in announcing that a seven-man panel of psychiatrists had been established by the New York County branch of the American Psychiatric Association to combat the confusion surrounding the subject of homosexuality (20). Its chairman, Charles W. Socarides, author of *The Overt Homosexual*, was quoted as saying, "It has gotten to the point where homosexuality has been put forth by certain groups as a normal form of sexuality alongside heterosexuality. We believe that homosexuality is a form of emotional sickness and that any attempt to glamorize it or elevate it or to condemn it as a moral offense is entirely beside the point and only clouds the issue of homosexuality as a form of illness."

In late 1967, however, the National Institute of Mental health had established a task force of nationally known experts for the purpose of encouraging research and clarity about homosexuality (21). Although no public statements have been issued about the work of this panel, it is clear that at least some of them do not accept the concept that homosexual behavior is the result of emotional illness or mental illness. The chairman of this task force, research psychologist Evelyn Hooker, found that comparable groups of homosexual and heterosexual males did not differ in overall patterns of adjustment, when psychological tests were used as methods of assessing that adjustment (22). A number of other controlled studies have come to similar conclusions, and Judd Marmor has suggested that traditional psychoanalytic concepts may well be based on a skew sampling of homosexuals who have been in therapy (23).

Clearly, these differences reveal that the psychiatrists are not expressing scientific medical judgments about an objective condition. At least at the present stage of knowledge, to stamp homosexuality as abnormal and a symptom of mental illness is to use a moral evaluation to foreclose on an open psychological and social question (24).

As the objectivity of each type of label—"sinful," "emotionally unhealthy," "abnormal," "immature," "pathological"—is brought into question, new ones tend to be substituted to achieve a less value-laden definition, although it does not take too long for each new label to take on the moral coloration of the earlier ones. One of the latest of such terms is "deviant" and it is often taken for granted that a given action is deviant because of a particular quality inherent in the act. In recent years, this view has been brought into sharp question by many sociologists. They point out that deviance arises by a process of labeling—people attach the label "deviant" to others and thereby make deviants of them.

"Social groups create deviance," writes Howard S. Becker in his book *Outsiders,* "by making the rules whose infraction constitutes deviance, and by applying those rules to particular people and labeling them as outsiders. From this point of view, deviance is not a quality of the act the person commits, but rather a consequence of the application by others of rules and sanctions to an 'offender' " (25) . "The deviant," he concludes, "is one to whom that label has successfully been applied; deviant behavior is behavior that people so label."

All marriage counselors are aware that disturbances are quite frequent among those persons whose behavior has been labeled as deviant. As sociologist John I. Kitsuse has noted: "An individual's sexual 'normality' may be made problematic by the interpretations and reinterpretations of his behavior by others . . . . The data suggest that the critical feature of the deviant-defining process is not the behavior of individuals who are defined as deviant, but rather the interpretations others make of their behaviors, whatever those behaviors may be (26) .

Thus, for example, the author of this chapter has received letters from couples such as the following: "My wife and I are over sixty-five-years old but we still like to have sexual intercourse very much. Please give us advice in this case? What should we do?" Here, obviously, behavior which represented no problem had been rendered problematic because of the prevailing stereotype of the "sexless older years" and the widely-held belief that having strong sexual desires in these years was evidence of deviance and abnormality.

Clark E. Vincent has pointed out that, because of the strength of traditional sexual mores, terms are changed more readily than attitudes and an ostensible change in attitudes may be only a substitution of terms (27) . Vincent notes the late Robert Lindner's argument that we have actually applied new terms to old attitudes about sexuality, e.g. the sexual deviant is now "sick" or "maladjusted," rather than "morally depraved" or "mentally deficient," but adds, 'And, although Lindner argued for a more understanding attitude, he too used a new term to express an old attitude when he labeled sexual deviancy as 'negative rebellion' and then proceeded to censure 'negative rebellion.' "

Kai T. Erickson notes that it is by no means clear that all acts considered deviant in a culture are in fact (or in principle) harmful to group life and that it is becoming more evident to sociologists engaged in this area of research that deviant behavior can play an important part in keeping the social order intact (28). Thus, for example, Fernando Henriques, in his recent three-volume study of prostitution, presents evidence to support the thesis, as many observers have suggested from the time of St. Augustine, that prostitution performs some functions as the guardian of the family (29). This view was best developed by Kingsley Davis, who argued that prostitution helped to maintain the family as an institution by acting as a safety valve for the expression of antisocial coitus that cannot be fully suppressed (30). Ned Polsky argues that from a sociological viewpoint, pornography serves a similar kind of purpose (31). Both prostitution and pornography "permit 'polymorphous perverse' and other sexual behaviors so highly stigmatized as to be labeled deviant even within the intimacy of marriage and morally inhibited from expression therein." Pornography particularly, he says, offers an opportunity for fantasy involvement in sex acts that society proscribes as "unnatural." To the extent that society, in restricting morally legitimate sex to certain specified acts within marriage, cannot count fully on the mechanisms of repression and suppression, to that extent it must provide stigmatized safety-valve institutions such as prostitution and pornography.

Certainly any experienced marriage counselor can cite many instances where couples have brought questions to them concerning the legitimacy of the husband's interest in pornography or in highly erotic materials either as an independent interest or as an adjunct to coitus, or of the legitimacy of the couple together using erotic materials to stimulate their sexual desires.

Alex Comfort notes that the sexual impulse is many-stranded in all individuals and that the range of typical heterosexual behavior in human beings is extremely broad (32). This range includes not only the oral and manual stimulation of the mouth and lips, the erogenous zones of the skin, the breasts and the genitals, but the whole range of custom relating to clothes, decoration of the body with paint and jewelry, variation in coital postures, and many other practices. It includes not just behavior but a wide range of fantasies as well.

Many cultures tended to develop the range of sexual practice as a social asset, producing a considerable erotic literature, and converting sexual behavior into a source of pleasure and recreation independent of its function of procreation. Cultures dominated by Judeo-Christian concepts have, on the other hand repudiated all cultural elaboration of physical sexuality, and severely limited and restricted most of its manifestations either by law or by a deep-seated public distaste. Narrow and restrictive concepts of acceptable behavior have also very much restricted the possibility of working out aberrant fantasies—involving, for example, minor manifestations of sadism and masochism—in a harmless form within the structure of husband-wife sexual behavior. In fact, says Comfort, "the total rejection of joy in sexual experience threatened at one time to become an official and moral norm."

Our entire culture is in a process of transition from the limited and restrictive attitude toward manifestations of sexuality toward a greater acceptance of sexual relationships as a rich and meaningful encounter between husband and wife completely independent of reproductive needs. It is the function of the marriage counselor to help rid his clients of the guilt that has been induced by their upbringing in a restrictive society and to help free them from expressing their various sexual desires and fantasies because of their fear of being considered "abnormal" or "perverted."

Thus, for example, Lester Dearborn has taken issue with a popular columnist who, in reply to a letter which described a wife's enjoyment at being spanked, contemptuously dismissed both husband and wife as "physical kooks" both of whom were "sick" (33). Dearborn noted that most people—including many professional colleagues—are so fearful of the word "sadistic" that they cannot be open-minded in assessing the effects of any behavior so labeled and dismiss it as "sick" and "abnormal" without engaging in the necessary careful and unbiased research. He reports the cases of five such couples where sado-masochistic behavior played an important part in creating and maintaining a harmonious sexual life and marriage. In none of these cases did the behavior create any unresolved emotional conflicts and there is no doubt that the wrong kind of attitude on the part of the counselor might have been very damaging to these marriages.

The term fetishism tends to inspire the same kind of reaction. Dearborn has related the case of a fetishist who could not attain sexual satisfaction unless his wife wore a black rubber bathing cap and whose wife was led to accept the behavior once she was reassured by the counselor that she was not the only one involved in this kind of behavior (34). Apparently, a completely satisfactory sexual and marital relationship could be attained in this marriage without attempting by prolonged and difficult psychotherapy (with little assurance of ultimate success) to change the behavior to a more "normal" kind.

It is obvious, of course, that many forms of behavior that have been labeled as abnormal and perverse are indicative of serious disturbances and require extended psychotherapy before the individual can function effectively in the marital relationship. But in a very large number of cases disturbance has proceeded from the process of negative labeling, rather than from the intrinsic nature of the conduct itself. The common denominator of this negative labeling is the downgrading of any but the procreative aspects of the sexual relationship.

The notion of the sex act as being primarily an act for the purpose of procreation becomes manifestly ridiculous when one contemplates the wide range of sexual experience and the fact that, out of the many thousands of times a couple engage in coitus during a lifetime, at most only a tiny proportion have as their purpose the production of a child. Thus, it is the pleasure or play aspect of sex that is the motivating force for most sexual relationships. And yet, as Nelson N. Foote has pointed out, the taboo against valuing sex as play has been so strong that even the more liberal moralists tend to boggle when they contemplate the recognition of sex as a legitimate form of play (35). The general prejudice against such recognition, he notes, is probably a result of the puritan tendency to frown upon play as well as the puritan tradition that sex is intrinsically sinful.

The marriage counselor can be of great help to couples who seek help about problems of sexual relationship if he helps the couple to shift their focus from worrying about "perverted" and "deviant" acts in the marriage bed to an emphasis upon valuing sex as play and upon learning to accept each other's desires and needs as legitimate. The mere use of terms like abnormal and perverted conveys a highly disturbing connotation. Seen through the lenses of "perversion" many acts that are basically harmless—whether they are the remnants of infantile tendencies, unconscious fantasies or learned compulsions—become threatening acts that provoke shame, guilt, and fear.

"The proper carrying out of the sexual act and the enjoyment of it," says psychiatrist Theodore Lidz, "involves an ability to give way to the irrational, the timeless, the purely animal in one: it includes a loss of individuality in a temporary fusion with another . . . Here one needs to be unabashed by the nakedness of impulse and drive by recrudescense of the infantile and the revealing of much that one has sought to hide from others" (36).

"The sexual act," Lidz continues, "contains a definite and direct relationship to infantile relatedness to the mother, with a renewed interest in sucking, in odor, in skin eroticism; and a reawakening of old forbidden desires to explore and play with orifices. So very much that has been learned needs to be undone; much that has been forbidden and long repressed and kept unconscious, but that haunted dreams and masturbating fantasies, needs to be released to permit sexual intimacy and enjoyment and to allow fulfillment rather than provoke shame and guilt."

When married couples see each other's needs and desires in this light, they are well on the road to achieving a genuine form of sexual intimacy and encounter. By clarifying the concepts of "normality," "perversion," and "deviance" the marriage counselor can do much to light them on their journey.

REFERENCES

1. Kisch, E.H.: *The Sexual Life of Woman*. New York, Allied Book Co., 1931, *passim*.
2. Newman, G., and Nichols, C.R.: Sexual activities and attitudes in older persons. *JAMA, 173:*33-35, 1960; and Pfeiffer, E.; Verivoerdt, A., and Wang, H.S.: The natural history of sexual behavior in aged men and women. I. Observations on 254 community volunteers. *Arch Gen Psychiat, 19:*753-758, 1968.
3. Masters, W.H., and Johnson, Virginia E.: *Human Sexual Response*. Boston, Little, Brown & Co., 1966, Section: "Geriatric Sexual Response."
4. Rubin, I.: *Sexual Life After Sixty*. New York, Basic Books, 1965.
5. Kinsey, A.C., *et al.: Sexual Behavior in the Human Male*. Philadelphia, W.B. Saunders, 1948, pp. 368-373, 573-574; and Kinsey, A.C., *et al.: Sexual Behavior in the Human Female*. Philadelphia, W.B. Saunders, 1953, pp. 257-259.
6. Hiltner, S.: *Sex and the Christian Life*. New York, Association Press, 1957, p. 102.
7. Cavanagh, J.R.: *Fundamentals of Marriage Counseling—A Catholic Viewpoint*. Milwaukee, The Bruce Publishing Co., 1962, p. 106.
8. Pomeroy, W.B.: Normal vs abnormal sex. *Sexology, 32:*436-439, 1966.
9. Ellis, A.: What is "normal" sex behavior? *Sexology, 28:*364-369, 1962.
10. Ruitenbeek, H.M.: *Psychotherapy of Perversions*. New York, Citadel Press, 1967, p. 13.
11. Kinsey, A.C., *et al.:* Concepts of normality and abnormality in sexual behavior, in sexual behavior, in P.H. Hoch and J. Zubin, Eds. *Psychosexual Development in Health and Disease*. New York Grune & Stratton, 1949, pp. 11-32.
12. Freud, S.: *Three Contributions To The Theory of Sex,* as quoted in M. Hoffman, ref. no. 14 below.
13. Szasz, T.: quoted by M. Hoffman, ref. no. 14 below.
14. Hoffman, M.: On the concept of genital primacy. *J Nerv Ment Dis, 137:*552-556, 1963.
15. Szasz, T.: *Law, Liberty and Psychiatry*. New York, The Macmillan Co., 1963.
16. Halleck, S.L.: *Psychiatry and the Dilemmas of Crime*. New York, Harper & Row-Hoeber, 1967.
17. Wooton, B.: *Social Science and Social Pathology*. New York, Macmillan, 1959, Chap. VII.
18. Davis, K.: Mental hygiene and the class structure. Social Science and Social Pathology. New York, Macmillan, 1959.
19. Willis, S.E., II: *Understanding and Counseling the Male Homosexual*. Boston, Little, Brown & Co., 1967, p. 203.
20. *New York Times,* March 16, 1969.
21. The homosexual patient. *Medical World News.* March 14, 1969, pp. 38-42.
22. Hooker, E.: The adjustment of the male overt homosexual. *J Project Techn, 21:*1-31, 1957.
23. Marmor, J.: *Sexual Inversion*. New York, Basic Books, 1965, Introduction, pp. 1-24.
24. Rubin, I.: *Homosexuality*. SIECUS Study Guide No. 2. New York, 1967, pp. 9-12.
25. Becker, H.S.: *Outsiders-Studies In The Sociology Of Deviance*. New York, The Free Press of Glencoe, 1963, p. 9.
26. Kitsuse, J.I.: Societal reaction to deviant behavior: Problems of theory and method,

in H.S. Becker, Ed. *The Other Side—Perspectives On Deviance*. New York, The Press of Glencoe, 1964, pp. 87-102.

27. Vincent, C.E.: *Unmarried Mothers*. New York, The Free Press of Glencoe, pp. 22-23.

28. Erikson, K.T.: Notes on the sociology of deviance, in H.S. Becker, Ed. *The Other Side—Perspectives On Deviance*. New York, The Press of Glencoe, 1964, pp. 9-21.

29. Henriques, F.: *Modern Sexuality* (Vol. III of *Prostitution and Society*). London, MacGibbon & Kee, 1968, *passim*.

30. Davis, K.: Prostitution, in R. Merton and R. Nisbet, Eds. *Contemporary Social Problems*. New York, Harcourt, Brace & World, 1961, pp. 262-288.

31. N. Polsky Pornography, in E. Sagarin and D. E.J. MacNamara, Eds. *Problems of Sex Behavior*. New York, Thomas Y. Crowell, 1968, pp. 268-284.

32. Comfort, A.: *Sex in Society*. London, Gerald Duckworth & Co., 1963, pp. 42-44.

33. Dearborn, L.W.: Wife-spanking. *Sexology, 32*:228-230, 1965.

34. Dearborn, L.W.: The man who needed rubber to enjoy sex. *Sexology, 35*:591-593, 1969.

35. Foote, N.N.: Sex as play, in J. Himelhoch and S.F. Fava, Eds. *Sexual Behavior in American Society*. New York, W.W. Norton & Co., 1955. pp. 237-243.

36. Lidz, T.: *The Person—His Development Throughout The Life Cycle*. New York, Basic Books, 1968, pp. 424.

Chapter 18

SEX EDUCATION IN THE PUBLIC SCHOOLS: PROBLEM OR SOLUTION?

IRA L. REISS

WITHIN the next decade the majority of our public schools will in all likelihood have some form of sex education program. Whether this change in our public school curriculum will be the solution to existing problems in the area of sex or whether it will create more problems is a vital question that we ought to face up to now. We still have time to assess the way sex education is being integrated today and arrive at a judgment on the wisdom of continuing or changing the present trends.

I have had the opportunity to become familiar with much of the material utilized in the public school sex education programs and with the way the courses are taught and integrated into existing school programs. I don't pretend to have taken a representative sample but I have become familiar with a great many sex education programs. The chief impressions that I have been left with are that the key characteristics of the sex education programs that exist in most of our public schools today are: 1) the courses have strong moralistic and propagandistic elements, 2) the courses stress physiological aspects of sexuality, 3) the courses are isolated and sexual materials are not integrated into other relevant courses in the school system, 4) the teachers of these courses are inadequately trained for an inadequately defined task. It should be clear that much of what is said critically about sex education could be said critically about many other aspects of the educational system, but I will leave that broader task to someone else.

The moral aspect of sex education courses is probably their most easily detectable quality. One has only to glance at course descriptions to find frequent references to teaching the students the "value" of chastity, or the "dangers" of going steady, or a list of reasons why one should avoid heavy petting, "excessive" masturbation, or premarital intercourse. On the positive value side one finds the emphasis on married life so strong that the clear implication is that those from broken homes are in a very "bad" situation. The specific values that are stressed vary somewhat, although they are almost invariably the *status quo* type. What is crucial is not the specific values but the fact that teachers are morally indoctrinating children in the name of education.

This raises the question that many public schools do not seem to have faced. That is the basic philosophy of education under which they operate. As an academician I can answer this question in a broad way quite easily. There is a general philosophy of education that is most accepted in the colleges among those who are in the education departments as well as among most others. The position is that education is aimed at teaching people *how* to think and not *what* to think. Education is not propaganda or indoctrination. If one teaches about politics, one does not teach that the Republican or Democratic party is the best party. Rather, one teaches people how the political processes work so that the students may be able to handle their own life in this area more intelligently. Similarly, if one teaches about American religions one does not teach that Catholicism or Protestantism is the best religion. Rather, one teaches how the religious institution is organized and how it operates in our society so that if the individual has questions regarding religion, this educational background may aid in his handling of them. The same should be true for teaching about sex. According to this generally accepted philosophy of education, we would not tell the student that abstinence or permissiveness before marriage is the best form of behavior. We would teach how sexual relationships occur and analyze this so as to increase the student's ability to think calmly and rationally in this area and thereby better handle whatever problems may arise.

Of course, no social institution such as the public schools is free of moral judgments. Judgments of value must be made to decide what is an important enough part of our cultural heritage and our current and future life to be included in the school curriculum. It is also a moral judgment that good education is education that is objective and impartial in its treatment of subject. But such judgments do not bias the way a particular topic is treated; they do not allow us to preach in favor of one political party, one religion, or one sexual standard. The moral judgments that schools allow are operational judgments concerning how the school system should function in our society—and that is quite different from moral judgments favoring a particular moral position on the substance covered in a course.

Granted, it is a difficult thing to be impartial and to maintain an interesting presentation and to avoid mere memorization of facts. In the area of sex, when an objective stance is not taken, when we resort to moralizing, the student's typical reaction is to tune out the teacher. Such indoctrination courses often bore the students who have heard the same thing year after year from other adult sources. Students may take such courses because they are easy and because they take little preparation, but they hardly take them for educational reasons. The goal of teaching people how to think without indoctrination is difficult and achieved at best in part only. But if we do not at least try for this goal, the likelihood of failure to be objective and the likelihood of our educational system becoming more propagandistic would increase greatly. The ideal serves to maintain approximation to standards. Such limitation on moralizing would naturally not apply to religious institutions. Sex education within a church would be expected to contain some moral commitment to the church's position.

The question arises here as to precisely how sex should be taught in order to fit into the public schools. At the present time, the heavy emphasis on physiology and the lack of an integrated curriculum regarding sex is in part a result of the fact that the physiology of sex is an area where teachers find it easier to avoid facing their own "hang-ups" on sex, i.e. their own emotional feelings. But the stress on physiology overlooks the crucial areas of attitudes and social pressures that mean so much in the full explanation of human sexuality. Also, the educational aids such as the charts showing the fetus during all nine months of pregnancy and the internal and external organs of the male and female, are readily available. Similar educational materials in the psychological, sociological, and anthropological aspects of sex are not so easily available. However, this is being remedied by publications issued by SIECUS and other groups. In addition, the National Science Foundation has given grants that will soon lead to revisions in our social studies offerings in the public schools. Some of these changes will include more materials on the entire area of family life.

Part of the question of content is the question of the level of sex education and the specific courses utilized. An isolated course on sex education at the seventh-grade level is hardly an effective way to handle the needs for sex education. If we have decided, as most Americans have, according to recent polls, that sex is an important enough aspect of our life that it should be handled in the public schools, then we have to do more than simply insert one course and feel that we have solved the problem. We must realize that the reason there is a felt need for sex education in the public school curriculum is that the curriculum has been denuded of its sexual content over the generations. Almost all disciplines have had the sexual aspects of their fields removed.

This "sex-ectomy" can be corrected. For example, in economics one of the most fascinating areas to study would be the economics of prostitution. To what extent do the classical laws of supply and demand apply here? In history one would gain much by studying the ways in which the sexual codes of society affected the political life of presidents and kings. The question of the illegitimate child of Grover Cleveland, the sexual interests of Catherine the Great, are but two examples of prime relevance. Social problems courses could discuss the relative effectiveness of various birth control methods in controlling population growth in countries like India. English literature is one of the very few areas where sex hasn't been removed as thoroughly as in other fields. This is predominantly so because to remove it would eliminate much if not most of the valuable literature that forms the subject matter of this field. This is one reason why it is in literature courses that some parents find books to which they object. Such parents lack the philosophy of education we have been speaking about and have more of a moral indoctrination philosophy of education.

My point is that the sex-ectomy should be remedied by putting sex back into all fields. In this way it can be viewed in social and cultural context and will not be given undue importance. After all, sex is not an academic discipline; one cannot major in sex. Thus it has no place as a separate course in a public school system unless one wants to take a kind of "driver's education" approach to it. If we want sex education to have the respect of the teachers and the students, then it would seem the best path to follow would be to integrate it into the legitimate existing disciplines. To do otherwise will make it likely to be taught in moralistic fashion. Of course, such total integration into various courses cannot occur without proper teaching materials and properly trained teachers. It is not something that can occur overnight. However, if we lack integration as a goal we may feel that the one seventh-grade course in sex education really is transmitting all the sexual awareness that is needed, and thereby we would fail to achieve an adequate sex education program. In the public schools as well as in other institutions, it is having well-thought-out, long-range goals that lead to progress.

This brings us to the last characteristic of present-day sex education— the poor quality of many of the teachers involved. Partly, this is due to the fact that what is supposed to be done is poorly defined and often is defined in ways that are nontraditional in American education. By this I mean that the course is defined as a kind of moral indoctrination which parents hope will cut down on VD, premarital pregnancy, and premarital intercourse. Note that such a demand for "practical" consequences would eliminate most of the courses in our current public school system, particularly those in the humanities area.

Why is it that when we add the "new math" to the public school system we use arguments regarding the ease with which the new math can be learned, its better integration with more advanced forms of mathematics, and so forth? We don't find many arguments that ask why bother to get so involved with mathematics, since most of us won't need to do more than count our change at the movie theater. We don't find such arguments because we have accepted the intrinsic value of mathematics as an area of knowledge that is important enough to our civilization for us to preserve a high level of awareness about it. Why don't we use the same reasoning about sex and justify the "new sex" by contending that such knowledge is an important enough aspect of our way of life that we should have a sound understanding of it? Such an approach would lead to better prepared students in our colleges. The answer is, I think, that in sex we allow our emotions to blind us to the educational philosophy that guides us in the case of mathematics. By doing this we take sex out of the usual academic structure; then it becomes a question of who is qualified to teach this unusual type of course. Often the coach or a friendly housewife is given the task. For a moralistic, applied approach to sex such people may well be relevant, but for an educational approach they clearly are not adequate.

From the point of view of educational philosophy, our basic mistake is to think that when we deal with sex in the public schools we must somehow treat it differently than we do all our other subjects. Different subjects may well require somewhat different pedagogical techniques, but the pedagogical requirement of sex is well within the limits of existing methods. Many classes handle emotionally charged subjects (often more emotional to the teacher than the student) when discussing social problems, novels, and cross-cultural differences. Is sex really so different?

The qualifications for teaching sex in the public schools should be the same as the qualifications for teaching in most other fields. A good teacher needs to be able to establish rapport with the class and needs to be sensitive to ways of clearly communicating to that class. A good teacher must know the subject matter thoroughly and must strive to communicate it at a level that can be understood. A good teacher must be able to handle all aspects of the field, and not be emotionally blocked from covering a particular part of it.

Ideally, sex education would be taught in an integrated fashion; materials could be added to the social science units at all levels. I stress all levels, K—12, because it seems best to start before emotional blocks are too strong and to treat sex as a natural part of all instructional levels. It would seem to be psychologically advantageous to discuss common events like menstruation, masturbation, and marriage before they occur. Children of all ages have a sexual quality to their lives and the discussion of sex is something they are "ready for." They are "mature" enough to handle it if it is presented in accord with sound educational principles.

A teacher whose substantive training is in psychology, sociology, and anthropology would be best equipped to see the obvious places that sex could be incorporated into the social science units. A few of the many ways that sex could be brought easily and naturally into the elementary classroom are discussions of the family, in comparisons of courtship in animals and man, in comparisons of different societies, in discussions of different customs regarding marriage, and in discussions of how our self-image affects our sex life. I stress here the social studies units, for the physiological aspects of sex can more easily and clearly be added to the biological science areas without as much difficulty. Home economics and health courses can incorporate the more applied aspects of sex—the problem-centered and direct role preparation aspects. Naturally, the knowledge of sex gained in a variety of other courses has implications for role preparation and should give greatly increased insight to the students, but home economics and health courses can focus more directly on this applied area. Nevertheless, sex education should not be conceived of as predominantly present in these applied fields, but rather as predominantly centered as one integrated part of many fields. This approach puts sex into a broad human context rather than singling it out as an isolated problem area.

The question of practical strategy necessary to get a sex education program adopted makes it likely that a school system may want to start with one course at a certain grade level. However, unless the person running that course plans to get educational materials and to help coordinate the integration of sex throughout the existing curriculum, the course will not really become part of the educational life of the students. One can, of course, have an interdisciplinary applied-type course on sex; but if that is all one gets into the school system, then sex has not been put back into our schools but rather has simply been fused onto the academic educational system. As long as that state of affairs remains, the course will have low prestige. It will thus be poorly staffed and students will take it for "laughs" and easy grades rather than for educational purposes. The faculty in college education departments will also not look favorably upon an applied course and will do little to further the preparation of competent teachers. The same holds true for "family life education" courses; they, too, most often have no disciplinary "home" and are no more readily accepted. Such family life education also needs to be integrated into existing disciplines.

The real danger in America today is that almost all of our schools will add a type of moralistic, unintegrated, and poorly staffed applied course in sex education and then feel that they have taken care of the needs for sex education. This is exactly what I see happening today in our country and unless we take a longer and more careful look at the matter we may have a sex education program on a national scale that really is an anti-sex education program.

Now let us briefly look at some of the key factors which seem to be pressuring sex education toward becoming an educational failure. One very crucial area affecting the popularity and the success of sex education programs today is the attitude of parents toward sex in their own families. An observer from another culture would be immediately struck by the fact that although parents will readily admit the great importance of sex to their youngsters' future lives, they have a noticeable tendency to avoid discussing sex with their children. It would be difficult to find a comparable situation in any other pattern of American socialization. For example, parents who feel that religion is an important part of their child's present and future life do not hesitate to talk about religion. They do not wait to be asked and then just answer a direct question and go no further. The modern parent seems to do just this on sex. He may rationalize this position by statements about the "readiness" of his child. He may feel that he will give the child "ideas" about sex if he raises the topic. The practical consequences of such an approach are to lessen the influence of the parents and increase the influence of one's peers on one's sex life. By minimizing talk about sex, one does not end the sexual interests of one's child. The child still plays the usual sex games of curiosity and exploration with other children. Sexual information, accurate or not, and sexual attitudes of various sorts inevitably filter down from the older boys and girls to the younger boys and girls. There is no way for parents to stop this; there is only the possibility of extending the parental influences by a more concerted effort to deal with the topic of sex even if the child doesn't initiate it.

Obviously, one key reason for the hushed approach to sex is that the parents haven't yet come to terms with their own attitudes. Also, the parent may feel he doesn't have the needed information. He may feel inadequate to cope with the possible consequences of initiating conversation about sex. Given such parents, it is clear that the consequences of talking about sex might be different if one had parents without such informational and attitudinal hang-ups. In fact, I believe it is the partial realization of this situation that has made sex education in the public schools popular and that has made it of the poor quality that it is at present. Let me briefly explain what I mean.

Many parents may have decided that since they cannot handle sex discussions comfortably with their children, maybe the public school system can help them. It is difficult to say why this didn't happen a few generations ago, but I think one reason is the fact that there has been a shift in the premarital sex partners of middle-class and upper-class males from prostitutes to the "girl next door," and so the parents of the girl next door are concerned. Also, many more children are in school now during their most sexually active years. There is increased awareness of the widespread nature of VD and premarital pregnancy even among middle-class and upper-class groups. Although the changes are too gradual to be called revolutionary, there has been a noticeable removal of adult heads from the sand. The difficulties of hiding sex becomes greater when it is occurring nearby and when historical and cross-cultural studies point out further its pervasiveness. All our evidence suggests that no culture anywhere at any time on this planet has brought up even the majority of one generation of males to physical maturity as virgins. The major historical shifts have been predominantly in terms of the partners of men—are they prostitutes or are they the girl next door? Such a factual situation needn't affect one's moral values. One can favor for oneself or others goals that cannot be achieved by all, but even so one must realize that the universality of premarital sex of some kind in a child's life experiences makes it an important area to include in a child's education.

Most parents are, naturally, not very conversant with educational philosophies. Thus they haven't generally internalized the idea that teachers should not be moralistic in presenting their subject matter. When social changes make parents think of accepting sex education in the schools, they tend to project their own parental roles on the teacher and feel that she should be moralistic. By this they mean, of course, moralistic in their own way; for they would object violently if the teacher's moralism were in accord with some other group of parents and not with their own.

Public school teachers do not have as highly developed a sense of academic freedom as do college teachers; thus they are more easily intimidated by these parental pressures. In fact, many of them have become so accustomed to pressures from parents, school boards, and principals that they have only retained a very watered-down version of the educational philosophy they were taught in college. Therefore, if one wants to obtain an academically respectable approach to sex in the public schools, it is essential to educate the parents and to strengthen the academic freedom of our public school teachers. They may then abide more closely with their original educational philosophy.

Such a closer adherence to accepted educational philosophy would force some parents into an uncomfortable situation. For if they accept the fact that the school is not going to teach their personal morals to all its children, then they cannot thereby escape from teaching sexual morals themselves. That means they will still have to transmit, directly or indirectly, their own moral values regarding sex to their children. Perhaps an adult education program on sex can help. It can aid the parents to understand their own values and the place of sex in their lives, to think through what they want to teach their youngsters and how.

Many practical problems are associated with any attempt to instigate a sound educational approach to sexuality in the public schools. As a sociologist, I realize that the social and cultural setting of the school cannot be fully excluded. It is obvious, for example, that Christmas and Easter and many other religious holidays permeate the school program and very often in obviously religious ways. Perhaps the best one can hope for is that at least films asserting the divinity of Christ will not be used in the schools. But if one does not aim at some objectivity, then such films and similar religious elements would surely permeate our school systems. Accordingly, perhaps certain widely shared values such as the vague notions of the value of love, respect, and responsibility will be endorsed in most all sex education classes. But this is still closer to our ideal of impartiality than would be the teaching of abstinence or permissiveness as the only moral way to behave. Sometimes we overestimate the public opposition to various educational endeavors. For example, I have seen reports that Catholic schools in some cities include more birth control information than do public schools in the same cities. While we cannot totally ignore social pressures, we can avoid exaggerating their potency.

It is also clear that different school settings will affect the emphasis on many school subjects, including sex. In a lower-class neighborhood with high VD and illegitimacy rates one can expect these factors to loom larger in the program. In an upper-class setting the psychological subtleties may well gain more attention. In both cases the approach could be objective. The question of whether to require sex education for all students becomes irrelevant in any school system that incorporates sex into its natural context in a wide variety of fields. Requirement is only an issue when one has but a single isolated course on sex education. The U. S. Office of Education announced in August, 1966, that funds were available to assist communities in the integration of sex into their public school programs and in the training of teachers. The specifics of the program are left up to the judgment of the communities.

One major point to bear in mind is that at least in recent American history the attempt to keep children ignorant of sex has rarely succeeded except in correlating highly with premarital pregnancy rates. The attempt to moralize about sex in public institutions has also not succeeded in changing major patterns of behavior. If we feel that sex is an important aspect of life, then it is important to enable people to think clearly about it. This the public school systems can do if the parents of America will let them. Sex education will not necessarily reduce to nothing our VD and premarital pregnancy rates, but it can, if taught in accord with accepted educational principles, make the sexual choices of our children less psychologically costly. A sound sex education can aid the individual student to choose his or her sex ethic in a more calm and less compulsive fashion. The choice of sex ethics is already an accepted part of youth culture. Young people feel that they have just as much right to choose their sex ethic as to choose their political party or their religion. They feel there are different ways suited best for different people. This is what is often called the "new morality." Parents may well favor one type of choice but ignorance or public moralizing will not achieve that goal. The parents have their chance to influence their child's choices by the values and attitudes they pass on. If they miss out there, they are not likely to change things by preventing a public discussion in a reasonably impartial manner of this area in the public schools. At least by having a sound sex educational system parents can assure a less compulsive basis for choice. Given the free courtship system we have, we cannot control sexuality directly, nor can we stop the flow of information and attitudes about sex. But we can add an element of enlightenment and control to our youngsters' sexual life by supporting an unbiased approach to it throughout the educational system.

As an educator I feel that we should adopt sound educational approaches to sex in the public schools. As a sociologist I feel that we should not distort by our moralizing the research findings that are available. As a father, I feel that I and not the public schools should do the moral teaching of my children in my own way. If we do not realize the distinct qualities of these various roles we play, we will have sex education in our public schools in a form that will not prepare our children for the sexual aspects of the lives they lead. We will have missed the opportunity to make the best case for our private moral positions.

Chapter 19

THE CONSCIENCE OR SUPEREGO IN MARRIAGE COUNSELING

BEN N. ARD, JR.

WHEN CLIENTS COME to a marriage counselor for professional help, they frequently are facing what have been called "moral dilemmas," or they need help in resolving questions involving very basic issues centering around "right" or "wrong" behavior. Because so many "moral" issues are raised in marriage counseling (3), the professional marriage counselor needs to be quite clear about how such moral issues are best resolved.

Some of the problems clients may face can involve such moral issues as: a) whether one should marry anyone of another faith or race; b) whether premarital intercourse is ever acceptable (if so, under what conditions); c) whether masturbation is wrong or not; d) whether certain, if any, birth control methods are right or wrong; e) whether certain "thoughts" are immoral, sinful, or not; f) whether certain forms of behavior are sins against God or not; g) what sorts of sexual behavior are "normal," "abnormal," "sinful," "perverted" or not; h) whether extramarital intercourse is ever justified or not (or whether it, in and of itself, justifies divorce); i) whether an abortion should ever be considered or not; and j) whether separation or divorce should ever be considered or not (if so, under what conditions).

There has been some recent interest in the area of values and morals in psychotherapy (7, 19) but there has not been sufficient discussion of what marriage counselors (who face particularly difficult value dilemmas in their practice) should do with regard to the conscience or superego in their clients.

There are several possible stances which the marriage counselor might take with regard to these moral issues so often raised in marriage counseling.

1. He may refuse to discuss "moral matters" and refer all such problems to the religious leader considered appropriate for the particular clients in question (i.e. the minister, priest, or rabbi).

2. He may strive by a variety of methods to reinforce or strengthen the clients' previously existing moral values so that the clients may have the moral resolve to decide what they already know (in some sense) is right.

3. He may teach the "proper" religious values which the clients may

not know and thus provide for the clients the means to resolve the moral dilemmas at hand.

4. He may try to always remain philosophically "neutral" and never say or do anything which would influence the clients in any particular direction on any moral issue.

5. He may strive to lessen the severity of the superego (following Freud's suggestions) and make it more "benevolent" or "tolerant." (But after the client has transferred the authority of his superego to the psychoanalyst, later the client reintrojects his own superego, according to this view.)

6. He may strive to eliminate entirely the traditional ways of deciding so-called moral issues (i.e. eliminate the conscience or superego) and help the client develop more rational ways of deciding ethical questions.

The first stance, or the "refer" stance, seems, on the face of it, to get the marriage counselor off the hook, so to speak, but it really is no ultimate solution. The marriage counselor simply cannot continue to function as a marriage counselor if he merely refers all moral problems to religious leaders. Sooner or later the marriage counselor is going to have to get down to brass tacks and wrestle with the moral issues raised by his clients.

The second stance of strengthening the clients' previously held values is no real solution either in many cases, since one of the main reasons why the clients are in the marriage counselor's office is because their previously held values have not led them to any resolution.

The third stance of teaching the proper religious values may be acceptable to those counselors who only see clients of their own religious faith but it is hardly a solution for the professional marriage counselor who sees a variety of clients in this pluralistic society of ours.

The fourth stance of trying to always remain philosophically "neutral" is probably one of the most popular among marriage counselors these days. Several authorities in the fields of counseling and psychotherapy have suggested that the counselor or therapist should not get involved in moral issues and should remain philosophically "neutral" on all such matters (6). However, to leave all moral decisions up to the client presumes that the client already has an adequate way of resolving moral dilemmas. Specifically, this means the counselor will rely on the client's conscience or superego to resolve all the client's moral dilemmas. In what follows the fundamental assumption that the conscience or superego is the best (or, as some assume, the *only*) way to resolve moral issues will be critically examined.

An extended discussion of the philosophical basis for making value judgments will not be possible in the present context but the interested reader may wish to consult several authorities in the field. Some authorities have suggested that all moral judgments are of an emotional (subjective) nature rather than a rational, cognitive, objective, or scientific nature (22). Others have maintained that it is possible to begin thinking about the development of an objective, scientific standard of ethics (20, 21, 15, 26).

In descriptions of human nature from ancient times there have appeared many concepts to explain a particular portion of man's personality, variously called his "moral reason," "divine reason," "moral sense," or *conscience*. Philosophers and religious writers have held forth at length about this "moral faculty." Some conceived of conscience as an organ implanted in man by God to guide man's conduct and show him what is right. The "voice of conscience" was thought of as the "voice of God." It was thought that man was born with this conscience, as it were.

Under such conditions, it is hardly surprising that little critical thinking was done about the conscience. Who could presume to criticize "God's handiwork"? But gradually, as a more scientific way of looking at man arose, closer, more critical views of man's conscience began to appear (4, 18).

Freud introduced a three-part division of the human personality. He conceived of the personality as divided into id, ego, and superego: the id being the unconscious part of the personality, the ego being the reality-oriented, conscious, cognitive part of the personality. The superego corresponded (in a loose sense) with the older concept of conscience. The superego is basically unconscious, although occasionally conscious.

Freud did agree, to some extent, with earlier religious views that the conscience (or superego) was the basis of morality (24). But this raises a very basic question: is the superego (or conscience) a good basis for morality?

As Grace Stewart has put it, we need to seriously question the superego or conscience as our only or best guide.

> For conscience has so often been called the voice of God that we might well examine it rather as the voice of the parent and his group and age. Conscience has, in such philosophies as Kant's, been exalted as man's greatest good. We might well ask ourselves whether it be not sometimes as much an evil as a good; whether there be not better guides, guides more reliable and more humane (23).

While Freud introduced some scientific thinking into how the superego developed (discarding the former assumption that we are born with a fully developed conscience), he too saw no other way to make moral decisions than through the superego. He described the superego as "a memorial of the former weakness and dependence of the ego and the mature ego remains subject to its domination. As the child was once compelled to obey its parents, so the ego submits to the categorical imperative pronounced by its superego" (11).

Freud was critical of former conceptions of conscience, for as he said,

> The philosopher Kant once declared that nothing proved to him the greatness of God more convincingly than the starry heavens and the moral conscience within us. The stars are unquestionably superb, but where conscience is concerned God has been guilty of an uneven and careless piece of work, for a great many men have only a limited share of it or scarcely enough to be worth mentioning (13).

But Freud saw no alternative to the superego in making moral decisions. He considered the superego natural, normal, and a good thing. And he also said, "The fear of the superego should normally never cease, since it is indispensable in social relations in the form of moral anxiety" (13).

The next basic question which each counselor or therapist must decide for himself is what shall be his goal with regard to the superego or conscience? Should he try to strengthen the superego or conscience (particularly if it is weak or nonexistent)? Or should he, along with Freud, try to lessen its severity? (This is the fifth stance we mentioned earlier.) Or should he try to change it at all?

What happens to the superego in psychoanalytic therapy is not always crystal clear, to say the least. And the final disposition of the superego in therapy should give us some better idea of its necessity for mentally healthy, psychologically mature individuals.

Judging from the literature on the subject, as one psychoanalyst himself admits, additional clarification is needed on the problem of assessing the precise results of analytic therapy in terms of the superego (5). The general agreement seems to be that the superego becomes milder, more "tolerant" or "benevolent." But Bergler has said the following:

> Personally, I doubt the direct applicability of the quality of benevolence to a monster such as the superego, whether the individual's state of health be that of health or neurosis. I would rather say that psychoanalytic therapy changes the technique of torture. The alleged "benevolence" of the post-analysis superego seems to me to be a mirage (5).

Another analyst, Erik Erikson, has spoken of a "workable equilibrium" or "balance" between the ego and the superego (8). Still another analyst, Flugel, has said that in psychoanalysis "the superego is required to undergo changes which result in a weakening in the power of at any rate its deeper layers" (10).

During therapy the patient is said to transfer to the analyst the authority of his superego (14). Eventually, however, in the course of treatment, the 'transference' is resolved, "so that the patient loses his dependence on the analyst, that is, he reintrojects his superego" (10).

Freud said that in therapy the analysts are, among other things, "attempting the gradual demolition of the hostile superego" (14). One might read this as an attempt to demolish the superego entirely, except for the preceding adjective "hostile." Perhaps Freud only meant to demolish the *hostile* superego. But this implies there is a nonhostile ("benevolent") superego, which is not so, according to Bergler *(vide supra).*

In another place, Freud said that in analytic therapy "we find ourselves obliged to do battle with the superego and work to moderate its demands" (12). In still another place, Freud stated that the objective of therapeutic efforts is, "to strengthen the ego, to make it more independent of the super-ego" (13). Here again we note the crucial word "more" in front of independent. Evidently Freud did not attempt to make the ego *entirely* independent of the superego. So it would seem that we must conclude that Freud considered the superego still necessary, even after successful analysis.

Apparently Freud was led to postulate the necessity of the superego by his conception of the nature of man in relation to society. According to Freud, the first society was formed by setting protective taboos against the so-called instincts of incest and murder. Man conformed only out of fear. Culture is thus a kind of rigid police system imposed upon man. Thus, *according to Freud,* man is "good" *only* because of his helplessness and dependence on others. This is certainly an attitude which is still prevalent in our society today, as Clara Thompson has pointed out. But, as she has clearly stated,

> It leaves out of consideration entirely the possibility that some things may be bad for man even though they are socially approved, and that some things socially disapproved may be good, and it implies that there are no socially constructive tendencies unless the police force and society insists upon them (25).

Thus Freud's view of the nature of man (i.e. that it is essentially, or ultimately, evil) led to the view that society must restrict man. This fatalism is reflected in the therapy of Freud and those who followed him unthinkingly. With the Freudian point of view, "the best that can be done for a man is to make him more able to accept the restrictions of society" (25).

But not all of those who followed Freud did so in an unthinking manner. And this leads us to the final stance for the marriage counselor, that of eliminating the conscience or superego. Some recent theorists have felt there is no necessity for following Freud's views of human nature slavishly, nor the goals of therapy following therefrom. A different point of view derives from the "cultural school," as exemplified by Erich Fromm and Karen Horney, for example.

> With the new point of view, the goal of therapy is different. The aim of the "cultural school" goes beyond merely enabling man to submit to the restrictions of his society; . . . it seeks to free him from its irrational demands and make him more able to develop his potentialities and to assume leadership in building a more constructive society (25).

Grace Stewart, in her book *Conscience and Reason* (1951), has provided a very insightful and critical review of the superego concept. At one point she seemed to feel that we would be better off without any superego.

> It would seem that if one grows up in a community which has no sense of sin, and if in consequence no stern parental rule makes one take into oneself and establish in one's own mind a stern superego, then a considerable amount of strain, anxiety, cominance, condemnation, competitiveness, ambition and war will naturally and inevitably be eliminated (23).

The next question is, what about the future? What should be the counselor's aim with regard to the superego? Freud, in stating the object of therapeutic efforts, said, "Where id was, there shall ego be" (9, 13) thought that this dictum should be supplemented. We should *also* say that *"where superego was"* (that is, the automatic autonomy of unreasonable guilt feelings, the principle of talion, revenge, and automatisms), *"there shall ego be"* (that is, a reasonable handling of reality). Fenichel commented that such an additional "shall" runs against socially determined barriers (9). That is a masterpiece of understatement.

Perhaps one of the clearest statements of what a counselor can aim for (if he wishes to adopt the sixth stance we mentioned earlier) is one given by Karen Horney:

> Freud can aim merely at reducing the severity of the superego while I aim at the individual's being able to dispense with his inner dictates altogether and to assume the direction of his life in accordance with his true wishes and beliefs. This latter possibility does not exist in Freud's thinking (16).

Some of these professional insights were anticipated somewhat by that perceptive young man, Mark Twain's Huckleberry Finn, who said,

> It don't make no difference whether you do right or wrong, person's conscience ain't got no sense and just goes for him anyway. If I had a yaller dog that didn't know more than a person's conscience does, I'd pizon him. It takes up more room than all the rest of a person's insides, and yet ain't no good nohow. Tom Sawyer says the same (17).

Since marriage counselors must deal with a variety of problems that clients bring in which are, ultimately, reducible in the main to *ethical* or what have been called "moral" issues, counselors must be explicitly clear in their own minds and in their relationships with their clients about how such issues are best resolved. Turning such dilemmas over to the client's conscience or superego is really not a very satisfactory solution.

Whatever the problem may be, whether it be one of divorce, extramarital relations, certain sexual behaviors within the marriage, the handing of money or other marital "rights," the superego or conscience may be the major factor in the client's *having* the problem in the first place. Turning the client back to his conscience or superego is of very little fundamental help to him, particularly if the reason he feels guilty and is in the counselor's office is because of the unquestioned assumptions of his conscience or superego.

Camilla Anderson, a psychiatrist, has suggested that man's propensity for making *moral judgments* is the basis for much of his human trouble (1). As the present writer has discussed in other contexts (2), counselors need to get away from such concepts as "sin," (Mowrer to the contrary notwithstanding), and help clients come to rational conclusions that will not be as self-defeating as turning back to the conscience or superego.

As Huxley has so succinctly put it,

> Once we realize that the primitive superego is merely a makeshift developmental mechanism, no more intended to be the permanent central support of our morality than is our embryonic notochord intended to be the central support of our bodily frame, we shall not take its dictates so seriously (have they not often been interpreted as the authentic Voice of God?), and shall regard its suppression by some more rational and less cruel mechanism as the central ethical problem confronting every human individual (17).

REFERENCES

1. Anderson, Camilla: *Beyond Freud.* New York, Harper, 1957.
2. Ard, Ben: Nothing's uglier than sin. *Rational Living.* 1967, Vol. 2, No. 1, pp. 4-6.
3. Ard, Ben N., Jr., and Ard, Constance C. (Eds.) : *Handbook of Marriage Counselseling.* Palo Alto, Science and Behavior Books, 1969.
4. Aronfreed, Justin: *Conduct and Conscience.* New York, Academic Press, 1968.
5. Bergler, Edmund: *The Superego.* New York, Grune and Stratton, 1952, p. 349.
6. Browning, Robert L., and Peters, Herman J.: On the philosophical neutrality of counselors, in Ard, Ben N., Jr., (Ed.) *Counseling and Psychotherapy: Classics on Theories and Issues.* Palo Alto, Science and Behavior Books, 1966, pp. 187-195.
7. Buhler, Charlotte: *Values in Psychotherapy.* New York, Free Press of Glencoe, 1962.
8. Erikson, Erik, H.: *Childhood and Society.* New York, Norton, 1950, pp. 367-8.
9. Fenichel, Otto: *The Psychoanalytic Theory of Neurosis.* New York, Norton, 1945, p. 589.
10. Flugel, J. C.: *Man, Morals and Society.* New York, International Universities Press, 1945, pp. 176-7.
11. Freud, Sigmund: *The Ego and the Id.* London, Hogarth Press, 1927, p. 69.
12. Freud, Sigmund: *Civilization and Its Discontents.* London, Hogarth Press, 1930, p. 139.
13. Freud, Sigmund: *New Introductory Lectures on Psychoanalysis.* New York, Norton, 1933, pp. 88, 111-112, 123.
14. Freud, Sigmund: *An Outline of Psychoanalysis.* New York, Norton, 1949, pp. 75, 77.
15. Fromm, Erich: *Man For Himself.* New York, Rinehart, 1947.
16. Horney, Karen: *Neurosis and Human Growth.* New York, Norton, 1950, p. 375.
17. Huxley, T. H., and Huxley, Julian: *Touchstone for Ethics.* New York, Harper, 1947, pp. 124, 256.
18. Knight, James A.: *Conscience and Guilt.* New York, Appleton-Century-Crofts, 1969.
19. London, Perry: *The Modes and Morals of Psychotherapy.* New York, Holt, Rinehart & Winston, 1964.
20. Maslow, A. H. (Ed.) : *New Knowledge in Human Values.* New York, Harper, 1959.

21. Otto, Max: *Science and the Moral Life.* New York, New American Library, 1949.
22. Stevenson, Charles L.: *Ethics and Language.* New Haven, Yale University Press, 1944.
23. Stewart, Grace: *Conscience and Reason.* New York, Macmillan, 1951, pp. 72, 146-147.
24. Symonds, Percival M.: *The Dynamics of Human Adjustment.* New York, Appleton-Century-Crofts, 1946, p. 292.
25. Thompson, Clara: *Psychoanalysis: Evolution and Development.* New York, Hermitage, 1950, pp. 138-139, 152.
26. White, Amber Blanco: *Ethics for Unbelievers.* London, Rutledge & Kegan Paul, 1948.

Chapter 20

REFLECTIONS ON THE SOCIAL CONTROL OF MAN

DAVID O. MOBERG

MARRIAGE COUNSELING by its very nature involves intervention in the lives of clients as individual spouses and as family units. The precise form of intervention varies with the background, training, and personal inclinations of the counselor, and the profession is still in process of development. It cannot be stereotyped glibly as either directive or nondirective, psychologically or sociologically oriented, a science or an art, for it is all of these and much more. The evolution of family therapy has seen:

> a change in orientation to basic issues: a shift of emphasis from biological heredity to "social-heredity"; from a one-way view of the effect of parent on child to a conception of circular interaction; from a trait analysis of parents to a consideration of total personality; from the isolated evaluation of each parent to the dynamics of marital and parental relationships, and from there to the study of the psycho-social organization, development, and adaptation of the entire family unit (1).

Despite modifications of emphasis and changing styles in thinking and practice, the goal of marriage counseling has continued to center around unsolved problems of husbands and wives, parents and children, and the family as a whole. These have been treated within the context of societal definitions of what is "normal" and "deviant," "wholesome" and "detrimental," "family solidarity" and "family disorganization."

Protection of the institutions of marriage and the family within their cultural context has been the primary objective of marriage counseling (2). The intervention oriented toward that goal is shifting its emphasis from the treatment of problems to prevention (3), but it remains "intervention" nonetheless. It is among the social control activities of mankind and may be labeled "manipulative," for it attempts to modify either the clients' external behavior or their internal emotional and psychological reactions to experiences in their environments. Whether the goal is change on the part of a client or helping him to adjust to his situation, the counselor is involved in manipulation (4). This undoubtedly has both functional and dysfunctional consequences for clients and their families, but generally it is believed to make an important contribution to the welfare of society (5).

REACTIONS TO MANIPULATION

Marriage counselors are potential victims of popular indignation, for Americans tend to react against anyone who is identified as a "manipulator." We fear such persons, thinking that they may use their manipulative influence upon us or upon our wives, children, and friends. People who are not members of labor unions hence tend to be highly critical of COPE, the Committee on Political Education of the AFL-CIO, in its efforts to get laboring people to the election polls and to stimulate them to vote for politically liberal candidates. When they pour large funds of money into key electoral districts, they are charged with "manipulating the vote."

Likewise, some have been very critical of the propagandistic activities of the American Medical Association, which has given its members extra assessments in order to pour millions of dollars into its campaign against "socialized medicine"; it has successfully prevented the passage of numerous pieces of proposed social legislation and thus has "manipulated" the political fortunes of our nation. Efforts of the National Association of Manufacturers, the Foundation for Economic Education (publisher of *The Freeman*), and *Human Events* to promulgate their interpretations of liberty are interpreted as propagandistic "manipulation" by those who do not sympathize with them, as are the publications and fulminations of Carl McIntire (International Council of Christian Churches), Billy James Hargis (Christian Crusade), and Howard Kershner *(Christian Economic)*. Meanwhile, the followers of these and similar "right wing" gentlemen are convinced that their movement is giving "the true facts," educating the nation and sounding a clarion call to freedom, and that the American Civil Liberties Union, Americans for Democratic Action, Southern Christian Leadership Conference, National Council of the Churches of Christ, and other organizations are subversively distorting information, suppressing truth, and stealthily "manipulating" the masses, moving them gradually into the morass of "creeping socialism."

The point I wish to emphasize through these illustrations is that *our own in-groups* (the groups with which we personally identify) *never manipulate;* they educate, inform, warn, guide, persuade, explain, edify, instruct, enlighten, disseminate the facts, disclose, unmask, clarify, affirm the truth, and defend the public weal. Our own group is honest, frank, plainspeaking, truthful, trustworthy, pure, scrupulous, and without equivocation. Our own group is consistent with history, with the welfare of our nation, and with the great traditional virtues of our faith.

It is only out-groups, groups from which we are alienated by aloofness or antagonistic nonmembership, that manipulate. They indoctrinate, propagandize, garble data, misinform, pervert the truth, deceive, misrepresent, cloak the facts, falsify, misinterpret, engineer consent, engage in pressure politics, lobby, and go about spreading lies in cunning craftiness. Their members are equivocators, propagandists, subversionists, masqueraders, brainwashers, or scoundrels who are anxious to stab us or our cause in the back. They are sly, stealthy, surreptitious, evasive, secretive, beguiling, double-tongued, hypocritical, and insidious prevaricators or charlatans.

In other words, manipulation is always an act of sombody else. We influence; others manipulate. We educate; others indoctrinate. We disseminate truth; others disseminate lies and half-truths. We give man the kind of education that liberates; other so-called educational programs are suspect because they tend to enslave their students in isms of one sort or another.

In general, men would much rather change others than change themselves (6). As Piet Hein, the Danish poet-philosopher, put it in his "grook" about *Mankind,* men are good to their brothers, eager to mend *their* ways but not their own (7).

There is a paradox in all this. None of us wants to be manipulated, but all of us are inclined to want the power, the status, the honor, and related results of manipulating others. The marriage counselor is seen as promoting family welfare by those who hold similar values, but he may be viewed as a manipulator by clients from a divergent subculture. His middle-class values are suspect among the lower classes and ethnic minority groups.

MANIPULATION IS INEVITABLE

Manipulation is not unique to marriage counseling and other helping professions, but is present in varying degrees in all areas of man's social life. Without it, there could be no order in society. It makes life tolerable (8). Parents manipulate their children. Spouses manipulate their mates. Teachers manipulate their pupils. Employers manipulate their employees. Social workers manipulate their clients. Parole officers manipulate their parolees. Medical doctors manipulate their patients. City planners manipulate construction firms. Political parties manipulate their candidates and prospective candidates. Governments manipulate taxpayers. Editors manipulate authors and reporters. Publishers manipulate their editors. Salesman manipulate the thought processes and actions of their customers. Clergymen manipulate their congregations. Young men manipulate their girl friends. In every instance, there is feedback, and attempts at counter-manipulation frequently become evident. Manipulative interaction is especially prominent among the "games people play" (9).

Anticipatory socialization is present in many realms of human activity. Expecting to become a businessman in the future, the student of business administration begins to act and think like a businessman. Hoping to become a college professor, the graduate student adapts his behavior and thought processes toward the professorial role as he understands it. Planning to be a mother in the distant future of adult life, the little girl acts toward her dolls as she thinks mothers should act or as she sees them act toward their babies. What people hope to become thus helps to make them into what they actually do become. Modification of desires is one of the manipulative goals of many marriage counseling situations.

There are wide methodological variations in the numerous patterns of manipulative social control. The robber uses a different set of methods for manipulating his victims from those of the blackmailer. The confidence man uses methods which differ from those of the shoplifter. The Don Juan who seduces "innocent" girls uses methods which are not the same as those of the pander finding clients for his prostitutes. The methods of group dynamics and sensitivity training diverge from those of the military drill sergeant. The evangelist's methods are not the same as those of the dictator to whom full political powers of censorship are added to conventional propaganda. A church's board of Christian education and the nominating committee of a professional society do not manipulate their "pawns" as readily as the sales manager reassigning territories to his staff. The parent cannot use the same techniques on his teen-agers as were used when they were of preschool age. The marriage counselor treats his clients differently from the priest in the confessional. Nevertheless, some form of manipulation is present in all of these activities.

MAN'S SENSE OF FREEDOM

The degree of manipulability varies greatly. It is a product of resistances internal to the person as well as of external conditions in his social situation. The more subtly and effectively men are controlled by their environment, the less is the degree to which they realize they are being controlled. The better they have learned to "follow the rules" and meet the demands of their social system, the freer they feel.

Every person is a product of his society as well as of his biological heredity. He is controlled by that society to a very high degree. The language he uses is determined by it. The basic customs, folkways, mores, and laws which regulate his behavior are given to him by society. His *Weltanschauung* is acquired chiefly from his society and the subcultural groups of which he is a part. The food he eats (and that which he refuses to eat) is culturally determined as well as culturally provided.

Some portions of these social pressures and influences are relatively easy to perceive, but others are not evident to a person until he has stepped actually or vicariously outside of his own culture and subcultures through study, reading, television, conversations with cosmopolitan people, and other experiences. One may readily perceive the work of a soldier of an occupying army or a policeman on the corner as controlling human behavior, but informal social controls are more difficult to identify. Men tend to cloak the latter under the guise of "naturalism"; they assume that their refusal to eat insects, snakes, or horseflesh is part of "human nature," for their own cultural ways of doing things normally are not questioned. But Hindus who refuse to eat meat because it is "contrary to human nature," use the same type of ethnocentric interpretations; they know that beef-eating is not only pagan and subhuman but that it also will make them ill. Both Protestant American values and those of the Hindus in India are products of social control; society has manipulated them.

As Alfred McClung Lee expressed it, "When things go well, we may like to dwell on how free and independent our will is" (10). We may even think that we personally are the masters of our fate and the captains of our souls. When, however, things do not move smoothly, we may blame outside determinants for our experience. Divine Providence, luck, heredity, magic, economic factors, society, or other influences are then assumed to control our ill fortunes.

The *feeling* of being autonomous or being controlled is not the same as the actual conformity or nonconformity with manipulaive social pressures to which all men are exposed (11). When social controls have become a part of our own personal internalized habits and values, we conform "of our own free will" without recognizing the fact that social forces modify and direct our behavior.

> The type of social control most difficult to sense . . . is that which operates by virtue of the fact that each person is a product of his society. To a considerable extent the society guides his behavior by virtue of having formed his nature . . . . The concept of the human as a person with a responsible and free mentality . . . thus appears to be sociologically inadequate because it fails to recognize the amount of control which the person cannot resist because he is utterly unable to perceive it (12).

This, nevertheless, does not remove all personal responsibility from the individual, for he experiences many pressures from diverse sources, and there usually are many alternatives of action open before him inside the scope of his "conditioned freedom." Within the range of freedom open to individual choice in his socially controlled and culturally determined situation, each person is responsible for his behavior (13).

SOCIAL LIMITATIONS ON FREEDOM

The degree of unanimity in society is related to the degree to which its members feel controlled. Those who wish to return to the mythical "good old days" when everybody presumably shared the same religious, moral, ethical, and cultural values actually are desirous of returning to an age in-which men, as a whole, were much *more* manipulated and controlled by influences external to the person than they are now. Indeed, contemporary interest in manipulation and control may be due to a considerable extent to the breakdown of the older forms of social control which has resulted from industrialization, urbanization, and other radical changes in modern civilization. No longer is every detail of a person's conduct scrutinized by next-door neighbors who are concerned about all areas of his personal life. No longer is he subjected to the restraint of a church that attempts to make conforming automatons out of its members by providing them with a changeless guidebook of rules and regulations that has clear black and white answers for every problem and thus makes it unnecessary to make any decision other than a "yes" or a "no" to any given opportunity. No longer is the child under the influence of a school that is closely linked with a church and that helps to control behavior in a manner and direction consistent with all other basic community institutions. No longer is the worker under the pressures of an employer who holds direct sanctions over family life and leisure-time activities as well as on-the-job responsibilities. The breakdown of order in some of the subsystems of our society is a result of pluralistic conditions that reduce the level of conformity to basic values and norms.

The degree of freedom and control varies, in other words, with social conditions. There are great differences among societies as well as from one community, functional grouping, or subculture to another within the same society. These differences apply, among other things, to the degree of manipulation, the forms or types of manipulation, the techniques of manipulation, the goals of manipulation, and reactions to manipulation.

The chief goal of social control once was uniformity. Today, with the great variety of groups and perspectives in our pluralistic society, the goal tends to be individual consistency within a general framework of societal welfare. Individuality is prized, and it can be exhibited to a far greater degree than in the past, for its acceptable boundaries have been vastly extended. Supreme Court decisions related to mass entertainment and freedom of the press reflect the expansion of personal liberty. They also increase the individual's responsibility for controlling his own behavior instead of being "protected" by the narrow conceptions of "public morality" which greatly limited personal choices under past conditions.

There are varying degrees of resistance to manipulative social control. We demand complete conformity of behavior from the convicted criminal who is undergoing a prison sentence. We expect little conformity from persons who are considered to be "creative" in the performing arts—yet actors who play the various dramatic roles created by these creators must conform strictly to the demands of their parts and the instructions of the producer; and the musician in an orchestra must follow the musical score and conform to the wishes of the conductor. We are free to resist the orders of our employers, but exercising this freedom is likely to free us from our jobs!

"Hippies" and other people who are labeled as nonconformists sometimes conform highly to one another; their subcultural group has become for them a manipulative overlord. Their nonconformity is restricted to limits by society which are gradually expanding with the legal breakdown of certain rules that have hampered the civil liberties of many minority groups.

The alternative choices that are open to individuals are themselves cultural products. They are not unlimited, and the exercise of choice even among the limited possibilities is subject to numerous restrictions that could be labeled "manipulative." I am free to fly to Australia, but financial costs, my sense of obligation to many duties, and other restrictions related to such a trip hamper my freedom.

One of the tasks before every society is that of "containing" persons and groups which are detrimental to social welfare. Thus, we imprison criminal offenders who are deemed incorrigible, and we place the bounds of probation and parole upon others. We lock up drug addicts while they are in process of physical withdrawal and psychological rehabilitation. Parents may "ground" teen-agers after they have indulged in conduct that the parents believe is inconsistent with their welfare or that of the family.

The most effective constraint of all is that which comes from within the mind or "heart" of the person—that which rests upon realistic self-conceptions, high moral values, and wholesome spiritual commitments. "Inner containment" of self-control, good self-images, and a high sense of responsibility must supplement and complement the "outer containment" of structural arrangements in society in order to have the most effective preventive and rehabilitative impact on deviant persons (14). Promoting constructive self-conceptions is a major goal of much marriage counseling.

MANIPULATION IN SCIENCE

The most advanced marriage counseling techniques are based upon insights and methods that have come from or were refined by scientific research. One of the goals of all sciences is the manipulation either of its subject matter or of human reactions and adjustments to phenomena as yet uncontrollable by man. The human aspects of this are especially significant in the social and behavioral sciences, which aim to develop principles of human behavior that will enable men to predict and thus to control individual and group behavior.

A great deal of manipulation is connected with scientific research. The funding agencies, whether government agencies, foundations, or universities, control the resources necessary for scientific research. By making funds available for certain topics and disciplines and not for others, they manipulate the growth and development of the respective sciences. In our society generally the physical sciences have prospered in this regard, for material things are much more marketable than the intangible principles for human behavior and social organization which result from research in the social and behavioral sciences. In recent years research resources for the social sciences have greatly expanded, but this has not applied uniformly to all areas. Certain types of family research, urban studies, analyses of military organizations and communications, and, more recently, medical sociology have moved ahead relatively rapidly, while such subjects as the sociology of religion and humanistic studies of group behavior have lagged behind. The marriage counselor therefore has only an uneven collection of scientific conclusions at his disposal, and evaluation research to test the effectiveness of various therapeutic approaches is almost totally absent.

Manipulation on another level occurs even in research and development projects to test the effectiveness of certain types of treatment. When an experimental group is paired off with a control group, one group gains the benefits or suffers the damages of the treatment, while the other does not. The research subjects are thus manipulated for the great goddess of science!

"The engineering of consent" through marketing research, advertising, and public relations work has become a major enterprise in our society; the sciences provide a foundation for it. Whenever we attempt through the media of mass communications, educational institutions, political action, and other means to change the attitudes and behavior of people, we are trying to manipulate them. We manipulate them even through the "technological fix" of making automobiles and highways safer, buildings less hazardous, parts of industrial machines more shielded, electric circuits better controlled by rheostats and protected by fuses, water supplies purer, aircraft guidance systems more efficient, and a multitude of additional changes. Most of the manipulation to which men are subjected in open democratic societies protects their welfare, enhances their individuality, and is desired by the majority. Yet by focusing upon the miscarriages of justice and abuses of human dignity and freedom, a strong minority feels that we reside in a nation that speedily is becoming a police state. "Coercion to virtue" through law and its enforcement is a tool that can be abused easily by the power structure of any society (15).

A MORALISTIC EVALUATION

In conclusion, let me add a few directly evaluative comments. First, let us face the facts. All men are controlled to a very high degree. Much of this manipulation is desirable. Order in society is maintained by social controls that necessitate manipulation; this order is a basic prerequisite to freedom even though it simultaneously limits liberty. Just as beauty in nature may be enhanced by man's manipulation, many beneficial consequences flow from the manipulation of man. Understanding the nature and extent of social control therefore comprises a first step toward appreciating and realistically appraising human freedom.

Second, we have self-consciousness and are not the passive victims of social pressures. We are autonomous beings with a responsibility to decide between the limited, yet in our society extremely extensive, alternatives before us. Our responsibilities to man and God flow out of our autonomy, our ability, and indeed our necessity to decide among the alternatives that lie before us at the moment of decision.

Third, understanding can help us control the social controls that constrain and manipulate us. Knowing the consequences of alternatives makes it possible for us to choose with greater liberty rather than less. Social science research reveals the limitations of cultural influence on our behavior (16), as well as its ubiquity.

Fourth, multiple memberships and orientations in our pluralistic society produce a high degree of freedom, for they promote recognition of alternatives of choice and in our open society allow a broader range of viable choices than was possible in the days of our grandparents. Dialogue between groups, the mingling of all social classes within many organizations, and a concern for all mankind, not merely those of our kin or nation, can help to balance our knowledge of which choices promote human dignity and which ones subtly erode them. Because we are "multivalent man," our freedom is enhanced (17).

Fifth, as far as our own attempts to manipulate others are concerned, whether in marriage counseling or other contexts, let us make certain that our goals are what they ought to be. Depersonalizing others by making them mere objects of therapy (doing *to* them) and degrading clients by treating them as if they are dependents on an inferior level of human dignity (condescending to do *for* them) are likely to have inferior results to therapeutic counseling which views them as autonomous and intrinsically worthy persons equal to oneself (doing *with* them) who have the right to make their own decisions.

When and if we have the proper ends in mind and use means that are fully consistent with those ends, our "manipulating" can uphold the welfare and dignity of man who is created in God's Image. It is wise to heed in true humility the biblical admonition, "Let not many of you become teachers, my brethren, for you know that we who teach shall be judged with greater strictness. For we all make many mistakes . . ." (18). Not only teachers, but also marriage counselors and all others who influence human conduct as members of the "helping professions," are in a vulnerable position of high moral responsibility. As we engage in various forms of manipulative behavior, we can easily harm others and heap condemnation on ourselves, or we can make significant contributions to the well-being of mankind.

REFERENCES

1. Ackerman, Nathan W.: The emergence of family psychotherapy: A personal account, in James A. Peterson, Ed. *Marriage and Family Counseling: Perspective and Prospect.* New York, Association Press, 1968, p. 157.
2. Mudd, Emily: The impact of the development of marriage counseling on the traditional and related professions, in James A. Peterson, Ed. *Marriage and Family Counseling: Perspective and Prospect.* New York, Association Press, 1968, pp. 171-188.
3. Peterson, James A.: Marriage counseling: past, present and future, in *Marriage and Family Counseling: Perspective and Prospect.* New York, Association Press, 1968, pp. 149-152.
4. Stein, Jess, and Urdang, Laurence, Eds.: Random House Dictionary of the English Language. (Unabridged edition), 1967, p. 872.
5. Evaluation research to test whether or not the actual results are in the desired direction is greatly underdeveloped in this as in other areas of activity of the "helping professions."
6. Berelson, Bernard, and Steiner, Gary A.: *Human Behavior: An Inventory of Scientific Findings.* New York, Harcourt, Brace and World, 1964, p. 664.
7. *Life,* vol. 61, no. 16, p. 61, Oct. 14, 1966.
8. Berelson, Bernard, and Steiner, Gary A.: *Human Behavior: An Inventory of Scientific Findings.* New York, Harcourt, Brace and World, 1964, p. 665.
9. Berne, Eric: *Games People Play: The Psychology of Human Relationships.* New York, Grove Press, 1964.
10. Lee, Alfred McClung: *Multivalent Man.* New York, George Braziller, 1966, p. 5.
11. Lee, Alfred McClung: *Multivalent Man.* New York, George Braziller, 1966, pp. 5-6.
12. Faris, Robert E. L.: The discipline of sociology, in Robert E.L. Faris, Ed. *Handbook of Modern Sociology.* Chicago, Rand McNally and Co., 1964, p. 6.
13. This statement is not intended to preclude neurotic and psychotic reactions over which the individual has lost control, the consequences of illness and injury, or other abnormal behavior. Society considers deviant behavior that stems from such problems to be exceptions to personal responsibility.
14. Reckless, Walter C.: A new theory of delinquency and crime. *Federal Probation, 25:* 42-46, no. 4, December, 1961.
15. Skolnick, Jeorme H.: Coercion to virtue: The enforcement of morals. *Southern California Law Review, 41:*588-641, no. 3, 1968.
16. Lee, Alfred McClung: *Multivalent Man.* New York, George Braziller, 1966, pp. 44-47.
17. Lee, Alfred McClung: *Multivalent Man.* New York, George Braziller, 1966, pp. 5-6, 19-21, 311-326.
18. *James 3:*1-2, Revised Standard Version.

SELECTED BIBLIOGRAPHY

1. Berger, Peter: *Invitation to Sociology.* Garden City, N.Y., Doubleday and Co., Anchor Books, 1963. This humanistic introduction to sociology includes many direct

and indirect references to the problems of social determinism and human manipulation.

2. Clark, Alexander L., and Gibbs, Jack P.: Social control: A reformulation. *Social Problems, 12:*398-415, no. 4, Spring, 1965. Conventional sociological approaches to the subject of social control are briefly surveyed and criticized in the course of developing a theoretical framework for the study of social control as reactions to deviant behavior.

3. Kelman, Herbert C.: Manipulation of human behavior: An ethical dilemma for the social scientist. *J Social Issues, 21:*31-46, no. 2, April, 1965.

4. LaPiere, Richard T.: *A Theory of Social Control.* New York, McGraw-Hill Book Co., 1954. This sociological textbook on social control holds that the strength of the control that is exercised by a group over an individual member is inverse to the size of the group.

5. Lee, Alfred McClung: *Multivalent Man.* New York, George Braziller, 1966. This textbook on social psychology emphasizes that the multivalent nature of society with its multiplicity of conflicting moral values makes its individual members also multivalent.

6. Queen, Stuart A.: Chambers, William N., and Winston, Charles M.: *The American Social System.* Boston, Houghton Mifflin Co., 1965. Social control is the central theme of this interdisciplinary social science textbook.

7. Shostorm, Everett L.: *Man, The Manipulator.* Nashville, Abingdon Press, 1967. Devices all men have absorbed to varying degrees for concealing their true nature, thereby reducing themselves and others into things to be controlled, are discussed together with the thesis that "actualization therapy" can resolve the problem of the life-style of manipulation.

8. Weisman, Irving, and Chwast, Jacob: Control and values in social work treatment, in Cora Kasius, Ed., *Social Casework in the Fifties.* New York, Family Service Association of America, 1962, pp. 252-262. Social work treatment is presented as one of society's ways of exercising social control over persons who manifest deviant behavior; problems, and value conflicts pertinent to applying these controls and yet keeping treatment a helping tool rather than another problem for the client are discussed.

Chapter 21

UTILIZING THE INTERPERSONAL RELATIONSHIP CONCEPT IN MARRIAGE COUNSELING

WESLEY J. ADAMS

T HE PURPOSE of this chapter is to stress the need and importance of marriage counselors to begin to reconceptualize the marital relationship and the type of counseling currently employed to help that relationship. This challenge suggests that counselors should begin thinking particularly about developing a truly distinctive type of marriage counseling which is both relevant and responsive to problems unique to contemporary marriage. Such counseling would be far different from that which now emphasizes primarily the client-counselor type of counseling as the best method for helping the marital relationship.

The client-counselor type of counseling which involves the counselor and only one spouse was the only model readily available when marital counseling first came into vogue during the early 1920's. It was satisfactory providing that the marriage relationship was based on traditionally defined roles which the spouses had somehow failed to learn adequately. In this case, a client-counselor type of counseling model would seem to be suitable as a way to help the individual spouse learn his or her role. However, as marriage now becomes less dependent on traditionally defined roles and it shifts more and more to an interactional pattern (1), a reconceptualization, of both the marriage relationship and that type of counseling which has been traditionally used, becomes essential.

To see the task in broader perspective, it should be noted that marriage counseling is carried on by several different professions. For example, the membership of the American Association of Marriage Counselors is composed of clergy, social workers, medical men, sociologists, psychologists, lawyers, and educators (2). While each counselor brings his own professional orientation to the counseling session, this factor alone is probably less significant in terms of counseling effectiveness than perhaps most counselors would be willing to believe or admit.

One of the most compelling reasons why the various professions probably differ little in their counseling effectiveness is that no counseling framework has been developed specifically for the marital relationship. There probably has been only scant attention paid to this problem because the majority of counselors have gained their counseling experience by having learned the skills and principles in a client-counselor relationship. This counseling model, a one-to-one counseling relationship, was simply transferred to the realm of counseling marriages with little or no modification. Yet, the situation now appears to demand the type of counseling skills, knowledge, and principles applicable to a dyadic or interpersonal relationship.

The needed change in counseling procedure may easily be ignored by those counselors reporting successful outcomes in working with one spouse. As a consequence they may feel, thereby, justified in maintaining the traditional client-counselor mode of counseling. It should be acknowledged, here, that there are times when the best approach to helping the marital relationship is by seeing one spouse for a particular reason. However, to counsel only one spouse as a matter of course is to perpetuate a type of counseling which serves the counselor's needs (as based on his training) and not those of the married couple.

In the meantime, trainees who wish to become marriage counselors must rely chiefly on a one-to-one counseling relationship for their training. For example, the casework method (3) exemplifies this situation in the field of social work. The casework method which has evolved over several decades is well grounded in knowledge and principles as related to a client-counselor type of counseling. Trained in this traditional method, these counselors then occupy counseling positions in the nearly four hundred Family Service Agencies (4) scattered throughout the United States. While having been trained to counsel principally a single client, it is most notable that their caseload is largely made up of problems involving marital relationships. Yet, nothing in their training has prepared them to counsel a couple, which would require the utilization of an interpersonal relationship framework.

If marriage counselors were to use an interpersonal relationship framework, then marriage counseling would derive its distinctive characteristic not so much from its content, as important as that is, but from its focus on an interpersonal relationship. The counselor's frame of reference would necessarily shift from a client-counselor relationship to the interpersonal relationship of the couple. To achieve competency in this new role, the counselor would need to be well versed in the psychology and principles which govern such relationships. He would have to analyze and determine the various aspects of marital interaction being hindered in their growth and development. In addition, he would need to maintain a keen appreciation of the part that roles, values, beliefs, and the couple's past experiences play in the dynamic maintenance of the marital relationship.

As contemporary marital relationships reflect an attempt to derive satisfaction and significance from an interactional process, they appear at the same time to become highly unstable and, therefore, perhaps more prone to dissolution. The use of traditional marriage counseling for such marriages seems inappropriate, when the marital relationship is viewed from this perspective. For example, if one assumes that a marriage counselor is concerned with the marital relationship of a couple, it seems rather odd that one of his first counseling decisions is to *separate* the couple. The reason for this action seems to lie in the unquestioning continuance of the client-counselor type of counseling. This incongruity between what the counselor intends to do (help the marital relationship) and that which he actually does (develop a client-counselor relationship) is quite striking. To illustrate this situation further, recourse will be made to both earlier and more recent counselors' writings.

For example, in an earlier writing, Rogers (5) recommended that marriage counselors should see the spouses separately, as a matter of procedure. One can easily understand this suggestion because his frame of reference has been the use of the client-counselor relationship for counseling. Yet, nearly twenty years later, this same recommendation has become more firmly fixed than ever. This point is clearly made by another marriage counselor who says: "Marriage counseling is essentially a matter of interaction between client and counselor. The client experiences an interpersonal relationship which is unlike the social interaction in his everyday life" (6).

When the possibility of counseling both spouses by the same counselor is considered, problems begin to arise in terms of how this might be handled. For instance, one writer takes the position that because marriage is a one-to-one relationship, the presence of a "third person throws the situation off balance" (7). Reasoning in this way, the counselor concludes that the client-counselor relationship, which is also a one-to-one relationship, would be disrupted if both spouses were present. So goes the reasoning.

The counselor mentioned above does offer a solution to the dilemma of having to attend to the marital relationship, and yet, still maintain the client-counselor type of counseling. He does this by suggesting that "wherever possible, ending interviews should be joint interviews to emphasize the unity of the two and the outsideness of the one" (8). These interviews would be arranged not so much for counseling purposes, but to emphasize the "unity" of the couple. Thus, by altering the counseling milieu in this rather mechanical fashion, the counselor apparently felt he had resolved the dilemma. From this article, one may infer that the counselor recognized the importance of counseling the interpersonal relationship of the couple and, at the same time, the incongruity of using the client-counselor relationship to accomplish that purpose.

While many marriage counselors continue to use what now appears to be an inappropriate form of counseling for marriages, i.e. client-counselor relationship, some counselors have nevertheless begun to see the need for change and are becoming innovative. For example, the term "joint interview" has come into vogue. This term means that both spouses or an unmarried couple are seen by the same counselor at the same time. One counselor, however, views the use of joint interviews more as a technique rather than a needed shift in a new counseling direction. Interestingly, although viewed as a technique, the very departure from the traditional mode of counseling must have been seen as a radical change. The counselor makes this observation: "It is a technique which should be used only by a skilled marriage counselor, as it is fraught with psychological dynamite (9).

This extreme caution in the use of joint interviews is shared by other counselors (10, 11). Moreover, this concern in one instance is listed as a "principle" in marriage counseling. For example, Karpf lists among his sixteen principles in marriage counseling the following one: "Joint conferences with both partners can be helpful but are difficult and extremely dangerous and should be resorted to only after careful consideration and planning" (12).

One can only speculate why such strong warnings of caution are given by these counselors in using joint interviews. Perhaps attempts at something new and different may indeed prove dangerous, *particularly if there is no theoretical framework or knowledge to guide one's behavior.* However, at the same time, there is no available evidence which indicates that joint interviews are any more fraught with danger than the client-counselor relationship. In fact, it could be argued that the client-counselor relationship suffers from transference phenomena, information distortions, and in addition, it provides no way to gauge the progress of the married couple since only one spouse is there to report such progress. Thus, strong admonishments to be cautious in the use of joint interviews because they are believed to be dangerous does not seem to be a very convincing reason for not using them.

More recently, there have been some attempts to reconceptualize contemporary marriages in terms of an interpersonal relationship. Because of this, several writers (13, 14, 15) have stressed the marital relationship as that in need of counseling rather than the individual spouse. By viewing the marital relationship as the counseling entity, this has become a turning point in helping the counselor to understand problems resulting from such a relationship. These writers have described the marital relationship as a social unit that is maintained by the on-going interaction of the two spouses. Through this interaction a relationship evolves which is more or less satisfactory as an end-product of this process. Therefore, according to this conceptualization, both spouses would need to be seen in counseling in order for the marriage counselor to better understand the interpersonal relationship of the couple.

Once the married couple is seen as a possible counseling entity, some type of justification is apparently needed by the counselor for counseling both spouses. For instance, one writer lists both the advantages and disadvantages seemingly inherent in the use of joint interviews. Interestingly, neither list shows concern with the couple's interpersonal relationship except indirectly, e.g. *advantages:* observe couple, assess motivation . . . *disadvantages:* hostility, premature plan or action of client . . . (16). Such listings provide some evidence that an interpersonal relationship framework is lacking.

While these lists compare advantages and disadvantages of joint interviews, none have been compiled which weigh traditional counseling in the same way, nor is there any attempt to compare the two types of counseling, i.e. client-counselor and joint interview. From this list-making activity, critical evaluations of joint interviews have, in some instances, produced very favorable reactions. For example, one writer, after compiling a list of advantages in conjoint interviews makes this poignant observation: "Marriage counselors have been slow to recognize the congruence of conjoint therapy with their basic orientation to counseling" (17).

Thus far, the need to reconceptualize the interactional type of marriage relationship that seems to be evolving, and the client-counselor type of marriage counseling now being used, has been stressed. In pointing out this need, it is not being intimated that the traditional client-counselor type of counseling is useless. Far from it. The concern here is that such counseling seems less appropriate when it is the marriage relationship rather than the individual spouses that need to be counseled. As marriages become less "traditional," and more "interactional," i.e. more concern with things like personality factors, ego satisfactions, self concepts, and companionship, then a type of counseling which takes these factors into account becomes appropriate. This would seem to require an understanding of the interpersonal relationship of the couple. While the use of joint interviews may be interpreted as a move toward meeting this need, the use of an interpersonal relationship framework would serve to strengthen and give direction to this type of counseling.

Marriage counseling, as is now being conceptualized, would involve and include both spouses in the counseling session. The interpersonal relationship of this couple would be the primary concern to the marriage counselor. To the extent that one could understand this relationship, it would be assumed that the counselor could consider himself in a truly helping role.

If he were to see only one spouse, as would occasionally happen, his concern would automatically center on the client-counselor relationship and how that relationship may help the individual spouse. With the presence of only one spouse, marriage counseling, in this instance, would derive its title solely from the *content* of the client-counselor dialogue which may be only indirectly relevant to helping the marital relationship. According to this schema, it would be sheer illusion to believe that the counselor was counseling the marital relationship without working toward the objective of having both spouses present.

In the remaining pages of this chapter, a number of principles depicting the Interpersonal Relationship Concept, will be presented which were developed by Kirkendall (18). These principles will not be new, radical, or unusual in any sense. Their sole purpose is to provide the counselor with a meaningful framework for perceiving the marital relationship as an evolving and growing entity. Content, then, would take on specific significance for that relationship. These principles are offered in the hope that the marriage counselor will become more effective in his counseling as he looks beyond the oft-held static concept of marriage with its prescribed roles, obligations, and responsibilities.

In setting forth these principles, as embodying the Interpersonal Relationship Concept, the following assumption is made: Interpersonal relationships in their development, growth, and decline are governed by certain sociopsychological principles. This assumption, that certain principles govern the growth, development, and decline of interpersonal relationships, allows one to analyze such relationships from a rational, logical, and systematic viewpoint. Moreover, the assumption seems to be supported from one's everyday experiences involving relationships. In addition, there is one most notable institution which relies on the orderly, stable development of an interpersonal relationship, i.e. marriage.

PRINCIPLE ONE

A relationship grows and progresses—it does not spring full-blown from a few interchanges.

1. It is built as a consequence of an investment of time and feeling.
2. This investment must, from time to time, be renewed and refreshed.
3. It demands courage and a *quid pro quo*.
4. It cannot be forced or developed by means which are essentially selfish, one-sided or dishonest.

This principle suggests that in understanding the growth and development of an interpersonal relationship, the length of time for which it has existed is one essential aspect. It also suggests some of the elements in the growing process, i.e. investment of time and feeling; a renewal of this investment; participants must give if they are to receive; and the relationship cannot be developed on the basis of deception or selfishness. Knowledge of this principle may help a marriage counselor to conceptualize the role that time plays in the development of a relationship. With this in mind, the counselor would quickly attempt to learn whether a couple have known each other for several months or several weeks at the outset of counseling. In seeking this information, he would also look for those particular elements in the relationship that were mentioned above.

A question the counselor might ask himself, as related to principle one, would be the following: In marriages of varying lengths, how many couples actually continue to invest and reinvest time and feeling into their relationship? Many, if not most couples fail to appreciate the importance of this factor in keeping their relationship strong. The counselor, to be helpful, would need to look for this reinvestment idea in a given relationship.

PRINCIPLE TWO

An individual needs relationships which vary in intensity and intimacy. One can support only a limited number of intense and concurrent relationships, however.

The second principle raises the issue of intensity and intimacy as conditions which vary from person to person in a given relationship and within the same relationship over a period of time. According to this principle, the marriage counselor would attempt to find what a marital relationship is contributing in this respect, for each spouse. Perhaps the relationship is too intense or not intense enough, particularly in its intimate aspects. This factor of intensity within the relationship would have to be thoroughly explored with both spouses. If changes were indicated, then this could be acted upon by the couple.

Principle two may also serve to sensitize the marriage counselor in the following way: He would need to assume that marriage is not necessarily the most intense and intimate relationship known. To assume otherwise, he runs the risk of tacitly accepting that assumption as being "good" for a marriage. For some individuals, an intense and intimate relationship beyond a certain point would be intolerable. That is, some individuals may have actually sought marriage to *escape* the continued premarital involvements with intense and intimate types of relationships. A marriage counselor cannot and should not assume that marriage offers an intense and intimate relationship simply because a marriage contract has been signed. One must look to the couple and learn what they are seeking and to what degree they have found satisfaction in their interpersonal relationship.

PRINCIPLE THREE

A relationship cannot engulf the individual. The individual must retain a sense of individuality and some privacy.

This principle is probably rarely honored or understood by most married couples. For many, marriage symbolizes "openness" and "total" involvement between two people. Yet, ideas such as these, when translated into acts, can work toward the dissolution rather than the strengthening of the marital relationship. Couples who do not agree with this principle intellectually, i.e. they see marriage as "joining two together," are often surprised to discover how necessity may prove such beliefs essentially invalid. For example, a common situation in marriage counseling is the one in which the husband feels betrayed (or left out) because his wife may adamantly insist on closing the bathroom door when in use. This is an act of privacy—repeated quite often.

This principle suggests, along with privacy, that one must retain his individuality while part of a relationship. The importance of retaining one's individuality may be challenged when a wife expects her husband to "devote" himself to her at perhaps the cost of not fulfilling some of his own needs and personal development. This last example applies to the husband who might make equally excessive demands on his wife. In either case, the relationship could become an oppressive one.

PRINCIPLE FOUR

Each party to a relationship must be permitted freedom in deciding how far he wants to go and how much he wishes to make of the relationship.

This principle must seem strange when viewed from the perspective of marriage. A more traditionally minded person would question this principle on the grounds that the relationship is made up of certain obligations, and responsibilities which are nonnegotiable and which both parties must perform. For example, the idea that a woman's role is one of passivity while the husband is the aggressive one in sex would represent this traditional position. Whether the couple wishes to, or are even able to, fulfill these prescribed roles would not be open to serious consideration. Principle four would challenge this static idea of marriage. Because men and women can interchange economic and other roles, they can also decide how their relationship might best serve their individual and relationship needs.

Many marital relationships, of course, are entered into in a predetermined, mechanical-like arrangement with roles, obligations, and responsibilities apparently assumed by both spouses. However, when ideas such as this are held, it need not mean that the spouses' behavior depicts the con-

sequence of these beliefs. In fact, in this day and age of technological advancement accompanied by rapid change in social and living conditions,
most couples probably would be surprised to discover that their marriage
has functioned according to principle four and not according to their fixed
ideas on what the marriage should be.

Principle four has particular importance to the marriage counselor. As
he analyzes how a marriage is currently functioning, he would also consider
how it could be otherwise. In such an analysis, should the marriage counselor use a traditional framework rather than the interpersonal relationship
one, he would probably fail to see unreasonable demands being placed on
the relationship by one or both spouses. For example, he might suggest
perhaps to the wife, who finds her marriage intolerable, that if *she* does not
change, i.e. change to satisfy the husband, then the marriage might dissolve.
In such a traditional framework, the counselor would see the maintenance
of the total relationship as being the responsibility of primarily one and not
both spouses. Had the counselor considered the total relationship, he might
well have realized that such a suggestion could actually hasten the relationship to dissolution, since it is already being threatened by having one person
assume most of the responsibility for its existence.

PRINCIPLE FIVE

*A relationship with genuine closeness must be based on certain qualities,
e.g. a human, outreaching motivation, mutual respect and trust, a capacity
for effective communication, a sense of empathy, a capacity for self-direction and self-governorship, and common goals and objectives.*

Principle five is probably the one that the counselor is most keenly aware
of and as a result, he spends a greater share of his counseling time in implementing this principle. Although it is only one factor, it is one which
both counselor and couple can easily discuss and translate into meaningful
relationship changes. For example, the idea of common goals and objectives sought by a couple can be evaluated and dealt with. Also, the counselor
may work toward helping a couple improve their communications.

It is probably accurate to say that in those marriages in which counseling
is involved, principle five is rarely governing the relationship. Whether it
ever did may be unknown to the counselor. However, the principle does
provide a basis for analyzing a couple's current interaction and of providing
a meaningful framework in helping them toward improving their relationship.

PRINCIPLE SIX

*The nature and extent of involvement in other relationships helps de-
termine the demands which will be made upon any particular relationship.*

Principle six is very important in alerting the marriage counselor to the need for exploring the many relationships each spouse may have exclusive of the marital one. It is important because the number and type of relationships any one spouse has may indirectly influence the couple's marriage. For instance, if a husband already has several other relationships, as seen in his place of employment, then he may demand less from his own marital relationship. That is, these other relationships may satisfy his relationship needs and, thereby, reduce the need for greater involvement in his own marriage. This condition may exist without either spouse fully realizing its impact on the marriage.

Another way of viewing this relationship idea may be seen from the perspective of the wife. If she has several on-going relationships outside of the marital one, she probably would be less concerned with putting pressure on her husband for satisfying her relationship needs. Consequently, the marriage counselor would want to know if there might be too many or too few outside relationships for either spouse and how that factor may be influencing the couple's current relationship. This may be easily determined, although it probably is often overlooked as being important by the counselor.

PRINCIPLE SEVEN

It is difficult to revive a weakened relationship, and very difficult to change one which has become fixated. It is practically impossible to restore a dead relationship.

When a marriage counselor sees a couple, who are seeking a divorce, the seventh principle is one the counselor must consider. The counselor probably feels most defeated when a relationship which is no longer meaningful for the couple, presents itself with little hope left for change.

Some counselors who see this type of relationship and observe that it is held together only by a marriage contract, may actually spend considerable time trying to revive this relationship, but usually to no avail. Paradoxically, these couples often appear to be rational, logical, and thoughtful in their interaction. This condition perhaps encourages the counselor to continue counseling sessions. However, the element of affection is often absent, and this, in turn, signals that it is a relationship without positive feeling or meaningful commitment for the couple.

PRINCIPLE EIGHT

Before relationships can be changed, there are certain requisites to the change: perceptions have to be altered and a wish to change must be present.

Crises very frequently serve the purpose of fulfilling the two requisites needed to change a relationship. A crisis, as defined here, could mean anything from an illness to an automobile accident involving, in some way, the relationship of the married couple. The significance and definition that the couple attach to the incident most clearly reveals whether a crisis has occurred. Through such crises, a relationship may undergo change which could be either negative or positive in outcome.

One crisis, which may facilitate change in a relationship is the threat of divorce. While such a threat may be welcomed by some couples and disconcerting to others, it often forces couples to reevaluate their relationship. Such an evaluation may lead to marital dissolution, but it need not.

Other crises, such as extramarital affairs, may create an opportunity to change what, up until then, was a weakened or fixated marriage relationship. None of these crises, of course, are recommended as ways to change a marriage relationship. However, the opportunity that these ready-made situations offer the marriage counselor should be recognized.

PRINCIPLE NINE

Relationships are growing, evolving entities which in the very nature of life will need to be altered and, in some instances, dropped.

This last principle should not be construed to mean that a relationship may run its course and then "naturally" dissolve. While any relationship may eventually be discontinued, such discontinuance need not "just happen." To the couple experiencing the end of a relationship, it may very well appear to have "just happened." However, if the counselor traces the history of the relationship he will usually discover that both people contributed to its demise. For example, many couples begin marriage with the belief that marriage *per se* is the act of insuring the continuance of a relationship. Of course, marriage is, in fact, only a symbolized promise for what is intended to be an enduring relationship. Believing that the relationship will automatically be maintained by marriage is to expect the marriage to care for itself. The value of principle nine is that people can be helped to terminate the relationship, when it is no longer viable, with mutual respect rather than as enemies.

With only nine principles being presented, the reader might well wonder why no principle covering the sexual aspects of the marital relationship was given. One reason for this omission would be that the quality of the sexual relationship commonly fluctuates as does the marriage relationship. Assuming that the marriage is satisfactory, the sexual relationship often serves as an expression of that fact. Where the marriage is languishing, one would expect a poor sex relationship, as well. While there are exceptions to this, by and large, the sexual aspect of the marital relationship seems to be a sensitive indicator of how satisfactory that relationship is for a couple.

In summary, as modern marriages become less concerned with the development of traditionally defined roles and are depicted by an interactional pattern, they also seem to be highly unstable and more vulnerable to dissolution. A need to develop a type of counseling which is relevant to that relationship seems essential. In response to this need, an interpersonal relationship framework embodying nine principles has been offered as a guide to the marriage counselor. As these principles become more refined, and as new ones are advanced, it is hoped that the marriage counselor will be aided in his endeavor to provide appropriate counseling for contemporary marriages.

REFERENCES

1. Bernard, Jessie: The adjustments of married mates. Chapter 17, pp. 675-739. In: Christensen, Harold T., Ed. *Handbook of Marriage and the Family.* Chicago, Rand McNally & Company, 1967.
2. The American Association of Marriage Counselors, Inc. Directory. 1968-1969, p. 7.
3. Brangwin, Lorna C.: Marriage counseling—The viewpoint of the caseworker. *Social Casework, 36:*155, 162, April, 1955.
4. Family Service Association of America. Pamphlet, New York, 1965.
5. Rogers, Carl R.: Counseling with the retired serviceman and his wife. *Marriage and Family Iiving. 7:*82-84. Autumn, 1945.
6. Johnson, Dean: *Marriage Counseling: Theory and Practice.* Englewood Cliffs, N.J., Prentice-Hall, Inc., 1961, p. 55.
7. Lane, Lionel: The entrance and exit of the marriage counselor. *Marriage and Family Living, 17:*58-61, 1955.
8. Lane, Lionel: The entrance and exit of the marriage counselor. *Marriage and Family Living, 17:*61, 1955.
9. Skidmore, Rex A.; Hulda Van Streeter Garrett, C. Jay Skidmore: *Marriage Consulting, An Introduction to Marriage Counseling.* New York, Harper & Bros. Pub., 1956, p. 313.
10. Crist, John R.: Marriage counseling involving a passive husband and an aggressive wife. *Marriage and Family Living, 20:*121-126, May, 1958.
11. Karpf, Maurice J.: Some guiding principles in marriage counseling. *Marriage and Family Living, 13:*49-51, 55, Spring, 1951.
12. Karpf, Maurice J.: Some guiding principles in marriage counseling. Marriage and Family Living, *13:* 51, 1951.
13. Ackerman, Nathan W.: *The Psychodynamics of Family Life.* New York, Basic Books, Inc., 1958.
14. Stroup, Atlee L., and Glasser, Paul: The orientation and focus of marriage counseling. *Marriage and Family Living, 21:*20-24, Feb., 1959.
15. Cuber, John F., and Harroff, Peggy B.: The more total view: Relationships among men and women of the upper middle class. *Marriage and Family Living, 25:*140-145, May, 1963.

16. Smith, Leon G., and Anderson, Floyd M.: Conjoint interviews with marriage partners. *Marriage and Family Living, 25:*184-188, May, 1963.
17. Leslie, Gerald R.: Conjoint therapy in marriage counseling. *J Marriage and the Family, 26:*65-71, Feb., 1964, p. 71.
18. Kirkendall, Lester A.: *Psychological Principles Governing Interpersonal Relationships.* (21 principles) Unpublished manuscript.

Chapter 22

SENSITIVITY ASPECTS IN COUNSELING UNWED TEEN-AGERS DURING PRENATAL AND POSTNATAL PERIODS

PATRICIA SCHILLER

P REMARITAL AND MARITAL COUNSELING has dramatically changed its focus during the past decade. If one is allowed a projection, it is reasonable to assume that the seventies will involve further changes and refining of the definition of premarital and marital counseling for unwed teenagers.

Traditionally, the premarital role of the counselor during the past twenty-five years was primarily concerned with engaged couples about to be married. Marital therapy and counseling was both general as a preventive therapeutic measure, and problem oriented. The couple often presented a concern related to their marriage. These problems ran the gamut and included financial planning, role concepts, personality problems, comminic-action, interreligious or interracial difficulties, in-laws, sex education, contraceptive advice, and child rearing.

During the past decade, premarital counseling has focused on the pregnant school-aged girl, unwed mother and father, group counseling, and interdisciplinary therapy dealing with drugs, commune living, and couple swapping.

In addition, sex counseling has cropped up in the literature as something separate and apart from marital counseling. The presenting problems in sex counseling are often treated as the problems and involve contraceptive counseling, abortion counseling, questions concerning emotional and social readiness for premarital sexual intercourse, extramarital sexual play, sexual identity problems, sexual difficulties between partners, and sexual practices involving the law.

It would be germane to those involved or planning to be involved in counseling with the teen-age unwed mother to appreciate and become sensitive not only to her psychological needs, but to the magnitude of the problems and the depth of insight and training required to meet these needs.

We need the power of premarital and marital sex counseling as no other modern generation has ever needed it. What premarital counseling should serve is our human understanding of our client's or patient's sexuality, of our relationship with them, and their relationships as man and woman, boy and girl.

Over the last five years there has been an enormous increase of illegitimate pregnancies among young people. New York State's illegitimate births have quadrupled since 1946. Nationwise, the Department of Health, Education and Welfare figures indicate over 300,000 illegitimate babies are born annually and that 245,983 of these are from mothers between fifteen and twenty-four years of age. With the number of young adults in the population rising steadily, government experts are predicting that by 1980, the number of illegitimate pregnancies may well reach close to 400,000.

Counselors need to be sensitive to the needs of young women, married and unmarried who obtain abortions each year and who are in need of therapy concerning their self image and their interpersonal relations. Doctors, who refer patients to the author, have advised her that approximately 20 per cent of young married pregnant women who come to them, conceive before marriage and deplored the lack of available counseling help at universities they attended or at social agencies in university towns.

There are also a million Americans between fifteen and twenty-four years of age, suffering from gonorrhea which has been increasing at an alarming rate. The cause of the apparent epidemic proportions of illegitimacy is not fully understood. Amongst the young, the reasons given are colored with notions romantic fantasy, rebellion, sexual identity crisis, and often sheer ignorance about contraception and the reproductive process.

It is not a surprise to many psychiatrists, gynecologists, and marriage counselors the amount of sheer sexual ignorance that exists among our supposedly "swinging" generation.

A recent survey by a medical student at a midwestern college that draws students from middle and upper-middle class homes indicated that although about 40 per cent of the unmarried girls had sexual intercourse, more than half reported they had not used any birth control method whatsoever. Even the girls who did not attempt to use some form of contraception generally, relied on techniques that had extremely high failure rates, such as foam, the rhythm method, or the male condom.

Among the low-income members of the younger generation, knowledge of contraception is abysmal. A survey of unmarried pregnant teen-agers at Sinai Hospital in Baltimore found that 25 per cent of the girls had not even thought about the probability that they might become pregnant from having sexual intercourse. Only 30 per cent of the girls used any form of birth control regularly. Among the answers to the surveyor's questions were such mournful comments as this one: "I thought you could only get birth control after you were married or had your first child."

There is strong evidence that parents need to understand the powerful emotional factors preventing too many young people (male and female) from using the theoretical knowledge about sex that they already possess.

The question, "Is the unmarried mother different?" is often asked of the author by colleagues. Amongst professionals this question is basic to diagnosis and treatment. My impressions of unwed, pregnant school-aged girls come from counseling with them as the clinical psychologist at the Webster School in Washington, D.C. This school was opened in September, 1963, in Washington, D.C. under a Childrens' Bureau, HEW Grant for pregnant girls at the Junior-Senior High School level. The project ended in 1966. The school was the first of its kind in the United States and served as a model for numerous other educational and medical institutions and agencies concerned with the unwed mother and father.

In her role as clinical psychologists and therapists, the writer pretested each of the six hundred girls concerning their social sex attitudes. These included attitudes towards self, dating, marriage, love, and relationships in their homes and in their peer groups.

The girls, in the main, reflected attitudes toward marriage that are commonly considered socially acceptable. The socioeconomic and educational potential constituted a cross-section of Washington, D.C. population. This is in line with the writings and research of others who have concluded that school-age pregnancies out of marriage cross socioeconomic and cultural lines. However, those girls and boys who come from broken homes appear to be more vulnerable to involuntary unwed parenthood. The term "broken homes" includes homes broken by physical separation or frought with psycological or social tensions to the point where hostile attitudes of the parents have created an atmosphere of anxiety and disintegration of the family unit.

According to the pretesting at Webster, the writer found the girls to be ambivalent about the role of the family and the father. The girls also expressed uncertainty about how a mother should feel and act toward her child when he misbehaves. Many of the girls had expressed limited options available to them in goals for marriage, job, and community relations.

The girls appeared to be uncertain as to the importance of love and companionship to child bearing and child rearing.

A major problem in the therapy related to the difficulty on the part of the girls in developing their sensitivity and insight to their potential ability to cope with their sexual needs in a way that would help them gain self-esteem and confidence.

Their ignorance in understanding the relationships between their sex hormones and sexual urges was an important factor in their faulty concept concerning their desire for sexual contact and play.

Some expressed the belief, due to lack of knowledge and understanding, that, "the devil got into me" or "that's nature and there is nothing I can do about it."

INTERDISCIPLINARY PREMARITAL AND MARITAL THERAPY

The results of interviews, psychological studies, and parent interviews crystalized the writer's impression that an interdisciplinary approach in therapy dealing with the pregnant girl and unwed mother's relationship would be a feasible approach. The apparent tensions and anxiety appear to stem from parent-patient relationship, boyfriend-patient relationship, and patient-peer group relationship, both at school and in her social environment.

Since the parent of the unwed mother or the parent-surrogate is a significant adult, it was felt that group counseling concerning the parent-patient role be included in any therapeutic program.

PROFILES OF GIRLS STUDIED

During the three years of the demonstration project, 487 girls were involved both in psychological studies and in group therapy for premarital and marital relationships.

Most of the girls were in the normal grade for their age. If out of place, they were more likely to be advanced in grade level than retarded. In other words, 8 per cent of the total group were advanced in grade.

Of the girls whose IQ's were known (80%), just about as many had an IQ between 90 and 110 as had a rating below that level, 188 and 190 girls respectively. Eight of those in the below normal range had an IQ in the 70's or 80's. Eight per cent had an IQ that was decidedly above normal grade averages indicated that 16 per cent were A or B students, 54 per cent had a grade average of C. Thirty per cent were D students. Only four girls had an F average.

With few exceptions the girls were pregnant for the first time and single when they enrolled in the therapy. However 11 per cent (54 girls) were married during the therapy process.

The girls were not promiscuous. As a matter of fact they felt that "love" as they understood it was the motivating factor for having sexual intercourse. They felt becoming pregnant was a mistake but having become pregnant, a majority felt it was their duty to see that the child had a home and was provided for.

The sterotype of male exploiter was not a valid description of the majority of the putative fathers. Most of the girls had known the putative fathers from one to three years by the time they became pregnant. Only one-fifth of the girls had known them a shorter time.

Three-quarters of the putative fathers were either the same age as the girls or within two years of that age at the time of conception.

From the studies, it was the author's impression that in many of the families there had been a long history of discord and poor personal relationships.

Although no uniformity existed in terms of contributing factors to teen-age pregnancies, some factors stand out, and may be useful to the premarital therapist in his diagnostic work with pregnant girls and unwed mothers.

FACTORS PERCEIVED BY THE PATIENTS

Although each of the factors described below were not common to all the patients they ran as an interlocking thread through a majority of the patients studied and involved in marital therapy. These were revealed during the individual interviews, projective tests, and during the individual and group therapy.

1. The girls felt a lack of overt affection from parents through non-verbal and verbal communication.
2. Many of the girls felt a poor relationship exists between themselves and their mothers. They were not sure that their mothers thought well of them or trusted them.
3. They felt uncertain of their pride and confidence in being a woman.
4. Many of the girls fifteen and older felt needed and wanted by the putative fathers, and felt they were expressing their "love" through physical sex play.
5. Most of the girls felt the pregnancy was a mistake.
6. They lacked adequate ego strengths to cope with daily problems.

GROUP THERAPY AND PEER GROUP NEEDS

Numerous studies and common knowledge among parents and teachers indicate that children and youth learn and are influenced in their sexual attitudes and behavior from their peer groups. This is applicable in various degrees with adult peers also. With this in mind, group therapy in premarital and marital problems amongst teen-agers is gaining support and proving a successful method with many professionals.

Teen-agers are concerned about their peer group relations. They want to be accepted, respected, and understood by their peers. This appears to be more significant than approval by adults. They want to feel part of a peer group and accepted by the group. This is sufficiently important to the point where the teen-ager may modify her sexual attitudes to conform to the group's values.

Several thirteen-year old girls reported to the author during individual sessions that in their social group their friends were pregnant, and this factor may have influenced them in "going all the way." The negative power of the group is very impressive too. During the course of one of my sessions with eleventh-grade girls, one of the girls asked the group how they felt about adoption. The student who asked the question had previously discussed her desire to give her baby up for adoption because she wanted to go to college and felt the baby would be better cared for in an adoptive home by parents who wanted the baby. She was no longer seeing the putative father and was looking forward to renew her social life after the baby was born. She wondered how the other girls would accept this decision because many had told her they disapproved of adoption. I suggested that she bring it up in the group where we could all have an opportunity to work out our feelings. She wanted very much to have the group approve of her decision.

As expected, the group was against adoption. Some were more adamant and hostile than others. The therapist sensed the feelings and reflected with the group "You appear to be opposed to adoption. I feel you believe 'Mary' should keep her baby." Their nonverbal and verbal responses indicated they agreed with what the therapist caught as their feeling about the situation.

It was important for the therapist to sense their need to express their negative feelings. The therapist was aware of the impact of focusing in on "Mary" rather than the problem, so she asked them to consider a problem of adoption which came to her from a teen-ager who lived in another city. The therapist filled the girls in on the girls needs and wishes. She asked their advice. Would they be counselors? She told them that as counselor they were free to explore all the angles and express whatever feelings or judgments they felt were real to them.

They gave expressions to many stereotypes. "She is selfish." "She doesn't love children." One said, "a girl who would give her baby up is a heartless mother." I suggested that they reflect upon her needs as a growing woman, on the baby's needs or her potential as a wife or mother, as a job earner, or her right to an education. Could they weigh all of these issues? Could they consider the baby's needs for attention, a home, and loving care?

The group felt the need to sort the issues. They felt they needed to think and understand what was involved. They wanted to hear more from one another. What was best for the mother? What was best for the child? Could a solution be found that would be satisfactory for both baby and mother?

The group members expressed anger and frustration. They argued back and forth and after three sessions they were more flexible, less emotional, and some were supportive and on good terms with the girl who wanted to give her baby up. They were involved and learning to check out their feelings and help their peers check out theirs. They really were desirous to understand more and to help each other. They were becoming aware—aware of themselves and each other as *feeling* people who could make realistic judgments.

Group therapy has been used with the unwed father with equal success. Some of the areas that both girl and boy invariably want to share with the group are the following:

1. How do you know it is love?
2. How do you know the boy respects you?
3. How much does it cost to bring up a baby?
4. What do you do on a date besides dancing and sex?
5. How do you say "no" to a boy without hurting his feelings?
6. Should young girls have an abortion?
7. Do you believe sexual intercourse makes you more of a woman or a man?
8. How can parents be helped to trust their children and know they are trying?
9. How do you gain confidence in yourself?

Current problems of the pregnant girl often involve the following:

1. Continuing school and baby care.
2. Financial problems.
3. Role of putative father on visitation, financial aid, and sex play.
4. Sexual activity during pregnancy with other men after dropping the putative father.

The questions the group asked each other and discussed are endless. The group therapist is the catalyst to spark discussion in order to help with "reality testing" and group support in sorting problems, and working towards realistic decisions.

The *marital* counseling and therapy with those girls who are married involves the following: a) financial problems, b) continuing education, c) separation from the school gang because of home obligations, d) changes in sexual patterns after the baby is born, e) fatigue and sexual performance, f) in-law problems, g) living with relatives, and e) extramarital relations.

TECHNIQUES OF GROUP THERAPY

During the years at Webster, the author experimented with several methods of introducing problems to the group that focused on their needs. It was important to bring them in touch with their feelings and to help them accept and understand them. The methods which appeared to appeal to successive groups included the following: a) role playing, b) reverse roles of therapist-patient, c) discussing a case related to their concerns, d) answering unsigned questions from a question box, and e) reacting to a film presented to the group or a newspaper or magazine story or article.

SENSITIVITY OF THE THERAPIST TO THE GROUP

It has long been recognized by professional therapists that such human qualities as warmth, understanding, permissiveness, and acceptance are relevant in promoting freedom to think, to feel, to err in judgment and to try again. This is further enhanced in a group where the therapist is understanding and well disposed toward individual members and to the group as a whole. This creates the beginning of a therapeutic climate that is conducive to trust and openness on the part of all the participants. Where the therapist communicates to the group the confidence that "all the group says is accepted without criticsm," the group then feels that in the relationship the therapist is cooperating in helping the group experience a nonmoralizing approach to understand the sexual-social behavior of human beings.

The therapist is sensitive to the fact that each member of the group is capable of assuming responsibility for his sexuality according to his age and social development and that within the limits of his development, he will in the group, make the right or best choices for himself.

How does the therapist in working with teen-age girls help the patients perceive the therapist in her supportive role?

1. She encourages group participation.
2. She accepts silence and other nonverbal forms of communication.
3. She intervenes in a manner that motivates a desire on the part of the group to explore the various options open for decision making.
4. She avoids projecting a "right" or "wrong" approach to a problem.
5. She reflects with the group their feelings of frustration, anxiety, disappointment, and also joy and satisfaction.
6. She does not push the group along at her pace, but accepts the rhythm and mood of the group, so that she is able to help them see it through.
7. She projects a feeling of maturity and support without being opinionated or judgmental.
8. She uses praise and sets limitations that are reasonable and conducive to the group's experience and self awareness.

Chapter 23

TO BE A WOMAN

CHARITY EVA RUNDEN

INTRODUCTION

Concepts in both marital counseling and in moral values continue to shift as psychologists and psychiatrists gain new insights into what it is *to be a woman*. The hundreds of books and the thousands of studies and reports relating to woman's sexuality do not at this date either singly or *in toto* show that anyone completely understands human femininity or "the function of the orgasm."

Studying reports of the scientific investigations and reading the writings in popular periodicals bring us to no clear formula for what comprises femininity or womanhood. *What is a woman? What is woman's role? What are characteristically feminine traits? Is the stereotype woman a beautiful madonna with her infant, a Salem witch, a member of a second sex or a lost sex? Is she a prostitute? A nymphomaniac? Portnoy's mother?*

Masters and Johnson, for all the scientific accuracy of their findings, have to date been able to report only on what can be seen and heard, what the physiology is. They and some of the rest of us must explore more into the mysteries of which poets have written through the ages.

The psychological and psychiatric counselors have had insufficient data for best helping womankind understand herself, her needs, her role. Even moral issues are unclear as long as such intense controversy rages over what womankind is. What are her rights, privileges, responsibilities, her needs, her capabilities?

It is the contention of this author that as more accurate studies and reports are published of woman's orgasm, moral issues in marital counseling will change, more happy marriages will ensue, and there will be less need of the marriage counselor, or at least his task will be easier, and the fortuitous outcome of the counseling more certain. We have almost arrived at a period in our civilization when woman need not be inhibited from her potentiality, her birthright, her full productivity.

WOMAN AND RELATIONSHIP

A group of psychologists and their journalist interpreters writing today emphasize woman's need for love, comfort, affection, being touched, hugged, cradled, and held close. These writers repeat what older interpreters of women insisted, "For few women is sexual deprivation such a fierce enemy as it is for most men," and "Women . . . are likely to see sex as a sort of bonus, something that comes along *after* a solid relationship is established," or "being held or cuddled may reduce anxiety, promote relaxation, and a feeling of security, and provide a distinctive type of gratification."

All this is, of course, near nonsense. What woman really wants, consciously or unconsciously, is orgasmic release. Her cry for affection, tenderness, hold-me-close is her defensive surrogate for what she has not been able to experience. For the woman who has no sexual partner available, or for the woman who has permanently assumed religious vows in place of masculine relationship, substitution or sublimation are no doubt necessary. These women deserve a different analysis and recommendation. For the woman living daily with a man, such substitution is demoralizing and debilitating. These little substitute niceties are often involved in the very cause of woman's failure to have complete orgasms.

The same writers who are saying, "Now for woman there are many interesting and happy little pleasures in sex just as rewarding, as joy-giving as orgasm," are insisting that woman's true pleasure and reward is in giving, giving, giving. She offers her sheathe and is to be delighted with having her breasts caressed, her ears bitten, her mouth kissed.

No! No! The woman who enjoys full and relaxing orgasm feels loved, needed, and secure. Closeness is good when it is interspersed with sexual mutuality of experience, but it is no valid substitute and no major need of hers in her physically active years. (Women in their nineties may be rejuvenated by kisses and tight hand holding.)

For woman it has been: apologize if you have an orgasm; apologize if you do not. Apologize if it is clitoral rather than vaginal.

The reports are in. Not everything is known. Enough is known. Women can be women. Men can help them be women and thus escape living with shrews and witches, Valkyries, Harpies, Moms, or Lesbians. Not all men will have to be taught.

Not all women are interested in orgasms. Some women would sooner dominate, reign supreme, be the Queen of the May.

Human sex works best in a partner—male plus female—relationship, but woman has been given the poor second place in the consummation.

Unsatisfied, needing, craving, anxious—she has been berated, labeled neurotic, nymphomaniac or frigid, when all she has needed is help in the completion of the orgasm.

Findings from the Masters and Johnson reports open the way for us to help rid the world of millions of neurotic, even psychotic women. These same women can become content, productive, creative, and loving beings. Women have been, then, literally warned that they must be satisfied with no afterplay, no completion. In many ways, their permitted experience has been comparable to the man's if that were limited to penetration, pump, pump, expectation, and then sudden withdrawal with no ejaculation and no hope of one.

Let us not cry for what has been; let us work for what can be.

A man has pronounced a woman frigid when she was not able to come to climax through their mutual endeavors. A woman who has learned to come to climax after the rejection of previous lovers will chortle both with glee and with bitter disdain for the former lovers.

To be a woman may be impossible without the understanding and cooperation of a man. Ann Landers quotes a French philosopher as saying, "There are no cold women—only clumsy men" (4). Julius Fast says, "It may well be a fact that there are no frigid women, just ignorant men" (5).

WHAT IS FEMALE ORGASM?

A new definition of female orgasm is needed. Some of the misunderstandings about female orgasm are misunderstandings because the authors are using varying definitions. Few adequate descriptions of orgasm are in the literature. The novelists, the writers in *Playboy, Adam, Modern Man,* and other of the more exotic men's periodicals have written better descriptions of women's orgasms than have the marriage manuals. This may, incidentally, be one reason women read such magazines, such novels, even while they raise protest at being the toys, the bunnies, the foibles, the abused ones.

Freud himself wrote, "If you want to know more about femininity, you must interrogate your own experience, or turn to the poets, or else wait until science can give you more profound and coherent information" (6).

Women are sexually starved today because they, their husbands, and their women friends do not know what a complete orgasm is nor how to achieve it.

Although Lombard Kelly, Albert Ellis, Alfred Kinsey, and other understanding men of science and medicine downgraded the superiority of the vaginal orgasm or declared that it did not exist, most writers on female sexuality had maintained that a woman was neurotic if she did not attain vaginal orgasm. Masters and Johnson have surely permanently shattered these assertions with their findings showing the clitoral glans and the lower third of the vagina both participate in the orgasm but are not "separate sexual entities" (7). Their report insists that it is improper to label clitoral orgasm immature or pathologic and that vaginal orgasm is impossible. They report, rather, that the clitoral glans initiates the orgasm which spreads to the outer third of the vagina.

Masters and Johnson in saying an orgasm is an orgasm—from nipples, clitoris, vagina—no matter how manipulated—by hand, vibrator, penis, etc. —may with this great new truth do damage. An orgasm is an orgasm, but a woman may need a larger one, a more devastating one than the quivers and relaxation she may have after, for example, breast manipulation.

Multiple orgasms? Of course, if one counts the orgasms, the larger and larger and larger orgasms that lead on and on and on until the last great convulsion leaves the woman as spent, as satiated, as relaxed, and as much in need of long hours of sleep as is the man. She could not possibly endure two such orgasms within an hour or two. If she has several close together orgasms, she has orgasms of degree or degrees of the orgasm.

Masters and Johnson have not differentiated between a shattering, crescendo climax which knocks a woman into immediate stupor and slumber and the involuntary but trifling climax she has when nipples are massaged or suckled or when the clitoris is stroked with penile penetration. They are quoted as saying that women "can often achieve as many as a dozen or more climaxes in rapid succession. Indeed, some authorities are now claiming that multiple orgasm is the natural birthright of all women" (8).

Phenomena called "multiple orgasms" by Masters and Johnson are bits and parts, much alike except in degree, of one massive, growing, building, and then, collapsing, shuddering, delectable crescendo.

In summarizing the data on orgasms from the Kinsey Reports, Paul H. Gebhard states that 59.4 per cent of wives who reach orgasm in 90 to 100 per cent of their marital coitus profess to have very happy marriages (9). Gebhard continues by saying that marital happiness and female orgasm correlate only at the extreme categories—very happy and very unhappy.

What women *say* they think or feel may not be quite the same as what they really think and feel, consciously and unconsciously.

THE FUTURE OF THE ORGASM

Emotionally a woman might wish for sexual satisfaction now, in the next ten minutes. Desire is avid, fresh, alive, insistent. But there is too much to do. The children are to be fed; the guests are coming; the house is in disarray. Yet most of all she knows satisfaction is not of the moment. She cannot become satisfied and be up, up, and away. She will fall into a deep, happy, untroubled and irrevocable sleep. She cannot leap up and go about her work. She is drugged; she is out. She does not dream. She has collapsed. She must sleep—not for minutes but for hours and hours.

A woman must be reduced to nothingness and obliteration—to full satisfaction, humility, completion. When she rises again it will be to creativity, full release.

Even women who can chuckle or shrug at their men's reading of *Playboy* or *Adam* or those girlie magazines may show themselves too greatly puritanical, reticent, or frightened to open the pages. These may be the women who are frustrated, nervous, unfulfilled.

Women probably need to see nude pictures and statues, to join nudist colonies more than men do. Women's frustrations and neuroticisms make it more difficult for them to accept a man's masculinity and their own femininity.

Writers on women's sexuality are quick to say the marriage manuals with their emphasis on sex instead of sex relationships have done more harm than good, while at the opposite extreme, other writers serenely repeat Masters' and Johnson's report that a vibrator causes woman to have a greater orgasm than she will have during intercourse.

While one notes with Masters and Johnson (10) that orgasm may follow any kind of natural or artificial stimulation to clitoris, mons, or other parts of female anatomy and that, in terms discussed "orgasm is orgasm" one agrees with most astute evaluators of the studies—Masters and Johnson included—that psychological factors have not been as yet adequately considered.

Some dream of love—candlelight, champagne, white roses, and pink sweet peas—London broil and fresh asparagus—moonlight streaming in from the doors of the balcony. Are such moments computed in the Masters and Johnson reports?

Warm wet grass on a summer's night—flickering fireflies, the long walk ends. Crickets chirp; new clover fields fill the air. New love, old love, warm love. Close to you, nostalgia for the old.

Was this a moment in the Masters and Johnson report?

To many a man, even today, the interest is over when his orgasm is over. Woman has little chance of a complete orgasm without the continued manipulation, lovemaking, fingerstroking of clitoris, vagina, vulva, and mons to bring *her* to the same shattering crescendo and destruction from which he has just emerged. Until he accepts this rhythm pattern, this need of hers, he may too early feel obliged to sink into the deep, ecstatic, fast slumber which she, too, needs or needs to need.

The man has an ejaculation and he is satisfied for ten minutes, an hour, two hours, a night, a week, a month. A woman has no satisfaction and so goes on and on seeking satisfaction. She is labeled a nymphomaniac.

A nymphomaniac and a frigid woman are similar. Neither finds sexual satisfaction. The nymphomaniac seeks and seeks and never finds it. The frigid woman does not want the satisfaction—or thinks she does not.

Men have called women either frigid or nymphomaniac when they were unable to bring them to complete and satisfying orgasms.

There is no doubt that some women are considered nymphomaniacs simply because they are seeking fulfillment of the orgasm which they could have if the knowledge of their lovers and their own knowledge and understanding were great enough.

Men have been asked to let women show them their masturbation patterns. This may be quite ridiculous for the woman who gets little satisfaction, try as she may, from masturbation. Is it, then, the ill adjusted or the well adjusted woman who can find little response to masturbation?

Psychologists, psychiatrists, and marriage counselors writing today do not, in general, become excited about masturbation as a moral issue. Many openly advocate masturbation for young people (11) or suggest that masturbation is, "positively good and healthy and should be encouraged because it helps young people to grow up sexually in a natural way" (12). Not all women learn to enjoy masturbation. The experience of masturbation can bring about orgasms that are as trivial to her full release as is the orgasm she may have from breast manipulation by her lover or husband.

For women, attempts at developing orgasm through masturbation may early be as frustrating as are her problems at coming to orgasm in her first genital experiences.

It is absurd that doctors tell women that, of course, it is all right to have sexual relations and orgasms during pregnancy. Who can jackknife, jerk, collapse when she is pregnant? Women who have complete all-over, all-through-the-body orgasms cannot have them when they are pregnant. If a woman used to such orgasms cannot restrain herself, she is going to prefer not to have sexual intercourse at all or to be afraid of it for the sake of the fetus. This has been understood by no one and written of not at all.

Suppose we forget the tag "cult of the orgasm" or obsession of the orgasm but take all positive steps to help all women have orgasmic, loving relationships. We will have a new culture. Hedonistic? Who cares?

Obsession with orgasm or the "cult of orgasm," please remember, has become important because of lack of orgasm, need of orgasm. When this great lack and need are fulfilled, the quiet, the productivity of after the orgasm will take ascendency.

When mistaken notions of woman's orgasms are no longer promulgated by marriage counselors, woman can be helped into her proper heritage and a human female will begin at last to comprehend how satisfying it is to be a woman. As the counselor continues to learn more about female orgasm, he will help woman work toward her real potential accepting whatever realities of her situation she must accept. He cannot morally help his client in terms of older information concerning orgasm.

REFERENCES

1. Collier, James Lincoln: Good sex without anxiety. *Pageant, 25:72,* 1969.
2. Collier, James Lincoln: Good sex without anxiety. *Pageant, 25:75,* 1969.

3. Liswood, Rebecca: New clues on how to satisfy a woman. *Coronet, 7:*40, 1969.

4. Landers, Ann: *Ann Landers Says Truth is Stranger* . . . Englewood Cliffs, New Jersey, Prentice Hall, 1968.

5. Fast, Julius: *What You Should Know About Human Sexual Response.* New York, Berkley, 1966.

6. Brecher, Edward and Ruth: *Analysis of Human Sexual Response.* New York, New American Library, 1966.

7. Masters, W. H., and Johnson, Virginia J.: *Human Sexual Response.* Boston, Little, Brown, 1966.

8. Masters, W. H., and Johnson, Virginia J.: *Human Sexual Response.* Boston, Little Brown, 1966, p. 131.

9. Gebhard, Paul H.: Factors in marital orgasm. *J Social Issues, 22:*88-95, 1966.

10. Masters, W. H., and Johnson, Virginia, J.: *Human Sexual Response.* Boston, Little Brown, 1966, p. 66.

11. Hamilton, Eleanor: *Sex Before Marriage.* New York, Meredith Press, 1969.

12. Pomeroy, Wardell: *Boys and Sex.* New York, Delacorte Press, 1968.

Chapter 24

MARRIAGE COUNSELING, POPULATION POLICY, AND AMERICAN POLITICAL INDIVIDUALISM

ETHEL M. NASH AND A. E. KEIR NASH

> In six and a half centuries from now—the same insignificant period of time separating us from the poet Dante—there would be one human being standing on every square foot of land on earth: a fantasy of horror that even the *Inferno* could not match.—Robert S. McNamara, speaking of the results of continuing the present birth rate, Address to the University of Notre Dame, May 1, 1969.

DURING THE FINAL THIRD of the twentieth century, no problem will weigh more heavily upon the world than the population explosion. No issue is likely to test more severely the capacity of the United States for international leadership. Responsibility for creating awareness among the American public of that issue's gravity and for thoughtful explication of its possible solutions will rest substantially upon those Americans whose professions involve them in influencing attitudes toward procreation, children, and families. Not the least among these are marriage counselors—whose professional activities include dealing with the significant hazards to the marital relationship of unwanted, and even of some wanted, children.

This chapter is concerned with the following:

1. The unpleasant facts of the population explosion.
2. Selected case histories whose common motif is marital or personal crisis to which unplanned childbirth has materially contributed.
3. An overview of current proposals for dealing with the population problem.
4. An examination of the difficulties of integrating each type of proposal with basic American tenets about the right relationship between government and the individual.

THE IMMEDIACY OF THE POPULATION PROBLEM

The present rate of population increase, when compared with that of past eras, is staggering both in its magnitude and in its implications. It took from the beginning of man to the Neolithic era for the world's population to grow to ten million. By the time of Christ, ten thousand years later, the population had reached three hundred million. When Columbus discovered America, there were five hundred million people. In the next three hundred and fifty years the population reached one billion. From 1850 to 1925 it in-

284

creased to two billion. The next thirty-seven years saw another billion added. Between 1962 and 1975, a mere thirteen-year interval, it will become four billion. By 1982 the population will be five billion (1). Before the end of this century, unless present rates of increase can be drastically curtailed, we will be adding to the world's population every seven years as many people as it took to reach from the dawn of man on earth to the age of the American Revolution. Clearly, even man's increasing capacity to utilize the planet's land and ocean resources cannot long keep pace. If voluntary or governmental effort cannot curtail population growth, a point will be reached in the not too distant future when natural or unnatural forces will take the matter out of our hands—be it through the natural forms of famine or disease, or through the unnatural forms of nuclear holocaust, homosexuality, or cannibalism.

Recognition by the leaders of foreign nations of the seriousness of the population explosion is considerably in advance of the general public's awareness among the nation upon whose technical resources the heaviest call will come—our own. On Human Rights Day, 1968, the heads of state of thirty countries—Australia, Barbados, Columbia, Denmark, Finland, Dominican Republic, Ghana, India, Indonesia, Iran, Japan, Jordan, Republic of Korea, Malaysia, Nepal, Netherlands, New Zealand, Norway, Pakistan, Phillippines, Singapore, Sweden, Thailand, Trinidad and Tobago, Tunisia, the United Arab Republic, the United Kingdom of Great Britain, the United States of America, and Yugoslavia—presented the Secretary-General of the United Nations with a declaration pointing out the economic, social, and psychological significance of the world's increasing population. Their declaration stated: "Too rapid population growth seriously hampers efforts to raise living standards, to further education, to improve health and sanitation, to provide better housing and transportation, to forward cultural and recreational opportunities—and even in some countries to ensure sufficient food. In short, the human aspiration, common to man everywhere, to live a better life is being frustrated and jeopardized" (2). By contrast, a Gallup poll taken in the mid-summer of 1968 found that less than 1 per cent of a national sample of Americans mentioned "population" when asked: "What do you think is the most important problem facing this country today?"

THE UNWANTED AND THE UNWISELY WANTED CHILD

The over-population menace can only be successfully averted if people realize that the consequences of not lowering the rate of population growth will be disastrous *for them, for their children, and for their grandchildren.* To confront all segments of our population with the urgency and immensity of the problem is not easy. As yet we are, to use Landmann's (3) graphic phrase, an "underdeveloped land in family planning." Action is necessary, but what action? What can be done to get the three-child family regarded as a large family? Is it possible to enable individuals to see the tragic cost to themselves and to children of conceiving for reasons other than those which can be good for the rearing of a child?

In the United States more marriage licenses are issued to girls of eighteen than to any other age group and more babies are born to girls of nineteen than to any other age group. Approximately three hundred thousand children are born out of wedlock each year. At least 80 per cent of all young women who marry during their high school years are pregnant at the time of marriage and 50 per cent of these marriages break up within five years. The Christensen (4) cross-cultural studies show that premarital pregnancy is statistically associated with divorce and that early postmarital conception is more frequently followed by divorce than is a delayed postmarital conception. This is not a short-lived problem. Rather, it continues from generation to generation: if research has made anything crystal clear it is the fact that the single most reliable predictor of a satisfying marital relationship is growing up in a home in which parents find love and joy in each other (5).

The following cases exemplify three distinct and frequently encountered types of male-female relationship in which the resultant child—while not always unwanted—is hardly the result of a mature and responsible decision to augment the world's population. In each, the child is not desired as an end in himself. Rather he may be classifed into one of the following types:

> Type 1—*desired as an indirect object* by one of the parents to further a distinct and direct objective (e.g. to compel or induce the other parent to alter his behavior pattern).

> Type 2—*wanted initially as a by-product* of a genuine developing inter-partner affection but virtually bound to become an involuntary contributor to the marriage's problem.

> Type 3—*an accidental by-product* of a sexual relationship.

In none of these does he begin life in anything like optimal circumstances. Nonetheless, the present structures of our laws and mores contribute materially to the frequency of such births.

The Case of the Beloved Pregnancy and the Unbeloved Child (Type 1). Mrs. R's reason for wishing to bear a third child at the age of twenty-six is a classic instance of preferring the getting to the begotten. An ineffective housekeeper, a shrewish marriage partner, and an erratic parent, she is given to episodic rages through which she controls her husband. Presently she is furious with him because he is stoutly resisting her wish for a third child.

This husband delayed marriage until his middle thirties. He loves order and peace, is temperamentally unsuited for, and, as an only child himself, is unpracticed in living comfortably with children. He recognizes that two children are more than enough for him and his wife to raise. However, unless marriage counseling can enable this husband to resist permanently and not to do what he usually does—give way in order to buy a temporary respite from attack—they will have another child. Only if Mr. R can learn to contain his shrew by becoming more confident in his own manhood can this marriage bring satisfaction to either and become an environment in which their two present children can hope to thrive emotionally. If counseling is effective and the marriage becomes more satisfying, then a third child will not be needed.

This is clear from the wife's story of why she wants another child. She says that she feels at her best when pregnant. In fact this is the only time she feels worthwhile as a person. Only then do relatives and associates (she has little capacity for friendship) give her favorable attention. She says longingly: "I would like to be pregnant all of the rest of my life." Being pregnant gratifies her infantile need for unconditional love, while being the creator of life provides a reassuring sense of omnipotence to her weak ego. If this young woman does not learn to deal with her own deficiencies as a person, she will alway resort to having another and another baby since this brings her temporary relief from the feeling of being useless and of no account.

The Case of Ovarian Roulette (Type 1). Mrs. Y is a much more competent person but her reason for becoming pregnant is no improvement on Mrs. R's. She wants to be able—if necessary—to wound her husband in a way that will really stick. They have four girls and her husband has always wanted a son. Now she too wants a boy desperately. She did not know that the chances of having another girl, under these circumstances, were less than fifty-fifty. However, she says that even if she had known she would have accepted the odds and gone ahead because of her particular motivation for this pregnancy. She is bitter because her husband Frank has given her little attention since the wedding ceremony. It seems to her that all that matters to Frank is his work and his athletic prowess. She says, "I was desperate. I decided that I was going to go all out for having a son. I checked the research about the time of the month that would give the highest possibility of conceiving a boy. I manipulated our love-making so we had intercourse at that time. If this baby is another girl, it does not really matter. I will just have played ovarian roulette and lost. If it is a boy, I will have given Frank what he most wants. Then maybe he will give me some of the attention I so much need. However, if he still remains indifferent to me, caring only for himself, his work and his son, then I will divorce him and be able to take away from him that which he has wanted most in all of his life—the boy."

Using the Child to Surpass Mother (Type 1). Sally's desire for children had yet a different motivation. She was determined to have four children so that she could outdo her mother who only had three. This competition was one that her husband, reared in an orphanage, could ill afford. Until Sally reached her desired number of children, four, he received the loving that his rearing made so necessary because he was, in a way, the child she did not yet have. When the fourth child was born, he was no longer important to this wife. She had all the children she wanted. Even as a "stud," her husband was no longer necessary. Not surprisingly, both are now under treatment for depression.

The Child as Healing Symbol (Type 2). There is another kind of "wanting" a child which has an emotionally healthier base but whose consequences are likely to rock once more a precarious relationship. In a period of three weeks it so happened that four couples, just when their marriages began to be more satisfying for the first time in many years, told me of a new pregnancy. I wondered why they had not used their customary contraceptive devices, since in each case it had become clear during the analysis of their marriage that none of these couples found it easy to accommodate to the multitude of complex relationships in their present family. Why then, at the time that the marriage took a turn for the better, should they add another child? The reply was essentially the same in each case: "We felt that we could only fully express the returning love we felt for each other if we had intercourse knowing that a child might result." These four marriages have so far weathered the crisis of the new baby, but each couple would have been able to discontinue therapy earlier and the marriage would be on a sounder foundation without the newest family member.

The Case of the Accidental Puppy-Dog-Child (Type 3). Linda is seventeen, pleasant, well-dressed, and plans to go on to college. She is four months pregnant by a boy whom she does not love. The conception occurred when they were both high on—to use her vocabulary—alcohol and grass. She says: "Grass alone couldn't have gotten either of us into it. It had to be the alcohol as well. But I'm glad I'm pregnant. Of course I am not marrying Bob. Our personalities clash. But being pregnant has given me something to live for. I work harder in school. I get better grades. I've always dreamed about having a baby and my three brothers and two sisters are all excited about my pregnancy. I know they will treat the baby like a doll. When my mother got over her shock she was sort of pleased because she would have a grandchild. She tells me that my stepfather wasn't really shook about my being pregnant because his own daughter was pregnant at fifteen. She says he is sort of glad there will be another baby around." The attitude of all these family members towards the birth of this baby is not in any way unkind, but it is more typical of feelings suitable for bringing a new puppy into the home. Clearly, Linda wants this baby, but is it the kind of wanting which should permit a baby to be born to her?

The Child as the Unintended Last Word (Type 3). Some children appear to be born as incidents in an on-going fight between their parents. The L's have four, born for no other reason apparently than that they happened. The L's relationship has been one of destructive warfare, covert and overt, from the time Mr. L preferred the engagement ring. Mrs. L considered the diamond inadequate in size but Mr. L refused to change it. During their sixteen years of marriage, this couple, both of whom are expert manipulators, have fought continually for dominance. Twice they have legally separated. Mrs. L initiated both reconciliations—ostensibly because she is afraid of their oldest child, a fifteen-year-old son who is grossly disturbed. Periodically and with increasing frequency, his inner volence explodes against his parents. Recently he has been in serious trouble for attacks on others. Two of the other children also need therapy.

In counseling with the L's it became clear that they could be taught to fight fairly and creatively. Yet, it is somewhat alarming to realize that at no time during their years of bitterness did the L's ever consider whether they ought to continue having children. They were not ignorant of contraceptive methods nor did they have religious convictions that would have prevented their using these. They just found satisfaction in climaxing their physically violent fights with spontaneous coitus. They had not given serious thought to not having children or even to spacing them.

The Case for the Crittenden Compromise (Type 3). Mrs. C, aged forty-two, sees herself as trapped. Jane, her sixteen-year-old daughter, whose I.Q. is around ninety, is pregnant by James. James is nineteen, a high school dropout of poor reputation, whose ability to keep a job seems minimal. He is one of seven siblings only two of whom have finished high school. Two of his brothers are selective service rejectees. One sister has two illegitimate children. Another has four children and the husband has deserted the family. James is a silent type who has come reluctantly to the counselor. His only contribution to the session is that he will marry Jane and live with her family, since that is what her dad wants. Jane wants marriage and a baby.

Jane's mother is desperate. She recognizes that her own tottering marriage cannot take this additional strain. Is there nothing, she wants to know, that can be done to compel Jane to go to a Crittenden home and put the baby up for adoption. Mrs. C's anxieties prove amply justified. Her husband, who adamantly refused to consider counseling, insisted that the couple join their household menage, but the strain of an unstable young man and a small baby were too much for him. Fifteen months later, he too joined the ranks of deserting husbands.

An Out of Wedlock Pregnancy with More Than Usual Potential for Af-

fecting Those Who Cannot Protect Themselves (Type 3). Thirty-eight year old Mrs. B's husband left her because she was too ill-tempered for anyone to live with peacefully. He has since remarried and is making similar complaints about his present wife, who in her turn has called the first Mrs. B to ask how she managed to live with him for fifteen years. The first Mrs. B has complete custody of the two children of her former marriage, girls aged eleven and fourteen. She has experienced two years of despair and loneliness. She has been eking out the support money by secretarial work. Her boss, married and with two childen, is a good listener. On two occasions the listening went beyond listening. The first Mrs. B is now two months pregnant. She desperately wants an abortion. Since the birth of a baby under these circumstances affects so many lives, ought not this woman be able to choose whether to carry this out of wedlock pregnancy to term?

ATTEMPTED SPACING THAT FAILED

In contrast to the foregoing situations, some conceptions occur even when great care is taken to prevent them. When such conceptions take place before the mother is physically ready to bear another child, the consequences may be tragic. The Bishop, Israel, and Briscoe (6) study of all premature births at the University of Pennsylvania Medical School Hospital revealed that if children were born with an interval of over twenty-three months between the births the incidence of prematurity was 7.8 percent. If the interval between births was from twelve to twenty-three months the incidence of prematurity was 10.3 per cent. If the interval between births was less than twelve months the incidence of prematurity was 18 per cent. Since prematurity involves a higher incidence of serious eye and ear defects, ought a couple to be compelled against their will to carry to term a pregnancy which has a high risk of deformity even when they have taken every precaution considered advisable by their obstetrician to prevent it? Is it fair to the child they already have to risk the health of the mother or the burden on the family that a deformed child or even another normal child conceived so soon would place? Is it fair to take such a risk for a baby who may possibly have to grow up seriously handicapped?

Even if the spacing interval is physiologically right, the timing may still be wrong for the birth of another baby. The D's, who married in the husband's freshman year of college, have, at the end of his sophomore year, one child. This circumstance makes it barely possible to keep the husband in school. Now, the contraceptive they have used since the first child's birth has not worked, and another pregnancy has occurred. To have another child at this time will require Mr. D to drop out of school. Should this couple be compelled to have this child in view of the inevitable consequences for their future and the future of their children? It will mean a tremendous income loss over a lifetime and almost certainly seriously prevent his potential developing as fully as it could in a job opening made possible by college completion. The possibilities for destruction of this already wavering family unit will inevitably be increased significantly.

AMERICAN INDIVIDUALISM, POPULATION CONTROL, AND MARRIAGE COUNSELING

An age is sometimes best defined in terms of its salient problem. And the viability of a political culture in that age rests heavily upon two characteristics: a) its capacity for timely perception of that problem as a problem and b) its ability to solve that problem within the political contours of its structure. Without perception and without solution, the society runs grave risks of disaster. At the very least, the society's politics must be able to temporize with the problem by handing it on, recognized even if only partially dealt with, to the succeeding generation.

That the phenomenon of nuclear power has been an overriding problem of the mid-twentieth century scarcely admits of doubt. That an equally important problem of the final third of this century will be the population explosion scarcely admits of greater doubt. The mid-twentieth century accomplished the minimum of deferring the nuclear issue. But there are at least two reasons for being less optimistic in prognosticating even such limited success with respect to the population explosion.

First, the nuclear problem had one great comparative "advantage"—its obviousness. After Hiroshima, it was inescapable. By comparison, population is a quiet issue that creeps upon us, particularly if we are middle class or upper class. If the nuclear age began with a bang, the age of the population crisis manifests itself with the intermittent distant whimper of a black baby starving in the forests of Biafra or (can we really believe it?) among the magnolias of Mississippi.

Second, grappling with the problem of overpopulation threatens to be gravely complicated by ideological factors. To put the matter bluntly, on its face at least there is something "un-American" about the notion of nonvoluntary methods of control. Furthermore, for significant sectors of the American population, even the idea of voluntary birth control is suspect. Thus a question is inescapably posed for marriage counselors, as for other professionals involved in opinion-setting concerning the population explosion: "To what extent can various proposals for population control be squared with American norms of freedom?"

In seeking an answer to this question, it seems fruitful to divide these proposals into four basic types. The first type is comprised of those proposals which would enable greater self-determination by individual couples. These include programs which seek—by contact with individual physicians, public health institutions, marriage counselors, and educators—to disseminate as widely as possible reasons for, and methods of, family planning and fertility control. Also included are proposals for the liberalization of abortion laws (7, 8, 9), since they share with information proposals the common objective of increasing the possibilities of autonomous individual choice. The one increases access to information, the other makes possible a greater range of choice based upon that information.

A second type consists of all proposals (10, 11, 12) for including population dynamics courses as a regular part of public educational curricula. It could be argued that this is merely a subdivision of the first range of proposals for better dissemination of information but there is an important difference. The first type merely "offers" the information to a willing hearer who presumably can "turn the information off" at will. The second requires "sitting through."

A third category of proposals urges governmental inducements to voluntary restrictions upon bearing children. The welter of such proposals may be subdivided into two sorts: a) positive incentive payments for limiting births (13), for voluntary sterilization (14, 15), and for spacing children through periods of nonpregnancy or nonbirth (16, 17, 18, 19, 20); and b) negative incentives built into the tax structure, for instance, taking away exemptions for exceeding "N-children" (21, 22, 23, 24) or levying fees on births above the Nth (25, 26).

Lastly, a fourth category of proposals would legislate involuntary controls, for instance, "marketable licenses to have children" (27), temporary sterilization of all females (28) or males or permanent sterilizations after N-births (29), required abortion of illegitimate (30) or post-Nth-pregnancies, and "general fertility control agents" (31) added to, say, the public water supply, with counteracting "agents" distributed to individuals who have demonstrated economic and emotional readiness for parenthood.

These four categories of proposals are listed here in increasing order of potential conflict with American individualism. That is to say, the fourth restricts free choice more than the third, the third more than the second, and the second more than the first. Both ease of acceptance and amount of change required in the contours of American political values suggest that the "best" solution to the population problem is that which relies as heavily as is feasible upon the lower numbered types. But time is clearly important here. Inaction while crisis builds may require greater reliance upon more restrictive governmental controls. The amount of free choice which would suffice today may not suffice tomorrow. In turn, therefore, it is imperative that opinion-setters give timely consideration to the real nature of the conflicts posed.

We believe that in the long run it is only the fourth set of mandatory proposals which entail terribly acute—and perhaps insoluble—attitudinal hostilities. The difficulty here can be put very briefly by means of analogy: granted the extent of antagonism manifested in certain sectors since World War II to fluoridation of public water supplies, what would be the reception accorded to anti-conception agents placed therein? *Ergo,* the importance of meeting the population explosion before such controls become inevitable.

In order to do so, it is crucial to meet quickly remaining hostilities to the first three proposal-types—hostilities which are as real as they are misfounded in some sectors of the public mind. Herein lies a crucial task for marriage counselors—making themselves aware of these hostilities so that they can perceive their manifestation, overt or implicit, in the attitudes of counselees.

In respect to the first type of proposal, we are not greatly concerned with a commonly raised issue—potential Roman Catholic resistance to abortion (32). If the American Catholic lay reaction to Pope Paul's Encyclical reaffirming traditional Roman Catholic abhorrence of interference with "natural processes" be any guide, it is hard to believe that in the long run the encyclical will have a significant effect upon lay behavior. Rather, we are more concerned with another type of resistance which until recently has gone largely unperceived—resistance to voluntary control among non-Catholic poor. Two related difficulties are manifest here. The first stems from lower-strata views of the optimal number of children per family. As Judith Blake has argued recently in a provocative article in *Science* (33), an inescapable fact remains when all allowances are made for religious views. All the statistics point remorselessly away from the "accepted wisdom" of family planners that poverty sector mothers have too many children simply because they are ignorant of contraceptive techniques. The second manifestation of resistance in this sector is an ideological justification of hostility to family planning schemes put forward by militant leaders of racial minorites: namely, the charge that such schemes directed at the poor are, in view of the coincidence of poverty and minority status, nothing but sugarcoated genocide pills. The point here is, of course, not the abstract merits or demerits of such interpretations of family planners' motives. Rather it is the "realness" of such attitudes among these sectors. On balance, we find it difficult to believe that such hostility will evanesce or even diminish in the face of persistent marginal standards of living. Surely, on the contrary, the increasingly ruffled racist waters of American politics during the late 1960's argue, if anything, for a short-run increase in such attitudes. That in mind, we find ourselves led to the view that the American populaton problem will require the satisfaction of at least three conditions before it begins to be met: a) raising the living standards of the poverty sector to a point where middle class mores have at least some possibility of "taking hold," b) structuring abortion laws so that couples have freedom of choice in respect to carrying pregnancies to term, and c) widespread adoption of the second range of proposals—integrating population dynamics courses into public educational curricula.

While it lies beyond the province of this essay to prognosticate concerning the first condition, we can venture judgments about the future in respect to the second and third. Barring a violent pendular swing toward right or left in American politics during the 1970's, we anticipate minor reactions among state legislatures against "sex education," and a stronger trend toward both more permissive abortion laws and incorporating population dynamics courses into public educational curricula. Essentially, we have two reasons for so anticipating. First, resistance to changes in abortion laws is primarily based on a combination of legislative inertia and a neo-Fundamentalist anxiety that "easy abortions" increase "sexual promiscuity." Such anxiety lies similarly at the base of recent movements to prevent or repeal sex education courses in the public schools. We doubt that such motivation for resistance can long endure in the face of the larger political truth of the relationship between large families, poverty, and urban unrest, and in the face of the obvious inability of such statutory structures to alter post-Kinsey sexual behavior, to prevent the acquisition of such knowledge in extracurricular fashion, or to prevent illegitimate pregnancies.

Second, as today's university students become tomorrow's opinion setters and as their generation swells the ranks of voters it is likely that more logical attitudes will prevail. Thus, samples of university student opinion in two states which have recently liberalized abortion laws suggest that the "present liberal" position requiring therapeutic judgment by the physician rather than decision by the couples involved will not suffice in a decade's time. Despite California's reforms, 83 per cent of a sample of University of California students wished further liberalization. Indeed, asked to judge the desirability of changing ten different types of present laws, including marijuana prohibitions, they came down most heavily in favor of abortion reform (34). Similarly, a sample of second year medical students at the University of North Carolina disclosed a heavy commitment to voluntarism (35). None of the forty-three sample members opposed family planning methods, but only nine predicted that they would be sufficient to solve the American population explosion. Over 90 per cent of the medical students favored abortion when carrying to term would threaten the *emotional or physical health* of the mother. It is important that these students would not require any showing of potential danger to life itself. One hundred per cent of the students would proceed beyond present statutory allowances for abortion in the event of *rubella*—with its very clear linkage to birth defects. All would permit abortion on a showing that *any parental condition* posed a substantially greater than average chance of a defective child. Lastly, and perhaps most indicative of the commitment to individual self-determination, 90 per cent would legalize abortion without interposing a "physician veto," if both wife and husband jointly desired one. This survey did not ask directly about compulsory courses in public schools on population dynamics. However, it seems fair to infer from the fact that less than one quarter of the medical students believed voluntary measures would suffice that medical opinion of the coming generation should be considerably in advance of present educational practices, as disclosed in a survey undertaken by G. D. Searle and Company (36) in 1967. Replies from forty-five of the fifty State Superintendents of Public Instruction from whom information was requested disclosed that, although only three states' laws prohibited sex education in the public schools, only one state—Oregon—required it. Further, only ten State Superintendents knew of even limited discussion of family planning methods in their state's high schools resulting from local level curriculum decisions. In sum, there are strong grounds for anticipating that, if medical students in a state hardly renowned as a "hotbed of liberalism" favor such voluntarism, general medical opinion among the coming generation of physicians will do so too.

The third range of proposals for positive and negative incentives to limiting childbirth raises issues of a more serious, yet soluble, political nature. In this respect we can only declare our perhaps too optimistic view that general attitudes will shift, in due time. Rather the question is—will "due time" be "in time"? The medical student survey (37) showed an interesting split of opinion on this issue—considerably greater support for tax incentives than for direct payments. Thus, twelve of the forty-three favored incentive payments for voluntary sterilization, while over a third favored reversing tax exemptions for exceeding a certain statutorily-determined number of children, and over half favored not reversing but limiting the maximum number of such exemptions.

On a purely economic basis, however, such a distinction is hard to defend. Just as there is nothing "procedurally" new in the relationship between government and individual in such tax exemptions, there is nothing really novel about direct incentive payments. In both, the government simply reverses a former "substantive" policy of reward for "helping the national interest" by having children, and promotes another "national interest" by rewarding restraint. Whichever way the exemptions run, or whether there are more or fewer child welfare payments, the government is carrying out policy through inducement. Additionally, there is no genuine economic difference between direct and indirect reward in terms of threat to the American democratic ethos. All such measures fall—like the progres-

sive income tax and unemployment compensation—in the realm of persuasion rather than statutory compulsion. On balance, the only viable distinction is in the specific terms of who is affected. Tax exemptions for not having children are more likely to take hold on middle or upper income
brackets. Unless there is a general minimum standard of affluence and concomitant pervasive adoption of middle class goals as to family size, direct
payments may be necessary if this third range of proposals is to be sufficiently effective to avoid ultimate recourse to the fourth—compulsory legislation.

CONCLUSION

The population crisis is already upon us, domestically and internationally. Marriage counselors, like others involved in leading opinion formation
concerning family structure, have at least two clear responsibilities. First, a
need to develop sophisticated positions of their own relationship to the
problem. Toward this end we have suggested four types of proposed solutions and offered our opinions concerning their basic compatibility with
American society. Second, all too often children are produced either as the
by-products of marital conflict, or as "accidents," or because the present
structure of American law discourages or prohibits planning of families in
optimal fashion—that the child be born only when he is wanted as an end in
himself *and* when his parents are "responsible" in their interpersonal and
community relationships. We feel that the marriage counselor should play
an active role in encouraging the acceptance of such conditions.

REFERENCES

1. Quoted from *Listen,* Vol. 14, No. 1, Harriman, Tennessee, 1967.
2. United Nations Population Division, *Population Newsletter, I:*44-45, April, 1968.
3. Landmann, Lynn: "United States: Underdeveloped Land in Family Planning,"
    Journal of Marriage and the Family, XXX (May, 1968), 191-201.
4. Christensen, Harold T.: Children in the family: Relationship of number and spac-
    ing to marital success. *J Marriage and the Family,* XXX:283-89, May, 1968.
5. Udry, J. Richard: *The Social Context of Marriage.* New York, Lippincott, 1966, pp.
    506-508.
6. Bishop, E. H.; Israel, S. L., and Briscoe, C. C.: Obstetric influences in the prema-
    ture infant's first year of development. *Obstet Gynec,* XXVI:628-35, November,
    1965.
7. Chandrasekhar, S.: Should we legalize abortion in India? *Pop Rev,* X, 17-22, July,
    1966.
8. Davis, Kingsley: Population policy: Will current programs succeed? *Science, CLVIII:*
    730-39, November 10, 1967.
9. Ehrlich, Paul: *The Population Bomb.* New York, Ballantine Books, 1968, p. 139.
10. Pravin, Visaria: Population assumptions and policy. *Economic Weekly,* August 8,
    1964, p. 1343.
11. Wayland, Sloan: Family planning in the school curriculum. *Family Planning and*

Population Problems. Bernard Berelson, *et al.* (Ed.) Chicago, University of Chicago Press, 1966, pp. 353-62.

12. Davis, Kingsley: Population policy: Will current programs succeed? *Science, CLVIII:* 730-39, November 10, 1967.
13. Enke, Stephen: Government bonuses for smaller families. *Pop Rev., IV:*47-54, 1960.
14. Samuel, T. J.: The strengthening of the motivation for family limitation in India. *J Family Welfare, XIII:*11-16, December, 1966.
15. *Approaches to the Human Fertility Problem.* Prepared for the United Nations Advisory Committee on the Application of Science and Technology to Development by the Carolina Population Center of the University of North Carolina, Chapel Hill, N. C.: Carolina Population Center, 1968, pp. 68-69.
16. Enke, Stephen: The gains to India from population control. *The Review of Economics and Statistics, XLII:*179-80, May, 1960.
17. Balfour, Marshall C.: A scheme for rewarding successful family planners, Memorandum, The Population Council, June, 1962.
18. Spengler, Joseph J.: Agricultural Development Is Not Enough. A paper prepared for the Conference on World Population Problems at Indiana University, May, 1967, pp. 29-30.
19. Summary of Michael Young's discussion by Margaret Snyder, A summary of the discussions, in The behavioral sciences and family planning programs: Report on a conference. *Studies in Family Planning,* No. 23, October, 1967, p. 10.
20. Leasure, J. William: Some economic benefits of birth prevention. *Milbank Memorial Fund Quart, XLV:*417-26, October, 1967.
21. Titmuss, R. M., and Abel-Smith, B.: *Social Policies and Population Growth in Mauritius.* London, Methuen, 1960, pp. 130-131.
22. Samuel, T. J.: The strengthening of the motivation for family limitation in India. *J Family Welfare, XIII:*11-16, December, 1966.
23. Ehrlich, Paul: *The Population Bomb.* New York, Ballantine Books, 1968, pp. 136-137.
24. Davis, Kingsley: Population policy: Will current programs succeed? *Science, CLVIII:* 730-39, November 10, 1967.
25. Samuel, T. J.: The strengthening of the motivation for family limitation in India. *J Family Welfare, XIII:*11-16, December, 1966.
26. Spengler, Joseph J.: Agricultural Development Is Not Enough. A paper prepared for the Conference on World Population Problems at Indiana University, May, 1967, pp. 29-30.
27. Boulding, Kenneth E.: *The Meaning of the Twentieth Century: The Great Transition.* New York, Harper & Row, 1964, pp. 135-36.
28. Shockley, William B.: Lecture at McMaster University, Hamilton, Ontario; see *New York Post,* December 12, 1967.
29. S. Chandrasekhar, reported in *The New York Times,* July 24, 1967.
30. Davis, Kingsley: Population policy: Will current programs succeed? Science, *CLVIII:* 730-39, November 10, 1967.
31. Ketchel, Melvin M.: Fertility control agents as a possible solution to the world population problem. *Perspectives in Biology and Medicine, XI:*687-703, Summer, 1968.
32. Potvin. R. H.; Westoff, C. F., and Ryder, N. B.: Factors affecting Catholic wives' conformity to their Church Magisterium's position on birth control. *J Marriage and the Family, XXX:*263-72, May, 1968.

33. Blake, Judith: Population policy for Americans: Is the government being misled? *Science, CLXIV*:522-29, May 2, 1969.
34. Nash, A. E. Keir, and Hall, Peter M.: Survey of a Random Sample of 300 Undergraduates at the University of California at Santa Barbara. University of California at Santa Barbara, Spring, 1968. Unpublished data.
35. Nash, Ethel M., and Nash, A. E. Keir: A Survey of Second Year Medical Students' Attitudes to Family Planning, Fertility Control, and Population Control. School of Medicine, University of North Carolina, April, 1969. Unpublished data.
36. Survey made by G. D. Searle and Company in 1967 at the request of Ethel M. Nash.
37. Nash, Ethel M., and Nash, A. E. Keir: A Survey of Second Year Medical Students' Attitudes to Family Planning, Fertility Control, and Population Control. School of Medicine, University of North Carolina, April, 1969. Unpublished data.

Chapter 25

COMMUNICATION AND CONJUGAL
SPIRITUALITY

JOHN O. MEANY

THE WORD "SPIRITUALITY" turns many people off; "conjugal spirituality" seems like an impossible puzzle. Rarely has something so valuable been so little understood.

Spirituality can be defined in various ways, depending on how history and culture have influenced the expressions of philosophical and theological truth. But today, many laymen feel spirituality is something reserved for monks or mystics, something unrelated to making love in or out of bed.

Although it is ultimately a mystery, conjugal spirituality exists as a *conscious psychological relationship* between a man and a woman who, in varying ways, consciously know and choose each other—before God and Man. Each spouse is a unique "being" who has the spiritual capabilities to think and to choose. It is too often forgotten that that which makes a man spiritual is his capacity to think and to choose.

As a child becomes a man, his awareness, his consciousness of the world around him, and of himself, gradually emerges out of what was previously unknown. Spirituality is like a large island gradually emerging out of a dark sea to form a land-mass of consciousness—to use an analogy of Carl Jung. The higher the top-lookout of this island, the further one can see, both out over the ocean, and down around the perimeter of the island and into its hills and valleys. Similarly, as Karl Rahner and H. Vorgrimler say in their *Theological Dictionary* (1), "Spirit" is that "entity which is characterized by an openness toward being and at the same time by an awareness of what itself is and is not." Thus, a "spiritual" person is psychologically "open" and has a broad nondefensive view of reality, as well as a clear, conscious, view of himself, what he is and is not.

The conscious, spiritual aspect of our "being" ever more deeply seeks an integration with our passions and our sensuality—so that, hopefully, a person rises up, like the island, to be ever more and more a unique and "individuated" person. This integration of our understanding and our choices with our emotions and our sensuality protects us from a splintering "schizophrenic" spirituality which is much too common today. As Carl Jung (2) says in his thoughtful essay on "Marriage as a Psychological Relationship" (Volume 17, *Collected Works*), "any attempt to create a spiritual attitude by splitting off and repressing the instincts is a falisfication." But when our instincts are respected as an integral part of our "being," then our spirituality is often subjectively experienced as "turned on," "feeling free," or "being alive." Integration or "wholeness" avoids the oppression of unresolved emotions as well as the wasteful ruminations of "intellectual" rationalizations, all of which are motivated by unconscious passions or instincts.

Good spiritual direction or marriage counseling can liberate a person, can deepen his spirituality by helping him "to be" more free and reasonable. With a clearer view of himself, a person can see what he is and is not. For example, I once worked with an emotionally explosive wife who learned through counseling, to talk reasonably about her feelings, and not to act compulsively on them. So that now she recommends: "Suppose you have the desire to throw dishes; express it verbally! Talking does two things; first you have it off your chest; and second, your good china and your spouse's head will remain intact, which is also nice!" She is freer and more reasonable now, which is also nice.

But it may be asked, "Where is God in all this?" He is in those actual graces which *illuminate our intellect* when we have meaningful spiritual insights into ourselves. He is also in the *strengthening of our will* when we choose what is really good for our whole being. He resides in us, in a sanctifying way, the more we are, nondefensively, our real selves. The more authentic a person we are; the more, in Him, "we live, move, and have our being."

Louis Bouyer, in his work *History of Christian Spirituality* (3), also sees spirituality as a "religious consciousness," and he clearly shows how the term is used interchangeably in the Gospels to include both the theological effects of grace and also that psychological "principle" which gives life to the human body.

Freedom and reasonableness are the spiritual capabilities in a person's nature which God's grace makes more perfect. Grace, in this view, perfects all the natural capabilities of each person in a marriage; it does not absorb, deny, or destroy what is natural. And since God works through what is natural, each spouse is the primary dispenser of God's grace to the other; not only at the wedding ceremony, but throughout their whole lives. Each spouse, working with and through grace, can perfect the other.

Jacques Maritain once said, in another context, that there are two ways of becoming secularistic: first, by so greatly stressing the spiritual, by so emphasizing abstract, or "angelistic" ideals, that the concrete environment (or human body) does not really matter; or, secondly, by becoming so preoccupied with the sensual, material world, that there is little awareness of the spiritual.

There is the error of the "angels." It is subtly secularistic to say that spirituality is unrelated to human experience; that is, "spirituality" in a marriage is something intangible; the fruits of spirituality cannot possibly be observed in the everyday behavior of married couples. Spirituality, from this point of view, would be so intimately bound up with God's Grace, that it would seem to exist only in God's mind. Too often conjugal spirituality seems to be identified only with some abstract concept of supernatural grace; thus, spirituality is not seen as something natural to man. But it is secularistic to separate grace from nature. In its worst forms, this "angelistic" view of spirituality would foster a "schizophrenic" spirituality which would try to separate a person's reason and choices from those basic joys and sorrows of his emotional life, as well as from the drives of his physiological functioning, like hunger and sex. It is impossible to divorce a couple's ability to be free and reasonable with each other from any long-term soul-satisfying sexual experience.

There is also the error of the "materialists." It is not so subtly materialistic or secularistic to say that "spirituality" is essentially a meaningless or "nonsense" word; in this view marriage and sexuality are basically matters of glands and physiology. If this widely held view is fully accepted then physicians, or urologists and gynecologists, are the only real authorities on marriage. Marriage then becomes only a matter of hormones and physical techniques, important as they may be.

Any view of spirituality which stresses only the ideal, or only the sensual, either at the expense of the other, is secularistic and schizophrenic. Because the Word was made flesh!

If it is basic to man's spirituality that he is also to make rational choices, choices that consider not only his personal "values," but also his sensual or physical well being, then an authentic spirituality presupposes some ability to look inside oneself. For only when we know honestly what we think and feel, can we be self-directed, and not guided by other people's values and "human respect." An authentic self-knowledge comes to grips with one's actual values—not those that others would like us to have, nor those we would like to have, ideally—but rather those values we actually use in making our everyday choices. An authentic self-knowledge is also aware of those unique emotional needs, feelings, and desires which are important to our total well-being. It is so easy to deny our feelings and then act on them. The spiritual man loves, not only with his intellect, but with his whole heart and whole soul as well.

But if, as Tom Merton says in his *Seeds of Contemplation* (4), an authentic spirituality presupposes a real self-knowledge, how do we come to know that spirit which enlivens us? How does a man know his own soul? Aquinas says that we know our own souls by reflecting on our own actions. If we know, really, why we do what we do, if we can see that our own real values and feelings are integrated into our actions and behavior, then we have the beginnings, at least, of real self-knowledge and spirituality.

Self-knowledge, or truth shall make us free. It is, of course, traditional that real self-knowledge is a prerequisite for an authentic spiritual life. But deep knowledge only comes from an understanding of causes, both immediate and ultimate. For example, to really know a woman, you must know her more than just physically. You know her better by knowing what she really "values" when she makes actual choices. But you only really know her, as the Bible says, when you share yourself with her, totally, in love. Thus, a deep knowledge of a person comes from an ever-deepening understanding and love of all of the causes of his whole being. But how does one uncover both the immediate and more ultimate determinants of one's own existence? By reflection and meditation on our "ultimate cause," God, and His present influence in our experience. But also by an understanding of those sociocultural determinants of our existence, like the unique personalities of our parents, or the significant teachers and the crucial life experience that we have had. A person's value and choices have been partially determined by his earlier experiences, his cultural background and his education. A warm Italian husband may place more importance on the emotional aspects of love than his spouse does, if she had been raised in a "cold" Jansenistic family. The uniqueness of our own existence can only be discovered by our own reflection on our own experiences. This reflection or "examination of conscience" can be enriched by discussing significant experiences with another person, a friend, a spiritual director or one's own spouse. But only a severe and ever deepening honesty with ourselves will help us to live our marriage without those erroneous assumptions or rationalizations about ourselves, or our spouse, which block love.

It is self-evident to any husband who has thought seriously about his marriage, that all of his "premarital" experiences, including his early experiences with his own parents, are vitally important for his present marriage. My experience as a psychotherapist has shown me that there are many more sexual nuances present in parent-child relationships than is ever openly admitted. Even in the nonsexual area, early childhood experiences lead to expectations and assumptions about one's spouse which can greatly affect the marriage. For example, if as a husband you had a mother who was an immaculate housekeeper in the Dutch tradition you probably came to marriage with the conscious (or unconscious) assumption that your new wife would also act much like your mother. But, if your wife came from a different tradition, where cleanliness is not necessarily next to Godliness, then there may be a conflict. By accepting your different expectations and values, you may have a home which is "clean enough to be healthy, but dirty enough to be happy." Thus the spiritual atmosphere existing in your present family relationships has often been largely determined by your earlier childhood experiences, which is why children from happy homes tend to build happy homes of their own. The more clearly and deeply a husband (or a wife) knows himself, the more he will understand how much of the past does really influence his present life. As Freud has said, "the first claim upon the feeling of love in a woman belongs. . .in typical cases to her father . . .whether the husband is rejected depends upon the strength of this fixation." Knowing the truth, a person is free to choose new and better ways of behaving.

From a psychological point of view, an authentic conjugal spirituality has a deeply shared intellectual and volitional life which, in turn, fosters a deeper and more mutual physical life. As Sidney Jourard says in *The Transparent Self* (5), "A healthy relationship between two loving people is characterized by a mutual knowledge, openness of communication, freedom to be oneself in the presence of the other without contrivance. When two people are thus open to one another, they will likewise have become able to be sexually open with one another. Openness before a person renders one open to sights, sounds, smells in the world, and also the riches of one's own feelings. The person who effectively guards himself against pain from the outside just as effectively ensures virtual sexual anesthesia." Like Jourard, many marriage counselors have found that "supposedly purely sex problems turn out inevitably to be problems that arise from fouled-up relationships." All of which proves the importance of the spiritual, even in sexual experience. The more spiritual we are, the more conjugal we can be, and vice versa. When the Lord said that a married couple is "two in one flesh," did he mean, among other things, that two spiritual beings are ideally united, physically and emotionally, in a mutually achieved climax of orgasm? I think so; sensuality and spirituality each draw life from the other in a marriage.

Ideally, one may describe a deeply spiritual couple as one which is characteristically open to their total experience of each other. That is, ideally, both spouses are nondefensive, or "game free," as Eric Berne describes it in *Games People Play* (6). A deeply spiritual relationship does not foster a "secret garden" which is selfishly reserved for one's self alone, while at the same time one does not get lost in the other, preserving one's sense of identity. Ideally, a deeply spiritual couple would live existentially, that is, they will be honest with each other at each moment, and will live as deeply with each other as possible, from moment to moment, throughout their lives; they would trust, love, and understand their own bodies, and all their senses so that they can ever more deeply and integrally share honest convictions, real feelings, and strong biological urges in an honest and meaningful way.

It is tragic to see an elderly couple who have lived their whole life together but have never really been honest and nondefensive with each other. For example, one wife pretended to be kind and giving when in reality she has been subtly hostile and the husband thought he was being charitable by constantly giving in to her every whim and not standing up for himself, and more truly respecting both her and himself. He was hospitalized eventually for being severely passive and dependent on her.

There are many different patterns and levels of psychological interaction possible in marriage. One very common pattern in our upward mobile middle class American society is an attempt by one partner, usually the man, to attain "self-sufficiency" through a "cold" type of emotional detachment and withdrawal into his work and/or intellectual pursuits; meanwhile the other partner, usually the wife, makes open and intense demands for emotional expressions of love, using all kinds of illogical arguments and false rationalizations to express her anger. But the more the woman demands affection, and emotional support, so she can feel dependent on his "strength," the more fear she arouses in the man, so that he becomes all the more withdrawn into himself and his work, justifying himself by his economic contribution to the family; but this, in turn, is interpreted as an even deeper rejection by the wife. Both blame the other, while each contribute to the problem. Meanwhile the satisfying sexual and really intellectual aspects of the relationship tend to deteriorate. Sometimes, the wife insists on having more children, so that small loving children will meet her emotional needs, which are largely unsatisfied by her husband; while he, in turn, may look for satisfaction in "affairs" and/or more and more "business successes." Victor Eisenstein's *Neurotic Interaction in Marriage* (7) says the problem with this kind of marriage relationship is that both spouses labor under an illusion. The emotionally dependent woman wants to be able to lean on a strong man; she saw, in courtship, his detachment as "strength" when it was, and is, really a fear of being emotionally involved. This is often due to the way he was raised as a child (e.g. Don't cry, be a big boy!!). The man, for his part assumes he is incapable of meeting the strong emotional demands of his wife, and children, and tends to withdraw without trying. He wants his wife to be as emotionally "independent" as he is; thus he wants to be free from "demands" for affection and emotional support because he assumes, with fear, that he will not be able to meet them. Each spouse wants to force the other into his (or her) own image of what they should be, rather than accepting them as they really are. Jung says, "a deep-seated unconscious tie to the parents" always creates an image which makes it difficult to be close in a marriage.

There are many other patterns in marriage relationships also. Sometimes one spouse spends much of his (or her) emotional and intellectual energy trying to dominate a more dependent partner. Each is furious with the other because the need for autonomy or "individuation" is frustrated. Such marriages are characterized by frequent quarrels and fights, where spouses attack each other, like angry children each wanting his own way.

In all these patterns, if there is growth toward more consciousness of what is really going on in the relationship, then the marriage contract, like a labor-management contract, is "renegotiated" from time to time; roles and functions can change as real motivations become clearer. But as Jung says, there is "no birth of consciousness without pain." However, the "midwife" is honest communication to increasingly clarify motivations. In this way, each spouse grows more and more away from unconscious infantile behavior toward a more mature and more deeply spiritual relationship.

If a woman is too much "wrapped up" or "contained" (to use Jung's phrase) intellectually in her husbands life and work, and the husband is, reciprocally, too much "contained" by his wife's emotions, then each, knowing this, can help the other to grow in the area in which they are limited. Thus the wife can more fully expand her horizons and develop her own intellectual interests, while the husband can more fully find a personal sense of unity and love in his family life. Only fear and prejudice block this in either spouse; but their mutual love can cast out each other's fears.

In practical terms, how can a couple work toward ever deepening their relationship, their spiritual understanding of each other? Carl Roger's book, *On Becoming a Person* (8), helps to point the way. If, for example, a husband wants to communicate more deeply with his wife, then he must attempt to express as accurately as possible, all of the feelings which exist *in him* at each moment at both the emotional and physiological level. He expresses these *as his own* feelings, not as statements about his wife or as a threat to her. This honest inward search on the part of the husband tends to encourage his wife to communicate more of her own real feelings; and she tends to communicate her feelings *more accurately*. The husband, having honestly expressed *his own* real feelings, is then more free and able to talk to her about her real feelings. How often we assume we know how our spouse feels, and really neglect to listen to her! However, often erroneously, we assume our spouse knows how we feel, but we neglect to inform her, and then feel hurt when she does not act understandingly.

For the same reason, a wife is more able to listen to her husband if she can express *her own* feelings about herself more openly. Thus, the honest expression of each one's own feelings, without blaming or threatening the other person, makes for a more genuine two-way communication. But the stronger the feelings, the harder this is to do; when really angry it is "easier" to blame your spouse than to talk about your own feelings. This honest sharing results in a greater depth of understanding of each other's emotions and physical state. If, for example, the wife honestly says she is tired, then her husband can better understand her irritability and do something to help her, perhaps take more care of the children for a while.

To help yourself control strong impulsive feelings, feelings that are hard to talk about, you can, as Carl Jung describes in his autobiographical *Memories, Dreams, Reflections* (9), "translate the emotions into images." That is to say, find the images which are concealed in the emotions, so that you can deal with them more reasonably. If you feel a strong anger, imagine, for example, that you would like to throw dishes, then you are much less likely to throw them, if you can think about what your imagination tells you. The process of sharing and discussing dreams, day-dreams, and imaginative fantasies with your spouse can deepen your relationship with each other, if this sharing is done in a constructive way.

Healthy lovers see and understand each other ever more deeply and accurately. An improved emotional life, a richer physical well-being results when deep and reasonable communication exists. Continued honest communication improves the relationship: it fosters personal growth and improves the spiritual functioning of both spouses. When poor communication prevails in a marriage, it promotes arguments and defensiveness; it fosters a deterioration of one's spiritual and sensual functioning.

Often it is one's deep need for one's spouse to change in a specific way, that makes it diffcult or impossible for him to change. Only when a person really feels free, and accepted as he is, can he be different. So instead of trying to change our spouse, *we can really only change ourselves,* change our own need for him to be different. Thus, in a Zen-like paradox, only by detaching ourselves from a need, can we be fulfilled. Only by losing our life, can we find it. Only by emptying ourselves can we become full. As Thomas Merton says in *Mystics and Zen Masters* (10), "there must be a 'death' of that. . .self-consciousness which is constituted by a calculating and desiring ego." But it is not easy to achieve. In this way, there is, or can be, a continuous existential interaction between personal growth and the reciprocal spirituality present in a marriage.

Actually, couples do, at times, feel the other is "distant"; perhaps, the other may feel like a stranger. But this is a choice point—for deepening the relationship by exploring the "emotional block"—or walling off that area, so that it becomes untouchable, a topic or problem that is never discussed. It is, of course, unrealistic, never to experience difficulty in discussing, say, mother-in-laws; but this is a challenge for mutual understanding; it is an opportunity for growth in the relationship. Psychologically, there seems to be a common fear of losing oneself in an ever deepening love affair; hence, there are periods of withdrawing where one "regroups" one's sense of identity in order to plunge again, more deeply, into the other. However, the deeper sense of one's own identity that one has, the deeper one can share oneself with the other. Even when spouses feel the closest during the act of love, each experiences sensations which may be very difficult to communicate to the other. However, "the mediative attitude (toward each other) can also be brought into sexual encounter" as Dr. Maupin, a psychologist at the Esalen Institute suggests in his monograph *On Meditation* (11). He recommends the use of "an intercourse position in which you can look at your partner and in which you can comfortably lie for a long time." Communication and "communion" with the other is an important part of a deep sexual relationship, although words can be a way of avoiding the sensual experience of love.

Obviously, deeply honest statements about oneself can provoke anxiety; it is hard to discuss a previously "unmentionable" item with one's spouse. But this fear of anxiety, too, can be discussed if one does not blame the other for it. The basic fear in the marriage relationship then, is the fear of fear itself; but "love casts out fear." So that, ultimately, real love in marriage is characterized by the absence of anxiety about the relationship; you trust each other, and the Lord.

The key to successful communication is, basically, the "good will" *to listen first to the other* although being willing to express oneself. Some couples insist on first being understood, before they will even consent to try to understand the other. But when "good will" and good communication exist, there is an ever increasing satisfaction with the quality of the real love present in the marriage.

There are various types of *spiritual direction* for married couples. Couples who want to deepen their spiritual lives, who want a deeper communion with one another, may find that the "spiritual" writers or directors are so "spiritual" that they may unconsciously extoll the virtues of a puritanical idealism because they themselves are so repressed or unaware of their own sexual needs. Another type of spiritual director may be unconsciously materialistic. He may need to convince his flock of how "savior-faire," or broadminded he is, so that offstage he may crack off-color jokes to impress his audience. But he also may be "rationalizing" about something that really exists in himself at a much deeper level. The good spiritual director for married couples will himself be an authentic person who has honestly and nondefensively searched to integrate his spirit with his body so he can usually be reasonable and free in expressing his own emotions and needs. An authentic spiritual director will be aware of his sexual emotions and biological urges as well as his limitations, "blind spots," and prejudices. Because he is working toward an ever deeper acceptance of these limitations in himself he can more truly love of his whole being; thus he can more objectively help couples to see their own intellectual, emotional, and sexual needs. One difficulty for a minister, priest, or spiritual director is to be truly objective, not to take sides in marital fighting—siding with one against the other. It takes two persons to have a good or a bad relationship. A spiritual director, like a psychologist, should be aware that if one spouse changes, the marriage relationship will change, or it will terminate. This is why when only one spouse receives psychotherapy, the marriage often ends in a separation or divorce.

A third person, who can bring differences out into the open, can help a couple to be more objective with themselves and each other. But in the absence of an authentic spiritual director or counselor, troubled spouses may have to depend on mutual friends, or each other, in learning how to help each other be more objective, more spiritual, and more loving.

Groups of married couples who are naturally friends can often be of great help to each other spiritually. Often they are of the same age and sociocultural background and may have similar problems, say, in rearing children. Also natural friendships tend to be based on "complimentary needs," to use the term of Dr. Robert Winch's *Mate Selection* (12). Hence, two or more couples can often help each other by talking things over—in an honest nondefensive way. This often involves a real feeling of risk, but the other husband may be able to understand the feelings of your wife, without becoming as defensive as you do, because he is not so totally involved; just as you may be able to appreciate the problems involving his wife, because you do not have to live with her intimately as he does. This mutual help and sharing such as is characteristic of deep friendships is a practical way of deepening conjugal spirituality. When a couple's love is deep, like the sea, then the surface emotional storms fail to disturb the peace and tranquility of the greater depths.

REFERENCES

1. Rahner, Karl and Vorgrimler, Herbert: (edited by Cornelius Ernst and Translated by Richard Strachan), *Theological Dictionary*. New York, Herder and Herder, 1965.
2. Jung, Carl Gustav: *Collected Works*. Volume 17, Marriage as a psychological relationship. (Eds.) Herbert Read, Michael Fordham, and Gerhard Adler.) New York, Pantheon Books, 1953.
3. Bouyer, Louis: *History of Christian Spirituality*. (Volume I, The spirituality of the New Testament and the Fathers.) New York, Desclee Co., 1963.
4. Merton, Thomas: *Seeds of Contemplation*. Norfolk, Conn., New Directions, 1949.
5. Jourard, Sidney: *The Transparent Self*. Princeton, N.J., Van Nostrand, 1964.
6. Berne, Eric: *Games People Play*. New York, Grove Press, 1964.
7. Eisenstein, Victor W.: *Neurotic Interaction In Marriage*. New York, Basic Books, 1956.
8. Rogers, Carl R.: *On Becoming A Person*. Boston, Houghton Mifflin, 1961.

9. Jung, Carl Gustav: *Memories, Dreams, Reflections.* (edited by Aniela Jaffe and translated by Richard and Clara Winston.) New York, Pantheon Books, 1963.

10. Merton, Thomas: *Mystics and Zen Masters.* New York, Farrar, Strauss, and Giroux, 1967.

11. Maupin, Edward: *On Meditation.* (Rev. ed., Esalen Institute, Big Sur, California, August, 1967.

12. Winch, Robert Francis. *Mate Selection.* New York, Harper & Row, 1958.

Chapter 26

COUNSELING PREGNANT TEEN-AGERS

ROBERT J. GOODSTEIN

THINKING back, I can recall the expression on my wife's face as she announced the happy news that we were expecting our first child. This was a time of anticipation and preparation to make all ready for the impending arrival. Family and friends delighted in the news of the prospective parents. A new dimension was added to our marriage with this shared experience.

Compare this event with the dilemma of a fourteen-year-old girl who has just been told by her doctor that she is pregnant. She feels that she has no place to which she can go—no one to whom she can turn. Home, once the secure nest to which she could run in times of trouble, is an unknown oasis. Her parents, once her source of comfort and security, may become condemning strangers. Her mother, she fears, will be crushed and humiliated; her father, she suspects, will be outraged. School, once a place filled with friends and exciting experiences, now is a place filled with fear and cruelty. Her principal will be forced to ask her to withdraw. This girl now is faced with having to make a tremendous number of important decisions at a time when she is far too young to cope with the seriousness of life. And the big question is "Why?"

It had started innocently enough: A birthday party at a friend's home; a little spiked punch provided by her parents ("After all, the kids are grown up now; a little nip won't hurt any.") and, before long, a pairing off of boys and girls. Suddenly, this girl, the youngest at the party, was experiencing emotions with which she never before had been confronted. Her boyfriend convinced her to show her "love" for him. He promised her that nothing would happen, and she did not have enough knowledge of sex or conception to know what she should or should not do.

In ever-increasing numbers, pregnancy is becoming prevalent among high school girls. More and more girls are abandoning their virginity as a sexual standard. Dr. Kinsey wrote that "among females born before 1900, less than half as many had premarital coitus as among the females born in any subsequent decade" (1). On the basis of his interviewing in the 1940's, Alfred Kinsey concluded that 10 per cent of all females become pregnant before marriage. In contrast, in 1966, staff officials of the Connecticut State Department of Health estimated that 17 per cent of the girls of that state, then in their teens, would become pregnant out of wedlock *before* their

310

twentieth birthdays, and the national rate is estimated to be about the same, or perhaps a little higher" (2) "If present rates of illegitimacy continue, during the next ten years we can expect 1,500,000 unwed mothers to give birth to a total of two million children" (3) .

A lot of time and energy could be spent on the *why* of this statistical information. But more important than *why* is the improvement of the lot of the unmarried pregnant teen-ager so that she can become a secure human being and a stable part of society after her delivery.

WHO WILL HAVE AN ILLEGITIMATE BABY?

According to Dr. W. Hugh Missildine (4) , there are three types of girls who will be prone to pregnancy out of wedlock. The first type is called the "impulsive girl." This is a girl who has lived with overpermissive parents. When parents are unable to say no to a girl, they establish a pattern in her life so that she, who has not been sufficiently disciplined, cannot impose self-discipline when necessary. Thus, when the occasion presents itself, this girl will be unable to say no. To better illustrate this point, let us examine the following case study.

A was in the eleventh grade when she became pregnant. School records indicate that she is of average intelligence. Her father is employed by their local Department of Public Works, and her mother also is employed. *A* started dating early, although her parents always had felt that she was too young. However, she was able to rationalize their objections away, and usually she got her own way. If she wanted additional money or the loan of the car from her father, he found it difficult to refuse her.

The alleged father of the unborn child, a single, twenty-three-year-old, has avoided *A*'s dilemma; and therefore, her parents have advised her to terminate her relationship with him. *A* would like to return to school and hopes some day to be graduated. She has indicated a desire to keep her child and has arranged for her married sister to provide day-care for the infant.

During the sixth month of *A*'s pregnancy, the school made its initial contact with the family. The attitude of the parents was one of inability on their part to comprehend how this ever could have happened to their daughter. With sober resignation, they had provided prenatal care for *A*, as well as an arrangement for light, part-time employment to facilitate monthly hospital payments prior to admission. After two months of counseling, the following character impressions evolved.

When *A* is speaking, she expresses a naive and overconfident attitude. She is unkind in her comments to people with whom she is speaking. With the birth of her child, she expresses a desire to remove herself from her pregnant "peers" and refers to them as "not normal" in her eyes. She has a tendency to act first and think afterwards.

A states that she knows how to persuade her parents into letting her have her own way. She often succeeds in doing what she wants. She has confided that, at times, she deliberately has disregarded her parents rules and regulations, hoping that they would put a stop to her "badness." She feels that they cannot really love her if they allow her to do things without regard for her health and well being, such as keeping late hours, doing no homework, and early dating—among others.

From her relationship with her boyfriend, she sought the much-needed love and affection which she did not feel at home. She describes her boy-friend as dominant and always able to make her do as he wants. "He's the only one who ever really loved me, even if it turned out to be only physical."

The second type is called the "rebellious girl."

The "rebellious girl" may spring from a home where the parents indicate, by their actions, that they do not trust her. Their demands upon her are extremely critical and difficult to satisfy. She also is meted out a goodly share of punishment. This type of pattern, evolving during the teen-age years, can lead to feelings of rebellion and rejection.

A case study which would more clearly illustrate the points to which we have alluded is the history of a girl whom we shall call *B*. *B* is seventeen years of age, in her senior year of high school; and at the initial contact with the social worker she was five months pregnant. She is one of three daughters in a culturally-deprived household. Her family life has been characteristically turbulent and financially insecure. The present household consists of the mother, father, two, older, unmarried sisters, *B* (now expecting her second child) , and her two-year-old daughter.

B is engaged and anticipates being married to the alleged father of her forthcoming baby. He is a high school graduate and, at twenty years of age, is the oldest of several children in his family. He had hoped that he would attend college. His parents recognize that he is still very immature and are violently opposed to this marriage.

B's parents had made it impossible for him to visit their household, and *B* was subjected to many beatings and lectures as a result of her relationship with her fiance. *B* always has had to meet her friends on the sly. She expects punishment for any act, great or small, which displeases her parents, and she is a very lonely child.

There are a great many problems awaiting *B* and her fiancé and it is hoped that group counseling will help both of them to adapt. They are anxious to learn from their mistakes and are trying to help themselves and one another.

The school social worker referred *B* to the hospital for pre-natal care and hospital admission. During a two-month group counseling session, the following character impressions were recorded regarding *B*.

She displays immaturity during her group counseling sessions; although, at times, she shows a mature attitude towards her daughter and her forthcoming baby. She feels that she was persecuted by her parents all her life, and she has no friends because of her parents' overbearing attitude. She is soft spoken, but willing to express her likes and dislikes freely and will disagree if she feels that she is right. She expresses a desire to remain in the group after the baby is born, and she is eager to go with her fiancé for counseling to help make a home for herself, her future husband, and her children. Shortly after counseling began, *B* was married and set up housekeeping in a rented apartment.

Here is a girl who feels rejected, who feels that there really is no place for her within her family unit. She cannot rebel against her environment openly and freely because she is afraid of the consequences. Thus, she has been able to use sex and her pregnancies to achieve the independence that she is seeking, and thereby punish her parents for their treatment to her.

The third type of girl who falls into the "theory of types" which will be prone to illegitimacy is called the "neglected girl." This is a girl who feels that she has received unfair treatment and is being left out. This can apply to the girl who feels outside the family unit. The most obvious types of situations where this is prevalent is in the case of a divorce. Here a girl can feel that she has hindered her parents in some way, that perhaps they would have acted sooner if she had not been around. If she lives with a parent who remarries and then has children of his/her own with the new mate, the girl may get the feeling that she is an outsider. Many complications can arise in dealing with an orphaned girl who may feel that well-intentioned relatives who raise her really do not want her. On the other hand, if she is raised in an orphanage, she may never get any feeling about home and family life. This feeling also can be implanted, unconsciously, by parents who favor one of their children over all of the others or by parents who are over-busy with their own personal lives and never really "see" their children at all.

Our case study relating to this type of girl is called *C*. *C* is eighteen years of age and, at the initial contact of the social worker with the home, she was six months pregnant. It was established that she was not receiving proper prenatal care, nor was she registered for admission to a hospital.

C has been living for the past six years with foster parents. There are presently five adults residing in this household, all gainfully employed.

After *C* attempted suicide and had run away several times, her foster parents resorted to seeking professional help. The County Court ordered that she be given close supervision and examined at the diagnostic center (a hospital for the care and treatment of potential delinquents), where she presently is being counseled on a weekly basis. The alleged father denies paternity.

C will speak freely if questioned directly. She seems to be more sophisticated and acts more mature than the other girls in the group. She is more knowledgeable about physical sex. Her statements seem to indicate a searching for other sexual relationships.

C expressed a desire to leave her home environment where love and affection seem to be lacking. Her search for love and security has led to multiple births. "Indeed, even the most promiscuous and aggressive pleasure-seeking girl is frequently using her physical equipment (almost always unsuccessfully) as a means to achieving acceptance and affection" (5). However, her lack of receiving love also has led to an inability or desire to truly give love and affection. Her desires are purely superficial. She has expressed no desire to keep this child or any others she may have. Feeling that she was unwanted in her foster home, she took an overdose of sleeping pills in a thwarted suicide attempt.

Each of the girls mentioned in these hypothetical case studies, as well as any other pregnant high school girls in Rahway, are recommended for placement in a class for pregnant teen-agers. This is conducted after the close of the school day in one of the local churches. Regular high school credit is given to the girls attending. Teachers give the girls the standard academic subjects, and education continues in as normal a setting as possible. There are also classes at the hospital on prenatal care and the signs and symptoms of labor, delivery, and baby care.

The author, serving as counselor, holds group counseling sessions encompassing family life and sex education. Motion pictures are shown, teaching about birth and contraception. The girls discuss the biological, psychological, sociological, and physiological aspects of their pregnancies.

In this environment, each of the girls can develop a sense of empathy with the others in the group. Here they are not alone. Together they can feel less like outcasts from society, and they can begin to divulge and share their pent-up feelings. The girls all begin to express curiosity as to how each one became pregnant. Questions are asked, such as, "Did you love the boy?" This question can prove to be a lead-in to a discussion of the differences between the male and female in their need for love and sex. "Because her total physical and psychic being reaches maturity earlier than the boy's, the girl often is the more sophisticated socially, and the better able to direct a relationship in the initial stages. Because of her orientation toward the permanent fulfillment of sexuality in marriage and child-bearing, she is far less interested in casual intimacies than the man" (5).

In a counseling session, this type of questioning also provides the opportunity to create an atmosphere in which to teach the girls about their physical needs as well as their boyfriends'. "It is of prime importance, if a girl is to be helped, that she understand that there is a profound difference between the man's interest and goal in sexual relations and that of many girls. It is this lack of understanding that contributes to producing highly-complex misunderstandings. For the man, advanced petting or intercourse is likely to be desirable, whether his feeling for the girl is deep or superficial. For her, it is more likely to be unattractive or even repugnant if no romatic relationship exists. Dr. Mary Calderone has written, The girl plays at sex for which she is not ready because fundamentally what she wants is love, and the boy plays at love for which he is not ready because what he wants is sex" (5).

There also are sensitivity-type groups conducted in which the girls can commiserate with one another. From these groups comes the realization that many of the girls are not at all certain as to exactly how they become pregnant. The findings of a sex knowledge inventory administered to the girls revealed that only 40 per cent of the questions were answered correctly. "Studies have shown that many teen-age girls, even after pregnancy, are still very confused about sex" (6).

Some of the following information was obtained by asking the girls pertinent questions and recording their answers.

Counselor: "Did your boyfriend use any means of contraception?" Answer: "My boyfriend used saran wrap." Counselor: "How do your parents feel about your pregnancy?" Answer: "Most girls do not know the real feelings of their parents."

The girls do share, with their parents, the same feelings of helplessness and rejection brought about by their pregnancy, but many of these feelings only are superficial, brought about by society; and, often with help, both the girl and her parents can develop a better understanding of what has occurred and why.

The counselor will ask the girls what their plans are for their babies. Some girls say that their children will be placed for adoption. "Much has been written and said about the alleged guilty, morbid feelings of a girl who gives up her baby for adoption—this has been vastly exaggerated. Unless those about her behave in a way to create guilt, I have rarely found it a serious or persistent problem" (7).

Some girls will send their babies to foster homes, and still others have relatives or parents who will care for the child. Some of the girls will marry and care for their own children, and many do not really know what they will do.

"A generation ago most clergymen insisted upon marriage of the pregnant unwed girl. In recent years, however, there has been a striking change. Now a large and increasing number of clergymen oppose marriage unless the young people are truly committed to each other and genuinely want the marriage" (7). Often, a young girl finding herself in this highly explosive and emotional situation is truly confused by all the standards and values she has been reared in, and it is really important that each girl be allowed to explore her own feelings and wishes as well as those of her parents before making any decision about her child.

During counseling, mutual rapport must be established between the counselor and the girls. This enables him to relate to the social worker the physical and emotional background of each girl. This information is essential if the girl is to be aided in her desire and ability to return to a life of normalcy after the birth of her baby. A social worker can arrange for placement of a child in a foster home, and she will help determine how the child's support will be handled. After delivery, the girls may return to this class before readmittance to school. They stay for several weeks, and they prepare to reenter their classes.

Of the number of girls who will become pregnant a first time, some will become pregnant again. These are the girls who, unless they are helped emotionally, are still punishing either their parents or themselves. A recent Yale follow-up study of a hundred unwed teen-age New Haven, Connecticut mothers found that they subsequently had an average of over *four* more illegitimate children! Only five mothers did not have a repeat pregnancy during the five-year follow-up period (6).

It is society's responsibility to aid in the rehabilitation of these young girls who become pregnant out of wedlock. We must be able to cope with the situation as it exists before we can create a better atmosphere in which girls and boys grow up. Concerned people are able to cope with difficult situations and meet crises as they arise without condemning the origin of the problem.

Each year, thousands of people disregard the Heart Association's admonitions against overexertion and fall victim to an attack. At that moment, their neglect to heed the warning does not influence the care and treatment they receive. The overriding concern of family, friends, doctors, and clergymen is the rehabilitation of this person and his eventual return to normalcy. Towards this end, they all unite.

Compare this with the young girl who makes a mistake and becomes pregnant. She also jeopardizes her future, perhaps quite unintentionally. We can readily see how differently the people around her react. Supportive measures are not as readily available as in the case of our heart attack victim.

What constructive measures can a community take to provide complete care for its pregnant teen-agers? A growing number of communities have programs specifically tailored for pregnant girls. One such program was initiated in Washington D. C.'s Webster School.

Washington, D. C., has a free, full-time public school for pregnant girls—the first of its kind in the United States. Started in September, 1963, with a U .S. Children's Bureau grant, Webster Girls' School today enrolls three hundred un-wed pregnant teen-agers, who attend seventh to twelfth-grade classes Monday through Friday.

During the regular sessions (plus a summer course), the school combines medical, psycological, and social services with the usual academic curriculum. In addition to the classroom teachers, the staff includes full-time psychiatric social workers, a clinical phychiatrist, and a registered nurse. The Department of Public Health supplies services of an obstetrician, a public health nurse, and several nutritionists. Prenatal and postnatal care and family living are highlighted.

Because the girls often do not understand the deep underlying emotional disturbances which led to their pregnancies, this professional team not only helps to rebuild their shattered self-respect, but aids in preventing a recurrence of the tragedy. Repeat pregnancies are unusual, thanks to the school's special physiological, psychological, and ethical instruction.

The Webster girls attend school until they are ready to deliver. Six to eight weeks later, they generally transfer to a regular junior or senior high school, but not the same one they were attending when they became pregnant. Most of the girls keep their babies; their families care for them while the girls continue attending school.

A recent Bureau of Social Science Research study compared 123 Webster girls with 123 other local teen-agers who had received no schooling during their pregnancies. Findings: the Webster girls' graduation rate (83 per cent if they had been in the twelfth grade at the time of the pregnancy) was sharply higher, and most landed far better jobs (6).

As parents, educators, professional people, and members of an even larger society, we must stop criticizing and start caring. Only when we reach this level of sophistication will we create an atmosphere which will encourage the help and care of "girls in trouble." Only when we all work together will we ever stand a chance to make this world a better place in which we all can live.

REFERENCES

1. Kirkendall, Lester A.: The problems of remaining a virgin. *Sexology*, 600, April, 1963.
2. Packard, Vance: *The Sexual Wilderness*. New York, David McKay Co., Inc., 1968, p. 493.
3. Schiller, Patricia: Sex attitudes in the ghetto. *Sexology*, 424, January, 1969.
4. Missildine, W. Hugh: *Feelings and Their Medical Significance*. Ross Laboratories, Vol. 8, No. 10, November-December, 1966.
5. Hettlinger, Richard F.: *Living With Sex: The Student's Dilemma*. New York, The Seabury Press, 1967, pp. 119-120.
6. Pollack, Jack Harrison: New help for pregnant teen-agers. *Good Housekeeping*. June, 1967, pp. 84, 160, 203.
7. Rubin, Isador, and Kirkndall, Lester: *Sex in the Adolescent Years: New Directions in Guiding and Teaching Youth*. New York, Association Press, 1968, pp. 160-161.

Chapter 27

THE WHOLE AND WHOLESOME FAMILY: YOUR HOPE AND THE HOPE OF AMERICA

DAVID GOODMAN

Lᴇᴛ's ᴛᴀʟᴋ ꜰɪʀsᴛ about you! You are a parent and a patriot. You want to do the best you can for your children and your country. You are also someone's marriage partner whose longing for love you sincerely desire to satisfy. Last, but far from least, you are a person with your own right to happiness. All these aims and purposes you can hope to realize as you bend your best efforts to building a whole and wholesome family.

What is a whole and wholesome family? And how do we achieve it?

It is a family united in its aims and purposes, with all its members soundly individualistic yet friendly and affectionate toward each other. It is headed by a father and a mother who love and enjoy each other and unite in giving love and guidance to their children.

Such families are unfortunately none to numerous in our society. Some of our most thoughtful psychologists, sociologists, and political leaders are saying that in this time of crisis, with a powerful foreign foe threatening to destroy us, the American family is not as strong as it should be to meet the crisis—that the enemy within, our own moral and spiritual weakness, may cause us to fall before the enemy without.

Surely you do not want that to happen. You want your children to grow up healthy and happy in a free America.

You would do well then to think hard and long on how you may assure this by contributing to an improvement of American family life. Accept the obligation with good nature and sturdy spirit, keeping always in mind that the whole and wholesome family is not only the hope of America, but also your own best hope of happiness, too.

Let us first understand the word "whole," the strategic term in our study.

The word "whole" is used here in the biblical sense as a synonym for the word "healthy": "Go, thy faith hath made thee whole."

The biblical idea of "whole" is more comprehensive than our modern idea of "healthy." It is the sad fact of much of our medicine that we treat the surface of the ill, its mere manifestations, rather than the sick person. How much wiser it would be if we kept always in mind that body, mind, and soul are one and must be treated as one. In some senses the very fact of di-

318

vision is the illness. The sick person is the divided person, unable to unite all aspects of his being in mastering the business of life.

In Shakespeare's great tragedy *Julius Ceasar,* we find a particularly poignant example of this when that very human character Brutus says of himself, "Poor Brutus, with himself at war forgets the shows of love to other men." How tellingly is the tragedy of modern man, divided in his ideals and allegiances, revealed in this sentence.

"Poor Brutus, with himself at war forgets the shows of love to other men." Poor Mr. Smith, poor Mrs. Smith, poor you and poor me, when we are divided, when we are fighting one side of our nature with the other, when we cannot decide—shall we, shall we not,—we are in no condition to give love, do our work, assume and carry out our obligations as a mate, as a citizen, and as a member of a family.

If wholeness is the health of the individual, so is it of the family. If your family is to be sturdy and strong, if its members are to achieve the good life, then your family must be united, it must be whole. It must never say: "Our poor family, with itself at war, forgets the shows of love to each other or to other people."

A useful symbol for the whole and wholesome family is the circle. In a circle there are no lines, nothing is broken off, nothing is separate. Every part is equally related to every other part. As you reflect a moment now, could you say that your family is a true circle, with everyone equally giving and receiving love, equally happy with each other? Then you can say that you have a whole and wholesome family. Fortunate you! Fortunate family!

Where does this whole and wholesome family begin?

It begins in the marriage of a truly masculine man and a truly feminine woman who out of their gender integrity understand each other's needs and are ready and eager to fulfill them. It is such sound mates who produce the whole and wholesome family.

Our study of how to improve family life in America should begin, therefore, with an analysis of what it is in our society that has prevented so many men and women from making that true marriage out of which can come a whole and wholesome family.

It is the parents who were unsuccessful in creating a true love relationship with each other who produced the children who for lack of a good example are, in turn, unsuccessful in their marriage. And so on through the generations! Somewhere, somehow, this evil chain must be broken. Let it be your aspiring thought that regardless of heredity it will be broken by you.

Many letters are directed to my column by parents protesting the most desperate love for their children, but no love for each other, who ask: "What can I do to assure my child's future happiness in spite of my poor marriage?" Usually one blames the other. Sometimes one is willing to condone the other, but not love him.

In either case the children suffer. While it cannot be guaranteed that your children will turn out well, just because you love each other, it is almost certain that the child who comes from a discordant home will grow up more or less neurotic. In fact, many of the ills that send people to the psychiatrist's office or the mental hospital can be traced to unwholesome factors in their early family life. Their immature parents were too confused and overwrought by their conflict with each other to give the children the loving care and sound guidance they needed.

Of course, over and beyond loving each other, husbands and wives need both knowledge and energy to carry out their full duty as parents. But in the home of marital harmony the proper rearing of children usually comes easy. The parents are full of vitality and enthusiasm; loving each other they instinctively love the product of their union. The children see in the behavior of their parents a perfect model of cooperation and so they cooperate too. They develop from this an easy instinct for good human relations, an invaluable asset for both business and social success. More valuable still, they carry out of the home sound family ideals and become good parents themselves when they marry and have families of their own.

Thus we see that good marriages produce more good marriages through the generations. The trademark of the good marriage is the true union of male and female.

All the books that have been written on building a successful marriage—and there have been a great number—could be summarized in their theme by one sentence taken from the Bible, "Therefore shall a man leave father and mother and cleave unto his wife, and they shall be one flesh." Notice again the idea of oneness, of integration, of unity, of wholeness. Never let this valuable thought out of your mind. All wisdom is in oneness. All folly is in division of self or family.

The emphasis on integration, on oneness running throughout all our spiritual literature is also the central theme of the modern science of mental hygiene, which we will call the mental health way.

The basic ideas of mental health should be of interest to every parent, for it is the sad fact of our society that mental illness is its number one health problem. More hospital beds are required for the mentally ill than for the ill of all other diseases put together. One child in ten will someday occupy a bed in a mental hospital. Make certain that that child is not your child.

Here are the six basic principles of mental health that can guide you and your children to achieve the blessing of a wholesome personality.

Work

Work is the great healer. When we are absorbed in our task we cannot be concerned with our worries and troubles because the mind cannot be in two places at the same time. Lose yourself in your work, therefore, and grief will not get you. Good work, furthermore, accomplishes things, makes us successful. How nourishing that is to our pride and self-confidence! Good workers are universally admired. The wholesome personality integrates around the task.

Persistence

For work to accomplish its healing influence you must persist at it. The ability to stick to one's job in spite of all obstacles and to the full extent of one's energy is one of the surest signs of a truly wholesome personality. Energy grows with the willingness to use it.

Objective Point of View

The great blessing of work is that it enables us to let go of the self, which in many instances is a weariness and a burden. The healthy soul integrating around the task, easily assumes the objective point of view. It is the sick soul that integrates around the self.

The self-centered, as we can readily observe, are in a continuous stew of fret and misery. Everything hurts them. Their work is always too difficult, their employer too strict, their mate mean and unfair. The weather is too hot or too cold; every passing word may offend them.

How fortunate by contrast are those able to take the objective point of view! Indeed, those who let go of self-centeredness, who live for their work and the welfare of others, find their higher personality, their whole and wholesome personality, and thus enjoy true mental health. "If you lose your life, you find it," is the profound spiritual summation of this wise philosophy. The commandment to love others, to work for others is thus seen to be no mere idealistic phase, but a true guide to the better life.

Democratic Household

It is the good fortune of Americans that we enjoy the great privilege of a democratic society permitting each of us to work out our own destiny. It is the great pride and satisfaction of the individual that he makes his own success, his own security.

If democracy is a blessing in the nation, it is also a blessing in the home. Parents must not only refrain from trying to dominate over each other, but also from assuming a possessive attitude toward their children. Your child, too, is an individual; he has a self and will be proud to make something of that self, if you let him. Not only love but a recognition of the rights of the individual give your child a true discipline. Children cooperate in plans they have had some share in making. A democratically run household is easier to manage because each individual feels proud to cooperate.

Genetic Viewpoint

The most important of all the rules for mental health is the principle of growth, of development, the idea that you can become a better person tomorrow because of what you did today. As long as you aspire to grow, you can work out of your present difficulties and become the competent person that commands circumstances, rather than is ruled by them. Ours is an ever-evolving universe. We feel at peace in it, not as we give up struggling, but rather as we strive to evolve, too.

"Man grows with his aims," said the great German poet-philosopher Johahn Wolfgang Goethe. Man is not a static thing but an aspiring spirit. His potential is as great as his belief in it. Our American poet Oliver Wendell Holmes expressed the same thought in his poem *The Chambered Nautilus,* one stanza of which is fortunately found in all school readers, serving to set forth to all American children the possibility of their high personal development.

> Build thee more stately mansions
> O my soul
> As the swift seasons roll
> Leave thy low vaulted past
> Let each new temple nobler than the last
> Shut thee from heaven with a dome more vast
> Till thou at length art free
> Leaving thine outgrown shell by Life's unresting sea.

Live One Day at a Time

This program of mental health may seem difficult in its totality. But not on a day by day basis! All the sages throughout time have urged the wisdom of living relaxedly yet constructively in the present. Learn to accept yourself and to live your life one day at a time and it will happily amaze you how easy it is to build that wholesome personality that will make you a better person, a better mate, and a better parent.

A group of psychiatrists in an informal discussion sought out the single sentence that could be considered most useful for the guidance of mankind. What do you think they came up with? It was the biblical quote: "Sufficient unto the day is the evil thereof." One day's troubles are enough. One day's troubles we can handle. It is when we burden our minds with regrets over what happened yesterday or over fears for tomorrow that we are overwhelmed. A modern writer has put the same thought in the jingle: "Life is hard by the yard, but by the inch it's a cinch." The most magnificent statement of this profound thought is found in the Hindu bible, *The Upanishads.*

> Look to this day,
> For it is life, the very life of life.
> In its brief span lie all the verities
> And realities of your existence—
> The glory of action, the splendor of beauty,
> The bliss of growth.
> For yesterday is but a shadow,
> And tomorrow is only a dream.
> But today well lived
> Makes every yesterday a dream of happiness
> And every tomorrow a vision of hope.
> Look well, therefore, to this day.

But in these days of national crisis you want to be not only a better parent but also a better patriot. The whole and wholesome family that you will build by following the ideas in this chapter is not only your own best hope of happiness, but also America's best hope of meeting the issues of the present time. Take any of our besetting problems, domestic or foreign, and where in the final analysis will you find its solution—only in an improvement of American family life.

Some of our keenest social thinkers are saying that the enemy within— juvenile delinquency, adult crime, alcoholism, drug addiction, sexual perversity, gambling, and so forth—is more to be feared than the enemy without. Each year the evidence of our moral corruption grows. Will a people so weakened internally be able to face up in a continuing battle to a dour, relentless, powerful, foreign foe determined to destroy us.

All of these ills have their source in the breakdown of American family life, and it is only as we will build a more wholesome American family that our society will renew its health and vigor.

Take juvenile delinquency, for instance, which some have called our number one social problem. For years the Senate Committee for the Study of Juvenile Delinquency aided by a corps of experts went up and down the land, through the cities and across the country, studying the source of this growing evil.

The conclusion of all their studies was this: "Better children can come only from better parents." All the conventional causes for delinquency, slums, lack of recreation, poor housing and so forth, were found to be of minor significance. The real factor is the mind and character of the parents. Better children can come only from better parents.

These findings were in keeping with the great research studies of other social workers, in particular, Drs. Sheldon and Lenore Glueck of Harvard University. In their monumental study, "Delinquents in the Making", they compared five hundred inmates of reformatories in Massachusetts with their nondelinquent counterparts, matching boy for boy in all possible factors of environment, heredity, intelligence, social and economic status, and so forth. And what was the difference between the delinquents and the nondelinquents? The nondelinquents had mothers who loved them, and fathers who gave them something of a social ideal. In a word, they came from families that were, to a degree at least, whole and wholesome.

The Gluecks have just published a new book, *Delinquents and Nondelinquents in Perspective,* showing what happened in maturity to the five hundred delinquent and nondelinquent boys, the subjects of the previous study.

The nondelinquents, in the main, stayed out of trouble and grew up to be wholesome, law abiding citizens. The delinquents, for the most part, grew up to be multiple offenders, arrested for every type of crime—homicide, robbery, rape, etc. Even those who gave up crime had other troubles, especially in family life, physical or mental health, job insecurity, etc.

The wise Solomon said: "Train up a child in the way he should go, and in age he will not depart therefrom." The Glueck study proves that this is exactly true for your child and mine, for every child. Give love and a good example and you get a dutiful, moral child, a child with his own sound conscience to guide him.

If we study any other of the social ills that beset our society we can see likewise that the source of the ill is the unwholesome family life, and the only sure remedy the building of a sounder and more integrated family.

It is the purpose of this chapter to suggest ways in which you can build, day-by-day, a more wholesome family of your own. Do not take this as a desperate task. In reality, easy does it, and it will be especially easy for you if you start out from the sure base of a good marriage, the one true joy of your mortal sojourn.

That many are disillusioned as to the possibilty of building a good marriage is seen in our ready recourse to divorce. One marirage in four in America ends in divorce. Some say the figure will soon be one in three. In addition, there is widespread marital infidelity, as well as widespread marital misery.

Is all this disintegration of marriage, this general disillusionment of man-woman relations really necessary? Frankly, I do not think so. I firmly believe that it is due more to ignorance than to malice. For love they have no talent, is the correct verdict on many an unsuccessful marriage. But love is an art that can be learned; marriage is an art that can be learned. If we realized the great rewards of that learning, we would give our best efforts to achieving it.

Here are four ways to make your marriage better and so ensure that your children will have a warm, secure home—so conducive to their mental health as well as a good model on which to build their own wedded life when they marry. These four constitute the art of marriage.

Give up Fault Finding

As we accept each other's imperfections we can enjoy each other's love.

A first fruitful step in the understanding of human nature is realization of the fact that we mortals are all full of imperfections. How could it be otherwise?

We came from parents who had their faults and who, in their life together, which we shared, exerted an influence that caused us to acquire many complexes and oddities of mind and character.

It is with these imperfections that we struggle, and it is in our triumph over them that we attain the spiritual growth for which we are destined. It is these same imperfections that each of us brought into the marriage causing conflict and distress.

But if, in mutual compassion and understanding, we accept each other's imperfections, a great comfort and satisfaction ensues. It is good to know that you are loved just as you are. Instinctively you feel grateful to the one who so loves you that he will accept and endure the weaknesses which beset you and which you have not yet learned to overcome. Life is peaceful and pleasant on this basis.

You do not have to pretend to be what you are not. You do not have to use subterfuge and trickery. You can be human and yourself. And in love for the person who allows all this to you, you try to improve— to be nearer what the other seeks and needs in you.

There is no luxury in the world like living without blaming. You feel relieved and happy, and you make others feel relieved and happy, too. And by it you make your marriage better.

The Spanish have a folk-saying, "You cannot love anyone unless you also love his faults." If you love at all, you love the whole person as is— faults and good qualities—just as you hope that you too will be loved as is.

If you apply this to your own marriage, you will be shedding a great burden. The real adventure of marriage, the thing that gives it zest for strong spirits, is in reacting to the reality of a marriage partner whose very human qualities mesh and meet in interaction with your own to produce two new beings who are stronger and finer and more deeply devoted to each other than before.

Always look at your marriage partner with eyes of appreciation. Praise, do not blame. There is plenty to praise if you look for it. So look for it. In all human relations, but especially in marriage, as we appreciate we prosper, but as we belittle we lose.

Be Faithful

The great wonderful experience of man-woman love can be built up with only one person.

Your sex life can be lived on any level. In its lowest form a prostitute is as good as a mate. But, if you seek in your sex life a complete communion with another being, in which body, mind, and soul are inextricably merged with another body, mind, and soul, you must concentrate on only one love. Such a full and complete union is a lifetime's endeavor and can be achieved only in a total loss of self in the self of the beloved one.

Have any achieved such complete man-woman oneness? Many have, although they would be the last ones to speak of it. But all of us may work toward this ideal, realizing that as we do we enjoy an ever richer experience, well worth the price of single-minded devotion that we paid for it.

In a society such as ours, where monogamy is often neglected, you will have to do some hard and clear thinking to resist the temptation of extra-marital sex.

Monogamy is not merely the product of moral and religious authority. Monogamy, like all moral ideals, is based on human experience. Through endless ages of trial and error, mankind has learned that the monogamous way of living one's sex life gives the greatest satisfaction to both mind and body.

In this, as in all other aspects of life, the moral law is your friend, and not a hostile opponent to be struggled with.

Morality in sex has for its purpose your own personal happiness. Its aim is not that you should enjoy life less, but that you should enjoy it more; not that you should have a thin and limited sex life, but that you should have a rich, full, and satisfying one.

Sex loyalty is also the best insurance that you could have against the break-up of your marriage. In sex loyalty you are able to overcome the petty irritations and annoyances that arise in all marriages. In the light of desire the faults of the marriage partner disappear; in renewal of *amour* you both regain your lost Edens. The unfaithful have no such insurance.

All wisdom is in oneness; all folly is in division of self or family. A thoughtful person readily recognizes the truth of this and sees in the sex code, not a harsh taskmaster, but a benign spirit and guide. Yet temptation besets us on all sides, and because of this husbands and wives must help each other keep faithful. Seek to understand your mate's sexual needs. They may be both greater and different than yours, but you will be well rewarded for trying to satisfy them. You will have a true marriage, a united family, and a happy home for your children.

The vast amount of sexual looseness in our society might call for much censure and blame. In a way, however, all sex seeking is also a seeking for love; it is the folly of promiscuity that we should emphasize rather than its guilt.

Would that all women understood their sexual responsibility in maintaining a monogamous home! No man deserts a wife with whom he feels sexually fulfilled. But how many wives are sexual misers, lacking the generosity of spirit to try to satisfy their man, and out of pure inertia and dullness failing to make good on their original marriage bargain. The man gave them security; why can't they give the man the satisfaction he seeks and needs?

Of course, there is another side to this story. As Dr. Anna K. Daniels, the noted gynecologist and marriage counselor, stated in her book, *It's Never Too Late to Love,* "The best cure for a frigid woman is a loving and potent husband."

Men who complain of the lack of ardor in their wives should take a good hard look at that sentence. All women long to be loved, and many of those who fail to respond are full of fears due to unhappy previous experience or the influence of mothers who told of their own unhappy experiences.

But a man who gives a woman the feeling that she is loved and appreciated for herself and not just for her body will sooner or later gain the response that he is seeking.

If spouses who go wandering and according to the Kinsey Report, this includes at least 50 per cent of the husbands and 25 per cent of the wives) understood the true luxury of monogamy, they would not fritter away their sexual energy in extramarital affairs. Sex divided is sex subtracted.

Consider Your Spouse, and Not Your Children, as the Primary Object of Your Affection

"I had a fine wife," said husband X, "until our first child was born. Then Mary became more mother than wife."

Husband X's numbers are many. The most common complaint of the American husband is that his wife cares more for the kids than she does for him. She fusses and frets over them all day long and is a tired and unattractive woman when the hour finally comes around that they can be alone together.

This is the great folly of the American wife—that she is more maternal than romantic. It is not for nothing that America is called the land of "Momism," a behavior pattern whose results are bad for both parents and children.

What children most need is to be judiciously let alone. They require a certain amount of care and guidance. We must keep a loving eye on them. But their truest and best development is in freedom; to act according to the needs of their inner natures; to dream and create a new reality out of their fancies.

The fussing fretful, oversolicitous mother destroys all this. She raises weaklings for sons, who are unable later when they marry to fulfill the obligations of husbands and fathers. Millions of them were found unfit for service in World War II, and millions more are the weak immature husbands who fail to meet their obligations as head of the family.

Children get along fine on a minimum of attention. "We take unto ourselves the strength of that which we have overcome." Let your children do their own overcoming, and give yourself in love and devotion to furthering the happiness of your spouse. The primary object of your affection should always be your mate and not your children.

Put Enthusiasm into Your Marital Relations

A mutual and equal ardor is needed to make a good marriage.

"Before I married I aimed to choose someone who would please me, but after I married I aimed only to please the one whom I had chosen." This paraphrase of an old-world idea of marriage is the fairest and wisest statement on the subject I have ever seen.

Once we have made our choice, presuming that we used the proper thought and judgment and acted under the inspiration of a deep love and not only out of mere infatuation, we should recognize that we are irrevocably committed to each other and that we must continuously strive to do better and better by each other.

A good marriage is not something that just happens. Nor is it a gift from Heaven. Always it is the product of effort. The French biographer Maurois, out of his rich understanding of human nature, put it this way, "Marriage is an edifice that needs to be rebuilt every day." You have to be your best and give your best today and every day, recognizing that total love, not 50-50 love, is what is needed to make a marriage.

It is an unfortunate fact of human nature, however, that while everyone wants love and nearly everyone is ready to respond to the love that is given him, very few of us have the spiritual grace, the gallantry of soul, to give love even though we are not getting it; to be ever ready to initiate affection.

In all marriages there are periods of stress and strain, of anger and conflict, of monotony and dullness. This is inevitable to human nature.

The fine men and women who have the heart to break the bad periods by renewing love, readily resolve these crises and restore the marriage to its basic joy and satisfaction. Sometimes, however, neither has the heart or the mind to make the first move. Then the marriage droops and declines for lack of the spiritual nourishment needed to sustain it.

In America especially, we note a sad state of conflict between the sexes, a struggle for dominance in the home and the family. The man should be the head of the house, as the woman should be its heart.

But many American women openly or subtly contend with their mates as to who controls the children, who manages the money, who is the symbol of authority in the home.

The results are bad for both.

The woman may triumph as an ego, but she is defeated as a woman. She finds herself married to a poor specimen of a man who gives no nourishment to her gender pride.

The husband feels defeated too, as a male, and lacks the energy and enthusiasm that a truly feminine woman could arouse in him.

A revaluation of values is long overdue in American marriage. The woman who knows how to build up the pride and spirit of her man will have a worthy head of her household. Half of a man's strength comes from what he sees in his wife's eyes. If you think you have a weak husband, put your strength behind him, not against him. Then watch him grow into the strong man you want.

But if you belittle him, soon all you will have is "a little guy" for a husband, little as a lover, too. Is that what you want?

The same holds true for wives. Treat your wife as if she were a princess and it will be a thrill to make love to her.

"Man goes from sex to soul. Woman goes from soul to sex." This is the basic sex difference between men and women, and what a world of misery might be avoided and what a wealth of happiness created if each understood this essential fact of the other's sexual nature.

The male attains his sexual peak far earlier than the female. Driven by desperate urges, he makes sexual demands that the as yet unawakened female cannot understand, much less respond to. If he could contain his urges and pay court first, he might happily discover resistance changed into ardor and then experience sex triumph rather than the sex defeat that so depresses him.

But women, too have to accept their sexual responsibility.

They have to understand that the demands of the male are not all pure egotism, but the expression of the needs of his own nature.

As women rise above their inherited inhibitions and gladly join in the sexual enthusiasm of their partner, they will not only win for themselves the warm appreciation of their mate, but also come to know and enjoy the realities of sex satisfaction themselves.

Thus, as each tries to serve the other, they meet in the middle ground of a mutual sex enjoyment, free of shame or blame and rich in the power to inspire strong and noble behavior. Thus they find that for loving people sex is good and can continue to be so for all their married lives.

The love of men and women develops like a pyramid. At its base is sexual desire, the purely physical need of male and female for each other on which depends the propagation of the race.

Above this is sexual-personal love, the desire to mix and merge with one particular person who seems to be the other half of oneself. No words can portray the exquisite joy of those who in immaculate loyalty attain this total oneness with another being.

But there is higher felicity even than this, sexual-personal-spiritual love. Completely one with your beloved mate, you feel related to all life, and thus happily at home in the universe. You are never alone any more. This is the ultimate lore of love for you to teach to your children. To teach it well you have to live it well yourself.

A hundred years ago, a British poet, Matthew Arnold, sitting at the seaside and seeming to hear in the lapping of the waters life's eternal note of sadness coming in, wrote a poem, "Dover Beach," which concluded with the following lines.

> Ah, love, let us be true
> To one another! for the world which seems
> To lie before us like a land of dreams,
> So various, so beautiful, so new,
> Hath really neither joy nor love nor light—
> Nor certitude, nor peace, nor help for pain;
> And we are here as on a darkling plain
> Swept with confused alarms of struggle and flight.
> Where ignorant armies clash by night.

How appropriately do these lines apply to the modern world, lost in the dark alley of doctrinal conflict between the Communists and the Democracies, and with the hydrogen bomb threatening us all.

In such a world, what happiness is there except in man-woman love, the one pure joy that earth allows us poor mortals in return for all our toil and trouble?

Yet how many in petty irritability or anger, in ennui or inertia, in stupidity or ignorance, throw away this dearest thing they own as if it were a careless trifle? In our divorce-ridden society how necessary is it that we should learn not to squander this joy, but to conserve it and make it grow into something ever finer and stronger.

Married love is an art, a great art, worthy for its rewards of our highest endeavors. It contains practical elements: a) generosity as well as good sense in money matters, b) unity in religious belief, parents and children going to church as one family, c) cooperation in the training of the children, d) acceptance of each other's in-laws in cordial hospitality, e) shared fun in social activities, f) friendship with other couples, and g) understanding of each other's sexual personality, so that each may give pleasure as well as receive it.

But love transcends practicality. Over and beyond these obvious practical elements that go into the building of a good marriage, there are deep spiritual feelings—the longing to join totally with another human being, to merge body, mind and soul—and so attain the exquisite joy of complete man-woman oneness.

Crudely we begin this task when we marry. With many a trial and error, we, in our ignorance, carry it on. Only those who hearken to the poet's words, "Ah, love, let us be true to one another!" finally accomplish it. Only those can build a whole and wholesome family.

Chapter 28

ARE MARRIAGE COUNSELORS QUALIFIED TO COUNSEL?

GERALD ALBERT

GEORGE and Helen M. were a married couple in trouble.

George was a forty-five-year-old police captain, college educated, highly intelligent, well-read and secure in his job. His bearing and his activities were clearly those of a man's man. Fishing and hunting were his delight, as was flying a plane; he had earned a private pilot's license, and was working towards becoming an instructor.

Helen was a young-looking forty-four-year-old brunette, attractive and well dressed in conservative style. She had never worked in a job, but had always been a very active and accomplishing woman, raising two boys (now twenty-one and twenty-three), participating as a leader in church affairs, and writing pieces for nonprofessional publications. She had dropped out after two years of college, to get married, and now had returned to complete her degree requirements, since she wanted either to teach or work professionally as a writer.

Their problem, as they saw it, was Helen's growing discontent with everything that George stood for. He had little interest in things artistic or cultural, preferring to spend his time fishing, hunting or flying—activities he would have loved to have Helen accompany him on but for which she had no tolerance. And, in spite of his "manliness," she complained that he was eternally indecisive and incapable of providing emotional support when crisis situations arose.

It was this problem they presented to the marriage counselor. Should Helen insist that George make an effort to use his intelligence in more academic and cultivated ways, or should she learn to accept him as he was, if possible? Did she have the right, at this late date, to try to make him over? What about *his* right to demand that *she* make changes in *his* direction?

Depending on his own training and background, the counselor to whom this couple went could have reacted in one of various possible ways. If he came from the field of education, or the older areas of marriage counseling (in which "counseling" essentially equaled "advising"), he might have been inclined to stress the ways in which people can learn to compromise their differences, and make adjustments to each other's needs. He might have pointed out that George and Helen had never developed techniques of compromise, and he might have tried to work with them on the specifics of such mutual adjustment.

If his orientation was primarily religious, the counselor might have been most concerned with the sanctity of the marriage bond, and his emphasis might have been on the usefulness of joint religious participation by the distressed couple, in the belief that this would combat the divisive forces in their relationship, and provide a unifying spiritual cement to hold the marriage together.

Counselors from the fields of social work, sociology, law, guidance, general medicine, psychology, and psychiatry might each have responded differently. Would they all have contributed equally to the welfare of the troubled pair, although in different ways?

As it happened, the counselor to whom they went was a psychologist, trained in psychotherapy, with a special interest in marital problems. Because of this background, his interviews (first with the couple together, then with each separately) developed the following awareness, much of it not in the consciousness of either of the partners.

Helen came from a family in which the father had been a dominating, highly educated man, an architect, extremely busy with his profession, with little emotional energy left over for his wife and two children. What interest he showed at home focused largely on Helen's older brother, producing in her a deep-seated feeling of deprivation and neglect, which she tried unconsciously to overcome by developing all the virtues her father valued— cultural interest, energetic participation in worthwhile activities, and neverending educational self-development. But her need to escape this impossible bind (for her father could never respond to her efforts) motivated her, unaware, to choose a man who seemed totally different from her father—a nondominant man in a nonprofessional career and with nonacademic interests. Nevertheless, her original unsatisfied needs, transferred from her earlier to her later family, seethed within, provoked her constantly to find fault with her husband—and had, unknown to him, driven her to an extramarital affair with a man very much like her father, a relationship from which she had only recently, desperately guilty, torn herself away.

George, on his part, had had his own problems in his original family. An only child, he had been the pawn of bitter conflicts between his parents, both stubborn, determined people, each seeking to dominate the other. Unconsciously, he had developed a total aversion to anything that smacked of this characteristic in close personal relationships. (Interestingly enough, it had not affected his capacity to exercise authority in his work activities.) Complicating the situation was the presence of a problem not altogether uncommon in very virile-seeming men—a latent strain of homosexuality, which his very masculine activities served to defend against and deny.

Deeper penetration of the couple's productions, as the interviews proceeded, evoked material revealing that George was (as a result of his latent homosexuality) not always fully satisfactory in his love-making, which was also a factor in Helen's response to another man's interest, and a reinforcing element in the inadequacy feelings which perpetuated George's characteristic indecisiveness.

How much of this vitally important material would have been elicited by a counselor not psychotherapeutically oriented? Very little, one would be safe in assuming. What likelihood would there be of resolving the couple's marital estrangement in a lasting way, if this material remained unexplored? Very little, one would again seem safe in assuming. A counseling poultice might cause temporary disappearance of the sore, but the underlying fever would still rage on.

The problem of what a marriage counselor actually does has been disputed for years. Karpf has written, "It would seem to be important to make very clear that marriage counseling is fundamentally different from psychotherapy and that the marriage counselor works on a different level from that of the psychiatrist or even the clinical psychologist. The people coming to the marriage counselor are normal people facing problems arising in normal human relationships. The marriage counselor does not and should not, unless he is working on that level, treat neurotics and psychotics. Nor should he attempt to make such diagnoses. He should, of course, be well enough trained to recognize when he is dealing with such problems and should refer them to those best equipped to treat them" (1).

It is a fascinating exercise in futility to speculate on how a counselor who should not attempt to diagnose the presence of neurosis or psychosis is expected nevertheless to recognize (through a sixth sense, perhaps?) that a marital problem is deeper than appears on the surface. How does one become well enough trained, for example, to detect the depths of the problems underlying the conscious presentations of George and Helen M. without tutelage in the field of psychotherapy itself? Their bearing, and the problems they outlined initially, certainly *seemed* to fall within the "normal" range—whatever that is.

As I have argued elsewhere, "Every effort is made by the defensive forces within a neurotic counselee to resist overt expression of the actual trouble source. If Freud gave us understanding of anything in the human personality, he made clear the existence of powerful unconscious motivations and the tremendous quantum of energy devoted by the disturbed personality to repression and the development of defense mechanisms.

> The most plausible-seeming causes of marital trouble may well be among the most deceiving in proportion to the amount of energy summoned up by the counselee to conceal the actual, but more painful, roots of the difficulty. Without

full knowledge of the broad range of illness possibilities and their underlying dynamics, the counselor would seem liable on many occasions to fail even to *recognize* that he is dealing with a deep disturbance—while on other occasions he might think he had a deeply disturbed patient when this was not so at all (2).

Bordin has pointed out that, while marriage counseling ranges from "giving instruction and information to handling emotional factors," where the emotional relationship between the partners contains the root difficulties, "then marriage counseling and psychological counseling seem to become one and the same thing" (3).

Even this statement, however, partly sidesteps reality, in its assumptions anent the accepted usefulness of instruction-giving. It *may* be true that some marital difficulties appear to have their roots in actual life circumstances, which could well be improved by following an objective adviser's suggestions, or acquiring helpful information about a better course of action. But one cannot help being reminded of the evidence so frequently adduced in another area of counseling, vocational guidance, where it has long been made clear to counselors that presentation of even the most convincing information does not affect decision-making when a prior emotional block or pressure is present.

Perhaps a few "pure" cases can be found, in which clients—no matter how exercised they may be by the pressures of their situation—are able to operate with complete rationality and logic, so that "contaminating" emotional factors do not intrude, but such instances seem likely to be rare indeed. Overwhelmingly more likely are those cases in which "marriage counseling and psychological counseling seem to become one and the same thing," because of the presence of underlying, hidden, often unconscious emotional factors.

Even closer to the point, perhaps, may be Green's contention that "Psychoanalysis has probably contributed more to the achievement of this understanding (of personality functioning) than any other single approach to the investigation and treatment of human mental functioning. . . The proper evaluation of ego structure and function offers the caseworker information that is essential to the understanding and management of marital problems" (4).

In other words, proper treatment of marriage difficulties requires the highly advanced and specialized knowledge offered in the findings of psychoanalytic psychology. When Green wrote this, in 1954, therapeutic approaches other than psychoanalysis were less fully developed than today, so that his stress was placed on that special form of help. At the present time, clinicians can also choose from such other modes of treatment as Behavioral Therapy (5), Ellis' Rational Emotive Psychotherapy (6), my own Identification Therapy (7), Reality Therapy (8), Multiple Therapist treatment

(9), as well as the various forms of group therapy (10) now more and more under investigation.

Whatever the psychotherapeutic mode employed, specialized knowledge and skill are required, with full understanding of the relevant psychodynamic principles and their application.

As I have indicated in another context, "Since each client is, to a greater or lesser degree, an integrated unit, all of his activities reflect and are affected by all parts of him. Excluding the unconscious, the defensively repressed, the irrational (which are parts of *every* personality, however minimal or well compensated) from the remedial efforts is excluding the parts which, even in 'normals,' may relate most actively to the difficulties under treatment. In more severe cases, such exclusion is like treating a brain tumor with a cold compress" (11).

In short, when we seek to aid a marital pair in trouble, we are dealing with a set of tremendously complex mental and emotional patterns, contributed separately by each partner's own personality make-up, and together by the interaction of the multiple factors brought to the relationship by each.

Consider only the comparatively superficial life history and personality elements identified by the scores of major studies of marital success and failure conducted by psychologists and sociologists over the past forty years. (I say "comparatively superficial" because the most subtle components, as well as those repressed in the unconscious, have been essentially beyond evocation for measurement in large-scale research endeavors.)

Tagged as especially significant in each partner have been the following: the importance of early family life experiences; the nature of early sex information acquisition; the duration of the courtship period; the age at time of marriage; premarital sexual experience; the motivations involved in marrying; the degree of conventionality and sociability; such personality items as criticalness, responsibility, humor, perspective, cheerfulness, self-respect, sensitivity, emotional adjustment; attitudes towards work and the use of money, and so on (12).

And these are qualities only of the separate individuals. What of the ways in which these and other elements *interact* in the pressure cooker of marriage? An attempt to understand some of these has been made by Winch in his studies of complementarity (13), by Tharp in his work on neurotic interaction patterns in marriage (14), and by Pickford, *et al.* in analyzing the effects of similar or related personality traits in the marital partners (15), but these have barely scratched the surface.

Practitioners actually working in this field have described in depth some of the maladaptive processes involved. These include the neurotic forces motivating the original choice of a mate (16), the unconscious meaning of marriage itself (17), reciprocal psychic injuries inflicted by the partners due to overdominance or oversubmissiveness (18), and a broad range of sexual problems, from frigidity and impotency through masturbatory diversion, perversions, and hypersexuality (19). Alcoholism is a special problem in a certain number of marriages: "He (the alcoholic) is driven by unconscious forces he does not understand and against which rational judgment and will-power are helpless" (20).

We face, then, the cold, hard fact that marriage counseling, rather than being a comparatively simple field of endeavor, in which a well-intentioned person with a moderate amount of training and experience can function helpfully as a qualified professional, is instead an activity which calls for a level of preparation at least equal to that expected of the most fully equipped clinical psychologist specializing in other treatment areas. Nothing less would seem appropriate, when we accept as reality what I have described elsewhere as "the magnificent complexity of the human animal and his mating interrelationships."

But who *are* the people actually working in this field?

As one authoritative publication puts it, ". . . marriage counseling has been carried on through the ages, by families and friends, doctors, ministers, teachers—informally, semiformally, and more recently formally . . . Specifically, marriage counseling has developed along a number of lines: as a by-product of the daily practice of professionally trained individuals—doctors, ministers, social workers, psychologists, and so on; as a development of already established community services, notably the family-service type agencies, child study and parent education groups, Planned Parenthood centers, social hygiene programs, university counseling services; as a service specifically focused on marriage counseling; and more recently full-time or part-time private practice of professionally trained persons in a variety of disciplines, who specialize in marriage counseling" (21).

And then, of course, there are the *self*-certified, those individuals with little or no training at all who—in the absence of laws in most states to protect the ignorant—have set themselves up as saviors of the maritally miserable.

Even the prestigious, standards-minded American Association of Marriage Counselors lists among its clinical members practitioners whose primary professional affiliations include substantial percentages in Sociology, Education, Religion, and various branches of Medicine, as well as the more expected fields of Social Work, Psychology, and Psychiatry (22). Although the requirements for membership in this organization insure that these individuals have had rigorous specialized training and supervised experience, the variety of backgrounds represented suggests how vague is the state of the art in this field to date. One can only view with alarm the large numbers of *non*members practicing marriage counseling—some perhaps quite good, others no doubt very awful!

If there is significance and validity in all that has been said above, concerning the complexity of the internal individual factors involved in marital difficulty, as well as the special nature of the interaction of these factors in the high-pressure intimacy of married life, then certain conclusions necessarily follow.

Just as individual psychotherapy deals with intrapsychic forces within individuals, and group therapy focuses on psychological interactions among several persons, so marital therapy has to do with the specialized considerations involved in the *dyadic psychology of husband and wife,* as well as the individual capacity of each to cope with life's requirements. These considerations call for recognition not only that a twosome is involved, but also that each twosome consists of a male and a female (with all the likenesses and differences, attractions and antagonisms, implied therein), and that each has subjective responses to his or her awareness of the social and legal implications inherent in the fact that they are *married.*

Psychotherapeutic help for individuals is considered a highly advanced field of specialization, calling for rigorous and extended training. Group therapy is generally viewed as another specialization area, with its own principles and body of knowledge.

Is it any less reasonable to perceive the treatment of marital ills as still another highly advanced specialty in the field of psychotherapy, demanding equivalent knowledge of all the forms of pathology involved, and the most effective modes of treating them? Must we not insist that practitioners treating marital patients (even those already practicing clinical psychology or psychiatry) be expected to receive training at least equal to that demanded of group and individual therapists? Anything less means permitting troubled couples to spend considerable time and money for help from practitioners really unable to provide it satisfactorily.

Should not the goal of everyone connected with marriage counseling be to supply the best possible professional treatment, rather than accept less because it is currently "practical" to do so? Should we not seek to insist that those who come to this field from other professions be required to become as skillful in this complex specialty, through freshly undertaken advanced study and supervised experience, as are individual and group therapists in theirs?

Should we not renew our efforts to upgrade the training of new practitioners, through the establishment of more and better graduate training programs, set up either as separate professional entities or as specialties within the broader field of psychotherapy in general? Should we not strive ever more vigorously to encourage the passage of laws designed to exclude inadequately qualified practitioners from "counseling" unhappy men and women whose married lives are sliding down the drain?

It would seem improper for us *not* to do.

REFERENCES

1. Karpf, M.J.: commenting on Albert Ellis' Legal status of the marriage counselor. *Marriage and Family Living, 13:*119, August, 1951.
2. Albert, Gerald: Advanced psychological training for marriage counselors—luxury or necessity? *Marriage and Family Living, 25:*183, May, 1963.
3. Bordin, E.S.: *Psychological Counseling.* New York, Appleton-Century-Crofts, 1955, p. 18.
4. Green, S.L.: Psychoanalytic contributions to casework treatment of marital problems. *Social Casework, 35:*419, November, 1954.
5. Wolpe, Joseph; Salter, Andrew, and Reyna, L.J.: *The Conditioning Therapies.* New York, Holt, Rinehart & Winston, 1964.
6. Ellis, Albert: *Reason and Emotion in Psychotherapy,* New York, Lyle Stuart, 1962.
7. Albert, Gerald: Identification therapy, *Psychotherapy: Theory, Research and Practice, 5:*104-107, June, 1968.
8. Glasser, William: *Reality Therapy.* New York, Harper & Rowe, 1965.
9. Spitz, H., and Kopp, S.B.: Multiple psychotherapy. *Psychiat Quart Supp, 31:*285-331, 1957.
10. Whitaker, D.S., and Lieberman, M.A.: *Psychotherapy through the Group Process.* New York, Atherton Press, 1964.
11. Albert, Gerald: If counseling is psychotherapy—What then? *Personnel and Guidance J,* October, 1966, pp. 124-129.
12. Albert, Gerald: Marriage prediction revisited. *J Long Island Consultation Center, 5:*38-46, Fall, 1967.
13. Winch, R.F.: *Mate Selection.* New York, Harper, 1958.
14. Tharp, R.G.: Psychological patterning in marriage. *Psychological Bull, 60:*2, March, 1963.
15. Pickford, J.H.; Signor, E.I., and Rempel, H.: Similar or related personality traits as a factor in marital happiness. *J Marriage and the Family, 28:*2, May, 1966.
16. Eidelberg, Ludwig: Neurotic choice of mate, in *Neurotic Interaction in Marriage.* New York, Basic Books, 1956, pp. 57-64.
17. Stein, M.H.: Unconscious meaning of the marital bond, in *Neurotic Interaction in Marriage.* New York, Basic Books, 1956, pp. 65-80.
18. Mittelman, Bela: Analysis of reciprocal neurotic patterns in family relationships, in *Neurotic Interaction in Marriage.* New York, Basic Books, 1956, pp. 81-100.
19. Eisenstein, V.W.: Sexual problems in marriage, in *Neurotic Interaction in Marrage.* New York, Basic Books, 1956, pp. 101-124.
20. Fox, Ruth: The alcoholic spouse, in *Neurotic Interaction in Marriage.* New York, Basic Books, 1956, pp. 148-168.
21. *Marriage Counseling: a Casebook.* E.H. Mudd; M.J. Karpf; A. Stone, and J.F. Nelson, Eds., New York, Association Press, 1958, pp. 28-29.
22. Membership Directory, American Association of Marriage Counselors, Dallas, Texas, 1968-69.

Chapter 29

VOLUNTEER WORK IN MARRIAGE COUNSELING

GERALD SANCTUARY

A MORAL ISSUE faces any society which regards the family as its basic unit, but in which one marriage in every four ends in divorce. That society must find the means to provide marriage counseling and processes of conciliation, and in the United States this aim has been partially achieved by the emergence of professionals qualified in these skills. It is generally accepted, however, that there are insufficient numbers of skilled practitioners, and this raises the issue whether it would be appropriate and possible to supplement existing services by using volunteer marriage counselors.

The purpose of this chapter is therefore to give an account of the way in which a national marriage counseling service was established and has developed in Great Britain, using selected and trained volunteer workers. It has been found that most modern societies, some years after they amend their law so as to permit divorce, recognize the need to create a service intended to reduce the incidence of divorce. Although divorce is regarded as an appropriate means of bringing a sick, or dead, marriage to a legal end, it is also thought of as a social evil and a personal tragedy, to be avoided if at all possible.

By 1937, it was generally accepted in Britain that the law was unsatisfactory, and it was then changed to allow divorce on several new grounds. Until then, it had only been possible to obtain a divorce on the grounds of the adultery of one or other of the partners, and in many cases the parties to a dead marriage, though agreeing to a divorce, had had to resort to manufacturing evidence of adultery when it had not in fact taken place. The change in the law resulted in a considerable increase in the number of divorces, and a group of men and women from the professions of law, medicine, the church and social work set up an organization to try to stem the growing tide. They gave this new agency the name of the Marriage Guidance Council. The outbreak of war in 1939 held back the Council's work for some years, and it was not until 1944 that it became possible to offer any kind of service to those whose marriages were in difficulty. At first, clients were referred to professional men and women who gave their time voluntarily to the Council as lawyers, doctors, probation officers, and clergy. On arrival at the London center, clients first saw a volunteer secretary, and were then referred to one of the professionals. An ever-increasing number of clients began to visit the new Council, many of them being casualties of the wartime conditions which separated so many husbands and wives; others had heard of the Council's work through the publication of its first booklet entitled, *How to Treat a Young Wife,* which had become extremely popular.

After a time it was found that many of the clients were saying that they had received more help from the volunteer secretaries than from the professionals to whom they were then referred. It seemed that, as the secretaries' function was to listen rather than to advise or treat, and as they had so much more time available, they were able to give a kind of support that could not be had elsewhere. Today, it is perhaps easier for us to understand why this should have been so, but at the time it came as a surprise to the Council members that its volunteer secretaries could be so helpful. The Secretary of the Council was then David Mace, later Executive Director of the American Association of Marriage Counselors, and now Professor of Behavioral Sciences at the Bowman-Gray School of Medicine in North Carolina. He suggested that the volunteer workers should be termed "counselors," a phrase by that time in common use in the United States. It was generally agreed that the counselors should be given some minimal training in marital counseling, and a program of evening lectures was instituted for all counselors working in the London area.

At this time, Marriage Guidance Councils were being formed in other parts of the country, and it soon became clear that some standards would have to be set for those who were to be accepted as counselors. Grouping themselves together to form a National Marriage Guidance Council, the people then involved took advice from others who had been concerned during the War with the selection of officers for the Army, and Selection Conferences were set up. In many ways this was the most significant development during the history of the Council, for it enabled a standard to be set for workers in a voluntary field, something that had not previously been attempted in Britain with this degree of sophistication. Selection is very necessary. There are many people drawn into this type of work, it has been found, who are concerned more with the salvage of their own marriages than with the problems of others. The predominant motive for wanting to become involved in marriage counseling may for some be an interest in the sexual activity of married people; for others, there is a need to work out some personal feelings of antagonism towards the opposite sex, or towards older or younger people. Very often volunteers are unaware, or at least only partially aware, of these motives, but they make it essential to impose a rigorous selection system between those who wish to become counselors and those who should be trained to do so.

It is the view of Professor Paul Halmos, as stated in his book, *The Faith of the Counsellors,* that the reason why most counselors are engaged in their work is that they have a fundamental concern for their fellow men. They disguise this concern, he says, by explaining in scientific terms the validity of the methods they use, but they do this rather than admit to a motivation that might cause others to throw doubt on the qualiy of their work. Certainly it is true that a high proportion of those candidates who want to undertake volunteer marriage counseling in Britain when asked about their motives, are willing to admit, sometimes a little shamefacedly, that they want to help other people to become more happy.

In the twenty-five years since its work began, the Marriage Guidance Council has grown so that there is now a branch in every major city in Britain, and over 1,500 counselors are now working, giving a total of more than 70,000 interviews annually to one or both spouses of 20,000 marriages. In the early stages, the work of the volunteers was looked upon with much suspicion by the professions, and by the press. National newspapers poured scorn on the efforts of the "voluntary do-gooders" who were charged with "meddling in the lives of other people." Had it not been for the standard of selection insisted on by the Council, and the consequent quality of the work done, it is doubtful whether the Council could have survived this barrage of criticism, but in fact its work caused it to receive more and more attention and approval from the public. A Government Committee set up to inquire into the Council's work recommended that it should receive official aid from public funds, and the annual Government grant to the Council now exceeds 100,000 dollars.

Local authorities also support the work of Councils in their own areas, contributing a total of 125,000 dollars towards the cost of manning and running the centers where counseling is carried on. In addition, the National Marriage Guidance Council and the local Marriage Guidance Councils receive substantial funds from individual, charitable, and business sources, which enables them to maintain an independent policy and to develop new fields of work without any need to refer first to official sources for permission. The Council has charitable status, and is therefore able to avoid payment of taxes, and to obtain additional tax benefits when individuals are willing to covenant to make regular payments to it over a period of time. Both the National Council and the local Councils publish regular Accounts and an Annual Report.

Although there are undoubtedly still some professionals in Britain who doubt the value of the work undertaken by volunteers, the majority of the clergy, doctors, lawyers, and others in regular contact with the counselors working for Marriage Guidance Councils think sufficiently well of their work to make regular referrals to them. During the past ten years, the number of marriages whose partners came to the counselors for help has grown steadily at a rate of nine hundred a year. As no means have yet been devised for measuring the effectiveness of marriage counseling, this is the only yardstick available for those who would place a value on the Council's work for the community.

It is one of the functions of the National Marriage Guidance Council to undertake the selection and training of all counselors, and to provide adequate supervision. Britain is a small enough country to make this possible, and a common system of selection and training results in a uniform standard of work throughout the country. In contrast, it is the local Marriage Guidance Council that recruits candidates for counseling, screens them, and makes provision for clients to be seen in suitable rooms near the center of the local town. The local Council raises its own funds, and runs its affairs through a local committee. In addition to the provision of a marriage counseling service, Marriage Guidance Councils also sell the publications of the National Council, which deal with all aspects of marriage and family life. Counselors are also provided to undertake regular group work with young people in schools and youth clubs under the general title, "Education in Personal Relationships"; marriage preparation courses are run for engaged couples.

Most volunteer counselors make their first contact with the Marriage Guidance Council through personal recommendation by a friend. They are not then sent straight to a national selection conference, but are encouraged to spend some time getting to know the existing counselors of the Marriage Guidance Council and reading some introductory material. It is explained to them that they will have to give up time for selection and for basic training over a period of two years; that they will be expected to attend regular case discussions at their local Marriage Guidance Council, to have tutorials and keep proper case notes, and to give a minimum of three hours each week to the counseling work. Many counselors give more time than this, but those who see at least three clients weekly find that they are in fact giving about five hours a week out of their spare time. For men, this means that they will normally work during the evenings, but women usually find that they can give at least one morning or afternoon regularly each week. There are about twice as many women as men working as counselors, which in fact is rather a high proportion of men for a voluntary service in Britain.

If candidates still want to go forward after reading the literature, they then see a local sponsoring committee and later will enroll for selection. Selection conferences are held in all parts of the country, but the selectors are appointed and paid by the National Council. The program is completed in one full day, on the following pattern.

9:00- 9:15	Welcome and introduction
9:15-10:30	Written work
10:30-11:00	Group discussion I
11:00-11:15	Coffee
11:15-12:45	Tape Session I
12:45- 1:30	Lunch
1:30- 3:00	Group discussion II
3:00- 3:15	Tea
3:15- 4:15	Tape Session II
4:15- 4:45	Group discussion III
4:45- 5:00	Closing Session

A Convenor is responsible for the smooth running of each conference; the Convenor welcomes the candidates, introduces the other selectors, and sets the written papers. Candidates are required to take a simple intelligence test, which uses progressive matrices, to complete an attitude questionnaire, and to write a self-description, first from the point of view of someone who dislikes them and then of someone who admires them. These written papers are reviewed by the selectors during or at the end of the Conference, as are the confidential references from two individuals who have known the candidate for at least three years.

During the group sessions, each candidate is given a subject to introduce for discussion by the group of candidates. These subjects are designed to produce controversy and to expose the attitudes and the value-systems of the candidates. The tape sessions are rather similar, but use is made of acted interviews during which "clients" describe their dilemma and invite comment or advice. The object is again to enable the selectors to discover what kind of people the candidates are, and to form a judgment as to whether they will be capable of being trained to work as counselors. During the working sessions, candidates leave the main discussion room from time to time in order to have two private interviews, each lasting thirty minutes, with a psychiatrist and also with another selector. During the meals the selectors make a point of sitting near those candidates whom they have not met, or about whom they still feel uncertain. At the end of the day, when both candidates and selectors are fairly tired, the former return to their homes, while the selectors discuss each of them for as long as it takes them to reach a decision on whether to accept them for training. In recent years, selectors have been selecting less than one-third of all candidates sponsored by local Marriage Guidance Councils. The selectors are looking for reasonably well-balanced men and women who are comparatively free from internal conflict, and who will be willing to accept their clients as they are, rather than try to change them. Most candidates are accepted between the ages of 30 and 50, though there are no rigid age limits. It is stressed that selection is for training, and does not operate as a certificate that the candidate is ready to begin an unlimited amount of counseling work.

Selection does not entitle a counselor to begin work immediately. The course of Basic Training provided by the National Council extends over a period of three years, one section of training being taken every school term, in spring, summer, and autumn. Sections last three days and are held residentially in centers hired for the purpose by the training department of the National Council. On completion of the first section of training, counselors may take their first case, and they do this under the supervision of a tutor, who is trained and paid by the National Council. During the Basic Training course the counselors have to complete a lengthy list of reading of published material and also of training booklets and notes produced by the Council. The training course covers the techniques and the difficulties of counseling, and as the course progresses the counselors bring in their practical experience of the work, sharing difficulties and anxieties with one another. By the time they have been selected they are beginning to feel more confident of themselves, and more ready to expose their own feelings of inadequacy and their lack of understanding of themselves and of their clients.

The Basic Training course also deals with the development of the human personality from childhood and through adolescence to adulthood. Many of these training sections are under the leadership of a psychiatrist, but there are also professionally qualified tutors available to deal with the medical and legal aspects of counseling. The work of the various social services, both statutory and voluntary, is described in some detail. Counselors are encouraged to make contact with these services, as they may frequently have to refer clients to them. Britain is a country where different social services abound, so much so that there are currently proposals for integrating some of them so as to provide a family-oriented service rather than a group of several problem-oriented agencies.

Counselors are not only expected to have contacted the local services, but also to know the individuals who are running them, as this makes for easier referral. In addition, the counselors are also expected to get to know the professional advisers to their own Marriage Guidance Council. Councils have legal, psychiatric, and clerical advisers, who give their time to help with the problems counselors encounter in their work. A client is always referred to his own professional adviser rather than to the adviser to the Council, but the counselors, not being professionally trained, frequently meet difficulties that they cannot handle. To give an example, a client may exhibit symptoms of behavior that the counselor does not understand, but that indicate a need for more skilled help than he is able to give. It is at this point that he will turn to the psychiatric adviser of the Council for guidance.

On completion of the Basic Training course, the responsibility of the counselor to the National Council for the standard of his or her work does not cease. Apart from occasional refresher courses, the counselors are required to attend regular case discussions which are led by professional tutors appointed and paid by the National Council. They also receive support and guidance from an individual tutor who has been assigned to them, visits them, and reviews their case notes. This in-service support is considered important for the maintenance of the standards of work on which the Council lays such emphasis from selection onwards, and there are many professional social workers who have expressed the wish that they had access to as comprehensive a system of in-service training or support as is provided for the marriage counselors.

A majority of the tutors working for the Marriage Guidance Council have received training for this work over a period of two years with a psychiatrist. They have started work as volunteer counselors and have been invited by the Training Department of the National Council to participate in the tutor-training scheme. They receive fees for tutorial work on a part-time basis. Tutors may, if they are dissatisfied with the standard of work being done by a volunteer counselor, require that he or she should have a formal assessment, in which case another tutor or tutors are brought in. Although this happens only occasionally it is a necessary safeguard, for the selection procedure is not infallible, and it is found from time to time that some counselors do not benefit adequately from the Basic Training course.

There is no doubt that this scheme whereby only a minority of individuals who want to become counselors in fact succeed, and under which some may be withdrawn during or after the training course, produces considerable strains within the organization itself. The great majority of people in Britain who want to do voluntary work have no great problem in doing so, and the tendency of the Marriage Guidance Council to reject around two-thirds of all those who have been sponsored for selection by local Councils undoubtedly results in stresses that are difficult for the organization to contain. In the first place, a fair amount of resentment builds up at local level when a series of candidates who were thought to be promising material turn out to be unacceptable to the National Council. Reasons are never given for nonselection, because the process needs to be entirely confidential, but the Council has sometimes to meet the charge that it is looking for superhumans, and that it is setting its standards unreasonably high. Even greater stress can be caused when a volunteer counselor, who has been working for some time within a local Council, is asked to withdraw from the work. These stresses have been known to result more than once in resignations from local committees, and in adverse comments in the press.

Other problems have arisen from the selective method of appointing counselors; in some communities people of influence, or their wives, consider that they are well suited to marriage counseling work, instancing the fact that people will frequently talk to them about personal problems. When they put their names forward, the local sponsoring committee, even if unconvinced of their chances of success at a selection conference, may be unwilling to prevent them from going forward, preferring to leave the decision to the National Council. All too often this process can result in a host of less suitable candidates taking places at selection conferences that might better have been reserved for others. Additionally, as the majority of these people are not selected for the work, much criticism can develop in the local community. It has been found that those who have been thought by selectors to be the least suitable for the work are often the most vocal in their criticism of the Council's methods of selection. It gives little satisfaction locally that this merely confirms the selectors in their original view.

In spite of criticism, the National Council maintains its insistence on rigorous selection and training for its volunteer counselors. The justification is said to be the experience the Council has in working with marital difficulties, and in using workers whose motive is essentially personal and unrelated to the need to earn a living. The Council says, in effect:

> We have been offering a marriage counseling service now for twenty years or more. Not only do we know how to do this, but we know who should do it. We are the right people, and we recognize others like ourselves.

How valid can a claim of this kind continue to be if no objective assessment is made of the work done by the volunteer counselors? The indication is that the service is appreciated and valued by the people of Britain, because more and more of them make use of it each year, but would it be even more effective if undertaken in a different way? Would the service really suffer if a higher proportion of candidates were accepted? Is there any difference in the quality of work done by the professional marriage counselor and by the volunteer? If so, can this difference be related to their motives for doing the work, to their training, experience, or personality? Other difficulties are posed by the insistence on selection: if selection is necessary for the volunteer marriage counselor, how much more necessary must it be for the professional, who is going to see far more clients and affect the lives of many more people?

It would now appear that there is sufficient experience in the work of volunteer marriage counseling to justify research in depth into the effect of this work. This is especially true at a time when there are far too few professional workers available to meet the needs of people in their community. Already there is a tendency for social workers to be involved in making exclusively material provision for the underprivileged, the effect of which can be to inhibit them from making the attempt to solve their own problems. Many doctors, certainly in Britain, are so heavily involved in dealing with lines of people at their daily surgeries that they must perforce prescribe pills and medicines, when what the patient needs most is their time. This very inability of the existing professionals to meet the personal and emotional demands of their patients points the need to create volunteer services whose workers have the time to listen, if not the skill to treat.

An experimental scheme has recently been instituted at the largest Marriage Guidance Council in Britain, in London, under which some counselors who have previously worked voluntarily are now receiving fees for a limited amount of marriage counseling. It was found that most counselors did not do much more than the required minimum of three hours counseling a week, and that in spite of the fact that the Council had over fifty counselors available, its waiting list continued to lengthen. The new scheme involves a selected group of counselors in a minimum additional six hours work each week over and above their three hours voluntary work. For this additional work they are paid a fee, and the first reports from their tutors indicate that a high standard of work is being achieved; waiting lists at the London Marriage Guidance Council are being reduced.

If this scheme develops further, what will be the relationship between the volunteer counselors and their colleagues who are being paid for some part of their work? To what extent does the professional represent a threat to the volunteer, and vice versa? Will the needs of society best be served by professionals and volunteers working together in the field of marriage counseling? It is suggested that it is in this area that experiments must now be made, that professionals must be willing to consider how their own skills can so be extended that they may reach into a much greater part of the community through the supervision and guidance of suitable volunteers who have been appropriately selected and trained for this task. Volunteers must be prepared to accept some degree of direction from those who have more experience and skill than themselves. In their turn, professionals will need to accept that the volunteer can offer their clients valuable support. It would seem that the time has come for us to reexamine our attitudes to competence in marriage counseling, unless we are willing to accept a state of affairs in which support is withheld from marriages that need it. To this end, there is an urgent need for research into the effectiveness of the work of the volunteer marriage counselors.

SELECTED BIBLIOGRAPHY

1. Sanctuary, Gerald: *Marriage Under Stress*. London, George Allen & Unwin Limited, 1968.
2. Halmos, Paul: *The Faith of the Counsellors*. London, Constable, 1965.

SECTION III
MORAL FACTORS

Chapter 30

MORALE IN MARRIAGE

WILLIAM L. CARRINGTON

THE TERM morale is generally understood to indicate a degree of emotional, moral, and spiritual self-mastery, a capacity to cope with even severe external and internal strains without being overwhelmed by them. It shows itself as the ability to react rationally and appropriately rather than automatically and impulsively in the face of all kinds of actual or threatened stresses. A good description of some aspects of morale may be found in Rudyard Kipling's well-known poem, "If—," the first verse of which may be quoted.

> If you can keep your head when all about you
> Are losing theirs and blaming it on you,
> If you can trust yourself when all men doubt you,
> But make allowance for their doubting too;
> If you can wait and not be tired by waiting,
> Or being lied about, don't deal in lies,
> Or being hated don't give way to hating,
> And yet don't look too good, nor talk too wise:

After many similar "ifs" the poem concludes with the following two lines,

> Yours is the earth and everything that's it is,
> And—which is more—you'll be a Man, my son! (1)

As many of the stresses to which we are exposed arise directly or indirectly from our varied and complex interactions with other people it would seem that our concept of morale will need to add the quality which we may term sociability to that of self-mastery. Sociability in this connection will include the ability to get on reasonably with many different types of other people in their varying attitudes, moods, and actions, as Kipling's poem implies.

On the wider scale morale has vital implications for all of the armed services, and for the civil population as well as their leaders in sudden and extensive disasters such as riots, earthquakes, explosions, fire, and floods; and in the extreme case of atomic war.

On the more personal, domestic, and social scale, not unrelated to the possible reaction to mass disasters, morale involves the ability to deal adequately and as constructively as possible with the many strains and

351

calamities associated with what has often been described as "the battle of life." And some of the most important, frequent and far reaching engagements in the battle of life are associated with the complex and often intense interactions of modern marriage and family life. They provide some of the greatest challenges to morale that the average man and woman is likely to face.

The traditional purposes of marriage: companionship, the begetting, nurture, and training of children, and the fulfilment of the reasonable sexual needs of each partner, are still generally accepted. But modern marriage has a further important function which is becoming more and more widely recognized, the absorption of emotional outbursts of either partner by the other, at least to a reasonable degree. This demands considerable maturity—or morale—but it is a most valuable service that either partner can offer. In today's world of tension and frustration and general insecurity it seems inevitable that some explosions of active or passive, aggression will become projected onto the person most available, the marriage partner, whether "deserved" or not. If the partner reacts destructively, by aggression or by sulking ("the silent treatment") the relationship tends to deteriorate and the children may tend to suffer. If the partner can accept the hostile feelings, even when unable to understand them, some real therapy will be offered for their resolution. This of course does not imply a complete acceptance of hostile behavior, to which, for most people there are limits.

Apart from this example of the need for morale in marriage itself, there is an important application of morale in the preparation for marriage, especially in the choice of marriage partner, the assessments of motives for marriage, and in the general exercise of responsible choice in matters of premarital sexual realtionships. It is assumed that, in a book dealing with "Moral Issues in Marriage Counseling," the counseling will include premarital counseling.

In the constructive handling of inevitable marital tensions and conflicts and the responsible exercise of premarital choices there is need for a considerable degree of morale, the capacity to act with reasonably mature consideration in spite of the pulls of sexual and aggressive emotion. The earlier maturing and greater freedom of young people have intensified the problem, and earlier marriage, while reducing the duration of the emotional difficulties, has brought further problems of its own in the interactive as well as the financial and vocational aspects of life. As we shall see the achievement of morale demands suitable training of sufficient duration, beyond all but the exceptional teen-agers. Marriage itself can bring remarkable growth if they can receive sufficient help.

SOME ESSENTIAL ELEMENTS IN THE ACHIEVEMENT OF MORALE

In attempting to formulate some of the underlying foundations of morale we may learn something from the experience of military leaders, to whom, and to those under their leadership, morale is literally a life-and-death matter.

In an address on "Morale in Battle" given to the Royal Society of Medicine in England shortly after the 2nd World War, Field Marshal Viscount Montgomery, one of England's outstanding generals, discussed the factors which contribute to the morale of the soldier in the heat of battle. He suggested four factors without which high morale cannot exist: leadership, discipline, comradeship, and self-respect. "A fifth factor, devotion to a cause, must exist but need not necessarily influence all the soldiers. Finally, there are numerous contributary factors which are of great importance but are not essential conditions (2). Among these he particularly noted success, regimental tradition, and personal happiness.

All of these may be adapted and applied to the promotion of morale in marriage, but in considering the application of marriage counseling to the problem it is necessary to remind ourselves, even allowing for premarital counseling, that most of the foundations of morale in marriage, as in the whole of personal and social life, are laid down, for good or ill, long before any of his clients come into direct contact with the marriage counselor. These foundations are laid and determined by each person's experiences and by the quality of his relationships, first with parents and then in widening circles with teachers and other influential people, peer groups—a strongly influential factor in these days, and the infinitely subtle and all pervasive influences that come through the mass media.

This opens up what may well prove to be a significant indirect opportunity for the marriage counselor to contribute to the promotion of morale through his influence in counseling and possibly in group leadership on parents and parents-to-be. The growing opportunities for Family Life Education in schools, colleges and churches, and the expanding services of family counseling are making a definite and valuable contribution to the whole project, one which may still be worthy of further evaluation and development.

One aspect of the promotion of morale in battle which was not covered in Montgomery's account of basic factors is concerned with the initial training of servicemen. If, for example, a company of volunteer soldiers receives a crash course of training, lasting only for a few months, the men will come to know exactly what is required of them and they will be able to carry out all that they are ordered to do with great efficiency on the training ground.

But in the heat of actual battle, with its overwhelming noise, danger, strain, and confusion, when orderly thinking becomes impossible, some of them may "lose their heads" and act in a manner contrary to their own best intentions and detrimental to the efficiency of the operation. If, on the other hand, the same company had been given a prolonged course of training, extending for more than two years, with continued repetition of all elements of their service, their reactions to orders would have become so ingrained in their habits that they are much less likely to be affected by the clamour and confusion. Their battle morale would have been established.

In civilian life what we may call character training is quite comparable to this. The prolonged training given in a good home and expanded socially through a good school and college, church and neighborhood, will contribute greatly to the development of the self-mastery and sociability which we have suggested as expressions of morale in marriage—and beyond marriage in total citizenship.

A particular aspect of this kind of morale seems worthy of special attention. In the modern highly competitive industrial and business life, and to a less extent in competitive professional life, many men appear to develop the cultivate the more aggressive qualities of initiative, drive, enterprise, toughness, and even ruthlessness through which they gain the necessary advancement; at the expense of the more "sociable" qualities of tenderness, thoughtfulness, flexibility, and graciousness which go to make a good husband. When these two sets of qualities are combined, as they can well be, in the male personality (and in the "career woman") they give balance and fullness to the personality. It is unfortunate that in our Western culture many men, senior executives of the highest integrity, intelligence, and wisdom, prove to be failures as husbands and fathers, and deprive themselves of some of life's deepest satisfactions, because they have given too little attention to the cultivation of these more tender qualities to round off the necessary aggressive ones.

These qualities of tenderness, consideration, and thoughtfulness are not, as is sometimes suggested, unmasculine qualities. They are essentially human, so much so that they may be regarded, not as distinguishing women from men, but rather as distinguishing men from beasts, as someone has suggested. They are not learned or cultivated in the market place, or in the tough impersonal world of industry. Men begin to learn them partly from their mothers, but mostly through an identification with a devoted father who possesses and shows them. Later they may be further encouraged through identification with other male objects of childhood and adolescent hero-worship. Women similarly make a good beginning in the development of morale through identification with a good mother and the encouragement of the first man in their lives, if he is a mature and gracious father, in loving and cooperative relationship with his wife.

Such considerations as these may serve to emphasize the value of well-planned and adequately conducted projects for preparation for parenthood, and particularly the need for much more than teaching as generally understood in this. Such preparation has so far been the missing link in most projects directed to improvement of marriage and family life, in spite of the fact that it may well be one of the most important and influential aspects of marriage counseling in the fuller sense of the term. One reason for this may be that it involves more deliberate and active organization, with less public motivation, than there is in the stress of marital conflict and the premarital desire to build a satisfying marriage.

This influence of identification is often very important in counseling. With a good counseling relationship the clients tend to identify to some extent with the counselor, and often to become "infected" with some of his calmness and steadiness in the face of emotional turbulence and confusion. "Counseling is the Counselor" has been a familiar slogan throughout the recent history of counseling, and this concept has spread more and more into the fields of teaching and many other areas of personal leadership. In the modern world people are much more immune to the influence of the spoken word than at any time in the past. They have been forced by all kinds of unscrupulous propaganda to become even negativistic to it. It has become clear that to have any constructive influence teaching needs to be underpinned and supported by example. But even this is not generally sufficient. People may deliberately refuse to follow the example of someone they find themselves unable to respect or look up to. Example in its turn needs to be further underpinned by a constructive relationship, a fact that many parents and teachers fail to recognize, or find themselves unable to offer owing to their own emotional tensions and conflicts.

THE COUNSELOR'S CONTRIBUTION

We are now in a better position to consider and to formulate the counselor's possible contribution to morale in marriage in fuller detail. It may be appropriate to begin by a brief consideration of the possible needs of the various kinds of people who may be open to help. Taking for granted the physical needs for adequate food, clothing, and shelter, we may describe the main needs of people in trouble, and incidentally also of children, as acceptance, direction, inspiration, and deliverance. Each of these "key" words may need some explanation and amplification.

Acceptance, a familiar term in counseling, involves unconditional acceptance of each person and his feelings (people are not responsible for their feelings) but not necessarily of all his conduct. With this essential proviso, however, there is a need for permissive and nonjudgmental attitudes to the inevitable mistakes, stupidities, and failures of clients, together with a readiness to look with them at possible consequences, and to encourage them to learn from experience. Above all the acceptance needs to be nonexploitative and "client-centered."

Direction will naturally find differing applications according to the age and general state of the person in need of it. With adults it will be more concerned with the offering of appropriate information than with advice. Information may cover essential facts about life and about productive and therapeutic personal relationships and about the normal range of feelings experienced by men and women. When dealing with questions of morality, the information will be more effective when it is about values rather than rules. People often rebel against or even reject rules, which they may regard as arbitrary or obsolete, but values may ultimately be seen as self-validating, even if there has been some scepticism about them at the beginning. Values also constitute the most dependable criteria for the necessary responsible choices for truly moral, as distinct from coerced, behavior.

Inspiration is needed by many people who may have a reasonably clear idea of what they ought to do but lack the emotional moral and volitional strength to do it. "Our chief want in life" wrote Emerson, "is somebody who shall make us do what we can. This is the service of a friend. With him we are easily great" (3). Inspiration at its best constitutes a kind of "spirit transfusion," which may do for the personality something comparable with what blood transfusion does for the needy body. It obviously demands a high degree of emotional and spiritual maturity and balance in the counselor. With the acceptance already discussed it provides an effective object for the client's identification. The biblical term, "abundant life" depicts an overflowing quality of life; the term abundant is derived from the latin word abundare which means "to overflow." Abundant life has an unselfconsciously radiant infectious quality, and as life itself can only come from life, so the mature personality is encouraged in its development by the inspiration of other mature and radiant personalities. Fortunate we are when we are privileged to meet and relate with them.

Deliverance is a universal need because of the universality of human fallibility, whether admitted or not. An important aspect of all therapy, including counseling, is in rendering it more explicit and more available to people in trouble, remorse, or despair, to assist in their liberation from the often heavy burdens and the lonely inner battles which are blocking or hindering their progress or recovery. In particular it is one of the most important recurring contributions of parents and other helping persons to the nurture and development of children, who so often fall into inextricable difficulties. For all people in trouble or in degenerating relationships deliverance involves the grace of forgiveness and reconciliation, not as a condescending offering of the "good" to the "bad," the "superior" to the "inferior," but rather in the recognition that we have all failed in all kinds of ways and are unfit to "cast a stone." In this recognition and awareness that we have been forgiven, delivered from the lifelong burden of our own failures beyond any of our deserving, we cannot properly withhold it from other people. The effect of such forgiving attitudes on marriage and family life can well be imagined.

In the context of these complex needs for acceptance, direction, inspiration and deliverance we may now turn our attention to some of the ways by which the counselor may apply the basic factors in the development or restitution of morale in marriage as previously quoted from Field Marshal Viscount Montgomery as applying to morale in battle. They were leadership, discipline, comradeship, and self-respect, together with devotion to a cause (2).

Leadership, for the counselor, is obviously different in some ways from that of the "top brass" in the services, which cannot afford to be permissive or even democratic. Discipline too in counseling is much more, though not entirely, a matter of encouragement of self-discipline. In common with the military leader the counselor needs to offer the kind of leadership which will win the trust and confidence of his people, and at the same time be prepared to give the adequate direction, inspiration, and deliverance already mentioned. This will need genuine acceptance and "caring." One of the most common "cries from the heart" of troubled people is, "nobody seems to care how I feel." It will need also to allow for some temporary dependence on the part of the disturbed client who will have "regressed" to some extent toward childhood. But like the good accepting parent, the counselor will keep his sights on the encouragement of growth back to adulthood, and will progressively throw the ball back into the client's lap as he becomes able to handle it. Like the good parent he will "love them and let them go," which is in marked contrast to the "lover" kind of love which "loves and hangs on," a very destructive relationship in counseling.

Another aspect of counseling leadership, especially in marriage counseling and in group leadership, is that leadership is at its best more than a relationship between the leader and each person under his care. Good leadership inspires some degree of comradeship, the third of Montgomery's basic factors, comradeship between those who are receiving the leadership. If the situation can be symbolized by a spoked wheel with the leader represented by the hub and the clients at the periphery, "attached" to him by the spokes, then the rim, through which the peripheral ends of the spokes are joined to one another can represent the comradeship, which, like the rim, gives much extra stability to the whole system. The aim of marriage and of group counseling of any kind is the promotion or restoration of comradeship, and this greatly depends on the quality of leadership.

Self-respect, the fourth of Montgomery's basic factors, is being more and more recognized as an essential element of constructive personal relationships, as it is an essential for morale in battle. Ideally the child has his own self-valuation generated in him through the experience of being loved and valued by his parents and other significant people. When he is frequently rejected in any way, or when the attitudes of his parents are inconsistent enough to be confusing to him he may well develop what Karen Horney termed "the basic anxiety," "the feeling of being isolated and helpless in a world conceived as potentially hostile" (4). If he is not helped to work through this he may well grow up with the kind of low self-valuation that seems characteristic of all grades of neurosis including many which seldom or never come under any professional therapy. When people carry such low self-esteem into adult life they can only depend, as the young child does, on what they think other people may be thinking of them, for any kind of inner poise. They are then constantly vulnerable, whether they attempt to cope with it (consciously or unconsciously) by undue dependency, by "chip on shoulder" general suspicion and hostility, by isolation and withdrawal, or by such other expedients as nonconformity, drugs, including alcohol, stinginess, extravagance, overambition, or even crime.

Many of the destructive and apparently irrational feelings, attitudes, actions, and interactions which are found in disordered marriages can be seen as "carry overs" from unresolved emotional tensions, frustrations, and conflicts in earlier life, and as expressions of the vulnerability that comes from low self-esteem. In the progressive "catharsis" which is facilitated by the counselor's genuine acceptance and caring many of these tensions are gradually relieved and the client grows progressively in self-esteem in a manner similar to that of the more fortunate "valued" child. It appears that as one comes to better and more rational self acceptance it becomes much easier to accept other people, "to love one's neighbor as oneself."

Marriage itself can be a most important training ground for morale, and in the multitudes of successful marriages the two partners help each other by expressing the qualities already mentioned. In many cases the two partners receive continuing help and encouragement from the constructive attitudes of relatives and friends, and from the experience of "being needed" by their children, a constantly recurring challenge to morale. Success in their domestic life and in any work or social service or sociability in general will also contribute to morale, as it does in battle. When these influences have been insufficient, or when the morale has been undermined to any extent by tragedy, illness, infidelity, loss of job, or other distressing experience, the situation may come under the influence of the counselor to an extent depending on the motivation of the troubled people and on the kinds of expectation they may have of counseling and of marriage itself.

This kind of expectation of marriage itself may be a very important factor in morale in marriage as it is in morale in battle (Montgomery's fifth factor). Many people in these days enter marriage with unduly high and even quite unrealistic expectations of what it should provide for them. Their pipe dreams are quickly shattered in a painful disillusionment, and they are often tempted to give up the struggle and separate when some expert help may have been able to give them renewed hope and "devotion to the cause" of marriage. Much of this unrealistic expectation seems to be consequent on the false idea that has taken root in western culture, and incessantly and subtly offered through all the mass media, that romantic love is sufficient to hold a marriage together. It is true that it brings two young people together very strongly and to their mutual delight and satisfaction, but it will never hold them together unless the "good feelings" are at least underpinned by "good will," a genuine concern for each other's welfare, even when the good feelings are replaced by considerable hostility, or combined ambivalently with it. With this good will there needs to be a strong enough belief in "the cause" (marriage and parenthood) to hold them as they go through difficult and confusing times, and even to inspire them with enough patience to give time for the counseling on which they may have embarked to exert its therapeutic influence. This of course may well constitute a challenge to the counselor to recognize and bring out such feelings of despair so that they can be worked through with patience and persistence.

This encouragement of endurance and the working through of the disillusionments may be very important for the promotion or recovery of morale in marriage. If the troubled marriage breaks up without any correction of the unrealistic expectations of marriage it may well be that one or both partners will venture into another marriage without having learned enough from their earlier distressing experience. Unless they are very fortunate in the choice of a second partner the inevitable disillusionment may again prove too much for them, and favor the growth of a cramping cynicism and the further lessening of morale. This may further reduce any motivation for counseling and their patience in going through the counseling process. They may then fail to learn that disillusionment, however painful, is essential, in that nobody can go on living effectively on the basis of illusions. Part of the counselor's task in this connection is to support his clients in such a manner that they can work through any disillusionments without overwhelming distress, and thus to prepare the way for the constructive and patient process of rebuilding on the strong and enduring foundations which make morale in marriage possible.

Finally, we may remind ourselves that for the preservation of morale in marriage, as in battle, an important element of good leadership and comradeship—and of self respect—is the preservation of constructive communication. The bonds of marriage and family life are living bonds, and as such they cannot remain fresh, or in many cases even survive, without regular "nourishment." This is in many of the marital difficulties encountered by the counselor an important part of his area of concern. Marriage is in this sense like a garden: it will not remain healthy unless it receives sufficient attention, unless it receives a high enough priority in the convictions of both partners, a sufficient "devotion to the cause." One of the elements of success in marriage counseling is the reestablishment of adequate communication between the partners, and if this continues the counselor's main task may well have been accomplished. But it will generally need to have become firmly and confidently established, and the partners convinced of its importance if the marriage is to go on improving (as one would hope it would do) after the termination of the counseling.

The most common factor in lack of communication seems to be some kind of fear of rejection, humiliation, or futile hostile argument, and here again the development of a reasonable standard of morale in marriage would do much to reduce such fears and release the ability and capacity to accept whatever comments the communication may bring forth. Here we have a situation, not unfamiliar to counselors, in which morale facilitates communication and vice versa. Fortunately the counselor's efforts can be directed to the promotion of both morale and communication. A comparable situation of course is in the reciprocal relationship between the personal and the sexual relationship between the partners, each of which again is related to morale, and with each of which the counselor can exert some therapeutic influence.

Insofar as morality is an essential element in the mutual trust and cooperation that make for successful marriage and for the promotion and preservation of morale in marriage, it is clear that morale is closely associated with morality. But it need not be identified with it, and in fact morale in either partner may well safeguard a marriage from being broken by breaches of morality. When we take account of the fallibility of human beings, the inadequate preparation given to most people for marriage and parenthood, and the magnitude and complexity of the strains that bear on modern marriage and the individuals who embark on it, the value of morale in marriage and of all efforts to achieve it, must surely be seen as beyond all doubt and beyond all measuring. As an expanding project it merits the cooperative planning and participation of all appropriate educational, religious, and therapeutic disciplines and all social welfare organizations. It provides an inescapable challenge worthy of all the wisdom, skill, and organizational ability of devoted men and women, with no less at stake than the welfare of the human race in the unknown future.

REFERENCES

1. Kipling, Rudyard: *Sixty Poems*. London, Hodder and Slaughton, 1939, p. 111.
2. *Brit Med J*, 1946, p. 702.
3. Considerations by the way, from *The Complete Works of Ralph Waldo Emerson*. Ward Lock & Co., 1898, p. 559.
4. Horney, Karen: *Neurosis and Human Growth*. Routledge & Kegan Paul, 1951.

Chapter 31

MORAL VALUES AND THE FAMILY

JOSEPH C. LANDRUD

A GROUP OF STUDENTS from an upper-middle class high school was asked to present a panel discussion at a family life conference on the topic "Teen-Agers Speak Out." From the audience of interested parents, a concerned father arose and asked the first question from the floor, "What do you on the panel see as the main reasons for the constant conflicts between parents and children in families today?" A handsome young man on the teen-age panel, who happened to be the student body president of his school, jumped to his feet and replied, "I think that there is only one main reason—a difference in *values* between parents and their children."

It is fascinating to know that this articulate teen-ager—a recognized campus leader at that—would answer the question as he did, in terms of conflicting values between generations. The use of the term "values" is hereby understood to refer to moral values, or the relative worth or importance placed upon "right conduct," however defined, depending upon the distinction between right and wrong. That is, a form of behavior described as acceptable or "right" by a teen-ager might well be deemed completely unacceptable, and therefore "wrong," by parents. And so the stage is set for all manner of tensions.

There is no doubt that a difference in moral values exists among generations today. But this difference is not only between generations, but also between sexes, and, very basically, between individuals. So every member of the family is involved. It will be the purpose of this chapter to examine the formation of these values, to see how they are dynamically transmitted within the personality structures of individuals, and expressed within the family constellation with growing children. The examination will then be focused upon learning how the adolescent within the family seeks to find his own values, which may conflict with those of his parents, as he strives to experience himself as a separate person, autonomous in his own right. Finally, the individual values of two separate people who find themselves married to each other will be investigated to learn what possible conflicts might arise within the context of a marriage relationship itself. Throughout this work the attempt will be made to gain fresh insight into the foundations of feelings: the values which underlie and motivate family relationships today.

In seeking to understand the formation of one's individual values, it is necessary to have a basic concept of man. A helpful framework has been advanced by Eric Berne, who described each person as having three distinct ego-states, or systems of feelings, each with a related set of behavior patterns (1). These three may be termed, colloquially, as *parent, adult,* and *child.*

The *parent* refers to that part of a person's personality which is directly received from one's own parents, along with other significant authority figures (family, teachers, clergymen, police) influential in formative years. These older people, whose approval and acceptance is valued by the growing infant for security, express a series of "do's" and "don't's" throughout childhood. Examples are the following: (parents) "Eat everything on your plate," "Don't be sassy"; (teachers) "Come to school on time," "Don't cheat on examinations"; (Clergymen) "Honor your father and mother," "Don't commit adultery"; (Police) "Observe traffic rules," "Don't rob the bank." Each of these injunctions, coming from powerful figures with the implied threat of "I won't love/accept you if you disobey," are first heard by the infant's *child* and gradually become integrated into the infant's *parent.*

The *adult* is that part of the personality which deals with the outside objective world. It is capable of logical thinking, planning, and predicting, based upon stored-away facts and learned experiences necessary in conscientious decision-making. It can be likened to a computing machine which processes the data fed into it through everyday living for ultimate use in effective, responsible functioning.

The *child* is the most interesting of the three ego states. It does not think, as does the *adult,* but is primarily concerned with feelings, and so experiences the full range of emotions. It may be happy, sad, impulsive, pouting, rebellious, joyful, trusting, or suspicious. It may feel very strong convictions ("I *love* the Beatles" or "I *hate* the Beatles") without any corresponding logical framework on which to stand. It is where creative sparks lie ("I've got a new idea!") and where sexual desires are experienced ("I'm really turned on by you"). The *child* should be understood in two forms: natural and adapted. The "natural" *child* is the spontaneous, uninhibited expression, while the "adapted" *child* is the modified reaction to meeting the real parent's demands, whether "acting like a good child," or "getting away with something."

Hence, by using this framework for understanding ego-states, the young married couple with their newborn baby might be graphically described as in Figure 1.

At the point in time of the birth of this child, mother and father already have their own *parent, adult,* and *child* ego-states in a relatively formed condition. Their *parent* ego-states tend to be rather fixed, as are their *child* ego-states, while their *adult* ego-states hopefully are more flexible, open to dealing with ever-changing outside realities of the world. The newborn infant,

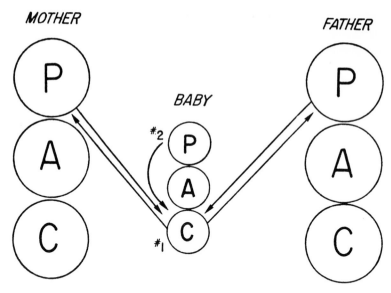

Figure 1.

on the other hand, primarily experiences himself in his *child* ego-state, with his *parent* and *adult* states only potentially present. That is, the infant is largely conscious only in terms of feelings, and the earliest of these is *fear*, as he experiences his separation from the security of mother's womb and his helplessness in controlling his environment. If he were to put these feelings into words his *child* might cry out (as in Figure 1 above): "Hey, I feel frightened and helpless to care for myself, so please protect me!" So when baby cries tears to convey this basic communication, the *parent* ego-state of mother and father responds with: "Sure, we'll protect you and care for you —we love you and want to help."[1]

As the baby experiences this loving response from his parents, especially from mother, his sense of security in the frightening world is strengthened, and he begins to develop his basic value of *trust*. Gradually, as these "caring for" reactions of parents are repeated, the baby's *parent* ego-state begins to form the message, "When I am unhappy, I can cry for help, and my parents will respond, so I can count on them." Hence, his *parent* learns to comfort his own *child* with this message (Fig. 2) just as his real parents did to him. As Erik H. Erikson states, "The infant's first social achievement, then, is his willingness to let mother out of sight without undue anxiety or rage, because she has become an inner certainty as well as an outer predictability" (2). This "outer predictability" of the infant is a function of his growing *adult* ego-state, which is emerging in increased awareness of the world around him. It should be noted that if this basic value of trust is not learned in these early months of life, or if it is experienced inconsistently, it will greatly affect the child's sense of well-being, along with hindering his progress in subsequent developmental stages.

Following trust, other basic values are also learned as received through relationships with parents and the "significant others" in the child's world. Dynamically, this occurs as communication between mother, father, and child is increased and new daily life situations within the family are encountered. Many of these values are communicated in terms of parental "No-No's" which is what makes growth painful, as per the phrase "growing pains." For instance, when the infant is three years old, his *parent, adult,* and *child* have all become actualized and are capable of being experienced, so the following transaction might take place (Fig. 2).

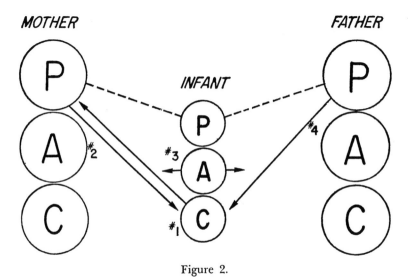

Figure 2.

1. *Infant* (from C) : "I like to play with water and pour it on the kitty."
2. *Mother* (from P): (Angrily) *"No,* don't pour water on the kitty!"
3. *Infant* (from A) : (Puzzled) "Why not?"
4. *Father* (from P): (Firmly) "Because the kitty doesn't like to have water poured on her. It's okay to play with water in the sink, but not to pour it on the kitty, as in our family we want to take care of the kitty."

As the infant hears the first "No-No" from mother's *parent,* which is challenged by the infant's *adult,* and then reinforced by father's *parent* in a consistent pattern, the infant's own *parent* receives a message for the future. This message may be challenged by further attempts of defiance, which points up the need for both mother and father to present a united front. Any inconsistency between them will *invite* further defiance, as the infant will

fight not so much out of rebellion as to get a consistent structure in his adapted *child* in which to operate securely. Gordon W. Allport shares a story
which describes how such messages become internalized:

> A three-year-old boy awoke at six in the morning and started his noisy play. The
> father, sleepy-eyed, went to the boy's room and sternly commanded him, "Get
> back into bed and don't you dare get up until seven o'clock." The boy obeyed.
> For a few minutes all was quiet, but soon there were strange sounds that led the
> father again to look into the room. The boy was in bed as ordered; but putting
> an arm over the edge, he jerked it back in, saying, "Get back in there." Next a
> leg protruded, only to be roughly retracted with the warning, "You heard what
> I told you." Finally the boy rolled to the very edge of the bed and then roughly
> rolled back, sternly warning himself, "Not until seven o'clock!" (3)

At first, internalization is quite unconscious, but later becomes more selective, as the growing person imitates values caught from heroes and "shining examples" that he finds in not only parents and family relatives and
friends, but also in beloved teachers, idolized athletes, entertainment personalities, and historical figures of all ages.

And it is during this period that all manner of family conflicts may
arise—and they arise *just because* the parents have been doing such a good
job! That is, from the baby's earliest infancy, the family transactions have
largely been between mother's and father's *parent* and the baby's *child*, as
shown in Figure 3.

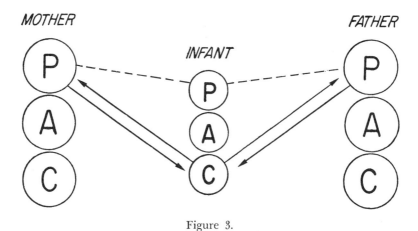

Figure 3.

And all through this period a good deal of internalization of the parents'
own values has taken place between the *parent* of mother and father to the
parent of the infant. (See broken line in Fig. 3.) But along with this internalization on the infant's part, he has been getting to know his mother and father
better. While he had originally known only their *parent* ego-state, he has in-

creasingly become aware of their *adult* and their *child,* as well, and so has
come to learn that they do not always practice what they preach! In other
words, the *parent* in mother and father may say one thing to him (e.g.
"Don't ever smoke, it's not good for your health"), while they actually, in
their own lives, follow separate codes (such as repeated chain-smoking). He
is going to be increasingly aware of such inconsistency and to wonder,
"What gives? What *is* right?" This questioning of appropriate moral values
on his part is going to come up more and more frequently, *just because* he
has heard mother and father say encouragingly, "Don't depend on us for
everything—*do* it yourself—try to figure it out on your own—*think* for yourself." They have done this in their endeavor to increase the child's own
autonomy, to encourage him to grow as a separate and distinct person. In
short, they have purposely been concerned for his growth to adulthood, and
so have stimulated him to use his own *adult,* to think, reason, compare, and
evaluate on his own. And because they have done so well in moving him in
this direction, the family communication transactions are taking place more
and more between the *adult* of all three parties concerned, as in Figure 4.

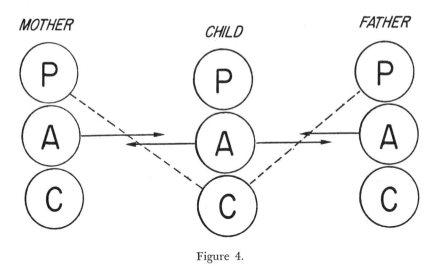

Figure 4.

To be sure, the growing child still remains their child (as the broken line
indicates), but he has a decreasing need for their Parental ego-state as he
gains more confidence in using his own *adult* and *parent.* And by using his
own powers of reasoning and logic, he is going to throw out some of the
values which were instilled in him from infancy, as his own world view expands, and he is going to be influenced by sources far afield from his parents' knees.

   This is the period of the teen-age rebellion, and it is a very necessary period indeed. It is the time when the growing youth is figuratively cutting the umbilical cord of dependence upon his parents and seeking to forge his own identity. This is no small task and is accompanied with much trial and error, particularly as concerns values, as they lie at the heart of selfhood. Consequently, as the teen-ager tries on new values for size, often in the face of grave opposition from his real parents, there is much occasion for tension, conflict, and anxiety. Indeed, as the teen-ager fights to be a person in his own right, to find his own values—to "do his own thing"—and yet feels the opposition from parents, from society, and even from other teen-agers, perhaps "anxiety" is the best word to describe how he feels. Rollo May even defines anxiety as, "the apprehension cued off by a threat to some value which the individual holds essential to his existence as a self" (4).

Out of this normal anxiety, which is healthy, although frightening for all concerned, the blooming adolescent is fighting to see himself as an individual distinct from his parents. Instead of merely accepting their values for self-definition (e.g. "Our family has always been Republican in politics and Lutheran in religion"), he will begin to say, "Well, that might be all right for *you*, but why should *I* buy it?" In the face of their admonitions to "study hard, work hard, and you'll make money and be successful," which were often forged in their own depression years struggle, youth of today, having been raised in the affluent society, are challenging these value systems by replying, "But maybe I don't want to simply make money—and, by the way, *just what is success* anyway?"

Consequently, young people of today are hard at work in hammering out a whole new hierarchy of values which has meaning to them. They do this in the continuous exercise of choices which arise in conflict situations. Many of these value decisions are fully conscious, growing out of the changing times in which we live, where it is increasingly difficult to make decisions in terms of blacks and whites, and vastly wide areas of gray invade their enlarged sensitivities.

On the other hand, many young people make value choices which are *not* consciously thought out, but which result from unconscious and irrational preferences sometimes designed to "get back" at their parents for suppressions experienced in early childhood. This "acting out" behavior is largely neurotic and often very destructive, both to themselves and their families. It may take the form of a simple "If my parents are for it, I'm against it" type of sentiment, which, if crossed or pressured by parents, may eventuate in great lawlessness and antisocial activity, with accompanying misery for all. More commonly, it is manifested in an obvious denial of parental job ambitions and their value interest in material creature comforts, as when young people renounce the family's "soft life" to embrace poverty, dirty clothes, and the hippie communes.

These new value hierarchies, whether set up consciously or unconsciously, have been fantastically influenced by youths' views of themselves in relationships with the world. New dimensions grow out of the tremendous impact of television to expand their horizons, along with what they see as the great hypocrisy of the adult "establishment" in dealing with such problems as the Viet Nam war and the American civil rights situation. These young people are not very different from any previous generation in questioning their elders, but changed modes of communication have made their outcries much more verbal, while the generally increased affluence of their parents has made them much more independent, more mobile, and, hence, more able to actualize their desire to choose values that "really count."

In setting up this new hierarchy of values, there is frequently great disagreement among young people themselves. (This "freedom to disagree" is by itself one of their cherished values.) For instance, the group of teen-agers on the panel described at the beginning of this chapter, when asked to name the specific values which they held to be important, came up with a list of six separate items. Yet, when discussing the list, the panel differed widely in their individual views and could come to a unanimous agreement on only *one* of the items as being important to them all. Significantly enough, this item was "the freedom to be an individual," which tends to be the heart of the matter today. This quest for individuality is not necessarily immoral or illegal, although it may take those expressions in its attempt to be heard in extreme situations. Hence, it is sometimes described as the "New Morality," with the connotation often being derogatory, as it appears to conflict with established moral views long held sacred by family and church. Yet this morality, frequently based upon a hierarchy with *love* at the apex, can also be descibed as rooted in a "Situation Ethics," which many responsible church leaders see as being framed within the New Testament itself (5) .

While the above discussion has focused upon the possible value conflicts between parents and their children, it would be unreal to assume that their relationships are the only sources of family tensions today. Husbands and wives can certainly have their moral value conflicts, too. In fact, the root cause of many marriage wars is *not* the relatively superficial (no matter how intense!) disagreements over money, sex, in-laws, or division of mutual responsibilities which fan tempers to blaze hot. Rather, more often than not, the source of great antagonisms lies largely in privately held but unexplored value systems of the individuals concerned. An example is the case of a young couple who shall be named Tom and Nancy, both in their early thirties, the parents of two young children. A series of marriage counseling appointments, while very heated, did not seem to be very beneficial in bringing about any increased communication. Instead, each session seemed to bring an ever increasing onslaught of attacks and counter-attacks from each side, with little or no understanding of how the other really felt as the specific items and events were hurled at each other with great gusto. Finally one day the counselor said to them both, "Well, now I know what things make both of you mad, and how you each can hurt and be hurt as we've talked about what's happening in your relationship. But this has all been pretty negative—that is, I know what you are both against, so let's look at the other side of the coin. What are both of you *for?* In other words, what things are most important to you in your individual lives? Let's list them on the blackboard."

This question resulted in a turning point in the entire counseling situation. Both Tom and Nancy hesitated at first, as if shifting gears, as indeed they were. Then Tom began by saying, "Well, what's most important to me is (1) my job, and (2) my advancement up the ladder into a better executive position. Of course, if I weren't married my job wouldn't mean as much, and I'd spend more time on my hobby of flying. But I *am* married and want to be, and want the best for my family—yet I get so griped when I don't get any support or encouragement from my wife at home to get the things which will make her happy."

As he said this, Nancy's jaw dropped in amazement, but before asking her to react to his "values" (that word never was used, but values *were* what was being discussed), the counselor said, "Okay, Nancy, now what things are most important to you?" She immediately replied, "I think the most important thing is (1) the atmosphere of the home, (2) the proper environment for our children, and (3) our ability to communicate."

Now it was Tom's turn to be surprised—and he said, "You mean it isn't important to you that I become president of the company some day and provide you with nice things?" She replied, honestly, "Well, that would be nice, but we are really doing fine with the things we have right now and don't need any more. Actually, I'm amazed that you thought I wasn't perfectly satisfied. I see you working so hard, and I try not to talk about it, hoping that you'll be more interested in me and the kids when you get home." Tom replied, "So *that's* why you do it! Why, I thought you talked about the kids because you didn't think I was providing well enough for them. It made me feel bad to think I was not satisfying you, so I couldn't stand any more discussion about it." Nancy was then close to tears as she said, "And all the time I thought you didn't care anything about us, but only about your old job."

Needless to say, this focus on values was the opening door to a much more fruitful therapeutic experience. Much work remained to be done, but the way was clear. And it never would have come, apart from looking at the foundations of the feelings individually held in their conflicting value structures.

It appears that the whole subject of values is an untapped goldmine as far as the resolution of family conflict is concerned. In the past, marriage and family counselors have placed such great emphasis upon understanding and clarifying "feelings," and the emotional dimensions of relationships that value structures may well be overlooked or ignored. When this happens it is evident that beneficial therapy may be blocked or even rendered impossible. Yet when the underlying values held by individuals are sought and held up for examination, great superficial misunderstandings can be eliminated. Hence, much deeper intimacy in marriage and family relationships is promoted.

In this chapter we have seen how values originate in childhood, as each of us integrates the learned values of our parents and the significant authority figures in our lives, in a gradual and almost automatic way. Then, as teen-agers, when each person is faced with working out his own unique identity, it has been seen how these values may be modified, revised, or altered completely, often in great family emotional turmoil. Finally, in marriage, even though these values are rarely expressed or identified as such, they continue to be tremendously influential. Even though they may now be integrated within the individual husband and wife, grave misunderstandings may exist if values remain unspoken and unshared. So, can any person say that he really *knows* himself or any other person, especially in marriage and family relationships, without a clear understanding of the personal values involved?

REFERENCES

1. Berne, Eric: *Transactional Analysis in Psychotherapy*. New York, Grove Press, Inc., 1961, pp. 30-36, 75-78.
2. Erikson, Erik H.: *Childhood and Society*. New York, W. W. Norton & Company, 1950, p. 219.
3. Allport, Gordon W.: *Becoming: Basic Considerations for a Psychology of Personality*. New Haven, Yale University Press, 1955, p. 70.
4. May, Rollo: *Psychology and the Human Dilemma*. Princeton, D. Van Nostrand Company, Inc., 1966, p. 72.
5. In this connection *see* Fletcher, Joseph: *Situation Ethics*. Philadelphia, Westminster Press, 1966; Pike, James A.: *You and the New Morality*. New York, Harper & Row, 1967; and Burtness, James H.: *Whatever You do*. Minneapolis, Augsburg, 1967.

Chapter 32

DIFFICULTIES DISTURBING MORAL VALUES FOR THE MARRIED PAIR

LeMON CLARK

ONE OF THE most necessary but sometimes difficult steps to achieve in marriage counseling is to get an individual or pair to accept the proposition that sexual activity should be purposefully pleasurable. It is necessary to gain acceptance of the proposition that to take very definite steps to increase the pleasure as much as possible is not only perfectly right but even highly desirable. Sexual activity should be regarded as play at the adult level. Where disappointment and frustration and a sense of guilt are a constant part of sexual activity moral values and precepts are readily abandoned.

Anything, be it physical, mental, or emotional, that interferes with the attainment of the greatest pleasure should be corrected. If you are having trouble in working out a completely satisfactory sexual relationship do not think that you are the "odd chicken," that nothing like this ever happened to anyone before. The first step towards the attainment of more satisfactory sexual relations is to learn to accept yourself as a sexual being. There must be no reservations. The second step is to accept your mate as an equally sexually motivated person. When such acceptance is complete each will feel perfectly free to disclose his sexual feelings and desires to the other. Each will then endeavor to display to the other the response and reaction that contributes so much to the attainment of the greatest ultimate saisfaction of both.

Mere acceptance of sexual activity as a duty or a necessity, or attempting it as a necessary physical experience without the overtones of emotional involvement on a loved and loving basis leaves far too much to be desired. There is the old story of the prominent Washingtonian who was embarrassed to meet his nephew going into one of the famous "houses" as he was coming out. Constrained to say something he remarked, "I can only tell you that the simulated interest and affection of these girls as vastly more stimulating than the dignified acquiescence of your auntie."

One cultural attitude, much more modern than the Judeo-Christian-Puritan-Victorian complex, contributes to sexual frustration. So long as women were there for the pleasure of the male and no one thought of questioning it, he, at least, could gain release from sexual tension as frequently as desired. True, he felt something was missing. There was little in the way of cooperation. Thus the male sought this from other sources. From the Greek hetaerae to the Japanese geisha girls to the modern call girl, men have sought a female who accepted them and made them feel welcome. Wives were instruments not participants.

Then came the movement of equal rights for women. Women had the same rights as men. That meant that if they did not desire coitus they did not have to submit to it. This set the stage for a constant "warfare between the sexes." If a wife did not feel like submitting to coitus when her husband approached her she could shake him off, tell him to go away, she was too busy or just did not feel like it.

In our civilization, at the present time, women are probably not as immediately sexually inclined as men. The male may be aroused by thoughts, sights, or sounds. The female takes actual tactile stimulation. If instead of pushing her husband away she would simply relax in his arms, and if he, in turn, had the wit to caress her gently and lovingly for a short time, she might then find that she was much more interested than she thought she possibly could be.

The most important part of the experience is that she must accept his advances at least neutrally. That is to say, she must not withdraw within herself. If she says to herself, "Oh! All right, go ahead. I'll be a good wife and let you," she has not remained neutral, she has backed off to a considerable degree. He is at the starting point. She is some distance back. If sexual pressure is great enough so that he goes ahead anyway, he will reach orgasm in due course. Because of the sexual stimulation she too will have advanced towards a climax, but is still some distance away from it. She has probably just passed the starting point. If now he would begin all over instead of rolling over and going to sleep she would welcome it. If a woman will train herself from the very beginning of her marriage to accept his advances, even passively to begin with, she will find that it turns out to be far more interesting in a short time than she thought it possibly could be. Then active participation on her part increases the enjoyment of both.

The male of the species is the seeking animal. He does initiate sexual play more commonly. The wise female appreciates this and adapts herself to it. Mutual satisfaction in such a situation is vastly greater for both. Where this is the usual action and reaction a man or a woman might try sexual relations with another but it can never exceed the satisfactions attained within the marriage bond.

The implication of the strain placed upon moral values by the disinterest of one member of a married pair is well illustrated by a recent letter in one of Ann Landers' columns. "Dear Ann," the letter read, "I'm a man who would like to sound a word of warning to wives everywhere. Including my own. Recent statistics indicate that one-third of America's working force is female. In my own office there are at least five attractive women who are getting to look better to me every day because: My wife is either too tired or she sits up until 2 A.M. watching T.V. and by the time she gets to bed I've given up hope and gone to sleep. Or she has a backache, a headache, or earache. Or she's getting a cold. Or I'm getting a cold. Or the children are still up. Or she's expecting a long distance call from her mother. Or she's mad at me for something I said last night."

One may immediately ask the question how much of this is his fault? If he went to her in front of the T.V. and gave her some affectionate attention might she not be quite willing to leave the show for a pleasant time in bed? Or does she have some actual physical or emotional difficulty that prevents her from letting herself take part in sexual activity?

A young woman came to the office complaining that intercourse hurt. She had been married for six months. A careful vaginal examination ruled out all the common causes of dyspareunia. There was no obvious vaginal infection by the common pathogens, monilia, or trichomonous. The vagina was normal in depth, the uterus normal in position. But during the bimanual examination the hymenal ring was definitely tight. It was like a strongly elastic rubber band. Two fingers could be inserted into the vagina but this ring constricted tightly around them. It was this that caused discomfort for her and for her husband as well. Elastic enough to permit intercourse it had not ruptured or torn. A cc. of novacaine injected at four and eight o'clock of the hymenal ring, and two small snips with a pair of scissors loosened the ring so that it gave no more trouble.

In counseling a young couple before or soon after marriage the importance of the attainment of orgasm for the bride should be emphasized. Sexual experience is so intense that emotional habits may be formed and become deeply ingrained in the individual's make-up very quickly. If a young woman becomes habituated to sexual stimulation without going on to the attainment of orgasm she may form such a habit that it becomes difficult to change it.

This is one of the problems of our day. With drive-in theaters and country roads far from home, young people may indulge in "heavy petting" with a tremendous build up of sexual tension. If she refuses to let herself go beyond a certain point for fear of going too far she may very well develop a definite psychological block at this point. After marriage she will enjoy stimulation to just that point and then interest and desire will simply die away. This can be disturbing to her and frustrating for her husband. She may feel vaguely that it is his fault and he may feel that she does not really love him. This may set the stage for sexual experimentation by both outside the marriage.

If young people are going to indulge in such sexual stimulation might it not be better for them to go on to the point of mutual orgasm without actual coitus? Would they not be better off emotionally and physically? Dr. Eleanor Hamilton in her realistic book, *Sex Before Marriage* advocates just such a course of action. If this is justifiable, even advisable for best emotional and physical health then young people should be taught to accept it without feelings of guilt.

After marriage the situation for the girl, at least, changes significantly. If they have not indulged in coitus prior to marriage but limited sexual activity to mutual stimulation to orgasm, after marriage she will be exposed to the possibility of pregnancy. If this is undesired at the time for any reason, it may seriously inhibit her ability to go on to orgasm in actual intercourse.

In addition to this, she is now available in bed. There is no longer the necessity to pet her for two or three hours. After a rather brief period of affectionate demonstration he will wish to go on to the act of coitus itself. She may be only slightly interested in so brief a time. One young woman came into the office and sank dejectedly into a chair burying her face in her hands and sobbing for ten minutes. She wore a diamond and a wedding ring so the ordinary cause, a premarital pregnancy, was patently not the reason. When she could finally talk I asked, "For Heaven's sake, what is the trouble with you?" Looking through her fingers she sobbed, "I don't know whether I love my husband or not." She had been married in August, some six weeks before. When I asked why didn't she know whether or not she loved her husband she sobbed, "I don't get nearly as excited as I used to." Of course not. He was ready for actual coitus in minutes. She was not. The two of them must keep open channels of communication and let each other know what is desired so that a mutually satisfactory adjustment can be achieved.

"Heavy petting" can take its toll in emotional complications for the young male as well. He may develop the habit of attaining orgasm with little, if any, actual physical stimulation of the penis. As a result, after marriage, he tends to reach a climax prematurely making it impossible for his bride to have the opportunity of attaining release from tension through orgasm. Only mutual desire and effort on the part of each to see that the other gains the same soul stirring experience can give the kind of satisfaction that will preclude desire to try other sources of satisfaction. Therein lies the real basis of family solidarity. Sexual experience, as Havelock Ellis said many years ago, is at least minimally pleasurable with anyone who is physically acceptable to us. But there is also no doubt that on the basis of a loved and loving relationship it has overtones of deep emotional satisfaction that other experiences never attain.

Our traditional attitude towards sex being what it is people, young and old, are hesitant about seeking help where trouble centers around the sexual organs. Only in the last very few years, and that due in large part to the prodding of Dr. Harold Lief, have medical schools begun to give medical students the kind of training and information that will help them to deal with the sexual problems of their patients.

There are several other possible causes for reluctance on the part of a young wife to indulge in sexual relations. One of the most common and most completely neglected is adhesions between the prepuce and the clitoris. At least 50 per cent of all young women have such a condition. In a fair proportion it is enough to lessen sensation significantly. Freeing such adhesions is such a simple matter it is unbelievable that more physicians do not give some attention to it. A blunt probe inserted at the apex of the hood and swept down and out, so as not to tear the mucosa, first on one side and then on the other quickly frees the adhesions. With a mirror the patient should be shown how to pull the hood up and back and put some unguent of any kind—cold cream, vaseline, on the area night and morning for eight to ten days so that it epithelializes and will not readhere.

Where there are clumps of epithelial cells beneath the adhesions stimulation of the clitoral area during sexual play, and even during actual intercourse, far from being pleasurable, may be actually painful, at least irritating. As one fifty-five-year-old woman with four grown sons said after a severe case of adhesions between prepuce and clitoris was corrected, "It's awfully hard to be a good wife to your husband when it hurts every time he touches you."

Many young women, during the years they are virgins, may suffer from a copious vaginal discharge. Brought up to be fearful of anything connected with the sex organs they frequently are afraid to call it to their mother's attention. Some think that it is normal, since it commonly makes its appearance after the onset of menstruation. If there is so much discharge that the panties are constantly soiled it is too much. If a little mucus is seen on toilet paper that may well be within the limits of normal.

There is no infection in the majority of cases. The discharge is due to a so-called cervical erosion. It is not necessary here to go into all the theories as to the cause of an erosion. A simple erosion are those cases in which the area is fairly smooth and bright red. "Histologically, one finds a single layer of columnar epithelium, few or no glands, and many thin walled vessels under the epithelium" (1).

Columnar epithelium is secretory where the flat squamous epithelium, which should cover the cervix, is not. This accounts for the increase in mucus. The cure is simple. Actual cautery of the cervix is necessary. The new cryo-surgery is being tried, but I personally have had no experience with it. The cervix is not heat sensitive. Cauterization can be performed in the office ordinarily with no anesthesia. There is little discomfort. If the patient is very apprehensive, 2 cc of 2% carbocaine injected into each uterosacral and each broad ligament will anesthetize the area and make it completely painless.

Excess vaginal discharge causes difficulties. It is a perfect culture medium. Hence vaginal infections simply cannot be cured unless the erosion is eradicated. The excess discharge favors the development of bladder infections. The excess mucus, carrying bacteria may be milked up into the bladder during the thrusts of coitus.

Last but not least, the excess mucus intereferes with sensation for both husband and wife. There is too much lubrication, and the skin of the penis does not come into close contact with the mucosa of the vagina, and vice versa. Women come for help when their husbands complain that intercourse simply does not feel right. This may occur after childbirth when there is an ectropion of the cervix, where it turns outward. Here again, deep cauterization is the only cure.

In some such cases, of course, where the vagina was overstretched some exercises must be instituted as advocated by Dr. Arnold H. Kegel (2). Where, however, there was a laceration or episiotomy that was poorly repaired, proper surgical repair is the only solution.

In some cases a poor repair may result in a vaginal introitus that is too tight, or too tender. A young Episcopal priest's wife suffered from such a condition. The mucous membrane of the forchette, or lower edge of the vagina, had been brought up to a sharp fold with no supporting connective tissue and muscle beneath it. Intercourse was intolerable until a proper repair was done.

One of the greatest hurdles each has to overcome is the feeling that somehow sexual activity is at best slightly sinful. Practically all males and many if not most females have indulged in masturbation. Anything that may be wrong with the primary sexual area, therefore, may be punishment for sin. To seek help would let the world know that you have been a sinner. All that is ridiculous. The sexual organs can have difficulties just as your eyes, teeth, ears, and stomach can.

Women put off coming to the doctor until almost driven to do so and then can scarcely bring themselves to more than hint as to why they are there. They will say, "Doctor, I want a complete examination." Whenever a woman says that, I know that she wants a vaginal examination but does not quite dare say so. I also know that there is something troubling her in that area and if possible I must get her to talk about it if it is not readily discernible by a vaginal-pelvic examination.

There may be a Bartholin gland cyst, a swelling in one of the labia. If this has become infected it may be an abscess. This would be so tender that she would almost certainly mention it.

Her uterus may be retroverted and bound down with adhesions from previous infection or from endometriosis. This may forshorten the vagina to such an extent that coitus is painful. The uterus may be up in normal position but endometriotic nodules may infiltrate the posterior culdesac and make intercourse painful. Endometriosis results from misplaced endometrium. Endometrium is the lining of the uterus. It is the menstruating organ. If endometerial tissue exists in other areas than merely lining the uterine cavity it can cause trouble. Each month it bleeds just as the normal area does. The blood cannot escape so the swelling incident to the bleeding causes pain and tenderness. The blood ultimately turns to fibrin and the fibrin to scar-like tissue. This causes adhesions.

Young people are not the only ones to have problems. Middle-aged and older individuals have them also. The mucous membrane lining the vagina during the menachme, or reproductive life of a woman, is tough resilient epithelium. Once through the menopause, however, this undergoes great change. From a membrane 35 or 40 cells thick it may regress to where it is at best only 8 or 10 cells thick. It is much more sensitive and fragile.

The husband has also advanced in years. Where he used to reach orgasm too quickly he now takes too long. Where she used to wish he could prolong the act now she wishes he would hurry up and get it over with to end her discomfort. This cannot fail to be apparent to him and he may be tempted to seek sexual activity somewhere else. The use of an estrogenic type ointment or cream such as Premarin Vaginal Ointment® or Dienestrol Vaginal Cream® applied to the vagina two or three times a week will restore the lining to the type it was during the menachme. Coitus will be much more pleasant to her and actually will feel much more normal to him, because the mucosa of the vagina is again normal and secretory in type giving more lubrication.

Much less common but still a factor in some cases is a very low grade bladder infection. Some women learn to live with such a low grade infection which seems to give them little trouble. There is no great amount of pain or burning upon urination, and very little excess frequency. But the bladder area, the anterior wall of the vagina, is unduly tender. She is inclined to avoid coitus whenever possible simply because it makes her so uncomfortable. This difficulty is missed by many physicians. It is found only when a catheterized specimen of urine is centrifuged and stained with Gram's stain and carefully examined under the microscope. Proper urinary tract antibiotics will clear it up and restore comfort.

The male of the species may also have trouble. A young man who is uncircumcized may harbor the monilia organism beneath the prepuce unless he takes great care to keep the area clean. If his wife has a low grade infection, one which does not cause her any discomfort, it may, nevertheless, cause him real distress. Under treatment for several days he may recover from his trouble. Following intercourse he will complain of little blisters under the prepuce or around the corona of the glans. This may occur again and again. Only adequate treatment of both will bring a permanent cure.

Men are more prone to disease of the coronary arteries than women, at least before the latter go through the menopause. When one or two of his friends dies of a heart attack, the husbands begin to feel that intercourse is too taxing and refrain from it, sometimes altogether. This may leave the wife very frustrated. As Havelock Ellis stated many years ago, and Kinsey and his co-workers restated some twenty-odd years ago, a woman does not reach maximum sexual capacity until about thirty years of age, but that her sexual desires stay at this high level for twenty-five years or more. A man reaches his maximum of desire in the latter teens and then slowly goes downhill for the rest of his sexual life. Some men, of course, continue sexually quite active until the seventies or eighties. But the fact that sexual capacity does decrease with age, moreso in some than in others, is undoubtedly true.

Some sexual activity, gaining release from sexual tension through moderate, restrained, or controlled sexual activity is probably better for the heart following recovery from an actual coronary attack than living in a state of frustration and tension. Of course there will be cases where it is contraindicated but under adequate medical management such cases could be reduced to an insignificant proportion of the whole. Doctors should discuss this realistically with their patients.

Do men go through a climacteric, a period of involutional change similar to the menopause in women? This is a very moot question. Authorities are divided in their opinions. Personally I am sure it is true. Somewhere between forty-five and fifty-five this may occur. During this time a man may experience a posterior urethral irritation and in many cases a mild degree of prostatitis. His sexual attitudes being as they are, he may very well feel that this difficulty is punishment for sin, some earlier indiscretions, masturbation, an almost forgotten case of gonorrhea, or a homosexual experience. He feels he dare not go to a doctor because he could not bring himself to confess his troubles. He may live in emotional turmoil himself and subject his wife to serious frustration because of his feeling that he must forego all sexual activity. Adequate treatment by a sympathetic physician would bring great relief.

Just as we no longer fear giving estrogen to women where indicated, to help her through the period of the menopause, it is possible to give testosterone to a middle-aged male with usually definite beneficial results. The usual care in examination, to rule out the possibility of other complicating conditions, must be observed.

Moral precepts cannot long be maintained where anatomical, physiological, or emotional difficulties interfere with the attainment of complete sexual experience and relief from tension. Anatomical and physiological difficulties can be corrected. It will take some time to overcome the emotional difficulties imposed by our culture. Sometime in the future we shall finally attain the point of view that completely satisfactory, emotionally thrilling sexual experience is the right of every adult. Realizing the restraints which the attainment of human intelligence puts upon us, we shall then undertake adequate training and education of the individual to help him direct his intelligence to achieve this end.

The era during which we attained our cerebrum brought all these complications. When we learned to remember and to foresee our primitive instincts could no longer be the one and only director of activity. We had to appraise our actions. Each individual had a built-in cause of internal conflict. And when the connection was finally made between sexual intercourse and childbirth, which probably occurred only late in the stone age period of human development, a whole host of new problems arose. Until the present era we have little in the way of intelligent appraisal of all the factors involved. But with the pressure of population now compelling a reevaluation of many of our basic sexual attitudes, fairly rapid progress should be made in the next few decades.

REFERENCES

1. Curtis, Arthur Hale (Ed) : *Obstetrics and Gynecology*. Philadelphia, W. B. Saunders Co., 1934, p. 537.
2. Kegel, Arnold H.: *J Int Coll Surg*, 25:487-499, 1956.

Chapter 33

CONSCIENCE-FORMATION, CONTRACEPTIVE BIRTH CONTROL, AND THE CATHOLIC CLIENT

JOHN G. QUESNELL AND PAUL MARX

INTRODUCTION

FOR TWENTY CENTURIES the Roman Catholic Church has condemned artificial, contraceptive means of birth control (1). Pope Paul VI reiterated that teaching with his encyclical *Of Human Life (Humanae Vitae)* of July, 1968. The hope for change in the Church's teaching engendered by Vatican II and by the writings of renowned theologians only enhanced the confusion and sharpened the psychological trauma observed by marriage counselors in their sessions with Catholic clients. These are often sincere parents who can find no satisfying way out of their agonizing dilemma.

This many-faceted problem of fertility-control is allied to many other issues such as a viable code of sexual morality, the Sexual or Erotic Revolution, Situation Ethics, the New Morality, preparation for marriage, chastity, sex-education, fornication, adultery, abortion, and the sexual perversions. The profundity and breadth of this problem tests the skills of the marriage counselor facing psychologically distraught Catholic clients. In a summary treatment of this enormous subject, the authors will briefly discuss: a) The Current Situation; b) Authority and Conscience in the Catholic Church and c) Conscience, Contraception, and Counseling.

THE CURRENT SITUATION

Even a brief listing of the various ongoing revolutions with briefest commentary brings home to one the often unique difficulties experienced by those who wish to be loving and responsible parents in a unique world tormented by an exponential rate of social change. Among the engines of accelerating change is the educational-informational revolution expressed in the explosion of knowledge. Human knowledge now doubles every eight to nine years. Instant, sight-and-sound, mass communications have made the world a global village seething however with international tensions. Anthropologist Margaret Mead remarks that "this is the first generation who have been brought up by the mass media instead of by parents." For the first time in human history there are no elders who know what young people know, she says of the generational gap.

Obviously the galloping pace of the scientific-technological and cybernetic-electronic revolutions is affecting our lives and modifying the culture enormously. Thanks to space science and the computer, for the first time man has *seen* the earth from the depth of outer space. Sophisticated nuclear, chemical, and biological weapons of death and destruction have made a shambles of the theology of war and peace. As a result of the agricultural revolution, we are no longer a nation of farmers and small-townsmen; almost 75 per cent of Americans now live in cities on less than 2 per cent of the land. Also helping to make the traditional generational gap into a grand canyon is the intellectual-philosophical revolution which fathered Situation Ethics and the Erotic/Sexual Revolution, striking at the very heart and center of human personality and the family. Closely allied is the New Morality which some have called all too simply "the old lust."

Then there is the medical-demographic revolution with its control of death at every level and the resultant, unprecedented population explosion. This has enormously affected parenting, occasioned a resurgent feminism with its accompanying role-changes between husband and wife, and produced what some call a contraceptive civilization or the pill-culture with its immense but unpredictable ramifications. Today women experience the menarche earlier and the menopause later. Never in the history of mankind has the human female been so fertile for so long! Meanwhile, the world population grows by some seventy million annually; the present three and one-half billion persons may double by the year 2000.

The impact of all this on the changing Catholic family, living mostly in an urban-industrialized society, is not hard to imagine. And this brings us to the "theological revolution" as it touches upon responsible family planning in a world where couples need ten-fifteen-twenty years of birth control.

Actually, artificial contraceptive birth control is nothing new in the history of mankind (2). Christianity condemned it for twenty centuries. The Lambeth Conference of Anglican Bishops in England in 1930 was the first Christian group to sanction contraception, but even then only under carefully stated circumstances. Other Protestant bodies followed. The decision of the Lambeth Conference occasioned in that same year the encyclical of Pius XI, *Christian Marriage in Our Day.* He wrote, "Any use whatsoever of matrimony exercised in such a way that the act is deliberately frustrated in its natural power to generate life is an offense against the law of God and of nature, and those who indulge in such are branded with the guilt of a grave sin." Pius XII supported and reiterated his predecessor's teaching, saying in an address, 29 October 1951, to the Italian Catholic Union of Midwives, "This prescription holds good today just as much as it did yesterday. It will hold tomorrow and always, for it is not a mere precept of human right but the expression of a natural and divine law." In this speech on rhythm and again in another on November 29, 1951, Pius XII spoke in favor of "birth regulation" by rhythm or periodic abstinence and again condemned birth control by artificial means. On the occasion of these two addresses on the liceity of timed abstinence or rhythm, he called for research to perfect the rhythm method beyond the pioneer Ogino-Knaus calculations, and express- ed the rather optimistic hope that science would soon solve the problem. Why Catholic universities, but especially the Catholic bishops of the world, did not instigate such research continues to be mystery. Were they that far removed from the practicalities of Catholic married life? In 1969, eighteen years later, the American hierarchy finally established The Foundation of Human Life to research the reproductive system in order to make fertility control by timed abstinence more workable. Incidentally, on September 12, 1958, speaking to an international medical meeting in Rome, Pius XII al- lowed the pill for therapeutic reasons only.

Although he repeated the teaching of his predecessors, Pope John's call- ing of the Second Vatican Council and his appointment of a small com- mittee in 1963 to study the morality of birth control by pill—a committee later enlarged by Paul VI—occasioned significant theological developments. The *Pastoral Constitution on the Church in the Modern World* urged par- ents to plan their families "with human and Christian responsibility and with docile reverence toward God," fostered "by common counsel and ef- fort." Thoughts like these from the same Constitution inspired theologians to give their attention to the positive development of the theology of mar- riage and conjugal love—a theology highly undeveloped:

> Let them thoughtfully take into account both their own welfare and that of their children, those already born and those which the future may bring. For this accounting they need to reckon with both the spiritual and material conditions of the times as well as their state of life. Finally, they should consult the interests of the family group, of temporal society, and of the Church herself. The parents themselves and no one else should ultimately make this judgment in the sight of God.

While sterilization, infanticide, abortion, and the "sexual perversions" were condemned, contraception was explicitly not condemned. The moral- ity of contraceptive birth control, while briefly discussed on the Council floor, was left by his own request to Paul VI, after being duly advised by an enlarged Papal Commission of experts from various disciplines who after four years of study and debate were, by an overwhelming majority, in favor of a new approach. At the end of the Papal Commission's sessions, reported- ly fifteen of the nineteen theologians favored the liberal position, while only four supported the conservative view.

Similarly, of the sixteen bishops including seven cardinals who had been added to the Commission for the final session and who examined the com- plete dossier—the minority and majority working papers and other special-

ized reports totaling some five hundred pages along with a special theological report drafted by the theologians at their request—nine favored the
more liberal stance, three opposed it, and another four expressed themselves as doubtful (3).

Meanwhile, theologians like Edward Schillebeeckx, Bernard Haering,
Hans Küng, Louis Janssens, and Charles Curran developed further the
excellent seminal ideas found in Vatican II documents for a positive conjugal love and mature Christian marriage, a sacrament perhaps the least
theologically understood. Also, the very existence of a Papal Commission
and some of Paul VI's instructions to it gave Catholics and the world hope
for a change in the Church's traditional teaching. Not least, the Pope's long
silence on the question he admitted "haunted" him encouraged further
hope, especially when a considerable portion of the younger clergy encouraged befuddled couples to make a personal decision in conscience.

Then came *Of Human Life* in July, 1968. This was really a more tightly
reasoned exposition of the conservative "Minority Report" without even a
serious attempt at rebutting the carefully constructed arguments of Papal
Commission members, bishops, and theologians, most of whom were prepared for a new approach to the resolution of the issue.

The international reaction of disappointment, frustration, and even
shock is well known. According to a Gallup Poll of American Catholics,
out of one-hundred adult Catholics in a representative sample, fifty-four
opposed the Pope; only twenty-eight percent supported him. The insistence
that the teaching was not irreformable or infallible although authoritative
and authentic by the Pope's spokesman did not lessen the confusion and con-
sternation. Even bishops were befuddled; many apparently did not see the
encyclical as the fruit of collegiality, a concept to be explained in the next
section. To quiet their people and to give some guidelines in a crisis brought
to boil, the bishops of Holland, Belgium, Germany, Scandinavia, France,
Austria, Bolivia, and Canada gave out official commentaries explaining the
theology of dissent and allowing for personal decisions of a rightly formed
and informed conscience for those responsible couples who could not solve
their problems by the teaching enunciated by Paul VI. Other hierarchies
were more conservative, including the American bishops who, however, took
a more middling position. But this very disagreement among the episcopal
commentaries only generated greater confusion (4).

The theology of dissent will be briefly explained in the next section in
terms of the nature and function of authority and conscience in the Catholic
Church as these relate to infallible and fallible though authoritative and
official moral teaching. Unfortunately, proper conscience-formation in the
religious education of adult Catholics had hardly been faced; they mostly
grew up thinking that no change was possible, that all the teaching of the

Church was more or less infallible and so unalterable, and that the Church had all the answers to moral problems as they came up. The anguish of many inadequately educated Catholics became pervasive and deep.

What is the factual situation in regard to ways and means of fertility control by Catholics? In the first place, the Catholic family is not notably larger than the non-Catholic Christian or non-Christian family. According to various studies, up to 50 per cent of Catholics in childbearing years have at one time contracepted, or are now contracepting, in ways and means forbidden by *Of Human Life* taken literally. Some one-third of such Catholics are still wrestling with rhythm, perhaps in some instances supplemented by other means (5).

Furthermore, in their preparation for marriage, young Catholics learned little about the physiology of reproduction and even about the pioneer, inadequate Ogino-Knaus rhythm method; nor was the more effective Sympto-Thermic method carefully explained to many; comparatively few even today understand that method well, including doctors. The Foundation for the study of the reproductive system set up by the American hierarchy in 1969 to perfect the rhythm method would seem to be evidence that rhythm is no answer for very many in the present context—as those have learned who have sincerely taught or knowledgeably tried it. Besides, it would seem safe to say that the majority of young clergy allow or help couples to form their conscience as to means. It is also well known that individual bishops have more or less kept a prudent silence in the matter, with notable exceptions.

Meanwhile, *Of Human Life* has been the occasion for the Church experiencing a deep crisis of authority and for the individual Catholic in many cases a gnawing crisis of faith, or at least a crisis of confidence in the proper handling of the Church's authority. However, they may be right who say that *Of Human Life* may be a blessing in disguise, for now Catholic educators and pastors will have to teach and emphasize the proper formation of conscience facing the whole moral teaching of the Church, that is, in the case of fallible but official doctrine. The end result of all this painful reassessment may result in much more mature, adult American Catholics. In that sense the Church is not breaking up but growing up (6).

AUTHORITY AND CONSCIENCE IN THE CATHOLIC CHURCH

Unquestionably, if the counselor is to help his Catholic client, he must understand the nature and function of authority and conscience as taught by the Catholic Church. Both are enormous subjects to be treated in limited space. Let us take up authority first, and then conscience, but throughout with a view to the birth-control dilemma.

To understand the nature and function of authority in the Catholic

Church it is necessary to grasp the Church as a unique, divine-human community, better known since *Vatican II* as the People of God. For Catholics the Church is Christ living and working in the baptized, with the Pope as the successor of Peter and the bishops as the successors of the apostles, by divine design and divine guarantees composing the Magisterium, that is, the teaching authority within the community of believers. The bishops do not merely act as emissaries of and for the Pope, mechanically handing down decrees from above. With the Pope as the first among equals and as successor of the apostles, the bishops teach and guide and rule their people as a loving service and not without taking cognizance of the Holy Spirit working and witnessing in the whole body of the faithful baptized into Christ. The traditional doctrine of collegiality was finely clarified by *Vatican II.*

> The order of bishops is the successor to the college of Apostles in teaching authority and pastoral rule; or, rather in the episcopal order the Apostolic body continues without a break. Together with its head, the Roman Pontiff, and never without this head, the episcopal order is the subject of supreme and full power over the universal Church (7).

In the careful words of Leon-Joseph Cardinal Suenens, "Collegiality remains an immanent factor in the structure of the Church. Life itself must find the balance between these two realities: integral respect for a divinely conferred primacy within the Church, and full realization of an authentically exercized collegiality" (8).

This collegiality, properly understood, of course refers only to the power jointly exercised in the Church by the Holy Father and the bishops. But as already intimated, this pastoral teaching and ruling is not exercised under ideal conditions without consulting the Christian experience of the faithful and the witness of the Holy Spirit working in them. Perhaps what has been said so far can best be summarized by quoting Acts 15:22, describing the Council of Jerusalem, "The Apostles, the presbyters, and the whole church decided . . ."

An even better view of the working of authority and decision-making in the Church presents itself in this official statement of *Vatican II:*

> A great many benefits are to be hoped for from this familiar dialogue between the laity and their pastors: In the laity a strengthened sense of personal responsibility, a renewed enthusiasm, a more ready application of their talents to the projects of their pastors. The latter, for their part, aided by the experience of the laity, can more clearly and more suitably come to decisions regarding spiritual and temporal matters. In this way the whole Church, strengthened by each of its members, can more effectively fulfill its mission for the life of the world (9).

Looked at from this viewpoint, *Of Human Life* and some of its teaching immediately presents some problems which will be discussed later.

The teaching of the Church expresses itself as either extraordinary, that is, infallible; or ordinary, that is, fallible though authoritative, official, and authentic. The doctrine of infallibility has been woefully misunderstood by Catholics and non-Catholics alike. Since 1870 when the doctrine was enunciated, there has been but one infallible statement. Obviously, the Church must speak to each age in the language of *that* age, not in the language of the past. Truth is always greater than our ability to capture it in human words. Papal infallibility is essentially negative: it merely says that on certain, very rare occasions, when the Pope officially speaks as the teacher of the universal Church to expound the faith of the Church, he will be prevented by the Holy Spirit from being in error—i.e. he will not betray the faith. This is unalterably Roman Catholic dogma. However, this is a far cry from the false notion propagated in many Catholic apologetic works and learned by so many Catholics in their past education: that the Pope is some kind of oracle with an answer to all religious and moral questions. This false view has been expressly repudiated by *Vatican II*, "The Church guards the heritage of God's Word and draws from it religious and moral principles, without having at hand the solution to particular problems" (10).

What about fallible though authoritative and official and therefore binding teachings? *Of Human Life* and all the Church's *moral* teaching is of such a character and binds in conscience. Exactly how any one such teaching binds and under what circumstances we shall see later. There are reputable moral theologians who maintain that the *moral* doctrine of the Church can never be once and for all infallibly stated, because in the very nature of the case, changing circumstance is always a dimension of such teaching. Every doctrinal pronouncement is conditioned by the age which produced it, and all the more so every moral teaching. With the growth of knowledge due to theological and Biblical research and also in response to changed historical and social conditions, there is development of doctrine accompanied by a better understanding of the moral demands of Christian living; and this explains how in the moral teachings of the Church there has not only been development but even reversals (11). To many Catholics such developments in teaching and such reversals come as a surprise. In like fashion they are puzzled that the Pope in *Of Human Life* should condemn all artificial, contraceptive birth control—this is the official though fallible teaching of the Church, no doubt about that—after which national hierarchies gave out statements explaining how sincere, loving, and responsible parents may make a decision of conscience to the contrary, a conscience rightly formed and informed. To cite a few examples—French bishops:

> Contraception can never be good. It is always a disorder, but this disorder is not always guilty. It occurs in fact that spouses consider themselves to be con-

fronted by a true conflict of duty. . . . On this subject we simply recall the constant moral teaching: When one faces a choice of duties, where one cannot avoid an evil whatever be the decision taken, traditional wisdom requires that one seek before God to find which is the greater duty. The spouses will decide for themselves after reflecting together with all the care that the grandeur of their conjugal vocation requires.

Austrian bishops: "Whoever acts against the spirit of the encyclical is not necessarily parted from the love of God and may accept Holy Communion without confession." Canadian bishops on a clear conflict of duties, e.g. the reconciling of conjugal love and responsible parenthood: "In accord with the accepted principles of moral theology, if these persons have tried sincerely but without success to pursue a line of conduct in keeping with the given directives, they may be safely assured that whoever honestly chooses that course which seems right to him does so in good conscience." Bolivian bishops: "If someone who is competent to form a sound personal judgment based on previous information, after a serious examination of the subject before God, arrives at other conclusions, he has a right to his convictions in that area, although he must be disposed to continue sincerely his investigations" (12) . Finally, as Bishop Christopher Butler, one of the great lights at the Vatican Council, wrote in the November 2, 1968 London *Tablet,* "If the Church has not committed her infallibility on a point of teaching, then she cannot require an unconditional assent to that teaching."

The heart of the matter is the following question. How does an official though fallible teaching of the Church bind in conscience in difficult and perplexing circumstances? Must such a teaching be followed by all in every possible circumstance? What is the theology of dissent? Before we can answer these questions, we must turn our attention to the important subject of the nature and function of conscience, its rights and obligations.

What is conscience? The very word conjures up a number of ideas such as God, law and authority, order, responsibility, morality, measure, guidance, freedom, and personhood. Austin Fagothey defines conscience as, "the practical judgment of reason upon an individual act as good and to be performed, or as evil and to be avoided" (13) . Note here the use of intelligence and will, knowledge and guidelines, and above all, responsibility. One is reminded here of Blaise Paschal's, "Let us endeavor to think well; this is the principle of morality."

For many, conscience may merely be a matter of consulting one's feelings. "Let your conscience be your guide" to a hippie may amount to "Do your own thing." Even for a Catholic, with a catechism knowledge of his faith, morality too often seems like something extrinsic to one's person, as if the Church manufactured it, and then clamped it on Her adherents, making religion a kind of strait jacket. Indeed, conscience is inviolate, but not a law unto itself; the individual conscience is not a teacher of doctrine, but must be guided by right doctrine. Briefly, conscience does *not* inform one about what is right or wrong but tells one whether a given act one intends to do or has done is in accord with what one *holds* to be right or wrong.

On the one hand, the sincere and educated Catholic not only sees the need for moral authority and guidance; he welcomes the Curch with Her teaching as his moral guide to shore up his reasoning (conscience). However, he must make that teaching by thought and prayer his own; through faith he cultivates a humble and generous docility to the teachings of the Church as coming from God. On the other hand, as Archbishop Roberts has pointed out recently, the important lesson which the Church still has to learn is that "the obedience of an individual is worth little unless his intelligence enters into it; otherwise a man's obedience is no different from a dog's." In this sense Martin Luther was right when he said, "Every man must do his own living and his own dying."

Ultimately, we must always follow our conscience, but we have the obligation to inform and form our conscience as well as possible by prayerful effort and by knowledge from various sources, and not least, the knowledge and guidance of the Church. In this connection it might be good to remember a famous saying, "No one lies more than to himself." To consult one's personal convenience only or to make moral decisions only by one's own fallible knowledge is to be guided by an uninstructed conscience which Cardinal Newman called "that miserable counterfeit." In another connection he said, "Do not determine that to be truth which you wish to be so, nor make an idol of cherished anticipations." An informed self-direction and maturity rooted in reason properly linked to faith and so captive to God, a healthy personal autonomy and thinking conformism—these describe a Christian who lives by an informed and formed conscience.

Perhaps we can eliminate all misunderstanding as to the nature and function of conscience, its rights and obligations, with this definition of conscience in the June 15, 1968 issue of *America.*

> Conscience is neither a dictator nor a slave. It is a discerning guide. Its freedom is not the same as isolation from all aid and enlightenment in its own formation (for this would be the slavery of abandonment to one's own limitations and appetites). On the other hand, competent guidance, to remain truly expansive and perfective of human liberty, must retain a healthy and realistic respect for the complexity of the individual situation and the interiority of decision. It cannot take over the function of personal decision; it can only guide it. The Church is divinely commissioned to enlighten conscience; not to prefabricate every decision.

Perhaps it is this kind of conscience that Shakespeare had in mind when he wrote, "Conscience makes cowards of us all." To take full and informed responsibility for one's life is no small task. But certainly a conscience formed by available knowledge, both human and divine, and a conscience captive to God by informed faith, gives us the kind of true Christian Guardini described, "A truly Catholic life is not the easiest and most satisfying, but the hardest, the least comfortable, and the most demanding. The more seriously we take Catholicism, the more tasks and obligations await us."

Space here permits only a mention but no description of the various kinds of consciences: antecedent or consequent; correct (truth) or erroneous (error), vincibly or invincibly; certain or doubtful; strict or lax, tender or tough, fine or blunt; and perplexed or scrupulous. Obviously, the ideal is to have a correct and certain conscience, that is, a delicate one, formed and informed. To paraphrase St. Peter, such a conscience can give an explanation for one's personal conduct and a reason for the faith that actuates the believer—faith seeking understanding being the oldest definition of theology.

We may now be prepared to return to the question of how an instructed conscience must be the mediating agency between an official and authoritative (though not infallible) teaching of the Church and one's responsible personal conduct. It has always been a part of the traditional wisdom of the moral teaching and guidance fostered by the Church that, in the case of a conflict of duties, while fully understanding because of thought and study the teaching of the Church and having full respect for Her teaching authority, one may consider himself exempt from a fallible, official teaching of the Church. This is the rationale behind the bishops' statements on *Of Human Life,* some of which statements we have quoted.

Too many Catholics in the past were more indoctrinated than educated; raised by and large not to think about the faith and rarely having been schooled in proper conscience-formation in the matter of proper dissent in individual difficult cases, and given also the abundant misinformation along with bad and conflicting advice, such Catholics now find making a conscientious decision as to responsible parenthood painful. Where they have made it, there is often lingering anxiety, as marriage counselors so well know. In short, even relatively well-educated Catholics know little about a healthy theology of dissent and so cannot find their way comfortably in the maze surrounding the whole question of freedom and authority today.

Undoubtedly many Catholics will continue to be willing, sometimes even eager, to hand their consciences over, as it were, to the crowd, to the priest who agrees with them, or even to a marriage counselor, for to do so seems to lighten the burden of risk and anguish that always accompanies personal decision. In this crisis of transition and this age of exponential change, the competent counselor, however, will know how to use his many skills in affording knowledge and guidance, by encouraging and by inducing thought, in bringing his client to a constantly greater personal self-direction. The contradictions and dilemmas and agonies generated by the birth-control controversy as these are reflected in the personality of his client presents the counselor with no small challenge. He may at times have to refer the patient to an informed spiritual advisor or priest.

In conclusion, the Church is moving through a "crisis of transition" from a concept of self-justifying authority to one of authority that must convince by the credibility of its message. As Archbishop Hurley of Durban, South Africa, observed concerning *Of Human Life:*

> The Pope is appealing to a human argument. The Catholic is not convinced by the argument. Here is the tension. Is it a creative tension? Yes, because the controversy is going to bring to the surface a much fuller understanding of Church authority, an understanding of the manner of exercising it in relation to the cultural attitudes of the time, and of the relationship between authority and conscience. The whole Church will be immensely enriched by these developments (14).

The competent marriage counselor will also have his knowledge and skills enriched if he understands the various points presented here, unfortunately all too briefly.

CONSCIENCE, CONTRACEPTION, AND COUNSELING

The helping professions have traditionally propounded the principle of self-determination. According to this principle, only the exercise of the client's own resources in problem solving develops the ability for self-direction and self-dependence. Hence each man has the right to be "master of his own soul" and of his fate (15). An examination of the literature shows that little has been written on the subject of self-determination as it relates to conscience formation and birth control; yet, the counselor faces the task of examining the role he plays in the formation of the client's conscience, and needs to evaluate the influence he has upon conscientious decisions made by a client. Although it is generally accepted that the client's choice of religious tenets must be respected by the counselor, it must also be recognized that some counselors regard adherence to religious tenets as part of a neurotic complex which must be worked through by the client. This bias becomes even more marked when the tenet espoused by the client is not universally adhered to by most religions; as a result some counselors tend to belittle the client who contends that contraceptive birth control is immoral.

When the counselor is confronted by a religious conviction which is peculiar to a particular group (such as the view that birth control is immoral) he needs to reassess his own commitment to the concept of self-determination. The present authors have noted the tendency for many counselors to embrace the principle of self-determination when the client's moral values accord with those of the counselor; if, however, the client espouses different views, some counselors are likely to change the rules of the game and to proceed to help the client work through his "resistance, neurotic dependency, and compulsivity." If the "resistance" continues, the counselor may conclude that the client is untreatable. Although a particular principle may not hold true in all circumstances, in matters of faith and morals, the concept of self-determination should have equal validity even when the client's decision is incompatible with the counselor's personal belief-system.

It is as necessary to develop a cognizance of the theological concept of conscience as it is to understand the developmental notion of the superego. Such understanding permits the counselor to differentiate between a decision made in conscience and one which stems from neurotic conflict. Although a conscientious decision can be influenced by neurotic conflict, the counselor must fastidiously sort out for himself and help the client to distinguish between the conscientious and neurotic components of his decision. In order to make this distinction the counselor must differentiate between the developmental concept of superego and the theological concept of consicience. On the one hand, the supergo is an internalization of societal norms, on the other, in *Theology for Beginners,* Frank Sheed states that conscience is the soul's way of indicating that the laws according to which its Maker fashioned human nature are being followed or ignored. Man becomes aware of moral laws through analyzing his rational nature and through authentic doctrine, i.e. through the exercise of reason shored up by theological faith. Conscientious decisions are practical moral judgments of the intellect—the intellect's judgment upon the rightness and wrongness of our actions.

The preceding section suggested that a counselor cannot approach the birth control question in the simplistic fashion exhibited by those positioned at either end of the continuum. There are those who contend that the Church has spoken authoritatively, even if not infallibly, on the matter of contraception and that there is therefore no room for dissent. Others contend that Paul VI's statement on contraception is fallacious and does not bind the Catholic. The controversies surrounding the means of birth control only serve to intensify the interpersonal and intrapsychic conflicts the Catholic client brings to the counselor. Obviously, instead of positioning himself at either end of the pole, the counselor should familiarize himself with the concept of conscience-formation and the fundamental nature of the controversy over responsible family planning. Such a familiarization enables him to differentiate between a conscientious decision and one which is a manifestation of neurotic conflict and/or ignorance. He should be capable of identifying misinformation and be more finely attuned to the possibility of pastoral counseling.

If pastoral counseling is indicated, the counselor will obviously refer only to a theologically informed clergyman. The competent pastoral counselor employs those methods and skills which facilitate self-directed choices. He seeks to further the development of the virtue of counsel and ultimately of prudence. Pastoral counseling entails the development of psychological insight plus an explanation of external Christian truths and the unfathomable influence of God's Grace. The pastoral counselor provides information and guidance within the framework of a formal belief system. He helps his counselees clarify and redefine puzzling and misleading religious and moral involvement (16).

In addition to differentiating between an informed conscientious decision and having a cursory awareness of the birth control controversy, it is helpful for the counselor to be aware of a typology which aids in an effort to understand the meaning the birth control dilemma has to a particular client. For some, the birth control question is a theological problem and the accompanying stress does not bring them to the attention of a marriage counselor; for others, the psychological distress is paramount, and the theological debate exacerbates the emotional conflict.

The authors have delineated three general reactions to the birth control controversy on the part of Catholic clients. Some clients decide to practice birth control and do not express any conflict about their decision; others are unable to reach a decision and although they believe they must control fecundity, they are unable to disobey the official teaching of the Church; and still others believe that the practice of artificial birth control is immoral. The specific approach of the counselor depends upon the meaning birth control has for his particular client. One client may explain to the counselor that the official teaching of the Church presents no problem for him and that he can practice contraceptive birth control with no qualms of conscience. In one situation the counselor may find that the client has maturely and conscientiously arrived at this decision while in other situations the client's attitude may be suggestive of a reaction-formation. When the latter possibility is found to be operative, it is often noted that religion was pushed and rammed down the throat of the client by his parents; the rejection of the Church's teaching in one area is often characteristic of a general rebellion against a past which was manifested by a submissive resignation to a dogmatic and autocratic parental and/or religious authority. This selective rejection of the teaching of the Church is often indicative of a larger "kicking over of all traces" and suggests a general "junking" of the client's faith. The counselee may have also decided that the Pope should get out of the bedroom. As much as counselors may view the inability to reject certain religious tenets as part of a neurotic matrix, they must also allow for the possibility that the rejection of certain tenets is suggestive of underlying pathology.

Other than the possibility that the rejection of certain parts of the formal belief-system may be representative of a more complex problem, the counselor should consider the attitude of both the husband and the wife. Sometimes spouses maintain diametrically opposed views in relation to responsible family planning. Here the counselor must help a couple to clarify the nature of their differences and provide them with an opportunity to decide upon a way in which the differences may be resolved or how they can adapt to their different perspectives and beliefs. The present writers have observed marriages in which the husband imposes his conviction upon his wife. A husband may realize that his wife's fear of pregnancy interferes with a rewarding sexual adjustment; he rejects contraceptive birth control while refusing to practice any kind of sexual restraint. Other husbands impose contraception upon their wives and intimidate them until they consent to take the pill. This violation of a spouse's conscience has serious ramifications for the individual and for the marriage. The couple cannot achieve a meaningful relationship if one spouse runs roughshod over the convictions and feelings of the other. Violation of one's conscience instills a resentment of the oppressive spouse, and the repressed anger may be manifested in the form of psycho-physiological reactions, conversion reactions, and reaction-formations. Compelling a spouse to violate conscience can precipitate more serious consequences than the use of coercion in matters that do not involve conscience, faith and morals.

The phenomena described in this category are typified by the *A* couple who were both educated in Catholic schools, considered themselves "Catholic to the core," and had completed their professional training prior to marriage. They encountered myriad problems, including severe disagreement about birth control. The couple gave birth to six children during their first eight years of marriage. The sexual relationship was rather exploitative and instinctual; they were unable to tolerate an intimate interpersonal relationship.

Before the couple sought counseling, they had parsimoniously defined their problem as resulting from too many children in too many years. Mrs. *A* insisted that they practice contraceptive birth control, but the husband was convinced that contraception was intrinsically evil; and submission to the will of his wife resulted in impotence. When Mr. *A* insisted that they discontinue birth control, she became frigid and developed psycho-physiological skin reactions when he demanded intercourse. A combination of marriage counseling and pastoral counseling enabled this couple to identify and cope with the problems underlying their relationship. They developed an awareness of the Church's teaching about birth control, authority, and the meaning of a decision in conscience. With this dual approach, the couple was able to develop a moderately meaningful marital relationship.

Other clients recognize their need to control fecundity, have an awareness of the teaching of the Church, and feel they cannot disobey this teaching authority. They realize that the quality of their marital relationship is adversely affected by the fear of pregnancy; they suspect that additional children will precipitate further psychological stress. The couple's adherence to their religious faith, however, prevents them from pragmatically electing to contracept. It is helpful to operate on the theoretical assumption that prolongation of a state of indecision is more uncomfortable than resolution of the conflict. The conflict may revolve around the moral dilemma of contraception while the situational problems may be manifested by a fear of pregnancy and an assumed inability to cope with the parental demands that would be caused by additional children. The couple may conclude that contraceptive birth control is immoral. In this instance, resolution of the state of indecision does not resolve the situational problem. Nonetheless, the couple becomes able to deal more realistically with the overt fear of pregnancy and their lack of confidence in child-rearing. Resolution of the indecision enables them to adopt an effective coping mechanism.

This conflict situation is depicted by the *B* couple who are in their midtwenties; they had four children in five years and had practiced contraceptive birth control for two years prior to the writing of *Of Human Life*. They struggled with the decision to practice contraception. They believed that there was sufficient doubt about the immorality of contraception on the part of theologians to justify a personal decision in conscience. During the course of these two years they experienced marital satisfaction, the sexual relationship was very rewarding, and they were more satisfied with their performance of spousal and parental roles. Subsequent to the appearance of the Encyclical, they became markedly anxious about their earlier decision; they decided that they could not disobey the teaching authority of the Church. Since the practice of rhythm had been unsuccessful for them, they decided to refrain from intercourse until they could establish the menstrual cycle and be assured that rhythm could be practiced without fear of another pregnancy. The quality of the marital relationship deteriorated, as did the performance of their parental roles. They sought marriage counseling in order to explore how they could adjust to the reality of their situation. They expressed disagreement with the Encyclical and could not understand its reasoning. They experienced a crisis in faith. The counselor felt that the psychological distress was precipitated by the theological conflict and referred the couple to a pastoral counselor who explained to them the difference between infallible and fallible teaching, as well as the nature of an informed conscience. They decided that their earlier decision to contracept was valid; again they began the practice of contraception and regained their previously satisfactory adjustment to marital and parental roles.

Since most counselors believe that responsible parenthood may entail the practice of artificial contraception, this final category presents them with the greatest degree of professional conflict. The client may neither agree or disagree with the teaching of the Church, but is firmly convinced that the authority of the Church may not be violated. It is evident to the counselor that the children already born are receiving inadequate care, that additional children would provide another opportunity for psychological and/or physical neglect, and that the fear of pregnancy interferes with the attainment of a satisfying sexual adjustment. If the practitioner's personal value system is syntonic with that of the client, the professional conflict is reduced, and he seeks to help them to rediscover ways in which they can adjust to the reality of the conflict between their conscience and life circumstances.

The authors have already explained that a truly conscientious decision must be respected by the practitioner, but if the counselor believes that the client has not made a basic decision in conscience and is instead submitting blindly to a teaching authority, he is faced with the connundrum of determining to what extent he will seek to interfere with an area involving faith and morals. We are then brought to ask whether the counselor is justified in arousing the client's anxiety by questioning his thoughtless submission to authority and by encouraging him to recognize the way in which his life-circumstances are affected by this submission. The Catholic Church currently stresses information, inquisitiveness, and informed consent. With this in mind, the present writers contend that the counselor is justified in initially exploring the client's beliefs and information in order to determine whether he sees the possibility of exploring other options to the birth control dilemma. The last word on means of birth control has not been stated. Hence, the counselor may not go beyond suggesting to the client that not everyone would agree that his approach to family planning was responsible and that this is a matter which is being furiously debated within the Church. The practitioner should avoid instilling anxiety over a moral dilemma as diffuse as the birth control question.

If the client conscientiously chooses to follow the teaching authority of his Church, the counselor must seek to aid the client in his effort to find the coping mechanism that creates the least amount of dissonance between his conscience and his existential situation.

This type of client is typified by the *C* couple in their early thirties with seven children in ten years of marriage, after practicing rhythm with only a moderate degree of success. They believed that the fear of pregnancy interfered grossly with the quality of their sexual relationship and that tension surrounding the effort to practice rhythm complicated the satisfactory performance of their parental roles. They were conscientiously convinced that the teaching authority must not be disobeyed, nor did they feel it right to question this authority.

Since it was guilt-producing for them to look inquisitively at this teaching authority, the couple was referred to a physician skilled in teaching the rhythm technique. The physician helped them to establish an understanding of the Sympto-thermic Method, they in turn developed more confidence in this contraceptive technique, and with the aid of prolonged marital counseling, established a satisfactory marital relationship. For the *A* and *C* couple, birth control was only part of the problem, but as much as the authors realize that financial problems, unemployability, or physical handicaps are contributing complications which must be remedied, so must counselors help their clients to find a remedy to the birth control dilemma.

CONCLUSION

This chapter has demonstrated the obvious necessity for continued cooperation between theologians, philosophers, and practitioners in the mental health professions. Counselors must recognize the importance that religious tenets assume in the lives of their clients; they must be aware of the pervasive implications of a particular belief. The nature and function of authority and conscience, as well as the developmental concept of super-ego must be properly understood if the counselor is to treat the total person as involving spirituality, physiology, and emotionality.

REFERENCES

1. Noonan, John T.: *Contraception.* Cambridge, Harvard University Press, 1965. Also in paperback: A Mentor-Omega Book, New York, New American Library, 1967.
2. Himes, Norman: *Medical History of Contraception.* New York, Gamut Press, Inc., 1963. Noonan: *The History of Contraceptives,* prepared by Beryl Suitters, Librarian I.P.P.F., published by and for 8th Conference of the International Planned Parenthood Federation, Santiago, Chile, April 9-15, 1967.
3. For texts of the Papal Commission reports, Pope Paul's encyclical, pro-and-con responses from bishops, theologians, and the laity, see Robert Hoyt (Ed.), The *Birth Control Debate.* Kansas City, Mo., National Catholic Reporter, 1968. For Edward Schillebeeckx' theological evaluation of *Of Human Life,* see Birth Control and the Papacy. *Herder Correspondence,* V:259-265, Sept., 1968. For a medical scientist's evaluation, see André E. Hellegers, M.D., A scientist's problems with the birth control Encyclical. *U.S. Catholic. XXXIV*:6-11, April, 1969, also Hellegers, Critique of an Encyclical. *Medical Opinion and Review,* Jan. 1969, pp. 71-87.
4. *OSV Documentation Service for Priests.* Huntington, Ind., Our Sunday Visitor, Inc.,

1968, *II* (Nov.-Dec., 1968). See also Charles Curran (Ed.), *Contraception: Authority and Dissent*. New York, Herder and Herder, 1969.

5. *Studies in Family Planning*. No. 34, Oct., 1968, Roman Catholic fertility and family planning; A comparative review of the research literature. A publication of New York's Population Council. This publication has a thorough analysis of fertility studies and a complete, up-to-date bibliography of pertinent literature.

6. Desmond O'Grady Interviews Archbishop Hurley, Letter of law and lesson of life. *Tablet*, Feb. 15, 1969, p. 152. Talking to John Jay Hughes. *Catholic Bookseller and Librarian, II*:21, Jan.-Feb., 1969.

7. *The Constitution on the Church*, ch. 3, pr. 32. All Vatican II quotations from Walter M. Abbot (Ed.), *The Documents of Vatican II*, New York, America Press, 1966, Angelus Book. Also, Hans Küng, *The Church*, pp. 444-80. For a good, popular yet solidly theological treatise of authority, see John L. McKenzie, S.J., *Authority in the Church*. New York, Sheed and Ward, 1966.

8. *Coresponsibility in the Church*. New York, Herder and Herder, 1969, p. 85. In thinking about authority and decision-making in the post-Vatican II Catholic Church, it may help to make these distinctions: The *doctrine* of collegiality which gives the bishops a more prominent status and places the Pope more solidly in relation to them, and the *principle* of collegiality which extends even to the parish level—as a principle of coresponsibility.

9. *Constitution on the Church*. ch. 4, pr. 37.

10. *Pastoral Constitution on the Church in the Modern World*, ch. 3, pr. 33. Even more striking: "Therefore, if the influence of events or of the times has led to deficiencies in conduct, in Church discipline, or even in the formulation of doctrine (which must be carefully distinguished from the deposit itself of faith), these should be appropriately rectified at the proper moment. *Decree on Ecumenism*, ch. 2, pr. 6.

11. Swidler, Leonard: Historian proves new popes reverse former. *National Catholic Reporter*, Oct. 2, 1968, p. 17. Since this chapter was written, theologian Hans Küng has authored *Infallibility? An Inquiry*. New York, Doubleday, 1971.

12. *OSV Documentation Service for Priests*. Huntington, Indiana, Our Sunday Visitor, Inc., 1968.

13. *Right and Reason*. St. Louis, Mosby, 1967, p. 35.

14. The crisis seen in perspective. *Tablet*, Nov. 2, 1968, p. 1100.

15. Perlman, Helen Harris: *Social Case Work*. Chicago, University of Chicago Press, 1957, p. 60.

16. Hagmaier, George, and Gleason, Robert W.: *Counseling the Catholic*. New York, Sheed and Ward, 1969, p. 32; cf., St. Thomas Aquinas, *Summa Theologica*. II-II, pp. 47-56.

Chapter 34

THE MEANINGLESSNESS OF LIFE AS THE NEUROSIS OF THIS GENERATION

JOHN J. O'SULLIVAN

IT WAS ONE of those nights on the runway, when planes were backed up by the dozen and people were still uncertain about getting off and into the sky. Conversations started which might otherwise have been left unspoken. Even confidences were volunteered. He was saying: "I don't understand them." He meant his sons in college. They kept refusing to tell him what they intended to do with their lives. He had a son in high school from whom he was also blocked off. You know the type. He admitted to ulcers when he was thirty-five years old and said he was president of his company at forty. He could never admit such things at home because the denial of any personal problems is a status symbol. Then he spoke his conclusion. It is almost an axiom. "I suppose you could say that I have had two lives. In business I hit the top, in the family, I hit the bottom."

One loser in a first marriage provides a sad autobiography: "The idea that I might merely get married and continue the human race was not, in our household, given much attention. My father was all his life wistful about people who had had a chance to get more education that he had, and I was under a good deal of pressure to get high marks in school. When I got them, I became too promising a sprig to be heaved without a second thought into the cistern of domesticity. Marriage was not ruled out, but it was clearly secondary."

One graduate reflected: "I have been educated to be a successful man; now I must educate myself to be a successful woman." She had a classmate who noted that "they taught us to love everything except what we would have to do."

A senior critic of this society asks: "How should a man caught in this net of routine not forget that he is a man, a unique individual, one who is given only this one chance of living, with hopes and disappointments, with sorrow and fear, with the longing for love and the dread of the nothing and of separateness?" (1)

There is a saying that modern man wants nothing and needs no one. One wife rebutted this by saying: "I am not married, I am only alone with someone." Her neighbor spoke and said, "Really, I am not married. I am only undivorced."

In the Wall Street Journal, you might have read: "Growing Job Demands Shatter the Marriages of More Executives." It would be difficult to overestimate the sweep of such problems, many sources agree that they are almost epidemic in proportion. Some companies realize what is happening. "We're ruining a lot of families," confesses the top medical officer of a big Pittsburgh firm. The staff psychiatrist for one of the nation's largest manufacturers concurs, saying, "The situation is really rough, and it's getting worse" (2).

This is how it looks for a French philosopher: "Yet this period of crisis in which love is involved does not affect love alone. Every sector of our life is experiencing a similar disturbance. The crisis is universal. The modern world finds itself, so to speak, in a state of permanent revolution. Conduct, institutions, and ideals have lost any kind of stability. Not only are the foundations of the old order shaken, but the elements of a new order are called into question as soon as they are thought of. We are present, not at a series of births followed by unified development, but at a series of abortions" (3).

A widow writes: "I had not considered myself happy; now I see the power of the feeling that bound me to Jo. There had been no love between us for—perhaps twenty years; but there was that tacit and irreplaceable habit that binds even a couple like us, who got along only on the condition of remaining silent on the essential questions" (4).

These instances are significant because "there is little doubt that our attitudes toward marriage, stemming as they must from our attitudes toward life and living are crippling, if not fatal, to be central relationship in men's lives . . ."

"This is the more shattering because there is hardly any activity, any enterprise which is started with such tremendous hopes and expectations, and yet, which fails so regularly, as love."

A universe of 210 million persons is vast, with many variables, limiting any author to tentative conclusions. This is mine, modest enough to be sure. It is almost true to say that *the meaninglessness of life is the neurosis of this generation*. While all persons are not laid low with this ailment, the infection is widespread.

Those who counsel couples, before the marriage or in it, may find it helpful to be reminded that the ordinary American does not have an articulate philosophy of life. This may cause unsuspected resonances in some lives on every level of this society. What is offered to the therapist as a marriage-problem may be a life-problem.

There is a theory (to which this author subscribes) that teachers would serve their students better if they would turn the sharp critical edge of their minds to their own biases. Here are some of mine, insofar as they relate to this chapter. It is not true that one is young only once. Life is not short. Man is not only human.

Youth is a part of life; its experiences accompany one the rest of the way. What is missed may never be supplied. The mistakes of the young can be crippling. For those living in a culture of planned obsolescence, this may be hard to admit.

Life is not short. It lasts forever and it has already begun. The best of people have argued that all the way to heaven is heaven. The Greeks reported that happiness was unregretted pleasure. Roues have confessed that all the way to hell is hell.

While a man is human, clearly he is something more and philosophies differ at this point. There is in him a touch of the immortal, a spark of the divine. How else account for the fact that every heart has its ache and every roof has its sorrow?

This can be made more specific. "Personal life is at a discount today. People work keenly, putting everything into their work, but many complain that their personal life is barren . . . it almost seems that work has come to have a value that is unreal and we take it as a drug, exciting and deadening . . . the relation between the child and the mother is the steady center on which the child's later development is based . . . only a close living relationship teaches the child loyalty to one person, thus giving it a sense of value in itself and in another and assuring it that a shared standard is worth serving even at the cost of suffering. Without this basis of human trust built up between a mother and a child, the child has no feeling that can be appealed to. It is also incapable of abstract thought, as only immediate gain satisfies its unappeased need, and no long-term meaning will be given heed."

Under another heading, there is the nine-year old girl who asked her father: "Daddy, why am I living?" He was the editor of a famous magazine with the notable fellow citizens as his intimates. To them sped his letter for their answers which could and did make a revealing article. He was urgent: "We cannot let this little girl down." Save for three or maybe four responses, there was little or no help in their thought about her question. Whether the father knew it or not, he had been answering it for nine years or more.

Harvey Swados wrote an indictment of this society a decade and a half before the campus explosions, riots, and revolutions of 1968-1969. He did this by studying their spring vacations around the southern beaches of this fair land. ". . . Thousands of college students have battled police, not for the dignity of their fellow men or the inviolability of human life, but for their own inalienable rights to invade these beach areas during their vacations, to carouse, to neck en masse, to litter the ground with the beer cans that are the vessel for their ambition, their esthetic sensibility, their rebellion . . . as long as it is possible for thousands of young people to call themselves students, and to demonstrate to the world that they have nothing more important to do with their time, nothing more important to do with their lives than to foregather for weeks on end at public playgrounds—for just that long *this society* will stand condemned as one which gives American youth everything except *a reason for living* and for *building a socially useful life"* (5).

This still seems to be true and the result is a foregone conclusion. Listening to complaints and studying those who make them, one can establish certain theories.

"Those who complain the loudest of the emptiness of their lives are usually people whose lives are overcrowded, filled with trivial details, plans, desires, ambitions, unsatisfied cravings for passing pleasures, doubts, anxieties and fears; and these sometimes further overlaid with exhausting pleasures which are an attempt, and always a futile attempt, to forget how pointless such people's lives are."

Man is a reflective animal, even believed by some to be rational, at times. In his literature, wherever and whenever written, there have been intimations that life was tragic, its burdens, heavy, and its meaning not always clear.

In the Old Testament, there is a literary form called the book of Job. There you can study an effort to come to terms with sufferings experienced with the just man. For this sorely tried man, "The life of man on earth is a warfare."

The student of the classics can match many lapidary gems of style revealing the bitterness that man experiences when he sees his life slipping away at ever increasing speed. *Carpe diem* (enjoy the day) directed Horace. What you identify as the pagan burial epitaphs, reveal this angst again and again.

> Do not laugh stranger, You will come here by and by.
> What you are, I was.
> What I am, you will be.
> I lived as I please.
> Why I die, I know not.

Much nearer our own time, Thoreau described the fact that all men lead lives of quiet frustration.

If art is holding a mirror up to life, one cannot like what he sees in the images of the theatre. From drama we learn what life is like for Tennessee Williams.

"There is a horror in things, a horror at the heart of the meaninglessness of existence. Some people cling to a certain philosophy that is handed down to them and which they accept. Life has a meaning if you are bucking for heaven. But if heaven is a fantasy, we are in this jungle with whatever we can work out for ourselves. It seems to me that the cards are stacked against us. The only victory is how one takes it . . ."

Walter Kerr, in *The Decline of Pleasure,* speaks of the images to be found in the theatre regarding sex and love. He begins with the following observation:

> One of the most disappointing things about the human condition is that the pleasures of the flesh offer no real antidote to the distresses of the mind. . . sensuality can provide him with a brief nirvana. . . but it cannot nourish what it tends, temporarily to obliterate.
>
> In a practical sense this should be clear enough to us from the fact that we live in an age that is highly permissive in sexual matters . . . but also conscious of its intellectual unrest. . . but the fleshpots, even when they are visited and not just yearned for, seem to brew very little in the way of sustained contentment; they give rise, rather surprisingly, to a fury. The most disenchanted face one sees in the newspapers is the face of the playboy who ought, by the standard enunciated in all of those commercial invitations, to have had the most fun.
>
> . . . we do lay some claim, in this century, to being relatively healthy in our attitudes toward sex. We do not hide it. . . We do not find sex embarrassing. . . We have been understandably eager to free our art forms from the artificial silences imposed by Victorianism. We have freed them But the reflection is most strange. What do our novels and our plays show back to us? Almost without exception an image of sex that is violent, frustrated, shabby, furtive, degraded, treacherous, and, more and more, aberrant.
>
> For the most part, as we spy upon sex we seem to be spying upon failure. . . Dante and Hell itself a more comforting place than this.

Ingmar Bergman is the cinema director who has turned his camera on our generation and come up with startling episodes. He explains a little of what goes on in the theatre or on the movie set in these lines. In explaining, he contrasts what was and what is.

> Today the individual has become the highest form and the greatest bane of artistic creation. The smallest wound or pain of the ego is examined under a microscope as if it were of eternal importance. The artist considers his isolation, his subjectivity, his individualism almost holy. Thus we finally gather in one large pen, where we stand and bleat about our loneliness without listening to each other and without realizing that we are smothering each other to death. The individualists stare into each other's eyes and yet deny the existence of each other. We walk in circles, so limited by our own anxieties that we can no longer distinguish between true and false, between the gangster's whim and the purest ideal (7).

From literature, there is a similar revelation. Camus is much read, widely discussed. It is clear that his philosophy had some constants but it is suggestive of the *absurd*.

For Camus in *The Fall,* the whole book is a bitter meditation on the worthlessness of man. In *The Stranger* (better understood as *The Outsider*)

Camus presents the idea of the *absurd*. "The meaning of the title is rather that all the circumstances of everyday living seem pointless or slightly foreign to him . . . He has no ambition, because there is no point in getting on in a world which is pointless . . . The lesson is that society has applied its meaningless conventions to someone who was, in any case, half paralyzed by the meaninglessness of existence" . . .

Allow your author one for the road before we begin our trek in the direction of some resolution of all this. "It's the whirling round of activities," complains one wife, "it's the many things that we do together that keep us from being together. I love all the entertaining we must do, but sometimes I can't help longing for the old days when we had lots of time alone with each other to ramble on about everything in the world. Now sometimes weeks go by without our having a real talk."

The woman, whatever her age, belongs to a large sorority. Perhaps there are ideas which can be shared and possibilities which may be held out to well-meaning partners like these.

Here are the members of the panel on whom the author will draw for clues to the bewildering confusion that surrounds us. Allow me to begin with John W. Gardner whose statements regularly make good sense.

"The present age is the first one in which large segments of the population have imagined that man might do without such a highly personal sense of the meaning of his life.

"And for a breath-taking moment, it did seem possible, in view of the glittering promises with which modern life offered to distract man's attention. Science was to cure his ills. The new technologies would conquer the physical environment for him. The new political philosophies would dissolve the social hierarchy and make every man a king. The destruction of old and unnecessarily rigid moralities would give him a healthier and freer life of the senses. In short, he would have security, opportunity, money, power, sensual gratification, and status as high as any man. He would be a solvent and eupeptic Walter Mitty in a rich and meaningless world.

"Comfort isn't enough . . . we need a sense of identity, enduring emotional ties to others, a vision of what is worth striving for. Most of all we need a system of values that we consider worthy of our allegiance (even if it is subject to revision) " (8).

And now Rollo May whose reflection complements the thought of Mr. Gardner.

Rollo May gives his explanation of what is happening in this time of crisis and revolution. In his judgment, our myths are disintegrating. "A myth is not a falsehood or necessarily a story . . . it's a description of a pattern of life arising out of the unconscious that carries the values for a society and gives a person the ability to handle anxiety, to face death, and to deal with guilt. It gives him an anxiety." You could say that, for many persons, the supporting props for a man's assumptions about life have been jarred, if not overturned.

Here is an author who confesses that, "I am much concerned with our national character in a culture increasingly feeling the effects of almost 150 years of lopsided preoccupation with amassing wealth and raising its standard of living. This may be somewhat less than it was when Tocqueville visited us in 1831, but it still constitutes a focus of such enormous interest that it raises the question, *"What had our great concern with raising our standard of living done to us?"*

"The fear of becoming obsolete is so powerful that the sense of being useless is *a common element in emotional crisis in America.* However this fear is rooted not only in the fear of obsolescence, but also in an industrial system that obliges too many people to do what they have so little interest in doing. In this respect America's industrial progress has made many people spiritually useless to themselves" (9).

Erickson contributes this thought about the human person and how he should function.

> Freud was once asked what he thought a normal person should be able to do well. The questioner probably expected a complicated, 'deep' answer. But Freud simply said, "lieben und arbeiten," ("to love and to work"). It pays to ponder on this simple formula; it grows deeper as you think about it. For when Freud said "love," he meant the generosity of intimacy as well as genital love; when he said love and work, he meant a general work productiveness which would not preoccupy the individual to the extent that he might lose his right or capacity to be a sexual and a loving being.
>
> Love as mutual devotion, however, overcomes the antagonisms inherent in sexual and functional polarization, and is the vital strength of young adulthood (10).

Victor Frankl has confidence in man. His own experiences under the worst possible conditions make his witnessing of special value.

> A human being is not one thing among others; things determine each other, but man is ultimately self-determining. What he becomes, within the limits of endowment and environment, he has made out of himself. Man has both potentialities (to be a saint or to act like swine) within himself; which one is actualized depends on decisions but not on conditions.
>
> Frankl distinguishes several *forms of neurosis,* and traces some of them to the failure of the sufferer to find meaning and a sense of responsibility in his existence (11).

It seems only a few years since Thornton Wilder wrote his work *The Skin of Our Teeth* which he meant as a love letter to the human family. However new the world may be, the human family remains the same, surviving just barely. The costumes change but the same actors and actresses wear them.

Man might have created a utopia but the elements that make life worth living seem to be lacking. The new man needs what man has always needed —some guarantees, some assurances, some granite foundations for his air castles.

Should this society have a debased conception of man, he is still a little less than the angels. There are in the human person three hungers: the hunger for meaning, the hunger for love, and hunger for creative craftsmanship.

> By feeding these hungers—or trying his best to do so—man can arrive at life of a sort that makes sense in spite of the frustration that ends every human career, in spite of death that comes surely, swiftly.
> . . . Every man asks, "Why?" constantly, wonders not only about the whyness of the world but also about the whyness of himself.
> . . . The hunger for love, that sort of love in the name of which men have dreamed great dreams, written poems, done heroic deeds, found consuming joy, . . .love which is the greater the more one has within oneself to give. By virtue of it the strong pours himself out for the week; the wise for the foolish; the good for the wicked. If deprived of the opportunity to develop and exercise such love, man crawls through life with hidden shame, making excuses to himself, rationalizing his failure.
> The hunger for creative craftsmanship. Unless man is prevented and thwarted he is always an artist. He is not satisfied inside himself unless he tries to do what is at hand and to do it as well as he can. . . Man has creative hunger (12).

There are therapists who believe that their clients have advanced and grown to the point that they can introduce them into reality. Hannah Green has such a paragraph which has given the title to her well-known book:

"Look here, I never promised you a rose garden. I never promised you perfect justice . . . and I never promised you peace or happiness. My help is that you can be free to fight for all of these things. The only reality that I offer is challenge and being well is being free to accept it or not at whatever level you are capable. I never promise lies and the rose garden world of perfection is a lie and a bore too" (13).

There are no perfect marriages because there are no perfect persons. The illusion that one can marry, and live happily ever after, dies hard. This is why we can reflect that "to live is to accept suffering. Its acceptance depends on some understanding of its hidden meaning—often seeing it as a guide toward potential growth. Suffering gives direction to one's freedom."

Who was it that noted, "unfortunately we are enormously clever about avoiding self-examination"? He would agree with the emphasis here that marriage "will not just serve the individual but give him an opportunity to serve. When people are serving, life is no longer meaningless; they no longer feel rootless. Without allegiance and commitment, individual freedom degenerates into sterile self-preoccupation."

The greatest treasure that anyone can have in this world is the undivided love of another person. In theory, this jewel lies within the competence of almost any married couple. Unfortunately, real life does not always correspond to the possibilities. It is a rare partner who has not suffered some degree of emotional crippling.

What does one offer a partner locked in a relationship which is far from ideal? Two facts apply to the situation. The first is self-evident. Ordinarily no one of us can *make* another do anything. But the situation does not stand as hopeless. There is an alternative, grim enough that one might hesitate to make the attempt without encouragement. One can change oneself vis-à-vis *one's partner*. Again and again a partner discovers that the spouse changes because of this act of faith.

In some marriages it may be possible to offer help with this magnificent insight.

> It is the rarest experience of our lifetime that we meet a man or a woman who literally drives us to the realization of what we really are and can really do when we do our best. What we all most need in our careers is the one who can liberate within us that life-long prisoner whose doom it is to remain a captive until another sets it free—our best. . . for we can never set our best free by our own hands; that must be always done by another.

Long ago Augustine of Hippo observed that there is some fatal flaw in man that prevents him from prizing a thing until he has lost it. Perhaps the final counsel should be this: Think of how many ancestors survived how many dangers to hand on this good gift of life.

Those who are able to be or to become successful in their marriages are those who find meaning in their lives.

REFERENCES

1. Fromm, Erich: *The Art of Loving.* New York, Harper & Brothers, 1956, p. 17.
2. *Wallstreet Journal,* May 3 or 10, 1967, p. 1.
3. Thibon, Gustave: *Love at the Crossroads.* London, Burns & Oates, 1964, pp. 43-44.
4. Gennari, Genevieve: *The Other Woman I Am.* New York, David McKay Company, Inc., 1961, p. 5.
5. Swados, Harvey: *A Radical's America.* Boston, Little, Brown & Company, 1962, p. 257.
6. Kerr, Walter: *The Decline of Pleasure.* New York, Simon & Schuster, 1962, pp. 304-305, 306-308.
7. *Four Screen Plays of Ingmar Bergman.* New York, Simon & Schuster, 1965, p. xxii.
8. Gardner, John W.: *No Easy Victories.* New York, Harper & Row, 1968, pp. 114-115.
9. Henry, Jules: *Culture Against Man.* New York, Random House, 1963, pp. 4-5, 24.
10. Erickson, Erik H.: *Youth and Crisis.* New York, W. W. Norton & Company, Inc., 1968, pp. 136-137.
11. Frankl, Viktor E.: *Man in Search for Meaning.* New York, Washington, Square Press, Inc., pp. 214 and IX.

12. Bell, Bernard Iddings: *Crisis in Education*. New York, McGraw-Hill Book Company, Inc., 1949, pp. 156-157.
13. Green, Hannah: *I Never Promised You a Rose Garden*. New York, The New American Library, 1964, p. 106 .

Chapter 35

SPIRITUAL VALUES IN MARRIAGE COUNSELING

LELAND FOSTER WOOD

MARRIAGE is largely a matter of attitudes. What we call spiritual is also: how we feel toward the sum total of things, how we feel toward our fellow men, how we feel toward those with whom we are bound together in the family. Attitudes are related to values. There are some attitudes such as kindness, love, forgiveness, and unselfishness, which are mainly not of the body but of the spirit. The spiritual is not independent of the biological and cultural, but transcends them, as a symphony transcends the notes that express it or a picture transcends the colors that make it up. Man is concerned with values as well as facts, and he is one who has come to a high degree of ability to appreciate values and to share them with others.

Marriage has problems, of course, as well as values, but it is not to be thought of as a rash of problems, or a series of question marks, rather as an accumulation of plus signs, a splendid creative undertaking in which people need to invest all that they have and all that they are, and together should receive dividends enriching what they are and what they can be.

In marriage counseling it is increasingly recognized that spiritual considerations need to be taken into the account as well as biological, psychological, economic, or sociological ones.

In his book, *Counseling in the United States,* a report of a three-year study, supported by the Walter E. Meyer Research Institute and published in 1967, Harrop A. Freeman says that people with religious affiliation come for counseling more freely than the general public, and that a clergyman is most often the first one sought. He says, "The counselees brought problems in this order of importance: marital-sexual, values, interpersonal. They sought and got reassurance, tolerance, forgiveness, a new perspective. They were aware that many clergy are now psychologically sophisticated." He finds it significant that ministers are especially close to marriage, and that they help people not only in the solving of particular problems, but in gaining a new perspective on marriage and on life.

Edward S. Bordin notes that religious beliefs are often an intimate part of the personality, and that warmth is a therapeutic ingredient, with desire to help and to understand. This, of course, would apply to any counselor, whatever the profession.

In many communities ministers, physicians, psychiatrists, and others are working together in an interdisciplinary way. In some cases ministers and physicians are involved by the very nature of the situation, as in case of death in a family. The fact that a doctor's contribution is primarily medical, does not mean that it may not also have a spiritual value. Good care of a doctor is a great comfort and his words also may be, but in the matter of giving comfort when a marriage is broken by death, not even the doctor is as close as the minister to the family. The first thing needed will then be comfort, and this means much to a bereaved person, but counseling also may be needed to help the person make drastic changes in the program of living. To supplement his comfort the minister may use such a book as *You and Your Grief* by Edgar N. Jackson.

PERSPECTIVE

Edward S. Bordin *(Psychological Counseling)* says, "Fundamental to good emotional health is a basic philosophy of faith: faith in the ability of ourselves and others to improve and grow; faith in the desire and capacity of human beings to work out problems cooperatively; faith in spiritual and moral values, and in the essential decency of mankind. This faith will carry us through stresses that might otherwise shatter us."

People need a sense of meaning for life and zest in their life together. They need to make their family living a part of the healing of the world, rather than its sickness, and when they encounter evil, to overcome it with good. As the idea of reverence for life has wide appeal, even more should the idea of sacredness of persons in the family. As such they should not be treated as married people sometimes treat each other. Feeling this the counselor will want to influence husbands and wives not to belittle each other, or attack each other, but rather to protect each other's self-respect, a precious thing which each has entrusted to the other.

FAMILY PLANNING

Something of this idea of the sacredness of persons should extend to family planning. Beyond questions of health and support, family planning is a matter of bringing new persons into the world, and training them to be workers for the good of mankind, not only as added members of the little group, but new forces for the betterment of the world. Somebody new to share our family love, and somebody added to bring good to others, this is the inspiring view which counselors can give parents, while physicians and clinics take care of the medical part.

According to the faith of many modern men and women we are not only products of evolution but children of God, in whom, "we live and move and have our being." It is true also that we live and move and have our being in our family relationships. Since the family is a manifestation of the spirit of man and woman, it will share their faults and their excellences, so the spirit of it may be sick or well. Its loving may be a joy and strength, or its hating may be pain and frustration. Such attitudes are not only consciously felt, but they also spread themselves in the unconscious, as in the case of a young wife, who said of her husband, "It hurts me even to have him touch me." This did not make sense in a bodily way, but it had to be taken into consideration.

Not uncommon are swings of ambivalence, bringing forth flashes of antagonism even in a loving relationship. An eruption of such feelings may terrify young married people with the thought that their good marriage is in danger. With anger, as with other poisons, there is, no doubt, a certain tolerance level which may vary with different couples, but it is to be held in suspicion.

It has been found by experiment that if an angry man breathes into a test tube, there is a brownish deposit on the sides, which, if scraped off and administered to mice, will kill them. Such breath of anger is not likely to do marriage any good, but kind and patient words, with pleasant looks and agreeable tones have often been found to lead toward reconciliation. In fact they will go far toward preventing any need of it, but without kindness a home is turned into a doghouse, as Peter Bertocci has said.

As a neurosis is a state of being at war within oneself, so continued conflict may be a sign that there is illness in the expanded self of the marriage, and the people may need help, as Carl G. Jung has said. "Man has always stood in need of spiritual help." He follows with words often quoted that of all his patients over thirty-five years of age, during many years, "there was not one whose problem, in the last resort, was not that of finding a religious outlook on life . . . and none of them has been really healed who did not regain his religious outlook." Many sincerely religious people, however, have not given enough attention to the fruit of the Spirit, which is "love, joy, peace, patience, kindness, goodness, faithfulness, gentleness, and self-control." Without these a marriage may become like a boat without a rudder on a storm-tossed sea.

The importance of spiritual factors in counseling is emphasized by the remarkable success of the so-called IRT approach: Integrity, Responsibility, Transparency.

In the marirage ceremony we say: "What God has joined together let no man put asunder." This is a continuing process, for we recognize that even God, in joining a man and woman firmly together, needs their loyal cooperation. "Do I not know that this is love, the offering and receiving of the warm wonder of spiritual greatness?"

PREMARITAL COUNSELING

Much help can come to a couple through counseling before they start their life voyage together. This has increasingly become standard procedure with up-to-date ministers, some of whom have as many as ten sessions, making use of books and check lists. The central question is whether these two have reason to believe that they can develop a fellowship worthy of perpetuating through a lifetime, "for better or for worse, for richer or for poorer, in sickness and in health." A valuable part of such counseling is to go through the marriage ceremony together, not as if in rehearsal, but in depth.

A young woman of good mind, fine family, and pleasing appearance had some misgivings about her engagement. The young man, a handsome person, who did things to her emotions, she said, was nevertheless a school drop-out and one whose job record was precarious. As he was then in the Navy and had a leave coming, he was insistent that they be married during this leave, while she, on her part, had begun to doubt whether she wanted to marry him at all. She hesitated to break their engagement, hoping to do it in some way that would hurt him least. The counselor felt free to look at the whole situation with her, not offering any definite advice but hoping to help her come to the best decision for her.

At that point there came into the picture another young man, who seemed as well suited to her as the other was ill-suited. She wondered whether it would be right to have a growing friendship with this young man while still engaged to the other. It was not long, however, before she was fully convinced that she must break her engagement to the first. She did so, and soon became engaged to the second. With her new fiancee she entered in time into an unusually fine marriage.

A counselor is often needed by mothers and fathers of young people making these great decisions. In one family the parents were disturbed about a daughter of twenty-two who had been active in interracial work and had become engaged to a black man. They feared that such a marriage would not work out well for any of them, or for children who might come. The daughter said that she could appreciate the concern of her father and mother, but that there were two sides to the question and she had chosen the other side. With the girl I tried to look at the matter from the standpoint of the parents, and, with them, to see it as their daughter did; hoping to help them all to move forward into the future with unimpaired love and confidence. The young people married, as they were determined to do, and their experiences, whatever they may be, are mainly ahead of them. In any case the counselor looks at the cultural background of the two and tries to help them draw on the best in both families for the building of a rich life of their own.

GOOD MARRIAGES CAN STAY ON A HIGH LEVEL

Abounding love is a fountain of life that need never run dry. In it are healing and renewal, and the stream of it flows over impediments along its way. If there are things that offend, on occasion, in one spouse, there will almost certainly be such things in the other, and both will need a love that will accept imperfections on both sides, with a joyous awareness of mutual excellences.

The Aldens had an unusually fine marriage, but the time came when they felt a lessening closeness and faced the problem together. When they came to me they did not indicate any specific trouble, and I did not press them. We took a careful look at their situation, going back to their childhood homes, their courtship, the establishment of their new home, the coming and growth of their children and the things they liked about each other —not overlooking their sex life, their financial cooperation, their relation to friends and in-laws, and their religious life in home and church. There was certainly no anemia in their marriage, but they wanted it to be full-blooded and growing. The outcome was that they felt much better, and invited me to have dinner in their home as a kind of graduation event for the completion of our sessions together. A message received at the following Christmas time said, "We think of you often and reread your books more than you know." So I was pleased to notice how face to face counseling and printed words can reinforce each other.

Such a couple might be compared with a person who feels quite well yet goes to his doctor for a check-up; and we hope the time will come when people will be more health-conscious about their marriages, so that such a thing will not seem so unusual. Hopefully the change from a sickness emphasis to one of health will come more and more.

THE SEX RELATIONSHIP

There are those who think that marriage is mainly a social device to make the sex relationship legitimate, sex being the end and marriage the means of reaching it. There was a time when the idea was spread abroad that if a husband and wife could achieve mutual sexual fulfillment, the rest of the marriage would take care of itself. There are still those who discuss marriage as if it were mostly a matter of night life, an idea that is not so much false as one-sided and inadequate. People are married for the days as well as the nights. The married pair are not merely two organisms, but two persons involved in with the whole of living. The sexual life of husbands and wives who admire each other, trust each other, and in their daily lives stimulate, reinforce, and complete each other, becomes incomparably more meaningful than a mere sexual encounter.

Their lives as persons become a structure of experience and fulfillment, of which their sex life can then be a symbol and expression. It is a token of their love, their trust, their belongingness, and their fulfillment in each other. A counselor may help couples to know that a good sex life is a part of the excellence of a good marriage, and the use of books is hopeful. But marriage as a whole is essentially a personal artistry in which the material is the substance of daily living. Sometimes a problem which seems to start as a sexual one is really connected with the psychological and spiritual aspects of life as well as the physical ones, so that facts and techniques of sex do not meet their situation. Often beneath the problem brought to him the counselor will find a deeper one.

Monogamy is not merely one-to-one relationship but a matter of the whole person with another whole person. I once met a man who was said to have fifteen hundred wives. In such a case, I suppose, a wife would have one fifteen-hundredth of a husband. Even with monogamy supported by law, a counselor may, on occasion, encounter a woman who has only a fraction of a husband, or a man who has only a fraction of a wife. Such people are fortunate if they can grow from half-heartedness to whole-hearted devotion.

In one case a wife, intelligent and attractive, with a big and impressive husband, felt that he was very careless in his treatment of her, except when he wanted sexual privileges; so she began to use sexual aloofness as a way of punishing him. Since he was being punished, he thought he would punish her also, so he told her that he was finding elsewhere what she was denying him at home. Their case is still a difficult one, but the counseling effort is, of course, to show each of them that sex is not to be had as a form of selfishness, but as a gift to be used with tender regard for the other.

MONEY IN MARRIAGE

To the counselor there come people who have carried over into marriage the habits of making final decisions about the use of money that they had as single persons. A man was making a good income, and using it freely on golf, while his wife had trouble in getting enough for household expenses. As a way of helping her to overcome her bitterness, and him to grow out of his immature attitude, I went with them into the history of their spending habits. He had been brought up in a well-to-do family of free spenders. She had come from one in which the income was used in a careful way and with great mutual consideration. She needed to realize that his spending was a life-long habit with him, and was not a proof of meanness so much as of thoughtlessness and immaturity. In the end she blamed him less and he was willing to sit down and work out a budget that would be fair to all of them, so that the use of money would not be a root of bitterness, but a means of showing their love for one another.

Money, like other things, needs to be related to the main objectives of family living, and the frustrations from its careless use can be greatly reduced. This is true also of careless spending in which a husband and wife may share equally in taking on so many installment payments that they are always in trouble. The counselor can help people plan a budget so that they can make both ends meet, and he can direct them toward help in setting up an insurance and savings program for great goals such as owning a home and providing for the education of children.

DIFFERENCES

No two people are alike, and people need to accept their differences gladly and for mutual benefit. One form of difference which the counselor meets is that between the extroverted person and the introverted one. The introvert, in the presence of a problem, tends to sit down and think about it, while the extrovert says, "Let's do something about this." Because of different ways of feeling, the extrovert and the introvert may be a strain on each other.

A woman came to me whom I soon assumed to be a very introverted person. When she told me something about her husband, I concluded that he was the opposite. Both were definitely religious. She had come to me, she said, because she was beginning to feel that she was no longer in love with her husband. She did not want him to know that she had any such problem, but she felt that she was in love with another man in their church. Her husband, she said, belonged to the worldly wing of the church, while she felt that she belonged to the more spiritual one.

Another difficulty was that they often disagreed in their ideas about guiding the children. She believed that strictness was needed and that he was so lax that it was bad for them. When they wanted something which was not immediately available, her view of discipline made her feel that they ought to learn to go without; but he would go far to get for them whatever they wanted. At the same time she felt that what she called his materialistic point of view would mislead the children as to the real values in life.

Meanwhile there was this other man. She was not closely acquainted with him, and did not know how he would feel toward her, but she felt when she heard him speak in church that there was a kinship of mind and spirit between them. She daydreamed about being free from her husband and being married to this man. In view of such feelings she wondered if it would be right to seek a divorce.

In response to my request that she tell me more about her feelings toward her husband, she said that she had nothing in particular against him, but that she wanted a fully happy life, and did not feel that she was having it with him. With the other she could have more harmonious times in the home, and could share more happily in the spiritual life of the church.

When I asked her if she felt that her husband had no real religious life, she said that he had, but that his kind did not mean much to her. "Well, what is the best you can say about his religion? I asked. She answered, "He will go out of his way to do things for people in need; people come to him for help and advice, and everybody has confidence in him." His religion, it seemed, was as sincere as hers, but he took it in an extroverted way: "Be doers of the word, and not hearers only."

Each had the potential of being a valuable mate to the other, and each was needed in caring for the children. The woman, attractive and intelligent in her way, needed a more practical person as husband. Her religion did help her in the end, for when she was faced with the question whether she would feel right about divorcing such a good man and separating him from his own children, she drew back from this. She had not seen clearly in detail where her daydreams were leading. In the course of our sessions she became more aware of what a good husband she had, responding also to the idea of learning to be the best kind of wife, and, with him, providing a good home for their children, who of course needed emotional security and a good parental example.

In the end she felt grateful that she had been helped to see her whole situation in clearer light, and that at last she realized that love is not so much an area of daydreaming as a way of living. She came also to feel that she could be closer to God in cherishing the sacredness of her family ties and making the most of them. The question, "Do I have the right person in marriage," can usually be changed with great profit to the question, "Am I being the right kind of person in marriage?"

Many a husband or wife who is asking, "Am I as happy in marriage as I deserve to be?" could be enormously benefited by being brought to change this into the question, "Am I giving in marriage as much happiness as I possibly can, and as much as my mate deserves, who after all, bet his life that I would be the best kind of companion?"

The neurotic person makes intolerant demands for perfection of the other: "Woe unto you if you are not perfect." Spiritual growth lessens this demand for perfection in the other!"

HOW PRAYERS MAY HELP

The wish to do right in spite of differences of feeling helped another couple who had a long history of good living, and an honored place in their church. Their daughter, then in her twenties, had become a bone of contention between them because she did not take her work very seriously at home or in her place of employment. Her mother believed that they should insist more strongly that she meet her full responsibilities and this seemed reasonable in its way, but the father felt that responsibility comes, not by nagging, but by growth in an atmosphere of love and kindness.

Along with the domestic strain that they were experiencing, their sex life, which might have been a strong and pleasing factor in binding them together, was suffering. When the wife had used sexual refusal as a way of getting back at him for his opposition to her methods in the home, he had come back by insinuating that she was interested in another man. This enraged her and each had come to a state of being unhappy with the other, but because of their aversion to the idea of divorce, and equally because of their place in church and community, they wanted to resolve their difficulties, if possible.

At our second session the man brought out a written prayer, in which he expressed the desire that they might do right toward each other and renew a good life together with God's help. At first she scoffed and said that if he really meant it he would show more concern for her feelings. When he replied that some of her demands were unreasonable, this led to such an explosion that it looked as if the marriage were falling apart right there, as they reverted to their habit of bitter words to each other. I tried to convince them that tongues are not for wounding but for healing, and so we continued with the counseling session.

The woman at last became more convinced of her husband's sincerity, and when we closed the session they gladly stood with me in a little circle, while I offered my prayer for them. For a couple to see their problems as in God's sight, and to feel themselves surrounded by a divine love often melts away the bitterness which they have felt. When they talk kindly and with mutual respect they are likely to make progress, and the counselor can help them in this.

By themselves they continued to work toward an understanding and presently reported that they were getting along better. So they went on together, and continued to be a credit in their large and highly honored kinship circle, while their minister was grateful to me for saving one of his outstanding families. It seemed that it was easier for them to come to me, a person with whom they did not expect to continue in a close relationship, than to their own minister.

Incidentally, such a case illustrates the way in which the social fabric and scaffolding of a family can uphold a couple in a precarious situation till they gain more security in themselves. The counselor is fortunate if he can get a couple into a group of couples in a church, who will be able to give one another their mutual support.

HOW PEOPLE CHANGE

A woman asked me with intense earnestness, "Can people change?" The background of it was that her husband had been unfaithful and had left her for a time. Now he wanted to come back, yet in her family there were those who urged her not to let him come. "He will never change," they said. She still loved him, she told me, and wanted him very much, as did the children. She feared that she would never feel right if she did not let him come. Naturally I said to her, "People can change, but I do not know whether this particular man will change as you hope he will."

Some feel that any sexual disloyalty creates a final break, and should lead to divorce, but that may be far from true. In such a case the injured spouse may be partly to blame, and there may yet be better possibilities for them both. Loyalty is of the essence, but so also is forgiveness. God himself sets the example in this, "As far as the east is from the west, so far does He remove our transgressions from us."

She may yet prove right or wrong in taking him back, but let us look at her question in a more general way. Probably we have all seen changes in people. John Dewey said that people change because of a reorganization of impulses around a new center. How good to organize them around the will to create an unusually fine marriage! The apostle Paul said more when he said, "If anyone is in Christ he is a new creature." The counselor believes that people can change and grow so that good marriages may become better, and some that have started to fail may be brought back to success.

RELIGION A DYNAMIC FOR IMPROVEMENT

"Conversion was once almost exclusively a matter of religious emphasis; now it is a daily problem of psychiatrists." Paul Tournier, eminent Swiss psychiatrist, tells of a surgeon whose wife felt so starved for love and attention that this was affecting her health. Tournier advised the husband to give her more of his company and to take her out at least once each week. This started them on in a better direction, and she began to improve, but it was not enough. "Then," Tournier says, "He received Christ as master of his life. Immediately he began to listen to his wife in a quite different spirit . . . He realized that while he was leading a most thrilling life at the hospital, performing operations, saving lives, doing research, writing for medical journals . . . his wife back home was dying of emotional starvation. And he had been blind to it all." He goes on to say, "Psychology may thus reveal problems, and suggest wise measures to be taken, but the real solution of problems demands a more profound change, one of a spiritual nature."

For the improvement of marriage, he goes on to add, "We need a new moral contagion, one which brings about change in deep-seated attitudes. We need . . . the breath of God's Spirit. No other force in the world can touch a man more deeply in his heart and make him more apt, at last, in understanding others."

Later he adds still further, "Every good happening is a gift of God, every deliverance from loneliness, fear, suffering or remorse is a result of the loving mercy of God." Some marriages are like a boat stuck on mud flats. They need not so much pulling and hauling as a new tide to lift them to a higher level. Faith can change otherwise drab details and episodes of daily life into splendid achievement. One has not only done his part but has enriched another life, and created a little unit of the Kingdom of God around his own life. "A person who believes that God is constantly doing all he can to enrich and dignify the lives of men, and who consistently accepts his personal responsibility to cooperate with God . . . finds his daily existence transformed by a sense of purpose and an inner joy which permeate and increase all his other values."

In pointing out how spiritual values help marriages to succeed, we know also how the lack of such values may doom a marriage to failure. A young mechanic, with a sort of rough-hewn strength and promise, came to me one morning to say that he had been living in wrong ways, but that he had spent a sleepless night and now wanted to repent.

I believe that he was sincere, but the question was complicated by the fact that he had been courting a girl of eighteen in a fine family, and her parents insisted that his repentance was only a trick to overcome their storng opposition to him. They even forbade him to come into their home again. He and the girl, however, continued to see each other in various places, and he was urging an immediate marriage. I tried to help them see that for the long journey together it would be worth their while to prepare the way carefully, to try to win the parents and to be sure that they themselves were fully ready for marriage. Their response was elopement. Following this they set up housekeeping in a place very different from the home in which the girl had been reared, and bought things on credit far beyond their ability to pay. Presently the young man lost his job and her wages were not enough to keep them going. Blaming each other for their plight, they not only quarrelled but fought.

One day they would be enemies, and another loving companions. I still tried to help them as much as I could, but it was not enough, and in time the girl was back with her parents. Of romantic love they had obviously had a due portion, but they lacked the qualities of maturity and inner development which might have enabled them to make something of their situation, and to bring out the best in each other. Their marriage had become desperately sick, but sick marriages are to be healed, if possible, and many are. People who may have lived together awkwardly can learn to be skilled marriage builders rather than bunglers. Dead marriages need to be buried, yet, as doctors use all the resources of science to restore the health of their patients, so we counselors should draw upon every possible resource for the healing of sick marriages.

Bitterness takes on an aggravated form when a spouse creates a false image of the other, believes it to be true, and then berates the other harshly. A wife, whose husband was a hard-working man in his place of business and even in the home, but had not reached the economic level on which her father stood, would call him a lazy loafer. Perhaps she was frustrated in that she could think of more things she wanted to buy than family finances allowed, and in her irritation threw at him the first verbal darts that came to her. She had some good points, and enough good intentions to bring her to me for counseling. There may have been a conscious or unconscious rejection of the husband, resulting in volcanic eruptions of domestic lava and hot ashes somewhat beyond her control. Doubtless she needed psychiatric help, but she rejected such an idea with indignation. "As a father pities his children," so the counselor must pity a person of that sort.

THE BIBLE AS A HELP IN THE IMPROVEMENT OF FAMILY LIFE

Rich sources of help in family living are to be found in the Bible. Again and again the ways indicated there are especially helpful to people who want to build homes of the best kind. How significant for marriage are the words of Jesus about building on secure foundations!

One man built his house on rock. "The rain fell and the floods came and the winds blew and beat upon that house, but it did not fall, because it had been founded on the rock." The other man built on the sand. There also, "The rain fell, and the floods came and the winds blew, and beat upon that house, and it fell, and great was the fall of it." Likewise some marriages give a warm shelter through all the storms of life, while others crash and leave people out in the rain and the cold.

"But the fruit of the Spirit is love, joy, peace, patience, kindness, goodness, faithfulness, gentleness, self-control," because "love is patient and kind, love is not jealous or boastful; it is not arrogant or rude. Love does not insist on its own way; it is not irritable or resentful . . . Love bears all things, believes all things, hopes all things, endures all things." The ideal is to love a person into an adjustment, not to try to make him comply.

Romantic love needs to grow into conjugal loving, which, like an irrigation system, keeps the fields of life green and fruitful. The same soil of circumstance may be a desert or it may be a garden, if love is there. This kind of love goes on when the spouse is most lovable, and still continues when the other is least so. Living together on such a basis helps each to grow into a person of splendid stature, and each problem will be an opportunity for a richer understanding.

DEALING WITH FAULTS GENTLY

The apostle Paul was speaking about life among church people, but his words might be very usefully paraphrased for husbands and wives, to read: "Now, husband or wife, if you find that your mate has faults, help him overcome them in a spirit of gentleness. Take a look at yourself, you are imperfect too. Help one another, for in this way you will fulfill the law of Christ." And, "Be kind to one another, tenderhearted, forgiving one another, as God in Christ forgave you."

As a recipe is not an arbitrary thing, but one which grows out of successful experience in preparing food, so "what's cooking" in a marriage will be more tasty if such good recipes are followed.

From my experience I am convinced that the healing of many hurts and bruises in marriage can come only through the willingness to forgive. A young mother reported that her husband had become angry and spanked the baby because he could not make her stop crying. The mother had rushed at him saying, "You brute, give me that baby." Then he had turned on her and slapped her. A little later he was very penitent and she forgave him. For long periods he would be a good husband and father, then he would lose himself in anger again. Brutality was followed each time by penitence, but the mother was asking herself how many times could she forgive this man. She wanted to continue with him, but, if so, an unusual patience, strength, and forgiveness would be needed. She said she had gone back again and again to the words of Jesus about forgiving, "I say to you, not only seven times, but seventy times seven."

Resentment of hurts great or small, real or imagined, may be like a boil, forcing its way to the forefront of consciousness, and needing to be lanced by forgiveness. How helpful it might be if when we say in the Lord's Prayer, "Forgive us our trespasses" we would think of the partner in marriage, as well as of others!

Both for counselor and counselee we need an ethics of mercy. Forgiveness is like sunshine on sour apples, changing them from puckery things that would give us a pain to things tasty and enjoyable. "Forgiveness is not a soft attitude toward a harsh fact: forgiveness is a vital action of love, seeking to restore harmony that has been shattered."

The forgiving heart is all the more needed because we all intend to do better than we sometimes do. We are like Paul when he says: "I do not do the good I want, but the evil I do not want is what I do." In line with this, family members may well be humble about themselves and gentle toward the faults of the others, taking to heart what is said, "Let all bitterness and anger . . . be put away from you . . . and be kind to one another, tender-hearted, forgiving one another, as God in Christ forgave you." We forgive not in a magnanimous "I-never-hurt-anyone" attitude, but with a sense of our own imperfections. Sometimes we can hurt another without even being aware of it. One might say that mutual consciousness of imperfections is one of the ingredients of an excellent marriage.

No two cases are alike, and this might be said of counselors also, who differ widely in personality, as also in the disciplines from which they come. Many problems that come to me seem to be in a somewhat different world from those which I hear some counselors talk about. It is taken for granted, also, that the measures which one counselor uses would not appeal to some others. My main purpose here has been to give expression to the faith that there are great invisible resources of strength for marriage, and that through drawing on these forces, marriages can not only be saved from disintegration, but may have a new birth of inner freedom and creativeness. Doubtless we might say of marriage what Fritz Kunkel said about life, that it is "to participate in the larger understanding of creation and to find a more appropriate place for yourself in it."

SELECTED BIBLIOGRAPHY

1. Ackerman, Nathan W.: *Expanding Theory and Practice in Family Therapy.* New York, Family Service Assn., 1967.
2. Bertocci, Peter: *Youth, Sex, Love and the Person.* New York, Sheed & Ward, 1967.
3. Bertocci, Peter: *The Human Venture in Sex, Love and Marriage.* New York, Assn. Press, 1949.
4. Bordin, Edward S.: *Psychological Counseling.* New York, Appleton-Century-Crofts, 1968.
5. Bowman, Henry A.: *A Christian Interpretation of Marriage.* Philadelphia, Westminster, 1946.
6. Cryer, Newman S., and Vayhinger, John Monroe (Eds.) : *A Casebook in Counseling.* New York, Abingdon, 1962.
7. DelliQuadri, Fred, (Ed.) : *Helping the Family in Urban Society.* New York, Columbia Univ. Press, 1962.
8. Duvall, Evelyn Millis: *Family Living.* New York, Macmillan, 1950.
9. Fairchild, Roy W., and Wynn, J.C.: *Families in the Church.* New York, Assn. Press, 1961.
10. Fosdick, Harry Emerson: *On Being a Real Person.* New York, Harper, 1943.
11. Freeman, Harrop A.: *Counseling in the United States.* New York, Oceana Publications, 1967.
12. Genne, E.S., and Genne, W.H.: *Foundations for Christian Family Policy.* New York, Abingdon-Cokesbury, 1949.
13. Horney, Karen: *The Neurotic Personality of Our Time.* New York, W. W. Norton, 1937.
14. Jung, Carl J.: *Modern Man in Search of a Soul.* New York, Harcourt Brace and World, 1934.

15. Kemp, Clarence Gratton: *Intangibles in Counseling.* New York, Houghton Mifflin, 1967.
16. Landis, Judson T., and Landis, Mary B.: *Building a Successful Marriage.* New York, Prentice-Hall, 1958.
17. Mace, David: *What God Hath Joined.* New York, Assn. Press, 1952.
18. McHugh, James T. (Ed.) : *Marriage in the Light of Vatican II.* Family Life Bureau, USCC, 1968.
19. McLaughlin, William G., and Bellah, Robert N. (Eds.) : *Religion in America.* New York, Houghton-Mifflin, 1968.
20. Morris, J. K.: *Premarital Counseling.* New York, Prentice-Hall, 1960.
21. Moser, Leslie E.: *Counseling: A Modern Emphasis in Religion.* New York, Prentice-Hall, 1962.
22. Mudd, Emily Hartshorne: *The Practice of Marriage Counseling.* New York, Assn. Press, 1951.
23. Nash, Ethel M.; Jessner, Lucie, and Abse, D. Wilfred (Eds.) : *Marriage Counseling in Medical Practice.* Chapel Hill, N.C., Univ. of North Carolina Press, 1964.
24. Peterson, James A. (Ed.) : *Marriage and Family Counseling: Perspective and Prospect.* New York, Assn. Press, 1968.
25. Raynolds, Robert: *The Choice to Love.* New York, Harper, 1959.
26. Rogers, Carl R.: *Counseling and Psychotherapy.* New York, Houghton Mifflin, 1942.
27. Rutherford, Jean B., and Rutherford, Robert N.: *The Personal Understanding of Marriage.* Chicago, Budlong Press, 1969.
28. Silverman, Hirsch Lazaar (Ed.) : *Marital Counseling.* Springfield, Ill., Charles C Thomas, 1967.
29. Small, Dwight Harvey: *Design for Christian Marriage.* Old Tappan, N.J., Revell, 1959.
30. Stewart, Charles William: *The Minister as Marriage Counselor.* New York, Abingdon, 1961.
31. Tournier, Paul: *To Understand Each Other.* John Knox Press, 1967.
32. Traux, Charles B., and Carkhuff, Robert R.: *Toward Effective Counseling and Psychotherapy.* Chicago, Aldine, 1967.
33. Turner, F. Bernadette: *God-Centered Therapy.* New York, Robert Speller & Sons, 1969.
34. Winter, Gibson: *Love and Conflict.* New York, Doubleday, 1958.
35. Wise, Carroll A.: *Pastoral Counseling, Its Theory and Practice.* New York, Harper, 1951.
36. Wynn, John Charles: *Pastoral Ministry to Families.* Philadelphia, Westminster, 1957.
37. Wynn, John Charles (Ed.) : *Sex, Family and Society in Theological Focus.* New York, Assn. Press, 1966.

Chapter 36

SIX LEVELS OF INTERCOURSE

JAMES R. BECHERER

Too many marriages are devitalized because woman has become more mother than wife; man has become more worker than husband. She has invested her spirit and body, her time and attention to being mother while he has given his all to being a success in his business in order to provide material happiness for his family. Meanwhile this once romantic suitor and this once idealistic wife have forgotten or forsaken their real interior needs and their youthful dreams and plans. They married mainly for love and fulfillment, not money, status, food, shelter, and clothing. But, where have all the flowers gone? They stand on their wall-to-wall carpet starved by wall-to-wall boredom and disenchantment.

They need what animals can never enjoy. They need mutual intercourse with God, intercourse of the minds and intercourse of their feelings. Sexual and social intercourse will then emanate from within. A vital marriage, therefore, is one in which the couple is serving each other's needs. They are satisfying each other's needs, consciously, conscientiously, thoughtfully, and actively. Far from leaving it to glands and instincts, they are really *working* at loving each other. They know the ingredients as clearly as the recipe for stroganoff or the parts of the engine. It is not guess-work.

Before the Second Vatican Council considerable emphasis was given to the hierarchical ends of marriage. Procreation and education of children was listed first, friendship and mutual help was second and the proper outlet for sexual desire was third. The Council included all these ends again in its treatment of marriage and the family,* but it no longer emphasized their hierarchical order of importance. Formerly people who married gave a great deal of emphasis to the bearing of children and their subsequent education. That education was religious, intellectual, and physical.

So, what is new in the Church's attitude? The Church is the People of God in this world and they are influenced by everything from outer-space to inner-city, from test-tube babies to youth communes. When life was shorter, women less emancipated, science less sophisticated, the world less populated, marriage and family life was less complicated. People knew their roles. They were more easily defined. There was a time when people had a choice of buying about ten different cars. Today, the variety of elections is

---

*Abbott, Walter M.: *The Documents of Vatican II*. N.J., Guild Press, 1966, p. 250.

innumerable. Modern marriage finds itself in a modern world where there is more and more emphasis on variety, choices, intensive and extensive needs. People marry for many reasons. What has not changed is the desire for happiness. Happiness is tangible, but less possible to describe. Beef, beer, and broads were once enough. Not today. Neither do people feel their lives must be mainly utilitarian. Human beings are not necessarily graded on human reproduction.

We sometimes got the impression that the Church was more interested in prenatal life and life hereafter than the span in between. Today we sing that we want to live, live *now,* that we want to *be.* "I gotta be me." We have realized that God is not dead, but our old ideas of Him and His expectations of us are dying. God just may very well be interested in quality as much or more than quantity; He may very well be interested in what we do while we are waiting to die. He cares what we become while we are living to live.

We have learned also that people who need people are the luckiest people in the world. We all need people. People grow in relation to other people. It is in relation to others, in interacting, reacting, and responding to others that we develop and mature. We have come to know too that maturity is the process of a lifetime and not something achieved at twenty-one and then statically lived with. Life is becoming. Life is dynamic. Stimulus and response are as much a human reality as a chemical one. With whom I live, whom I love, and who loves me changes me. With whom I live, interact, and love for a lifetime is profoundly formative and intensely related to my growth, happiness, health, holiness, and fulfillment as a person and as a Christian. Life is, indeed, what I do *with you* while I am waiting to die. And it is what you do with me while you are living with me.

All this strikes a contrast with people who married mainly to produce offspring. People marry surely to bring forth new life. But, they marry very much to produce new life in each other, to continue growing, maturing, cultivating, blossoming, and frutifying the life in each other. People are happy when they are growing as human beings. Arrested development on any level of our being is unhappiness for ourselves as well as others and it reveals itself in some form of pain. When marriages are in trouble we have to investigate the pain. "Where does it hurt?" we ask.

Unknowingly some people are feeding their children while they starve each other. The emphasis on procreation and education of children has historically deemphasized the husband-wife relationship. People have not always known that their own cultivation of each other is indirectly cultivating the children. They have tried so directly to train their children and mold them into good children, good citizens, good Christians. But we all know, if we stop to think about it, that the children are formed far more by

what the parents are than by what they say. The children are subtly influenced by what they experience daily. They learn what a man is by living
with a real man who is their father. They learn what a real woman is by
living with a real woman who is their mother. They learn what a husband
and wife are and what a father and mother are by living with their parents
who are these things, who play these roles constantly.

It would be well if a man and woman could realize that they cannot give
to their children what they themselves are not. If parents are not mature
and maturing men and women, husband and wife, they cannot be mature
and maturing parents. They steal nothing from the children by the time
and effort they take to love each other, to cultivate each other, to feed each
other's needs. There is no better way to become a real man or woman than
to live with one throughout infancy, childhood, and youth.

If we were to emphasize, therefore, between the husband-wife relationship and the parent-child, it would be better to choose the former. The
children will be the recipients of the results and they will not become
mature men and women, husbands and wives if they see their parents only
in the role of parents. The husband and wife relationship came first and it
was because of this loving relationship that the child was born in the first
place; the child should not break it up. The husband-wife relationship is
permanent until death; the parent-child relationship is temporary in reality
until the child leaves the home. Children should be raised in such an
atmosphere that they can take their place in the world independent of the
parents knowing that they do not need their parents and their parents do
not need them because they have each other. The child must develop his
own identity, individuality, integrity, and independence.

Many a youth has not felt free to leave the home because he knows he is
keeping the parents together. And many couples have nothing but a gaping
canyon between them when the children have all left the nest. So, for the
sake of the couple, as well as the children, the husband and wife need to
keep growing throughout the marriage. They need to keep feeding and feeding on each other. What are these needs and feeds?

There are many ways of listing human needs. These needs cannot be
supplied exclusively by the spouse, but to a high degree they can be and
should be. When people say they are not communicating, that their marriage
is suffering and listless, they need to examine these needs to locate the starvation.

The needs are spiritual, intellectual, psychological, physical, sexual, and
social. We may also refer to these as levels of intercourse. There is a dynam-
ism in this approach. There is an intake and output supplying life and
growth. A marriage that is taking nothing in on a particular level is not
giving out on that level. When the couple are conscious of these needs, this

intercourse, they have something definite and concrete to work on together. If there is no food on the table for a few days it becomes quite evident and the hunger shouts for bread. The same is true of our other needs. If there are no truth, wit, wisdom or ideas on the table for a few days the soul begins to hunger for some.

It was St. Augustine who said, "Our hearts were made for Thee, O Lord, and they will not rest until they rest in Thee." Whether one is a person of Faith or not, this still applies. No one human being can totally satisfy another. The cravings of the human heart are satiated only by the infinite. Two people in marriage should realize this and admit it to each other. They will not expect more from each other than is humanly possible to give. They should come to realize more and more in their marriage that their love is a reflection of the love of God for them, that the source of their own love is Infinite Love. Together they can look out to God and back to each other and deepen this conviction. God becomes the efficient and final cause of their union. They grow beyond formal, recited prayers together, and beyond self-conscious "made-up" prayers. They speak aloud to God before each other about God, about themselves and about each other. They speak the truth, the sincere hopes and dreams, disappointments and failures, praises and thanks, pleas and pardons. They pray it as it is.

This spiritual intercourse is not done at Mass or in the recitation of a family rosary. It may be done while sitting on a bench beside the sea, in a parked car in a municipal park or in their beds at night. But it is done and it must be learned and practiced. It would seem that even the most devoted couples rarely, if ever, practice such a prayer or intercourse. Yet, what richness, vision, strength is neglected or never known.

When people are asked whether God is in their marriage, they usually reply that they do or do not go to church on Sunday, received the Sacraments, say the Rosary, send their children to catechism classes—all the formalities of religion. It seldom occurs to them that this is hardly a living faith, any more than the learning of spelling makes one an author. There is such a distance between formal religious practices and the living, loving involvement of two souls entwined with God as simply an abiding reality. The religious-type people can be so forbidding, so holier-than-thou and unattractive to real people. Real spirituality, on the other hand, sets two people free and releases their inhibitions, scruples, and fears. "Perfect love casts out fear,"* says St. John. Two souls pray honestly when, in their own words, they express their desire to love and be loved, their gratitude, their need for pardon, mercy and understanding, their failures, hopes, disappointments, their promises to start anew, to try again to love and grow and give and surrender. This religion is quite another phenomenon that reaches the

*New Testament. N.J., St. Anthony Guild Press, 1941, I St. John, Ch. 4, vs. 18.

depths of being. This kind of soul-loving in God does not replace formal religious attendance. It is the outgrowth of it and the preparation for it when these souls return to the Community of the people of God.

Our next need is intellectual. The next level of intercourse between husband and wife is intellectual. Some day perhaps one of the legally acceptable reasons for divorce may be "intellectual non-support." It deserves to be.

A young married couple may come in to the counselor and say, "We just aren't communicating." An older couple will come in and say, "Our communications have just broken down." The couples have usually used up whatever they have of intellectual food and they are boring each other to death. The once cool cat on the beach really has not much depth of thought, conviction, and originality after all. The luscious bride is, after all, just a dumb blonde. They sit across the breakfast table staring into space. They have eaten, they have slept, they have had intercourse. "So what else is new?" Another way to ask the question is, "Can man live on bread and sex alone?" No, he cannot.

If education does nothing more than teach us how to pursue truth, knowledge, and wisdom throughout our lives, it has succeeded. But has it? How many people really search for truth instead of a degree or a diploma? How many couples do serious reading, discussion, attend lectures, pursue more education after they marry?

Still, too many do not want to pay the price of learning and serious study. It is enough for most to read the newspapers and magazines and discuss current events with their high school minds. Our world is so rich with thought, opportunities to learn about everything from Art to Zoology and still people are listless and boring. They hold the same trite conversations with the same insipid words. They have the same circular, routine thoughts and reactions. They soon learn to anticipate each other's word patterns and responses. It is true to say, "Why talk?" It has all been said.

What are the alternatives to this intellectual desert? Take the index of *Time* magazine for an examination of your own intellectual life and interest: Art, Behavior, Books, Business, Cinema, Education, Law, Letters, Medicine, Milestones, Modern Living, Music, Nation, People, Press, Relation, Television, Theater, World. How many of these areas do you care about, know about, pursue, discuss with your spouse? No one should be allowed or allow another whom he loves to settle for Kolbassi and beer, or comics and sports in a world of moon landings, social injustices, assassination, ocean science, Disneyland and Helen Keller.

It requires discipline of some of the lower appetites to pursue the higher, but it is worth the effort. If we have nothing to say to communicate it may be because the cupboard is bare. Where there is no intake there is no output. People would have a lot less trouble if they had a lot more truth, they would have a lot less friction if they had a lot more fiction, they would have a lot less worry if they had a lot more wisdom, and a lot less boredom if they had a lot more books—that they read. What the world needs now is love—and also truth.

Even more important than the sharing of academic, artistic, cultural, and scientific truth is the need to share the real truth about each other. Husband and wife need to continue to explore each other's minds, feelings, and history. They need to talk about themselves and listen actively not passively from behind the evening paper. Does anyone ever really know anyone else? Only to the extent that one is able to reveal and the other to comprehend. We reveal to the extent that we will be accepted and understood. And when this exchange is mutual and the waters that once kept the lovers hidden from each other are lowered mutually around two naked souls accepting, embracing, sharing, communing, and uniting, we call it love.

A man and a woman experiencing spiritual and intellectual intercourse are bound to recognize each other's psychic needs and attempt to feed them. Aristotle lists eleven emotions: love, hate, joy, sorrow, hope, despair, courage, fear, anger, desire, and aversion.

Unlike the angel, man is a physical being; unlike the animal, man is a thinking being; unlike the plant, man is a sensitive being. He feels. She feels. They do not usually feel alike about the same things. A man and woman living together must surely learn about each other's feelings and how to relate, balance, supplement, alter, console, and lift their feelings. This is psychological intercourse. They must learn about the daily, weekly, and monthly rise and fall of their emotions and nourish each other. If he is lying on the floor with a bleeding gash in his chest she does something to cure it. If he has an unseen gash in his feelings it may go attended or vinegar may be poured in. We care so about physical well-being, but is psychic health less important or less a part of us? The public is well aware of psychosomatic illnesses and the reciprocal effects of psyche and body.

Husband and wife need to become para-psyche therapists to each other. Far from a clinical atmosphere, it is simply the sensitive overflow of love in the mutual exchange of studied caring how the beloved feels. And, while caring they behave appropriately. They notice that it is not the time to bring up the subject of money or family conflicts. It is the time to complement, to encourage, to say nothing but only look, to touch the hand, to offer a kiss. They are in tune, in rhythm, in harmony; their emotions dance together leading and following, following and leading. They respect each other's moods, the need to be alone, and need to speak or to be silent, to be angry and even to pout for a while. Like Tom Sawyer and Becky Thatcher they need to explore the caves of their emotions and discover each other.

It is up to the woman to decide if five o'clock in the afternoon is going to be the end of the day or the beginning of the evening when her husband comes in. It is his responsibility also to be aware of what his wife has endured all day as well. She determines it very much by her own mood, appearance, and warmth. It is not the hour for both to unload the cares and frustrations of the day.

A woman can use a word of thanks for a good meal, a whistle when she has primped and a bit of praise for cleaning a room. A man can use the same food for his aching soul, his unsung efforts, his underpaid toil, and his thwarted dreams for the woman and children he loves. How sincere it should all be. How spontaneous and from a heart that really cares. Two hearts really caring make it all seem worthwhile. If the children do not seem to notice or care and the boss has little regard there is the reassurance from each other that nothing has gone unknown or unrewarded because it is done out of love. Heart to heart love. Heart to heart intercourse.

When people are asked what they do for each other to show their love, they frequently refer to the fact that they supply each other's physical needs. He works for money and supplies food, shelter, and clothing. She prepares the food, cleans the house, and does the laundry. This service is, of course, not to be overlooked. It can be love. It is not always. It must surely not be a substitute for all other needs or considered the primary reason for living together in the name of Christian love. After all, in our society, if the husband does not provide food, shelter, and clothing, the government usually will. And a woman who is a housekeeper prepares food, cleans rooms, and does the washing and ironing. She is a hireling. So, in itself, it is not marital love unless two people make it that.

They make the food, shelter, and clothing a part of their love, their physical intercourse by their intentions, artistry and methods. We all need these necessities of life, but there is some difference between feeding a dog and the man of your life, between a kennel and a man's castle. There is also some distance between an employer who pays his employed and a husband who provides for his beloved wife. This is all rather obvious, but it is this everyday supplying each other's physical needs that can most easily be taken for granted.

It has taken some of our modern movies *(Tom Jones)* to show us that eating together can be rich in sexual overtones, powerful in communication. It is not incidental to mention that Christ chose the process of eating to provide a love-ritual for his followers. How, what, where, and when two lovers eat is not unimportant. A woman who does not know how to cook does not love enough to learn. There is all the difference in the world between eating at a drive-in and a gourmet restaurant. Every woman should know this and make reasonable attempts to provide good food in an attractive atmosphere with a variety of recipes and ingenuity. A man should learn how to use a fork, a napkin and to ask for the butter.

A man's house really is his castle. He usually cares very much how it looks, how it is kept and respected. It is his trophy. He won it by working. It breaks his heart to see it abused. But it is her home too and the world in which she spends most of her life. It should project her abilities, her refinement, her talents, values, interests, and respect for things and the people she loves most. It is her trysting place with the man she loves; it ought to seem so.

The history of man could be studied by simply a study of the clothes he wore, how he decorated his body. Clothes are still a projection of one's self. They communicate. A man and a woman in love care about each other's bodies and how they are decorated. Appropriateness, cleanliness, and good taste with an aim to please each other sets the stage. Man is very much attracted by beauty and a woman must not forget that she is competing with all the women her husband sees all day. A frowzy appearance day after day is no way to love a man. And a man who loves a woman will care enough to dress with self-respect and pride.

Usually when the word intercourse is used it refers to sex. For its effectiveness here we have used the word to describe a man and woman relating, sharing, expressing love on a spiritual, intellectual, psychological and physical level. Love is just love. We have dissected it here in the hopes of exploring the hierarchical levels of human needs and feeds. There is a course running back and forth between a husband and wife. We call it intercourse. The isolated act of sexual intercourse, apart from the areas we have been describing, is simply an animal function in which two physical beings receive and give excitation and pleasure with a deposit of male sperm in the vagina. We know that this act, as just stated, can be for two people nothing more than that. It is nothing more than prostitution for the release of sexual urge and the payment of money in exchange. This is sex, but it is not love.

Sexual intercourse, ideally, is the ultimate expression of love that stretches out from God through the spirit, the intellect and will, the emotions, parts of the body to the entire body. The two become one: one in mind, one in heart, one in affection, and one in body. It is the mutual giving and accepting of all of two people—all they are and have to give—not merely their genitals.

So much damage has been done in this area either by excess or neglect. Society has treated it so strangely and secretly. Ignorance, silence, repression, guilt, shame, scruples, fear, disgust, hostility, sin, perversion, anxiety—all have characterized so much of our sexuality.

This is not an in-depth treatment of the subject. A few salient points should be made. The sexual life of a husband and wife is both an important cause and effect of the vitality of the marriage. Two people relating wholesomely as sexual partners are likely to be nourishing all their other needs: spiritual, intellectual, psychological, and physical. On the other hand, if the couple's spiritual, intellectual, psychological, and physical intercourse is vital and healthy, their sexual intercourse ought also to be thriving.

Formerly we treated marital intercourse very juridically. It was called a duty (another name for a tax). Women were threatened by the teaching that it was a mortal sin to deny one's husband his marital rights. It was also taught that the husband would sin if he denied his wife's request for sexual intercourse, but what woman then felt it was ladylike to ask? So the burden was more the woman's. It was a man's world and women often thought they should not really like sex; her duty was to satisfy her husband. In practice this led to such abuse as a husband asking the priest to remind his wife of her duties to him. (If any man needs the priest to get his wife to go to bed with him, he is, indeed, a desperate man.)

Women reluctantly complained that they did not want to have intercourse as often as the husband, or did not really want it at all if it were possible to escape it. Men would tell other men how often they "get" it like boys getting their father's car or cookies when they were younger. Women were made to prostitute themselves in their own homes by bargaining with their husbands for clothes or appliances. All this is not yet resolved, but it is in the process.

It is no longer a man's world of sex. Some time ago the modern American wife combined the former two types of women, the sexual mistress and the respectable wife and mother of children. And she is learning to be comfortably mature. She need no longer fear being the aggressor in bed or the initiator of love play.

She speaks out openly about what she is and likes and wants and does not want. She seems to have a more soulful kind of sexuality. That is, she seems to need to be loved as a whole person, from the inside out. She will not be a thing, will not be abused as an instrument of a man's pleasure. By her needs, now more often expressed, she is teaching her man more about sex and its totality. Her needs become his needs to satisfy her and finally himself. He is learning that what he gives to her, he receives back a hundredfold. His own sexual happiness exceeds that of yesterday.

A woman needs to be loved spiritually. She needs to experience the reflection of God in their love and an expression of her love for God in their union. She needs to be told that she is loved. She needs to have an intellectual conviction that she is loved as a person, that her mind matters, her thoughts and values, judgments and opinions. She needs to be talked with and not at or to. She needs sentimental love—those little things that mean a lot: a phone call in the day, a gift on a special occasion, an anniversary card, a Christmas gift that *he* picked out. She needs sensual love; she has five external and four internal senses all waiting to be nourished, wooed, and brought to life.

Then she can be loved sexually. This is loving her sexually. And the male who develops all these responses becomes much more of a male, of a man, of a sexual lover. His pleasure is in giving more than getting, in seeing her not just satisfied, but brimming over with loving appreciation of such a noble man "whose left hand is under her head, and whose right hand embraces her."

All this does not mean that the man's sexuality has always been selfish or genital sex alone. It is simply necessary to emphasize the above in contrast with the history of woman in our culture. There have always been outstanding, selfless husbands and wives enjoying the blessings of mature marital love.

Social intercourse is the by-product of all the other modes of intercourse described briefly above. We bring to the world what we are. And we are what we have done, what we have achieved, the love we have given and the love we have received. A husband and wife who have experienced often the love of God through each other, who have nourished each other with truth and wisdom, whose emotions are tuned by sensitive care, whose bodies are well fed in a warm atmosphere of beauty, charm, and good taste, whose love has exploded in sexual embrace have much to offer their children and other members of society. They are full and their cup runneth over to the world around them.

In turn they are open to the world in which they live and work and recreate. They give to the world individually and together. Like square dancing they start with each other as partners and fan out to touch the lives of others returning always to the person of their first choice. They give and also take from the world its riches and treasures in order to supply each other as they part and return to each other. They experience God, truth, emotion, food, possessions for their home, clothing, and sexuality. They see life. They see these realities because they are these realities themselves. Sensitively and with acute minds, hearts, and senses they ferment the world around them.

Husbands will recognize that wives need to be with other women just as they at times need to be with their own male friends. In this there is no jealousy. They do not compete but rather complete each other by encouraging "outside" friendships, hobbies, and pursuits. These enriched couples will value also the friendships they share with other couples. It stimulates the mind, the emotions, the personality, and social graces.

Emphasis has deliberately been made on the husband-wife relationship, their needs and feeds and the resultant six levels of intercourse. If the children seem to have been omitted in this treatment it was done deliberately. As was stated at the beginning of the chapter, we believe the children will become what the parents are, rather than what they tell their children to be. Maturity becomes the parent of maturity as much as poverty, hostility, suppression, and ugliness become the parent of all these. Happiness, health, and holiness will become the parents of happy, healthy, and holy children. At least the chances are much greater than if the parents are anything less.

Chapter 37

ABORTION: SHOULD THE PHYSICIAN BE THE CONSCIENCE OF SOCIETY?

E. B. LINTON

THE DICTIONARY DEFINES CONSCIENCE, in part, as "a feeling of obligation to do right or be good (11). Although conscience is a private and individual characteristic, society itself derives its "obligation to do right or be good" from the collective emotional intellect of its human constituents. While it is true that, often, group thought and action does not necessarily reflect individual conscience because of the effect of that mysterious thing called mass psychology, social conscience is a composite of individual consciences. "Moral Issues in Marriage Counseling" could hardly be a discussion of morality or of marriage if the subject of human reproduction and its control were not examined in depth. The milieu in which man lives dictates that contraception and sterilization can no longer be matters solely of individual conscience, but are concerns of society. The even more provocative subject of abortion has now become a matter attracting the attention of lay and medical public alike, reflected in the deliberations of legislative bodies. The physician, inadequately qualified to serve as theologian, sociologist, or even expert in family life, finds himself in the position of attempting to define society's conscience, and to act on the basis of that definition. It is quite obvious that society itself will have to more clearly understand its collective conscience and provide better interpretation of its will.

What has prompted the physician and the society he represents to concern himself with both the qualitative and quantitative aspects of human reproduction? The answer, of course, lies in the fact that man is threatening to annihilate himself by the very mass of his numbers; the fact that he is increasing exponentially and is rapidly shortening the time interval required to double his numbers; the fact that population growth rate far exceeds increase in food production; that even now in some areas, starvation is the rule to which there are few exceptions; the fact that at our present growth rate, man will be forced either to starve himself or to kill his neighbors.

However, not only has man been provoked to look at human reproduction because of its threat, man has also been permitted to view more critically all the aspects of reproduction because of his scientific achievements. Modern technology has brought with it the knowledge necessary to an understanding of human quality and numbers and the tools by which at least a measure of control can be achieved. It has also afforded to man the leisure to consider, alas to agonize over his morality, ethic and behavior as it relates to sexuality, prevention of unwanted pregnancy, and interruption of established pregnancy.

What has man's response been to the threat and to the opportunity afforded him by his technology? Japan has perhaps taken the greatest step forward, or backward, depending on the reader's viewpoint. Through contraception, sterilization and legalized abortion (662 per 1000 live births), the birth rate has declined from 34.3 per 1000 in 1949 to 17 per 1000 at present (7). This means that the population of Japan will increase from 100 million to 113 million by 1995, then begin a decline. Japan offers abortions legally on demand and is to date the only country in which abortion is placed in the same category as any other elective medical or surgical procedure.

A number of countries in Europe on both sides of the iron curtain have sought to liberalize abortion practices to varying degrees by writing into the law specific guidelines. Many of these countries have found reason to change these laws from time to time, e.g. a recent change in British law has made termination of pregnancy dependent only on the consent of two physicians. It should be noted here at least in British society, at the present, the physician is the key to abortion practices. This change has caused the number of legal abortions to skyrocket, necessitating the expansion of medical facilities to accommodate the demand. This suggests that where physician and patient are permitted greater latitude, interruption of pregnancy is carried out in increasing numbers.

The response to both the challenge of population growth and to the new look at morality and custom has varied considerably in the United States. Colorado was the first state to initiate permissive legislation regarding abortion. A recent study in Colorado shows that 72 per cent of legal abortions were performed for psychiatric reasons (3). One would suspect that there was some element of emotional disease involved as a reason for many of the remaining 28 per cent, indicating that termination of pregnancy solely because of a direct threat to the mother's life is becoming increasingly rare in that state.

That there are inconsistencies in the application of existing requirements for "therapeutic abortion" in this country is well documented. Hall has shown clearly that the higher socioeconomic group find it much easier to obtain a legal termination of pregnancy than the lower strata of society (5). In other words, the unmarried daughter of a professional man can obtain an abortion for "psychiatric reasons" when abortion, all other factors being equal, would be denied the unmarried, young, slum dweller.

That man does seek and does find abortion, albeit illegal, as a solution to unwanted pregnancy is well-documented by many authors (10). Paradoxically, laws governing abortion probably have little bearing on the rate of criminal interruptions, a contention supported by the study of Huldt in Sweden (8). As the number of legalized abortions increased, the number of live births declined, and the abortion rate, which includes both spontaneous and criminal abortion, remained the same.

Maternal deaths as a result of criminal abortion is probably not nearly as high in the United States as statistics often quoted would indicate. The figures 5,000 to 10,000 deaths per year is one cited by those proponents of more liberalized abortion laws (1). A study by Barno at the University of Minnesota (1) involving maternal morality in the state of Minnesota shows very clearly that the number of deaths caused by criminal abortion is quite low. Using these figures to calculate the number of deaths from criminal abortion in the United States indicates the figure quoted is far too high. Stevenson (1) in discussing Barno's paper quotes statistics from Michigan's large urban center, and though the rate compared to live births is considerably higher than the figures from the state of Minnesota, it is still far below the figure of 5,000 to 10,000 per year.

Thomlinson (10) estimates that there are between 700,000 and 2,000,000 criminal abortions annually throughout the United States, figures difficult to prove for obvious reasons. Interestingly, abortion is resorted to more frequently by married women than unmarried, perhaps only a reflection of the fact that there are more married women in the child bearing age group who are becoming pregnant. Whatever the actual number may be, even one death at the hands of an abortionist who is completely untrained seems an unacceptable penalty to pay in the light of the medical sophistication available in American society today.

Medical and personal factors notwithstanding, and in this day of mass media, man is forced to recognize and confront the inconsistencies which are the product of the variance between his teaching and his practice. It is only logical, then, that man question theology in his search for interpretation of his thoughts and actions.

Western society has evolved under the influence of the Judeo-Christian system of moral teaching. Indeed, Common Law, in large part, evolved from canon law. Historically, the church considered abortion a sin only after quickening. At this occasion, the soul was considered to first enter the body. In England in the 19th Century, the first abortion law called for condemnation and penalty only after fetal movement had been felt, or after the fourth month of gestation. In Roman Catholic history, the first act was issued on October 29, 1588, by Pope Sixtus the fifth. "All abortions and all contraception by potion or poison were to be treated as murder." The ultimate ecclesiastical penalty of excommunication was invoked for this sin; and to make the penalty more stringent, only the Holy See could release the ex-communication unless the sinner were in articulo mortis (9).

This act was repealed only two and one half years later by Gregory XIV (9). It was not until the 19th Century that the official stand of the Church against all means of birth control became clear. In the interim there was a wide divergence of opinion among church leaders and of practice among church members.

There is no argument that one of the basic tenents of the Judeo-Christian religion is the limitless value placed on human life both collectively and individually A superficial reading of the Bible makes this quite evident. It is remarkable, however, that in the entire Bible there is only one passage dealing with the worth of the fetus. It is *Exodus, 21,* 22-25. "When men strive together and hurt a woman with child, so that there is a miscarriage, and yet no harm follows, the one who hurt her shall be fined, according as the woman's husband shall lay upon him; and he shall pay as the judge determines. If any harm follows then you shall give life for life, eye for eye, tooth for tooth, hand for hand, foot for foot, burn for burn, wound for wound, strife for strife." It would appear from this quotation that the Old Testament makes a considerable difference between the worth of the fetus and that of a human being.

The New Testament has no passage dealing directly with the subject. It would seem, then, that there is no purely theological basis upon which one can support the concept expressed by Hardesty (6) that abortion is equal to murder.

It is obvious, then, that theological, sociological, and psychological views of the human conceptus permit no absolutes. At what point in time and in size, the developing embryo becomes human is an abstraction and is beyond finite interpretation. The answer to the question, when is life human, exists, only in the mind of he who contemplates the question; it is arbitrary and variable.

Man's inability to define and give limits to life and humanity does not, however, permit him the luxury of ignoring the question or of failing to respond to the needs of society. The increasing utilization of contraception and abortion, both legal and illegal, and the world's requirement for self-control dictate that man find some solution to his problem that he can abide. As one looks at what is now occurring in society, and the way it currently deals with the problem of population control, there appears one common denominator—the medical doctor. It is he who has the skill and knowledge to provide contraception, sterilization, and to perform an abortion. He is the central figure, either because he performs an abortion, or because he refuses, and the population must turn, individually, to illegal means. It is the physician who is expected to decide which patient deserves to be aborted and which one does not. A negative decision by a physician regarding abortion, however, does not relieve him of any responsibility since his decision many times does not offer his patient the medical care which the patient seeks, and is even sometimes responsibile for forcing the patient into criminal action.

Historically, in the eyes of the law, for example the North Carolina statute, an abortion performed by a licensed physician illegally is considered a felony punishable by imprisonment (4). In the eyes of the law, an operation of any other type performed on an individual by a licensed physcian is felony only if the individual sustains an untoward result, and if it can be proved that the physician was negligent, unqualified, or willfully did wrong. In other words, the fetus is considered in this context to be more than just an appendage of the mother's body. However, the penalty for illegal abortion is far less than for murder. It is quite obvious then that there are inconsistencies within the law regarding attainment of life by the fetus. Before the fact, the physician is guilty of a felony of taking life; after the fact, he is guility of something less than murder.

It should be obvious that physicians, individually and collectively, face the same moral dilemma as does the population as a whole. The physician, as a member of society, responds to the same trends in mores, customs, and behavior as the general population and is no better equipped to make these decisions than anyone else in the populace. It is small wonder, then, that the physician experiences the same anxious indecision as does his fellow man when the inconsistencies of both collective thought and law are so prevalent.

The physician must ask himself and because he is unqualified to answer, society must, perforce, ask itself these questions and many others. Should the interruption of pregnancy be considered any differently from any other medical procedure? Should a woman be forced to carry a pregnancy she does not wish? Is it feasible to legislate sexual standards by placing penalties on the natural results of these acts? Is the physician qualified to make the decision as to who should be aborted and who should not? Or is any one group of people qualified to do this? It would seem that society is actually avoiding the issue if it attempts to force one segment, the medical profession, to be its conscience in these matters.

Considering the course to be followed in the future, there appear to be three alternatives. The first is to continue along the present path, gradually liberalizing the law with the concomitant ambiguity and inconsistency, changing the laws only as medical practice changes. Even today, some large well-recognized medical centers have taken an extremely liberal view of the psychiatric indications for termination of pregnancy with a hundredfold increase in legalized abortion, while other institutions literally perform no abortions for other than strict medical reasons.

The second is to design a procedure by which the physician performing the abortion would not actually participate in the decision; that there would be members of several professions—medicine, psychiatry, sociology, religion, law, and psychology—who would serve as a board of review to make the decision. The objection to this would be that it would be difficult to find many physicians who would wish to act solely as the agent by which the unwanted pregnancies of society would be disposed. The physician would question whether this were not a reintroduction into our culture of the professional executioner. From the point of view of the woman involved, how many would hesitate to reveal their lives to a bureaucracy in order to obtain help?

The third alternative would be to do away with all laws relating to abortion and to reduce this procedure to the same level of medical practice as any other therapy. The decision would be up to the individual couple and the involved physician as to whether a particular abortion should be done. This would also leave free choice to the physician to participate in this type of medical practice as his own conscience and beliefs dictate.

In conclusion, society is asking the physician collectively and individually to be its conscience in human reproduction, specifically in the matter of abortion. Yet the physician faces the same ambiguities, inconsistencies, and hypocrisy in his own mores and customs that society confronts. Because the physician has the skill and knowledge to perform the act does not imply that he is better qualified to pass a moral judgment on the indication for that act. If abortion is to become a medical matter, devoid of morality and ethic, the physician will then be able to make the decision, for in this area he should be at ease. Should society elect to make abortion a purely medical matter, the physician will no longer be required to attempt to interpret and act out society's conscience, but will be able to perform the function for which he is qualified. If, on the other hand, society arrives at any other conclusion, it must attempt to define both for itself and for the physician the ill-defined. It must provide arbitrary interpretations to life, health, and philosophy. Otherwise, widespread hypocrisy and self-deceit will remain and prosper.

REFERENCES

1. Barno, A.: Criminal abortion deaths, illegitimate pregnancy deaths, and suicides in pregnancy. *Amer J Obstet Gynec, 98:*356, 1967.
2. Clark, T. C.: *Birth Control and the Christian.* Wheaton, Illinois, Tyndale House Publishers, p. 359.
3. Droegemueller, William: The first year of experience in Colorado with the new abortion law. *Amer J Obstet Gynec, 103:*694, 1969.
4. General Statutes of North Carolina, G.S. 14-45, General Assembly of North Carolina, Article 11, Chamber 14.
5. Hall, Robert E.: Therapeutic abortion, sterilization, and contraception. *Amer J Obstet Gynec, 91:*518, 1965.

6. Hardesty, N.: Should anyone who wants an abortion have one? *Eternity, 18:*32, 1967.
7. Hart, T. M.: Legalized abortion in Japan. *Calif Med J, 107:*334, 19.
8. Huldt, Lars: Outcome of pregnancy when legal abortion is readily available. *Lancet, 1:*467, 1968.
9. Noonan, Jolen T.: *Contraception: A History of Its Treatment by the Catholic Theologians and Canonists.* Cambridge, Harvard Univ. Press, 1967.
10. Thomlinson, R.: *Population Dynamics.* New York, Random House, 1965, p. 198.
11. *Webster's Seventh New Collegiate Dictionary.* Springfield, Massachusetts, G. & C. Merriam Co., Publishers, 1967.

Chapter 38

THE MORAL AND ETHICAL PROBLEMS IN PASTORAL COUNSELING

ACE L. TUBBS

KAREN HORNEY has said that inherent in man are evolutionary constructive forces which urge him to realize his given potentialities. This causes man, by his given nature and of his own accord, to strive toward self-realization, and from such striving is evolved his set of values. Although man is not essentially good, he strives to be truthful to himself; to be active and productive; and to relate with others in the spirit of mutuality. He begins to grow when he assumes responsibility for his behavior.

Most people feel that such moral striving has a religious base, and when they fall short they tend to take their personal problems to their minister, priest, or rabbi. Perhaps they feel that their basic problem is theological or they feel guilt-ridden and wish to deal with their guilt in a religious manner rather than first to seek medical, psychological, or psychiatric help.

For the most part, those who come for pastoral counseling do not hesitate to state the exact nature of their problem, freely acknowledging their weakness or the error of their ways. In others seeking help, however, this self-recognition is lacking. Some appear to be blaming someone else for their behavior or attitude. Others seem to be looking for some sort of psychological out from their counselor. They are seeking an excuse or an extenuation to conceal or disguise the enormity of their fault or crime rather than a constructive course of action. This sometimes calls for detective work on the part of the counselor. Drawing on his experiences as a counselor and on the special training he has received in the field of counseling, he must try to help the counselee get down to the roots of the problem. The counselee is doing something that keeps him from an optimum physical, emotional, social, or spiritual development. He needs help, and that is why he has turned to his spiritual mentor.

Herein lies the crux of the problem to be covered in this chapter. How should the pastoral counselor handle the illegal, immoral, unethical, or even criminal material presented to him in counseling? Some counselors seek the easy way out. They say: "Let us pray" and proceed to ask God for his guidance for the counselee. Others are shocked by the behavior described and convey the feeling of disappointment in the counselee or even manifest shame for him. These pastoral counselors attempt to get the counselee to

442

repent and promise not to sin again. The story is told of one such clergyman who, when told of a serious drinking problem by a remorseful parishioner, asked the man to get on his knees while he, the holy Joe minister, stood and prayed in sepulchral tones: "O Lord, have mercy on this poor drunken bum." Whereupon the counselee tugged at his minister's trousers and exclaimed, "Don't tell the Lord I'm a drunken bum. Tell him I'm a sick alcoholic."

BE SHOCKPROOF

Well, what does the pastoral counselor do about what to him is sinful activity? If he follows the rules of the game, he is shockproof. This means that no matter what he hears in counseling, he does not convey condemnation, judgment, or even surprise. He is the doctor. He must be objective and rational. He cannot afford to treat the "wound" excitedly or emotionally. His first reaction to the counselee is that he is sick and has come for treatment. The counselor is as professional, effective, and thorough in his treatment as a medical doctor. As in medicine, diagnosis precedes treatment. Thus he probes for the exact nature of the wrong. Sometimes this appears to be too personal for the counselee, but the probing, however painful, is necessary if the problem is to be treated adequately.

For example, one of my ministerial friends told me of a man who was an officer in the church; a church school teacher; a man who was respected in the community as one of its spiritual leaders; one who on numerous occasions gave talks to church groups on moral and spiritual topics; and a family man whose wife and children happily joined with him in church activities, one of the daughters being in training for full-time church work. This man came to see his pastor one day and simply said that he was in love with another woman. The pastor was shockproof. He began to seek the nature of this relationship, finding that the man spent much of his "out-of-town" time as a salesman with the other woman, that their sexual relationship was deeply satisfying to both, and that the man wished to leave his wife and marry this woman. The counselor inquired further and discovered that this man had been in love with other women living in various towns in which he worked. All the details of these love relationships were elicited without any difficulty. The counselee seemed to regain peace of mind and to experience great relief as he poured out every detail of his secret life. In line with the tenets of pastoral counseling, his pastor never once rejected the man and was careful not to give him any feeling that their relationship was marred.

HATE THE SIN BUT LOVE THE SINNER

The pastoral counselor is taught to recognize that the behavior problems brought to him manifest a sickness rather than sinfulness. The counselee is fully aware of his sinfulness if he has had any religious training at all. He need not be reminded that he is living an abnormal life. He knows this. He needs help with his problem. Undoubtedly he has prayed for forgiveness a thousand times, only to find himself right back in the same old pattern again and again.

An interesting case will illustrate. A brilliant young man sat crouched in the corner of his kitchen in a drunken condition. When his pastor came the man said, "Preacher, if you have a kind word, come talk with me. If not, there's the door, because my wife doesn't have a kind word, my father and mother don't have a kind word, and you should hear what I'm saying to myself." He was saying that he condemned himself much more than those who loved him had condemned him. He knew how shiftless, irresponsible, and no good he was. He did not like it any more than they did. He needed someone to love him for himself; someone to accept him and help him rather than berate him for his drunkenness. He expected his minister to hate the sin and its effects but also to love the sinner in spite of it.

WHAT'S BUGGIN' OLE PHARAOH

After the nature of the problem has been revealed the trained pastoral counselor should explore with the counselee the cause of his behavior. This is the difficult part of counseling because often the counselee has no idea why he acts the way he does. He can easily justify or excuse himself, but he has difficulty understanding himself and his behavior. Therefore, much questioning and exploration of life situations and early childhood experiences is necessary to help the counselee discover the etiology of the problem.

A wife came to her minister one day to inform him that she had taken her husband's bizarre activities as long as she was going to. She was going home to her mother. She reluctantly told her minister that some of the housebreaking going on in the town was being done by her husband and that the attic and basement of their home were filled with stolen merchandise. The last straw came when, as usual for no reason, her husband stole several packages of cedar shingles from a house construction job. There was no room for them in the basement. She was at her wit's end. She got only abuse when she pleaded with him that they did not need these stolen goods, that he made more money than most of the people in town, and that they would never be able to use most of it, nor did she wish to use any of these things that he had stolen.

The minister's first reaction was to notify the police. This was clearly his legal and moral duty. His next inclination was wiser. With the man's help he discovered the underlying causes of his stealing. A referral was made to a psychiatrist, who helped the man break the behavior pattern and return the stolen goods when it was expedient to do so. An interesting insight this man received was that his overly strict parents had deprived him of many of the things his friends had and had also given him a distorted view of God. Consequently, he got back at his parents and God, who is against stealing, by stealing. The stealing stopped. So did church attendance. But the counselor saw that the man had found a measure of peace and, free of this incubus, was now better able to realize his full potential as a human being.

SITUATION ETHICS

In the counseling process it is essential for the pastoral counselor to see that the "most loving thing," as Fletcher* terms it, is done. There are situations when it is best for persons to break the law. A wise counselor is able to accept such a decision on the part of the counselee rather than to be rigidly moralistic. The pastoral counselor then should treat rules, codes, principles, laws, or maxims of society as illuminators of a particular problem rather than as precepts to be blindly followed. Any law can be set aside if it would be more loving to the most people to do so. A wise counselor is sensitive to variety and complexity in the lives of his counselees. Nothing is rigid. Love is for people and not necessarily for principles. It is personal. The counselee must decide for himself according to his own estimate of conditions and consequences. The counselor should not decide for him nor condemn the decision to which the counselee comes.

An unmarried girl returns from a year abroad to discover that she is pregnant. Eventually this young woman must make a decision. She enumerates and weighs all the relevant factors with her pastor and discusses the possible courses of action. She could write the man for consent and return to Italy and marry him. She could grab the first available guy and marry him, telling him their baby is a month or two early. She could put on a ring and announce her marriage to an American soldier of Italian background, later announcing his "tragic" death. She might decide to have the baby and give the infant to her mother or put the child up for adoption. Or she could decide to go to New York and have an abortion under clinical conditions. She decides the latter is the most loving thing to do. The pastoral counselor concurs.

But what if the pastoral counselor does not agree? In his opinion the counselee should not do what he is doing or plans to do. In this situation it is the counselor's ethical and spiritual responsibility to state his case, giving concrete reasons why he feels a mistake is being made. In other words, the pastoral counselor takes off his nondirective hat and simply states there is a more loving way, a way he, the counselor, feels will be more effective in developing the full human potential. Even if the counselee persists in his

---

*Fletcher, Joseph: *Situation Ethics.* Philadelphia, Westminster Press, 1966, p. 57f.

intention, at least the counselor does not have to bear part of the responsibility if indeed a wrong course is followed. This is particularly important when a counselee tries to convince the pastoral counselor that suicide is the only answer to the problem. It may be that there are things worse than death, but a pastoral counselor would hardly concur with a counselee who plans to take his own life.

Under no circumstances should the pastoral counselor actually participate with the counselee in the behavior that is in question. For example, every counselor encounters sexually frustrated women, who may taunt or openly seduce him. But if the counselor is to be the doctor, he cannot be a part of the problem. He must be a part of the solution. Therefore, he does not engage in sexual activity in any form with the counselee. As a rule the effect would be iatrogenic for the counselee, that is, the counselor by his words or actions would be contributing further to the sickness of the counselee, thus going directly counter to the ends of counseling.

Chapter 39

SOME PNEUMATICS OF THE PSYCHOSOMATICS OF MARITAL COUNSELING

ALFRED VAIL

In the yeast at the bottom of the vat there is a mix of residual power that stands ready to bubble up and energize a new batch of brew. The title is a frank spin-off of Seward Hiltner's *Ferment in the Ministry*. Hiltner makes the point that the time *(kairos)* is right for bringing to a close the fermentation-like process in the ministry. Out of all of the agitation and unrest around the minister's many functional roles, Hiltner brings a cartoon-like description of nine aspects of the ministry, namely Preaching, Administering, Teaching, Shepherding, Evangelizing, Celebrating, Reconciling, Theologizing, and Disciplining. After capping his nine images and unifying his case, he leaves the vat ready for a new batch of grapes and more wine.

Since I am writing this chapter in Cincinnati, a city that used to be proud of its vineyards and now favors it malt products, it seems appropriate for me to use the analogy of the "yeast at the bottom" to bring into focus some questions that relate to marital counseling. This is a role that has particular significance not only for clergy-counselors but also for the other professions and agencies working to help those who have needs for marital counseling or family life education.

I am no biologist and make no pretense of fully understanding the function of yeast in a culture. The yeast analogy of the leaven in the lump calls to the attention of religious people a sense of the boundlessness of the creative possibilities which result when people of good will work together in the mix. Indeed, "the whole is more than the sum of the parts."

Yeast also has a temporal dimension. In brew making and in bread making in rural areas, the yeast provides continuity with the old and expression in the new. Part of the bottom of the vat is held over and kept fermenting, to be used from one baking day to the next throughout the years. In addition, the analogy of the yeast relating to the quantitative and temporal dimensions of bringing marital counseling and education to purpose, carries with it a dizzy and bubbly quality that sparkles with novelty, reaching toward the future and surging with energy to serve each new generation.

I will consider some of the problems and opportunities that I see in approaching my own work in a church-community setting and entailing, of choice and necessity, all of the ministerial functions described by Hiltner.

I will organize the material in the classical pattern for describing *Man* as Body, Mind and Spirit (i.e. *Soma, Psyche,* and *Pneuma*). From within each of these basic categories I will try to relate the ministerial marital counselor to the world in which he lives, the minds with which he works, and the moral implications of both. If what I say appears to be personal and limited, it is meant to be. On the other hand, I hope that some of the questions raised will be answered and will provoke new questions; that some of my opinions will be countered by those who have had more extensive or intensive experiences; and that whatever can pass for wisdom or warning will be put in the yeast of those who have a professional interest in marital counseling and family life education.

That the yeast at the bottom, passing from one batch (or generation) to the next, was a messy looking mix would be denied by no one who brewed his own beer or baked his own bread before Mr. Fleischmann put out his convenient little tin foil packages. Besides being messy, the yeast increased in proportions that outgrow household need. It was rural wisdom that taught early plumbers that the waste product (still alive) had a beneficial effect in septic tanks. It kept them from crusting, thereby becoming impervious and losing their "drain-off" function through the walls and nitrogen fixation function at the bubbly top.

Yeast proves useful not only in the leavening action in the generational process of the new batch but also in transforming what might become distructive waste, moving it into the cyclical routine of nature. It is in this double sense that the considerations below are presented.

Ministerial Marital Counseling and Family Life Education is not new but most certainly needs to be studied again so that the yeast at the bottom can sparkle with the new and leaven that which is discarded.

IN THE YEAST AT THE BOTTOM

The Ministerial Marital Counselor and Family Life Educator	Some Considerations for
1. Body	The World he lives in A. Environmental Matrix (Ecological-Sociological) B. Functional Matrix (The Body Politic)
2. Mind	Interpersonal Relationships A. Identity Struggle (Psychological factors) B. Stochastic Approach (Feedback necessity)
3. Spirit	Moral Implications A. Issues and Dimensions B. Priorities and Direction

BODY—THE WORLD HE LIVES IN

The ministerial marital counselor lives in a world that is increasingly understood to be a unity in itself although part of a universe that is beginning to open up the secrets of its own interdependent nature as part of creation. Neither the counselor nor anyone else can have all of the knowl-edge he desires of himself, of others, or of the world in which they all live, but he can and he should maintain his desire to increase his understanding of himself as a person and professional in relation to the others of his life and their common world.

The idea of man as a *many-leveled unity* related to others has been part of the Judeo-Christian heritage from the beginning. This concept is con-firmed constantly by scientific observers. We do not see the counselor as a mere body in the considerations that immediately follow, but rather as a self-acting, feeling, dreaming, willing, and thinking self-in-community. As a counselor he is shaped by his relationships, and as a counselor he shapes his relationships. This mutually reciprocal function is described by Ian Barbour, who says, "The dominant image of person-in-community empha-sizes this corporate dimension of selfhood without absorbing the individual into the collective" (2) .

The counselor is involved in many relationships, but lives, nevertheless, in a limiting environment. His environmental matrix or envelope is literally a womb in a social context that both expands and limits his own possibilities for growth and meaning.

The body among bodies is understood first as contained by a world or house. Ecology means "knowledge of house," from the Greek *Oikos,* and is used in a social context. The body functioning as a marital counselor is further understood as working in a *functional matrix* that supports the life of his profession in the socio-political context of work. Whatever environ-ment provides for the counselor in his world and the population in it, must also concern him about the covenants of relationship or rules that govern the administration and ethics of his profession; with respect to others who also would help marital pairs, nonmarital pairs, their offspring, single adults, their social and spiritual generators, and their physical progenitors.

We will look at the outline of the bodily aspects of the ministerial marital counselor before moving on to the more subtle concerns of the life that takes place within, through and around the physical organization of the counselor. Probably the physical is easier for most of us to see. The body is usually defined traceably, if not always clearly and brightly. We can almost always delineate the "hard data," the demographic, geographic, and organi-zational material. We can even bound, from history and rubric, the body politic.

Again noting that the physical body is not separated from the mind or the spirit, we proceed to look at a few considerations which concern the body of the counselor and his world.

ENVIRONMENTAL MATRIX

Ecology—Sociology

As we move into the telescopic and macroscopic universe of the year of the moon shot, the marital counselor begins to see brewing a deep concern for the ecological balances of the universe. This is especially true of the ministerial marital counselor who must orient his life to matters other than the microscopic interaction of marital pairs. If the counselor settles for the "Malthusian" expectation that war and famine will cure things for a while, he probably can save himself some worry as "things happen anyway." If, on the other hand, he can begin to see some real possibilities for rational intervention in the affairs of the universe because of the moon shot, I believe he will be able to see more possibilities for rational intervention and problem solving within each family constellation and human galaxy. The problem-solving techniques and energy that bring orbiting modules together and keep them apart can certainly provide some clues to help people move together and apart with more human and creative concern for each other. This is not to say that the possibilities are not also there for mere mechanical achievement and the unleashing of destructive power and manipulative control.

What happens within the limits of time, space, and energy of the lunar year can be expected to touch the lives of man in the future. When the counselor looks at only a few of the changes in family life and marital dynamics in the United States since colonial days, he can plan to see changes in the patterns of tomorrow. Bundling boards and buggies—motels and automobiles; chaperones—group standards; father around the place, in town, or at sea—father on the road, commuting, and in some groups absent; church and town hall centers of community life—spectator sports, television, and campus separate the generations; races separate on the surface—races intermarry openly; the expanding apron and delivery with social consequence—the pill and abortion with relative anonymity are some that must be considered.

The paths men travel to do their work and get their food have shaped the style of their marriages. The houses and dormitories they sleep in have patterned their sex lives and attitudes. The people with whom they relate have helped to draw the perimeters around their lives and institutions. The environmental matrix needs to be studied and new life planned with care. Men need not be victims of chance and misdirected power. Mother Nature need not be raped and robbed of her bounty and beauty.

The ecology and sociology of the present will give us options for life in the future.

The questions are now asked, "Who should study the house and its people?" "What business is it of the marital counselor and the ministerial marital counselor in particular?" "If Hiltner describes the ministerial profession correctly, don't the members of that group have too much to do now?"

I do not propose that the counselor presume to take the responsibility for extensive study of all of the ramifications of the ecological and sociological problems that could be projected on the drawing boards. Such a global approach would take him out of the counseling business to say nothing of destroying this listening ability through the deaf "third ear" of *hybris,* that is, overweaning pride. Neither do I propose that the counselor be irresponsibly eclectic as he looks at problems in this vast and largely unexplored area. I do plead that counselors be encouraged to see beyond the problems of counseling as such and look into the fields where others work more deeply. We can not all be proficient in every discipline or even outstanding in the required ones. Great preachers spend many more hours on sermons than do great pastors or administrators. There will be some who become so proficient in one area that they can successfully turn a part of the business into a full-time focus for work.

As I write these remarks, I remember the consistent and constant example set by Kenneth Appel for psychiatrists, nurses, social workers, and marital counselors while teaching case conference sessions. Working as a physician-psychiatrist at the University of Pennsylvania, he encouraged the scientific people to read in the arts, religion, history, myth, and novel. He raised the issue that mathematics and physics, granted their place, are not substitutes for the other disciplines for those who would work in human dynamics.

I raise the issue that those who work in human dynamics, and family life in particular, need to study some of the physical and cultural ramifications of the Space Age. I suggest that some of the subjects below are more than just cerebral popcorn and that the list could be expanded greatly.

Time and acceleration.
Role conflict in changing world.
Space and living space.
Renewal and Christian community.
Photography and agriculture.
Diet, populations, and family planning.
Vocational pressures and body needs.
Differing styles of life and human rules.
Free time (nonvocational) on our hands.
Cybernetics and who steers for whom?
Education.

Automation and the effect on families and sexuality.
Man's responsibility over nature, including procreation.
Family patterns in different social settings.
Mixed marriages—intercultural.
New language and symbolic thought.
Really one world and no doubt about it.
Race and family.
Are there common moral standards?
National budgets and family life.
Space medicine and sex.

FUNCTIONAL MATRIX
The Body Politic

If the environmental matrix of the world of the ministerial marital counselor needs to be studied, so also does the functional matrix, the womb of the body politic that supports the life of the profession. The counselor who works as a marital counselor and family life educator in any depth in a parochial setting must understand the politics of his working priorities in his own church. In addition, he must also relate to people and organizations in the other helping disciplines. As he relates to the organizations in his community, he might keep in mind a point that Drucker makes: "Organizations are legal fictions. By themselves they do nothing, decide nothing, plan nothing. *Individuals* do decide and plan."

The minister-counselor does not just relate to the "psychiatric community," a "social work agency," a "Family Service Agency," a "power structure" here or an "establishment" there. He needs a reciprocal-covenantal-collaborative-ethically responsible communication with particular human beings who function in the service and referral organizations. He needs to have the same communication with supervisory consultation and within his own church staff.

I used to think loyalty was the key word in building a consultation team and working employment lines to pull along the case load. Loyalty here has all of the connotation of referrals to friends and seniority organization lines rather than a functional matrix through the midst of organizational lines.

I now agree thoroughly with Drucker as he looks "Toward a Theory of Organization" in *The Age of Discontinuity.* The claim for loyalty in the employment contract is impermissible and illegitimate. Service to the client or parishioner is without question the key.

The lines of relationship for working in ministerial marital counseling should be based on the best plan for help that can be obtained for the client. Whether referrals are made and to whom they are made are judgments that should be reviewed with consultation from time to time. Clebsch says that the best available studies show that half of the troubled Americans who seek professional help turn initially to ministers, priests, and rabbis. He refers to all pastoral contacts and not just to marriage and family clients. There is reason to believe that a significant proportion of those persons seeking help are referred to others for help more appropriate than can be provided professionally by the minister.

Those seeking pastoral help in my own experience, excluding the hospital patients and shut-ins, are for the most part persons who come in with a presenting problem that is directly focused in the marital counseling area. Others present alcohol and vocational problems but even these often reflect pressure in the marriage. Much of the youth counseling done at the parish level is also family-life connected. The minister-counselors are also called upon periodically to counsel persons contemplating marriage, and most require this of their own membership prior to marriage in the church.

Most clergy consider the role of "pastoral" counseling as part of their ordination responsibilities. Relatively few clergy have received postseminary training as marital counselors. With the recent push in several major denominations for an increase in emphasis in continuing education, Marital Counseling will get its share of trainees. Clergy who have received supervised training are generally expected to know the limits of their competency as marital counselors. As more states set standards of training for marital counselors, more clergymen will make the effort to get the training, and more seminaries will find ways of helping their graduates build the marital counseling skills.

We are a long way from the early Church when, as Hiltner points out, "The communities were so busy performing the necessary functions of ministry that they handled the structural aspects informally, without constitution and bylaws." Although I see a real need for the "evils" of certification of training and the cost of continuing education in the marital counseling field, I am certain that the work should cross professional barriers as an interdisciplinary cooperative community function and proceed toward licensing and certified training as outlined by The American Association of Marriage Counselors in 1958.

Not all ministers are marital counselors, nor are all psychiatrists, psychologists, social workers, or lawyers. Some are and should take some responsibility for the work. "The competence is ultimately functional, that is, the combination of abilities that can best get the job done."

Hiltner raises some questions of ethics concerned with ministers taking fees for counseling. I am inclined to agree with him. I would caution against too rigid guidelines, however. There is a growing group of non-

stipendiary clergymen who, for one reason or another, have left the parochial scene. If the marital counselor who is qualified gives up his other
ministerial duties, he should be treated as any other counselor of equal
training. It is also interesting to note in this connection that several well-
trained marital counselors in the last few years have established busy marital
counseling centers in the parochial setting, the official boards consenting
and all finances being run through an official set of books in the parish.
Other marital counselors are working under judicatory auspices and at least
partially supported by fees from clients. I see this only as a problem that
ought to be handled in an ethical and businesslike way. In this age of discontinuity there will be innovations in how many men work.

Clebsch sees a trend away from the generalist clergy in the healing and
guiding functions of pastoral work with the client system turning increasingly to the medical doctors and psychiatrists. On the other hand, he sees the
clergy counselors retaining certain advantages over the other helping professions as sustainers and reconcilers. These latter two functions would fit
well into the marital counseling role.

I do not agree with Clebsch's concluding remark in his article which
appears to attack the prophetic role of the minister who might also be a
pastoral or marital counselor. He sees the clergy as "a profession which
presently seems fascinated by matters of public policy to the detriment of
its potency in evincing spiritual health, education and welfare." As a
ministerial marital counselor and a family life educator, I have been constantly impressed with the need for large-scale political and educational
measures that will innovate a public policy bringing marital health to more
families than all of the counseling we can provide.

Ministerial marital counselors who play a careful and passive role in
dealing with such problems as housing, sex education, and abortion retard
the community family health. It seems to me to come dangerously close to
being like the "close-minded" professionals who impeded the work of
Pasteur and Freud and scoffed at Ehrlich's "trial and error" attempts that
after the 606th try found a medicine for syphilis. We need strong voices
and public witnesses when they are sincerely working for the common good.
If we do not have the voice or witness, we need to support those who do.
Think if you will about the family dynamics in large urban ghettos that
would be significantly changed by housing and welfare programs or employment policies that support family life in constructive ways. We all know the
community price for the absence of one father in the home. Apply the
multiplier principle for monetary savings on that problem alone and my
point is made. There is more than one way to leaven the lump in the body
politic.

MIND—INTERPERSONAL RELATIONSHIPS

As the yeast is needed to leaven the body—the environmental matrix and functional matrix, the physical and political structures of life, so also is the yeast needed to keep alive the mind as it interacts with the minds of others. The interaction of minds is obviously not in a vacuum but very much a part of the body. Physical signals meet body receivers and describe what is going on with the minds. What is received and described in one mind tends to shape the receiver equipment in another. Either learning and growth takes place in a positive sense or plateaus become stopping places, minds are set, or, in an even more negative sense, deterioration sets in.

Storehouses are built that hold the treasures we value for good or ill. We become in one sense an institution, or maybe a character. Each ministerial marital counselor is a character and each client or associate is also a character and, in the sense above, institutionalized.

I will never forget an offhand remark that was made quietly during a lull in the North American Conference on Church and Family back in 1961. One notable expert who had delivered a paper the previous hour on homosexuality, after listening to and watching another notable read his paper on infidelity and walk up the center aisle of the meeting room, said, "Now *he* is all male!" Her mind had received the signals that described affectionately and with some professional expertise a character who is in a real sense an institution. The minds of each of the notables had interacted, and I, as a listener, could discern something new bubbling into my mind that made both the papers and the people more alive. A yeasty remark made a difference in perception of male sexuality and the memory carries forward a picture of very real people and yet very fixed institutions.

Carlyle Marney says, in a chapter appropriately entitled "The Padded Cell," "modern man is as he is by virtue of his institutions. These are frames, cells he has constructed or inherited to hold his valuables." He goes on to quote Winston Churchill who put this notion in a sentence: "We shape our dwellings, and afterward our dwellings shape us."

There is a danger of becoming institutionalized or a mere character or mind-set to the others in our lives. Life is more than impressions, descriptions, certifications, fixed roles, and tightly limited performance expectations. The rebel Roman Catholic priest, Ivan Illich, described this idea when he advanced his radical, humanistic point of view against the norms of middle class aspirations: "The world finally is divided between the biophilic and necrophilic, between those who love life and those who worship possessions; between those who can laugh and those who can't; between those who want to deepen life and those who only want to lengthen it."

I see the ministerial marital counselor obviously on the side of life and obviously and constantly engaged in an identity struggle which is described by Seward Hiltner and also by Clebsch. The latter delineates the struggle saying, "Little of the restlessness which presently infects ministerial ranks in America springs from a jealousy that more specialized helpers are performing functions which once belonged to religion. Few clergy resent their calling's having lost the honor of representing the community's most learned man. Rather, basic ministerial frustrations arise from concurrent demands for expertise in many areas of work—areas which compete for time and energy but also reinforce one another's potency. The catechist wants to become a theologian, the preacher a poet, the administrator an executive, the liturgist a Thespian, the pastor a psychiatrist, and, compounding the problem perhaps by geometric progression, the exemplar a saint.

There is no question that the ministerial marital counselor needs to bring certain personality equipment to his work. He needs to be, among other things, sensitive, objective, flexible, and empathetic. For those who would read further about these qualities of the mind in interpersonal relationships I would suggest Wolberg, *The Technique of Psychotherapy*. Holt and Luborsky describe more comprehensively some of the qualities needed short of expensive psychiatric training in *Personality Patterns of Psychiatrists*. Holt and Luborsky reinforce in detail the need expressed earlier in this essay for the counselor to be reasonably eclectic and well-rounded.

It is obvious that the marital counselor needs to bring in not only personal qualifications but also a reasonable understanding of the sociology and psychology of family life. These subjects have been thoroughly covered in Silverman's *Marital Counseling*.

IDENTITY STRUGGLE

Psychological Factors

Nobody wants to be a cog in a wheel. Everyone, including the counselor, the client, and those in the helping professions, holds his own self-image close and protects it as best he can. Each man wants to be known, loved, and valued. Rollo May speaking of Camus' *Values of Being a Rebel*, shows how important it is to force the "impersonal authorities" or the "too systematic system" to look at each person, to recognize him, and to admit that he *is* and that his *power* is taken into account. "I mean, literally, that unless I can have some effect, unless my potency can be exercised and can matter, I inevitably will be the passive victim of outside forces, and I shall experience myself as without significance."

Now the minister has, without question, a fundamental task in bringing this kind of significance to each member of his congregation. At the same time, he has a very real task in bringing this kind of significance to a marital counseling client who expects to be related to him in a dyad or in a triad with his spouse or possibly sharing his significance in a group session with other members of the family constellation.

Without self-pity, I make a plea that each of us who works professionally in the marital counseling field, consider the load that each carries and try to pave the way with good reciprocal communications within the profession. The clergy counselors with whom I have talked have made literally hundreds of referrals to agencies and specialists in the other helping professions. They find reciprocal follow-through on either a report-back or referral-back basis inadequate.

Trust levels are important. When trust is high the work goes on as constructive business, with each person benefiting from the trust. When the trust level is low, the work becomes painful, threatening, and a general aura of pessimism prevails.

With whatever aggression or passivity and character profile we bring into the marriage counseling relationships, it can usually be worked with in a constructive way. In this connection I am impressed with the word "fusion" which is described by Schafer in *Aspects of Internalization*. "Fusion refers to a quality of projective experience or action that depends on the presence of aggressive and libidinal tendencies and yet cannot be reduced to anything like a juxtaposition or aggregate of these tendencies; it is as if, in a context of compatibility or mutual reinforcement, they have blended into one tendency, often with ego-syntonic, pleasurable results. Commonplace instances of fusion are observed in the loving sex act; in unanxious competition in games or sports with friends; and in responsible assertiveness against loved ones, such as the fond parent's firm control of his child when that control is in the child's interest. The aggressive and libidinal sides of these acts are not in a tug-of-war, as they are in the acts we term ambivalent. In general, the aggression in fusion appears to contribute to dominating and controlling rather than to destroying or being cruel."

Yeast keeps the action in the identity struggle moving in a way that permits each person to maintain his dignity and self-respect. Yeast in the identity struggle permits that which is useless to be cast aside and circulated back in the nitrogen cycle.

STOCHASTIC APPROACH
Feedback Necessity

Where yeast is constantly moving and bubbling in the mix, it builds its power quietly and subtly. In order to highlight the need for constant movement and evaluation in the interpersonal relationships involved, I have chosen the word "stochastic." Stochastic is used for its particular emphasis in moving with a constant plan for change in the rapidly changing world. Like a fencer holding on the "stocho," that is, target, moving toward his opponent, the decision for being on target may depend on the last flick of the wrist. The fencer can participate, as a gentleman, with no anxiety in the outcome of the competition, but with the desire for self-expression.

I suspect that I shall be criticized with some justification for using the symbol of an adversary system rather than one of love. Those who would speak in terms of "love and marriage" can find the same principle described by Watson giving an account of Margaret Mead's new role patterns as "a ballet in which each couple must make up their steps as they go along. When he is insistent, should she yield, and how much? When she is demanding, should he resist and how firmly, who takes the next step forward or the next step back?"

The ministerial marital counselor has many opportunities for training in the use of feedback and a stochastic approach as a style of life. The National Training Laboratory system, the Indiana University Plan for Adult Education in the Church, and much of the group life theory that is described in many texts and at many educational centers is available to clergy in short courses and palatable doses.

As I write this paragraph on the eve of the Apollo 11 moonshot, the feedback concept seems particularly significant to me. If men can plan for the shifting scene and universe in teams of thousands, in teams using two million or so parts in a mechanical device, it would seem not so monumental to me that men of good will, who work to counsel people in relationships of love, could find ever-increasing ways to use themselves and the knowledge at their disposal for the betterment of the families of the world.

"Stochastic" is a yeasty word and counsels one to be light on his feet, looking out with a clear eye and moral courage in a moving and vibrant scene. The counselor must be able to see the movement or lack of movement in the client he counsels. The counselor who either gets ahead of his client or conversely, does not recognize that the client is ahead of him, has lost his effectiveness in the relationship.

There is also another danger which requires a stochastic approach in this profession—that counselors do not evaluate their work. Emily Mudd points toward this need in "A Philosophy and Method" in *Man and Wife*. She uses the term a "cultish apathy" as the warning symbol that thoughtful persons check their work and put it under the scrutiny of others in the professional field. Indeed, the brewmaster must check the mix just as Hiltner asks the vintner to bottle the wine before it turns to vinegar.

SPIRIT—MORAL IMPLICATIONS

The religious metaphor of yeast was frankly cast into the brewer's vat not with the intent of being arrogant or impious. It seems to me that the brewer's vat signifies an earthiness that I intend in order to make the point of this essay. We need to allow growth and sparkle to come into every aspect of family life and in every aspect of our work as ministerial marital counselors. Even that which we discard or rebel against must have the yeast added. The cycles of nature go on, we know, and life goes on in God and His people, we believe.

For the Jew, the Shekinah, the continuing presence of God, goes forward and abides. For the Christian, what was seen through the eye of faith to be dead and closed is alive and open, moving in the Spirit. Yeast is in the lump of life, all of it! Ministerial marital counselors with this faith and knowledge should not feel the necessity for having to solve anyone's problems, but they do need to respond appropriately to any of the people of God who need what he can share. This brings us back full circle through the considerations of the body and the mind. The following questions will always be there: What are the issues for us to work on and what are the dimensions of the problems we can handle? What are the priorities for work and which direction do we take?

These two questions bring the religious issues into focus. What are we really called to do? And where does the Spirit lead us?

In very secular terms we ask the ministerial marital counselor to bring definition to his problems and to set his priorities aright. For Drucker the last question comes first. ". . . action decisions are rarely made on the basis of ideology. The crucial question is: 'What comes first?' rather than 'What should be done?' There is often substantial agreement as to what should be done, but there is always disagreement as to what should be done first."

For the man-of-faith, prayer and openness to the creative possibilities in every decision, may be the answer. This does not mean, at least for me, that prayer should be a part of counseling sessions except as one's own interior life is committed to God and as one prays for the best possibilities to come out of the session. Prayer can be a very real part of a hospital or sick call routine for the pastor, but in the counseling session it stands the risk of being manipulative. The prayer intention can be expressed to the client nonverbally as the counselor gives his very best to the task at hand.

Prayer is always important but it should not lead to "religious isolationism" or "other-wordly quietism." Prayer belongs at least in the community life of church and synagogue and hopefully in the world outside those doors. Nature and life itself have no meaning if religion is radically interiorized.

The ministerial marital counselor need not put aside his scientific training or his psychological insights to bring the religious dimension into his work. His deep concern for the personal integrity of the client and professional associates will be the yeast at the bottom that sustains his life, giving him the moral courage even occasionally to reset his priorities and take the leading of the Spirit.

SELECTED BIBLIOGRAPHY

1. Barbour, Ian G.: *Issues in Science and Religion.* Englewood Cliffs, N.J., Prentice-Hall, Inc., 1966.
2. Clebsch, William S.: American religion and the cure of souls, in Cutler, Donald R., *The Religious Situation.* Beacon, N.Y., Beacon Press, 1969, p. 933 ff.
3. Drucker, Peter F.: *The Age of Discontinuity.* N.Y., Harper and Row, 1969.
4. Goodall, Norman, Ed.: *The Uppsala Report of 1968.* Geneva, Switzerland, World Council of Churches Press, 1969.
5. Hiltner, Seward: *Ferment in the Ministry.* N.Y., Abingdon, 1961.
6. Holt, Robert R., and Luborsky, Lester: *Personality Patterns of Psychiatrists.* N.Y., Basic Books, 1958.
7. Marney, Carlyle: *Structures of Prejudice,* N.Y., Abingdon, 1961.
8. May, Rollo: *Psychology and the Human Dilemma.* N.Y., VanNostrand, 1967.
9. Mudd, Emily H., and Krich, Aron: *Man and Wife.* N.Y., W. W. Norton & Co., Inc., 1957.
10. Neubeck, Gerhard: The dimensions of the "Extra" in extramarital relations. Hirsch L. Silverman, Ed., *Marital Counseling.* Springfield, Ill., Charles C Thomas, 1967.
11. Reevy, William R.: Educational and professional training of the marital counselor. Hirsch L. Silverman, Ed., *Marital Counseling.* Springfield, Ill., Charles C. Thomas, 1967.
12. Reik, Theodore: *Listening with the Third Ear.* Chapter XV, N.Y., Evergreen, 1948.
13. Rokeach, Milton: *The Opened and Closed Mind.* New York, Basic Books, 1960.
14. Schafer, Roy: *Aspects of Internalization.* N.Y., International Universities Press, Inc., 1968.
15. Schrag, Peter: Ivan Illich, the Christian as rebel. *The Saturday Review,* July 19, 1969.
16. Silverman, Hirsch L.: *Marital Counseling.* Springfield, Ill., Charles C Thomas, 1967.
17. Watson, Goodwin: *Social Psychology/Issues and Insights.* New York, J. B. Lippincott Co., 1966.
18. Wolberg, Lewis R.: *The Tecnhique of Psychotherapy.* N.Y., Grune & Stratton, Inc., 1954.

Chapter 40

SOME THEOLOGICAL IMPLICATIONS IN MARRIAGE COUNSELING

MERLE R. JORDAN

URING A WOMEN'S GROUP therapy session that was discussing sex, an insightful woman, whom we shall call Claudia, shared her story with some awkwardness and embarrassment and yet with courage. "My husband Bruce never wants to have sex relations with me, and I feel like some kind of nut because I'm so frustrated. It seems strange to me that most of the women I talk to about intimate things complain because their husbands want too much sex. But that is not true of my marriage. My husband never wants to go to bed with me. That shatters me. What is wrong with me as a woman? Am I not enough of a woman so that he would desire me? Or am I such an oversexed woman that I cannot accept what Bruce says are 'the normal sexual patterns of married life' . . . . . . Sometimes I am afraid that I am abnormal or perverted because of my sexual desires. My mother made me feel that sex was dirty and sinful. She said that men were animals and that a woman had to put up with sex as a marital duty. But my doctor has told me that mother's attitude was not right. A woman has a right to expect sexual fulfillment in marriage. He says that I am not abnormal because I want to have sex relations and to enjoy them. He has even suggested a number of times that I have some affairs so that I can find sexual fulfillment that way. I wonder what you all think about that suggestion. I must admit that at times I am tempted to follow the doctor's advice just to see if I could really be happy in a sexual relationship and perhaps even to show that husband of mine that I could get along without him. But I'm afraid that I'd feel so guilty that I'd be in a worse mess if I had an affair."

During the discussion, one of the group members asked, "Did you have any clues prior to your marriage that your husband would be like this?" Claudia replied: "Yes, I realize now that there were some indications of this, back before we got married, but I didn't see it that way then. I remember how I had a number of fellows who dated me, and they all tried to go as far as they could in making out with me. But my upbringing caused me to dislike aggressive men and to think that those who tried to make out were sinful and dirty and didn't really care about me. They only wanted sex. Then along came Bruce and he was so different from all the rest. He was so nice and gentlemanly. He didn't try to make me; in fact, it was only after many months of dating that he even kissed me goodnight. I felt that he respected me and that he was a person of high moral and spiritual character. So I married him. Now I know that I misread his 'virtue.' I thought that it was all noble and good, but now I can see that much of it was fear, inhibitions, and sexual problems."

There are a number of moral and ethical questions that are involved in Claudia's story. Of course a major issue would deal with the pros and the cons of the doctor's advice to her to have an affair. Or the question of what is a healthy attitude toward sex could be another moral concern. Another issue might be whether she should really stay with her husband who is not fulfilling some significant needs in her life. As important as these and other issues are, let us focus on a theological implication that is too often overlooked in many marriage counseling situations. This issue has to deal with the question of who is functioning as the ultimate authority in the superego or conscience of the person and thus dictating many of the attitudes and patterns of the marital relationship. In other words, who is functioning as the final authority or "god" in Claudia's life. From the brief material presented above and other evidence it was clear that in her childhood Claudia had accepted her mother as the ultimate authority in terms of the development of an attitude toward sex. She had internalized what she had perceived to be her mother's values so that she saw aggressive men as all bad and a passive man like Bruce as good. (In all fairness it is important to point out that the child's image of the parent may be somewhat different from the real parent. Claudia's mother may not have been as prudish, puritanical, and moralistic as Claudia thought, but nonetheless she acted according to the image of her mother as she saw her. As Dr. Eric Berne wrote: "A person acts and feels, not according to what things are like, but according to his mental image of what they are like.")

Now the significant theological point is that the internalized image of the parent functions like a god or idol in the individual's life. The word "idol" is being used here in the sense made meaningful by Dr. Paul Tillich that an idol is anything relative that is made into an absolute. Thus a parental image that is made into an absolute functions as an idol in the person's life and may not only have significant authority in the determination of the choice of a marital partner, as in the case of Claudia, but also in determining many of the attitudes and patterns of behavior in the marital relationship. Claudia had rationalized that her mother was the good and true ultimate authority and that her advice in regard to boy-girl relationships, sex, and marriage was the gospel truth. Usually the idol who is creating such a disruptive influence in the person's life has, to some extent, been rationalized as good. The idol's authority has not been questioned too seriously and the person tends to identify the idol's attitudes and teachings as good and his own needs and feelings as bad. Thus counseling needs to provide an opportunity for Claudia and others for confronting the idol image with the harmful messages and deceptive lies, masquerading as truth, that have been destructive of personal and marital harmony.

This truth about the effects of the idolatry of parental images in marriage is depicted in a cartoon showing a newly married couple lying timidly in bed with a sense of awkwardness. Hanging on the wall above their double bed are four individual portraits of their parents looking down with judgmental scowls upon the couple below. The deep and profound influence that the images of parents can make on the marital relationship is impressively clear in this cartoon. The frowning parental faces imply "you are a bad boy and a bad girl for wanting to indulge in sexual relations." The observer can see the resulting shame and guilt emanating from the faces of the man and the woman who desire to have intercourse. This is also similar to the experience of the middle-aged married woman of a highly moralistic background who could not go to church on Sunday morning if she and her husband had intercourse on Saturday evening since she pictured God to be like the frowning and disapproving parents.

The crippling effects of fixation, especially around parental influences, have been recognized for some time. But it has been through the work of Dr. Wilfried Daim that it has been acknowledged that what Freud referred to as the object of fixation is really an idol that operates in the psyche with the power of the divine. Daim states: "Empirical research of analytic processes confirm that Freud was right in seeing the real root of neurosis in a fixation of the human being on a object of childhood. At closer examination we found that in every case the object of the fixation possesses an absolute character. The object of fixation in Freud's system is what we call an idol."

This chapter seeks to take this concept of idolatry and show how the psychic idol often plays a significant role in disturbed marriages. If the hang-up with the internalized idol-image is not worked through prior to marriage, it will create problems in marriage. In fact, the original relationship with the idol may be approximately recreated in the relationship to the spouse.

Let us look more concretely at the ideas about idolatry through a counseling situation. A woman in her middle forties, whom we shall call Eleanor, was unhappy in her marriage as well as suffering from ulcers and depression. She had a very difficult time communicating with her domineering and authoritarian husband. She bottled up her feelings, and most of the time she was a passive and submissive marital partner. In discussing some of the origins of the difficulties of sharing her feelings, she told of a pattern that she had developed in childhood with her mother in regard to the expression of hurt feelings. Interestingly enough, her mother had regularly read the Beatitudes to her. One of these sayings of Jesus is, "Blessed are they that mourn for they shall be comforted." Or one can paraphrase this thought in these words "Blessed are they who can let themselves experience and express their hurts, disappointments, and grief for they shall then find healing and comfort." However, when this woman was a little girl and she would be hurt or disappointed and show any of these feelings either verbally or nonverbally her mother would say, "Shut up. Go to your room. Don't be a cry-baby." Now which authority would we expect Eleanor to have followed? Naturally the impact of the mother's attitude was greater when she was scolding than when she was reading. Thus in relationship to dealing with hurt, Eleanor had followed the authority of the mother rather than the spiritual authority of Jesus. In her psychic life Eleanor had set up the image of her disapproving mother as the "god" who taught her what was right and wrong, and she had persisted in her married life to follow this same kind of repressive authority. In fact, she had married a man whose repressive attitude to the communication of her feelings was similar to her mother's original attitude toward her. The internalized mother image acted like "god," and the role of the dominating husband fell right in line with Eleanor's idolatry of such authority. Even though Eleanor felt trapped and frustrated, she had also developed through years of experience a feeling of "at homeness" with such authority. She both resented and depended upon the authoritarian directiveness of the idol and her husband. For example, she had found advantages in the safety and security of having someone else make decisions for her and maintain control over her intense feelings rather than face the risks and anxiety involved in asserting herself in decision making and in the expression of her feelings. So while she wanted to throw off the yoke of the idol and the tyranny of her husband she also clung tenaciously to this "security blanket" of dependency on such authority.

H. V. Dicks expresses this basic intrapsychic fixation around the bad internal object and the resulting marital conflict in this way: "The individual remains unconsciously still at grips with the object of conflict and with his own complex of feelings surrounding that figure (termed the bad internal object) . . . . Marital problems arise, sooner or later, when the interaction does not permit the working-through of relations with bad internal objects through the marital relationship. The partners choose each other because in the other they sense the promise of such a work-through but also, paradoxically, as a guarantee that it will not need to be worked through, because there is an unconsciously shared deterrent figure." Thus prior to marriage a person may have some clues, which have been ignored, denied, or not taken seriously enough, that there are characteristics in the future mate's personality upon which he can project the image of the original bad object. Likewise, between the couple there may be an unconscious collusion or neurotic complementarity of the fixations so that a working-through of the bad object relations is not possible in the marital interaction. In the courtship one individual may idealize the other as the opposite of the bad inner object or idol and deny to himself that the other has attributes or qualities similar to the psychic idol. In fact the beloved may even be seen as a kind of romantic savior figure who will deliver one from all of the deprivation and hurts of the past. Later in the process of living and interacting together in marriage the couple may find that the idealized images fade and negative images are aroused and projected. Then a reactivation of the unresolved conflict with the psychic idol may develop and may be unconsciously reenacted in the relationship with the spouse. The partner is then perceived as though he is the bad object himself. This mate receives the projection of the bad parental image and all of the complexity of feelings that are associated with such an idol. Thus the basic unresolved problem of idolatry originating in the child-parent relationship is reenacted in the marital relationship. However, while a person may say in anger to his spouse "Oh, you're just like my father (or mother)," he does not realize that he has participated in structuring the marriage relationship in terms of the unresolved idolatrous relationship with his internalized image of father or mother. In the Sullivanian concepts of Interpersonal Psychiatry the idea of the "self-perpetuating organization of the central paranoia" is related to this idea of the recreating of the unresolved idolatry problem in the marriage relationship. The marital partner unconsciously organizes his interaction with his mate to conform with the patterns of interaction that he had with his mother (though idolatry is not limited to the mother image)." It is the intent and goal of the central paranoia to recreate in the patterning of the adult's relationships the specific unpleasant emotional interactions that characterized his situation during infancy. This period represented the most direct and intense interaction with the mothering figures. The central paranoia became the condensation of all the negative and frustrating aspects of this early interaction. . . . As the infant becomes an adult he organizes the patterns of his primary integration, of interactions with those people who are of particular significance to him, in such a way that they will have the same attitude toward him that his mother had when he was a baby." The main point in this discussion is that the marriage counselor needs to be aware of the real possibility that the conflictful marital relationship before him may be the result of the recreation of unresolved idolatrous relationships from childhood. The marriage counselor needs to consider the holy deadlock of the couple as having profound meaning when understood through the perspective of the idolatrous relationships being reenacted in the marriage. Thus the marriage counselor may have to consider idolatry as a central issue with which the therapy has to deal. In fact, one can hypothesize that this reenactment of the idolatrous relationship in the marriage is an unconscious attempt to come to grips with the problem with some hope of resolution (this perspective in parallel to that of Ferenczi in dream interpretation wherein he believes that dreams are an attempt to master and settle traumatic experiences). Unfortunately the spouses involved are not able to have this positive perspective of the marital conflict presenting an opportunity to resolve the idolatry problem.

In a larger framework than marriage, it is possible to see that an individual so projects this idol-image that in his psychic world view he perceives and experiences the ultimate core of reality or the central nature of the universe as being just like the idol. Though he may be an agnostic or atheist intellectually, he still has a subrational view in terms of imagery of some ultimate authority. Similarly, many persons who intellectually would say that the nature of God is love, nevertheless live in the depths of their psyche with an ugly image of the ultimate, such as a wrathful father or depriving mother, and it is this latter authority which most truly directs their life. Such a view of the central nature of reality or ultimate authority as unloving, wrathful, indifferent, impotent, unreliable, etc. will have significant effects upon the individual as well as upon his perceptions and interaction in marriage. While some marriage counselors may feel that this dimension of idolatry should be left in the hands of pastoral counselors, it behooves all of us to look seriously at the implications of idolatry both in terms of the effects of idolatry upon individuals but also upon the marriage relationship itself.

A related concern to the issue of idolatry in marriage counseling is guilt. The dynamics of guilt are complex as are the possibilities for its resolution. However, it is worth looking briefly at one facet of guilt in terms of idolatry and marriage counseling. People who are fixated around a parental image take their cues for guilt from their psychic idol. It is this object of fixation that dictates to the person about what he should and should not feel guilty. To obey the idol is to be without guilt; to disobey the absolutized image is to be guilty. For the marriage counselor to be aware of this connection between the idol and the person's struggle with guilt may prove to be helpful. For example, in the previous case of Eleanor, in which the idolized mother prohibited expressions of hurt and grief, Eleanor would feel guilty if she felt like crying and more guilty if she actually did cry. Her husband, who could not tolerate the expression of such tender feelings, was sensitive to his wife's guilt about such feelings. He could control her by his reinforcing of her guilt about sadness through his showing anger or displeasure if she dared to begin to express these feelings. Thus Eleanor had been conditioned to feel that she was bad if her hurt or sad feelings began to surface and that she was a "good girl" if she did not expose such feelings. She had literally taken her mother's negative attitude toward grief as the gospel truth, and she would feel guilty if she broke this commandment of her idolized mother. She had internalized this negative attitude toward grief as though it were a scriptural truth with all the weight of divine authority and to violate this authority was to commit a sin of considerable import. She experienced her husband as being on the side of the "god" who sought to prohibit the grave transgression of grieving. Most, if not all, theologians and psychotherapists would attest to the therapeutic importance of being able to grieve in situations of loss, and they would affirm that Eleanor need not feel true guilt for her expression of authentic grief. But Eleanor's point of reference for determining her guilt was her mother image acting as the ultimate authority.

The concept of idolatry provides a framework whereby the counselor may view the question of true and false guilt. For a person like Eleanor, who is fixated around an idol, experiences her false guilt as being real and her true guilt she may not experience at all. From a theological perspective of the Judaeo-Christian tradition, the person is not aware of violating the commandments against idolatry, such as, "Thou shalt have no other gods before me" or the first love commandment of Jesus. Eleanor did not realize that she was guilty in the sense that she was literally worshipping and obeying a false god in the form of her mother image functioning as the divine. She did not realize that she was guilty of not being true to her real self because she was not able to be true to the authentic ground of her being. While the person is not fully responsible for causing the idolatry to happen in childhood, nevertheless he does need to own up to the idolatry as his. While he has not consciously projected the idol onto his mate and willfully participated thereby in structuring marital disharmony, he does need to come to the point of accepting responsibility for the fact that his projection of the idol has been an important factor in the marital discord. The person needs to come to the point of accepting or affirming his own guilt of orienting his life around a false god so that he may move beyond the idol to a new center of his existence. Formerly the person has felt guilt for disobeying the idol, whereas what he really needs to feel is the true guilt of having participated in the idolatry that has distorted his perceptions of himself, others, the world, and ultimate reality. This confrontation with the guilt of one's idolatry is not to be seen in the spirit of condemnation but rather in the spirit of therapeutic confession so that one may be free to move beyond the idolatry.

The concept of idolatry may also deepen the counselor's understanding of guilt. For example, this concept may help to guard against a danger in the recent emphasis on responsibility, integrity, and confession of guilt to significant others whereby superficial guilt may be accepted as the real guilt. Thus the confession of guilt may not be at the deepest level that is really necessary for healing. Take the case of a married man who tested out women by subtle flirting. On one occasion when a woman responded passionately and there was some sexual play between them, the man was wracked by guilt. He struggled with the question of whether he should tell his wife or not. For a counselor to deal with this issue basically on the sexual level or to see the moral issue in terms of whether he should confess his involvement with another woman to his wife are simplistic approaches. At a depth level this man may be struggling with the problem of idolatry of the exciting but rejecting mother image around whom he is fixated. He has acted out this struggle at the sexual level to test out whether the female is really cold and rejecting or warm and receptive. In his marriage relationship he may also have unconsciously married a woman who is attractive but frigid, and thus the core of the idolatry is embedded in the marriage. In such an instance, the man needs to come to terms with his guilt for centering his life around such an idol. While many other dynamics need to be explored also, the counselor should not overlook the significance of idolatry in relation to guilt. Otherwise in numerous situations, the counselor may be doing band aid therapy when psychic surgery is indicated to deal with the real guilt.

In light of this brief discussion, let us look in a summary fashion at some of the ramifications that the concept of idolatry poses for marriage counselors and marriage counseling.

Marriage counselors need to recognize the significance of how the absolutized object of fixation functions like an idol in a person's life and plays a significant role in the neurotic selection of mate and in the marital interaction. Not only are the intrapsychic dimensions of this phenomenon important to recognize but also the projection onto the mate of the idol and the complex feelings and patterns around the idol is important to recognize and explore in marital therapy. This reactivation of the child's unresolved struggle with the absolutized parental image projected into the marital relationship offers a frame of reference or another perspective to the marriage counselor in his attempts to understand some of the unconscious meanings of the hangups in marital relationships.

At some appropriate time in the marriage counseling, the counselor may interpret to the couple or to a spouse that the structuring of the deep conflicts in the marriage has been an unconscious reenactment of the unresolved problem of childhood with the idol-image which offers an opportunity to deal with that problem in the present. As a spouse can see that he has projected the idol-image onto the mate, he may become more open to seeing the mate as he really is. He may be able to accept that his image of the spouse is different from the real spouse, although there may be some ways in which the mate has really been like the idol. Also if a partner can see that there was some meaning to his selection of a mate with whom he has developed such a conflictful relationship and that he himself participated in setting up the misery of the marital relationship as a way of restructuring the core of the idolatry problem, he may be less prone to feel that he will solve his problem by divorcing the spouse. In other words, divorce in such an instance may be a way of avoiding facing the idolatry by seeing the spouse as the bad object and leaving him. In any event, whether a couple decide to divorce or to reconcile it is important to try to have them look at the idolatry of images and the projection of these images in the marriage for they are liable to do the same thing in another marriage if the idolatry is not explored.

Resistance to change in the marital relationship and in the counseling relationship may be seen as a part of the person's commitment to the idol. As much as the person may dislike being held psychic captive by the idol, he also is dependent upon the idol and he would expose himself to risk, guilt, and anxiety if he were to change according to the values of someone else. The counselor needs to appreciate that the person has held his psychic world together through the style of life that he has developed around the idol. The marriage counselor needs to help the partners to confront and acknowledge their idolatries and the profound reasons (such as avoiding anxiety) why they want to maintain their commitment to the idol and thus resist change.

The techniques for analyzing idolatry and for helping people to synthesize their lives around a new center need to be explored and clarified much further than can be done here. The variety of images that become idols and the defensive strategies of living that seek to cope with such idols is a fascinating study in itself. The meeting ground of theology and psychology at the point of true and false guilt in terms of idolatry offers a fruitful area for further research. The work of Roberto Assagioli in psychosynthesis and Wilfried Daim in depth psychology offers some guidelines, but further explorations must be made in relating both theory and techniques to marriage counseling.

The marriage counselor needs to come to terms with the question of the ultimate authority in his own psyche. For if he is hung up with his own idolatry, he may not be able to deal meaningfully with the problem of idolatry in his counseling. Also the counselor needs to look at the ultimate source of his own values in terms of what he would see as the therapeutic goals for those marital partners who may seek a new authority and new values to replace an idol and its values. Does the counselor take his final source of authority from the rational thoughts of his own mind, from the criteria for mental health or marital happiness in his profession, from the therapeutic principles of one of the fathers of psychology, from humanistic ethics, from the historical revelation of the nature of man and God in the biblical tradition, or from some other source? The ultimate authority for the counselor will play a part, however hidden and subtle, in his counseling. Also a related concern is that while people in counseling may become free from a former idol and function more effectively than before therapy, they may also gain a new idol that may be more sophisticated and deceptive, which they have incorporated from the therapy or perhaps from their therapist. For example, there is the case of the former bible quoting fundamentalist who through his analysis experienced himself as being free and mature; only now he quotes Freud as dogmatically as he once quoted the scriptures. Thus it is imperative that the counselor takes seriously, both personally and professionally, the implications of idolatry.

SELECTED BIBLIOGRAPHY

1. Berne, Eric: *A Laymen's Guide to Psychiatry and Psychoanalysis.* New York, Grove Press, 1957, p. 16.
2. Daim, Wilfried: On depth-psychology and salvation. *J Psychotherapy as a Religious Process*, *II*.1, January, 1955, p. 26.
3. Matthew, *5:4.*
4. Dicks, H. V.: Concepts of Marital Diagnosis and Therapy as Developed at the Tavistock Family Psychiatric Units, London, England, in Ethel Nash, Lucie Jessner, and D. Wilfred Abse (Eds.). *Marriage Counseling in Medical Practice.* Chapel Hill, North Carolina, The University of North Carolina Press, 1964, pp. 261 and 266-267.
5. Pearce, Jane and Newton, Saul: *The Conditions of Human Growth.* New York, The Citadel Press, 1963, p. 385.
6. Exodus, *20:3* and Matthew, *22:37.*

Chapter 41

RELIGION AND AGGRESSION

FRANK A. SARGENT, JR.

> So long as our society is more concerned to prevent strife than to
> prevent humiliation, its moral status will be depressing indeed.
> RABBI ABRAHAM HESCHEL

Rᴇᴠ. J. ɪɴɪᴛɪᴀʟʟʏ contacted the counselor because he was becoming over-whelmed by his need to control all of the activities of a medium-sized church. His presenting problem was his struggle with severe depression, perfectionism, and resulting compulsive behavior in the administration of that church.

The client appeared to the counselor as neatly dressed and meticulously groomed, exhibiting little affect, and very controlled in his speech. He began to relate his religious background. He grew up in a very religious Roman Catholic home, with a father who gave little warmth and a mother who was overprotective and compulsively concerned with her only son's health. Apparently under the influence of a friend he was converted to a fundamentalistic* denomination of the Protestant church. Shortly before his conversion he lost his father and his mother remarried only to lose her second husband before the client was twenty. He is now twenty-seven years old, married with one infant son.

Rev. J. was very theological in his early conversations with the counselor. He felt inadequate spiritually, focusing often on eschatology. He could not enjoy the present and would look forward to the second coming of Christ as the solution to many of his problems. He would awaken in the morning saddened that he was not in heaven and anxious about the planning for that immediate day and week.

When the counselor inquired whether the reverend had any negative or angry feelings, the client responded by quoting a New Testament passage that said, "Let all bitterness and wrath, and anger and clamor, and evil speaking be put away from you."† He claimed that it was not Christlike to be angry and he made a conscious effort to avoid predicaments that involved angry feelings. Later as he described his marriage he asserted with

---

*The term "fundamentalistic" refers to a trend in the Protestant church that emerged in the early nineteen hundreds. It stressed the fundamentals which were a series of pamphlets advocating orthodox theology. It later degenerated into a movement stressing separatism, a negative ethic of prohibitions, and an anti-intellectualism.

†King James Version of the Holy Bible, Ephesians, 4:31.

some pride that he and his wife *never* argued. Whenever she would get angry or whenever he was in danger of losing his temper he would deliberately walk from that room. The result was a neurotically motivated clergyman and as the counselor later discovered a very depressed wife.

Rev. J. was typical of the many clients that sought help at a pastoral counseling center in Philadelphia. This article is the result of both my perplexity and my supervisor's, Abraham Schmitt D.S.W., at the high number of marital partners exhibiting depressive symptomology that come from a very religious and often very conservative background. Out of roughly one hundred clients or couples that came from a religiously conservative background approximately 56 per cent exhibited clear depressive symptoms.

Often they came with great despair over their "spiritual" problem. They found themselves feeling out of touch with God or wondering whether God has continued to accept them, only to discover in the course of counseling that they were in reality alienated from their children and their spouses. When the family and marital relationships improved, often the "spiritual" problem would disappear.

A great many of our clients had tremendous difficulty with the expression of aggressive or negative feelings. They came from a religious background that contained a built in prohibition against anger, this is what I have chosen to call a "heritage of denial."

In this article, which does not presume to be a comprehensive statistical and empirical study but rather my ruminations regarding this counseling experience, I want first to examine the relationship between aggression and religion. Presenting the positive function religion can play in controlling aggression and then examining in detail a neurotic and sick interpretation of Christianity, an interpretation which seeks to avoid any negative or angry elements by advocating their complete rejection. I hope to illustarte this thesis with ample case material.

Secondly, I would like to discuss the pathological support this theology gives to the neurotic interaction in marriage, suggesting that the result in the marital partners is alienation and loneliness, inadequate problem solving, inability to express warm feelings, and depression. Truely this sick theology contributes to sick marriages.

Lastly, I would like to suggest a possible therapeutic approach that in our experience seems to promote quicker resolutions of the problems.

Religion has been seen to be a positive force in controlling aggression. Karl Menninger in his book *Love Against Hate* says, "The position I have maintained throughout this book is that the problem of life is the problem of controlling and directing aggressions. If religion enables us to do this realistically, it is no illusion and not a neurosis."*

---

*Menninger, Karl: *Love Against Hate*. New York, Harcourt, Brace and World, Inc., 1942, p. 191.

Early in the history of psychoanalysis Freud implied that religion was derived from fear and he related this infantile fear to a realistic comparison of man's own weakness to the immensity and power of the universe. Menninger suggests that man is not so often afraid of the immensity of the universe as he is of the immensity and malignity of his own aggressive instincts. He also suggests that a healthy religion may very well be and excellent defense against this internal danger. Menninger also draws a comparison between the religious act of atonement and the psychotherapeutic act of undoing. Both acts are directed toward making an organism whole. Where there has been hatred and aggression expressed, the religious person may need atonement† and restitution. In therapy the counselor tries to *undo* the patterns that have resulted in dysfunctioning and mishandling of aggression. Menninger concludes with an affirmation in the possibility of religion and psychiatry both making major contributions to the mastering of aggressions and the promotion of love.

Likewise Leon Saul has a chapter on hostility and religion in his classic work, *The Hostile Mind.* He sees the handling of hostility as the central problem in human affairs. In the individual as well as in societies the failure to mature, or fixation at an infantile level of functioning is the basic source of hostility and of a deficient capacity to love. A religious *feeling* is related to a depth of a closeness to maturity of motivation. It involves humility and an ability to love in more selfless motivation. These are two goals espoused by both religion and psychotherapy, that is the freeing of the mind from infantile egocentricity, and the subsequent decrease in destructive hostility and increase in mature creativity. He sees hostility as the true evil or devil and indicative of immaturity. Therefore, "this hostility is the central problem for religion as it is for science."‡

It seems clear from much that dynamic psychology has to say that religion can play a very positive function in both the controlling of hostility and aggression as well as in the promotion of a proper motivation based on love. However, the tragedy appears when we discover that much of Christianity is infected with the misconception that aggression is not only to be handled but that it is, in and of itself, in any form, evil and unacceptable. Even Saul notes that aggression (from the Latin meaning moving actively) has a constructive dimension. In distinction to aggression he defines hostility as a destructive tendency toward another organism or toward oneself. Hence, aggression when sublimated, directed constructively can be extremely beneficial. Perhaps, one of the reasons for Senator Robert Kennedy's

---

†By the term atonement I mean the act of the covering of sins, thereby treating them as nonexistent and the sinner as if he had not committed them. It is not that our sins are condoned and conveniently forgotten, but we confess them and find absolution and forgiveness.

‡Saul, Leon J.: *The Hostile Mind.* New York, Random House, 1956, p. 149.

popularity was his attempt to deal with the ills of our society with constructive aggression. Whether one agreed with his political program or not one had to admire his drive that sprung from his proper use of aggression.

The pattern for the denial of any legitimate aggressive feelings was articulated and institutionalized in the third century with the rise of monastic Christian asceticism. Monasticism and asceticism were not prominent in the first two centuries of Christianity. However, those in the Christian tradition of the third century believed they found injunctions in the teachings of Jesus and the New Testament to lead the life of self-denial. The accuracy of their interpretation is open to question. The ascetics felt that they must remove themselves from the world and deny any bodily pleasure. The focus of their life was to be peace and communion with God. Hence the idea of fasting and celibacy grew prominent. Along with the deliberate suppression of the legitimate sexual drive, there was a stress on the controlled life and therefore a denial also of any carnal feelings such as anger. Thus both of the basic drives postulated by dynamic psychology, the life or creative drive and the death or aggressive drive were denied as permissible in the experience of the true Christian.

Jesus did, at times, enjoin his followers to live a disciplined life. In one notable instance he commanded a rich young man to sell all he had and give to the poor, yet in contrast to John the Baptist who was clearly an ascetic, Jesus was accused by his critics of eating and drinking with the sinners and neither he nor his disciples fasted during his lifetime. The Christian tradition has never completely transcended the negative way of life introduced in the third century.

Throughout the history of the Christian Church in both its Protestant and Roman Catholic forms there have been significant numbers that have advocated the life of self-denial. This was particularly true in America with the rise of frontier pietism and later American fundamentalism. However, it is quite clear that a denial of aggressive feelings is not limited to the more conservative wings of Protestantism and Catholicism but infects the whole of Christianity and other religious beliefs. The articulation of this motif is most clearly heard in the more conservative traditions. For the therapist dealing with a person of strong religious convictions it is very necessary to recognize and treat this "heritage of denial."

All too often therapists have felt that they were immune from dealing with the value systems of their clients or patients. It seems clear that many values are implicitly or explicitly involved in the therapeutic process. Carl Rogers has noted that just the presence of an accepting, empathetic, and genuine counselor can communicate to the client the positive value that he is of worth. This is the same religious value that Christianity has been declaring when it has asserted that man is in the image and likeness of God and that man is therefore invested with a dignity and worth.

It would seem that a weight of responsibility rests on therapists coming from a religious orientation and particularly on the new breed of clergymen specializing in pastoral counseling to call to awareness in the therapeutic community the fact that therapists are, in fact, dealing with the religious systems and beliefs of clients as they are doing therapy. One clear example of this is the neurotic person from a religious background who is desperately struggling with his aggressions. This is not to say that religious values or beliefs can cause or cure a neurosis or a neurotic interaction in marriage but it does mean that religious values are often found in the structure of neurosis and neurotic marriages.

The Group for the Advancement of Psychiatry in report number 67 titled "The Psychic Function of Religion in Mental Illness and Health," suggests that the religious values and beliefs are present in neurosis either as the result of a defensive attempt to resolve intrapsychic conflict or because they are incorporated into the ongoing neurotic process. Hence they can influence the characteristics of the neurosis, its course, and intensity. The same thing might also be said about a neurotic interaction in marriage. The person with a rich religious background might certainly use attitudes of a religious nature in aiding repression, in attempting to overcome intense but unacceptable impulses such as anger and to justify self-righteous anger.

The case of Mary richly illustrates the neurotic who used her religious beliefs to deny her anger. Mary is a thirty-year-old housewife and a mother of three who complained about what she called "depression." She experienced periods of depersonalization, anorexia, and has contemplated suicide. She talked much about how she "lives her thoughts around herself," which pretty well describes an obsessive symptomatology. She seemed not to be primarily depressed but frightened of her anger, exhibiting the paranoid-omnipotent type of thinking of the individual who as she said, has to "make things right." Along with this she suffers from feelings of inferiority and worthlessness.

Her father was an alcoholic who never related to Mary in an accepting fashion always causing her to attempt to prove herself and her love. However, she can never feel that things are done right no matter how hard she works. As might be expected she married a man on the surface vastly different from her father, calm, poised, and very steady, yet beneath the surface quite insecure. Her husband never allowed her to argue with him stating that as man of the house she was to be submissive to him. Often he would quote Ephesians 5:22,23, "Wives submit yourselves unto your own husbands as unto the Lord. For the husband is the head of the wife even as Christ is the head of the church: and he is the savior of the body." Hence because of his insecurity he would never allow her free vent of her aggressive feelings toward him and males in general.

Mary would await the time when she could do religious battle with her husband. Whenever, she could marshall an army of Biblical passages and theological constructs that would prove a particular point she would feel free to get angry at her husband, however, these times were few and far between.

Mary first entered conventional psychiatric therapy for six months. She felt she was getting no help and turned to the pastoral counselor. After a psychiatric evaluation and several joint interviews with both parties the therapist tried in a kindly and firm way to interpret Mary's anger and her efforts to defend against it. This was unsuccessful until the counselor spent some time dealing with Mary's neurotic interpretation and use of Christianity. She felt she could never get angry unless she was absolutely justified and even then she would feel guilty about any aggressiveness. The counselor suggested to her the example of Christ who used his aggressiveness constructively in relation to the Pharisees of his day and the money changers in the temple. He also spent time examining the angry feelings expressed by Job and numerous of the psalmists. After this digression Mary began to see a much more positive side to her religious beliefs. They did not hang as a millstone around her neck, judging her and echoing an eternal "no" to any differing with her husband. In the course of counseling Mary was better able to work out some of her old hostilities toward her father and began to use her aggressiveness more constructively in relation to her husband. He was at first threatened but after several joint sessions saw and appreciated his wife's new found assertiveness and confidence. As a result of this freedom Mary gained weight, had fewer bouts with depression and became less obsessively concerned with herself and more truly concerned with her family and friends. The intense neurotic interaction in the marriage as well as the intrapsychic conflict were eased not only by dealing with Mary's feelings directly but by also dealing with the religious system that fed and supported these conflicts.

The total rejection and the labeling of angry feelings as sinful has grave repercussions for the marital relationship. One negative result is the promotion of loneliness and alienation in one or both of the marital partners. Our suspicion as we worked with these clients was that both were, in fact, alienated from each other and that the defensive systems of both parties dovetailed.

T. S. Eliot expresses the aching loneliness of modern man as one of the characters in *"The Cocktail Party."*

Do you know—
It is no longer worthwhile to speak to anyone . . .
No . . . it isn't that I want to be alone,
But that everyone's alone . . .
They make noises, and think they are talking to each other;
They make faces, and think they understand each other.
And I'm sure they don't. Is it a delusion?

Loneliness is an intrinsic condition of human existence and it can be a time of creativity, reflection, and a time of asserting one's self-identity. However, many of the clients I saw were not involved in creativity but in the process of alienation from their partners and personal stagnation. Often they would "spiritualize" this experience and speak of losing communion or fellowship with God and with their families.

Because religiously they rejected negative feelings as legitimate they were unable emotionally to share them with each other. Hence the only solution was to create enough distance between pairs in order that the negative or aggressive feelings would not be stimulated. It is a given fact that when two people come into proximity, feelings are aroused and often the very fact that the two are of different personalities will create the condition for disagreements and conflicts. As Rev. J. walked from the room where his wife was for fear of having an argument, he created the ideal atmosphere for estrangement and alienation. In the case of the good reverend this feeling was also articulated spiritually by feeling his status in relation to God had become precarious and if he continued feeling depressed God would eventually reject him. Without intensive ties in the marriage which have genuine meaning, the marital partners will maintain an essential anonymity and the relationship will become contractual with the partners treating each other as objects, not persons.

When there is this alienation there is obviously little or minimal need satisfaction and hence frustration. Frustration of needs often leads to more anger and hence the neurotic cycle of interaction in the marriage is completed.

It also follows from this that marriages that contain a prohibition against angry feelings also contain little true warmth or love. So often therapeutically when someone can feel freer in handling and expressing constructively aggressive feelings the dam that has been holding back warmth and love is broken. Where there is alienation and loneliness there is not the deep sharing and expressing of love. When negative feelings cannot be shared often positive feelings cannot be shared. Perhaps, the case of Mrs. O. will illustrate this.

Mrs. O. is the thirty-year-old wife of a minister doing inner-city work among the poor. She came because of an inability to control her actions when she became angered, and a general feeling of depression. She was apt to react to her husband's criticisms with anger out of proportion to the situation, and she found herself withdrawing by leaving the house in anger driving around in her car struggling with some mild suicidal thoughts and feeling she had done something very wrong. She was never able to successfully argue with her husband because she entertained a very perfectionistic image of him. She admired his faith, his ambition, his talent, and his ability to "do anything good." She struggled with feelings of inadequacy all her life, centering often around her own sexual identity and femininity. Obviously her husband's perfectionism made her feel more inadequate and as a result she did not feel she had the right as a person to argue with him.

As we progressed in the counseling relationship Mrs. O. admitted to great guilt feelings about masturbating as a child and while she was initially dating her husband. She felt this might have bearing on the fact that she has never enjoyed sexual contact with her husband. In the early years of their marriage she would pretend to be enjoying intercourse but inside she would be completely revolted. She said her husband was tender and often would spend a good deal of time in foreplay and she would be physiologically excited and ready for intercourse, yet inside she would be screaming for him to hurry up and be done with it. Now with the arrival of two children she was more tired at night and found herself increasingly unable to control her disgust at sexual relations. Interestingly enough Rev. O. would often want sexual relations after an argument, at a time when Mrs. O. was feeling especially inadequate and frustrated.

Mrs. O. was unable to express negative or angry feelings in any constructive way to her husband and as I later discovered was really unable to express the warm feelings to her husband which she internally experienced. As we explored the marriage in both conjoint and concurrent interviews we found that because Mrs. O. was unable to resolve her negative feelings through constructive discussions she tended to act them out sexually. As she grew in feelings of adequacy she began at first to be able to tolerate sexual relations and later began to have regular orgasms. One of the significant turning points in the counseling was the assurance that she had a right to try to resolve her anger "in relationship to her husband" not out in the car alone. As with many of our clients, Rev. and Mrs. O. honestly felt it was a sin to become angry. Many times with the highly religious person an appeal to their own authority will aid the process of counseling. I asked in one instance in a conjoint interview in which both had become angry and made no attempt to deal with this anger whether they were aware of some of the teachings of Scripture that advocated creative anger. In the New Testament book of Ephesians 4:26 it says, "Be ye angry and sin not: let not the sun go down on your wrath." This is an imperative, a command to be appropriately angry and contains the implication that it must be dealt with and expressed not suppressed. If the sun goes down on the anger it is apt to degenerate into bitterness and resentment. The experience of anger is even ascribed to God in numerous Old Testament passages.

After Mrs. O. began to deal creatively with the differences between herself and her husband the wealth of warm, loving feelings that had been bottled up was released and the sexual activity increased in quantity and quality. Of course, this is not to say all that this couple needed was training in arguing creatively, because I spent over a year dealing with both in individual, conjoint, and finally group counseling. However, this was one of several significant turning points in the counseling process.

Not only does this "heritage of denial" promote alienation and an inability to express warm feelings but it also inhibits a couple's ability to solve problems which they as a pair face. Problem solving is a necessary skill for good marital interaction, and it involves a number of steps. The first is that both must recognize a problem exists. The problem is better handled if some of the feelings surrounding it are also raised rather than left to fester. However, if anger is unacceptable and inappropriate often the problem itself will not be raised. When a "problem" is raised one of the chief dangers in a very religious home is that one party will attack the other partner's ego with religious terminology and concepts. Instead of focusing constructively on the problem facing the couple the argument ranges far and wide and focuses often on religious issues. In the case of Mary often the argument would degenerate into accusations of a lack of spirituality and Christian obedience on the part of the wife. When this happens either the parties mobilize their defenses and a hot war is on or alienation and withdrawing occur and a cold war has begun. The object of attack should be the problem at hand rather than the other person and the couple's creative anger at this problem should be utilized in obtaining a solution.

Along with my findings concerning loneliness, lack of warmth, and inadequate problem solving I would like to reflect on the depressive symptom that provided the impetus for our study. All of the cases presented thus far have contained elements of depression. Rev. J's depression was presented in religious terms. He wanted to "go to heaven" to escape the pressures of life on earth. Certainly this preoccupation with death and the life hereafter masked suicidal wishes. The suicidal wishes and excessive self-depreciation were clearly evident in both the case of Mary and Mrs. O. In these cases there was undue sadness, dejection, and self-depreciation out of proportion to the given situation, as well as great difficulty in sleeping and some early morning awakening. However, the common way for the extremely religious person to handle these feelings was to "spiritualize" them. The Christian is a sinner and of little worth, life is a constant battle, hope does not reside in the present but only in the life hereafter, were common statements made by the clients.

Of course, where there was alienation and little warmth in a marriage and constant frustration over inadequate problem solving there would be extreme frustration and an intensification of infantile needs and drives. When these were consistently unsatisfied there would naturally arise anger. However, with this prohibition against anger and even shame over ones basic needs, a vicious cycle was begun. The frustration led to anger and the anger stimulated anxiety which would lead to a further intensification of the need for love. With the inability of the partners to deal with this anger and frustration in any constructive way and the prohibition against even expressing it and the guilt over feeling the push of these negatives, the individual would be left with no object toward which to direct his anger except himself. Freud and Abraham in particular have noted that depression is a response of the ego to loss, frustration, helplessness, and damage to the ego ideal. In these marriages which contained a great amount of loss and frustration, the anger was inverted. Obviously these clients had developed a predisposition and prototype of this type of reaction from childhood losses and this infantile pattern was reactivated in their marriage. The important thing in dealing with this reaction in someone conditioned by this "heritage of denial" is to note that their neurotic religious attitudes, and beliefs tended to sustain and intensify this reaction and prohibit any satisfactory resolution in their marriages. I began to feel that while it was necessary for the individual to gain some insight into the basis of this pattern of reaction, and to help them appropriately deal with the "here and now," it was also necessary and very helpful to deal with their religious systems. Many times it is frustrating and self-defeating to deal with the rationalizations that clients use as defensive measures against their impulses and conflicts, but in these instances some religious reeducation tended to promote a faster movement of the counseling process. This approach strengthens the ego and helps ameliorate the harsh superego, without taking away the much needed support that religious systems can provide.

When a nonreligious therapist, encounters a patient or client that has been profoundly influenced by a religious system similar to what I have called a "heritage of denial," it would perhaps benefit his work with the client for him to consult with an accredited pastoral counselor, and even in some instances refer to one trained to not only provide the needed therapy but also appropriate religious help.

SUMMARY

The following statements are very tentative conclusions I have reached after reflecting on this counseling experience. Perhaps, someday there will be some solid statistical and empirical work that will give us greater understanding of the function religious attitudes and beliefs play in the neurotic process.

There is within some religious circles an ethic that advocates the complete rejection of angry feelings. I have called this a "heritage of denial."

This religious tradition provides rationalizations that are used by the very religious person to control his anger.

These attitudes tend to sustain and intensify the neurotic process both in the individual and in the marriage interaction.

Many of these people suffer depression, loneliness, inability to express warm feelings, and inadequate problem solving.

Often these symptoms are expressed in religious language.

Many times in the course of counseling significant turning points were reached and the counseling process moved more quickly when the sick religious attitudes were handled.

Chapter 42

BASIC VIEWPOINTS IN COUNSELING AS A FUNCTION OF THE CHRISTIAN CHURCH

MATTI JOENSUU

MOTIVATION

Dᴉꜱᴄᴜꜱꜱɪᴏɴ ʙᴇᴛᴡᴇᴇɴ ᴛᴡᴏ ᴘᴇʀꜱᴏɴꜱ, support given by an experienced person to a young one, care of souls, and counseling—this is in miniature the development of the counseling in the work of the church. It is so essential and natural that hardly any question has been raised in the past whether *this* kind of functioning is relevant or what are the motives for *that*. The expression "care of souls" has often been understood mainly as a clarification relating to religious life and problems of a person. Usually the word "counseling" has much larger contents. In counseling there are possibilities available for clarifying whatever areas of life. Thus in family counseling the emphasis is on a certain area of human life.

Usually these kinds of services are available for everybody in spite of their relationship to any church or religion. In the present situation the counselor makes a profitable use of the knowledge of science, especially of behavioral sciences to be able to understand better the dynamics of human beings and human relations and also the skills and experiences reached not only in the field of care of souls but also in social casework and psychotherapy. A new phenomenon is, too, that there are secular counseling services available in present society. It is difficult to imagine any modern social services without counseling or casework functions at least as a part of the work.

In some countries such as Scandinavia the trend is that state and municipalities take more and more responsibility for all services for individuals and for families. In a situation like this it is really necessary to raise the question whether it is relevant that the churches found and support specialized counseling functions and train workers for that.

The question has been raised if the task of the church is not essentially a religious one. Does that also include counseling? These questions are raised by serious members of the churches and also by outsiders criticizing the work of the churches. Moreover, it has been asked whether the church should not act in the opposite way inspiring society to take more and more responsibilities for counseling. Some people have asked if the motivation of the churches maintaining functions like counseling is to increase their influence to show that they still are indispensable or is the basic motive to convert people and so to increase their membership. In other words, is the church exploiting people or honestly serving them? These kinds of questions have been raised in Scandinavian countries, probably also in North America, and in other parts of the world. It is very necessary to take these questions very seriously and to investigate what the motives really are.

One cannot deny that the churches may have conscious or unconscious motives or in any case possibilities for the motives mentioned above. In the pluralistic society the churches, also feel that they are in a competing society like the other communities. That is why it is very necessary for the churches to clarify their motives. The motives of the churches should be ethically correct and honestly based on the foundations of the churches. They should also be able to clarify honestly the motives of their functions to society in which they are working.

If a church limits its counseling function to serve only its own members, then there are no special problems about them. In that case the purpose of the special counseling function of a certain church is to help, in the best possible way, people with roughly similar values of life and ethical and religious principles. In practice the situation is most often not like that. The counseling functions of the churches are available for all people in spite of their membership to any church or if they do not belong to any church or religious community at all.

Family counseling in Finland has developed mainly as a work of the Lutheran Church (90% of the population). It has been repeatedly emphasized that the only motive for this work must be love of one's neighbor. A counseling center must never be a place for converting clients. It must be ready to help people with the problems for which they are asking help. If a client is an atheist and does not like to hear or mention any word about religion he is accepted as he is. His belief and views of life must be respected. If he belongs to any other church, no attempt is made to convert him but, on the contrary, he is helped to come to a better contact with his own church if necessary. This means that counseling is and should be an ecumenical function whatever church is maintaining. It is most often based on an ecumenical structure in the beginning especially in developing countries where family counseling is beginning to develop and is being maintained by several churches together.

Thus it is possible to summarize that, in principle, counseling is diaconia. Its purpose is to help people where help is needed. In the present situation, especially in industrialized societies, the greatest need for help is most often related to family life and to other human relationships and personal problems. The help given in counseling must be as unselfish as the help given to a person injured in a car accident on the road—without asking what he believes in.

The need for counseling looks so great at present and well-trained counselors are so few that church counseling is hardly unnecessary in any part of the world. But one can ask, what is the trend for the future? Is it not so that the churches had done pioneering work in many other fields such as school education, social work, and maintaining hospitals? But later on when society had developed to take care of these services, it has been relevant that the churches have left their responsibilities of these tasks to the state and municipalities. Will this be the trend also in the development of counseling services? One can say that presently the churches are doing pioneering work, diaconia, in the field where distress is burning as long as societies will be ready to take responsibility for all kinds of counseling work and then the churches can withdraw from these kinds of tasks and concentrate on more religious functions.

One point of view seems to be very clear. The churches must not monopolize counseling services. The need for counseling is really great. Wherever people are served by counseling, especially by skilled workers, it must be welcomed and it is something which is worthwhile to promote the philosophy behind the institution concerned. It is clear that scientific knowledge and skills reached by different groups and schools of counselors mean that people can obtain help in their sufferings and better fulfillment in their life.

On the other hand one can observe that problems faced in counseling are combined with the whole personality of the human being. One cannot isolate a person's religious life from his everyday problems. If the Christian Church believes that the phenomenon called "the message of the gospel" is a functional element of power in the practical human life, it cannot withdraw from the counseling services. Clinical experience shows how religious resources often indicate meaningful and new possibilities in the process of crisis clarified in counseling. It also sometimes appears that some people have distortions about religion which reflect to their whole personality and human relations. The clarification of these special problems plays an important role in the process of counseling. Although a counselor employed by the church must never be missionary-minded, he must understand religious life and be available for clarifying problems related to that, if necessary. It is true that counselors who are serving in secular agencies may have readiness and abilities to handle these problems, too. An open-minded attitude towards all kinds of human problems is the principle of counselors in general. But in practice it seems that the counselors and clients as well often isolate religious life from other problems which means that they will not be handled in the counseling process. This is understandable because this part of life does not in a way belong to the program of a secular agency. It is true that in church work one can never ensure that the counselor is always sensitively aware and able to hear the appeals related to a person's religious life.

This ability depends mainly on the counselor's personality. But in any case the situation is different if this part of the work is essential, if it really belongs to the training program of the counselors and in the practical world. It means that the counselor's sensitivity towards religious life and problems is continuously under training. That is why there are great possibilities of this part being taken care of in the counseling process.

Sometimes an attempt to solve the problem of how to handle the client's religious life has necessitated a practice of inviting the priest or pastor for discussion with the client. It seems that these kinds of arrangements have not been very successful—probably because an outside clergyman who often has not any special training for counseling has difficulties understanding the total process of counseling, in which the client is involved in his life situation and to which the religious problems relate.

On the other hand, the experience gives evidence that clients avoid discussing any religious problems in an agency in which he feels or knows that it does not belong to its function. This is often the case although the client has very great needs for that. In addition the clients' appeals in these, as in many other problems, are most often indirect and are not heard by a counselor who is not especially trained for that.

The counseling agencies of the churches with well-trained full-time counselors are functioning like laboratories where better understanding of people's problems is continuously being gained and better skills of how to help people are reached. These agencies usually influence the clergy serving in local congregations and other church workers serving the experiences and more or less training them. It means that all the church functions are developing to serve people better and more concretely in their personal problems as a whole. It is hardly believable that any society would ever have enough specialized functions to be able to give counseling services for everybody. That is why it is very important that the attitudes and, if possible, the skills of helping people will spread as far as possible.

THE IDENTITY OF THE COUNSELOR AND HIS DEPENDENCY ON THE CHURCH

Who is the counselor and how does he define his own profession in relationship to other more traditional professions? This is a problem which is continuously under consideration although there already exist some definitions. Pioneers who have begun to function as counselors have most often belonged to some traditional professions like that of physician, clergyman, social worker, psychologist, or even lawyer. In the counseling work of the churches the main line, yet not the only one, has been that some clergymen have a special training in counseling. This is continuously the trend in the pastoral counseling services in North America. The American Association of Pastoral Counselors is an important and influential organ, not only in the training of pastoral counselors but also as a factor and group strengthening and clarifying the identity of the pastoral counselors.

If we study the development of professional identity in an individual case of a clergyman we can recognize that most often the ideal is that the person concerned has clearly identified himself to the role and profession of a clergyman in his church. He sees his vocation to be bringing the message of the gospel. But then he has realized how much people need personal counseling in their life. He has also realized that his own abilities and special talents give evidence of him serving people probably best in specialized counseling work. If his background is something like that, it is probable that having received a training for counseling he can honestly be solidary towards his own church and function as a good counselor. Functioning as counselor, the surroundings and people's expectations do not formally locate him to the peculiar role of a clergyman as it happens when he has served as pastor in a local congregation. That is why in serving as a counselor it is significant that he himself is clear about his identity. He is continuously a clergyman. His role as a counselor relates to the role of a clergyman although in this specialized work his role somehow differs from his role at the time he served in a local congregation.

Sometimes a clergyman has, in fact, more or less great conflicts about identity to a clergyman's profession. It is understandable that these kinds of persons have a need to find a job in which they feel to be less clergyman-like. Acting as a counselor seems to be one possibility for that less clergyman-like job. This means that they bring with them confusion in the identity problem in this new kind of work. In this position the identity confusion easily multiplies itself. Persons like that very often feel conflicts between the work as a counselor and the dependency on the church. But in fact the confusion in this case is not based on the role of counselor in the relationship to the church but on the confusion in their own personality. Naturally this confusion is also a burden and a disadvantage in their work as counselor. Training and personal supervision which most often bring about personal process may help them to clarify their relationship to their church and religious life and to find a new orientation.

There are prejudices of outsiders that the counseling function of a church is always limited. One can say that there is always a burden of the doctrine and of the ethical views of a certain church. That is why there is not the necessary freedom of a secular agency in a counseling function of a church. The above-mentioned confusion in the identity problem may mean that a counselor feels these kinds of limitations or feels to be dishonest in some way functioning as a church worker. But in this conflict it is in the personality of the counselor, not in the situation itself. That is why it is important to remember that in the selection of counselors the counselor's profession should not become some kind of a refuge of pastors confused in their identity problem. On the contrary it is very necessary that specialized counselors are very clear about their professional identity problem. If this is the case then the work can develop in such a way that the doctrines and ethical thinking of a certain church do not bring about any limitations or burdens in the counseling work.

Clergymen are not the only counselors employed by churches. For example, in the family counseling system of the Lutheran Church in Finland roughly 50 per cent of the counselors are clergymen and 50 per cent have their basic training in psychology or in social work. All of them receive roughly the same specialized training in counseling. In Germany and in Switzerland there are many psychiatrists employed by churches, acting as family counselors. In the selection of counselors one aspect among others is to investigate that the candidates are not in a conflict situation with their relation to their church and how much insight they have into their own religious development. It is not possible to measure how much they have grown in their own belief. Everybody has their freedom to grow and to develop according to their own time-table and in the way which is natural to their own personality. It is important that in his work the counselor has clarified to himself his own personal religious life as far as possible. If he has serious blind spots in his own religious life, it will hinder his work as is the case in other areas of the personality, for example, conflicts in his relationship to his own parents.

In the training of a counselor employed by a church general training for counseling enables him to deal with all kinds of life problems of the client and in addition problems related to religious life. This means that if the counselor is a clergyman or has a basic training for some other profession there are no great differences in the role of the counselor in church agencies.

Another problem is that a person who is continuously working as a counselor is all the time in a process of evaluating his own attitude and that of his church towards various kinds of problems and people. This leads also to theological reevaluation and gives a chance to bring the aspect based on counseling experience to the theological discussion in the church concerned. This is not exceptional because freedom for theological reevaluation is open to every worker of the church whatever his special task is. The counselor's challenge is to bring clinical experience to the discussion which means that education and preaching as a whole relate to the life of modern man.

SPECIAL ASPECTS IN THE COUNSELOR'S ATTITUDE

The principles in social casework as well as in counseling, acceptance, respect of self-determination, and belief in the possibilities of every human being do not conflict with the thinking based on Christian belief. One can say that the roots of these principles are in Christianity.

It is possible to base the arguments of the principle of acceptance on fully secular or human thinking and experience. Acceptance is a profitable and helpful attitude according to the experience in the process of helping people in various kinds of problems. One can find psychological clarification and understanding for why it is possible to help clients effectively if the counselor is able to accept him. But it is also possible to understand the principle of acceptance as a result of the Christian belief. In other words, one can say that acceptance means preaching the gospel by attitude without using any religious words. One can find a pattern of this attitude in the New Testament.

One example is how Apostle Paul describes his own attitude in 1 Cor. 9: 19-23: "I am a free man, nobody's slave; but I make myself everybody's slave in order to win as many as possible. While working with the Jews, I live like a Jew in order to win them; and even though I myself am not subject to the Law of Moses, I live as though I were, when working with those who are, in order to win them. In the same way, when with Gentiles I live like a Gentile, outside the Jewish Law, in order to win Gentiles. This does not mean that I don't obey God's law, for I am really under Christ's law. Among the weak in faith I become weak like one of them, in order to win them. So I become all things to all men, that I may save some of them by any means possible. All this I do for the gospel's sake, in order to share in its blessings."

It is possible to find these patterns also in Jesus' attitude towards different kinds of persons. One example is his discussion with the woman by the well of Sychar (John 4:5-29). One can understand that since Jesus had no condemning elements in his attitude towards the woman, this atmosphere created the possibility for the woman to discuss her delicate personal problems. It would have been really dangerous for her to express these problems to her neighbors.

If the counselor does not have any needs for condemning, it means that the counselee is able to see his own problems and guilt more clearly, because he does not have any need to defend himself. This means that he can free himself from the guilty feeling and is able to find new possibilities to go on in his life.

It is very significant for a person related to the church to understand his freedom from any condemnation according to the principle based on the

Christian belief. This means that he is able to accept the fact clearly and with a good conscience that his client may have quite a different system of norms and values from what he has. In that case it does not make the counselor hesitate although the client is sometimes making immoral decisions according to the counselor's way of thinking, not only in the past but continuously.

The fact that some churches have strict doctrines in some ethical questions like divorce, remarriage, abortion, and family planning does not indicate any hindrance to a pastoral counselor being able to accept a person who does not respect the norms of a certain church.

Again it is quite another problem if a counselor who has experience in his clinical work raises a discussion in his own church and suggests that the ethical norms of the church should be rethought and investigated, if it seems that these views do not support the healthy human life.

The fact that a clergyman who has begun to act as counselor has met conflict with his own church or become aggressive, does not necessarily mean that he has understood the principle of acceptance too well. On the contrary this conflict is often caused by the fact that the counselor has not been able to accept his clients soundly. Sometimes it happens that especially young counselors, who have not yet advanced very much in their skills, begin to identify themselves with some of their clients. In fact it has been too difficult for them to accept the client and his thinking although he does not agree with him. Sometimes a young counselor begins to agree with the principles of the counselee which very often relate to the philosophy caused by the defensive mechanisms of the client. Sometimes it is clear that, agreeing with the client, the counselor begins to fight for some very confused philosophy or ethical thinking.

Basically the differences in the philosophy or theology of the client and counselor are compared with the situation in which the counselor can accept an alcoholic although he hopes that the alcoholic can be healed. Or one can accept that a person decides to apply a divorce although the counselor may hope that he will still find possibilities for a more satisfactory marriage than at present.

It is possible to accept the fact that the client is atheist or moslem and his different thinking of ethical problems in spite of the fact that the counselor is very clearly Christian. The more clear and more secure he is in his Christianity, the easier it is for him to accept that another person is different and respect him as he is.

Essential in "the message of the gospel" is that it influences inside a human being and will cause some changes as a result of his behavior. That is why compulsion or pressure are not based on the gospel. This also means that it is logical according to these views to respect a person's self-determination, thus a person has the right to make mistakes and to develop and grow according to his own personal time-table.

One of the basic principles of case-workers is that the worker should believe in the possibilities of the human being although the worker, or the client cannot realistically observe the possibilities in the situation concerned. Some pastoral counselors may express this principle by saying that God has possibilities for everybody. No one is a hopeless case. In practice this leads to the same attitude. This optimistic but realistic belief in the existing latent possibilities plays a very important role in counseling work. It is much easier to express this principle than to really behave in a difficult practical situation accordingly. It is essential and most meaningful in the work if the counselor is able to stay with the client without any answer to the open problems, if they cannot envisage any realistic answers or possibilities. But it is also essential that the counselor stay in this kind of situation without becoming hopeless. This kind of situation or atmosphere often leads to a creative situation where the client is being encouraged to consider the problems more deeply than in other situations. The counselor's personality and belief creates a necessary security for him.

Several elements may help the counselor be optimistic in a situation where he does not have any answers. A psychoanalyst may trust that he has a right theory which will lead to result at the time being. The experience gained in practical work increases this necessary optimism of counselors and of all workers. To a counselor to whom the belief in God plays an important role, this is an element which gives him basic possibilities to stand in a situation described above without becoming hopeless or avoiding the usual temptations to reject the client or to offer irrelevant advice or comfort.

COUNSELING AND RELIGION

As mentioned above, it is possible to deal with the problems relating to a person's relationship to God without using any religious words. It is just as natural that in the counseling process it is possible to discuss religious problems directly. It seems to be common that many people have hindrances in raising questions relating to their personal belief in God. Many people easily isolate these problems to a special part of life. There is a threat of a confused atmosphere as soon as certain people begin to deal with their religious questions.

Very often the clients' appeals for help for their religious life are indirect and not really conscious. That is why the counselor's sensitive ability to hear the client's appeals plays an important role in counseling. For example, the client may say as first words to the counselor that he is an atheist and will not touch any religious problems but is asking help for his marital conflicts. An experienced counselor hears in this expression a signal of conflicts relating to religious life in the client's personality. That is why he is aware that this client will later in some way ask help for his religious conflict, if the relationship between the counselor and the client becomes secure enough to feel free without a fear that the counselor will not convert or recommend any philosophy or belief which he will not accept. Sometimes a client begins to criticize the church or christianity. Very often the criticism is only to test the counselor's attitude and a preface to his real personal problems such as his hopes and disappointments in the past relating to his existential problems and religion.

It may happen, too, that the client introduces to the counselor his problems in a religious form, problems which are basically connected with his human relations. For example, a person describes God as a powerful, violent, inconsequent phenomenon who continuously means threat to him and causes fear. In the discussion it may become clear that this is based on what he has experienced in the personality of his father in his childhood. A clarification of his relationship to his father may mean that the relationship to God later becomes something which means to him security and resources and increases his possibilities to tolerate fatherlike authoritative persons.

Sometimes the starting point in the counseling process is obvious. The client asked to get help for his family problems. For example, the wife has earlier been very much dependent on her husband. He has represented to her security and a person who makes decisions. Her expectations from her husband are continuously on that line. But he is now different. He has withdrawn; he is isolated, insecure, and unable to make decisions. The wife seems very insecure and hopeless. In the discussion the wife also expresses her confusion to what God means to her and genuine expectations from that area. In the course of few weeks development and clarification appear in her religious life which means that an inspiring personal belief to God is strengthening. This again means that she begins to feel much more secure and independent. Her independency seems to transfer her towards a relationship to God. The result of this again is that she begins to behave in a more mature and independent way in her relationship towards her husband and children. She finds enough resources to become able to understand also some of her husband's problems. The change in the wife's attitude causes a positive experience to the husband. The communication begins to function. The roles of husband and wife in their mutual dependency relationship begins to change. But they are more and more encouraged and able to understand their roles and to clarify their relationship.

This is an example of how the clarification and strengthening in relationship to God often means new resources to the practical life situation in which people are living. Thus, in practice, "counseling" in a wide meaning, and "care of souls" belong together. In most cases it is artificial to isolate these functions apart from each other.

All counselors have experiences about how an alcoholic is able to take care of his own life and his family after a religious renewal. It is also not rare that a person who continuously lives in a very difficult life situation is getting a new view through a religious experience. He can now envisage his sufferings like a sensible task instead of having earlier felt it as a meaningless burden. He can accept the life situation as an important call and get satisfaction about his exertion. The life situation may be as it was earlier. But the client has a different insight towards that and he sees it with different colors which means that the contents of his life have changed a great deal.

One can never indicate that the counselor has permanent clarifications in his own religious life. This means that he cannot always have the same sensitivity and readiness to be able to hear the weak and indirect appeals of the client. There are different periods in the counselor's life, too. That is why his effectivity to help people varies from time to time. A counselor may experience a serious crisis in his own religious life, too. But he should be aware of his own problems as much as possible so that he can really be of neutral and sympathetic help to other people.

Chapter 43

AN ANALYSIS OF PSYCHOLOGICAL IMPEDIMENTS TO LOVE AND THEIR RELATIONSHIP TO PERMANENT MARITAL AND RELIGIOUS COMMITMENT

SISTER M. CATHERINE DERICCI KILLEEN

> I shall be telling this with a sigh,
> Somewhere ages and ages hence
> Two roads diverged in a wood, and I—
> I took the one less traveled by,
> And that has made all the difference.
>
> ROBERT FROST

IT WAS THREE days before the annual Christmas holidays and I had just completed the final chord of the last song of the Christmas Pageant Chorus, composed of fifty excited little first-grade choristers when the little youngster who had patiently and efficiently turned my music during the practice, leaned over very softly and said, "When I grow up, I am going to be a Sister just like you."

I was partially distracted by the fact that the other members of the small-fry group had to descend the side stairs of the stage, but I was curious enough to probe the cause of the decision which had taken place in the mind of my little friend at this time.

I replied, "Oh, you mean God has something special for you to do?" "I don't know Sister," said my little friend, "but my mother said I could be a Sister when I grow up, because then she would never have to worry about my being unhappy or crying."

"Don't you feel Sisters are ever unhappy or cry?," I asked.

"Well, my mother said Sisters don't have any men around to be mean to them or holler at the little children."

The dialogue went on, and I, as the teacher, tried to reshape the negative attitude of this particular child by incorporating true values which demonstrated more positive roles of husbands and daddies in other homes and families, through the classroom reading situation (Bibliotherapy). I knew, however, that this incident was only a random sample of all the little boys and girls who begin their lives psychologically infected more than affected with negative ideas about members of the opposite sex because their parents made poor marriages or failed in their capacity to work at them. Children living in such homes without opportunity to learn correct views of sex or

493

family living become disaster specimens of conflicting emotions, and when they contemplate marriage as a natural vocation later on, bring with them distorted psychological attitudes.

This initial observation was later confirmed many times by other similar incidents during my twenty years of teaching children, adolescents, and young adults. I also found significant correlations to male and female religious, who became emotionally disturbed during the course of their religious lives because a proper understanding of the role of the male and female in the home, which is essential to the development of a mature personality in any walk of life, had been a neglected part of their childhood or early adolescent education. I know of cases where individuals thought a fear or dislike to risk marriage was an indication of a religious vocation.

I have been a member of a religious community for the past eighteen years, and one might easily say that my insights about marital stability are bred from the point of view of the "road not taken," and therefore tend to be more idealistic than realistic, but the memory of my own childhood experience reinforces my thesis that early childhood concepts of parental relations in marriage form the nucleus of correct psychological attitudes later on, whether one enters the state of matrimony, virginity or celibacy, and these in turn determine the moral issues involved in the break-up or possible annulment of a marriage or a religious commitment. Homosexuality, severe cases of neurosis or psychosis produce crippled personalities which are incapable of carrying out the responsibilities of marriage or religious commitments.

I was one of the more fortunate children of this world. My parents manifested to me an obvious, mutual trust in one another, an open tolerance intermingled with humor for each other's failings and a dynamic faith that welded their lives together on earth and culminated in their deaths which occurred within nine months of each other.

The last part of the above statement, as I pondered it when I made it, brought to my mind the beautiful words of the poet, Tom Moore in his poem "Believe Me, If All Those Endearing Young Charms,"

No, the heart that has truly lov'd never forgets
But as truly loves on to the close,
As the sunflower turns on her God, when he sets
The same look which she turn'd when he rose.

I feel that the death of my father so shortly after that of my mother was hastened by a painful isolation of spirit, part of his life had departed, the other hastened to follow.

Elizabeth Barrett Browning alludes to the same aspect of the strength of the marriage bond when she states:

I love thee with the breath,
Smiles, tears, of all my life—and, if God choose
I shall but love thee better after death.

Poets tend to convince the romantic of the eternal quality of love, but real experience proves it to the ordinary person as he measures the effects love produced in his own personality and adjustment to life. Might we not conclude that the last two generations of "Newbreeds" and "jet sets" and other misfits, are the products of misfit marriages? There is evidence that if the hearts that have truly loved, give their children positive attitudes from their own marital happiness, therefore those who love only themselves breed selfishness in their offspring.

Therefore, one is inclined to believe that there is both psychological disturbance and damage which takes place in the person of estranged marriage partners. Feelings of hostility, guilt, and sometimes antipathy for the opposite sex become a part of the defense mechanism of the adult personality and very often breed confused attitudes and values in the offspring. As an educator, I feel it is the responsibility of all teachers to provide means of growth in the development of mental health in their students that will enable them to become happy adjusted adults. A good society has its roots in a good home, but today the concept of a good home is more the ideal than the real situation, and the values, attitudes, concepts, and behavior that are sometimes distorted in broken homes must be diagnosed and rehabilitated by competent members of the school and church.

My original thesis is that early childhood concepts of parent relations in marriage form the nucleus of correct psychological attitudes about sex roles and become a part of the philosophical make-up of the individual in his relations with men and women in adulthood, whatever his state. These attitudes in turn determine the moral issues involved. If these attitudes are pathological in origin and are diagnosed as such, without hope of rehabilitation that would enable such persons to carry out the responsibilities of marriage or religious life, they may be classed as impediments to a valid marriage or religious vocation, and should be considered apart from a particular theological position.

Erich Fromm in his book, *The Art of Loving*, claims love to be "a capacity of the mature, productive character"—the psychologically immature person therefore, would be incapable of reaching this capacity in terms of the love required to maintain a marriage or the type of loving dedication necessary to handle the demands of a celibate or chaste life.

Father Anthony Padovano, in his book, *The Estranged God,* claims the following:

> Modern man is really afraid of love. He wants desperately to communicate, this is true, but he cannot or will not. One of our difficulties today stems from the fact that we desire the state of being loved rather than the challenge of loving. We want all to come to us, yet if they do, we remain imprisoned within ourselves. We must burst out of this prison and overcome the separateness from each other which is at the very heart of all human anxiety. If we do not overcome the separateness, we cannot love ourselves or believe in God.

"Love then," states Father Padovano, "is an act of faith in someone else." It is my position, however, that in order to maintain this love in spite of many difficulties, one must be a mature person that can sort the wheat from the chaff in human nature. A neurotic, for example, who is psychologically immature is incapable of such consistency because of his deep feelings of inadequacy.

"Basically, weakness is most often nothing but destroyed power of thinking and doing," claims Doctor Silverman in his chapter, "The Philosophical and Psychological Implications of Marriage and Womanhood, "but if this weakness to weather through conflicts in marriage was from the beginning destroyed power to love, or arrested power to love, caused by rejection in childhood or adolescence by disturbed parents, the chances for such people making any kind of a stable relationship, let alone a stable marriage are poor. Unrequited love in childhood is not displaced in a psychic vacuum, but is often confused with sex in early adolescence and even in early adulthood, especially if the psychic energy finds no way to displace itself in creative enterprises such as art, music, dancing, poetry, creative writing. Masturbation in young children or homosexual alliances sometimes indicate these disturbances. The example of Estella in *Great Expectations* demonstrates the child who was made incapable of love by an unhappy guardian who taught her to use sex attraction as a tool for the destruction of another human being in the person of Pip.

One of the most tragic things one can say about another human being is that they are incapable of love, for without love, there can be no growth.

Fromm states that "if two people who have been strangers, as all of us are, suddenly let the wall between them break down, and feel close, feel one, this moment of oneness is one of the most exhilarating, most exciting experiences in life. It is all the more wonderful and miraculous for persons who have been shut off, or isolated without love."

Most psychologists would support that a deprivation of basic needs causes an emotional imbalance in personality. People who are deprived of basic love in childhood become easy targets for sexual promiscuity in adolescence or homosexual relations and are prone to contracting poor marriages based more on infatuation rather than love, unless the other partner concerned is most perceptive and understanding. In cases of unsuccessful marriage partners, disturbed priests or Sisters suffering from unresolved love deprivation or unrealistic sex identification, how does the counselor help them to resolve conflicts or make decisions? Is there a moral issue involved in such decisions or is it psychological rehabilitation that must be involved before any decision can be made? Does the school have a responsibility for teaching sex education, the cornerstone of family living? Is there a relationship between a lack of information relative to human sexuality in childhood or adolescence and a person's total response to other people and society in general when they appear as adults?

From my experience as a teacher, I would say yes. Sex education for correct family living as a part of the ordinary school curriculum has been one of the most provocative questions submitted to local school boards all over the country. It is a continuous observation to note, however, that there are as many valid arguments proposed against the teaching of sex education as there are valid arguments proposed for it. Yet the teaching of sex education is not new. The sensitive teacher has been developing the sex roles of men and women in all areas of the curriculum for many years, especially when negative attitudes have been expressed or repressed by children in the classroom situation. Such attitudes, similar to the one I described in the beginning of this chapter are easily diagnosed in compositions or verbal responses to characters in reading or language situations, on any grade level.

Much of the controversy provoked by the term sex education, is spawned, I think, because many people feel that sex education is an introduction to physiology and anatomy with the emphasis placed on the technical aspects of the reproductive process detached from its proper place in life and would remove it from its consideration as an expression of deep permanent love and a privilege of those who are married. The object of sex education is to help youngsters accept and understand their own sexuality as I propose it, as a potential man or woman with a significant role to follow in relation to the opposite sex in friendship, love, and marriage. Understanding the feminine or masculine nature of one's self is a definite component of developing the total personality. Possession of this knowledge will pave the environment for more mature and responsible relationships to take place between young boys and girls in courtship and then in marriage. A quick survey of examples in literature, modern novels, and plays provide us with excellent material to detect the personality failures which lie at the root of a person's incapacity to understand one self or to learn to love maturely. Films such as *Alfie* and *Georgie Girl* present the modern dilemma of such people very well. *Goodby Columbus* points out the acute anxiety of children of confused emotions who flaunt parental mores.

Marriage cherished as a permanent state is the culmination of the mature expression of love, but like the nature of love as Fromm states it, marriage too becomes an art in theory and practice. Marriage requires the intelligent cooperation of two mature people who value the "we" more than the I or you. I do not mean to indicate here that masculine or feminine individuality must be sacrificed to meet the demands of matrimony, but that they should be fully understood and enhanced and sometimes even transcended by the marriage union.

People who are products of similar religious convictions and who have integrated their religion into their personality in consistent patterns of behavior should have a better foundation for a stable marriage than people who do not, for faith in God stabilizes faith in another and sometimes faith in another stabilizes faith in God. This is true, however, of mature people. Many times people who have poor sex orientation or people who have been made incapable of love because of deep seated psychological factors and who need psychological rehabilitation, cling with neurotic tenacity to religious principles as an escape from decision rather than as a means of insight into their problems. The same fears, insecurity, and anxiety that blocked proper sexual attitudes, robbed them of the capacity to love, also robbed them of the opportunity of loving God unreservedly with trust that He who made them would understand them in their hour of need.

A marriage contracted between individuals who are psychologically impaired or defective in their capacity to love cannot be regarded as a useful marriage and the morality of terminating such a marriage is contingent on the investigation of psychological forces in the past that tend to make the marriage incompatible if not impossible. I am not a Theologian, but I do feel that holiness must be conceived in wholeness and that Theologians of all religions are beginning to see that a lack of psychological wholeness can be a real impediment to marriage. The behavioral sciences have contributed much to a better understanding of the individual as he moves through the various paces of life, and no state is more important to the status of mankind and country than the marriage state.

I began this chapter with a story of a little girl who wanted to be a Sister because her mother told her she would never be unhappy or cry, and that there would be no mean men around who would holler at little children. This true story, perceived through a seemingly simple dialogue, illustrates the very beginning of both a negative aspect of early childhood sex orientation and the formation of a very unrealistic foundation for entering the religious life. I see here a very strong correlation for failure in marriage and failure in the religious life. Psychological "hangups" are formed many times by negative parental attitudes caught by children which become deep-seated. It is almost sad to note that when these attitudes are uprooted later by adult learning, more positive heterosexual exchanges, or experiential insight produced by a more mature perspective havoc sometimes classified as a serious psychological trauma occurs within the individual who feels he has been betrayed in life, and must make an emotional or intellectual adjustment in his thinking or living. In some cases there is a complete breakdown or disorientation of the personality.

Sometimes more mature considerations and convictions demand another course of action or way of life more compatible with the contemporary knowledge of the individual. To annul a marriage or break a religious commitment demands spiritual maturity as well as psychological maturity with a rational basis for future action. As an educator, I feel many of these delayed growing pains which cause so much anxiety, sorrow, and sometimes apparent disgrace to so many people involved as in the cases of divorce or the ex-priest or ex-nun who runs off and gets married instead of operating through proper channels, could have been avoided if not altogether prevented if proper sex education had been initiated and integrated in earlier years as part of family living education.

Today we live in a disturbed society. Children are the products of this disturbed society and if we are going to help them adjust or better adapt themselves psychologically, we must first help them to know themselves and then teach them how to love other people.

Genesis really gives to us the opportunity to probe deeply the earliest beginning of the paradoxical nature of all human love. I have mentioned consistently throughout this chapter the influence of childhood experiences on the formation of psychological attitudes and personality development. Childhood experiences reinforce self-rejection but rejection itself is predispositioned in man and was first brought about by his fall.

Eve rejected God when she ate of the forbidden fruit. Eve loved God but she loved herself more when she rejected His will. The whole trauma brought about by her sin has many interesting psychological implications. With her sin, Eve knew the horror of guilt, felt the isolation of anxiety as a result of her guilt and the insecurity that overtakes one's psyche when one knows he has been betrayed by misplaced faith in the deceit of another.

Adam also sinned and also rejected God but in turn rejected his wife, his only neighbor when he blamed her as the cause of his sin. Self-love displaced God and self-love displaced neighbor. It would be interesting perhaps to think what might have happened to the whole human race had Adam said, "Eve sinned and I sinned, Eve is my wife and I love her and I don't think we ought to be deprived of Paradise because of one mistake." Maybe God, who is love, would have pardoned them both because of Adam who had loved and shielded his neighbor. As it happened, man and woman were both cast out of Paradise. If the failure to love one's neighbor more than one's self put the human race out of Paradise, then perhaps learning to really love will help us to find the way back.

Fear, mistrust, anxiety, doubt, and feelings of guilt stifle the great capacity of love to accept, tolerate, redeem, and make whole. The capacity to love can be a redeeming force but this capacity is bred in a sound psychological frame of faith and trust. Men and women who for some reason or another do not possess psychological wholeness are not capable of love that accepts and redeems. They must first be made whole. The message of the perennial Christian is joy because we can say to Christ, Although we have sinned, you have become a part of us, and have redeemed us and made us whole. And in the words of Shakespeare we can see the wisdom of the sonnet perhaps learned in the pages of human experience by the descendents of the first man and woman.

> Let me not to the marriage of true minds
> Admit impediments. Love is not love
> which alters when it alteration finds
> Or bends with the remover to remove.
> O, no! it is an ever-fiexd mark
> That looks on tempests and is never shaken
> It is the star to every wand'ring bark,
> Whose worth's unknown, although his height be taken.
> Love's not Time's fool, though rosy lips and cheeks
> Within his bending sickle's compass come.
> Love alters not with his brief hours and weeks,
> But bears it out even to the edge of doom.
>   If this be error, and upon me proved,
>   I never writ, nor no man ever loved.*

Life without love is impossible. Love is a man and a woman and their ability to share in the eternal love theme of creation. Love begins with understanding and reverence for the beloved so we must teach our children to love other people and to see love as respect for the total person. With this vision our children will see sex, love, and marriage as part of the harmonious blending of life, and as Chardin says, "Nothing is profane for those who really see."

In Summary:

During the twentieth century human institutions have been evaluating themselves in an attempt to improve society. One need only to look at the divorce rate and the corresponding rate of disturbed children who are the results of these broken or unhappy homes to see that there must be some provision made in the curriculum to provide for the rehabilitation of these children. Psychologists, sociologists, and educators have traced emotionally

---

*Shakespeare, William: *Sonnet 116.* New York, Dodd-Mead and Company, 1966.

disturbed children to disturbed parents of unhappy marriages and found the cause to be poor sex education and education in family living in childhood.

The attempt to implement sex education or Family Life programs into the school has been caught in a savage crossfire between uncritical lovers of the American educational system and unloving critics all over the country. On one side we have those who love the system as it is and they prevent it from the opportunity to change and expand, by shielding it from life-giving criticism. On the other hand we have a new breed of critics without love, skilled in demolition but untutored in the arts by which human institutions are nurtured and strengthened and made to flourish. More than ever, we must understand in our human institutions of which the American educational system is a strong counterpart, that love without criticism is not love, for its silence brings stagnation, and criticism without love brings destruction. Moral aspects of anything determine intelligent decisions. Is is not immoral to omit that which is essential to the betterment of society, as much as it is considered immoral to commit a grave offense against society itself? Marital stability is the cornerstone of society, civilization, life itself. Can we afford to be unloving critics of its present critical state?

> Two roads diverged in a yellow wood,
> And sorry I could not travel both
> And be one traveler, long I stood
> And looked down one as far as I could
> To where it bent in the undergrowth;
> Then took the other, as just as fair,
> And having perhaps the better claim
> Because it was grassy and wanted wear;
> Though as for that passing there
> Had worn them really about the same.

Throughout this chapter I have presented significant correlations between failure in marriage and failure in religious commitment due to psychological immaturity and the crippled capacity to love. It is the task of humanity to design institutions that are capable of continuous change, continuous renewal, and continuous responsiveness. Love is a basic need essential to human survival and characterizes every human being that is born. Love is the eternal teacher and from it education must be born if it is to last.

It is love that expands and can hold and motivate individuals as well as social organizations. It is the very nature of love then, its promise, its message and its effects that must be taught to our children, because as the popular song says, "What the world needs now is love!"

SELECTED BIBLIOGRAPHY

1. Browning, Elizabeth Barrett: *Sonnets From the Protugese.* New York, Pyramid Publications Incorporated, 1967.
2. Fromm, Erich: *The Art of Loving.* New York, Harper Brothers Publishers, 1956.
3. Frost, Robert: *The Road Not Taken.* New York, Harper Brothers Publishers, 1955.
4. Padovano, Anthony: *The Estranged God.* New York, Sheed and Ward, 1965.
5. Shakespeare, William: *Sonnet 116.* New York, Dodd-Mead and Company, 1966.
6. Silverman, Hirsch L.: *Marital Counseling: Psychology Ideology, Science.* Springfield, Illinois, Charles C Thomas, 1967.

Section IV

COMPREHENSIVE EVALUATION: MARITAL THERAPY CONCEPTS

Chapter 44

ABSTRACTS OF CONTENTS

HIRSCH LAZAAR SILVERMAN

As intimated in the Preface, this book contains original essays written especially by scholars and thinkers from America and other nations. It is not the usual "book of readings" consisting of reprinted journal articles. Although the writing styles and approaches vary greatly, each contributor has tried to do his best to present in brief form a response to the Editor's originally posed question, which was almost the only guideline for their work. The question: "What would you say to an intelligent layman and to your fellow practitioners in marital therapy if they asked you to tell them about the main points in the field, and what influences seem likely to shape it in the foreseeable future?"

As the Romans stated, "Art is long and time is short." At the risk of the charge of "superficiality" (the easiest of all charges to level against any sort of summary or synthesis), each person has done his best, within the space allotments assigned by an unbending Editor-organizer, to present the picture as simply as possible. No mere knowledge of professional jargon on the part of readers is presupposed; no uncertain knowledge of therapy psychologically, sociologically or moralistically, is presupposed beyond the "general" knowledge of an intelligent layman. Naturally, some authors have succeeded for certain readers better than others.

Again, in general, the Editor has tried to retain the maximum amount of the individual Author's own words consistent with readability. While such a practice does not always contribute to editorial niceties, and may indeed lead to criticism for "loose" editing and inconsistency, the Editor believes that these matters are of small consequence to most of the intended audience and will upset primarily purists who psychologically—even psychiatrically!—make a career of being upset anyway.

Every attempt has been made to be true to the meaning of each contributor. The editorial prerogative of shortening, omitting, rephrasing, and toning down biased and unnecessarily unkind statements has been exercised. Some of the printed "asides" which have been cut editorially are in themselves most interesting, but they added little to the assigned task and might have detracted unnecessarily from the main points of the chapters.

The volume was produced over a period of three years. It suffered all the pains of any international writing venture of such scope—deaths, sudden

505

changes of responsibilities which led to withdrawal by some, too many commitments to meet deadlines, physical illnesses of some duration, even international incidents, and other hindrances. Thus, some of the chapters are unavoidably more current than others.

The contents of this volume are multifaceted, diverse and various. The contributors have written as individuals, each a specialist in his own discipline. The result, it is hoped, will add to knowledge in the broad area of marital therapy and counseling. The Editor in this concluding chapter briefly summarizes, in abstract, each of the chapters. To avoid any semblance of partiality, the abstracts appear alphabetically by contributors.

Chapter 21

Marriage counseling, which began as a professionally concerned response to the increasing divorce rates shortly after World War I, was undertaken by many counselors who were previously trained to counsel individuals rather than couples. This counseling model was used, although it automatically excluded one of the two spouses with its focus on one client. The marriage counselor, then, derived his distinctive title from his counseling emphasis on marriage problems rather than because he counseled a married couple.

What apparently began as a "stop-gap" procedure has, according to Adams, over the past decades become the preferred way of conducting marriage counseling. While this historical precedent has set the marriage counseling pattern, there are some who now recognize that it is the marital relationship that needs counseling and not just the individual spouse. Moreover, there is some evidence that the marriage relationship itself is moving away from a traditional type with its prescribed roles and responsibilities, to an interactional type with concern over such things as ego satisfactions and companionship qualities.

Adams' chapter, therefore, is written with two needs in mind relative to the marriage counseling field. First, is the need to reconceptualize contemporary marriage as developing toward an interactional type relationship. Second, is the need to place marriage counseling within an interpersonal relationship framework. Both needs are presented as important issues in marriage counseling today.

Chapter 28

Married couples in difficulty often seek help from practitioners designated as "marriage counselors." These practitioners, in Albert's view, as the professional stands today may come from such varied fields as education, religion, social work, sociology, law, guidance, medicine, psychology, and psychiatry. Some have had extensive training labeled "marriage counseling," others insufficient training. Even those with adequate training may be somewhat inadequately prepared to deal with the real, perhaps serious, difficulties lying beneath the surface of presenting problems. Apparently "normal" marital partners frequently conceal unconscious determinants of their difficulties, in the service of neurotic defenses of which they themselves are unaware and which insufficiently qualified counselors are unable to detect. Marriage counseling is then seen as a specialized branch of the art/science of psychotherapy, calling for psychological training in dynamics equivalent to the specialized background expected of psychotherapists practicing individual or group therapy.

Chapter 19

After a brief listing of some of the sorts of moral issues in marriage counseling which the marriage counselor must typically deal with, Ard discusses six possible stances the marriage counselor may take with regard to the client's conscience or supergo. These stances range from building up the conscience or superego, through a philosophically "neutral" position, to trying to lessen the severity of, or even eliminating, the conscience or superego. Each of the various possible stances is examined critically with the limitations pointed out. Examples are drawn from various points of view, e.g. client-centered and psychoanalytic, as well as others.

A critique of the conscience or superego as the "only" or "best" way to resolve the many moral issues in marriage counseling is offered by Ard. The marriage counselor is urged to think through very carefully which stance he takes with regard to the conscience or superego.

Chapter 15

Bardis' interdisciplinary and primarily socio-historical study combines description, theory, and quantification. Its main objectives are four: one, to systematize most of the important ideas regarding sin which have dominated the Western world, and thus supply counselors with that kind of knowledge which facilitates insightful and creative thinking about some of the problems with which they deal; two, to formulate various hypotheses and theories concerning the history of the concept of sin in the West; three, to utilize such generalizations in the construction of a device for the quantitative measurement of attitudes toward morality; and four, to present this device as a partial index of modernization.

After discussing numerous religious systems among the Hebrews, Greeks, Christians, Moslems, and others, Bardis formulates twenty-seven hypotheses and theories. Ten of these are then modified and presented in a technique for the measurement of attitudes toward morality, as well as a partial index of modernization.

Chapter 36

Becherer treats human needs and how these are mutually nourished by husband and wife in a vital, health marriage. The needs are spiritual, intellectual, psychological, physical, sexual, and social. These areas make up the six levels of intercourse telescoping and influencing each other. The treatment is necessarily brief, but furnishes the reader with a kind of outline by which to examine communications between husband and wife. It serves also as an ideal toward which to strive concretely from day to day.

Becherer believes that formerly religion had treated marriage more in a juridical manner, that justice was more the tone of the marriage rather than love. The emancipation of American women has created more equalitarian relationships between spouses and has made greater demands on the male to satisfy his wife.

A particular belief of the writer is that parents have attempted to cultivate and train their children too directly and at the expense of their own husband-wife relationship. He believes that marriage furnishes the profound relationship which produces not only new life, but new life and growth in the spouses themselves. Children share the abundant and fruitful results of their parents fulfillment in each other.

Chapter 1

Young human beings have to be taught the proper use for their faculties, and the sexual faculties are no exception, according to Calderone. Man will not, can not, use his sexual faculties any better or more responsibly than he has been taught in childhood and youth. If we wish man to use his sexual faculties constructively, creatively, responsibly, maturely, lovingly, then we must so construct the education institutes of society (home, school, church) as to produce constructive, creative, responsible, mature, and loving human beings. Of all man's universally-endowed and psychological functions, this one, his sexuality, is the one that is the most likely to be used, or misused, in such a way as directly and consistently to reflect either the distortions, the deprivations, the brutalizations, or the joys, the securities, and the wonders of his life surroundings during his first fifteen years.

Thus, truly responsible parenthood requires of the marriage partners investment of *themselves* as persons in the person who is their child. Today this is a most awesome responsibility. To enter into parenthood should therefore be in full awareness of the high moral commitment that this requires of man and wife.

Chapter 30

Morale, the capacity to cope with even severe external and internal pressures without being overwhelmed by them, is of great importance in the complex and often intense interactions of modern marriage, in the view of Carrington. Beyond the traditional functions of marriage, the capacity of each partner to absorb the emotional outbursts of the other has emerged as a most valuable service when it can be provided in marriage.

Morale in marriage is somewhat comparable with morale of the soldier in battle, which has been described as based on four essential factors: leadership, discipline, comradeship and self-respect—together with a fifth factor, devotion to a cause, which may not necessarily influence all soldiers. These are generally applicable to the promotion of morale in marriage, but most of the foundations of morale are laid, for good or ill, long before his clients come into contact with the marriage counselor, even for premarital counseling, as Carrington sees it.

Apart from his direct contribution to the promotion of morale through premarital and marital counseling, and in many cases through family life education programs, the marriage counselor may be able to offer an indirect contribution in the training of young married people for parenthood, so that they can play a more efficient part in laying down the foundations of morale in their young children. Such a service, mainly offered through group counseling, would seem to be worthy of increasing attention in the future.

Chapter 32

Anything, be it physical, mental, or emotional that interferes with the attainment of the greatest pleasure in the sexual experience of a couple may ultimately pose a threat to their adjustment within the framework of marriage. Individuals need reassurance, in Clark's thesis, that they are not the only ones that have trouble. Many troubles can be corrected through the help of trained counselors or physicians. Acceptance of sexual inclinations and activity by each member of a married pair for himself or herself, and for the other as well, is absolutely essential. Then with open channels of communication and a real desire on the part of each to work through any difficulties which might occur, most can work through to a satisfactory relationship.

Chapter 11

Crandall examines the nature of the authentic marriage from the standpoint of Heideggerian ontology. Starting from the structure of the existence, or the human nature, of the persons in the marital group, criteria of authentic marital life are propounded having to do with a variety of associated phenomena. The criteria are organized about the teleology of marital life (what a marriage ought to be), the instrumentalities of marital life (how a marriage becomes what it ought to be), and the positive mood accompanying instrumental success (what marital partners experience as positive emotion as their marriage becomes what it ought to be).

The primary teleological criterion is the development within each marital partner, as a result of his marital experience, of an authentic style of life as characterized by an openness to being. A marriage where this occurs is called a marriage lived in the truth.

The principal instrumental criterion is understanding, Crandall believes. Here marital partners awaken to their unique human capacity to disclose being, to be a servant and shepherd or being. As they do, the authentic style becomes possible.

The positive emotive-consequential criteria are related to the concept of joy (a mood arising in marital partners as they fulfill themselves) authentically. Joy is defined as homecoming, or the feeling of fulfillment in the presence of being.

Chapter 43

Marital stability is the concern of the educator today, for psychological wholeness in children depends upon the initial education they receive in the home. The natural course of action for most people in the world today is to get married and the whole stability of civilization has its cornerstone in the family unit, in Sister Catherine's presentation. The rapid increase in the divorce rate and the rising ratio of disturbed children coming from broken or unhappy homes demands consideration and planning on the part of the educator if he is to educate children to make adjustments in life. A better understanding of the sexuality of persons as a part of the total personality has been found by many psychologists and marriage counselors to be a significant factor in marital adjustment; therefore, whatever facilitates better adjustment in life created by societal needs must be integrated within the educational system.

Does the school have a responsibility for sex education? This is one of the most provocative questions submitted to local school boards all over the country today, but it is the author's opinion that most of the controversy concerning the implementation of sex education programs is caused by a lack of understanding concerning the objectives of sex education. Sex education has, as its subject matter, understanding one's own sexuality as one of the many areas involving the total personality of any human being, not an orientation on the proper functioning of the reproductive process inside or outside of marriage.

Proper sex instruction cultivating the importance of developing the capacity to love in children is another positive factor insuring marital success later on in life. Individuals who are classified as incapable of love because of rejection or thwarted emotions experienced in childhood are psychologically impaired. Many times these people develop neuroses that impair normal performance in marriage and must be rehabilitated before mature decisions involving life commitments are made. Basic to the nature of every man and woman is the ability to love in spite of all the elements of human frailty present in one's self and in the beloved. It takes a mature person, however, to increase this capacity to really love another person because self-love is so strong in human nature.

Chapter 12

An initial two-year experience of marital and premarital counseling within a university health service is examined by Eastman and Reifler. All evidence indicates that on college and university campuses marriage will be a continuing phenomenon. The responsibilities carried by the university health service for its married students and their dependents are underscored, including the provision of a specific marriage counseling source and participation in a major medical and hospitalization insurance plan. Within this framework the student-clients and their nonstudent spouses who utilized the marriage counseling service are described. This premarital and marriage counseling service has served a need not otherwise met on campus, and the total experience confirms the recommendation of the American College Health Association that a successful college health program must be responsible to, or originate from, one department charged with implementing the program—the college health service. The range and quantity of opportunities for preventive, nonclinical campus consultations and programs are limited only by time and energy. In support of the unique opportunities for prevention and education among the single as well as married students, consideration is given the creation of a faculty position of marriage therapist and family life coordinator.

Chapter 5

The view is taken by Ellis that the first principle of morality is the following: To thine own self be true; or be, primarily, kind to yourself. The second principle is the following: Do not commit any deed that needlessly, definitely, and deliberately harms others. Other corollaries of this view of morality are discussed in Ellis' chapter. From these principles of general morality, rules of sexual conduct are derived, particularly in regard to masturbation, petting, premarital intercourse, adultery, sex deviations, and sexual assault and rape. It is noted that sexual acts are immoral when they are generally immoral and that they are not unethical simply because they are sexual. It is also held that when an individual commits an immoral or wrong act, he is still a basically good person; and that although his *act* may be deplorable, *he* is not reprehensible or wicked.

Chapter 27

The whole and wholesome family is the product of whole and wholesome people as parents, in Goodman's view. They produce and raise whole and wholesome children. The whole and wholesome person is the man (or woman) who is not at war but at *one* with himself. He is united in his aims and purposes, clear in his conscience, direct in his dealings with all people. He is free of self-centeredness, readily understanding the other fellow's point of view. He is attentive to his daily task, which he accomplishes easily because he can apply his whole strength to it. He is devoted to his marriage partner and thoroughly enjoys her because he gives her his whole love. If she is similarly united—in herself and in her love for him—they will make a whole and wholesome marriage: a whole and wholesome family.

Chapter 26

Goodstein provides an insight into the "types" of girls who are more prone to premarital pregnancy, what forced them there, and how their problems were met. Case studies are used to illustrate points. A recommendation is made at the conclusion with a description of a well-engineered program for these girls. Cooperation is essential between home, school, physician, psychologist, social worker, and any other community agency available to help in these problems. The ideal solution would be a centrally located residence containing all of the aforementioned services which would aid in the rehabilitation of these girls while they are in residence there and when they reenter society, thus permitting them to continue their schooling so they may resume as normal a life as possible.

Chapter 42

The motive of the churches to found and to maintain counseling services must be based on the love of one's neighbor. This means that it is basically diagnostic without a trend to convert clients, in Joensuu's viewpoint. In some countries there are more and more developing secular counseling services. The churches should promote and help these services. In the general task of counseling, the churches have a special duty to offer possibilities to clients for strengthening their spiritual life whenever needed. It is important for the counselor to clarify his professional identity as a church worker. Conflicts relating to their dependency relationship with a certain church, which some counselors feel, is often based on their personal confusion, not on the structure and doctrine of a certain church. The principle of acceptance which is one of the basic elements in the counselor's attitude towards his clients is based on the message of the gospel. This means that the counselor is able to deal with clients having a different philosophy or set of morals from counselor or from the doctrines of the particular churches.

Chapter 40

While there are many theological implications in marriage counseling, Jordan seeks to focus on the concept of idolatry as a key to the understanding of some of the dynamics of marital interaction. Idolatry is to be understood in the sense of making anything that is relative into an absolute. The idol is the object of fixation, in Freudian terms. In marriage counseling the idol often appears as the internalized image of a parent who has assumed the role of ultimate authority and dictates attitudes and behavior for a person in his marriage. (This truth is depicted in the cartoon showing a newly married couple lying timidly in bed with the individual portraits of their parents glaring down judgmentally from the wall above the bed.) Many persons have internalized the picture of a parent of the past into the superego, and many attitudes and patterns of interaction are dictated by the internalized parental image functioning as the ultimate authority or idol in the person's marriage. This psychic false god may create problems of neurotic or false guilt, which may also hamper the marital relationship. A marriage counselor needs to help marital pairs to become free of their hang-ups with psychic idols so that they can develop a more creative and loving relationship.

Chapter 31

Based upon the Parent-Adult-Child structure of personality as developed by Eric Berne, it can be seen, argues Landrud, that moral values are originally formed in childhood. They are learned in relationships with parents and the "significant others" of one's formative years. Then, as the youth moves toward adolescence, his world view expands. His search for a personal identity, apart from his parents, leads him to question and challenge the values of his family background. This process is intensified due to the influences upon him of changing modes of communication (especially television), the easy comforts of an affluent society, and the questionable commitment to the Viet Nam war—all of which involve him without any decision-making on his part. As he forms personal values of his own he may experience great emotional conflicts, not only within himself, but most directly in terms of family relationships. His own sense of growing individuality leads him away from neat black-and-white decisions, as he perceives fewer absolutes and more possibilities. He may embrace a "new morality," which has been described as not too new at all, but rooted in the New Testament. In the marriage relationship each mate brings his and her own value structures, which, if not openly discussed and acknowledged, can lead to grave relationship conflicts on a feeling level, for personal values can themselves be seen as providing the foundations of feelings.

Chapter 37

Linton examines the provocative question whether the physician should be the conscience of society; and finds that the physician is being placed by society in an untenable position. He is asked to make decisions, not because he is truly qualified to make these decisions but because he has the medical skills and knowledge to implement the control of reproduction through contraception, sterilization, and abortion. Linton further points out that at this point in history there are many inconsistencies, ambiguities, and out-right hypocrisy surrounding society's attitude toward these very subjects.

Chapter 14

A concept of marriage is explored by Mace based on the degree of inter-personal involvement of the spouses, and ranging from minimum involve-ment in the traditional marriage, through various stages of limited involve-ment, to maximum involvement in the close, intimate relationship that is coming in our time to be regarded as the ideal. Three modes of involvement in marriage are explored—that of *communication,* which is primarily the means by which the spouses come to know and identify each other as per-sons; *sharing,* the process by which they seek to unify their lives by accepting each other's values, goals, relationships, and possessions; and *cooperation,* in which they engage together in carrying out their common obligations and tasks. Obstacles to the attainment of relationship-in-depth in marriage are considered, and means of overcoming them discussed. Finally, attention is drawn by Mace to some implications of this concept of marriage for the marriage counselor—its use as a framework for diagnosis and therapy, and the need for marriage counselors to shift their emphasis from the remedial to the preventive and facilitating role.

Chapter 10

McGinnis reviews the reasons behind the pressures on school systems to incorporate sex education programs into the curriculum. He explains why he feels that sex education is best taught in the public schools, but admits that those responsible for carrying out this urgent public demand were forc-ed to jump hastily into an undeveloped area of education and move with very limited tools. Inadequately trained teachers, uncertainty about course materials, and insufficient time to bring about informed community support all were factors that created an atmosphere of confusion and concern. Right wing organizations seized the opportunity to go into action with fear campaigns that labeled sex education as a plot to pervert and destroy American youth.

The importance of going forward carefully, laying firm foundations under good, qualitative sex education programs is then discussed in view of concurrent opposition that is both undermining and potentially destructive. McGinnis offers guidelines to communities on how to assess their individual situation in terms of degrees of community support and opposition and in light of the unique cultural and economic characteristics of each location. He categorizes the various organized and unorganized groups that oppose sex education and their reasons for doing so. The characterological style of the paranoid personality found in extremist organizations is delineated so that it can be dealt with in the most effective way. Suggestions are made as to how and where community support for sex education can be found. School districts are urged to develop action programs of positive information that can be carried out by the joint efforts of school administrators and community leaders. In conclusion, the prediction is made that future focus will move from preparation for marriage and family life to preparation for human experience and that teachers in this field will be the most creative and effective in the field of education.

Chapter 25

Meany is concerned with a psychological and religious definition of spirituality, as this relates to communication in marriage. Presenting alternative views of spirituality, the chapter stresses the need for self-knowledge, seen from the point of view of sociology and depth psychology. The relationship of communication to sexuality is discussed from the point of view of psychological defenses and inner growth. Some typical patterns in marriage relationships are analyzed from the point of view of unconscious motivations and psychological needs. An existential approach to communication in marriage is stressed, following the Rogerian model. The Jungian translation of "emotions into images" to facilitate communication in depth is illustrated, as is the use of meditation to facilitate communication. Spiritual direction, by both an individual and by groups, is presented with some of the practical implications for marriage counseling.

Chapter 20

Marriage counseling involves manipulative intervention and is one form of social control, in the view of Moberg. Most people react negatively to the idea of being manipulated, but much human behavior is aimed at manipulating others. The need for order in society necessitates social control over individual and group behavior. The greater its effectiveness, the less the person feels constrained and the greater is his sense of personal autonomy and freedom. The goals of social control in every society include the "containing" of persons, perspectives, and groups which are interpreted as being detrimental to societal welfare. In a pluralistic society, according to the author, the problems of social control (and hence of marriage counselors and others involved in enforcing it) are accentuated. Understanding the inherently manipulative nature of counseling and the ubiquity of social control can help to promote human dignity and freedom.

Chapter 4

A direct relationship exists between the lack of sufficient sex education and some peoples' inability to free themselves from an unpractical and visionary morality which impedes their progress in life's adjustments, according to Moore. There is also a close relationship between the need for a revised sex ethic and the lack of adequate sex education. Because marriage places people in modern life's most intimate relationship, marriage counselors are in distinctive positions to help clients help themselves (and their children) in this critical area of learning.

Moore's chapter seeks to define sex ethics, sex education, and morality and to describe the intricate relationship among all three, while lending the greater emphasis to sex education *per se*. Some attention is also given to the problem of guilt as it stems from, and is pertinent to, inadequate sex education.

People who have mastered information about sex early enough in their overall adjustments seem to feel more confident about their own sexuality. Those persons who do not gain the information early enough are often filled with guilt and shame about sex; they are reluctant to admit to any confusion (or ignorance) ; and they are often painfully indecisive about their own sexuality.

Chapter 24

During the final third of the twentieth century, no problem will weigh more heavily upon the world than the population explosion, in the analysis of Nash and Nash. No issue is likely to test more severely the capacity of the United States for international leadership. Responsibility for creating awareness among the American public of that issue's gravity and for thoughtful explication of its possible solutions will rest substantially upon those Americans whose professions involve them in influencing attitudes toward procreation, children, and families. Not the least among these are marriage counselors whose professional activities include dealing with the significant hazards to the marital relationship of unwanted, and even of some wanted, children.

This chapter is concerned with the following: a) the unpleasant facts of the population explosion; b) selected case histories whose common motif is marital or personal crisis to which unplanned childbirth has materially contributed; c) an overview of current proposals for dealing with the population problem; and d) an examination of the difficulties of integrating each type of proposal with basic American tenets about the right relationship between government and the individual.

Chapter 9

In their dialogue, Neiger and McCulloch contend and agree that in sexually oriented marriage counseling there is a gap between the reality and the commonly perceived ideal of the "full unbiased" marriage counselor, who is supposed to be a "neutral facilitator" helping people to clarify what their own positions are. After attempting to define counseling in common sexual marriage problems, the authors identify at least three sources of bias which, they submit, every counselor carries with himself into the counseling process, to a greater or lesser extent. The sources are the following: a) the counselor's concept of what counseling is all about; b) the counselor's concept of what marriage is about (Is it exclusively, primarily or mainly a sexual union?) ; and c) the counselor's concept of what sex is all about.

Questions are posed by Neiger and McCulloch, but no answers are offered as to how these biases could be eliminated. However, it is suggested that an effort by the counselor to become at least aware of where he stands on these and other factors on which personal value systems tend to differ, may yield at least two benefits: a) more explicit initial communications with his clients about the *type* of counseling he is offering; and b) greater tolerance for other points of view.

Chapter 6

Marriage counseling is seen by Phillips as an "interpersonal influence process" by which clients are helped to make decisions, but in the light of all the influences which have been brought to bear by the counselor. It is argued that the counselor has power and uses it far more frequently than may be believed. The basic source of the counselor's power is seen in the fact that it is given to him by the client; and the continuance of the counselor's power depends on the perception the client has of the counselor as the process continues.

Several ways of using power are examined and it is asserted that the central issue for the counselor in any given counseling situation is the determination of how he should use his power. The counselor's responsibilities are then considered and it is concluded that the kind of person the counselor is, in fact, will determine whether his power is used with responsibility. Finally, it is suggested that an adequate selection process for all counselors is necessary.

Chapter 34

There is no limit to those things that can cause problems in the human psyche: The self, the partner, child (children), others, plus the circumstances of life in which one is living combine possibilities of explanation that are almost unlimited, in the view of O'Sullivan. He suggests that a thread worth pursuing is the meaninglessness of life as some citizens experience it in this revolutionary time. There are crises; there are confrontations; there is a revolution. Change is widespread, which is always threatening to some degree.

O'Sullivan's chapter has two parts. In the first, there is the effort to cite and to detail some of the many forms this suffering takes. In the second, there is a series of quotations from authors whose thought seems to coalesce into a pattern which may be helpful in offering guidance to some who come for assistance.

Chapter 33

Quesnell and Marx deal with the basic problem facing the counselor who is working with a Catholic couple who wishes to be true to their conscience, their faith, and the teachings of the encyclical, *Of Human Life,* and who yet also realize that their marital and family relationships as well as their individual emotional health will be in jeopardy if they have any more children. The first part of the chapter traces briefly the Church's past and present ban on contraceptive birth control, describes the rapidly changing conditions impinging upon the family today, and briefly outlines some facets attendant to the birth control dilemma for Catholics. The second part discusses the nature and function of authority and conscience according to the latest teachings of the Catholic Church. The authors deal with the differences between infallible and fallible though authoritative teaching, and the implications of these for the individual couple caught in the birth-control dilemma. The conclusion: since *Of Human Life* is not infallible teaching even if it is the official teaching of the Church and so binding in conscience, yet such teaching does not bind in every possible circumstance, and therefore the properly formed and informed conscience may dissent, and the couple involved should be able to dissent without anxiety. The stage is then set for the third part, which discusses counseling theory and client self-determination in relation to proper conscience-formation, and a variety of troubled couples and their problems as illustrative cases.

Chapter 18

Sex education in the public schools, indicates Reiss, is becoming increasingly popular. The author's examination of present-day sex education programs in the public schools reveals four major characteristics: a) a strong moralistic and propagandistic characteristic of such courses; b) a stress on purely physiological aspects of sexuality; c) a lack of integration of such courses with the existing disciplines; and d) inadequately prepared teachers for an inadequately defined task.

The generally accepted philosophy of education in the public schools involves a belief that teachers should teach the students *how* to think and not *what* to think. Education should involve learning how to use one's intellectual and analytic powers by reasoning, and calmly examining various aspects of a phenomenon. Education, in this accepted view, does not involve indoctrination to a particular moral view.

The key areas of sex that need expansion, according to Reiss, are those involved with the social sciences. Sex has been kept out of these fields and it can best be put back in an integrated fashion so that history, economics, and sociology will talk about sex when it is relevant to their topic. Teachers prepared in social science background can best help in this reintegration of sexual matter into the K-12 curriculum.

But, according to the author, parents have a major influence on their child's sex attitudes and behavior whether or not they talk about sex directly with their child. Conflict can be avoided if parents realize that the public school has a specialized role and is not a parent-substitute in the area of sex. Sex education can be justified on the grounds of all curriculum, that is, it is a key part of our cultural heritage and helps us understand the world in which we live. Such courses may or may not cut down on VD or premarital pregnancy but they will reduce the psychological costs that young people pay in the course of finding their sexual identity.

Chapter 17

Large numbers of individuals who seek marriage counseling are concerned about whether their various sexual desires and actions are "normal" or "perverse." In handling these questions, Rubin emphasizes that marriage counselors face a number of problems: confusion brought about by the many meanings of the term normal; the difficulty of defining normality and perversion, particularly in terms other than socially accepted behavior; and the strong possibility that attitudes dealing with "perversions" are value judgments disguised in scientific terms rather than medical judgments dealing with objective conditions. It is essential for marriage counselors to be aware of labeling and dismissing any form of behavior as "sick" and "abnormal" without engaging in the careful and unbiased research necessary to determine its meaning and effect in the marital relationship. Counselors must help couples shift their focus from worrying about "perverted" and "deviant" acts in the marriage bed to an emphasis upon valuing sex as play and upon freeing themselves to accepting each other's needs, desires and fantasies as legitimate.

Chapter 23

Marriage counselors must continue to develop an understanding of womankind. Runden's thesis is that, in spite of great numbers of studies and an abundance of publications about woman and her sexuality, some concepts of woman's orgasm and woman's needs have been little or errone-ously comprehended. Concepts the author declares as still wrongly empha-sized are those concerned with relationship, closeness, tenderness, and giving. Runden briefly cites historical arguments concerning clitoral or vaginal orgasm, and agrees with Masters and Johnson on the impossibility of purely vaginal orgasm. She is not fearful of a cult of the orgasm and stresses that obsession with orgasm is important only because of lack of orgasm.

A new definition of orgasm is needed, in Runden's view, one which will clarify the near impossibility of multiple orgasms and admit woman's need for hours of prolonged rest and sleep after her cataclysmic experience. The author suggests orgasm during pregnancy has not been adequately studied and wrong advice may have been given by supposedly enlightened coun-selors. To those recommending men study woman's masturbation patterns, she suggests that the best adjusted women may have had little pleasure from masturbation.

Chapter 16

Samejima believes that gathering of facts and insights can not be separ-ated theoretically, that they could be divided into two concepts: the gather-ing of facts and the establishment of insights. The establishment of insights would be the goal and content of the adjustment activities of marriage and family counseling. The establishment of insights could be facilitated by the gathering of facts. Furthermore, if this could be done under the rule of law in the authoritarian setting of the court, marriage and family counseling would be recognized as the technique of legal interviewing and counseling. Facts and insights are the soul and essence of family law practice.

Chapter 29

At a time when marriages show an increasing tendency to break up and thus to affect the quality of family in society, it is suggested by Sanctuary that an examination should be made of the extent to which volunteer work-ers could and should be enlisted to help those marriages with problems that are at present without support. Details of the work undertaken by volunteer marriage counselors in Britain are given, with an account of the historical development of the National Marriage Guidance Council and of its selection, basic training and in-service training procedures. The motives of those wishing to work as marriage counselors are discussed, also the need for research into the effectiveness of the volunteer worker who has been carefully selected and is adequately supervised. It is further suggested by Sanctuary that effective support could be given to far greater numbers of marriages if both volunteers and professionals could accept the validity of one another's roles, and work in cooperation without feeling mutually threatened.

Chapter 41

Sargent attempts to draw some tentative conclusions about the relationship between religious attitudes and beliefs and a neurotic interaction in marriage. The viewpoints grew out of the author's counseling experience with a group of religiously oriented people that had been influenced by a tradition that rejected angry feelings. The chapter explores the relationship between aggression and religion, focusing first on the positive function it plays in controlling aggression and, secondly, on a negative over-control and denial of aggression. This repudiation of aggression as a legitimate experience for the Christian often results in loneliness, inadequate problem solving, inability to express warm feelings, and depression. This last symptom, depression, was found in fifty-six out of one hundred cases handled at a pastoral counseling center and provided the impetus for this emphasis.

The author found that this religious background, called "a heritage of denial," provided religious rationalizations used to control aggression. These religious rationalizations tended to sustain and intensify a neurotic interaction in marriage. Many times in the course of counseling with these partners, significant turning points were reached and the counseling process moved more quickly when the religious attitudes and beliefs were dealt with directly.

Chapter 22

Teen-age pregnancies are increasing with the advent of the pill, the increase in population of youth, and the new freedoms afforded young people, Schiller emphasizes. With these changes, new responsibilities and decision making for the young, male and female, come into focus. The confident young person can more easily sort out his feelings and pressures in arriving at feasible solutions. Those young people whose family, personal and social life style have tended to weaken their ability to make decisions that work, who lack ego strength to cope with sexual pressures, and who relate to the opposite sex without awareness and confidence tend to be more involved with unwed motherhood and fatherhood than their peer group.

Group therapy concerned with the interdisciplinary array of personality and family relationship appears to help young people work through their frustrations and concerns. Teen-agers gain much through such techniques as role playing, discussing case problems, reacting to films and stories, reversing roles with the therapists, and general encounter situations with which they can identify.

The therapist's role as catalyst is effective where youth sees him as an open, trusting, and accepting person. He accepts the anger, judgments, and ambivalence of youth, in turn; and is aware of their need to grow in self awareness as sexual human beings.

Chapter 13

The woman has always played a special role in human society, in the viewpoint of Schwartz and Leder, perhaps because she is the bearer of children and the source of nurturance for the child. The mother offers structure to the family and is the recipient of the aggression from its members. No woman, no mother can fulfill the idealized role ascribed to her. Neither can the husband nor the child satisfy the expectations multilaterally projected. Conflict and tension exist in every family.

The authors hold to the position that every human contact provokes anxiety in the participants. In order to bind the anxiety, the mental mechanism of familiarization, or as the psychoanalyst calls it, *transference,* is utilized. The projection of fantasies on the other converts the interpersonal situation into a familiar one, into a repetition of what occurred in the past. The presence of a third person always adds anxieties and complications. One of the characteristics of transference is ambivalence.

Male-female and parent-child relations are made difficult by the real and fancied expectations projected multilaterally. Storm and strife are to be expected in all family relations. Where help in a marital crisis is necessary, short-term psychotherapy is more appropriate than prolonged treatment. But even in brief treatment methods, transference work must be stressed. The marriage counselor, therefore, must be equipped to recognize, evaluate, and interpret transference phenomena in intrafamiliar behavior.

Chapter 8

Basically, Seymour deals with techniques in marriage counseling that involve sexual morality; and he also includes a discussion of counseling practice that might violate the rights of the client. The first portion of the chapter is concerned with systems of counseling that tend to inject the counselor's attitudes and value systems directly and consciously into the work with the client so that he feels impelled to make sudden changes which could cause considerable loss of ego identity. It is felt that not enough respect is given to the individual as he has developed up to this point in his life; and the therapist's notion that only his morality is the proper one, is really a counter-transference problem relating to an inordinate need of power and control.

Then a brief history is given of the development of sexual morality in the United States. Concise descriptions of value systems related to sex of the major religions are presented by Seymour, in order to indicate to the counselor that he should know something about his client and the origins of the development of his sexual values; then work within this religious framework, helping the client to make gradual changes in his religious beliefs if he so desires, but otherwise respecting the counselee if he wishes to remain within the confines of orthodox doctrine.

So-called sexual deviations are discussed in reference to what should be the counselor's need to obtain background about legal implications which could be communicated to his client; and it is indicated that our knowledge is incomplete in many areas relating to sex so that forcing our own notions upon the client might not only be morally uncalled-for, but could be informationally incorrect.

The final section of the chapter deals specifically with counter-transference problems, and states that the first generation of therapists, despite their own insights, are still combating the effects of long-standing psychological problems, and therefore must be ever-cautious of their own lack of objectivity towards clients, for this could lead to a relationship which might be dubbed immoral rather than therapeutic.

Chapter 2

Marriage therapy is regarded by Silverman as a specialized field of family counseling which centers largely on the interpersonal relationship between husband and wife. It involves many disciplines and is interprofessional in character. Those who wish to qualify for this field, whether psychiatrist, physician, clergyman, psychologist or social worker, require a common body of scientific knowledge, techniques, and qualifications.

The "practice of marriage counseling" means the rendering of professional marriage counseling services to individuals and marital pairs, singly or in groups, whether in the general public or in organizations, either public or private. Marital therapy also includes premarital counseling, pre-divorce and post-divorce counseling, and family counseling which emphasizes the spousal relationship as a key to successful family living. The practice of marriage counseling consists of the application of principles, methods and techniques of counseling and psychotherapy for the purpose of resolving psychological conflict, modifying perception and behavior, altering old attitudes and establishing new ones in the area of marriage and family life.

In its concern with the antecedents of marriage, with the vicissitudes of marriage, and with the consequences of the failure of marriage, marriage counseling keeps in sight its objective of enabling marital partners and their children to achieve the optimal adjustment consistent with their welfare as individuals, as members of a family, and as citizens in society.

All the factors that are indicated in textbooks as being pertinent to counseling situations in general are relatively pertinent to marriage counseling—the counselor's knowledge, training, and philosophical orientation, his maturity and image of himself in the counseling relationship. There are, however, additional factors to be considered in dealing with a couple and their marriage problems, according to Silverman's view.

In contrast to individual therapy in which the counselor centers his attention primarily on the individual, the marital therapist must keep track of *two* personalities with not only the *intra* conflicts but also those between the two; there are two sets of inconsistencies, indecisions and interpretations; and there is a whole array of perception in the interplay of feeling and action between the spouses.

Discussion, dialogue or communication, in short, the *therapeutic process* in marriage counseling, takes for granted, Silverman emphasizes, that the persons concerned and involved have experiences and insights which may contribute something of value to the overall problem. In brief, dialogue in marital therapy uses the language of the experimenter, the individual trained and competent to confront new things, seeking enlarged areas of understanding, expanding knowledge, deepening insights. Dialogue and therapy then consist of both *transmission* and *reception*.

Marriage is based on characterful living. We may mass-produce almost everything in America, but we cannot mass-produce character, because that is a matter of personal identity. It belongs to those who have found the part they are to play; who are doing the work for which they are best endowed; who are satisfied that they are filling a vital need; who are meeting their obligations and standing up to their tasks. Character is a positive thing. It is not protected innocence, but practiced virtue; it is not fear of vice, but love of excellence, especially in the marriage relationship.

Chapter 7

The counseling gynecologist is faced with a multitude of issues, calling for both medical and philosophical evaluation. Stern discusses typical cases taken from his daily practice, and their many-faced, problematical nature is analyzed. Foremost among the issues which test the counselor's and the counselee's scale of values are those dealing with fertility and sterility, contraception and insemination, abortion and childbirth. Illumination of such problems and juxtaposition of possible attempts at their solution may enhance the adviser's acumen and serve thus as a future guide, in Stern's viewpoint.

Chapter 3

The relationship of sex to marital incompatibilities is outlined by Trainer from the standpoint of the physician as a marital counselor.

The natures of the Sexual Urge, the Domestic Urge and the Territorial Urge are elaborated. Frustrations of the Urges produce secondary related emotional disturbances, he points out, which interfere with the communicative relationships of the couple. It is convenient to examine the sexual incompatibilities in terms of their association with the following three stages of marriage: *Early marriage* is marked by problems deriving from gender orientation differences, from sexual ignorance, from new paired-relationships and from fatigue states. *Middle marriage* is a period of definition of the personal incompatibilities. Progressive alienation develops, exacerbated by emergence of some disease states, and producing others. Preoccupation with careers, money and child-raising compound the sexual losses. *Advanced marriage* is one of aggravated incompatibilities and the common existence of relatively severe disease states. Iatrogenic dyssexuality occurs as a consequence of our new and useful medications. Mutual dysattraction is at its maximum, related strongly to our overfed, overalcoholed life style.

The specific ways in which the physician can function are summarized by Trainer as: a) individual sex education; b) group, or public sex education; c) the proper conduct of the premarital examination and counseling; d) relating other disease states to sexual problems; and e) the elaboration of a sexual history comparable to those used in disorders of other systems.

A suggestion of some of the kinds of problem presented is given by Trainer; and the chapter concludes with a statement of obligations and duties deriving from the expectations of the society and the rights it accords the physician.

Chapter 38

The pastoral counselor is usually the first to be contacted for help because of the moral aspects of the problem, or the desire to deal with it from a theological, rather than medical or psychiatric point of reference, in Tubbs' viewpoint.

The pastoral counselor should be shockproof when confronted with any moral or ethical situation in counseling. He should recognize the behavior problem as a manifestation of sickness rather than sinfulness; he should attempt to discover the basic problem rather than deal with the presenting problem; he should seek to help the counselee find the optimum spiritual, emotional, and physical adjustment, and this is ordinarily done by helping the counselee to behave in the most loving way possible for himself and others.

The pastoral counselor must never contribute further to the sickness of the counselee by going along with attempted suicide or any other violent "activity," or by taking advantage of the possible weakness of the counselee for his own gain or pleasure.

Chapter 39

Largely personal, autobiographical and to some extent homiletical, Vail leans heavily on his experience as a clergyman, who having received training at the Marriage Council of Philadelphia now functions as a parish priest, family life educator, and marital counselor. Questions he raises suggest the nature of man, being what it is, Body, Mind, and Spirit, must be recognized in its unity and celebrated in its ever-growing, ever-changing, ever-unifying process. The "yeast" metaphor carries the Biblical theme in an earthy way that further suggests that religion and counseling can be side by side, the psychosomatic bolstered by the spirit (Pneuma) as the spirit leads in setting priorities and focus of relationship.

Chapter 35

Marriage is essentially a matter of attitudes. These are related to values. What we call spiritual is concerned with the meaning of life, and with its highest values. People need training for marriage, and couples also premarital counseling. Essentially this is Wood's thesis.

We need to see marriage in the perspective of the whole person: psychophysical, social, spiritual, and with reverence for personality. Family planning involves not only questions of health and economic support, but of producing and training new persons to serve the highest values. Persons whose marriages have been broken by death may need counseling as well as comfort, Wood also points out.

Counseling involves not only specific problems but deep-seated attitudes and values; therefore, religious feelings are of great importance. It helps people when they see their problem as in God's sight, and also see any problem from the standpoint of the life companion. The Bible has rich treasures of insight and inspiration for couples. Wood argues that no two cases are alike, as no two counselors are. Different counselors attract different types of cases, and vary in their methods, but all counselors seek to help people achieve higher levels of cooperation and creativity in marriage.

*   *   *

Thus we bring to a close this text on marital theory. I take the liberty now, as Editor, of a few final comments and viewpoints.

This concluding chapter certainly is not intended as a comprehensive treatment, even in outline, of the contents of the book but rather as a provocative introduction to the material.

It is the Editor's opinion, moreover, that no one text can provide enough information in an area such as marital therapy. Practitioners, teachers, clinicians, and students are therefore urged to supplement this book with appropriate collateral and supplementary reading and research.

The point of view dominating this entire volume is that the best clinical and theoretical experiences must be provided for those being trained and working in the ever-expanding, multifaceted, broad, and comprehensive profession of marital counseling and therapeutic services.

AUTHOR AND CONTRIBUTOR INDEX

SUBJECT INDEX

and obedience, 365
and protection, 364
and sexual fulfillment, 372
and sexual response, 40
as basic need, 501
capacity for, 500
nonexclusive, 101
sexual-personal, 330
working at, 407

M
Male climacteric, 379
Manipulation
　in science, 251f
　morality of, 252
　social, 245ff
　function, 482f
　functional matrix, 450f
　interpersonal relationship concept, 256ff
　intra-conflicts, 15
　joint interviews, 259, 260
　one-to-one relationship, 257
　origin, 13
　prejudices, 176f
　preventive, 14
　psycho-therapeutic, 335ff
　relationship fantasy, 90
　religious issues, 459f
　the schizophrenc client, 20
　sexually oriented, 93f
　skill, 14f
　spiritual direction, 300
　spiritual values, 409ff, 411
　theological implications, 461ff
　therapy, 13ff, 18ff, 20, 21
　traditional, 258
　value positions, 98f
　volunteer workers, 340ff
Marriage
　advanced, 36f
　arranged, 150
　attitudes, 409
　authentic, 123ff
　child-centered, 424, 425
　conjugal spirituality, 301ff
　control factor, 131f
　cooperation, 166f
　dependency, 171ff
　disintegrating, 324
　early, 134f
　emotive-consequential dimensions, 130
　ethics, 81
　existential aspects, 123ff
　expectations, 149f

happiness, 425
hierarchical ends, 424
"homecoming," 131
ideal, 123ff, 124ff
interactional pattern, 256
master-slave relationship, 129
middle, 35f
mixed, 42
modern function, 352
monogamous, 33, 326f
perfect, 406
personal involvement, 159ff
prediction information, 17, 18, 286
Marital counseling, 13f, 93ff, 97ff, 142
　and political individualism, 284ff
　casework method, 257
　church, 482ff
　client adjustment to, 19ff
　client-counselor relationship, 61f, 256, 257
　client expectations, 61
　conjoint, 20
　countertransference, 89ff
　ecumenical approach, 485
　environmental matrix, 450ff
　etymology and definition, 179
　privacy, 128f
　psychic safety, 131
　psychological barriers, 170f
　religious aspects, 498
　sharing, 165f
　societal aspects, 14, 259f, 501
　successful, 406
　traditional, 256, 352
　types, 159
　understanding, 127ff
Marriage Council of Philadelphia, 13
Marriage counseling, *see* Marital counseling
Marriage Counselor, 15f
　biases, 104
　catalyst, 98
　clergymen, 486ff
　individual-centered, 99, 447ff
　institution-centered, 99
　leadership role, 357f
　ministerial, *see also* clergymen
　motivation, 341f
　orientation, 332f, 337f
　personal concepts, 99f
　power, 57ff, 62ff
　professional, 51, 58
　professional diversity, 256f
　psychoanalytic orientation, 16
　qualifications, 67, 332ff
　rationalizing, 80